BISON
BOOKS

A Doctor's Gold Rush Journey
to California

by ISRAEL SHIPMAN PELTON LORD

edited by NECIA DIXON LILES

with a foreword by J.S. HOLLIDAY

UNIVERSITY OF NEBRASKA PRESS
LINCOLN AND LONDON

Copyright © 1995 by Necia Dixon Liles. Published by special arrangement with
McFarland & Company, Inc., Publishers, Jefferson, North Carolina.
Manufactured in the United States of America

∞

First Bison Books printing: 1999
Most recent printing indicated by the last digit below:
10   9   8   7   6   5   4   3   2   1

Library of Congress Cataloging-in-Publication Data
Lord, Israel Shipman Pelton, b. 1805.
[At the extremity of civilization]
A doctor's gold rush journey to California / by Israel Shipman Pelton Lord; edited by
Necia Dixon Liles; with a foreword by J. S. Holliday.
p.   cm.
Originally published as: At the extremity of civilization: Jefferson, N.C.: McFarland &
Co., 1995.
Includes index.
ISBN 0-8032-7990-6 (pa: alk. paper)
1. Oregon Trail.   2. Overland journeys to the Pacific.   3. West (U.S.)—History—
1848–1860.   4. California—History—1846–1850.   5. California—Gold discoveries.
6. Panama—Description and travel.   7. Lord, Israel Shipman Pelton, b. 1805 Diaries.
I. Liles, Necia Dixon.   II. Title.
F587.L86   1999
978'.02'092—dc21
[B]
99-38773   CIP

Table of Contents

◆ ◆ ◆

PART II : DESERT AND THE SIERRA

PART III : SACRAMENTO CITY AND THE MINES

Foreword
by J.S. Holliday

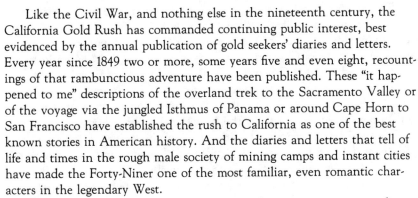

Like the Civil War, and nothing else in the nineteenth century, the California Gold Rush has commanded continuing public interest, best evidenced by the annual publication of gold seekers' diaries and letters. Every year since 1849 two or more, some years five and even eight, recountings of that rambunctious adventure have been published. These "it happened to me" descriptions of the overland trek to the Sacramento Valley or of the voyage via the jungled Isthmus of Panama or around Cape Horn to San Francisco have established the rush to California as one of the best known stories in American history. And the diaries and letters that tell of life and times in the rough male society of mining camps and instant cities have made the Forty-Niner one of the most familiar, even romantic characters in the legendary West.

While professional and amateur historians have written many studies, monographs and historical narratives seeking to recreate the gold rush experience, the gold seekers themselves have been most responsible for keeping the story fresh and compelling.

Writing with a literary ability beyond that of today's average American (including most college graduates), these ordinary folk of 1849 and the 1850s scratched onto the cramped pages of their diaries and letters vivid depictions of scenery and daily life on the overland trails and later "in the diggings." Their commitment to what was in effect a journalistic effort derived in large degree from the fact that they knew they were engaged in a great undertaking, a vast migration of thousands of young men across the wilderness half of the continent, on a journey imperiled by disease, hardship and mortal danger—much like a war, with the nation anxiously awaiting news of their progress.

This self consciousness explains why so many coupled their good-byes with promises to "write home" from the western frontier and then from

Fort Kearny and Fort Laramie and thereafter to keep up their diaries. They looked forward to returning in six months or so, not only with a "pocket full of rocks" but also with a record that would prove their fortitude and rectitude and would preserve the wonder of all they had seen and endured.

As they and their families, friends and creditors shared a consciousness of the gold rush as a historic event, so they shared a sense of what would be encountered on the overland trail—for publications of explorers like Fremont and travellers like Parkman in the 1840s had reported predatory Indian tribes, vast herbs of buffalo, deserts and mountain passes. And from California, writers like Bryant and early gold seekers had written about astonishing fortunes dug from river banks and sinful temptations of gambling, drinking and worse in San Francisco. Believing they knew something of the dangers and the wonders that awaited them, the gold seekers felt all the more intent on chronicling their heroic enterprise.

With the entire nation, thirty states, aware and excited during that first spring of the rush to California (President Polk had announced the gold discovery in his December 1848 message to Congress, newspapers had printed descriptions of California's streams "paved with gold," and ministers had sermonized on "that Golgotha of sin"), literally tens of thousands of families, from Maine to Texas, were emotionally and economically involved. Wives ("California Widows"), fretful creditors and many who wanted to join the rush but lacked the funds (or the gumption) stayed at home in villages and farms and cities, anxiously awaiting news of the arrival of their husbands, sons, fathers, brothers and friends in El Dorado—and then reports of their success in digging nuggets from that astonishing soil.

The story of the gold seekers' westward trek and later their experience in the mining camps and boom towns was a matter of public record in the first years of the rush and has remained so for 145 years. At the beginning, letters sent home were shared with local newspapers, dailies and weeklies, so everyone could see, through hometown eyes, the prairies described as "oceans of grass" and the majestic sidewheel steamboats on the Sacramento River. Later, when the Forty-Niners and their successors returned home, their diaries were published. Before long more diaries, edited for a wider audience, began to appear and continue to this day. Thus, thousands of Americans through the decades have vicariously walked beside the ox-drawn wagons and forded icy streams and thirsted on endless desert crossings and then "seen the elephant" in Sierra canyons and San Francisco gambling palaces.

That is why the gold rush remains such a vital part of the ever-increasing awareness of the American West—because hundreds of young men (and a very few women) sought to talk to their wives and sweethearts, mothers and fathers when letters and diaries were their only means of communication. How lucky we are!

For many years I have spent a part of my life studying gold rush diaries (and collections of letters), both in manuscript and published form—more than 500 as of a few years ago. (I do not include the many reminiscences written years after the events and therefore less reliable.) Each year I read the annual production of newly published gold rush books, with a more critical eye and greater degree of expectation than most readers, even most California historians. And I am each year reinforced in my judgment that at this late date in the business of recreating and studying the gold rush years, only the very best diaries/letters can be justified as deserving publication.

In a review of a gold rush diary published in 1989 by the University of Nebraska Press, I suggested: "There are probably not more than a dozen presently known manuscripts that justify preparation for publication— several are at the Huntington, Bancroft and Yale libraries. They should be offered to the public and not anything of lesser quality. For example, the diaries of Isaac Lord at the Huntington, Joseph Hamelin at Yale and E.H. Patterson at Bancroft are each worthy of publication.... The California Gold Rush story cannot survive many more years of being used. Rather it must be respected as a challenging opportunity to be bold, even innovative, like the gold seekers themselves."

How delighted I am that Isaac (actually Israel) Lord's remarkable diary has now been brilliantly prepared for public enjoyment. That preparation has been accomplished by a bold and innovative editor/researcher, Necia Dixon Liles. She deserves great praise and respect for her indefatigable effort to create a gold rush book that will truly be a major contribution to the literature of that familiar story.

My praise of Ms. Liles is based not only on reading her manuscript but also on my recollection of the many hours, even days I spent (in 1958) laboring to read Lord's manuscript diary at the Huntington Library. Her transcription of Lord's massive account was a feat of patience, perseverance and scholarship. She tells that story—and so much more—in her lively, humorous and thoroughly rewarding introduction.

I want to add that Lord deserves publication because his is one of the most detailed, opinionated (how enriching) and informed of all gold rush diaries, offering not only a superlative day-by-day description of the overland experience (with escape via Lassen's Cutoff) but as well his vigorous recounting of life in mines and in Sacramento City. Few diarists remained as devoted to their task as Lord; many simply gave up on reaching the Sacramento Valley or gradually became less and less attentive, more and more wearied and bored and boring. But not Lord.

More than that, he continued his diary-keeping on his return home via the Isthmus of Panama. Here too his account is sustained at a high level of descriptive power and, as always with Lord, moral indignation.

Necia Dixon Liles has chosen and done well for her initial effort. Even Dr. Lord would praise her work.

Preface
by *Necia Dixon Liles*

———— ◆ ◆ ◆ ————

Some people fall in love at first sight. Others take years to realize that there is a smouldering spark waiting to flare and brighten a dark corner. The affair between Dr. Lord and me was both.

Dr. Israel Shipman Pelton Lord came into my life in 1964 when a college friend found three volumes of a handwritten medical journal in the attic of her dilapidated rental house. I noticed them on her bookshelf one day and began to thumb through the heavy, musty smelling journals. Hundreds of entries, dated from July 1856 to November 1863, clinically described diseases like dyspnoea, brash, anasarca, hysteria, and page after page of ague, cholera and typhoid fever.

I quickly became fascinated with a doctor so opinionated that he would make clinical notes that "this woman has hardly brains enough to have idiopathic headache" or "the physician who has ordered the [allopathic] remedy, or rather directed the inhuman application three or four times and not seen any mischief come of it, has not common powers of observation, and had better hire himself out to skin live eels, as he is never likely to learn anything from his own experience."

I was enchanted with his objective bedside manner which seldom cracked ["this child was murdered"] and wanted to know more about him and his life outside the practice. But, meticulous as he was about other documentation, there was not a single mention of his own name or the location of his practice.

After a few weeks of laboriously deciphering the small, sepia handwriting, I began to recognize patients and families. I was hooked. I couldn't wait to get back to my friend's house to read more about these contemporaries of my great, great grandparents. When the school year ended, I asked my friend what she planned to do with the books when she moved. "Who cares?" she answered. "You're the only one who's ever even read them. Why

5

don't you take them?" The owner of the house was a large corporation whose sole interest in the property was to put up an apartment building, scheduled to begin construction immediately. I had a deep involvement with the patients in these books, and even though they all had been in the great beyond for many years, I couldn't bear to let them be buried again by a noisy bulldozer.

For the next few years, the heavy volumes sat like a quiet graveyard in my bookcase while I produced and raised three children, started and managed a couple of professional businesses, decorated several houses, spent a few months in Europe, moved a dozen times, and divided my free time between political activism, needlework, gardening and half a dozen other loves. During those years, probably because of my latent interest in the journals, I sporadically collected ancient looking medical books which took my fancy in used bookstores or library sales. I seldom read them, but just tucked them on a shelf as if their purpose for existence were to collect dust.

In 1989 I began transcribing the journals. I couldn't believe, as my husband told me, that I was the only one on the planet interested in them. Here was the torment of long painful deaths. Here was the agony of families losing two or three children in a week. And here the exhausted relief when someone near death was brought back to health. I loved these people and rejoiced and mourned with them. Why wouldn't others feel the same way?

Because I originally read the journals randomly rather than in chronological order. I had missed an early clinical entry written in the first person. This was the first real hope that I might find out about this man who had embedded himself in my heart and my daily schedule. (It was about this time I found myself dating checks "1861.") The patient's name appeared to be I.W. or J.W. Lord. The entry observed "my" eye burning after having rubbed it with "my" finger which wasn't washed after mixing a remedy. I finally had a name—or part of one—and it inspired me to accelerate my transcription work to two days a week. A few weeks later I found an entry stating, "Went to Springfield yesterday. Saw Mr. Lincoln."

Later that year, I went to visit my son, Jason, who was working as a congressional director in Washington, D.C. I brought with me ancestral data, thinking that, if I had time, I might piece together some more of my family's nebulous genealogical puzzle. I hadn't given much thought to researching Dr. Lord, but the old dear had his own way of manipulating my life and he was tired of being neglected in the dusty heights of my bookcases.

I was born a bibliomaniac and the Library of Congress has been my concept of heaven since I first heard of it, so I set aside a full day to spend there. After a brief tour of the literary wonderland, I went to see if I could find some of my ancestors hanging out in the Genealogy section. Dr. Lord was incensed and demanded time. He wanted to be found. After nearly a century of patiently waiting for this moment, he led me straight into the trap he had baited for me.

I began by casually looking for doctors named Lord who practiced in Illinois in the mid-nineteenth century. I found several who washed out quickly. The possibility that I might actually find him began to stimulate me and, with growing excitement, I soon exhausted my minimal research skills. I approached a librarian and told her about Dr. Lord. I should have recognized Virginia Wood as a guardian angel, so sweet was her manner. She accepted the challenge with enthusiasm and a vast amount of knowledge. She immediately found an obscure book of nineteenth century physicians from Illinois which listed an I.S.P. Lord in Batavia, Illinois. Could this be my J.W.? We pursued it. We hunted in biographies of Illinois, medical histories, county and state histories. Bit by bit we confirmed that, indeed, I.S.P. was our man and his flowery penmanship confused the letters. His full, ostentatious name, Israel Shipman Pelton Lord, was soon revealed in the Library of Congress stacks and slowly he reached out from books not opened for half a century, and leaped onto the center stage of my life.

Israel S.P. Lord was born in Hadlyme, Connecticut, on September 16, 1805. He began his medical career in 1830 as an allopath and continued the traditional practice until 1842 when he "had a terrible attack and the doctors came near killing me." Distraught at the death of his infant daughter and feeling as if the harsh remedies of current medical treatment had failed her, he turned to homeopathy. For the rest of his life he eschewed allopathic medicine with its noxious remedies, such as the mercury-laden Blue Pill and calomel. He was appalled by the use of quinine and blood letting, both high on the list of remedies in that day.

The man was stern, severe, cantankerous, opinionated, officious and adventurous. He was also caring, gentle, patient, compassionate and honorable, and I was eager to finish transcribing his medical journals and make them available to anyone who might be interested in the homeopathic medical treatment or genealogical data, or just want a fascinating swatch of nineteenth century life untainted by social considerations from the twentieth.

As soon as we confirmed that his practice was, indeed, homeopathic, Ms. Wood gave me the name of the National Center for Homeopathy in Washington, D.C. I had completely forgotten my own family history by then. The Lord research was exciting and falling into place so easily that I seemed to feel Dr. Lord dragging me around by my nose. I wasn't surprised to find the homeopathic center just three blocks from my son's apartment. (During this week I saw very little of Jason, but, at 22, he really didn't mind.)

Filled with anticipation, I walked to their offices on a bright fall morning. They showed me the library and invited me to spend as much time as I needed there. Over the next couple of hours I found not a single biography or even a mention of Dr. Lord. Frustrated, I sat down on the floor and leaned against a bookcase to ponder my next move. After a moment I turned my head to the left and saw, six inches from my eye, primly standing in alphabetical order, a brown leather book with gold leaf lettering entitled *Intermittent Fever*. The author was Lord. He might as well have tapped me on the shoulder and said, "Look, Stupid."

I stared at the book for a moment, then took it off the shelf and opened it to the cover page and read "I.S.P. Lord, M.D." I felt like an orphan who had just found her birth certificate. I opened to the middle of the book and there were what appeared to be the same case histories that I had so carefully transcribed over the past nine months. The work, it seemed, already had been done—and published in 1871. I couldn't decide whether to laugh or cry, so I did both.

The passion of the hunt dried my tears quickly. I saw that all the cases in the book were malarial and dated from January 1849 to November 1854. No brain fever, no childbirth, no horse accidents or phthisis. The book's title, *Clinical Medicine, Vol. I, on Intermittent Fever and Other Malarious Diseases* told the story. Since my handwritten journals began in 1856, were case numbered and annotated, it was clear I had the unpublished volumes three, four and five. In a biography I found later, I read that Dr. Lord had meticulously prepared ten of these volumes for publication.

Of course I asked the center if I could buy the Lord book and of course they said no, but they gave me the name of Bill Kirtsos of the Homeopathic Resources and Services in Old Chatham, New York. I called him immediately and he said, yes, he did have a copy of the book, and, yes, I could buy it from him. I could hear Dr. Lord humming in the background.

As soon as I arrived home (in Santa Rosa, California) I wrote to the Kane County (Illinois) Historical Society. They had very little information on Dr. Lord but sent me a letter written to them in 1968 by a man named Noel Stevenson asking for information on Dr. Lord. He mentioned that he had just retired from his law practice and wanted to spend the next few months researching Dr. Lord. Stevenson's home address was Santa Rosa, California. I immediately checked the phone book but didn't find his name. Since he had retired 21 years before I got the copy of his letter, there seemed little chance even that he would be alive.

On my lunch hour (I had a full time job) I dashed to the library and found the Parker Directory of lawyers licensed in California. I flipped through the book, county after county and finally, in Orange County, found Noel Stevenson—name, address and home phone number. Back at the office I dialed his number. "I want to talk about Dr. Israel Shipman Pelton Lord," I said.

"Oh. It's been a long time since I heard that name," he said. We talked for a long time and he told me he had gotten interested in Dr. Lord through a gold rush diary written by Lord and now housed at the Huntington Library in San Marino. This clarified several entries in *Malarial Fever* which were datelined California. Stevenson had done years of research on

Dr. Lord, and had "massive amounts" of information on the man. What was more, he told me, I was welcome to it all.

While at the local library, I checked the indexes of several books on the California Gold Rush and found one which listed "Lord" as a reference. This book was the quintessential gold rush chronicle, "*The World Rushed In,*" by J.S. Holliday. In it, several passages were quoted from a gold rush journal written by "Isaac Lord." The instant I read them I recognized the acerbic, articulate Israel Lord and checked out the book.

My adrenaline was rising. I made plans to go to Southern California and visit Mr. Stevenson. I called the Huntington and talked with Dr. Peter Blodgett, assistant curator of manuscripts, who, when asked if I could see the Lord diary, regretted that, since I was not a professor or working on my doctorate, I could not have access to the private library.

But Dr. Blodgett is a reasonable (and sweet) man and when I explained my fervor and research and told him about the medical journals, he graciously acquiesced and we set up an appointment for me to see the actual manuscript on my trip down to see Mr. Stevenson.

Meanwhile, I was still spending two days a week transcribing the medical journals. By this time I had more than a thousand pages typed and Dr. Lord was taking up as much space in my life as two or three live people. There were dozens of obsolete and obscure medical terms which I needed to research in order to transcribe the case histories. In each case, I found the appropriate reference book in my own collection, sitting within six feet of my computer.

During this time I contacted Julian Winston, a homeopathic historian who lived then in Philadelphia. He read me the first real biographical data of Dr. Lord from an 1873 *Cleave's Biographical Cyclopaedia of Homeopathic Physicians and Surgeons.* (This biography of Dr. Lord is reprinted herein in its entirety as Appendix A.) I asked him if the publishers of Dr. Lord's book, Bourecke & Tafel, were still in business, thinking they might have some more information on Dr. Lord in their deep archives. I had searched through lists of publishers and had not found any variation of the name. Mr. Winston told me that Bourecke & Tafel was not a publisher, but a large old homeopathic pharmacy. I wouldn't be able to reach them soon, he said, because they were in the process of moving and it would be a few weeks before they were settled into their new place—in Santa Rosa, Calif. Dr. Lord was at it again, pulling the wagons in a circle with me in the center.

My visit to Mr. Stevenson was informative but not the intense satisfaction I hoped to find. He and his wife, Mary, had recently moved to a retirement community and the research from all his prolific years as a lawyer and genealogist was stored in boxes, jammed to the ceiling. There was no way to know where the Lord material was, and, since Stevenson was quite ill, he did not feel comfortable having me rummage through his entire history, which now silently shared its existence with the family car. A year later, after he had passed away, Mary invited me to find the material and allowed me to copy some documentation. Noel gave me an index he had made of the journal and told me that Dr. Lord had returned to California in the early 1870s and was buried in the Eastside cemetery in Los Angeles. This news alone would have made the trip worthwhile. After our visit I headed quickly for East L.A.

I arrived at the huge Eastside cemetery at 4:45 on a Friday. The office was closed and in fifteen minutes the gates would be locked for the night. I decided to spend the few minutes familiarizing myself with the cemetery, but Dr. Lord was in no mood to waste time. He led me straight through the convoluted acreage and in less than three minutes, my daughters, Koran and Joie, spotted a large stone labeled "LORD." I stopped and there he was, with his first wife Mary, his second wife, Mary Case, his son, daughter, infant daughters, grandson and several other members of the family. I left the car and sat down on his grave, hoping for more information. Dr. Lord smiled quietly.

The next day at the Huntington, the gracious Dr. Blodgett handed me the diary. It was heavy and lacked the musty smell of the medical books, but holding the manuscript was a fulfilling emotional experience for me. This was history in its purest form, not a palimpsest of modern research and editing.

Much of the manuscript was in very small type, having been printed in local Kane County newspapers, *The Western Christian* and *The American Baptist*. Interspersed with the printed pages were at least as many handwritten pages, written in the same meticulous, sepia penmanship so familiar to me from the medical journals.

Virtually every day of his expedition, Dr. Lord scrupulously mapped the route, scenery, feed, water and road conditions as a guide to future emigrants. The acid and the sweet, the repulsive and the beautiful all are there to entice or warn those who lusted for adventure and California gold. On August 7, 1849, three months after he left home, Dr. Lord proffered his reasons for the assiduous work:

> I have been adverted to the need of a definite guide. With one the emigrant is at home. In entering upon this untried and therefore under-scribed route I have determined to furnish the future emigrant with this great desideratum. The courses will in general be given, land marks described, crossings of streams noted, springs marked down, and distances estimated. The latter will only be guessed at from point to point, and will probably not vary much from the results given by the road-ometers, which are not to be depended on entirely, as they occasionally get out of order. I shall endeavor not to make the miles too long, that the traveller may be disappointed, the right way, (i.e., pleasantly), if at all. One must travel in this road, to form any idea of the importance of knowing exactly

where he is, and the distance from water to water, wood to wood, and grass to grass.

No more meticulous and exacting physical account of the expedition can be found.

For years the gold rush journal was credited to Isaac Lord because Isaac's name is scrawled in huge letters several times at the end of the journal. Noel Stevenson corrected the Huntington records and gave authorship back to Israel. I might offer that, given the age of Israel's son, Isaac (probably in his 50s at the time Dr. Lord compiled these notes and newspaper articles into chronological order), it more likely was Israel's grandson, Isaac (Ikey, born 1875, died 1897), who scrawled his young name so grandly on the empty final pages of the journal.

I sat in the Huntington Manuscript Room fondling the fragile pages, carefully turning them a few at a time, reading long passages like, "The course is next west, N.W. three miles turning west across a ravine, then N.N.W., winding down and up and through and over the ravines and hills, not very bad nor steep, one and one half miles to the north side of a semicircular sand hill forty feet high. Then by a very crooked route N.W. by W. toward the south point of the island like range."

These word maps go on for weeks during the first third of the journal, and seemed mundane to me until I drove the trail, looking at scenery described by Dr. Lord the same year my great grandmother was born. He wrote of a huge stone, on the pinnacle of which is "the appearance of a man sitting astride." Just words. But it came alive for me when I drove to the City of Rocks (in southern Idaho) and faced that same huge rock which looms up out of the road exactly as he saw it.

Interspersed throughout the directional tedium are rewarding entries like Lord's description of the typical gold rush participant:

> Imagine to yourself a biped five feet four inches high, with big whiskers, red mustachios, steeple-crowned hat, buckskin coat done up with hedgehog quills, belt, pistols, hatchet, bullet pouch, bowie knife twenty inches long, red shirt, spurs on left heel eight inches long, with a burr as large as a small sunflower, at least three inches in diameter, mounted on a small four-legged piece of mule flesh of the most obstinate quality, and you have some idea of things that are—for there are many such. It seems to me that the boys take considerable pains to make themselves ridiculous. The most disgusting feature is the hair on the upper lip.

Later there appears an eleven-stanza ode to a dying ox preceded by a descriptive paragraph of the animal whose "bones seemed to bend out and his wrinkled skin to swell, and a sound like the shrill whistle of the wind through a broken casement, changing to the low prolonged rumble and roll of a bass drum, became a low muttering articulation and ended in a tremulous tone of sad repining. . . ."

Who could resist? This was poetry from the man I loved. Never mind
that he had been dead for nearly a hundred years. Never mind that I had
no idea whether he was short or tall, fat or thin, bald or toothless. Never
mind that he was a hard-core fundamentalist Baptist and I was not. I knew
that he was a homeopathic physician who had walked all night through
snow blizzards to attend sick and dying patients. I knew he was a clean-
shaven teetotaller, a nonsmoker and a man who never gambled, swore or
indicated a lust for women—completely excluding even a brief mention of
longing for his wife.

Lord was appalled by the cultural phenomena catalyzed by the promise
of easy wealth. He held little hope for the future of California and despaired
that the entire state seemed so plunged into moral depravity as to never
emerge. Writing for theological newspapers, *The Western Christian* and *The
American Baptist*, probably influenced his discernment and encouraged him
to feel justified in ranting uncharitably about his fellow miners, though he
seemed to need little prompting once he got started.

Many of the gold rush journalists boasted of adhering to their prudent
Christian mores in the face of iniquity and disillusionment. Without doubt,
Dr. Lord felt the same way. His moral structure never seemed to falter in
the face of rampant, enticing sin. Indeed, his convictions appeared to have
become stronger on contact with their opposites.

He leaves no doubt about his revulsion of bars and gambling casinos,
refusing even soft drinks to avoid the appearance of sin. He consistently
submitted detail about churches and Sunday services, either to assure his
readers that they would have no lack of religious oration in the wilds of
California, or to remind them of his Christian piety.

Dr. Lord's deepest profanity is a Twainesque comment about the store-
keepers of St. Joseph, Missouri: "The merchants are clever and accommodating. They charge large profits, at least now; but they do it without
telling you to go to hell, or any other celebrated place."

The Huntington copied the journal for me (and later granted permission
for it to be published) and I spent nearly a year poring through hundreds of
pages of words written by a man who generally was filled with enthusiasm,
frequently was appalled, and sometimes had "hardly spirit left to write." But
write he did. Every day for nearly two years.

Dr. Lord was always nearby during the transcription of his journal, and
when a word was unclear, I needed only to close my eyes and open my
mind. Within a few moments the words would become as obvious as if I
had written them myself. In nearly seven hundred pages there are fewer
than a half dozen words which are illegible, even though some of the handwriting is smaller than a subscript type.

The text of Dr. Lord's journal as it appears in this volume has been left
just as it was originally written, with peculiarities of grammar and punctua-
tion intact. The only changes that have been made are those that were

needed to improve the readability of the prose without interfering with the tone or style of Dr. Lord's writing. These changes are limited to standardizing his inconsistent capitalization of placenames and inserting apostrophes in contractions when he omitted them. In the interest of preserving the original flavor, archaic and idiosyncratic spellings have not been altered. When explanatary notes are needed, they have been inserted within brackets in the text. Footnotes are used for editorial remarks and occasional background material that supplements the text.

I'm glad to have this done. I'm glad that Dr. Lord's graphic descriptions of the Oregon and California trails, Northern California and Panama can now be added to the histories of his era. There are literally dozens of journals of this era, but none so clear, so concise, so articulate as I.S.P. Lord's. J.S. Holliday did a massive job annotating the William Swain journal, *The World Rushed In*, which is almost without doubt the best-referenced book written on the California Gold Rush, and I am confident that it need not be done again. Although I have spent literally thousands of hours researching Dr. Lord's trip, and could, indeed, footnote, annotate and document it until it reached twice its own length, that is not what I want to do with his work. The few footnotes I have added are there at the whim of my own interests without any attempt to "prove" his existence, his observations or his opinions.

I have not the desire, inclination or life expectancy to duplicate the thirty years' effort that Holliday put into his book. I feel that Dr. Lord's articulate journal stands very well on its own with little help from me and I, simply as a messenger, present his book in its purity. To do it any other way would be to qualify his disciplined genius.

I feel about Dr. Lord's diary the way I feel about my children: I am the vehicle that allows them to get here. From there, my job is simply to nurture them, try to make them presentable, and send them out into the world to fend for themselves.

I offer you Dr. Lord.

The editor
Fall 1994

Chapter One
May 6–June 24, 1849:
Kansas, Nebraska

———◆——◆——◆———

MAY 6TH, 1849. We left a dead man by the name of Middleton on the
levee at St. Louis, and thought that we had left all the cholera with him.
We were grievously disappointed, however. At noon, a deck passenger from
Tennessee, a boy, was taken and died the next day. On the eighth a
fireman died. On the ninth a deck passenger, and a negro below died. On
the eleventh a deck passenger from Alabama, by name of Leventon, died.
On the twelfth, G.W. Evans, of St. Louis and Ephriam Treadwell, of South-
port, Wisconsin, died.

We found that it was not confined to the boat. Several of the inhabitants, at the obscure hamlets of one or two houses where we stopped to
wood had died of cholera. The town of Kansas was nearly deserted, and no
goods were received at the ware-houses.

The cholera is a rapidly fatal disease, when suffered to run its course
unrestrained; and more easily controlled than most diseases when met in
time. I speak of it as I saw it. It commenced with a diarrhea in every case. A
single dose of laudanum [tincture of opium], with pepper, camphor, musk,
ammonia, peppermint, or other stimulants, usually effected a cure in a few
minutes. If pain in the bowels was present, another dose was required. If
cramp in the calves of the legs had supervened, a larger dose was given. If
the skin had become cold, and covered with sweat, which did not happen
unless the diarrhea had run several hours or days, the doses were frequently
repeated, until warmth was restored. The medicines were aided by friction,
mustard plasters, and other external applications.

If to all these symptoms vomiting was added there was no more to be

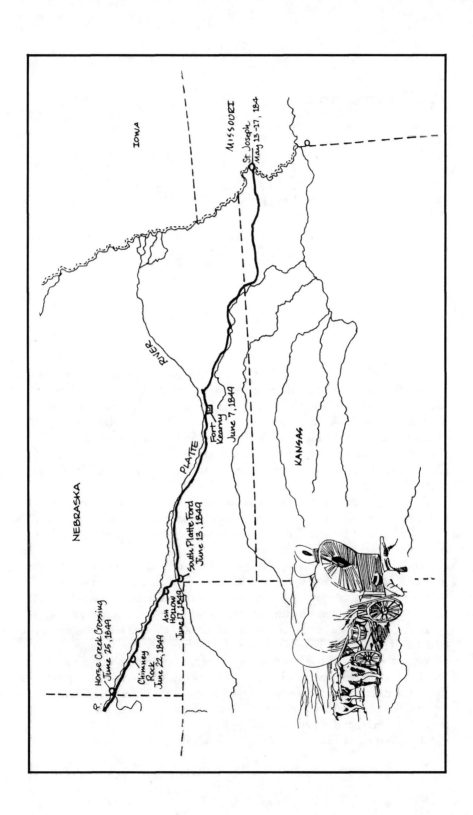

IOWA

MISSOURI

St. Joseph
May 13-17, 184

NEBRASKA

PLATTE RIVER

KANSAS

Fort
Kearny
June 7, 1844

South Platte Ford
June 13, 1844

Ash
Hollow
June 17, 1844

Horse Creek Crossing
June 25, 1844

Chimney
Rock
June 22, 1844

R.

done. Vomiting was the worst symptom, and every case proved fatal where vomiting, purging, cramp, and cold sweaty skin were present. Better put medicine into their pockets than stomachs in such a case. I tried Homeopathic remedies, in all cases where they had taken other medicines previously, and with uniform success. One drop of tincture of camphor every five minutes will restore warmth to the skin more certainly and speedily than a larger dose, or than any medicine we used; and I presume we had on board ten or twelve different medicines, put up and labelled "Cholera Specific."

If cholera with you is like cholera on the Missouri, I have only to say, keep clean. Do not eat too much, take capsicum in the morning and Veratrum [Hellebore Root] in the evening. Homeopathically, carry a vial of tincture of camphor and on the first symptom of diarrhea, cramp, or cold skin, take a drop every few minutes till relieved, and you have only to mind your business, and thank God that cholera is no worse.

MAY 13 – Arrived at St. Joseph at 5 o'clock. Found all my company but [George] Sharp, [Sammy] Ball, [D.] Darling, Whipple and [Ben] Wilson. They came in next day. Saw Mr. [Samuel] Ambrose. Elder Wisner preached twice during the day in the Baptist house, (a log one by the by). In the evening attended at the Presbyterian house, and heard a Methodist minister preach. The house is a large brick one, plainly furnished; the pulpit a little better than the body of the house, or slips; with a porch, and gallery over it for the negroes. A rather small pattern, I should think for the large proportion I saw of that class; but perhaps they are very wicked and wouldn't come if they had room. I presume the folks here understand all about it, as they seem very intelligent and hospitable.

There was a very good attendance at church. Indeed, if I did not know to the contrary, I should deem myself at the center, rather than on the verge of civilization. The people are mostly from the middle and Southern states; open, frank, friendly, and of course easily approached and readily known. The merchants are clever and accommodating. They charge large profits, at least now; but they do it without telling you to go to hell, or any other celebrated place.

The town is pretty well built; that is, the portions last put up. The principal buildings are of brick, and not very well done. I have not seen a good brick wall in town. They need a few good bricklayers here. Mechanics of all kinds would I think find profitable employment. Lumber (pine) is very scarce here, and high. There are two steam saw mills, and three flouring mills in the place. There is plenty of most kinds of timber to saw, except pine. The churches I leave to Brother Wisner [see Wisner letter, Appendix B] to describe. They appear to be in quite a flourishing condition.

I have not yet made up my mind as to the very best way of getting to

Opposite: Map 1. First leg of journey.

California. Some pack mules, others horses. Some drive mules, some oxen, some horses. All kinds of vehicles are en route for California—buggies, carts, boats on wheels, arks, etc. etc. Some wagons are a load for two yoke of oxen. I am certain of one thing, and you may put a mark there—all load too heavy. What can be best left I shall learn hereafter.

I saw some of the Chicagoans on the move at noon for the ferry, six miles above. Among them, I learned the names of Hamilton, Getzler, Kimberley, Mann, Sweet, Churchill, Cook, Elmer, Brewster, Bird, the Haywards, Knight, Grubb, Weisencraft, Dean, etc. etc. All well. Potter and Williams of Warrenville, have been here and returned East. Samuel Ambrose leaves for Council Bluff this afternoon in search of his team. He has heard nothing from it. I have seen many caricatures of gold diggers; and if the future develops such facts as the past, the designers must have been endowed with the gift of prescience.

Imagine to yourself a biped five feet four inches high, with big whiskers, red mustachios, steeple-crowned hat, buckskin coat done up with hedge-hog quills, belt, pistols, hatchet, bullet pouch, bowie knife twenty inches long, red shirt, spurs on left heel eight inches long, with a burr as large as a small sunflower, at least three inches in diameter, mounted on a small four-legged piece of mule flesh of the most obstinate quality, and you have some idea of things that are—for there are many such. It seems to me that the boys take considerable pains to make themselves ridiculous. The most disgusting feature is the hair on the upper lip.

There are plenty of teams in town to sell, as emigrants are constantly returning and selling out. Shall write on and send by every safe conveyance.

ST. JOSEPH, MO., MAY 15, 1849—My last was mailed at St. Louis. In it I said nothing of slavery, which may perhaps excite the wonder of those who are acquainted with me; but really I saw nothing of it, and heard nobody speak of it. Mum's the word, I should think.

In passing up the Missouri, you see extensive sand banks, from one to three or four feet above present water mark, and entirely bare: banks somewhat higher, covered with a thick growth of cottonwood from three to thirty feet high; and banks still higher (perhaps ten to fifteen feet), covered with a heavy growth of timber, mostly cotton wood. The shores are occasionally diversified by a high rocky bluff on one side of the stream; never, I believe, on both at the same time. The bluffs are generally on the left bank in ascending, and sometimes rise 300 or 400 feet. The bed of the river is constantly changing, the banks washing away, and trees by thousands falling into the water every year. They wash nearly perpendicular, and the sand lies in regular strata, with soil generally, but not always, between each layer. One stratum is pure sand, white and nearly three feet thick, and extends the whole distance I have travelled. The flood deposit of 1844 lies irregularly spread upon the surface sometimes twenty inches thick and again only an inch or two.

The towns on the river are miserable, dull, ill-built, unpainted, wretched looking affairs (so far as I had an opportunity of seeing), with the exception of Lexington, Boonville, Weston and St. Joseph.

You are perhaps aware that Independence is several miles from the river; how many I cannot say. Some said three, some five, some eight miles. I reckon the threes have it. By the by, let no man put his trust in maps, or "Traveller's guides." They are born to deceive, and made to sell. When anybody volunteers information, I take it and lay it away, serve all alike and when I get a heap, overhaul the whole, find it worthless, and dump it down. So the world goes.

I believe that they have nearly all the saints in the calendar between St. Louis and St. Joseph, and yet they cannot prevent the most unbounded lying and frauds. You cannot ascertain anything to be depended on, about any place on the river. The river is full of snags, and every few miles we ran on a sand bar. They are of no account in going up as the boat is backed off without difficulty. The water is filled with sand; literally muddy like water running down a sand hill in a heavy shower. When settled it drinks very well with ice in it. Without, it is bad.

MAY 16, 1849—N.B. We leave today at five o'clock and cross tomorrow morning six miles above St. Joseph. I have been up this morning on foot to examine the road and ferry boat. All the boats in this vicinity are worked by men with oars.

ABOVE ST. JOSEPH, MAY 17, 1849—We left St. Joseph yesterday evening at six o'clock and camped four miles above, under the bluff, in the timber. The road to the ferry two and a half miles above us is pretty good, across the bottom land, on the west side at St. Joseph ferry, it is very bad. As a rule, the best road is where the ferry is least used.

Just before we started yesterday a Californian of the Virginia company was shot by a constable in tow. They had a quarrel, passed the lie, and followed it with the revolvers. Neither of them would probably have given the lie, if they had not been well, or rather ill, armed. Most of the Californians make a very ridiculous display of fire-arms and other weapons. From what I have already seen, I should think that there was less need of revolvers here than in Illinois.

Young McClure, of Dundee is in town. Cushing and Wilson of Aurora, are here waiting for their teams. The latter is making money in ferrying across the river, with a small boat—ten cents a passage. He probably takes from two to four dollars a day for his half, the boat taking the other. Rosencrantz is in town. We intend to cross the Missouri, and launch on the broad prairie today.

*SUNDAY, MAY 27, 1849, CAMP, 32 MILES FROM THE ROAD
FROM INDEPENDENCE TO FORT LARAMIE*—I wrote you last from St.
Joseph. We moved off up the river six miles to a new ferry, and crossed on
the 17th, camping three miles west under the bluff. The company from
Chicago lay camped north of us some fifty rods. There are some rattle
snakes here; have seen one lynx. The bottom land here is rich, and covered
with timber south and east of us, but north of us is an extension. The hills
back are high and abrupt.

We lay in camp arranging loads, and ascertaining all our wants, until
the morning of the 22nd when we left for the "far west." While in camp we
learned the value of water-proof coats and pants. The common articles, such
as are usually made, are of but little value. They soon wet through. Perhaps
it might be different elsewhere, but here when it rains, (and that has been
some part of every day so far), *it rains and no mistake*; and such thunder.
Our wagon covers are not perfect. I have not yet determined what would be
better; but ours leak some. More of that when I have more experience.

The men wanted canteens. We also found that we must have more rope
to tie our cattle. Every creature ought to have twenty-four feet of 5-8 rope,
or larger if thought necessary; twelve feet is none too long for a halter.
Every man should have a small watertight match case to hold five or six or
more matches.

The country for the first twenty miles has very recently been covered
with timber, but is nearly destitute now. It is very rough, though there are
no very steep hills on the road, which runs on the dividing ridge between
the waters running north into the great bend of the Missouri, and those
running south into some of its tributaries. In travelling thus far we have
only crossed some five or six streams and those of the smaller kind, having
followed the "divide," as the hoosiers call it, on an excellent road, with no
hills of any consequence. The whole country is very destitute of wood and
water, unless you leave the road.

Every two or three miles is timber in some ravine, on one side of the
road or the other, generally not more than a mile distant, sometimes much
less. When you have travelled as far as you wish, take the first road that
leaves the main one, and it will lead you to timber and water at once.
When you find good drinking water, however, lay in a supply. Fill your canteen, and put a gallon or two, or more, in your water keg. As for a guide,
you need one much more to go to Chicago. Indeed you cannot go amiss, for
every road that turns out comes back again into the main track. Where you
cross streams you find wood.

From sixty to eighty miles from the river we passed over the most beautiful prairie I ever saw; sometimes no timber in sight, and scarcely any elevation worthy the name of hill. We are now camped on a spur of hill, facing
a long range of hills on the south, with a small stream of water at its northern base. The feed has been excellent so far. Millions of cattle might be

pastured within two miles of the road, on our present route, instead of a few thousands. We have plenty to eat – flour, meal, rice, sugar, coffee, bacon, ham, plenty of milk, tea and hard bread.

Our hard bread is admired by all who have examined it. It was made by H.C. Stewart of Chicago, and packed in dry goods boxes. We paid about 3s each for the boxes in Chicago, and sold them in St. Joseph for 4s each. Barrels would not sell at all. The boxes ought to have new hoops put entirely around the ends and well nailed, as they handle them roughly on the steamboats. I saw several barrels of bread broken open. I saved by buying in Chicago 4s per hundred in price, besides the quality.

Today we had gooseberry pie. We have good bread, rice pudding, bread pudding, warm cakes (Indian and wheat), beans, baked and stewed, apples and peaches and make a moderate supply of butter. We put our morning milk into a tin churn, holding two or three gallons, being merely a cylinder, stopped at both ends, and having a hole in the side with a cap cover. A handle on each end finishes the apparatus. We fasten it to the "hind part" of the wagon, and the motion from side to side throws the milk from one end of the churn to the other, making butter in the course of the day. The whole need not be more than two inches across, as the butter gathers in lumps of the size of a walnut, and may be poured from a small hole.

The cholera has made sad havoc with the doctors on the route. Some government men took supper and breakfast with us since we camped. They have been hunting horses back sixty miles or more, and report fifteen of the faculty buried at the different camps. M.D.'s will be scarce in California at this rate. We saw a number of graves by the road side, and at the few camps we visited. I minuted down the names of J.B. Densmore, C.F. Adams, Mo., Coterill, St. Joseph. We passed on the route the Rev. Mr. Stibbs, Capt. Dentz, Howlett, Herr, Cox and Robbins, of Franklin Co., Ohio. Saw George Crocker and two men from Niles, Michigan with pack horses, and met several teams and men returning – some from sickness, but most on account of too heavy loads; I find noted also the graves of E. Spencer, Mich, aged 28, died May 19, and Charles J. Porter, of Lockport, Ill. We have seen several cases of small pox.

The weather has been generally cool; sometimes uncomfortably so. We have found our tents very useful in cold and rain. We sometimes tie the cattle, sometimes leave them loose. We have a night guard for cattle, of two watches; one to twelve thirty, the other to daylight, when the cattle are out; when tied, we have only a camp guard of the same number, three to a watch. The boys like this, as it saves an extra duty as a camp guard.

We have seen Indians but once, and those with the glass, since we left the mission, some twenty five miles from the Missouri. There are Indians, however, through the country, but probably at a considerable distance from the main route. Indeed, I cannot see how they could live here unless a few turkey buzzards, small birds, black birds, crows and lynxes furnish sufficient food. I have seen no fish larger than three inches, except in a small stream seventeen miles back, where was say some bill fish, two feet long. They are not eatable.

Four miles east of the mission we were met by three big Indians who came out of the huts at the base of a hill, and levied black mail. They have a field with a fence partly round it but rotting down. One was a Sac chief. He presented a paper from Col. Vaughan, the government agent I suppose among the Sac and Fox Indians, to the following purport: that the Sac and Fox Indians were kind and peaceable and had not meddled with the whites, and recommended that the emigrants pay them a small amount as compensation for the timber they used in crossing the country. The whole is a gross imposition. The timber used is worth nothing at all to the Indians, being mostly dry wood which would burn the next time the prairies burn over.

We paid $3.00 for twelve wagons—25 cents apiece—and all the timber we used before we came to the encampment would not be worth one farthing one mile from the town of Batavia. The third day's travel, I observed that very little of the timber had leaved out. I did not discover the reason but certainly the timber is fast disappearing, and what the emigrants use can be of no possible use to the Indians.

The more I see of land monopoly, the more indignant I am at the supine carelessness of the masses, in allowing the government to impose upon them such oppressive laws. The "idea" that an old Indian should lay claim to a tract of land as large as all the New England states and levy black mail on all passers is sufficiently absurd; but when it is done by the connivance of the U.S. government, and all the title they have is derived from that source (they, the government, never having the shadow of a title), language becomes useless, and men had better think. I would like to inquire,

1st. Is not all government inherent in the people?

2nd. Has one man any more power to govern than another?

3rd. Can two men, of equal political power and rights, increase that power and those rights by associating together?

4th. Can any individual, or number of individuals, delegate to others, powers which they themselves do not possess?

5th. Had any inhabitant of the United States any title or right to the soil of the territory west of the Missouri unless he occupied it?

6th. Could he give Congress power to do that, or dispose of that, which he had no right or power to do or dispose of himself?

7th. Where is the government or Indian title?

Now, answer these questions honestly and candidly, and I have the same right here as any other man, and no more. What I occupy is mine, while I do so—and no longer.

The earth was the Lord's; he gave to man—not a man, or an Indian—dominion over it, and he who occupies, and he alone, has a real title.

JUNE 2, 1849, CAMP ON PAWNEE RIVER* 100 MILES FROM THE JUNCTION WITH THE INDEPENDENCE ROAD – My last reaches to the 28th ult. That morning we left camp early. By the by, it is necessary to rouse every man as soon as it is light enough to see to work, else we get a late start. By being at work early we are able to make 20 miles a day without hard driving. Our cattle are in good condition, the feed abundant, and weather cool.

About nine o'clock, we found a man by the side of the dry bed of a ravine, four or five feet deep at the crossing, lying on the ground, with a bag of clothes and some bread under his head, and an old bruised tin cup within reach. He had the cholera and was abandoned by his company (from Hannibal) to which he had attached himself. He called himself T.R. Waring from Andrew, Iowa. He wished to go back and had lain two days expecting to get on board some team going east. We have and had met more or less every day. We filled his cup with coffee and left him another cup full of water and some medicine; offered him some clothes to keep him warm, which he said he did not need, and went on our way. We have since heard that he was taken up in three or four hours by a light team, and thence transferred to an ox team and forwarded on his way. We cannot even hope that this will be the last instance of extreme suffering we shall meet with.

We have already passed a considerable number of teams which have not the remotest chance of reaching the mountains by the first of November, even; and those who are thus belated must either remain in the plains, or perish in the mountains, or return before reaching Salt Lake. The great difficulty seems to be too heavy loads. No amount of team will compensate for that. Many are half loaded with chests and boxes alone. This is worse than useless. Every thing which can be put in sacks should be. You want bags of different sizes and lengths for convenience in packing. Many of the wagons look much as though they put in all they could think of, and hung everything else on the outside. No caricature of the print shops can give more than a faint idea of the realities we are every day passing or meeting.

We made one of our best camps at night on a branch, 2½ miles east of the Big Blue to the left of the road. On the east and north high hills, on the west the Big Blue Bottoms covered with timber and on the south, across the Branch (a pretty stream five yards wide) a nearly perpendicular bluff, 100 feet high, backed by high hills and faced with cedar and elm. We drew our wagons in a line across the bend of the stream and made a field of half a dozen acres or more, into which we turned our cattle at night. So far we have camped when the sun was about one and a half or two hours high, let the cattle feed till dark, or as long as they will eat, which will be nine o'clock, if it be pleasant and bright star and moon light and then take them up and tie to trees or stakes, or watch them at large, or do as I have just

*Lord uses the name Pawnee interchangeably with the Big Blue River.

described. It is absolutely necessary to look well after them. Many have lost cattle, and charged the Indians with stealing them. They will steal horses or mules, but seldom working cattle.

The Big Blue is a considerable stream 35 yards wide and takes its name from the appearance of the water in the stream. It is so blue that the reflection of the light above the stream in the morning appeared so much like blue smoke that the men insisted that the Indians were camped along its banks. The color is occasioned by the broken bits of blue limestone which seem to form the bed of the river. The water is clear and excellent for drinking.

The lower ford comes into the wagon boxes some five or six inches, and I ordered the men to raise them by putting blocks of wood under the bolsters, but before they had raised more than three or four we discovered a way dug to the river, some five rods above, by the government train. We drove through and the water just cleared the wagon beds by an inch or so. A couple of teams are now drying their bread by our camp. They wet it in the lower ford of the river. Damaged bread is unwholesome. It is necesary to overhaul all provisions except beans, sugar, salt or bacon, often.

We struck the Independence trail at half past three o'clock on the 29th. The junction is a high elevation, and commands an extensive view of the country. On the 30th we had a tremendous shower of wind and rain for an hour, and it rained some throughout the day. Passed a number of graves as indeed we do every day. One was J. Landon, Oxford, Ohio, aged 23.

Camped on Fox Creek, a contemptible little stream but with beautiful banks and scenery around, with considerable timber. Part of one of the Ottawa companies camped near us. Noticed the grave of Jason Abbott of New Albany, Indiana. Saw four prairie hens yesterday. Up to this time (June 3rd Sunday) we have seen but little game. No Indians except one yesterday morning on the banks of the Pawnee concealed behind a tree, some mile and a half off when discovered, and nearly a mile from the road at the nearest point.

The Pawnee or Blue River has been in sight on our left since we came upon the Independence trail. We have camped on it twice. It is not the one we crossed some twelve miles east of the "junction." It runs through a most beautiful prairie country in an easterly direction, with hills on either side, and extensive bottoms. The hills on the south are mostly smooth, and seldom broken by ravines, presenting a continuous range of green and brown. The northern side is higher, extends farther back from the river, and is broken by ravines. Of these, only Wolf, Fox, Elm, Pool and Sand Creeks had running water in them when we camped. We had to carry water from these streams, or camp on the Pawnee. We found water for the cattle at two or three of the other streams and found scattering trees in most of the large ravines would furnish wood to camp if one were obliged to stop.

There is some timber (cotton wood, elm and ash) on the river. The soil is like that of the whole country from the mouth of the Missouri as far as I have travelled: i.e., sand, sand, sand, of all colors, but still sand, with just clay enough to make a perpendicular bank when the water washes it. We are now camped on a bank of this kind; I just counted the deposits, and find twelve layers; one of which is eight feet thick, of pure white sand. The water is constantly washing these banks away and depositing them on the opposite shore, or carrying them into the Missouri. The hills are many of them washed, bare of soil, and of course, almost destitute of grass, present-ing a brown or parched appearance. I shall send the first opportunity.

JUNE 3RD 1849, ON THE PAWNEE–The country has no other timber than I have described, and so far as the surface is concerned, is very much like Northern Illinois, especially above Elgin, across the state. It can hardly be of use except for grazing. The river bottoms are extensive and dry with good grass, and would raise fine grain, I should think, unless the drought should destroy it. There are very few springs. The rain water settles in pools in some of the ravines, and furnishes a temporary supply for a few wander-ing buffalo, deer, antelopes or perhaps elk.

We have seen hundreds of the horns of the latter by the road side, and our hunters report the bones of six or seven buffalo with some of the meat and skin on the skeletons. They brought in the meat of an antelope day before yesterday. Ball shot it. The meat is better than venison, something like lamb. They are the size of a small deer.

On the evening of the fourth we had a Sergeant U.S.A. in camp. He stayed all night. Had been after a deserter from Fort Kearney. Did not catch him. Had fifty teams in company in the morning, among whom was Mr. Whitney and daughters, from Quincy, Ill. Passed the grave of a negro man, Charles, near which we found a tree on which, among many others, was written, "Beloit Wisconsin Company passed 29th, all well." "John Gilson, Batavia, Ill. 26th." Met a buggy wagon, covered, with an escort. Sent letters to the Western Christian by them. (Probably burnt on the Algoma, as they were never received–Ed Chr.)

Left the river several miles for the highlands on the right. Found a regular Illinois slough, but a beautiful prairie country. No timber. Turned down to the river again, and camped. Water better and river eight yards wide. Excellent grass across the river, where we turned the cattle to.

JUNE 5, left the Pawnee "for good." When leaving it, take in water. No more good water till you get to Fort Kearney. Passed the grave of W. Belcher, Boon Co., Ill. At noon came to a branch of the Pawnee. Take in wood here, no more short of Fort Kearney, though some stinking water in the bed of the stream. Passed another branch, and some very good looking prairie and camped three miles short of the hills on the south of the Platte. Here we found water for the cattle five or six inches deep in some sloughs. The weather is cool and pleasant. Have seen no strawberry vines for sixty miles at least. In a dry season there is no water in this region. The road must have been very heavy here as it is cut into deep ruts. Even here I can see no particular difference between the broad and narrow track wagons. If any, the latter have the preference.

ON THE 6TH—passed the hills, and came in sight of the Platte. The hills are of sand, arid and barren, but may be easily passed with a loaded wagon almost any where. It is where the road crosses, two miles from the prairie to the plains below, which are three or four miles wide on each side of the river. The sight of green timber on the islands of the Platte was cheering. Five or six miles on from the pass, we found very good grass.

An Arkansas train came up from down the Platte while we halted at noon. They reported that seventeen Indians came into their camp last week,—that they gave them something to eat, in return for which the rascals stole two of their oxen at night, and butchered them. They found the scamps cooking the meat and in routing them were fired upon; and in returning the fire, killed five and wounded five; one of their own company being wounded by an arrow. The Indians who could run, now took the hint and "put out," deeming discretion the better part of valor. Two soldiers, just come up, confirmed the above.

About four o'clock a tremendous hail storm swept over us. We had much difficulty to keep the cattle from turning the wagons over. They ought to be taken off before the storm comes. The thunder and lightning were continuous for at least an hour, and the hail stones as large as an ounce bullet, or larger.

Camped between Fort Kearney and the river. Wood very scarce, none but willow brush on this side of the river. The island has plenty of timber, and the channel between it and the fort is not more than twenty-five yards wide, and fordable. The musquitoes are very troublesome, for the third time only on the route.

JUNE 7, Reached Fort Kearney, 260 miles from St. Joseph last night, and the mail goes so early that I was obliged to enclose at once. The fort is elevated, perhaps fifteen feet above the river, about one mile distant. The country is quite level back to the hills, as far east and west as the eye can reach. The ground between the fort and river is low and wet. At the fort, as it is maintained, (for there is neither wall nor picket, nor fortification of any kind), they get very good water only three feet below the surface. The grass is all fed very short and but for having some blacksmithing done, we should have left early.

By the way, if we had no blacksmith we should have to wait a day or two. The government shop was at our service, gratis. The officers and soldiers very polite, gentlemanly, and accommodating. Almost every thing we had done should have been done at home, such as lock chains, rivets, linch pins, cold shuts, nails, (wrought) staples, keys, small staples for mending a broken skein, filing a notch in each side and driving it over, irons for the end of the tongue, etc. etc.

The place is built of turf with two or three exceptions. It was commenced last fall, and the buildings look well considering the material. Some of them are shaved down so true and smooth as to look really well. The largest are perhaps twenty five or thirty feet wide, and seventy or eighty long—and there may be twenty in all. One frame building is now nearly completed, and a great number more will be erected this season. They have a steam saw mill in operation and are making large quantities of brick. The soldiers have extra wages if they choose to work, which most do. There are a great many tents pitched about, and altogether it is quite a busy place. They have one store filled with goods, and they were just receiving a large supply by land from the Missouri.

Vegetation is backward. The gardens have been planted three or four times and the seed has mostly rotted. Potatoes were two inches high, and peas in full bloom, five inches. Rope sells for 4s. a pound, salt ten cents, four quart pans fifty cts.; cheapest suspenders, four to six shillings; etc. etc. The weather has been so cold till the last three days, as to require overcoats in the middle of the day. Take wood and water from Kearney for two days. You will find plenty of water for cattle almost anywhere. The river is full of islands, sometimes covered with wood.

ON THE 8TH JUNE, camped on Mobile Creek where there are some large cottonwood trees and good water. This creek is 34 miles from the fort, grass short all the way. Today the brown line of hills has changed to an almost unbroken range of beautiful green, only a mile or two at most from the river. Went on to the hills and found it a boundless rolling prairie. Saw the first prairie dogs here, a very large village, some 200 or 300 acres. They are a small animal and quite shy. The earth dug from each of their holes is heaped around its mouth, and prevents the water from running down. Their bark resembles that of a prairie wolf, and they kept it up nearly all night.

Our cattle have been lame with cracks in the hoof. Cure it with hot tar, and drawing a tarred string through the slit. One ox cracked the hoof nearly through to the bottom an inch and a half from the point, cut it off with a bowie knife and hammer, which cured the lameness entirely. Took wood and water from here.

After leaving the camp, on the 9th, the boys amused themselves shooting at prairie dogs. The hills here appeared near the river, and are more abrupt, broken by ravines, and almost destitute of grass. Watered our cattle at noon at a small channel, forming an island, where are a few small cottonwoods. Weather cool. Broke a chain hook; ought to have extra hooks. This afternoon, ground almost marshy. Saw a Buffalo, twenty or thirty antelopes and several mallard ducks. No timber since noon. Hills gradually receding, more barren, and getting tumbled into heaps, and cut by ravines, with here and there a solitary tree of a small size. Weather so cold that a great coat feels comfortable.

JUNE 10, 1849, SUNDAY. Had to break camp and go a few miles for water. Found a good spring on the right of the road, thirty miles from Mobile Creek. Took in water, and camped one and a half miles beyond, near the hills on the left. No wood, except a few straggling trees in the ravines at some distance. The road is on much higher ground today. Hills more broken and barren.

Passed the grave of J.J. Hardy, Winchester, Ill., age 33. Have passed a great many graves, and seen any quantity of clothing, bedding, wagon tire, old iron, etc. thrown by the road side. The cholera is only a few days ahead of us, and the clothes of all who die seem to be thrown away. Wood should be taken in at the fort, and Mobile Creek, as you can get nothing but green cotton-wood elsewhere unless you go two to four miles out of the way. Went on to the hills.

It is impossible to give an adequate idea of the scene which presents itself from the highest summits. The whole country is cut into all manner of uncouth, fantastic shapes, without regard to form, regularity, or beauty, though there is certainly variety enough. Peaks of sand, 300 or 400 feet high, with steep sloping sides, sometimes cut into terraces — ravines with sides fifty to 150 feet perpendicular, extending up into the range for miles, with a narrow bottom, smooth and green like a well-mowed lawn, and easy enough for a carriage road, these are the most striking and interesting features. Had a tremendous thunder storm with hail in the evening.

JUNE 11—MONDAY MORNING. Broke up camp and in two miles over muddy road, came to some large cotton-woods on a low bottom. Cool and pleasant. Saw several varieties of cactus, or prickly pear; one shaped like a pin-cushion, and from the size of a cent to that of a coffee cup, composed of little cylinders from an eighth to three-eighths of an inch in diameter, and bearing a brilliant red flower; another of the same species, or variety, had a straw colored flower, which looked like satin. There were several other colors and shades of color.

At four o'clock this afternoon, the plain has an elevation of forty to sixty feet. If you want wood, camp near the hills, follow up the ravines and you will find plenty of dry oak and cedar. Camped after passing a deep ravine on the west side of a second one, where are some large cotton-wood trees and two good springs just below the crossing. Grass very short today. Passed Cedar Creek without knowing it.

JUNE 12–TUESDAY. In two miles crossed Pako Creek which comes inland eight or ten miles through the most broken, tumbled up country I ever saw. It drains half a hundred square miles, and yet I dare say has not a drop of water, except from rain and melting snow. Many of the hills seem composed mostly of marl lime, and are some of them white as snow, and like an ash heap to tread upon.

Camped at four o'clock on the right of the road, and almost before we were ready on came another thunder gust with hail. Had to use Buffalo chips for lack of wood, not taking it in at the last camp, as we supposed Pako Creek must be some twelve miles ahead. The chips make a first rate fire when dry. The hills are gradually falling off towards the south fork of Platte, and the Plain is about two miles wide here.

General directions: After leaving the Pawnee the second time and before leaving it finally, take in wood and water for two days, and make it a rule ever after to have, if possible, two days' wood and water on hand. It is impossible to know, from any map or guide, or even person I have yet seen, where to get wood and water, or anything else, between Fort Kearney and the South Fork. The difficulty seems to be the impossibility of describing that which is constantly liable to change.

For instance, one traveller finds wood and water in a ravine. The next finds the wood cut down, and the water sunken in the sand. The first marks it as a creek, the other passes it without note or comment, and marks the very next as a creek, where the first found no water; and yet one might have been but a month, a week, a day, or a single hour behind the others. That time is sufficient here to change a dry ravine into a creek. These dry ravines are very numerous, and so difficult to distinguish that I got several miles ahead of my reckoning in two days, notwithstanding the most careful attention to a map I have heretofore found entirely accurate.

I will add further, that when you come to where the plain is not more than a mile wide, forty or fifty feet above the river, very beautiful, a marshy bottom between it and the river, covered with timber, a deep ravine across the road, with trees on the right, you will go on one mile, cross another without timber, and in three-fourths of a mile find wood and springs, the timber mostly cottonwood, and extending to the hills on the left. The springs are at the right, below the crossing. You soon cross another ravine and leave wood till you get two days beyond the Platte Ford.

WEDNESDAY, JUNE 13, 1849. Left camp late and reached the ford of the south fork at 5 p.m. The road was generally good, crossing the long spurs of the hills as they gradually descend to the north and west. Two miles of bottom before reaching the ford was wet from the recent rains. The ford is a very good one considering the width of the river—half a mile or more. The water did not come into the boxes of high wagons. Low wheels dipped a little. To guard against accident we raised our boxes two to six inches.

Had a fair chance to see a buffalo this morning. As we raised the long low spur of one of the hills which fill with a gentle slope towards the river, we discovered some three miles off. Three dim, dark looking objects moving down the river's bank. My glass showed at once that we were looking at 2 horsemen in full chase of a Buffalo bull. In a moment all was excitement. Sixty wagons were in full view, and when the word, Buffalo! was passed, the men seized their guns and started hot footed for the scene of action, or for some more elevated ground to get a better sight, leaving scarcely enough to keep the teams in the road.

It may not interest your regular prairie hunter reader to hear of a chase after a single Buffalo, but to us at least it was eminently exciting. There we stood, more than 200 men, along those low hill slopes; before us a plain two to four miles wide, bounded by a broad ribbon of water stretching east and west thirty miles and shining like burnished silver in the morning sun; beyond, a long strife of green backed by high, brown hills.

The Buffalo seems only a black speck slowly moving toward the river, and the horsemen mites trying to intercept him. On, on, he goes, gradually increasing his pace, and faster the miles skim along after. There he turns; the miles are on his flank. And now he comes. How black he seems. Harder and closer they press him, and now he turns directly back and towards us. Hurrah! Hurrah! On, on he rushes. See one of the horses plunges into a ravine. Horseman and horse, gun and pistol all roll over and over in the splashing water. The horse is out, and the rider—yes he is out too—and the Buffalo—goes through above. Splash! Splash! Splash! and away he goes again. We shall lose him. No; there he meets the mounted man. Hark! No report but the rolling smoke tells us a sure tale. He turns, he turns. Hurrah! Hurrah! he comes, he comes—and wounded too, see how he limps—and on, and on he rolls his heavy bulk along, pressed closely by the panting horse and his excited rider. Now he turns and glares on his pursuer. Now he comes madly on, dashing and splashing through the water courses. And how he turns again. He hesitates. Will he rush upon the horse? No, no. See the smoke—crack—hurrah 'tis a noble fellow. Now for him boys! And down rushed the crowd, a crooked wavy line of moving rifles.

Van Wormer on the pony and "our Ben" [Wilson] on his own legs take the lead. Ben got in first ranging along side of the animal a few feet distant, as he rushed for the hills.

Next comes Van with the pony and gives him one—two—three deady shots—after two or three more from various hands he went down within a quarter of a mile of our train.

I was not in at the death, but stood by him before he ceased to quiver. He was a noble and withal a wicked looking beast, though he had very little more hair than an elephant except on his head and neck.

In an hour the place was left desolate. Nothing left that a man could eat. We had a "hind quarter," some ribs, the liver and part of the skin. Before he was dressed another one came across the river and in less than ten minutes twenty men were in full chase. After all had gone and the last was at least half a mile off, Van Wormer seized his rifle, and without a saddle or bridle, hat or coat, mounted the pony and was off like a bomb shell.

Away! Away! Go it Van! See how he gains on them all. There he comes up—he passes—and then he goes over the hill.

Listen—Crack! That's Van's rifle and the Buffalo bites the dust. We had meat enough so he was left to the next passers. We have seen several today. They say that more than 300 were feeding about the ford this morning, early. Camped three miles from the ford. No wood. Some musquitoes. Very cold this afternoon.

THURSDAY, JUNE 14. Left camp before breakfast. Saw a Buffalo a mile off on our right. Travelled six or seven miles and found some willow bushes on the Islands in the river. Very scarce. Took breakfast. About two miles farther on crossed the hills over to the other or north Platte. Hills not very bad. Made ten miles after halting at noon and camped three or four miles above where the bluff comes down the river, on this side. Sixty wagons camped in sight. Feed short. No wood. Very cool. Lost several whip lashes yesterday, some in the river. Ought to be several lashes to each wagon and whip sticks should be brought from home. None can be found west of the Missouri River thus far. We need a bellows very much. Passed a village of Prairie dogs in the morning.

FRIDAY, JUNE 15. Took the first left hand road up the hill and gained a mile and more of those who camped beyond. Ascended the hills and found a heavy rolling prairie and very good grass and water. The last only immediately after rains. Probably there is plenty now. In the afternoon again descended to the north fork, by a tolerable road. Made about 15 miles and camped. Road on the hills much cut up.

One mile south east of our camp is a tent made of hides. It stands very prettily and is well shaped, round, pointed and very high. The boys have been there and report five dead Indians lying in the tent, covered by a bed quilt and Buffalo skins. They have moccasins on. There is no smell from them. A dead horse and colt lay there and the remains of a buffalo. There were also eleven dogs, one of which had a kind of harness on him. Very cold. I was on guard last night.

SATURDAY, JUNE 16. Left camp. Travelled over long low spurs, sloping toward and to the river—rough hills, ravines with sandy beds, in which streams of water rush to the river when it rains—and level plains a mile or two in width, sometimes answering for the channel of a river. At 3 p.m. came to some large cedars and a few ash trees—just past a deep rocky ravine. This is the first wood we have found since we left Pako Creek beyond the ford.

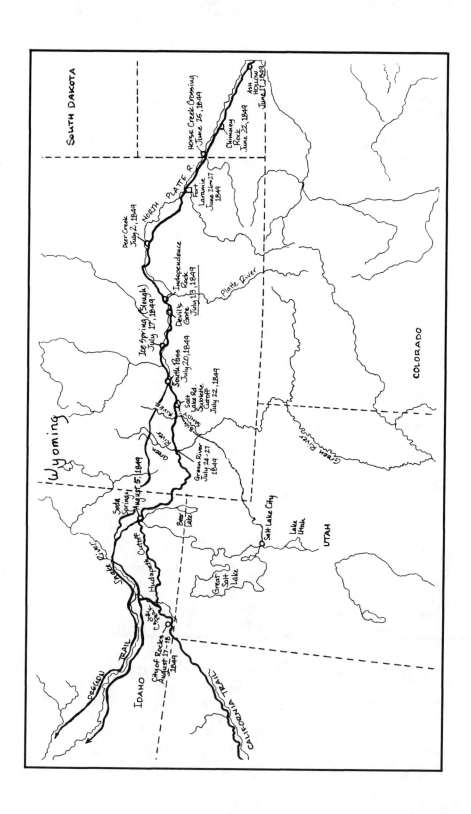

Took in wood. A mile beyond found springs on the left under the bluff. Took in water and passed on, and camped in a broad deep and rocky ravine. Feed very short today.

Cattle look gaunt. Plenty of good cedar on the hill sides among the rocks. This ravine is forty or fifty rods wide for a considerable distance up. Find today that the hill sides were covered with flowers, being almost the first we have seen that made any show. Passed several graves today, as usual. The Elgin Company are two days ahead. I notice that most of those who die are under 33 and over 60. Most from Missouri, next Indiana, next Kentucky, etc. etc.

SUNDAY, JUNE 17. Left camp before sunrise and went directly up the hills to the left. The worst hills this side of the Missouri. Descended into the ravine of Ash Creek. It is broad and rocky. Perpendicular lime stone bluffs on each side was by the water and excavated by frost into nobs and caves. There are cedars stuck into the bluffs and several hundred ash trees, low and scrubby with trunks of considerable size.

Some water still runs in the broad, level, gravelly bed of the ravine, but all disappears in the sand and rock far short of the river. Drove out of the ravine and, turning up the river a mile, stopped for breakfast and to feed the cattle.

The bluff here is rock nearly perpendicular with the narrow plain between it and the river, and very little feed for cattle. The head of a "ring bolt" came off yesterday and put in a new one in a few minutes. A spare ring bolt saves a wagon. Road continues under the bluff which here is rather regularly every quarter of a mile crossed by ravines. The hills seem 200 or 300 feet high and most of them have more or less cedar on the sides and at the edge of the summit, which is crowned by a broad table of lime stone usually projecting like a cornice over the wall of sand stone or clay underlying it.

Some of them appear to be limestone from the base. There is generally a mass of earth and rock with a scanty growth of grass sloping from mid-height to the plain. In the clay beneath the tables of limestone (for there are commonly three or four layers with a thick stratum of clay or soft sand stone between) the swallows have innumerable nests. The holes through which they reach them make the face of the bluff for yards square appear like a honey comb. Some of these bluffs are singularly beautiful.

The stone caps projecting over and forming a heavy cornice, the upper layers being thick, perhaps ten or twenty feet and rather compact, resisting the action of the elements, while those beneath, less dense, have wasted much more. One rock which I named the "Bastion" may be seen more than two miles. It has the appearance of a round lower at the angle of a high wall

Opposite: Map 2. Second leg of journey.

though its summit is even, or nearly so, with the top of the wall. The wall itself extends eastward quite a distance, terminating abruptly as though cut down to its base by a sharp instrument, the section as you approach directly from the south east presenting the figure of an acute pyramid.

East of it and doubtless once forming a part of the same range is a very regular pyramid, presenting rather the form of an eight-square tent, rather loosely put up. I ascended to its summit but could not stand there, the wind blew so strongly. It is composed of clay with a very little sand and at the extreme point is about three yards long east and west by one foot wide, giving a rather precarious foot in a windy day. It may be 200 feet high, perhaps more. Pushed on nine miles to a spring of good water and camped two miles beyond where we found good grass, on low wet bottom land.

For several nights we have had no dew and no rain since I last reported it. Trappers say that the grass this year is much better than usual. If so, from Fort Kearney here, another as large emigration can hardly subsist. A part will have to cross the Platte there. There is an abundance of good grass on the north side of the Platte, and just across from here we can see the green meadows but cannot cross to them. The water is not more than three and a half feet deep at the most, but the sand is too loose and constantly shifting. If there was only a ferry at Fort Kearney so that a part of the emigrants could go up the north side it would help the matter wonderfully.

Within ten miles there are no less than 150 wagons on this side the river and fifty or sixty on the other. About 400 teams have passed up, and at least 500 more are on the way from Council Bluff, making about 1,000 in all on the north side. Add these to the 500 which have and will pass Fort Kearney, this season and we have a total of 6,000 wagons, or at least 21,000 emigrants, "en route" for California by the South Pass.

Give one half the amount for all other routes and we have a grand total of 31,000 in all, overland to California and Oregon.

This is the common estimate. I think it too high by some thousands. Both yesterday and the day before two men forded the river on foot. They report that the company ahead of theirs have lost fourteen head of cattle by the Indians, and that a man by the name of Rowe from Plattville, I think, Wisconsin, was killed. He was alone and on foot when the Indians met and attempted to rob him. But he wouldn't be robbed no how and so they shot him. We have seen no Indians since the dead ones. Today two skeins broke in one wagon. There should be extra skeins with every wagon.

Since we came into the Buffalo country we see comparatively few elks though Buffalo's skulls lie scattered in profusion all over the country, white as marble. Today I saw at the foot of a perpendicular bluff six skeletons entire, bleached white and piled promiscuously in a heap, as though they had tumbled off together. We frequently see half eaten corpses by the road side. One lay in the road at "Ash Creek" this morning. Had evidently lain several days and yet had very little smell.

MONDAY, JUNE 18TH. S. Hawley sick this morning and all night. Has diarrhea—Cholera. The men are busy, washing, making boots for the cattle, etc. etc. Mended the two broken wagon skeins by filing a notch in each side and driving a staple over. Each wagon should have staples of different sizes. We also shall need more tacks. In the afternoon a trader and hunter came into camp. Gave him some dinner.

He said he had not eaten bread before in four months. Had had nothing but coffee, sugar, and Buffalo since he came out.

He says that he eats it raw for his breakfast. Lives now with the Sioux warriors. Has three wagons and four men left. Sent five loads of Buffalo and otter skins down to St. Louis last month. Seventy miles S. east and only a few miles south of our route 800 Sioux warriors camp and are hunting.

He pays for a prime Buffalo Robe, two pints of coffee and one pint of sugar or two plugs of tobacco. Original cost at St. Louis, twelve cents. The Indians are peaceable and charge nothing for being so. The cupidity of the traders serves us much better than the tame subserviency of the government officials. They say to the Indians, "If you trade with the emigrants we leave your country and you get no more coffee or tobacco." "They will give you the cholera, too." Of course we never see an Indian unless in company with a trader.

Eighty three teams passed us before 3 p.m. and twenty after before we broke camp. In the afternoon went south on to the hills. Shot a wolf and a skunk. Saw neither Buffalo or Deer. Country very rough. Some good prairie in patches. Lay all day in Camp. Saw several wolves in vicinity of the camp.

On the hill the wind blew almost a gale and had a small shower in camp. Strong wind for several days.

TUESDAY, JUNE 19. Wind died away about midnight and then the musquitos became very troublesome. Shot a wolf about twenty rods from camp.

Cloudy and lowering at day light but cleared off at sunrise. No dew and warm. Left camp and travelled over a heavy sandy road, broken by ravines and the sandy beds of dry creeks. The hills have been washed into all manner of shapes. Sand is very deep. No good. Those marked as such on my map are unfit for use. Musquitoes very troublesome all day.

Occasionally a few cedar trees appear on the bluffs at a distance where wood if needed may be obtained.

Towards night road was better, hills fall off lower—finally came to a creek with a broad sand bed and a fine stream of water running down it. A large tree stands on the west bank half a mile south of the road and seven others half a mile above that. There was a smart shower in the afternoon and probably most of the water is from that. Just over the hill south there is a bottom several miles long and quite wide. Rained in the night.

JUNE 20TH. Cloudy and plenty of musquitoes; but cleared off cool with some wind. The prevailing wind since we reached the Platte has been south east. Left camp and travelled over a low spur of the hills two or three miles, some of the way through deep sand or gravel. Passed several ravines, one with a rocky bed of considerable width. A great many fine looking trees stand in sight on the left, among the hills, apparently eight or ten miles distant. No wood near the road.

For several days have seen wagon tires, hubs, boxes, old irons, etc. scattered along the road. Had a shower at two o'clock, p.m. The country where we were at noon was very handsome, and the hills, which are at a considerable distance from the river, seem green and smooth like a rolling prairie. The river plain lies in gentle swells. On the other side, two or three miles distant, are rocky bluffs. At 5 o'clock came to a stream, the Ninewa, six yards wide and 16 inches deep, very good looking water. Scattering trees, probably cedar, in great numbers, are spread over the green hills, and stuck against the rocky bluffs, some miles off at the left. Passed the creek, crossed a spring brook, and soon after a spring, in two miles, and camped a mile beyond. A beautiful prospect. High rolling prairie, and high hills on the opposite side of the river, which runs smoothly and quietly along, without a tree, or rock, or island to impede its course. The prospect up and down the river is boundless.

There is a spring of good water a few rods south east. Every two or three wagons should have a tin funnel, and a bushel basket. Ants, of almost every color and description, and lizards in any quantity, abound on the route. The lizard is about three and a half inches long, silver grey, occasionally yellow, or orange, where the soil is red, and has fine, sharp, shining scales. They move about very swiftly and we sometimes see a dozen at once.

JUNE 21, 1849. THURSDAY. Left camp early. For two or three miles the road was a little broken, and deep sand in portions of it. Passed three graves on a little hill at the left. One was Samuel P. Judson, aged 49. Died June 15th 1849. N.G. Phillips, aged 32, 17th and Ellis Russel, aged 53, 14th, all from Elkhart County, Indiana – Bristol Company.

Here first saw a dome-like hill, on the left and ahead some distance, and very soon after, Chimney Rock came into sight. Its tall spire pointing to the sky, looks in the clouds of dust at a distance, like a pillar of smoke. Beyond this, and a little to the right, is a large conical shaped hill of a yellowish grey color. From this point I see several ponds of pure looking water on the right, and one on the left.

Two or three miles farther on, the river bottom sweeps round to the south, and makes a wide opening. Through this depression runs Quicksand Creek, a shallow stream, several yards wide. This and the Ninewa are probably the only streams which have durable water after we leave Ash Creek. There are doubtless other springs than I have mentioned, but not easily found. We have taken in water at every good spring.

Halted at noon opposite the Court House, as the dome-like rock is called, which stands behind a low range of hills in the bottom of Quicksand Creek, some four or five miles from the road, but apparently but two. It seemed to be isolated, lying between the range I have just spoken of, and a long, high, broken range some miles farther back. This back range keeps distinct and distant from the river range and presents a face and summit covered and crowned with cedar and pine, or fir, through its whole extent, which may be fifty miles. The rock from the road looks very much like a court house, with a low dome on the centre, and two wings. Its sides are irregular in reality, but appear smooth and round.

Beyond the Court House the road passes over a rolling prairie, with some sand, not deep. Chimney Rock rises into view as we advance, and occasionally we get a glimpse of its base, which seems a slightly irregular pyramid. The upright part appears very much like the tall chimneys of some steam propelled manufactory. Four miles this side, as we were descending the hills into the plain in which is the chimney, an express overtook the train, asking my services for a young man accidently shot, in a train from Jackson Co., Mo. Rode back nine miles, and found him dead. He was shot through the chest. Tarried for the night and was roused up to visit a patient in a train 40 or 50 rods off. Found three cases of cholera, one past cure, the others will get well. All were taken just before sun down.

Left at sunrise, the 22nd for camp; the Court House on the left, and the morning sun shining brightly on Chimney Rock, Castle Rock, the high bluffs beyond, the silver riband in the broad green plain below, and the distant hills on the opposite shore. Nothing short of the pencil of another Banvard [Joseph Banvard, Baptist clergyman and history writer, 1810–1887] can give even a faint idea of the extreme delicacy, beauty, and romantic gorgeousness of the scene. In the distance, twenty-five miles to the right, rolled up the gigantic form of Scott's Bluff, towering in marble whiteness toward heaven, and without an effort of fancy, indeed despite of reason, presenting the outline and filling up of two contiguous cities, of miles in extent. Long ranges of buildings, of vast height, and uniform architecture, seemingly interminable, dome and spire, and tower, and wall, and battlement, and cedar trees scattered over the whole like living moving men, might well deceive himself in the vicinity of civilized man.

The whole range of river hills, from the Court House to Scott's Bluff, are cut down and worn by the elements into almost every shape that clay and sand can be conceived to assume under such circumstances. There seems to be first, at the base, clay, sand and marl, light yellow; next a layer of white lime stone, several feet thick and vitrified; next, clay, sand and marl, the first predominant, whitish and compact. Then loose blue or gray lime stone. Then a bluish grey clay, or sand stone, quite compact, and splitting or peeling off in perpendicular plates, or masses, while the lower layers split horizontally. The upper portion, or that which appears on the summit of every cliff and hill that has not been washed down, is arranged in regular strata, each of different thickness, and shades of difference in color.

The whole of the perpendicular part of Chimney Rock is composed of this gray mass, and is two sevenths of the whole height from the base of the flat cone on which it is elevated. The best idea that I can give of its appearance, four or five miles off, is either a glass funnel inverted or a huge gourd cut across, leaving one third on the stem, (which is slightly indented where it joins the body) and set down with the stem up. This is rather a descent, but still it is nearer the truth than any other comparison I can think of. For the rest (i.e.) except the form, nothing of the kind anywhere on this route can touch it; and as regards the whole scenery, the liveliest imagination would be sobered directly in looking over these freaks of nature. They are fancy tamers. If all had read Stephens' [John Lloyd Stephens, 1805–1852, *Incidents of Travel in Central America, Chiapas & Yucatan*] travels in Yucatan, I might yet reach the idea. His plates of those ancient ruins, the works of man, have here on every side their "facsimiles," but in form, size, locality, variety and perfection of architecture, these bear away the palm. (I speak of a distant view.) Still the likeness is so striking, the resemblance generally so close, that even a careless observer could hardly fail to recognize it on the instant. These are, however, anything but ruins. Most of them appear to have been finished but a day or two, and some are yet unfinished.

Came into camp just as the cattle were being hitched on. It was on the right side, toward the river, at the point of the hill where it breaks down on the plain from which rises Chimney Rock. North of the camp are several excellent springs. Filled our kegs. Chimney Rock stands in full view, apparently one and a half miles distant, but in reality four or more. Let the traveller not deceive himself in matters of distance or height, here. If he does his legs will pay the penalty. Hunting after curiosities, here, is like chasing. The farther you go the less likely you seem to catch them.

Went to the rock, and ascended to the base of the tower or perpendicular part. The last twenty feet of the ascent is rather difficult, and but few of the many who go up reach that point. There are perhaps a hundred names inscribed here, while thousands have left their autographs below.

The road is excellent from our last camp to Scotts' bluff, a distance of perhaps twenty miles or more. We camped four miles south east, turning off the road soon after surmounting the hill and going nearly to the river on the right. Here we found good feed. The grass has been very good for several days past, till four o'clock this afternoon, when it began to be short, probably owing to the emigrants' trains stopping here to "rest and look."

Beyond Chimney Rock is the grave of Dr. Macbeth of Buffalo. One of the boys brought in an ivory brush, and tooth pick, with three points which evidently belonged to him. The plain today has been several miles in width, and almost entirely level. Halted at noon nearly opposite Castle Rock and paid it a visit. Its summit is difficult of access. Its sides are perpendicular half way from base to battlement. Its form is an oblong square 40 or 50 rods wide, and perhaps 80 to 100 long. It is surmounted by three dome-like eminences, connected at the base, the eastern being the smallest, the west, the largest and highest.

South of it are several similar "structures," one a very regular like elevation, with perpendicular sides of the same height of the others, and covering 50 or a hundred acres of ground. Another is a regular, level platform half a mile long. On the north at the base we found the cactus growing luxuriantly and in full bloom, the flowers being straw and pink colored, and as large as hollyhocks. Sometimes there were fifty flowers in one bed. Cool in the night and uncomfortably so in the morning. No dew except in low grounds.

SUNDAY, JUNE 24. Made three miles and camped on the east side of Little Creek where was a pool of water.

Chapter Two
June 25–August 1, 1849:
Wyoming

———◆——◆——◆———

MONDAY, JUNE 25. It is better to cross Horse Creek here and go up it one mile on the west side for a camp. Little Creek is a bad crossing. We made it good with a few bundles of juniper brush and a few minutes work with six spades. Horse Creek is a pretty stream of grey good water, shallow and thirty yards wide.

There are some living trees at its mouth, and limbs, roots, trunks and fragments of dead ones are scattered along the bottom of the road or buried in the alluvion.

Indeed this whole country seems to have once been a high smooth level plain up to the river on either side and covered with pine, fir, cedar, etc. It has been blown by the wind, torn by frosts, and washed by water into its present form.

All the broad valleys seem to have these different woods buried in them or lying on the surface. The destructive process is still going on and may be seen on any of the hills where there is a comparative level. The surface is first broken. The wind then drifts out some of the sand. The water runs in and washes it down, and again the wind seizes and whirls it away. When the water gets a fall of five or six feet the process must be carried on with astonishing rapidity.

They have storms here which will pass for the second edition of Noah's flood, and if the water does not find an outlet from the basin where it accumulates, through the limestone below, it will fill the basin to the depth of ten or a hundred or two feet and breaking over the rim sweep away acres and miles of soil—making little account of lime stone, loose sand, or slacked lime or clay.

I saw on one high level summit with nearly perpendicular sides a basin 300 feet in diameter and fifty feet deep, with no outlet unless a filter in the bottom through the rock. It was no doubt blown out by the wind and it would not take long at the rate it rolled out while I stood beside it.

A single year and the curious traveller may enquire of himself while looking at the place, "how many hundred years did it take to wash out that ravine 200 feet deep," and the trees that now adorn the hill side will be crushed and buried beneath the rushing mass to be exhumed by a slower but equally sure process.

The lighter particles are swept into the Platte by wind and water whirled down into the Missouri and rolled into and down the Mississippi into the Gulf. We have already passed washings enough to make such a state as Louisiana if its bottom was reasonably removed from earth's center.

Horse Creek is about 25 miles from Scott's Bluff, and so excellent is the road that an ox team can easily make it in a day. From the creek the road ascends gradually over rolling land some six miles and then falls off to a spring four miles. A long range of bluffs lie stretched and toward the south 15 or 20 miles. There is the river with a narrow bottom on the right bank and barren sand hills on the left. One mass of them is entirely destitute of grass. This is rather scarce here, unless in the valley to the south.

Before rising the last hill, came to some masses of granite. The spring here is very large. Took a supply of water and halted a little beyond at noon as usual.

Four miles beyond the spring the hills approach the river and the road runs along the bank at the base of some barren hills of clay, sand, gravel and sandstone. Cotton wood trees plenty on the Island, and flood wood in the river in abundance. Four miles beyond we camped in a broad plain. Feed poor. Very cold night after a very hot day but it makes the musquitos budge, and no matter where they go so that they don't come back.

The plain around our camp is level and very handsome and hills around low. Abundance of small cotton woods on the islands in the river and some kind of trees scattered over the high hills ahead and on the opposite side.

Some of the boys brought in an antelope.

TUESDAY, JUNE 26. Left camp, and in three miles came to the river, watered the cattle and immediately turned off among the hills which are not steep. Road good. The highest peak of the Black Hills was in sight as we descended a mountain gorge on the 23rd and seems no nearer yet. Passed over the hills a mile or two and came upon a plain where the road is like a pavement for several miles. Bluff in full view ahead on the left.

Halted at noon just past the point of the first bluff with a fair view of a mountain gorge which extends south west between the several ranges. The grass is good, better than any for the last twenty miles. Two miles farther the road strikes the river bank again and the scenery is precisely like that when we came to it last before, the road however is better.

Passing over the "flat" the road turns to the left and two miles travel up and down hill brings us in sight of "Laramie Fork" or river where we now are. Found the Buffalo Company here breaking up and part of them going back. The river bottom is here narrow and broken, the ford very good, but six inches too deep for a common wagon. Raised our boxes and went over dry. One wagon which had a double reach, uncoupled in the deepest part. It took two hours to get it out. Nothing wet. All this for lack of a key in the bolt. The Platte comes down from the west through a high range of barren black looking hills. On the north side is a large fine bottom land on which a number of wagons are waiting to be ferried over. They came from Council Bluff on the north side and have come to the end of the road.

There has been a scattering of provisions here. Flour has sold for 1.50 per cwt. Bacon, no sale. Wagons 2.50 to 6.00 and other things in proportion. Large and heavy wagons have been broken up and sold for firewood or burned and small and light ones bought. The big loads have exchanged for little ones and the little ones to pack mules.

The surplus goes overboard, and such a scattering. We are camped a half a mile north of the new fort, but no one has yet been up as it was late and rained when we got in. The old fort is a high square mud wall and a mile or more north. Is now abandoned. Sent letters home and journal to W. Christian.

FORT LARAMIE, JUNE 27, 1849. Remained in camp till late, for the boys to mail letters and get the horse shod. The road passed directly by the fort, which is quadrangular, its sides 150 to 180 feet with square towers at three of the angles, and a large square building at the north east corner. There is a gate in the centre of the south wall with a square wooden tower over it, and a door in the north wall, opening into a passage under a building, used as a store and dwelling house. The walls are from sixteen to 22 feet high, built of sun-dried brick, which are from four to six inches thick. On the west is a range of rooms along the wall, and a like line of workshops on the south.

On the east there seems to be two suites of rooms, the whole leaving a large open court in the centre of the quadrangle. This is paved with gravel. There is a company of U.S. soldiers camped opposite the fort, and the officers are now negotiating the purchase of the whole concern for the government. It will probably belong to us in a day or two. The whole country around is strewed with wagon irons, bacon, boards, old clothes, leather straps, bits of harness and fragments of every portion of an outfit.

After leaving the fort, soon began to ascend the hills by an easy road, along a high rolling prairie. The grass is thin, and very short, or occasionally tall, course and mixed with weeds, cactus, etc. Every green thing seemed withered and dying, and the ground is covered with grasshoppers and a large, fat, reddish brown cricket, which devours like the drought itself.

From the highest point, I had a splendid view of the whole country. On the north runs the Platte, with a range of black hills beyond, sparsely covered with evergreens. On the east and south the Laramie, with its green hills stretching broadly on into a great rolling prairie, lost in the distance. On the west is a broad valley, with low hills gradually rising in the distance, till the eye meets the Black Hills, scarcely yet distinguished from a dark blue cloud, and the passage of the Platte through one of its spurs, all of which are covered with evergreens.

Halted at noon half a mile to the left of the road, in a valley where was grass but no water. Three miles ahead are some hills like those just described; and on the right some sandstone bluffs. Passed up the hill and over into a deep rocky ravine, where was a spring of warm water in the west bank, half a mile below the road at the right. Considerable water runs through it at certain seasons. Grave of Dr. McDermott (Fairfield Iowa, aged 28) on the right, as you go to the spring. His own sign was nailed to the head stone. There is plenty of cedar and pine, or fir, for fire-wood here. Turned to the left, up the ravine three fourths of a mile, and then to the right up a branch and steep rocky hill. On the hill, at the right, is the grave of A. Hammond, Winchester, Ill., aged 36.

Kept the right hand track over a rolling prairie, till we came to the forks of the road: a deep ravine and trees on the right of the road with good grass, but no water. Took the right hand track, and passed up the hill through a gentle depression. From the top of the hill the scenery is magnificent.

The hills which looked dark heretofore, now appear bright and covered with a variety of evergreens, about as thick set, to appearance, as an apple orchard. The view was extended in some direction more than fifty miles. The Black Hills lay at the south west, like blue clouds, and Laramie Peak was densely buried in one half way to its base. It began to rain when we were at the spring and continued for half an hour. It rained on the mountains, however, for hours; and has rained there at least half the time since we came in sight of them. The Platte lies hid among the hills, a mile or two at the north, shut from sight except in one place by perpendicular walls of red sandstone. The country lying between us and the Black Hills seems to be a rolling prairie, cut up by deep ravines, lined with cedar.

Descending the hill and turning to the left, we reached Bitter Creek, twenty four miles from the fort, at dark. Turned up the east bank half a mile, and camped. Just before we came to the creek, found a man desperately wounded and another dangerously injured in the spine, and otherwise bruised. There were eight wagons on a train descending the hill, when a pack mule running by them, the oxen got frightened and ran away, tearing the wagons in pieces, and dashing the men among the fragments. Bitter Creek is a small stream of very pure water and has considerable cotton wood on its banks. Vegetation is tall and rank, but good grass scarce. The ravines in all directions are covered with evergreens. It rained hard just as the wagons got in. We were late because the teams stopped at noon without orders, bringing us in behind another train or two, and hindering us an hour in watering at warm springs.

JUNE 28. Heard from Dodson in the Pioneer train. He has been very sick of cholera. Left camp late. Went up hill and down, crossing a ravine; pretty steep. From the hills the view is fine. They are spread around in all directions, covered with evergreens and the heights overhung by thunder showers all the time. Just before noon came to Horse Shoe Creek, a deep ravine and very little water running—but very good. The west bank is high and bluff. The road turns down the creek a mile or more and then round the hill, on the flat, to another stream, where you may find good water up the hills to the left, among some cotton woods. The Platte is in sight at the north.

Camped at the edge of the cotton wood grove, in the creek bed. Thunder showers in all directions. Went on to the high hills west, and the skirt of a cloud swept past just over head. I sought refuge under a handsome thin ledge, projecting some ten feet over, and itself entirely overhung by a couple of pine trees. While lying here secure from wind and rain, a bird much like a martin dropped down from a tree and settled on a dry twig. They are very numerous here and desirous of examining one, I brought my revolver (a five inch barrel) to bear upon him and winged him at seventeen paces. I believe it was a very good shot.

JUNE 29. Left camp late. A number of trains in sight on the road. The probable average where we are is four to five teams to the mile. Passed a large dry ravine, and up and over a hill, by a very gradual descent. Came to another ravine, without water, but with cotton wood, which usually indicates it. About eight miles from camp came to a wide stream, where was abundance of cotton wood—probably this is Buffalo Creek. Plenty of water here, and a wide bottom.

Passed on to the right and down to the plain below, where we have a sight of the Platte, which is here lined with cotton wood and has low banks. In different directions I notice hills of red sand stone. Ahead is a wide plain, bounded on all sides by hills; and directly so, is a sloping bluff, where a dry, wide stream bed comes from the south, and falls into the Platte forty rods north of the road. The Platte here makes a break through the hills, and a noble one it is. I much wished, but had not time, to examine it.

Passed south of the large bluff, through an easy ravine, into a broad plain. On the right is a range of high hills, at the base of which is the river: and on the left, a range of low hills. There has been plenty of grass today, but generally since leaving Laramie it has not been of the best. Two miles from the bluff we camped on the plain, at the left of the road. Two miles on, the Platte runs up to the bluff on the left, where are plenty of cotton-woods.

About the camp we pick up plenty of small pieces of cedar wood, which has washed down from the hills south, though there is none growing in sight in that direction. The road is excellent. North northwest of camp, across the river, on the bluff, which here is perpendicular and much worn, there is the appearance of a large ruin, which an Englishman says looks like an old dilapidated castle in England. It has the form of a mass of sharp pyramids and cones, thickly set down, with considerable order, over a large area of ground.

JUNE 30 – Broke camp, and passed the cottonwood bottom under a sharp bluff. The best of the trees have been cut down, probably to browse cattle. Two miles on, after passing the heaviest grass we have seen on the whole route, turned to the left, up the largest hill we have ascended since leaving the Missouri. Our course for five or six miles was due south, (between two ravines some considerable distance apart, and lined with cotton-wood) toward Laramie's Peak. Directly ahead, a high hill with barren sides presents itself, on the west end of which are a large number of cedar trees. One of them has the exact form of a cross. The road here gradually turns west, leaving Laramie Peak at the left; and about six miles from a large clump of cottonwoods, on the side toward the peak, and the last or nearly so in that ravine, this one enters the southern road – or the straight one.

From the junction, the road descends gradually into a deep ravine, the head of some creek, probably Buffalo. It was dry where we struck it, but we found a small spring on the left and soon after came to La Bonte, a fine stream five or six yards wide, and ten or twelve inches deep. I notice willow, ash, and cottonwood on its banks.

Turning down the ravine a mile and a half, we left it, and bore off west, up a slope to a natural turnpike, only wide enough for one wagon to pass for several rods. From this we turned north over the hill, and down by a spur of the Black Hills, within a few rods of its eastern point, on the left. From this position the scenery appears to be very nicely painted. In the bottom of a broad ravine runs a stream, that is when it is wet weather; in dry it sinks in the sand every few rods.

The spur just noted is a sharp, bomb-like ridge, running off to the west and south and composed, I should think, of brown sandstone, which lying in large masses, loosely scattered over the sloping sides and ridges casts a strong shadow below, and with the small green bushes, short grass, and cedars sprinkled over the surface, fixes upon the mountain masses the dark, and sometimes even black appearance, which has given them the cognomen of Black. Passing this point, several sharp descents (the brows of one of which exactly resemble the bed of a huge lime kiln) bring you to a dry ravine, steep in and out. Turning across the bottom, covered with willow, ash and cottonwood, and up the ravine south west, we camped under a high bluff, composed entirely of red sand stone, and at the right of the road.

From the top of this the whole country looks like a modern map, colored to order, and made to sell. And (I speak it not irreverently) I should think that all we have yet passed through was made to sell, or give away and not to buy, or take. Here, although it is painted with every shade of color that red can yield, it is little else than a mere daub, after all. The truth is, it wasn't worth painting anyhow. The whole is made up of white sandstone, piled on red, and very little workmanship displayed in the getting up.

Some of the hills are made up of piles of stone, and stone-like brick, dumped down at a venture; others seem to have been corded up, but no regularity; nothing smooth, no joints, no carving, no angles, no lines, no anything that is beautiful. Even the elements seem to have neglected their duty, or in their discharge of it made matters worse, for points are not half rounded, and the half rounded are not half smoothed, and these last look the worst of all. Even the valleys are just no valley at all, being merely the tops of other hills, sticking up from below, with a crooked groove in the top, (where water makes a pretense of running) and even this may be only the shell of another hill, turned bottom upward. It is just no country at all, (I mean now all of it, back, back, back to the Missouri) I had rather take the raw material, stone, sand and clay, than have Uncle Sam's title to the whole of it. I shall recur to this subject again, when I get through in reference to Whitney's project.

I ought perhaps, in justice, to note here that the roads, or rather the road, is good; as good, perhaps or better than any other country can present, with the same labor, or rather neglect of labor. The only fault from here to Laramie is a hill or two, and a few places where the sharp gravel wears the feet of the cattle. No feed at all for the cattle except a very scattering growth of grass, or want of growth rather, for it looks as though it had been always here.

JULY 1ST, 1849. Moved off west, up hill, and down, the road is red as rose pink. Indeed, everything is more or less so. Some of the hills look like a mine of Spanish brown, others, rose pink, others salmon, chocolate, flesh color, cream, etc. The north sides of the Black Hills are purple, and even the wild sage and grass is colored with all the pervading pigment, which, pulverized under the wagon wheels, rises in clouds and settles again upon everything for a mile or more, on either side of the road.

Crossed at a ravine, in which on the left, were three small pyramids and a large one, 100 feet high, close beside the road, with a small projection on the road side, between which and the base is a large rock nine feet high. Beyond these a hill is washed into quite a regular pyramid, and just beyond another is decently rounded, the only attempts of the kind (which I observed) in the whole range. By the bye, the pyramids are only masses or blocks of stone, heaped up, like potatoes, as long as they would lie on.

The road is up hill and down and down and up, (for there is sometimes two to one and vice versa) lock chains, and backing and whoaing and stopping, and yelling and (I am sorry to say it) cursing, from beginning to end and no grass, but plenty of grasshoppers, and wild sage and crickets and horned toads, with tails and ears. The horns are on their sides, and as for ears, all I can say is that they look like ears; but I shall speak of them again when I have examined them more. I would only say that they appear to be hybrids; half lizard, half toad, and a touch of the snapping turtle.

We see or hear but few wolves. Occasionally a pair of elkhorns or a buffalo's white skull, may be seen glistening in the sun, but the musquitos "are gone, all gone" "to the cane brakes lone and dreary." Well, joy go with them. The hum of their departing wings sounded a welcome jubilee to us, and right sorry shall we be to meet them again, as friends or foes. They followed and stuck by us faithfully to the last, but even musquitoes seem to have some sense, and cannot stand every thing. I reckon they knew too much to come up here. Some half a dozen pursued us from Laramie for a while, but finally backed out, or were killed. They are very great pests, and have caused me, at least, more trouble and suffering than everything besides since we left the river. Hunger, thirst, cholera, cold and heat may be endured or cured, musquitos never: and the only sure remedy I can prescribe is, "put for the Black Hills."

Camped on the east side of a small creek, four and a half miles short of the Fauche La Boise. Plenty of cottonwood and a spring of good water in a deep ravine, of considerable width. Some grass up this ravine. Left camp at sundown and rode over to Boise Creek, to visit Mrs. Cameron of the Oskaloosa Iowa train. Had the cholera. The road is very crooked and passed two ravines, one of which had running water and a bad crossing. The La Boise ravine is very beautiful. The stream is two yards wide and a foot deep. Grass all fed out. All day the Black Hill range has been on our left, only a few miles distant. Remained all night with the Oskaloosa train, and rode on with them in a covered carriage, drawn by horses. On the morning of the

2D JULY, 1849, Leaving the teams to follow, we drove on, and passing up and over a hill, got a fair view of the Platte, and teams almost without number moving or lying upon the river, waiting to cross. A long, gradual descent through, or rather between the low hills, brought us to the first ferry on the upper Platte. The emigrants are being ferried across the river for $2.50 per wagon. Passed up a very good road five miles and camped on Deer Creek. Here is a wide bottom, mostly covered with cottonwood, and a fine stream of water. Plenty of anthracite coal here, but it will not weld iron. A blacksmith by the name of Ford, just now travelling with the Oska-

loosa company is at work shoeing horses and oxen already. He will be setting tire directly, I presume, as he has promised a number to do so. Bought
a boat in company with Cameron's train, to ferry ourselves over, when we
get ready. Drove our cattle seven miles up the creek for grass. None nearby.

JULY 3. Lay over. Cold night and frost.

JULY 4. Knoxville company came in; forty wagons and one hundred
twenty seven men. Miles, a Salt Lake man, brother in law of W.E. Bent,
pilots them through. There are now at least two hundred men camped here
on one hundred acres of ground. In the evening they nearly all assembled,
and we had any quantity of speeches, and sentiments, and firing of guns
(and for that matter you might hear them in all directions, for miles around)
and one man had a thumb shot off.
    The Pioneer train is lying on the east side of the creek on the hill, and
Dodson is in our camp. He looks like anybody but himself. It would be the
refinement of flattery to say that he looked human, when I went out to
meet him coming into his own camp, after falling behind the train. They
told me that they sent the carpenter back two or three times to make a box
for him. Cold night, frost.

JULY 5. Crossed all our wagons by a little after noon, and the other
train before night. At 5 o'clock started the teams up the Platte, and first
went up a hill bearing a little to the right, through loose sand, in some
places a foot deep, one mile; then a tolerably smooth descending road, two
miles to the river; sand not as deep. At the river crossed a ravine with some
water running into it; a spring up half a mile. Camped one mile from this
point, where there are a large number of cottonwood trees, mostly dead,
scattered over a level, handsome bottom. The whole road is very heavy.

JULY 6. Left camp, and made about ten miles over the heaviest and
worst road we have yet found. It is very near the river, passing a succession
of ravines, and often running along the hill sides, near the base, and through
deep sand. Camped on a handsome bottom, directly at the head of a large
island, with timber, and a clump of cottonwoods on either side of the river
immediately above camp. The road here turns a little to the right over the
low spur of a hill, the river making a bend to the left. The day has been exceedingly hot. No grass on either side of the river near it; all fed off, but
back over the hill a mile it is very good. The route which we took through
the Black Hills, after leaving the Platte, was nearly destitute of grass; but I
learn that, by going three or four miles off from the road to the foot of the
hills, we could have obtained feed for the cattle every night. Again some
teams came up the Platte, without leaving it all the way to Deer Creek, and
had, of course, plenty of feed. So large an emigration, however, must

necessarily sweep the feed from any one route; but divide it equally among three, and there will be grass on all.

McCollum, from Leroy, N.Y., of the Pioneer train, is in camp. The U.S. troops passed us about 6 o'clock; they looked jaded, dirty, and inefficient.

JULY 7, 1849. From camp passed over the low spur of a hill, and came to a stratum of coal showing itself for half a mile or more on the side of the bluff at the right. Passing on two miles, turned up the hill to the right, and over into another bottom covered with a growth of young poplars. From this the road is alternately on the bottom and over the hills to the camp. The hills are steep and long, and the wheeling heavy, a deep coarse sand.

The sand in places seems filled with particles of iron. The edges of a magnetized knife blade will be completely covered with the particles by passing a handful of the sand over it. There is some timber on the river bottom, generally in clumps, sometimes scattered. The grass seems to improve, though the hills are nothing but sand, at least on the surface.

Some masses of sandstone on one hill were covered with names carved in the rock. Camped four miles below the upper ford, and twenty eight above Deer Creek.

Saw Asa Canfield, from Dupage county. This road is a little longer than that on the south side, rather heavier and no springs or streams of water, with one exception; but the grass has not been as much fed down, as fifteen hundred teams crossed the upper ferry before we came up, and there are ferries every two or three miles to Deer Creek. The Platte here is crooked, and the bottom green, and covered with scattering cottonwood, and two or three kinds of bushes or shrubs. One mile back from the river is very good grass.

JULY 8. SUNDAY. Lay over all day. Wind blew a gale. Saw Miles again, and talked with him. A great many persons have been drowned in the Platte, at the different ferries and fords this year. The current is so bad, and the water so cold, that he who swims it must be a swimmer indeed.

JULY 9. MONDAY. Left camp early. Ascended the bluff immediately. Road sandy to the upper ford—grows better beyond. Four miles on passed some ponds on the left. A triangular one was one hundred rods long, the water muddy, and the shoal sandy beach covered with a white efflorescence, probably carbonate of soda: I tasted some, which appeared to be glauber salts. (Sulph. soda.) It is said to be strongly laxative when taken or drunk by cattle or men. From here the road gradually rises with occasionally a gentle descent, several miles, and is hard and good. On the summit, four or five miles from the ponds, are some piles of brown sandstone, lying in ranges on the left. The descent from this summit is crooked, and a little rough in two or three places, but generally quite good.

From the ravine at the bottom you rise again, bearing south, and passing some hills, showing shelly slate in the sides. Here the road turns more to
the left, and runs down into the bed of an abrupt ravine, and soon by a
very crooked road reaches some springs, and a semi circular pond, on the
left, and contiguous to the track. The water is accounted poisonous, and is
bitter to the taste; and though clear when at rest to the very bottom, yet as
soon as stirred it becomes black as though mixed with cobalt or gun powder.
Even when at rest, the bottom is covered with some substance having the
exact appearance of cobalt. Perhaps if the water was carefully dipped out, it
might be drank with impunity. I have no doubt that the poison is nearly or
quite insoluble, as some water their cattle and lose none, while others have
lost many. This pond is five and half miles from the top of the hill, and on
the bottom, about the spring, is the first green grass we have seen since we
left the Platte.

Five and half miles on, over some long ascents and descents, by an excellent road, though rather too hard and gravelly for the cattle, came to the
avenue; which is a broad find wagon road down a gradual descent for more
than a quarter of a mile. The low hills on each side of the pass, are crowned
with a range of irregularly piled rocks. Another ascent and descent carried
you down to a ravine, with a bed of deep sand, and hard pulling for a short
space. Soon after the dry white beds of some alkaline ponds show themselves
on the right.

The general direction is south west. From thence, a good road four
miles brings you to some springs at the left of the road, the upper or farther
one being sulphurous. By this we camped at half past 11 p.m. making a drive
of thirty miles without grass or water. From the poison springs you can
reach the Platte in five miles, toward the Red Buttes and find plenty of
grass. We have passed thirty five dead oxen today, several dead mules, a
number of wagons, and clothing, provisions, stoves, etc. Generally, every
thing left is broken or otherwise rendered useless. There is no grass here of
any account. A narrow strip by the spring brook is all that looks green,
except a shrub that grows with the wild sage. The latter is no longer green,
and seems entirely destitute of moisture, burning like seasoned wood. The
Red Buttes are merely the red sand stone bluffs, where the Platte breaks
through the hills from the south. They were in sight from eight o'clock a.m.
to half past four p.m., when we passed leaving them several miles at the left.

JULY 10, 1849. Left camp late, on account of the cattle straying away in
the night for want of watching, and reached willow springs through a break
in the hills and across the bed of a stream, at eleven o'clock a.m. There are
several springs here, and quite a quantity of willow bushes enclosed in a
large basin. A broad green ravine comes down from the west, the south side
of which is lined with springs, now filled up with mud. One mile brings you
to the top of Prospect Hill, at the bottom of which on the other side is a

moist piece of ground, with green grass, and three and a half miles from the top is a large, springy, miry piece of land, on the right hand covered with good grass. They say that cattle cannot run over it to feed. Perhaps they cannot; we did not try it.

Four and a quarter miles farther on, at the foot of a hill, came to a small stream, nearly dry, and passed half a mile along its right bank, and one and a quarter miles from the foot of the hill came to Grease Wood Creek, now six or seven feet wide and eight inches deep. Camped on the west side. No grass here.

WEDNESDAY, JULY 11. Left camp at sunrise with five teams, the remainder did not picket their cattle, and of course could not be ready. Passed over a sandy plain, ascended a little rise of a hill, turned to the left by the grave of J. McCumber, Park Township, St. Joseph County, Michigan, and halted for breakfast. The Pioneer train lies below, on the creek bottom where we turned out our cattle and found very good feed; the best we have seen since we left the Platte. While at breakfast, the Pioneer train left, and passing down the creek, leaving the main road at the right, went straight on by the eastern base of some granite or sandstone mountains, and camped on their southern base on the west side of a spring near the Sweetwater. We soon followed on the west bank of the creek, till within half a mile of a high irregular sandstone hill, the east part detached and bare.

Here we turned our cattle down a quarter of a mile to the creek, where the grass was tall enough to mow, and very fresh and green. This is the best grass we have seen since we left the little Blue, or Pawnee. The valley extends down the Sweetwater here a long way, and the feed is excellent, and will be till future emigrants shall use it up. Very few teams have passed this way. Most go straight through by Independence Rock.

Two miles on we passed round the mountain, and camped just below the Pioneer train. The mountain is of naked granite, with a few small cedars and tufts of grass and sage brushes scattered over it. On the south side of the Sweetwater are more hills of the same character. North west, around the mountain, are a large number of ponds, whose surface and shores are encrusted with carbonate of soda, but not thick enough to be easily gathered. The idea of getting saleratus on the road is all a humbug. One might get enough for a plate of biscuit directly, but to gather any great quantity in a reasonable time, and free from sand or stinking mud, is entirely out of the question. It may have been done, but cannot now. The smell around these lakes is very offensive.

JULY 12, 1849. THURSDAY. The Pioneer train is engaged today in reducing the passenger baggage, etc. Yesterday they had rather a stormy meeting, which resulted in the appointment of a committee of high ways and bye ways who resolved that Captain Turner should throw away five passenger wagons, some of the baggage wagons, and the passengers reduce their baggage to seventy five pounds each; all the doctors, three or four of them, together to be allowed seventy five pounds extra.

They are now weighing and throwing away or selling all manner and sorts of traps—pins, needles, law and medical books, crowbars, spades, shirts, shovels, basins, matches, collars for horse and man, handkerchiefs, vials, medicines, trunks, buffalo robes, boots, shoes, novels, nails, screws, clothing of all kinds, gold washers, screen cloth, blacksmith's, joiner's and carpenter's tools, soap, picks, writing paper, brandy, tobacco, hatchets, rifles, shot guns, etc, etc, etc. The property thrown out was worth, probably, $5,000. Some was sold, some burnt, and the remainder picked up by the emigrants. Our train took as many as twenty trunks and discharged as many boxes or trunks of less value and more weight.

The proprietors of this train promised their passengers, at Independence, that they should hold their Fourth of July at Sutter's, in California and the Fourth overtook them before they were half way. Something of a mistake, but time waits for no man, much less for overloaded and overdriven and badly selected mules. The passengers pay $200, and cook their own food, watch the camp, harness and drive their own teams, and generally go on foot. This is paying pretty dear for the whistle; working their passage on the tow path and then falling behind some of the ox teams.

They ought to have known that one mule can never take a man to California. Three is certainly the very lowest mark at which it ought to be attempted. Anything less will probably always prove a failure; at least if they attempt to make good time. The mules are pretty well used up now, and they cannot lighten as the mules fail; hence the necessity of reducing the baggage. What they will do hereafter is a problem yet unsolved. Many are leaving and probably others will do so until there will be but a remnant left, who will be likely to go through because they can do no better. Dodson goes with us. They are a hard set, are the Pioneers, for sure. Half of all, I should think, perhaps more, are gamblers and hard drinkers, men without character and perfectly reckless. There will be too many such in California. May we not meet them in desperate circumstances this side.

JULY 13, 1849. FRIDAY. Left camp early, and made directly for Independence Rock, five miles distant. Ball and I were ahead of the teams, in search of a camp for the night. From a distance the rock is hardly perceptible, being so much lower than the high rocky mountains on the south east, south and south west. The rock itself is nearly half a mile long and thirty rods wide on an average. I should judge it to be about one hundred fifty or two hundred feet high, and the surface of hard brown granite is handsomely rounded over, appearing from a distance quite smooth. About one third of the way from the north east end (for it runs from north east to the south west, the road passing around the north east end and between it and the river) there is a deep depression, and a slighter one another third. The south side is deeply indented in two places, where the rock is easily ascended.

In many places the rock seems formed of immense masses of granite, piled up irregularly; in others it is as smooth as a floor. If it stood alone, it would have a very imposing appearance. The whole of the east two thirds is covered with names, mostly done with black paint. Another rock of the same character nearly as large, and much higher, stands only eighty or a hundred rods east.

Leaving the rock, we crossed the river one mile above, here about thirty yards wide and eighteen inches deep; and then over some moderate elevations four and a half miles, and saw the road some little distance ahead passing between two granite hills. Turned toward the high Sweetwater Mountains on the right; in half a mile came to the opening in the mountain, called the Devil's Gate, where the river rushes down, tumbling through the deep kanyon. We found the pathway on both sides obstructed by huge blocks of granite and after going up on the south side as far as we could without danger, we went below, forded and tried the north side.

Above us hundreds of swallows were flying in all directions, chattering and twittering and dodging into their nests, which stick on the sides of the rock, and seem made of clay of the size of a great bottle, with a hole just large enough for the bird to go in. The wall on the south is perpendicular, perhaps leans to the north and is from four hundred to six hundred feet high. The north wall leans a little from the gap. I should judge that the width at the narrowest part might be one hundred feet; and yet from a short distance only it seems scarcely more than ten feet.

Camped three and a half miles above, under a low sloping, grassy bluff, on the south side of the Sweetwater. Before reaching it we crossed a small spring brook and a larger one of clear good water. From the camp directly east is the mountain seen south of Independence Rock and intermediate is the passage for the road, which cuts off a spur of the chain lying on the north side of the Sweetwater.

Half a mile north of the road appears the slit in the mountain, the ascent to it being very gradual. Half a mile farther north it rises to nearly twice the height. From this onward up the river as far as I can see, immense hills of granite protrude themselves at different angles with, and almost, and sometimes quite, to the river. Such is the scenery above the Devil's Gate.

The river bottom is of considerable width, and furnishes abundance of grass. South, for several miles, the land is sandy and barren, furnishing little but wild sage. The road runs on the upper level some miles above the gate and is sandy as it has been all day. The Black Hills lie beyond, looming up into the clouds. The mountain north of camp has a remarkably smooth surface, and slopes from the top to the river at an angle of forty degrees.

Yesterday was quite cool; today hot, and no wind, but the nights are uniformly cold. Passed twenty three dead oxen today. Some of the men report finding saleratus more plenty in a pond north of Independence Rock. The Sweetwater is fordable now at almost any point.

JULY 14. Two miles from camp, crossed a dry, deep stream bed. The hills south fall down quite low, back to the foot of the mountains, which opposite here, are broken through by a broad ravine. Eight and a half miles on, the road comes to a good watering place on the river bank, and the old road leaves the river here for six or seven miles. The new one, which we took, leaves the river, and after running over a hill or two, turns toward the river again, which is a break through a spur of the mountains very much like the Devil's Gate. The gap, however, is not very bold, nor the rocks high or perpendicular.

Passing through the spur, half a mile south of the river, we came upon its bank again, and turning south, passed up a very steep sandy hill, with a high sloping bluff at the left. Above, and at the right, the river bottom lies broad and green, bounded by the bare granite hills, which seem to have just been projected from below, clean and fair, without time to wear down or vegetate.

Directly ahead, a long spur as naked as the rest, slopes down to the plain, from one of the two highest points in the whole range. The first is conical, the other is split down from the top, leaving a wedge shaped gap, and has been in sight all day. Directing our course for the point of this hill, we passed over several high ones, and through a very deep ravine, Sage Creek, and turning to the right, camped on the river bank directly below where it passes the point of the hill. The grass has been fed close, but answers very well.

Saw the feathers of some sage hens here. We have killed a few, and those who eat them say the flesh is good. They are the color of the prairie hen and much like them in shape and habits, but larger. I have been told that some of them are as large as a half grown hen turkey. Mountain sheep are said to abound here, but I have seen none, except a dead one lying in the Devil's Gate. If he fell from the top, and no doubt he did, I reckon he lay quiet; though he might exclaim with much truth, if not poetry,

> "Oh what a fall was there, my countrymen,
>   When all alone I fell within the gap."

Passing it hastily, as it lay there, one might easily mistake it for a sheep. From an examination (slight it is true) I should think it more of a deer than a sheep. I have seen some of their horns, as much as five inches in diameter and two feet long, and resembling the goat's horn in structure and form.

SUNDAY, JULY 15, 1849. Obliged to travel for grass. Ordered the teams on, and taking Stebbins with me, crossed the river and ascended the high peak I have just mentioned as being split from the top. From the base two

thirds of the way up, we found immense masses of loose rocks piled promiscuously, with pine and cedar (some of the first twenty inches, and the
latter four and a half feet in diameter) growing between or among them, and
water trickling down under in several places, furnishing fountains, caverns
and hiding places for wild beasts.

From this mass of confusion we followed up a ravine with a good growth
of pine or fir and cedar, an almost perpendicular smooth rock on our left
four or five hundred feet high and rock which seems never to have been
moved on our right, till by dint of hard climbing we reached a nearly level
space on the east side. Passing around north into the notch or gap, we
found it a deep ravine, heavily timbered with a fine growth of pine and
cedar. Turning directly south through a cut in the rock, we came to another
level from which we turned west up the rock, winding our way along—in
one place through a crevice scarcely a foot wide, till we came to a cedar ten
or fifteen feet to where the top was broken off.

Placing one foot on the stem and the other in a crevice running from
above down the smooth perpendicular face of the rock, a smart spring of
three feet gives the hand a precarious grip of a sharp edge above, and a pull
or two, with a bruised knee and a scratched elbow, places you on another
level, from which the ascent is quite easy to the pinnacle. The whole time
occupied in reaching it was one hour and thirty five minutes. The depth of
the notch is about two hundred feet.

Seated on the very pinnacle, the prospect is almost boundless. Mountains and plains are spread out in all directions. Cattle and men, wagons,
mules and horses are scattered twenty or thirty miles along the river, which,
like a snake, winds lithely away between its green banks, a line of vegetative
life seemingly painted across an immense field of barrenness and desolation,
a field covered with wild sage, greasewood, and kindred plants, with scarcely
a blade of grass on its withered sun dried surface.

East, west, north and south, I see hills of rock, or sand, or clay, or
gravel, of every size and shape and height, seemingly thrust up from the
midst of an enormous plain. The only appearance of a continuous range of
hills is on the south, and that is often broken through. The rest seem to
have come up out of the earth much like thistles.

Far to the west are mountains, whose summits for a considerable way
down seem covered with snow. They must be the Wind River Mountains.
They are to be passed, and so we must leave here. Our descent was by a
winding way one hundred fifty feet south east, then westerly by a fissure in
the rock, which rapidly widens to a ravine, with trees of considerable size.
About three hundred feet down we found a spring of most excellent water—
the very best I ever drank.

Following the channel till it spreads out into a comparatively level (i.e.,
not perpendicular) space, we turned to the right down into the main ravine
which makes down from the gap or notch. Down this the descent is easy,

obstructed only by fallen trees, to the base of the mountain. The whole height, I should think, might be from one hundred to twelve hundred feet. We consumed an hour in the descent. Striking off south westerly, we intercepted the teams at Bitter Cottonwood Creek, five miles from camp. This creek is now dry. Half a mile beyond, turned down to the river to noon, and after hitching on, crossed the river and went round and up on the north side of some high rocky hills, expecting to find better grass as the old road runs three miles south and does not come to the river again for six miles. Not more than fifty wagons have passed this way.

I have been thus particular about the hills, that your readers may form a better idea of the country, and the best or rather, the quickest way to "get up in the world." If I get tedious, please knock off a page or two occasionally.

Camped four miles from Bitter Cottonwood Creek, south of the river, on the north side of an immense pile of rocks. Good grass and of excellent quality, most of it the red-top of our own land, abounds here. It is fresh and green and stands ready for the scythe, a foot high. This is the first of the kind that I have noticed on the route.

MONDAY, JULY 16TH, 1849. Half a mile from camp passed a point of a hill at the left, and a pile of rocks at the right, across the river. From this up to the ford, three miles, is level, and a good road. The south, or old road is a heavy, sandy one, and only three fourths of a mile shorter, and no grass. Crossed the ford at the foot of the high granite hills, and turning to the left up the river, skirted their base (they being on the right) for one and a quarter miles, and in the last quarter crossed the river twice. The rocks on the road at the right are covered with names, like Independence Rock. On the left is the river, with a narrow bottom, partly covered with high willows until you come to the upper fords, where it is nearly shut in by the rocks.

From the last ford, you pass up the right bank, leaving a large mass of rocks five or six rods at your right, with a lake behind, and the green river bottom with alkaline water at your left—and turning south, ascend to a handsome, level, gravelly plain: a most excellent road; which continues to the next ford, seven miles. The route for this distance has the high hills (which here seem to be sandstone) on the right, and the river, with its broad green bottom, at the left; the long range of black hills ten miles south, and the snow capped Wind River range fifty miles west. Camped one and a quarter miles below the lower ford. Grass good, but has been fed considerably—better than we have generally found it lower down. Probably there has been more rain here. It has been cloudy all day and threatened rain, but only sprinkled on the plain, though it rained on the hills. The weather is quite cool.

By the rock-line telegraph, the Napierville company passed here two weeks since, and the Elgin four days.

TUESDAY, JULY 17, 1849. After leaving camp, crossed the ford, and ascended a hill to a broad plateau, which gradually became more and more uneven until it broke up into hills. Six miles on, in a valley directly by the road-side on the right, we found plenty of most excellent ice one foot below the surface. It lies in a bog or spring hole, forming a slough forty rods wide; which has been gradually approaching the road for the last mile, and just beyond the spring crosses it, although the crossing is now dry and stretching off south west, loses itself among the distant gravel hills.

Passing over these, which for the next nine and a half miles constantly increases in height, we crossed the Sweetwater again and immediately fording one of its tributaries, passed up the north bank of the river nearly to a high hill, crowned with loose rock, and camped. The road has been hard and good, but no grass except at the ice spring—where it is abundant. No use is made of it for oxen as the water is accounted poisonous. Water for drinking must be taken in at the river, as there is none fit to drink between the fords. You can let the ice melt, or have the river water iced. Grass is scarce, as the river bottom is somewhat narrow and trains have generally laid over here a day or two.

At noon today a big buffalo came over the hills from the south and from the distance of a mile reconnoitred, for some time, two or three trains which had halted on the road. Having apparently become satisfied of our hostile intentions, for a dozen men were loading their rifles and make preparations to pay him their respects, his prairie majesty wheeled round and showed us a clean pair of heels. They move off with a motion peculiar to themselves, and combine with great strength, much dignity. It has been very warm. Some of the cattle have cracked or chapped feet, from travelling so much in the soda. Very cold in the night.

WEDNESDAY, JULY 18, 1849. Cold morning. The road was up a long hill, making a long turn from the river. Descending this again, we came upon the river bottom, and three and a half miles from camp forded it again, and back in half a mile. Three miles farther up the stream, crossed a small spring brook, with abundance of willows, and halted. Good springs here at the opening of the ravine from the hills, which shut down pretty closely upon the river.

Two miles from this, the river pours down through a narrow gorge at the left, and the road diverges to the right, passing through a narrow deep ravine, over one hill, and then up another, long and steep; turning left; and directly a still farther turn, half round, and down again, brings you to the bottom of another; the road bearing here to the right. Here it begins to be rocky for hitherto it has been smooth and excellent. At the top of this hill, where the road bends again to the left, it passes over several ridges of rock which seem like stone walls thrown down and half buried in the earth. There is no way of getting round, as they extend the whole length of the ridge. Passing the last of these, we turned directly to the left forty rods, and camped, driving the cattle down a ravine where is good feed, now, and a spring of pure fine water. Killed a couple of musquitoes. They look starved and weakly.

JULY 19. THURSDAY. The road today is excellent, over plains and long slopes, gradually ascending. After crossing two small creeks in going five miles, came to the Strawberry, a beautiful stream. Usually plenty of grass here, but now have to go three miles up for it, or three miles down to the Sweetwater. There is a snow bank just below the ford on the east side. One mile brought us to Quaking Aspen Creek, no grass on the road. A nameless branch of the Sweetwater follows in two and three fourths miles, and Willow Creek two and a quarter farther. All these streams afford good grass, but near the road it is all fed out. The water is abundant and good.

Four and three quarters miles on, forded the Sweetwater for the last time, and camped on the south side. The Wind River Mountains lie off northwest, the sides half covered with snow. South west and south are some long ridges, covered with a scanty growth of grass and wild sage—and east, down the river, is a broad green bottom, with excellent pasture, and immense clumps of willow bushes. It rained a little here this evening, and heavy clouds lay on the mountains, where it snowed. There is a snowbank forty rods from camp, under a bluff, some eight rods long and two rods wide and three or four feet deep. The evening is very cold.

20TH JULY. FRIDAY. Left camp early, and went up the south side of the river alone. On the broad, long hills at the south are two somewhat remarkable rocky bluffs, or hills. The nearest is rather irregular, but the most western has nearly perpendicular sides, and appears level on the top. They were in sight all day yesterday. Saw a flock of sage hens. By the bye, the boys brought a number of chickens into our mess yesterday. They are excellent eating, and have no taste or flavor of the everlasting sage, which we consider strange as it forms a part of their food. This shrub seems to pervade the whole country—sometimes, though rarely, six inches in diameter and ten feet high. There is a variety of other shrubs; but all are aromatic, and the combination of all the sweet scents is absolutely overpowering.

Three or four miles up the river came across a flock of wild geese, and gave them four charges of shot from my double barrelled gun, but could neither kill them nor make them fly. They finally ran and tumbled and rolled into the river.

The whole country seems one vast plain, rolling in heavy swells, except in the immediate vicinity of the river, where it is broken and abrupt for a short distance on each side. Eight miles from the ford the river is only a short distance from the north road, and perhaps a mile from the south, and has a broad fine bottom, extending several miles north west and north, and

down toward the ford. In one and three quarters miles you reach the summit, or divide of the south pass, by a very gradual, yet perceptible ascent.
The descent from the summit is more considerable, though not by any
means deserving the appellation of a hill.

Three miles on you come to a marshy, green looking, level, slough like
piece of land on the right of the road, in which is what is called "The Pacific
Spring." From this, a small stream makes off southwest. The musquitoes
were very troublesome on the Sweetwater all day. Shot two sage hens, and
went down one and a half miles to the crossing of the Pacific Creek, passing
at the left the west end of the southern range of hills, which here terminates
rather abruptly, in two bluffs and a table land between. Stopped on the
creek three miles below, with Armstrong of Ottawa who came up the
Missouri with me. Plenty of grass and water here, the latter highly alkaline.

SATURDAY, JULY 21. Went back to the spring, and waited until after
noon for the wagons, which passed the camped half a mile below where
Armstrong camped last night. It rained smartly two or three hours in the
forenoon and was cold.

SUNDAY, 22 JULY. Left camp by a road which in two miles intersected
the main road, running west over a plain and some low hills seven miles
from camp to the Dry Sandy, a miserable excuse for a creek. There is a very
little alkaline water in the bed now, but it sinks half a mile below the road.
Here the road turns nearly south for four and a half miles, down the creek,
one mile distant—then one and a half miles over the hill to the junction of
the Oregon road, which we followed two miles, then turned to the left, and
in three miles reached Little Sandy, here three feet deep and three rods
wide. Good water—grass all fed out for five or six miles above and below.
Some bunch grass appears among the sage, which here is not more than ten
inches high. The crossing is good, but the hills on each side are rather
steep. From this there is a nearly level plain two miles, and then a gradual
descent between two ranges of hills on to a broad level, through the west
side of which the Big Sandy winds its way to the south. The two streams
are about six miles apart.

We camped forty rods east of the river, and turned the cattle north
where is a plain and a large shallow sink, with grass. It is several miles in
extent, stretching off apparently almost to the mountains, which yesterday
were snowed under during a tremendous storm. Ball and myself were ahead
of the teams on the Little Sandy, when it swept across from the north, with
strong wind, rain and hail.

The stream here has a very narrow bottom—the plain is elevated some
forty or fifty feet above it on the east, and the hill on the west rises gradually
to a considerable height. A few trees are left standing (i.e., if any more ever
stood there) alone in their glory just above the crossing, which is here six or

eight rods wide, and two feet deep—a fine stream. The whole country is one vast sand bed, poorly covered with sage and bunch grass.

MONDAY, JULY 23, 1849. The northern part of the Wind River range is white with snow. It is melted from the southern side of those peaks which the storm of yesterday did not reach. The hills in this section are mostly of sand stone, low, with washed sides, and extensive plains on the tops. They seem to be the remains of a former and higher level; the parts where the valleys now are having been washed away. It is rather a miniature representation of the Chimney Rock region.

Have fixed on 4 o'clock, p.m. to start for Green River. As there is no water for forty three and a half miles to Green River, we drive it in the night, the cattle suffering less from thirst. We are on Greenwood's or Sublette's cutoff. Seventy teams have left already since noon. The Auburn (N.Y.) train have passed on with the others. The cattle wandered off, from carelessness in watching and were not brought in till eight o'clock. Started at ten o'clock from the Big Sandy. Drove all night and reached Green River at sunset on the evening of the

24TH JULY, 1849. TUESDAY. The distance from Big Sandy to Green River is forty three miles. The first twenty miles are comparatively level, like a heavy rolling prairie, but destitute of vegetation except the usual quantum of wild sage, greasewood, and a few tufts of bunch grass, at rare intervals.

At or near this point the country is broken by a deep irregular basin, succeeded by others in a few miles with steep hills down, and gradual and long ascents, with one exception, up. Long swells, with broad shallow valleys, and considerable good grass, succeed until within ten miles of the river where the surface becomes much broken, and at the river mountainous. There is not a drop of water in this whole distance as far as I could discover. All is dry, dry, dry. Let those who are troubled with water in their cellars move their houses up here. Ground rent free, and no drainage.

We carried from Big Sandy about half a pail of water for each creature. It was undoubtedly a considerable relief. We stopped soon after sunrise, for breakfast, and an hour at one o'clock, p.m. The cattle travelled through well, but did not eat very well till they had rest.

JULY 25. Turned our cattle up under the east bank of the river last night and drove them across this morning and up an affluent to the north west, some three and a half miles, where there is plenty of grass. There is none on the east side of the river, the bluff coming close down for several miles, except some small pieces of bottom land. The bluffs are very high and resemble the scenery of Castle Rock, the dome being the most common form. Most of them are rounded off by the action of the elements. The valley is several miles wide and there is some timber on the river, and some willows. The water is very cold. A few fish have been caught. Sage hens abound.

There is a camp of Indian traders two miles above us. One of them was formerly from Chicago. There are two hundred wagons here now. Their cattle and mules generally look bad; ours are in good condition. Only one has died, one left, and two strayed and lost. We have brought one yoke of oxen. The road is strewed or rather lined with dead cattle. The scent of these is very offensive. We sometimes pass five or six in a mile. A long beastly charnel yard; the house must be ahead.

Horses and oxen bear a high price. The traders ask as high as two hundred and fifty dollars for a pony for which they probably paid the Indians fifteen pounds of coffee, or half a dozen shirts; and oxen in good condition, seventy five to one hundred dollars.

Green River must have several large branches just above here. One two rods wide and three feet deep comes in from the west, where we herd our cattle. From this point a broad valley, through which rushes down the main fork, opens a fine view of the Wind River Mountains, almost to their very base. They are yet covered with snow and there are a few patches on some peaks at the north west. The days are warm, and the nights very cold — freezing — and plenty of musquitoes between ten in the morning and eight in the evening. The whole land through which we have passed is one vast sand bed, desolate and barren except on the banks of the water courses.

JULY 26. THURSDAY. Lay by all day.

JULY 27. FRIDAY. There is said to be a ford down the river two miles. At a lower stage of water it is probably passable, but there has lately been a rise of eighteen inches, which is gradually subsiding. One mile below is another ferry, which carries a wagon entire, with the load, at two dollars. We bought a small scow boat brought on by the emigrants, as a wagon box; and ferried ourselves over. It cost ten dollars. I gave it to a young fellow from the North River, who was left destitute by the train he came with.

Left camp at ten o'clock and our course for six and a half miles was down the river, about one mile distant. At the end of the first three miles ascended the bluff by a long, steep hill, and two or three less ones carried us over in two miles to a small stream with a bad, muddy crossing. One and a half miles on, turned to the right, up through a deep ravine, and in one mile reached a high elevation. Turning east, and then south, by a very gradual descent reached Ham's Fork in three miles. This is a beautiful stream coming down from the west. The broad bottom, green with the richest grass and scattered clumps of willows was a cheering sight. We camped one and a half miles west of where we came in to the valley. Made eleven and a half miles.

The water here is cold, and doubtless has been stocked with fish, but the harvest of game has been reaped and even the gleaners have passed on before us. There has been a ferry six miles below the upper ones and a ford at low water just below. By going down the river on the east side some had hills may be avoided. To make the great drive right, teams should start from the Big Sandy at two o'clock, p.m. and they may reach Green River by noon next day. They can then get their cattle over to feed the same day, and perhaps their wagons. They should tarry on the river but one day as the grass is better on this stream, and it is so far on the way. It will require two or three days rest to put the cattle in order for moving off again. Let me try to give you some idea of Green River scenery.

Imagine a section of twenty miles on Fox River, in the region of St. Charles and Elgin, entirely divested of timber except on the islands; which should be numerous; and some willows on the small streams. Raise the hills to double their present height and wash them bare and steep—put on their sides a few small cedars and a few tufts of sage with here and there a blade of grass, and diversify the whole with a snow white incrustation of soda, or immense patches of red sand stone and you know all that I can tell you of Green River scenery.

SATURDAY, JULY 28, 1849. Crossed a ford three miles above camp, course west, up a long hill and into a deep hollow and on and on and up and over a long ridge to the foot of the mountain, which I could see distinctly, before we reached the Big Sandy. There are a few detached clumps of fir on the mountain side, and large groves of dwarf poplars which stand thickly, the whole ground underneath being covered with a dense, tangled, luxuriant growth of rose bushes, and other flowering shrubs and plants all in full bloom. There is also a rich growth of grass wherever it finds room to spring. I found a few ripe strawberries at a high elevation as I ascended, and pure water from springs and melting snow runs rippling down through the dense thickets and shallow ravines. In one place, exposed to the direct rays of the sun, I found the snow six feet deep.

The ascent of the mountain is very gradual, and the view from the top is magnificent. Passing over a number of bad hills, in nine miles the road descents into a deep valley by turning to the left, but we kept directly ahead toward the base of the mountain west, and camped on a small stream. Plenty of grass here. Made twenty three miles.

The weather is intensely cold for the season, and one needs a great coat. The wind has blown strongly from the west all day, raising a cloud of dust, covering cattle, wagons and men, and involving the distant hills and mountains in impenetrable obscurity.

JULY 29, SUNDAY. Elder Wisner sick of a fever. Ice half an inch thick this morning. Went over west, on the mountain with Dodson. One half the mountain side we found green with grass, where the snow has lain till late before it melted. The other half is destitute of grass as is the whole of trees or bushes, except when a ravine runs up and terminates in a point near the top. The spurs that spring from the east side and run down to the valley are also bare, or only covered with a scanty growth of sage and dry grass.

Between these spurs are broad patches of timber, poplar and fir, some of the latter not more than six inches in diameter, running up sixty or eighty feet. The top is a very pointed cone making a beautiful tree. The undergrowth is like that described on the mountain yesterday. The ascent is very easy except the last five hundred feet, where the angle is some 75 degrees. The view from the summit is splendid. The range stretches to a great distance north, and at the right, the Wind River Mountains and the South Pass are clearly in view, between the white castellated ranges of the Green River Valley.

At the right of the pass, three or four elevations slightly interrupt the long, low range, stretching south west until it rises into a high, abrupt range covered with snow, and glistening in the sun. Sweeping round to the west, mountain rises beyond mountain, until the weary eye returns to rest on a broad green valley at the western base of the mountains, and almost under our feet. The ranges here are north and south and some of them are crested with a sharp edge of comb-like rock. A few are broad, and for miles level enough for a wagon road, but generally they present a thin ledge, standing up at an angle of forty five degrees or more. Two high rocky ridges, almost bare from their base, lie between the camp and mountain—a small spring brook coming down from the west dividing them.

Behind, and parallel are two similar ridges, which are joined with them till within one third of the top. The south one of these has a stratum of coal, apparently ten feet thick, and extending its whole length—nearly a mile. I pulled out pieces with my fingers as large as a man's fist. Evening very cold.

JULY 30. MONDAY. Road runs west of south, ten miles, round the southern point of the mountain—then westerly to the crossing of Black's Fork, a fine stream of clear water, twenty yards wide, which come down from the north, and on the west side of the mountain range and runs south east into Green River. Here is the best grass we have yet seen on the route. The valley is long and wide and the hill sides covered with grass. Camped one mile above the crossing.

Ball and I made a cut off over the mountain. Saw no large game except antelopes, and they were too shy for a shot. Killed eight sage hens, one of which we roasted and ate without salt at noon. The whole country abounds in squirrels, which burrow in the ground. They are of two kinds, one like our chip squirrels—the other as big as a large rat, very fat, dark dun color, with a short bushy tail. Sometimes as many as twenty or thirty are in sight at the same moment. Road excellent. Made twelve miles.

JULY 31. Left camp late, and ascended a high, long, bad hill, from whose top a long gentle slope runs down west on to an elevated plateau, which ascends very gradually, north of west, seven miles, between ravines from one to four miles distant on either side. Here the road turns west a mile or two then west down a hill (leaving some springs and timber, the head of a ravine at the right) and up again, turning south through a grove of poplar and fir and on to the top of a high hill, or mountain rather, overlooking the whole country back to the high range east and the Salt Lake one on the west. From this point the road winds south west down the largest and roughest kind of a rocky steep hill, one and a half miles and finally turning sharp north, lands on a small stream of excellent water, running south, where we camped. The valley is very narrow, but there is good feed north, as few have camped here.

For a wonder, the whole country we have travelled through today is covered with grass; the like of which has not been seen since we left some place beyond Laramie, which has escaped my memory—for I don't mind where it was. The road was good, except the hills.

Dodson and I went up a ravine north of the wagon road some miles and intersected it just before reaching the springs. North of the fir grove, which we passed in the afternoon, is a very good camp, and water in a ravine below. There are some traders scattered over the country and occasionally an Indian (Snake) comes into camp. This evening three or four were in with horses. They are a little bodied, big headed race, little better than the animals they ride. S. Hawley sick. Made nine miles.

AUGUST 1ST. Ice, as yesterday morning, nearly half an inch thick. Very cold, and the sun was two hours high before it peeped in here. Half a dozen Indians in camp. Traded the gray mare for one of their ponies.

A squaw on horseback had two children with her; one about three years old clung to her shoulders in some inexplicable manner; and the other, a year old, with a handsome little buckskin shirt on, was by some means equally inexplicable, fastened to the pummel of the saddle (a Spanish one). She had beside a gun lying before her in a buckskin case with horn and pouch, and led a horse in the bargain—all not only without difficulty, but with perfect ease.

One of the Indians seemed quite shrewd at bargain. The horses had no bridles or saddles, except the one just mentioned. Instead, a hide rope is tied round the neck and slipped with a turn over the lower jaw.

Leaving camp went directly up a long hill, not very steep, and then down another, steep and long, into Bear River valley which here has a bottom several miles wide, intersected with dry channels, long shallow ponds, bayous, and green with rush and luxuriant growth of fine and excellent grass. I noticed twelve different kinds. There is but little timber, but there are plenty of willows on the river bank. The stream is crooked, muddy and full of sand bars. Its average breadth may be six or eight rods and its depth very variable, from one to three or six feet and a slow current. Ducks and plovers abound here and I notice a number of meadow larks and robins.

Between the river bottom and the mountain, on the east, is a range of irregular hills perhaps three or six miles wide, on the west side of which, long parallel ranges of stone wall run as far as I can see. Their course is north and south and some have the appearance of a perfect wall. The road turns north west over these hills and skirts the western base, leaving the river at the right some two miles.

Made eleven miles and camped on Smith's Fork, a beautiful stream, eighteen yards wide, coming down from the east. We passed an isolated mountain directly on the right just as we camped; and north east three fourths of a mile, and across the stream is a singular one, being the extreme point of a long spur coming from the north. It rises boldly from a level bottom, and looks as if a number of rocks, one hundred feet wide and from four to ten feet thick, had ages since been inserted into the mountain side from bottom to top and the crests serrated or jagged by the action of the elements. The mountains on the east are not as high as those on the west, very sloping, and present irregular patches of green and brown and yellow and red, with out timber. Indeed there is none in the whole country except in the ravines on the mountains. Made eleven miles.

Chapter Three
August 2–August 18, 1849:
Idaho

AUGUST 2, 1849. The fords here being deep, went up where are several channels. The road runs along the base of the south mountain and comes round under that of the jagged one. It is a bad road and a new ford might be easily made. We ought to have made it.

Four miles below the river breaks through a narrow pass. The long low spur of the western range pushing it over to the east. Immediately the bottom widens to several miles, extending up Thomas' Fork twelve or thirteen miles, while it sweeps round to the west and south and turning the point of a spur from the north, pushes on to the north west again. This is a beautiful section of the valley, covered with excellent grass, and the river and streams fringed with willows. Almost every mountain gorge has its little streamlet, some of which reach the river. Most of them, however, sink sooner and make their appearance in springs or ponds on the river bottom.

I ascended one of the highest peaks of the eastern range. It was quite smooth, but very steep and forests of poplar and fir lay deep below and stretching up almost to the very top. Some of the fir trees were two feet in diameter. I found a number of delightful streamlets from which I drank with a relish. The prospect was as usual—mountains—mountains—mountains— and little else to attract notice. On account of the wet, flat land at the bend of the river, the road sweeps round three or four miles north and turning south again crosses Thomas' Fork a mile or more above its mouth. Camped on the fork a mile above the ford. No fire wood but willows, and those scarce. Better bring wood from Smith's Fork. Saw John McMillen (and sons), uncle of Joseph McMillen, "of our ilk." He made many kindly inquiries about his relations, all which were answered, apparently very much to his satisfaction. Made seventeen miles.

AUGUST 3. Crossed the ford, and turning first down on the west side of the fork and then directly west into the hills, passed as the teamsters report over a very bad road—hills very steep and long and camped on Bear River, not far from where the road turns north down the river for Fort Hall. If you pass the road west any considerable distance you will perhaps have to swim the river for wood.

Ball and I went northwest from camp directly over the mountain spur and stopped on a small stream to fish, some seven miles north of where the teams halted. Caught a few trout, and as the teams did not come along, were obliged to foot it back to camp, which we reached about ten at night.

Bear River gets into this valley by a very crooked channel, winding among the mountains until it opens into the most romantic and beautiful valley we have yet passed, or that I ever saw. It is probably thirty to sixty miles long and twelve to twenty broad—shut in by mountain hills on the east and real mountains on the west and south which are covered with timber half way down from the top and dotted with patches of snow.

A large lake [Bear Lake] with its deep blue waters occupies more than one third of the whole valley, in the south, and a marsh stretches up several miles north, on the west side, at the base of the mountain, covered with black rushes, through which the river winds and turns and finally emerges from seemingly inextricable confusion, to wander north, we know not where, as yet. Made ten miles.

This valley is very fertile—so much so that a human [illegible] called "Peg Leg Smith" (from having a wooden leg, I suppose) and who lives in a log house four or five miles east of camp, conceived the idea in the spring of '48 of raising vegetables and grains, and packed a plough, tools and seed from Salt Lake, bringing a Mormon to assist him. From various causes he failed in everything except a few messes of peas. The wheat which promised fair, and had reached eighteen inches in height

> "Had not yet filled its husk, when from the hills
> A swarm of fierce black crickets rushing down,
> Swept it away."

At Salt Lake, when they make a descent, the Mormons meet them with the whole population and drive them back or kill them. I give all this on the authority of Smith and his Mormon, not vouching for the truth, for Smith is a "customer," and they are ready now, to shoot each other—indeed did threaten it only day before yesterday.

AUG 4, 1849. Left camp early, and passing down the valley sixteen miles, camped within a few miles of its lower end, half a mile west of the road, by

some willows and a beautiful spring. Eight rods below is a clump of poplars.
The highest peak of the Bear River Mountains bears almost directly west
from camp, and the river is about a mile off in the same direction. Course
today more north than west. See Fremont's report and colored map of Bear
River in the book. This is the best watered region we have yet seen. Within
ten miles we have passed nearly as many mountain streams, some of them
two yards wide. Some run between low ridge, stretching down from the
east, and others merely wander over a level plain. Our camp is in a shallow
valley, which is itself divided down as far as the camp by a ridge with a
brook running on its north side.

Just before sundown, an Indian appeared on the ridge south of us, and
nearly down to the river, whipping his horse to the highest speed, and
careering on to our camp. Directly another, and another, and another on
the same trail, until a dozen, large and small, were amongst us. They
appear quite active, intelligent and good looking. One of them is quite a
wag, full of fun and frolic. They seem very poor, and beg for everything
they know the use of. Powder, lead and guns are in good demand, though
we gave them but little. One of them was entirely blind, and had a little
boy ride before him to guide, while he put on the steam in the shape of a
whip.

AUG. 5. SUNDAY. Elder Wisner still sick and not able to be about.
Moved on to get rid of the Indians, with whom the less we have to do the
better. Came near having a "blow up" with them last night. One of the men
showed him who seemed to be the chief a pair of scissors, and clipped off a
lock of hair to give an idea of the use. He was very angry, and it cost the
boys two biscuits to heal his wounded honor. They wear their hair as long
as it will grow, sometimes four or five feet.

Three miles from camp crossed Tullicks' Fork, and a mile beyond and to
the left, went up a high, smooth peak, by a very gradual ascent, much like a
wagon road; and indeed from camp it looked much like one. Another lower
peak on the west is connected with this, at whose base, on the west side,
Bear River finds a channel; the mountain rising from its western shore or
bank, peak after peak, until it reaches a height where the snow still lies in
broad patches, under an August sun.

At the northern base of the peak I ascended, lies a very pretty, nearly
triangular valley, of more than a mile in diameter. A small stream runs
across the road down by some poplars and willows through this bottom
making it a good camping place. The river here sweeps round to the west
two or three miles, and then turns northerly again. The road passes over a
mountain spur, steep and long, keeping nearly the general direction of the
river till it gets about half way between that and the eastern range of mountains. The river bottom in the valley is hardly a mile wide, and all on the
west side, but a succession of low hills or ridges, running west from the base

of the eastern mountains down to the river, occupies a space of four or five miles, gradually narrowing as you approach the bend of the river north.

There are numerous roads leading down to the river, one of which we took, and camped on a bluff thirty feet high, facing directly south, under which the river forms a remarkable eddy. There is a very good spring forty rods east of camp, high up on the north side of a ravine, and plenty of dry wood under the bluff up the river. Abundance of grass all about—indeed, there is no lack of grass anywhere we have travelled on Bear River.

There was not much ice this morning. Made twelve miles. I have noticed the common blue flax in full bloom for the last one hundred miles, but in the valley, the flower is already gone. In fact, we have only just kept up with the flowers—scarce anything seems to have matured except a few early grasses.

AUG. 6. MONDAY. Broke camp and made for Beer Springs, ten miles. The first four miles brought us to volcanic remains. Small piles of black rock, appearing very much like blacksmith's cinders, with deep fissures in the earth where they have been thrown up and burned, appear in different directions. Here, as you approach the mountains, which seem to block up the valley on the northwest, there appears to be a broad plain like a prairie stretching north to a great distance, and having in spots the same black masses. Spread out on the right of the road, a few miles ahead, and at the opening of the plain just described, are two large patches of cedar, willow and alder, interspersed with a variety of shrubs and bushes, among which I noticed a large quantity of currents—the yellow variety. The timber stands on limestone, deposited in successive layers—some of them very thin, others thick; and the whole surface broken or excavated into shallow basins, ledges and holes.

In the south west part of the grove (if I may call it so, for the trees, except willows, are much scattered) is a large spring, covering, perhaps, a surface of three rods by four—the water being from six to ten inches deep, quite cold, clear as crystal, and very good to drink. There are two Indian lodges here, and about five and twenty Indians, great and small.

One of them was grinding something on a large, thin, smooth stone, with a small round one not much larger than the fist. He manifested a good degree of dexterity, rubbing, by pushing the stone from him. The flat stone lay on a large piece of buffalo skin. I inquired by signs what it was, when one of the Indians showed me some grass and the unground seed and then gave me some that was ground to taste. It was a very fine, almost impalpable powder, very much the taste of parched corn. Indeed it must have been roasted before grinding.

They are a very filthy race, and hardly removed from the brute creation. I notice that many of them have guns, and begin to know the use of them. The emigrants furnish them, and the temptation is surely strong, when

an old rifle not worth three dollars in the States, and a little powder and
lead, and a few caps, will bring a pony worth one hundred dollars—yet so it
is. They are constantly begging for powder and caps. Some future emigration may have trouble from these guns yet.

They have a pretty high opinion of their national importance. A short
time ago the traders took one of them down to St. Louis, and like most
travellers he had his long yarns to retail when he returned. Among other
things he asserted that there were fifty times as many whites as snakes. This
was an unpopular and of course unpalatable truth. The fellow was silenced
at once, and barely esaped with his life. "What?" said the wise ones, "as
many whites as snakes?—no, no, ten snakes to one pale face." I reckon they
know better now. They can hardly number as many men, women, children
and horses, as the pale face rifles that have passed through their land in the
last eight weeks.

To return, I did not visit a large patch of trees east of this, but it seems
to be of the same character, while in all directions the water is oozing from
the ground, changing grass and sticks and everything to stone. As you
approach the first grove, another directly ahead springs into view, on the
side of which, towards you two singular looking red and white mounds arise
from the plain. Turning directly toward these, you cross a small stream that
runs down from the timber, above through a sloughy piece of ground,
where willows grow in bunches. Among these willows in a deep hole, eight
or ten feet across, the best drinking water to my thinking is to be obtained.
It boiled like a kettle of water over the fire, but is cold.

Crossing the slough brook one road leads to the first mound. We took
the left, leaving the mound at the right, and soon after crossed a creek a
rod wide having boiling springs, (though the water is cool I believe) on the
north bank just below the road. Pass on half a mile through the cedars
almost to the last, and you come to Beer Spring, where we camped. It is a
break into the rocky bank of the river ten feet in diameter and the water
boils up in two very large rocky spring holes. The largest and best is above
the other at the right hand as you face the bank and opens with an orifice
above two and a half feet in diameter—the rock projecting over, and
enlarges as it descends. The first spring up among the willows, and this one,
are the only ones I visited which were at all palatable. From the first I drank
two quarts in a few minutes. Some put in sugar, and others sugar and acid,
but I preferred it fresh from the well.

I visited the mounds, which are real curiosities, but they, like every similar thing here, have been deposited from water. Fremont has described them
accurately, and they who wish to amend had better come to view them for
themselves. There is a great curiosity on the north slope of the mount nearest the road. It is a rock, of the shape and size of a barrel, elevation four or
five feet, with a small hole in the top out of which the water boils, almost
too hot to hold the finger in.

The mountain range which has been on our left through the last valley slopes down four miles west of Beer Springs, by irregular peaks, to Sheep Mountain, fourteen hundred feet high, where it terminates abruptly. The river, sweeping round its base and turning to the south, runs down its western side six miles, and then, turns west, coursing across the plain, here eleven miles wide, through a deep fissure in the solid basalt, one hundred eighty feet wide and from one to three hundred feet deep.

At the bend under Sheep Mountain, the opposite bank of the river is nearly one hundred feet high, perpendicular. North of the bend is the terminus, four and a half miles broad, of a range coming down from the north. The peaks are irregular, and the central ones high, very jagged, and covered with scattering cedars. The pass or valley between them and Sheep Mountain is perhaps a mile wide.

On the west side of the north range the Oregon road runs up to Fort Hall, the fork being just beyond the bend of Bear River. The other road runs west. Hudspeth left, four weeks since, with a train of forty seven wagons, taking this route, and most of the trains have followed. If they could not get through some one would have returned before this. It is now a bourne from which no traveller has returned; yet I intend taking it, as there is a path in the same direction which has been packed through with mules. I learn also that Hudspeth has himself packed through.*

At noon, seven of us started for a hunt on the mountains, south west, and fording the river above Beer Springs, where the water was only knee deep, and boiling all over the surface like the springs, steered for the hunting ground on the mountain side. We found it four or five miles to the nearest base, and by different routes reached the highest summit, except a snow capped one some twelve miles south.

Three of us descended on the west, and leaving the two, I struck off south west, and came up Bear River five or six miles south of a large circular mound, or hill, mentioned by Fremont, and west of Sheep Mountain three miles. Following the river up on the east side to the base of the mountain,

*This "cut-off road" was known by various names—Emigrants', Myers', and Hudspeth's Cut-off. It was first used by emigrants in July 1849, when James Hudspeth and J.J. Myers led over it a company they were guiding. Henry Mann's diary (the manuscript of which belongs to Mrs. Adeline T. Cox), includes this entry for July 24, 1849: "Messrs. Hudspeth and Myers of the Jackson Co. Mo. Co. have just made their appearance through a gorge in the mountains. They left the main road at the point where we left Bear River, going west through a gap in the mountains. They intended to come out at the head of Mary's River, but not understanding their true latitude have struck the old road before it crosses the dividing ridge to the Basin. They would have made some 200 miles on the old road had they succeeded, but as it is they have made nothing. They were almost thunderstruck, when upon emerging they found they were only 70 miles from Fort Hall"—Gold Rush, J. Goldsborough Bruff, p. 621.

where the bank breaks down on to a small bottom by a steep, bold ledge, one hundred feet high, I crossed the river forty or fifty rods above, where the current was three feet deep, and very strong, running over and between huge masses of basalt. It was not more than one hundred fifty feet wide and yet I was half an hour in crossing. Let no one attempt it again, unless he wishes to be ducked.

It was after sun down when I reached the top of the bluff on the west side, and taking the direction for the circular mound, or crater, pushed on, determined to visit it that day. The whole plain abounds with deep fissures filled with loose rock, and between the mound or crater and the river is a long depression, extending several miles generally north and south, of the same width as the river channel, and into which the river breaks four miles below the bend. The east bank of this curious ravine, or crack, is fifty feet high in some places, a huge pile of rocks, lying loosely tumbled together, and sloping from the top, forming underneath immense caverns and holes, in one place two hundred feet deep. I saw snow and ice in two of them. They form convenient dens for wild beasts. Reached the mound after dark, and could see but little. From here to the road was one and a half miles north.

Reaching this, I turned east and came into camp at 11 p.m. heartily tired. I stopped a few minutes three quarters of a mile below camp, on the river bank among the cedars, to see Steamboat Spring. It comes out only a little above the water, boiling, foaming, white as snow, frothing, roaring, and whirling the water three feet high, from an orifice a foot in diameter.

AUG. 7, TUESDAY. Visited the same spring again this morning and it presents precisely the phenomena which it did last night. I could not find the little stream pipe spoken of by Fremont. Started late, and passing Sheep Mountain, and leaving the crater on the left, steered for a gap in the mountain nearly west, over a great plain, and entered a pass one mile wide between a very high sloping hill covered with grass on the left, and a number of high peaks covered with cedars on the right, fourteen and a half miles from camp. The road next turns south west, gradually and sometimes rapidly rising by a very smooth way four miles to the summit. (Here the road turns north west half a mile, and then nearly west one and a half miles to a fine stream, two yards wide, running across the road north.) Instead of turning to the right, we descended one and a half miles down a broad ravine of easy descent and camped at a small spring, one of the heads of the stream just spoken of. This is the first water after leaving the bend of Bear River. Take in water before you leave, or suffer with the thousand thoughtless ones who have gone before. Made twenty miles.

I have before adverted to the need of a definite guide. With one the emigrant is at home. In entering upon this untried and therefore under-scribed route I have determined to furnish the future emigrant with this great desideratum. The courses will in general be given, land marks described, crossings of streams noted, springs marked down, and distances estimated. The latter will only be guessed at from point to point, and will probably not vary much from the results given by the road-ometers, which are not to be depended on entirely, as they occasionally get out of order. I shall endeavor not to make the miles too long, that the traveller may be disappointed, the right way, (i.e., pleasantly,) if at all. One must travel in this road, to form any idea of the importance of knowing exactly where he is, and the distance from water to water, wood to wood, and grass to grass.

AUG. 8. WEDNESDAY. Left camp early, and going almost directly and nearly in a straight line, intersected the main road on the hill, saving by the whole cut off two miles, and getting much better grass. The grass was good every where except on the mountains, but near the camping place below it has been fed down. From the intersection the course of yesterday was resumed south west, and ascending gradually a mile, began to descend the most difficult hill we have yet found. Many teams have been overturned here, but we escaped uninjured.

At the foot of the hill, five miles from camp, came to a creek three yards wide, running like the other north, and uniting with it two miles below. Half way down the first hill is a spring on the left hand. From this stream the road continues, the same general course, up and down hills not very bad, and rapidly descending four and a half miles more, when we came to the bank of the main stream, which is here ten to twenty feet deep, and two rods wide, being dammed up below by a dike of basalt, or limestone, or both.

Took in water and camped one mile and a half below, at the eastern base of the mountain, the stream at our right one mile running south west, through a deep kanyon, and the road turning south up a valley which has a dome-like hill almost exactly in the centre. Made eleven miles.

AUG. 9, THURSDAY. Left camp before sunrise, and passing the eastern base of the dome-like hill, course south, reached the extremity of the valley and turned west on to the hill, distance three miles; then swept down the hill into a broad valley, and bearing to the left, in two and a half miles came to a stream running north through a grassy marshy bottom partly grown up to tall rushes. On the opposite side is a good spring.

Turning up the stream two miles S.S. east, came to a very good ford, one rod wide and two feet deep, muddy bottom and banks. From this point, S.S. east, a high double peak, from which the stream seems in part at least to arise, bounds the valley on the south. S.S. west is a like very irregular peak, and north the valley stretches off twenty or thirty miles between two ranges of high irregular mountains. West, a deep rocky kanyon cuts the mountains in two.

Six miles south of this, a wide, deep depression appears, leaving an isolated, low range, smooth and covered with grass and crowned with scattering cedars. From the ford the road ascends to a plain, and gradually rising, course S.S.W., reached the base of the mountain, and by a gentle ascent passes it midway between two kanyons just described, distance nine and a half miles. The descent is steep, and two miles, to a brook running south east. Passed several springs at the left on the way down. Here is a very pretty grassy valley, but it is close fed. Plenty a mile and a half above or below. Cedar for fire wood. Made nineteen miles.

The current news is, that an Indian attempted to steal something last night from a train, and was fired upon. In revenge he shot arrows into three of their cattle, wounding one badly. By a careful inquiry, I ascertain that the guard was asleep, and the Indian coming into camp waked him suddenly and in his fright he scared the Indian so that he ran away, and then he was fired on, both by the guard and from camp, but without effect. Our guard must keep a sharp lookout tonight. We are now among the Pannocks, two lodges of whom were by the spring where we stopped this morning. They seem very friendly, and want guns with flint locks.

Musquitoes have not troubled us any for two nights. Quite cool. Have noticed dwarf maple on the west side of all the mountains (in the ravines) this side of Sheep Mountain till today. Days as usual very hot, and roads covered with clouds of dust.

FRIDAY, AUGUST 10, 1849. Road from camp is one and a half miles S. West. Crossing two small streams, very bad crossings; then turns south and, passing over and down a mountain, crosses a small stream running from the north west, seven miles from camp.

This is the first water since leaving Bear River, which runs into the Great Basin. Of course the river is on the heights back of this ford. The ascent and descent are easy. From this point the road continues to descend ten miles, coming within a mile of the stream again and crossing a small branch just before reaching the foot of a mountain. Here five teams camped and the other seven went on making a night drive over the mountain. Made 17 miles.

SATURDAY, AUGUST 11, 1849. The valley where we left camp yesterday morning sends from the north part a small stream through the rocky kanyon, spoken of yesterday, and the stream running south by the camp winds around the hills south and east, receiving small streamlets from the west and south and pours through the south depression, and both of them then run into the small rushy stream where we halted in the morning. Ice this morning a half inch thick.

From the camp the road winds first south then west and then S. west through and up a ravine by an almost imperceptible ascent over the mountains and down by a precipitous descent into a valley at the bottom of which the road turns south round a considerably elevated hill ten miles from camp. One mile north of this turn the rim of the Great Basin crosses the valley, which is here some four or five miles wide and extending north until it sinks out of sight, two-thirds of the right side being occupied by the mountain in the distance. The track is now directly south six miles on the low level valley bottom, when it turns suddenly west, and by a very gradual ascent in four miles reaches the summit of a very high hill. The descent due west is tolerably good and easy over small elevations five and a half miles to several springs and a small stream which comes in from the S. west below them.

No wood but plenty of grass three or four miles up or down. It is all fed down any where near the springs.

Men and teams suffered a great deal for want of water on this route as they always do when neglecting to take a supply. The heat in the valley is excessive and the dust suffocating. Men frequently lie down by the road side, with black parched lips and dry swollen tongue and wait till some passing team can spare a cup of water, or till the sun goes down. We travel in the dark, bound to that bourne from which no traveller has yet returned. No one has yet come back by this route.

Yesterday Ball, Dodson and myself were on the mountains all day hunting. Dodson left us at 2 p.m. and got into camp but Ball and I wandered too far to get in. We got into a Hoosier camp and stayed with one Dr. Bradford from Southern Illinois.

We saw no game but a fox. It is all driven away if there ever was any. We hunted till noon today, cutting off several miles by going over a mountain and overtaking the teams in the dusty hot valley I described. When we got into the valley and came up with the five wagons in the rear we found they had no water. We had had nothing to drink since the day before at noon, as Bradford has only enough in the train to make coffee. We got part of a cup of coffee each and lay down without eating. So we had been without water 24 hours. And it was really annoying to not find it in the train when the standing order was never to leave a spring without a 24 hours supply of drinking water.

Seven teams had gone ahead and reached the springs I have described but the five which we overtook stopped three miles short at 12 p.m., it being too dark to drive, and it was uncertain if they were in the road at all. The cattle were turned loose and ran off south where I was satisfied that there was a considerable stream. The boys turned into the wagons. I told them that I was satisfied that there were springs within three miles west and I was determined to find them. If any one wanted water and supper he could follow.

Ball said he would go and so we started off. We soon came to a deep ravine with rocky sides. We made several attempts to cross it and did not succeed. The whole plain was uneven, rough and covered with sage brushes and cut up with ravines. Finally Ball caved and fired his rifle in the air, a signal agreed upon when we left, if we should wish to return. It was some time before the signal was answered and then it was a good distance away and not by any means in the direction that Ball expected. He turned back and I pushed on for a place that I could only imagine the existence of.

It was dark and the stars did not seem to give the least light. I plunged into ravines and through clumps of sage brush and stumbled over rocks but still kept on, with no guide but the stars. It was after 2 a.m. that I came to the brink of a precipice several hundred feet high and looked down on a scene that seemed little else than enchantment.

There almost under my feet, was a grand encampment. Several hundred human and inhuman beings were congregated in one of the most delightful spots on the route. A deep valley, a level bottom—a large area mostly floored with a large flat rock as large as a dozen dancing halls—a massive rock in the back ground dark with cedars. The lamps and candles and huge bonfires turning night to day. A group there laughing and swearing and gambling. Another trying a criminal for a murder recently committed. A hundred males and a half a dozen females dancing cotillian on the base rock to the music of flute and hautboy and clarinet and violin and horn. The loud laughter from that little group where some wag is retailing some ridiculous misadventure comes up here distinct and clear and quite refreshing—and yonder little squad sure as I live it is a prayer meeting.

All were busy and all enjoying themselves. With a good deal of difficulty I succeeded in getting down and soon I stood before the wagon in which I had slept so many nights in the wilderness. Sharp was on his taps in a hurry. It was a welcome. The boys all gathered round. They thought that the Indians had us. 20 minutes and I had as a good a supper as man need to ask.

But after coming so far and fasting so long I could only eat very moderately and as for drinking I was satisfied with half a pint, though I should have bargained for half a gallon at least three hours before. I slept well though. I was told in the morning that the dancing and singing and all the noises were kept up till day light. The mountains over which we travelled the last two days are rounded off mostly, and many of them covered to the top with grass. Some have cedar on their tops. Most have groves of poplar in the ravines and are sparsely covered with service berry bushes, the fruit of which is now ripening. They are very much like whortle berries, perhaps a little larger. We find acres and acres of rose bushes. I saw one double leafed rose three inches in diameter. Made 25½ miles.

SUNDAY, AUGUST 12. This place has not the gorgeous splendor this morning, that invested it last night. It is quiet now as a New England Sabbath and beautiful indeed. North high mountains, rough and timbered, East a high bluff, south and east a broad plain and mountains in the distance. West gradually rises to rounded, smooth, grassy mountains: here rock and tree and grass and water and men and women and tents and wagons and busy life.

And death is busy too. A young man, I.A. Wood, age 23, died this morning and was soon buried beside another, F.M. Bates, age 32. His train had to leave, hence the hurry to bury. There are a great many trains here and probably two hundred wagons and five or 600 men and a few women.

The reason for such a congregation is first Sunday, next the beauty of the place and the excellent grass and water, and lastly the distance back to water; the long drive having greatly exhausted the cattle. Several trains have passed today without stopping. They will miss it. I think we shall have a desert country and hard drives ahead. No use hurrying. By my reckoning Fort Hall is 75 miles directly north and the extreme N. west point of Great Salt Lake twenty miles south. I intend to see it tomorrow from some of those peaks west of us.

MONDAY, AUGUST 13. The road from camp is west up not much of a hill, two and a half miles, making a detour northward around the head of a ravine and crossing to the north side of the rim of the Great Basin again. Then west and S. west until it enters a mountain gorge at the northern base of a mountain range or rather clump of mountains, lying west and south of our last camp, and between the road and the Great Salt Lake. From camp this morning I marked the highest peak bare of trees, smooth and apparently gravelly, bearing west south west and determined to get a view of the lake from it. [This probably was Cache Peak on Mt. Independence, between Almo and Elba, Idaho.] I told the boys that I was bound to see it and anyone who wished could have a chance. But no one believed and laughed at the idea. So I was alone.

Leaving the train and road three miles on I immediately began to ascend the mountain due west on a smooth rounded spur which descended from near the top. At first the ascent was very gentle and I walked bravely and rapidly for more than two hours. It gradually became steeper and the scattering shrubs and green sword gave place to gravelled clay and a very light covering of grass.

Sharper and sharper was the ascent and slower and slower my progress. I persevered, and never stopped or looked back and, at broad 12, reached the summit. I was richly rewarded for all my present and previous tramps to get a good mountain view and the long tedious hours I have put on this, for I began the ascent just after sunrise. The mountains are piled in heaps all around me. It is like getting on the highest stack of an Illinois farmer and overlooking all his stacks and ricks and cocks of hay. South 25 miles lies the Great Salt Lake in full view.

One glance and I look again at my feet and down the mountain side

and on a perfect nest of mountain peaks smooth as the one I stand upon
but much lower and gradually receding and lessening in height until they
become a part of the plain which seems to occupy nearly half the space this
side of the lake. Across this plain I see a constant succession of little whirl-
winds like water spouts. They rise up suddenly and sweep along for a mile
or more and vanish only to give place to another. Sometimes there are
several at the same time. It is a barren desolate waste. No tree, no grass, no
sign of vegetation after the first two or three peaks. All beyond looks utterly
desolate. And all here is a dreamy, empty silence. I do not hear a sound.

But the lake — there it lies, white as the driven snow, with now a dark,
now a green, now a blue spot in the center, stretching away toward the S.
east directly against a high, black looking island. Beyond the white expanse
rise high black barren looking mountains. The white expanse is pure salt.
The dark streak is the water which is blue, green or black as it is more or
less ruffled by the wind. It is a sublime but melancholy sight after all. There
is not a dimes worth of anything here, if we may except the salt.

North are two or three miles of mountains and beyond a broad plain
cut up by ravines, and here, right under my feet, is something moving like
ants or some sort of insects. As I live my glass reveals my own train. There
is Ball and Stebbins and Elder Wisner's teams; and Hawley's. It is the road
which runs at the base of the peak, directly under my feet. They have
[made] but little progress or I have travelled far. There they stop and are
about to take dinner. I scream. It seems that I could jerk a stone down on
their stupid heads and yet scream as I will they don't hear me. I discharge
six barrels of my revolver. No, they don't hear yet. My rifle with three
inches of powder — Bah! how deaf. I can hardly hear it myself. No wonder
they don't hear. If they had any curiosity they would look up at least.

The place where I sit and write is only a level, smooth place nearly circular and two yards in diameter, and composed of clay sand and bits of flint
stone. From this the slope is rather gradual a few yards and then down it
runs steep, steep and smooth, half way to the base without a shrub and
only stunted grass.

In the center of this place or table is a cactus of the size and shape of an
old fashioned quart bowl on which I first placed my leather portfolio and
here I sit. Equidistant S.E., S.W., N.W. and N.E. are four others of the size
and shape of tea cups and there are two or three lesser ones.

In the gorge up which runs the road, seven miles from camp is a spring
sending a small stream down near the road where it sinks. I can trace it as
distinctly with my glass as if it was worked on a map. It can afford but a
scanty supply of water. One mile and a half farther on the left of the road
there is a well. (This, I learned from the boys, supplied but little water and
is about four feet deep.) Indications of water may be seen through the gorge
on its southern side for two miles in the vicinity of the springs and well. A
short distance from the well, west, you reach the rim of the basin. Thus far

I can see from here, though up the gorge the shrubs and trees interrupt a perfect survey.

I enjoyed my perch for two hours and when the teams were again in motion I reluctantly left, descending a smooth spur several hundred yards in a westerly direction parallel with the road, and then as it assumed a more nearly level course I followed it slightly descending, in nearly a straight line a half mile when it was no more than two feet wide, rapidly descending on either hand hundreds of feet among the stunted bushes into a deep ravine seemingly walled in on every side. The hog back soon grew wider and gradually ascended and turning south west, seemed to melt into another mountain peak similar to the one I had just left, and to become a part of it. Here I left it and made my way along the north side of the mountain as best I could. I was several hours working my way through and finally reached the road 80 or 100 rods east of the rim of the basin. It is much farther here than I had estimated from my elevated observatory. But I made slow progress among the smooth mammoth stacks, sometimes going two miles to get a hundred yards.

Oh, what a solitude. Not a bird or beast or sign of one. Not even a cricket or a worm. Utter silence reigned. And the chirping of a cricket at the spring where I first found the road was music to my ear. From the rim of the basin there is a sharp descent south west and, a short distance below, found the teams and a spring with a plentiful supply of water. It is ten or eleven miles from camp of the morning. From here the road again ascends a few hundred feet, again crossing the rim of the basin, and then descends into a valley which opens broad towards the north west and Snake River and south east and Great Salt Lake.

The ascent is long, gradual and easy and the descent almost equal to it. It is all mountain behind us crowded and jammed together between the bases of which are extremely narrow and crooked valley abounding in rich grasses. Little or no timber. Camped at a spring on the left of the road, just beyond a small mass of basalt on the right, four miles from the "summit" and turned our cattle back for grass two miles into one of the narrow ravines on the south side of the road. The grass here has just been burned off through carelessness or wantonness of the emigrants. I should judge, the latter from the number of points at which the fire has started. The brush is still smoking.

Today, at noon, Ball and Darling had a dispute and exchanged a few blows. This is disgraceful, but such and similar scenes occur often on the route, though not in our train. I have forborne to speak of the conduct of the men thus far, hoping that I might be able to give the picture a better coloring, but I haste to do it now lest it should become worse. And

1st, the Devil seems to take full possession of three-fourths of all that come on to the "route," within one hundred miles after leaving the Missouri River and when they reach the "South Pass" all restraint seems to be at an end.

They are by turns, or all together, cross, peevish, sullen, boisterous, giddy, profane, dirty, vulgar, ragged, mustachioed, bewhiskered, idle, petulant, quarrelsome, unfaithful, disobedient, refractory, careless, contrary, stubborn, hungry and without the fear of God and hardly of man before their eyes.

Nothing seems to have any influence on them except the elements and physical force united with strong moral and mental power. The remaining fourth are very much in the position of Driesback with his animals, controlling and yet always prepared and expecting an outbreak and by associations becoming half animalized himself. Made 17 miles.

TUESDAY, AUGUST 14. Road west, S. west down the ravine with the creek formed by the springs on the left (a few rods). Crossing a branch from the north three-fourths of a mile on and another three and a quarter beyond near a large quagmire also on the left. Here it turns S.S. west two and a half miles and then W.S. west three and a half miles and crosses the main stream. The last three and a half miles runs through a broad and handsome valley, the creek still on the left side. The road, till it emerges from the ravine into this valley, crosses the extreme points of several low spurs only a few feet elevated and sometimes not more than one or two feet above the stream. Springs are numerous and the water good. Grass everywhere if not fed down or burned. The ravines passed on the south yesterday and this morning have fir trees in considerable number and some of them of large size but back some distance from the road.

Halted for dinner two miles before reaching the ford where the water sinks into the ground just as it reaches the track. From hence the road runs S. west, six and a half miles on a higher level covered with sage bushes, the only vegetation, and then descends to a lower one covered with weeds and greasewood, runs eight and a half miles W.S.W. to a stream a yard wide and a foot deep. I suppose it to be one head of Raft River as it runs north. Distance from the sink, 15 miles. The Fort Hall trail should come in here. Feed good. Water plenty. No wood.

We are outside of the Great Basin now. The rim or divide is several miles S.S. east and the road seems to cross the head of the valley at a very low point of the two breaks in the mountain west. Seen from camp, at noon, the narrow right hand one must be the route. This is a beautiful valley and the ground rises gradually toward the S. east for several miles covered with three or four kinds of grass of excellent quality and appears like an extensive meadow.

It is intersected by two or three dry channels several feet deep, and one which has occasionally a pool of water. The bottom is very miry. The valley narrows as you go north. Made 25 miles.

WEDNESDAY, AUGUST 15. Lay by all day. A couple of men in a train just over the stream had a quarrel last night. One struck at the other with a large knife, and then both took their rifles and went out to shoot each other. But it all ended as it began, in nothing. This quarrelling is almost universal. Broke up Hill's wagon and divided his load and team to two other wagons. The load weighs 1074 lbs. Kan's baggage made it about 1300. Van went off north with his team without orders. Showers with thunder on the mountains yesterday and today and strong gusts of wind with a few drops of rain occasionally.

THURSDAY, AUGUST 16. Left camp at 8 a.m. Course west five miles to the creek here ten feet wide with gravelly bottom. Grass all the way four miles to the ford, and above it as far as I can see. Courses west. A short distance above the ford the Fort Hall road comes in. One and a half miles west from the ford is a bog on the left and a small warm spring rises from a truncated conical heap within two yards of the road. Thunder showers hang over the mountains in all directions but no rain in the valley.

This range of mountains is, geologically, like those hills described as painted in the Black Hills. In many places a substance similar to slacked lime has the exact appearances of snow so that most are deceived by it. On the peaks south there appears to be several precipices or walls of basalt, (columnar). The mountains are generally smooth with grass and scattering shrubs to their summits, but no trees. The slopes to the creek bottom, which has nothing but grass, and the plain to the mountain gorge is covered with sage or greasewood.

Shortly after leaving the bog and warm springs we came to a second of considerable size and probably impassable in a wet time, dry now. Three miles west, where the southern mountain slopes to the valley and a small stream comes down from the north, the road turns S.W., crossing several little rills coming in from the north, and then south across the main stream four miles. Camped on the south bank after crossing at the ford. The stream here is larger than ten miles below.

The route after crossing the first ford this morning is a few rods north of the main stream which skirts the base of the southern range. It runs along the slope of the northern range just above the creek bottom which is sometimes only a few rods wide and then again a quarter of a mile. There is abundance of grass and plenty of dry willows for fuel. Springs abound everywhere. The ascent has been very gradual today. Scarcely perceptible. Made 17½ miles.

FRIDAY, AUGUST 17, 1849. CAMP. A small stream comes in one mile above here from the N.N.W. and two miles and a half above one from the mountains south joins one from the valley west. Left camp early. Cloudy morning and pleasantly cool but not cold as it has been. Some musquitoes. The road for a mile and a half is south, passing some springs, then three miles S.S.W. crossing the dry bed of a streamlet which comes down from

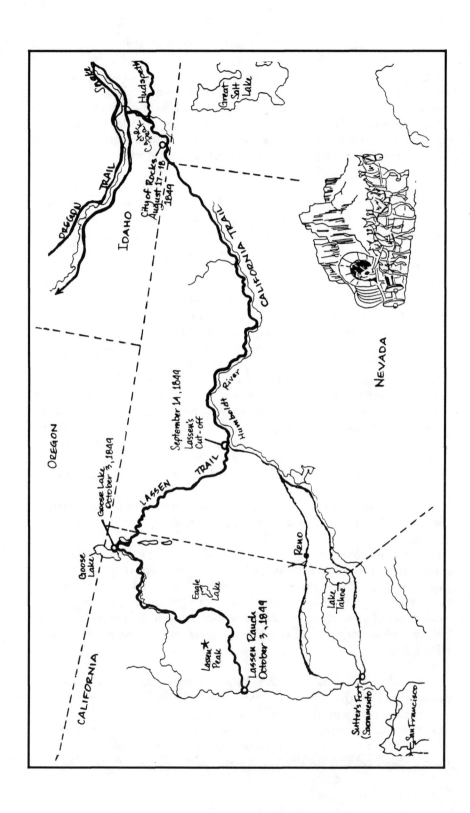

the south, and then ascends more rapidly to a much higher level. Two miles from this point, W.S.S., are several rounded mountain peaks with a clump of willows and a spring at the base, and S.W. there is an isolated one looking like a pyramid. The plain between is smooth and beautiful.

On the left a short distance is the dry bed of the stream, running parallel with the road, bounded on the east, without an intervening bottom, by some low, irregular, brown, gravel bluffs, partially covered with dwarfed cedars and cut through with deep ravines, which commence three or four miles back at the base of a range of mountains extending north and south, and presenting a jagged and unequally broken ridge. Its crest, indeed, looks more like a saw with broken teeth than any other thing.

The route is next nearly south one and a half miles and then we cross the river of the Great Basin again, and are once more in it. The descent is very gradual; course due south. Mountains obscured by smoke, right ahead and on our right, in the distance. Three and a half miles on, the road angles slightly to the right and crosses two little branches, where we take dinner. (9 miles.) After leaving we gradually descend east of south one mile when the road turns S.S.W. leaving the little stream at the left. 2 p.m. A heavy shower with some thunder.

Nearly due west from this last angle are some singularly appearing rocks, and in a valley beyond some isolated hills. Towards these I directed my course and found them located in a valley from one and a half to three and a half miles broad and abounding in grass. On the east side is a small rivulet from one to two feet wide. Another, one and a half yards wide, comes down from the N.W. east of the rocks, and a third, two yards wide runs among them on the east side, while a fourth takes its rise from the base of an isolated rock, south, all uniting below three miles, on the west side of the last hill in the chain around the southern extremity of which it sweeps and then passes our camp, then turning east, runs several miles down the valley. I know not what it empties into. The road from the turn continues to descend (passing some springs and low, wet ground where several small branches sink) and crosses the main stream one-half mile below camp and six miles from where we took our nooning. Made 15 miles.

The rocks I have just mentioned lie in a delightful valley, and at a distance have the appearance of water thrown up into the air from numerous artificial hydrants forming irregularly pointed cones.

Nearby they display all manner of fantastic shapes. Some of them are several hundred feet high and split from pinnacle to base by numerous perpendicular cracks or fissures. Some are dome-like and the crack runs at different angles, breaking up the masses into huge blocks, many of which hang tottering on their lofty, painted beds, ready to tumble when the elements shall have undermined them a trifle more. Some of the smaller rocks

Opposite: Map 3. Final leg to California.

are capped with a single stone, to appearance scarcely larger than a man's
head, though probably weighing several tons. One huge dome capped mass
on the east standing alone, has the dome split down, leaving a fair, smooth
face forty or fity feet in diameter, and maybe one hundred. On the very pinnacle of this is the appearance of a man sitting astride, and from the south
the resemblance is so perfect, that you see the shape of the left leg extending
down the smooth surface in due proportion to the body and head above.

   Another rock on the south side after crossing both streams has a deep
cavern on its S.W. side. I have not time to write the hundredth part of the
marvels of this "Valley of Rocks" as I have named it. It is worth a long journey to see but for an hour suffice it to say that of the 100 points and spires
and domes and masses, etc., no two are alike, and the effect in the aggregate
is absolutely indescribable. [City of Rocks was called various names by pioneers, including Silent City of Rocks, Fountain Rocks, Cathedral Rocks,
Cottage Rocks and Steeple Rocks. Lord may not have been aware it was
already named, or may simply have preferred his own name for it.]

   There is a singularity about the mountain range. All its peaks and rocks
have a pyramidal form. I should judge from appearance that the rocks are the
remains of washed away mountains. They are formed of a loose, coarse sandstone which yields readily to the action of the elements. The valley and the
hills are strewed with a white rock resembling marble but in reality is quartz.

   It lies scattered about in blocks, masses and broken into small fragments.
It is sometimes now with green or red, and in some localities lies so thick that
it has the appearance of a snow bank. I did not discover its location in the
mountain masses but it probably lies in layers among the sandstone.

   The beds of the streams are lined and filled with them, worn so smooth
and polished so nicely that one can walk across barefoot without any pre-
caution.

   This valley opens into the main one directly between our camp and the
pass where we next plunge among the mountains. A branch of the Great
Valley comes sweeping down from the south, with its willow-fringed mountain stream which gains the other affluents far away to the east. On the
south side of this stream, some seven miles distant S. east, there is a smoke
of a camp fire, doubtless the new Mormon "cutoff" round Bear Lake comes
up the creek formed by these streams.

SATURDAY, AUG. 18. Left camp; crossed the ford—course from ford
two and a half miles S.S.W. Next course west two and a quarter miles to
the "gap." Here the road turns W.S.W. around the base of a hill down
across a small stream and on to a cluster of rocks—one mile. Very crooked.
This valley is small and rough but remarkably interesting. The formation
and general appearance the same as in the Valley of Rocks, and the range is
far more extensive but does not possess the extreme beauty of the first. From
the form of stone on the right of the road a few rods, and its remarkable

similarity to a thatched cottage even to the very eaves and chimney, and being surrounded by other large cottages and tent-like rocks, I have ventured to name the place Cottage City though I found "Castle City Hotel" painted in large letters on the front for a sign. I do not think the last name appropriate and I shall retain my own. The cottage, or "hotel" covers a quarter of an acre and has a chimney top five and a half feet in diameter and six feet high.

These singular rocks extend more than a mile north and south, and the whole looks like a village with two or three long streets. I ascended the "hotel" and climbed up and sat upon the chimney. This perch where I now sit to write is 80 feet high though from a short distance it appears no more than 25 or 30. It is very difficult to attain, a regular break-neck performance. South east is a rock which presents the transverse section of an aqueduct. From the cottage the road is south and S.S.W. two and a half miles crossing a shallow valley and gradually ascending to a considerable elevation, passing between two remarkable masses of rock by a narrow opening. On the left a few feet above the road lies a rounded rock five or six feet in diameter with a large excavation from the road side into it, and some body's name painted in the cavity on the rock.

I also read the following: "Baird and Tucker of Elgin passed the 11th inst."

The road here descends a narrow and rather rock way for a few rods and then the descent is easy though winding and crooked one mile and S.S.W. Then the road turns west and the one from Salt Lake, a new route, comes in from the east up a ravine.

This route is worse than ours and fifty miles longer. It passes up the east side of Salt Lake, crosses Bear River and runs along the north side through a barren desolate region and enters the old Fort Hall trail here.

From this junction of the roads the course is west one mile and a half, to the valley, five miles S.W. across it to the entrance of the "gap" and one mile and a half W.S.W. to the summit of the ridge. The ascent is easy for so considerable an elevation. The hills on each side of the road are sloping, and at some one third of the way up are some good springs. The main valley which we have crossed runs nearly S. east and N.W., and has abundance of springs on the west and south.

Leaving the summit which seems to be the rim of the basin we descend rapidly to Goose Creek, six miles. The hills are steep, bad, and stony, and some to ascend, too, and in many places the wagons were in imminent danger of over turning. The road is crooked beyond description but the general [direction] is about S.S.W. We camped on a brook a mile and a half short of Goose Creek. The hills through all this region are sparsely covered with dwarf cedars. It is very rough, but there are no very high peaks. There is a small stream and some springs on the route. Made 22 miles.

Part II : Desert and the Sierra

Chapter Four
August 19–September 8, 1849:
Nevada

———◆——◆——◆———

SUNDAY, AUG. 19. It was dark when we camped last night and this morning we discover that there is no feed here. It is gnawed down into the ground. Some ice this morning on the streamlet where we camp. Hitched up and drove down to the creek, near two miles, then up the creek two and a half miles S.S.W. and halted. The feed is nearly gone though the bottom is nearly a half mile wide. The stream is muddy, four yards wide and eight or ten inches deep. Course of the stream nearly S.S.W. From the halting place went up the creek one mile and a half nearly. South, two miles nearly S.W. and two miles S.S.W. and camped by the creek. It is here very crooked, abounds in willows, and the feed has been plenty and good but is now eaten and dried up. Found some good feed in a ravine one and a half miles south west of camp.

The road along the creek passed at a little distance from it through the wild sage. The hills and mountains are not high and in ridges rather than peaks. The white rock and red sandstone run in strips or layers through some of them or their fragments paint their sides in alternate patches of white and red. Made ten miles.

MONDAY, AUGUST 20, 1849. Ice three-eighths of an inch thick. Left camp as late as usual. Course one and a quarter mile S.S.W, two miles, S.S.E., one half mile W.S.W., one and a quarter S.W.W., one quarter W.S.W. Then four miles S.S.W. general direction. This section of the road has several detours to the left to avoid a very large marshy bottom, with hot springs and cut up by numerous little streamlets.

87

The course is next two and a half miles W.S.W. Then two miles S.S.W. at the turn are some curious excavations in loose sandstone. They are scooped out with so much regularity that one might suppose it to be artificial. A species of bee or wasp has pierced it with innumerable holes for nests and the swallows have attached their mud domiciles to one section.

The main branch of the creek we have followed on the east and south side, so far comes in at the beginning of this two mile section, and at the end of it the road turns up the creek one mile W.S.W. and enters a deep kanyon.

The sides are high rough and steep, and the summit crowned with basalt, which also covers the sides, and blocks of scoriated basalt lie at the base, and in the bed of the branch which runs through its whole length. The first one half mile the road is rough, crooked and rocky and crosses the stream. Soon after it opens into a small valley and running a considerable distance along the creek enters another section similar to the first, though not as rocky. General course, W.S.W. three miles. Here we cross the branch and turned S.S.W. one mile and camped, driving our cattle south up the valley, which here is from a quarter to half a mile wide.

Scarcely any feed after turning up the branch toward the kanyon. Two or three springs under the mountain on the east of the camp. The ascent up the creek to this place is very gradual, scarcely appreciable. The width of the valley varies from one mile to where it is pinched in between two hills almost touching together and this too in a number of places. Some small streams come in from the east and south and make two or three bad crossings. Made 17½ miles.

TUESDAY, AUGUST 21. From camp course is west two and three-fourths miles winding up and over a hill the first three-fourths. Not very steep but rocky and the other two smooth, crooked and nearly level. From here the road runs S.S.W. crooked one mile up hill but not high nor steep; then a little east of south one and three-fourths miles. The mountain ranges in all directions are smooth and covered with grass to their summits.

The hills and valleys below as far as vision extends, present nothing but sage, greasewood, and weeds with a scatting or sprinkling of cedar. The last section winds down into a shallow valley and up another hill, rather rocky, and turns S.S.W. in a winding tortuous course, with very gradual descents and quite steep ascents two miles to the summit. From here it runs in a winding way S.W. a quarter of a mile. Then south, down a hill and over the point of another, with east descents and ascents, one and a half miles. Noon. Here is the eternal "river" again.

From this one and three quarters miles S.S.W. and one and a half south winding over gentle hills brings us to the summit of a hill from which you look down into a valley where the road winds along south among hills crowned with cedar one and three-fourths miles. Mountains on either side, right and left at some distance. No vegetation but sage yet and no water. Road down easy though somewhat rocky at first. But no place at all steep. Just at the bottom of the little hill course changes to S.S.W. and runs one mile up and down but a smooth road.

Then we descent three-fourths of a mile south and one mile S.S.E. to a small stream and a spring one quarter of a mile to the right under a mass of basalt. Water not very cold. Plenty of feed two and a half miles east on the hills. Made 17 miles.

WEDNESDAY, AUG. 22. Had a company meeting last night and the men conducted most scandalously. They (i.e., is a majority) are great rascals. Of the greatest are Van Wormer, Hanby, McCauley, Morgan and Darling. Whipple (crazy?) Hill, G. Hanby and Ballard are only less rascals because they are greater fools or cowards. Such is human nature. Van pitched off 200 pounds of provisions day before yesterday and the company took no notice of it. May everyone that refused to do so starve before they die and God's curse of the wanton rest on them.

From camp the road descends all the way for ten miles. First three and a half miles south, then one and three-fourths S.S.W., then four and three-fourths south, skirting the base of the hills on the right. The stream from the spring runs three and a quarter miles along at the left as we came down, the bottom being of considerable breadth and mostly covered with sage and greasewood, which also covers in part the hills on the west and altogether on the east. On the first section (of three and a half miles) the water sinks and some wells have been dug at the beginning of the one and three-fourths mile section. One mile from the beginning of the third section it reappears, or at least there are some springs.

Very little grass anywhere except several miles distant on the hills. The road next turns to the right at the point of a hill and passing an alkaline bog or spring hole and over a hill and up another, good path one and a half miles S.S.W., it turns south and enters another valley, three miles over gentle hills, to the valley bottom, in which there are signs of water. From this the road runs S.W. four miles, and a road that turned off to the left after sweeping round into the foot of the valley, where is water, comes up the dry bed of the stream and enters the main road.

Numerous pits are dug in the stream bed, now dry, in various places, for water. Some of them are dry and some have water in them, but muddy generally. It is the opinion of all I ask that this valley descends to the south. But it certainly descends to the north. Through the whole valley, which will average nearly a mile, there is a luxuriant growth of tall bunch grass, but it has been much eaten and trampled.

Next course is nearly S.S.W. to camp. This is one mile and a half below where a mountain sends a stream from the east down to the valley. The water makes its appearance in pools every few rods in this section, but it is alkaline, and will certainly entirely disappear in a few days.

The hills are whitened with patches of soda, and to appearances, very barren. The bottom mountains a considerable breadth, and the bunch grass contends for mastery with the all-pervading sage and greasewood. Some times one prevails and sometimes another and sometimes they all grow peaceably together. Neither has much to boast of in the contest. Whether the hostile onset of the numerous herds pastured on it this summer will lessen its chances of a final triumph remains to be seen. I should judge the chances much against the grass now, and the future traveller may look for the promised feed in vain.

The days are as excessively hot as the nights are uncomfortably cool. Still the fine dust from the track rises in the clouds covering men and wagons and cattle and grass, and every green or dry thing. Made 21½ miles. Good water may be obtained here by digging a hole on the side of the stream bed. As yet there is enough standing in the channel in pools.

THURSDAY, AUGUST 23. Left camp early. Course one and a half miles S.W.W. then one and a quarter south then S.S.W in general three and a half miles up the wide grass-covered valley bottom, to a number of spring holes in an extensive slough. Then one mile and a half and turned to the left on to the grass and camped to adjust the loads. After all were weighed found the loads of those who had made the loudest complaints the lightest. These fellows are great fools, delaying the train to alter loads when not one reached 1100 lbs for three yokes of cattle. Showers in the afternoon and drizzling, cold rain in the evening and through the night. Beautiful road. Made 7¾ miles.

FRIDAY, AUGUST 24. Clouds passing away. Sun out. Not cold—only pleasantly cool. This is a beautiful valley. There is, however, a scarcity of wood and the water is alkaline. From camp the road passes over a long level sage plain and strikes on to the grassy bottom near the sink of some hot springs. Distance 12 miles, and course nearly S.S.W. by south. Road winding. From the hot springs a fine stream of hot water rushes down growing less and less to the sink. Near the boiling is a spring of cold water.

The only scenic variety here is the sage and a solitary clump of willows, here and there at long intervals. The mountains on either side and ahead are very pretty but not at all remarkable. Everything is quiet and that is about all. Near the middle of the western range is a peak with a big rock perched nicely on the top. It bears about west of the sink.

The road comes to the stream two miles below Boiling Spring, and does not leave till we reach cold spring on the left one-third mile beyond the hot one. The springs are all on the left and the hot springs cover nearly an acre in all, the whole surface being cut up into channels, each several feet wide and partly covered with masses encrusted with soda or lime and iron. The water is clear, of a bluish cast, and in many of the springs so hot that the hand can be held in it only a moment without scalding, and one is absolutely boiling hot. The water boils up in hundreds of places from mere heat and not gas, and the stream more than two miles below is as warm as dishwater, and warmer than the hand, four miles, though the stream is five or six feet wide and two feet deep and quite rapid. They are situated on a fine level plain covered with good grass but destitute of wood.

But that is little needed as the boys are washing their clothes at the spring without fire and it takes but little soap as the water is alkaline. Still they say that it does not wash very well.

Camped at noon by the cold spring and broke up a wagon. The loads now all weighed and adjusted weight 1300 to each wagon with three yokes of cattle and thirty head of loose cattle, to relieve. Had no fire wood this evening but the wagon.

SATURDAY, AUGUST 25. This morning Col. Wm. Hamilton, son of Alexander Hamilton of Revolutionary memory passed our camp. He is a small, active, smart looking man, apparently fifty, and was once undoubtedly a very handsome man. His exterior is now not of the smoothest, though a decent hat would much improve it. He is wearing, or rather is capped with, an old, rusty, torn, shockingly dilapidated, part of a straw hat – the major part it is true but a very considerable minority has seceded.

He has a four-horse team of fine looking animals, and has oats to feed them, brought from Salt Lake at one dollar a bushel and threshed them himself at that. Success to the enterprising Col. Conde and Hawley bought a horse last night for a blanket, a half pound of powder and five pounds of lead.

Left camp late. Course nearly S.S.W. to a spring on the left nearly a mile short of the entrance into the "pass" and nine miles from camp. A small stream runs down into the valley, this end of which is a broad plain half covered with sage. The grass is all eaten down, back to within two and a half miles of the cold spring. A small part of Burnham's train is here as pioneers. The most of it winters at Salt Lake. These have come from there in twelve days and intend to go through any way and examine the gold region by the time the others arrive next summer. They report all kinds of vegetables plenty at Salt Lake, but very dear.

I have said nothing about dead cattle lately but it was not from forgetfulness, for a carcass is passed oftener than a mile post. The mountains here are neither high nor steep, but barren and smooth and generally gravelly.

Some of them are sparsely clothed with scrubby cedars. The road is surpassingly excellent. No turnpike equal to it. From this spring the road turns the spur of the mountain at the left, and takes a S.E. direction one and three-fourths miles to the top of the hill; then S.S.E. down into a ravine and up. This is a winding way generally, no part steep, two miles. There is yet grass enough to camp in all the route and some springs, with sage for fuel. From the top of this mountain the descent is easy three-quarters of a mile S.S.E. Then S.S.W. up one hill; over and turn to the left down a steep place, then on gradually descending eight miles to a number of springs and some willows. Water bad.

The stream that runs from these springs, sinks and appears again repeatedly, at short intervals for quite a distance, taking in other springs from a sloughy bottom, forty yards wide. One mile from the upper springs there is no sign of water, though the dry bed of a stream remains and a grassy bottom as above on each side of it. The whole country from the other valley abounds in grass which grows among the sage to the mountain tops.

The valley itself is nearly circular, from eight to ten miles in diameter and descends to the east where is a long narrow bottom with a strip of willows, and also to the south towards a high mountain range with an irregular jagged outline buried in a blue mist. The road descends the same course from the upper springs on the west side of the bottom, one and a half miles, and crossing a "swell" covered with sage one and a quarter miles down to the bottom where we camp by some willows. The water is better than above. Last night the wind blew a gale for a few minutes and it became as cold as a November night. Cool today except about an hour after 12 a.m. Made 24½ miles.

AUGUST 26. SUNDAY. Very cold this morning. Feed very short—water neither plenty nor good, and no wood but sage. Left camp; course S.S.W. half a mile; then S.W. five miles over a sage plain, valley bottom some distance at the left, and two steep short hills to go down. From this the road turns short south two miles then S.S.W. three quarters of a mile, then one mile west on to the bottom, where is grass and plenty of water; the road rapidly descending, and two steep places. The mountain at whose base we are has snow on its summits, and seems quite precipitous towards the top. The valley opens broad to the west and the grassy bottom, which seems full of spring holes, is more than a quarter of a mile wide. Halted for noon here.

From this the road runs west N. west by west one mile and a quarter down the bottom, winding north under the bases of three singular looking hills, having the appearance of being formed of pipe clay and turning at the last N. west three quarters of a mile, then one mile and a quarter W.N.W. down the valley to a large spring, where the grassy bottom is nearly a mile wide. This spring is merely the reappearance of the springs which have sunk so often in the valley above.

From the spring to the sage plain, to which the ascent is gradual, is one mile and a quarter having the bottom sweeping round to the north and west. Next course is W.S.W. by west, two and a half miles through a valley; very fair descent and ascent, and down again into the valley which we left a few miles back and which is here more than a mile wide, and runs south west. A large portion is covered with grass, but no water, for at least five miles from the top of the hill where I now sit to write. The hills on either side of the valley are low, covered with sage, and on the west not much broken. The scene is one of quiet beauty. A mist covered, snow clad mountain rears its solitary form on the left of the road. From this point it is very distinct.

The owner of the horse which Conde and Hawley bought night before last, was after it last night, and this morning took it away, paying them as much as they paid the Indian, who, its seems, stole it. There are mountains in all directions except S.S.W. but they are at a considerable distance. The prospect for feed is now much better. From disaster, casualty, and disease, the breaking off of trains, and detention at Salt Lake, and the time gained by taking Hudspeth's cut off, we have 8,000 less cattle ahead now than at the South Pass, which is one fourth of the whole number. Our chance is nearly fifty percent better than if the whole had come through.

Met three Indians on the bottom. They are very saucy, grovelling, animal looking scamps. Their bows are not more than two and a half feet long. One of them reached out his hand, I grasped and found it soft and nerveless as a woman's. It seemed that I could crush every bone in it with one brotherly grip, and I had more than half a mind to try. When we reached the willows, found our old enemies the musquitoes, ready for the onset. Camped one and a half miles below, and six miles from where we came down on the bottom, course W.S.W. Grass is excellent, and very abundant here, and will average one and a half miles in width. No wood but a scanty supply of dry willows. There are a dozen trains in sight. The sun pours down his hot rays without stint, and he who would save the backs of his hands from blistering must wear mitts. Made 21¼ miles.

MONDAY, AUG 27. Ice three quarters of an inch thick this morning. Course from camp south west four and a three quarters of a mile. Here is quite a stream, and some willows, but the water soon sinks again. Then S.S.W. six and a half miles to a stream bed with abundance of willows, and water standing in pools. Crossed and stopped to noon one mile below. The road all the way down this valley is as smooth as a plank. This stream comes down from the north, and is probably one of the branches which constitute the north ford of the St. Mary's River. From noon halt, course is S.W. seven miles.

In this section the water reappears, augmented by the streams from the Blue range heretofore spoken of, and which extends south forty or fifty miles. The stream is lined with willows of large size, and is several yards wide, and in places several feet deep. In a place where it is three quarters of a mile from the road, I went down to the stream, and found a grave. On the board at its head was inscribed, "Samuel A. Fitzsimmons, died of a wound inflected by a bowie knife in the hands of James Remington, on the 25th day of August 1849."

At the end of the seven mile section, turned down S. east and camped on the creek, which is here at the shallowest place only a "ripple," four yards wide and six inches deep—just above it is eight yards wide and six feet deep; water clear and current rapid. Some men from a camp just above state that two of their oxen were wounded last night by the Indians with arrows, at the springs which we passed in the afternoon yesterday. They can assign no reason but wantonness. One of the arrows hung in the skin of the animal in the morning.

AUG. 28. TUESDAY. Not as cold this morning. Cloudy. Took the after cattle watch alone. This watch is from twelve to sunrise. I expected to have trouble with the Indians as they are somewhat saucy, and very numerous in the mountains east. I preferred the after watch as they would be most likely to disturb the cattle just before day, if at all, and to watch alone, that I might be more sure to detect them. I saw nothing of Indians, and probably should not if I watched twenty times, but heard a solitary wolf, howling short and sharp as he went sneaking down the valley. These scamps creep round in the tall grass, and are not easily seen. Eight miles below camp, passed the camp of a train from Missouri, which had all but a dozen of its cattle drove off in the night by the Indians. They left one, which probably lagged behind, with an arrow sticking in him.

Capt. Pierce had volunteered, with twelve men, and with the owners, to go after the cattle. They had not returned. On either side of the valley bottom is a sage plain, broken by ravines reaching to the base of the mountains. The course for ten miles from camp is S.S.W. and here the sage plain slopes down, and the river sweeps round to the west, only thirty or forty rods from the plain. Between the two runs the road, close to the base of the hill. For the last mile the road has turned S.W. A broad valley comes in from the east, down which flows another and larger branch, which unites with this some distance below.

From noon halt road continues one mile S. west, then four miles W.S.W., and one mile west to a stream which I shall call Soda Creek, from the abundance of the article on its banks. This creek comes into the fork from the north, through a considerable valley. It joins it just before it enters a kanyon, through which it passes at the left of the road into another valley, which the road runs over a hill, the descent steep. Distance one mile.

This valley is less than half a mile wide, and the grass is fed down close. Crossing this one mile W.N.W. and over a hill and down into another valley, we camped. The river winds round the hill south through a very rough kanyon, at the northern base of a mountain which may be seen thirty miles back, standing solitary at the south end of the great valley which we have been so long travelling down.

The road this afternoon has been for the most through greasewood, or sage. I suppose the bottom is wet and muddy early in the season; and to avoid this the road is crowded off the grass, towards the base of the hill. The great valley abounds in rich grasses and the banks of the streams are heavily lined with tall green willows, giving the whole a very beautiful appearance. At the junction of the two upper branches the valley is five or six miles wide. South there are no mountain peaks in sight, only long ranges of hills running east and west; one appearing just behind another as far as the eye can reach.

About 8 o'clock in the morning the wind began to blow, though not violently; and shortly the wagons were involved in a cloud of smoke and dust, and men and beasts half stifled. A similar cloud soon obscured and finally completely hid the mountains from view, and so things remain now we have camped. It is only half an hour, and all is clear again. The eastern range appears almost fearfully near and distinct.

Ball, Van Wormer and Dodson went under the mountains for a hunt this morning, and brought in a large antelope this evening about 8 o'clock. They report plenty of red clover on the mountains, and a great many deers and antelopes. No news from the lost cattle.

This valley is small, and like the other, closely fed, but no doubt had plenty of grass two weeks since. A valley comes into it from the north, nicely carpeted with greasewood and sage. The south side is bounded by the base of a considerable mountain. At the western part of the valley this base forms a high bluff, the upper half of which, facing N. west, is a jagged, broken, rough almost perpendicular wall of basalt, round which the river sweeps south, and plunges into a deep kanyon; then turning west, rushes into the next valley while the road runs down the valley. Made 20 miles.

AUGUST 29, WEDNESDAY. After leaving camp, the course was one mile and a half west to the bottom of a hill, then three fourths of a mile over; ascent not steep, but sandy, and a little heavy. From the top, road turns to the left. Course from the bottom of it S.W. three and a half miles, touching the river at the end of the second mile. This valley is similar to the other, only much larger. Greasewood and sage encroach on the grass considerably, but there is plenty yet. A range of rough low mountains stretches along on the west, at a distance of eight or ten miles. There seems to be grass to the summit, but not a tree or bush. The range at the left is similar, and the river runs at its base. This is a very pretty stream.

At the camp this morning where the current was rapid for four or five rods, it was nine yards wide and six inches deep. It is generally much wider, and several feet deep. The road in the valley bottom is cut down in one place three feet by the action of the wind, which blows the dust out of the track.

I would here observe, once for all, that where you find greasewod, with or without sage, you will find more or less depth of fine dust, which hardly affects or retards the rolling of the wheels. When you find sage alone, or nearly so, there will be more or less sand, sometimes causing a heavy drag, or a hard gravelly or flinty track, wearing and cutting the cattle's feet.

Since leaving Green River there has been much more gravel than sand among the sage. The exceptions to these facts are only enough to prove the rule. At the end of the last section the road turns to the left, a small part over a greasewood plain, three and a half miles S.S.W. to where we halted for noon, at the bend of the river, between which and the hill west the valley is not much more than half a mile, but immediately beyond both, it widens to two miles.

Directly ahead the eastern range sweeps round to the south west; the river running close under its base; on its side and summits are bushes of some kind. Above us the stream is very crooked, and seems loth to leave the beautiful valley, crossing it six times in half a mile. The men have returned from pursuing the Indians, and succeeded only in part. They brought back fourteen head, which the thieves abandoned ten miles on the route; probably because they did not drive fast or well enough.

From noon halt the road runs south one mile and W. by south half a mile, then S. west three miles part of the way through greasewood, then W.S.W. one mile and a half to camp. The valley bottom on this afternoon's route will average one mile and a half in width. The stream enlarges gradually, though it receives no tributaries. Occasionally a stripe of willows may be seen on the western range, but the water sinks long before it can reach the river. Willows about on its banks, and some reach a height of twenty feet.

The report is current now, and generally believed, that it was not the Indians who drove off the cattle, but somebody from the direction of Salt Lake, as the trail leads that way, and on the trail was a shoe track among the moccasins. Two horses also joined the trail some ten miles on. There are plenty of ducks on the river, and occasionally we see a lark, and a few birds unknown in the higher regions. We have ice every morning. I call the Great Valley the Valley of Thieves. Made eighteen and a half miles.

AUG. 30. THURSDAY. From a long distance above it may be seen that the valley is shut in at its south western extremity by the junction of the two ranges of mountains. Toward the lower end of the valley, at the left hand, may be noticed a pyramidal mountain peak which from the distance of a few miles presents the appearance of an Indian pagoda. The whole upper section seems formed of thick layers of earth, alternating with thin plates of stone, at very regular intervals. The layers of rock project considerably beyond the slope, with rather sharp ragged edges, the whole gradually and regularly diminishing to a point and dotted with dwarf cedars.

As you pass round to the west, the point appears to stretch off into a ridge. Beyond this, as seen from a long distance up the valley, and a little to the right, is a similarly shaped peak, but lower, smooth and without vegetation except grass. It slopes toward the north, and rises again gradually into a ridge. At this depression the mountain side seems bare and rocky, except a few patches of cedar, with a notch cut down right and left at an angle of 45 degrees, and this is a kanyon through which the road passes. I have called it Yellow Stone kanyon. It is fifteen and three quarters of a mile S.W. by south from camp, the road making considerable of a detour to the right three or four miles before turning down toward the kanyon to avoid a bayou and some long bends in the river.

Halted to noon below the bayou, and above the first bend, eight and a half miles from camp. East south east is a deep rocky kanyon, which admits a large stream into the valley from the east; probably the South Fork, some where below this, where I could not determine, comes on the old Salt Lake road. Beyond this kanyon over the mountain top the range east of the Valley of Thieves may be seen, pushing its rough, bare, snow patched peaks high into the air, and others may be seen stretching away a long distance at the left. This valley I shall call Pagoda Valley.

The river here is very crooked, and very deep where it is not rapid; and the bottom, which will average two miles, is much cut up by dry channels. One mile and a half above the kanyon, the road, which for the last four miles has been sweeping round to the south, crosses the river and descends S.W. on its south side over the slope of the mountain for the last half mile to the next ford. The bottom here is not more than a quarter of a mile wide, and at the south a broken plain sweeps up to the mountain base, while on the north the mountain terminates abruptly, and a part of the way presents only huge masses of basalt, or broken and crushed fragments, spotted with sage and greasewood.

A short distance above the pass are some singular yellow colored rocks. I shall not presume to attempt a description, as they have no particular resemblance to anything that I ever saw. Any one who can remember what he saw sometimes when he has the night-mare can get a fancy sketch from the recollection. Perhaps such an one might liken them to an assemblage of rude, uncouth monuments, set up by the unfinished inhabitants of a half formed world, such for instance as the wise ones would have the moon. The largest and tallest may be between one and two hundred feet high. This much was written under the shadow of the rocks, at 4 o'clock p.m.

Passing down along the base of the mountain, I turned for a farewell look, and was surprised and highly delighted to see an admirable and strikingly correct likeness of a lady, in full riding dress, apparently walking up the hill behind the enormous rock I have just mentioned. The best point of view is sixty rods below, but it may be seen from the road between where it is crossed the second time, (for it is crossed again here), and the entrance of the gorge.

The soil of this valley does not seem to produce as well as that of those above. There are large patches of course bunch grass and greasewood, and the same may be said of wild flax and weeds. It suffers much from drought and vegetation is now withered and dried for want of water. The soil appears to be finely pulverized clay and sand, and is full of holes where all kinds of insects and reptiles burrow, and the mole mines to such an extent that in many localities the earth is as porous as a sponge, and oxen or mules sink half way to the knee. Earlier in the season, I suppose the growth must be luxuriant—now feed is very scarce, though the bottom is very extensive.

A mile or more back from the first crossing, the old Salt Lake road winds up a ravine over a mountain south east. From the second crossing the road ascends a hill, not very long or steep, but a little rough, and descending to the river again passes down its north bank one mile and a half north west. The bluffs on either side are rough and irregular. On the north are some cells or caverns, high up in the rocks, and below is a mass of red stone, blackened as by fire, on the other side.

The gorge is thirty or forty rods wide. Next turns is N.N.W. half a mile, just at the end of which the road crosses the river where is but little room and none to spare. The bluffs on either side are masses of basalt, covered with small fragments sliding down from above. Just below the ford, the road, which is rather rough, turns round to the left a quarter of a mile W.N.W. then a short distance west, then round a low rocky bluff, a high jagged bluff on the right, course S.S.W. then round S.S.E., a high rose-pink colored rocky bluff on the right, to another turn, (three quarters of a mile in all), just before which the river is forded again. Here is a very singular and very picturesque valley.

At the first point of the bluff, where the road turns, is a tall plate of stone standing upright, having the appearance of an enormous curb-stone. A rocky mass just above is composed of huge plates of basalt, set up against each other almost perpendicularly, like a row of books. On the top of the mountain east is a range of bare rocks, with several large caverns in them. A close examination discovers the right hand bluff to be pierced with innumerable holes, or cavities, large enough to harbour or conceal all kinds of wild beasts that infest this section of country. The road next sweeps around the point of the bluff, and takes a general direction of west; the river on the left. The mountains have diminished to hills, and the river bottom is half a mile wide and has plenty of willows, which had nearly disappeared in the kanyon. On the whole, the road through it has been pretty good. But little feed yet. There are a number of musquitoes round again, which is rather strange, as the ice in a pail was three quarters of an inch thick this morning. I should like to find the place where they put up at night, if it is any warmer than our camp.

East of camp this morning, at the base of the mountain on the slope, were some hot springs smoking like large fires. The inquiry is "who finds them in pipes?" The men who went to visit them report, among other marvels, a pool several rods in diameter, boiling like mad, and real hot — scalding hot water too. There were large quantities of soda, which lay thick enough to be easily gathered.

A card at the first crossing stated that on the evening of the 27th, eleven head of cattle were stolen from a train at that point. They recovered four and found some of the others butchered. Very cold this evening; though the days are excessively hot; and the teams getting a late start, and stopping two hours at noon contrary to orders, did not reach camp two and a half miles below the kanyon till 9 o'clock p.m. Good enough for them. If men will be lazy in the morning, they must make it up at night, though it is much better to camp early as a rule, to give the cattle time to feed before dark.

The road on the last section runs mostly over a large sage plain, and rises a short steep hill just before we turned down to the left to camp. Feed is very good in this part of the valley, which is a very irregular one, and might not inaptly be named Crooked Valley. It is impossible from this point to see its direction, or the way out of it.

AUG. 31. FRIDAY. Cold again this morning and ice. Lay over. Ball and I went ahead to examine the mountain where the road passes over. Found no grass. All fed down for twelve miles, and no grass to speak of beyond, to the top of the mountain, eighteen or twenty miles. So returned, and will start early in the morning and make a long drive for it.

About nine miles below this, the road leaves the bottom and winds over a high mountain range, while the river sweeps around it to the south. The valley bottom gradually widens from camp, where it is a mile wide, to the turn where it is two or three, and continues so until it terminates in a deep rocky kanyon, through which the river finds its way. The grass had been fed down for three miles, and between this and the kanyon there is plenty.

SEPT 1ST, 1849. SATURDAY. Left camp at half past 7 o'clock. From the top of the hill from which we turned down to camp, the road runs south west, probably twenty miles, through a high mountain range, and is very crooked. The descent from the hill is easy, and two and a half miles on is a dry stream bed, and another one mile and a half farther, both having willows on them. Two miles from the last is a fine stream, three yards wide and one foot deep, swift current and clear water, which I shall call Yellow Stone Creek. It comes in from the north west. From this to the foot of the hill, touching a bend of the river by the way, it is three miles, the last mile running nearly west to the foot of a deep ravine, through which the road winds up over the first hill by a tolerably easy ascent, and smooth, hard beat, not flinty track. From the foot of the ravine back the route is mostly through a greasewood plain — ahead to the pass is sage, with very little grass.

There is a very large spring half a mile from the road at the left; to find which you have only to turn down a ravine after crossing the first hill, and follow it until it is intersected by one from the south. Immediately below this, turn to the right directly over the hill twenty or thirty rods, and you have some good spring water, though not quite cold enough. There is a range of boiling sulphur springs at the water's edge, under a low bluff, just east of the road, nearly half a mile before the final turn up into the ravine. A shallow rocky ravine, with a low mass of rough rocks below, runs down to the river at the place.

To determine the course of the river I left the road where it turns off towards the mountain and went down to the spring just described. From that I ascended the first peak and followed the ridge down, generally in sight of the river and the road, until I reached the summit of the farthest range, which from the valley back seems about one mile east of where the road descends through the mountain pass. I say descends for the road does not attain anything like the elevation which one would naturally expect from a cursory survey, but begins to descend about a mile before reaching the highest range and actually cuts through its very base.

The whole road across to it is tolerably easy, so say teamsters. As viewed from the height, I should judge that long ranges of low bare hills lie parallel, on the right, and the eastern mountain slope broken into ridges by deep rocky ravines on the left, the greater part of the way.

In many of the ravines I discover considerable grass. Directly in the gap is a spring, and a number of others a mile or more below. As to the river, it runs south five miles and then turns S.S.W. A large stream seems to come up from the south, turns S.W. and then a mile west and empties into the river two and a half miles below the last point.

The scenery is very bold, the banks in many places are perpendicular, the mountain peaks ragged and abrupt, and the valley only wide enough for the short turns of the stream. The whole country to the extent of vision is broken into ragged mountains. There is hardly a spot anywhere on which the eye can rest with pleasure. It is sometimes difficult, even from the highest point, to get more than a glance at the river, so deep and so narrow is its valley. It would seem that the senseless, shapeless masses of earth really grudged the beautiful little willow decked stream free passage through their sterile, thirsty domain.

The course of the road from the summit is still nearly south west. The ravine, after leaving what I shall call Spring pass, [Thousand Springs, Nev.] about one and a half miles, is narrow and rocky and has some very rough places requiring careful driving, and winds down among the mountain peaks, much like a snake. Three and a half miles down, the road turns short to the west nearly half a mile, and then resumes its course again, running over on the east side of a high hill, very rocky along the summit. Two and a quarter miles on the road forks. The main and direct one goes down to the

river; we took the left and reached camp at nine o'clock p.m., two and three
quarter miles from the fork. The distance from the foot of the ravine where
we began to ascend the mountain to Spring pass is eight and a half miles,
and from thence to the river eight and a half more. Made twenty-six miles.

SEPT. 2, SUNDAY. Not as cold this morning. Crossed the river immediately on leaving camp, and rolled down on its south bank. It is a noble
stream here, clear water, gravel bottom, and a wide plain. It is so smoky,
however, that I can hardly see how far it does extend on the south. On the
north is a range of high hills, and I perceive a road winding over one five
miles below camp. Night before last the watch of a pack mule train above
camp was attacked by Indians, and one man shot, and another said to be.
They drove off nine mules; so runs the story.

Met a man by the name of Rhodes, from Sutter's Fort, forty eight days.
There was a long train of fourteen or fifteen wagons with him. He says the
feed is short. Met the first packers the second day, then mule trains, then
mule and ox trains together and the second week met little else than ox
trains. He advised to throw away every thing but barely enough to get there
with. Henry M. Clure drove into camp this morning, with part of the Elgin
boys. Knows nothing of McCawley or Calvert. A large number of wagons,
perhaps fifty, were in this morning. The Indians have been busy among the
trains below—so says report.

Our course the first five and a half miles is west S. west, till nearly
opposite the southern terminus (a high rocky bluff) of the right hand mountain range. Then W.N.W. two and a half miles, and pass a mountain which
comes in from the south. So far there has been but little grass; most of the
valley, except immediately on the river, being covered with greasewood or
sage. Below the mountain the valley widens on either hand; on the right I
can only discern the dim outline of mountains through the smoke. On the
left nothing is to be seen but a level plain covered with bunch grass, now
dry, and dotted with greasewood, sage, or low willows. The river is lined as
usual with these last, some of which are twenty feet high. Nooned on the
river two and a half miles below the last section; course N.W. From noon
halt course N.N.W. three miles then north three quarters of a mile, then
N.N.W. two and three quarters miles to the river, and camped, turning the
cattle south on the sage plain, where is very good feed.

This is the first tolerable feed since yesterday morning. Some papers in a
stick by the road side (the P.O.) state that a man was wounded here last
night by an arrow, and one man had all his mules but one stolen, leaving
him destitute. The Buckeye company took his family along, and some others
his goods, leaving his wagon, harness and sundries, scattered by the road
side. Ordered the men to shoot every Indian they may see, until we come
into a section where they will come into camp in the day time. These fellows
are really the Arabs of America. They are thieves, destitute of gratitude;

nothing conciliates them, and no amount short of all will satisfy. Their
hand is against every man, and every man's hand will be against them. The
valley is nearly closed here, on the left, by a low broken mountain range,
and a small one seems to have been dumped down on the other side of the
river, just to obstruct the valley. An immense space here has been covered
with grass, but it is now pretty well fed down. Made sixteen miles.

MONDAY, SEPT. 3, 1849. Course from camp west half a mile; then N.
west one and a half miles; then N.N. west by west one mile to the foot of a
hill, where we turned to the left, and went over the spur of a high hill,
W.N.W. half a mile; hill smooth and rather steep—not very high. At the
foot on the other side, turned N.W. to the right, past the base of another
spur, the river immediately on our right, which we cross in half a mile: then
W.N.W. half a mile, and turned down to the left to noon. A road crosses
the river below where we camped last night, and comes in again at this
point, avoiding the high hill. Not much difference in the distance, and
probably little chance any way. The next course, the general direction of
the road is W.S.W. eighteen miles, sweeping to the south to touch the
different bends of the river, to the extreme southern point of the right hand
mountain range. Camped five miles from noon halt, at the left, in a deep
bend of the river. Made ten miles.

SEPT. 4, TUESDAY. Left camp early, and nooned nearly down to the
point of the mountain. To it is thirteen miles. The road is very crooked for
a mile and a half, and at the end and the last half mile winds round under
the base of the mountain among the rocks, crowded to it by the river on
the left. After passing the bend, turned down and camped on the river. A
broad valley comes in here from the south, which, like the one we have
passed through, appears to be almost entirely level, and abounds in grass. I
cannot see the mountains on the south and south west up the branch
valley, from this point; but could doubtless if it was clear of smoke and
dust. The great valley, through which this river runs, seems to be divided
into a large number of valleys, forming a kind of chain, by the protrusion of
the mountain spurs from either side into it. One from the right and another
from the left, approach here within three miles; (they usually approximate
much nearer); but above, the valley is from ten to fifteen miles wide; this
may be twenty or thirty wide, and perhaps no more than fifteen long and
perhaps thirty or forty. The mountains above here are high and bold, and
generally have a dark or reddish brown color, and frequently in parallel
strips running toward the base.
     Among the stories of Indian misadventures, some of the watch from
McElvain's train peeled a part of the hair from one of the dark prowlers'
shaggy polls, night before last. I believe this is one of the latest. The gun
was charged with buck shot. There is considerable excitement about these

days, and the scamps will have to be on the alert, or some of them will get
shot (at?) yet. No body hits one yet, for they are invulnerable, I suppose,
and the bullets bound off; as no one can presume even that the men are so
frightened as to miss them. The trains now generally haul in near together
much more so than heretofore. Made fourteen and a half miles.

SEPT. 5, 1849. WEDNESDAY. The river here makes a long detour to
the left, and the road a similar one to the right through a greasewood plain
eight and a half miles to the river again. Through this section the road is
somewhat heavy. Some men who went round on the south side of the bend
report that a deep bed eight or ten yards wide, lined with willows, with scattering pools of water, comes in from the south.

In this section, the plain or river bottom is covered with a thick incrustation of soda, mixed into a paste with the dust and the rain which has
lately fallen, and baked in the sun, crushing under the feet like ice. The
grass is light and thin in this bend, though it was excellent where we camped
last night, and for miles above and below on the south side. The river itself
is very crooked, with abundance of bayous and dry channels, all of which
are lined with willows.

The blue or rather green water varies from fourteen inches to fifteen feet
deep, and the main channel is usually found with one bank (sometimes
both) clay, perpendicular and several feet high, the other shoal, sand or
gravel. The width varies from eight to thirty-five yards; the widest places
being usually the deepest. There are abundance of sage hens about and
ducks in the river. After reaching it the road turns W.N.W. by north six
miles, touching the river several times the last half of the distance; then
north west seven miles, touching the river in the first and last portions;
then west one mile and turns down to camp. Very good grass.

The boys had something of a "stampede" this morning. They put a bell
on a cow, and she, not fancying the noisy thing, set off like mad after the
train, with a dog at her heels. There were two or three trains mixed in with
ours. The first team she came up with was Gilpin's and

> "Away went Gilpin, and away
> Went Gilpin's hat and—"

Not wig, but wagon and oxen. He was walking when they started, but
jumped on the tongue, and after a small run succeeded in calling a halt.
The next belonged to an old gentleman by the name of Nash; and away
they went, not brought up until the wheel cattle were dragged down. Charley's started next, but he stopped them at the risk of breaking his neck. The
scene was intensely exciting for two or three minutes; as no one could say
that the whole fifty eight wagons might not be in racing order before five
minutes expired. A card in the P.O. today reads that the Indians got five
steers from a man last night. Met a government train of eleven wagons,

some horses, and "lots of cattle" for Fort Hall. The cattle were from Oregon, very large, and finely built. Made twenty two miles.

SEPT 6, THURSDAY. From camp course N. west three and a half miles, touching the bends of the river and then one and a half miles N.N. west; then one and a quarter west, leaving the river; then N.N.W. five miles over a sage hill, across a greasewood plain, covered with alkali, and no grass, to a low, round flattened hill in the middle of the plain. Several camp roads turn down to the river on the left before you come to the hill, which, at its southern base, has an alkaline bog grown up to deep green rushes, and forty rods south of the river, with a wide grassy bottom. From this hill top are to be seen mountains in all directions, generally broken and rough, with ragged peaks.

North the plain extends at least thirty miles, and a thick greasewood blanket overspreads its whole barren surface. Northwest is a high mountain range, stretching far south and west and beyond a long low spur which runs down from the south, forming a kind of pass for the road, which turns down between them, leaving the spur at the left, and a couple of miles south turning the mountain range, leaving it at the right. From where the road passes the northern base of the green rush hill, the course is N. west, through the same barren plain in part, and in part on the grassy bottom, touching the river by sweeping a little to the south, and passing its most northern bend in the valley twelve miles on, and nearly to the base of the mountain.

Camped seven miles on. The grass is grazed to the ground on this side of the river, from where we left it this morning.

I notice wagons broken up at almost every camping place on the river. The irons are generally thrown into the water. I have said nothing lately about dead oxen, but they lie along the road, with a much larger sprinkling of horses and mules than heretofore. The rumors of Indian depredations, though thick as blackberries, are not much to be relied on.

It is impossible to give much of an idea of the palpable annoyances we have to encounter. The heat is fiery, intense, sultry, oppressive, suffocating; parching and scorching earth, and water and air and every green thing, (Californians included). The air itself, when it does not whirl along the plain, wantonly twisting the dust two hundred feet into the air, rolls, lazily about in any, or rather in no particular direction, and before you are aware, pours slowly and hesitatingly a stifling cloud of vaporish powdered earth, from the rolling wheels, above, below, and all around you, at the very moment you were congratulating yourself upon having escaped by dodging from where you deemed it was sure to go.

And then the sun's blinding reflected rays, glaring from the broad silvery horizon, the pale blue sky, the pointed peaks, and rocks and bluffs, and domes and up from the soda whitened earth, and out from the misty, smoky, mountain sides, gives to the whole the visionary, unearthly appearance of a monstrous, unmeaning, vacant, lustreless eye, staring at you from every point of the compass, or rather the whole range of vision. Add to this the constant listening to the everlasting hum of imaginary sounds, which cease with your own motion, and by their monotony give one a feeling of loneliness, which half a dozen trains creeping along over a wide plain at a snail-pace and two hundred mites miscalled men crawling around them, tend rather to increase than relieve.

Who says "hurrah for California?" Not many here, for most are heartily tired of the journey. If there was game it would be much pleasanter, but the constant chasing by thousands has driven them so far, or rendered them so shy, that it is not worth the trouble to hunt, as you can seldom or never get a shot.

There are abundance of lizards on the St. Mary's and of many different kinds. Some are of the size, and almost the shape of small toads, with rough hard scales all over them, terminating in sharp triangular points on their sides all around; and some are eight inches long, and not more than half an inch (some even less) in diameter, of all colors from red to ash, and many are parti-colored; for instance, half brown or yellow and half deep green; sometimes yellow and blue, mixed up in patches or streaks. Their motions are so exceedingly quick that one can scarcely see them as they dart from place to place. I first noticed the long variegated kind in Crooked Valley, near the Boiling Springs, and saw one today. I have seen several hardly an inch in length, of a light brown color, darting about.

There is not as much water in the river at camp tonight, seven miles from the hill, as at the camp of night before last, and the water is not as good. At home I should hardly think of washing me in the water, and here we have no other. Hang it up in a canteen all night, when it is cool, and it is quite palatable in the morning, or in a stone jug, and it does well all the forenoon if kept in the wagon. After all, one cannot help thinking of the dead cattle which, unfortunately for them, have fallen into it, and worse still, could not contrive to get out. Canteens and jugs are soon drained in these hot, dusty times; and then we take it sweet, and nice and warm from the fountain. Oh, for a drink of cold spring water, the greatest luxury in the world. Made eighteen and a quarter miles.

SEPT. 7. FRIDAY. From camp three and a half miles crossed a wide dry channel coming in from the east. The bottom is level and covered with soda, and must be very muddy when there is water enough to moisten it. One mile and a half on through greasewood and heavy road we passed the bend, from which the course is W.S.W. eight miles to the foot of the hill. A road comes in here, crossing to this side half a mile below and running down the river. It crossed two miles above our camp of night before last, and runs down on the south side of the river to this point. I know not which is the best road of the two; but the south is five or six miles shorter, runs farther from the river and grass, and is much heavier and more hilly.

This section is much in the shape that a sickle would be if a sickle was a great deal more crooked, beginning at the point and passing round to the heel. It first sweeps down a little to the left, and then curves far to the west and north, finally to the south and then the most travel turns up the hill W.S.W. by a heavy sandy road, while the remainder goes down on the west and then the north side of the stream. At the north bend of this semi-circle are several roads running down to the river; one or two of them to a ford crossing to the south road. Unless you wish to cross, keep the entire circle to the north, as any attempt at a cut off will involve you in a net of bayous, or dry channels, with steep banks. You can water cattle almost anywhere after the final turn S.W. or south.

At the turn at the foot of the hill we kept down the river south three quarters of a mile, and then S.W. by south two miles, when the road turns sharp south a quarter of a mile, then S.W. under the base of the mountain, which is more broken but not so high as the right hand one, three miles, to where the river runs, on the very bank of an open bend, and camped. The valley where it turns south is three or four miles wide, narrowing down to a mile where it turns between the mountains S.W. by south until the average is not more than a quarter of a mile. The heat today greater than yesterday.

Not a living thing to be seen at 12 o'clock, except what belonged to the trains. The lizards disappeared, and the ants, which usually run over one by dozens every time he lies down on the ground, left the sleeper undisturbed under the willow; the only cool, or rather not hot, place to be found on the whole plain. The valley through which we have just passed I shall call Greasewood Valley and the pass we are not in is called the Panta Pass. Made nineteen miles.

SEPT. 8. SATURDAY. From camp, after running a short distance west, the course is west N. west eleven miles on the south side of the river, partly through greasewood, then west one mile over the hill. So far the grass is fed pretty close, and there is barely enough left to travel on. The valley appears to be very large, stretching off farther than I can see to the north and N. west. Perhaps I might see the end were it not for the cloud of smoke and dust covering the mountains, which appear through it on the west; the white sides dimly shining in the sun.

We passed some springs, apparently alkaline, four or five miles from camp, and far to the left under the hill. The water comes out at the water's edge under the south bank of the river opposite these springs. The river has a much deeper, narrower channel, and not as much water at camp of this morning as at that of yesterday morning. Just below camp the valley grad- ually widens, and the river separates into two channels, the north one being much the longest. I shall endeavor to ascertain and note down where the two come together, whenever I come to the junction. There has been an immense quantity of grass here, as the two streams run a mile or two apart, but what has not been fed down is nearly dried up, and it is very scarce now. From the last section the course is W.S.W. by west, over a low hill to camp three miles.

Before the cattle were turned over to feed, we heard that one mile below they were cutting grass with scythes. Hitched up again and drove down to camp, nearly half a mile at the right of the road, in a very handsome bend of the river. Got our hay cut, or rather found it cut, and dried or drying. It clouded up just at dark and sprinkled, but did not rain. A train of three wagons, camped a hundred yards below, favored us with some most delightful singing in the evening. There were two or three ladies and several gentlemen. They had some large musical instrument, I did not go down to see what kind. The boys who went down report that it looked like a piano. It sounded like an organ at the distance from which I heard it. The music was very fine, anyhow, and kept up till midnight. Made sixteen miles.

Chapter Five

September 9–October 2, 1849:
Farther into the Desert

SEPT. 9, 1849. SUNDAY. Lay over. The men brought in some very excellent hay this afternoon, completely cured. We are laying in for a long drive without grass. The wind blew very strong for some time this afternoon, and scattered clouds of dust over everything. Report here says that there are four routes, the old one, across the desert; another, striking Truckey River twelve miles north lower down; a third north of Pyramid Lake, by Mud Lake, crossing over to Feather River; and a fourth, still farther north, called the Government Road. The last two leave the road about sixty miles below, at the next great bend of the river. The first of these two is called the Cherokee route, and promises so much that, if I mistake not, it will be found a humbug. A Cherokee who resides in California has been through to this point, and started back with the great Cherokee train, as it is now called, of one hundred wagons. The real Cherokee train was reduced to a dozen wagons, I should think, before this new manoeuvre. This man reports a good route across the desert, and water and grass at some points.

If there was not a northern route besides this into California, I certainly should not venture. If it should fail, the Government route is sure, though certainly far round. I shall consider it. All the men, I find, are determined to go that way; and probably any attempt to take the old route would lead to a division of the train. There are one hundred and fifty wagons in sight, preparing for hard times, and others rolling in hourly. I call this valley Meadow, or Island Valley. Look well to your cattle here. The watch dragged a dozen out of the west channel yesterday where they were mired.

SEPT. 10, MONDAY. Left camp with Ball. Ordered the teams to start at 11 o'clock, a.m. Course one mile W.S.W. touching the river; then curving to the left over a slightly elevated greasewood plain, down to a bend of the river bottom, and forty rods across where are willows and an old dry channel — and on and over the plain again two and a half miles W.S.W. by south, touching a bend of the river again. Then south west, touching the river at the end of the first mile, four miles to the river bottom — the river three quarters of a mile at the right. This section has a sprinkling of sage, and is crooked, and most of the way heavy.

On the left the plain extends five or six miles to the base of the mountain, which is rough and broken. On the right is the river bottom, the two channels cutting its wide surface into numerous squares and angles, and dividing it quite equally into patches of grass and patches of rushes. In one place about a mile above here, the bottom is very narrow, and all the channels run into one. West from this point the river runs at the base of a high mountain. The road runs S.S.W. down the smooth grassy plain four miles to where the eastern mountain sends down a long slope to the river, leaving only a few rods for the road, which runs through greasewood and sage for some distance, very near the river, and then through greasewood alone down to the river bottom. Course S.W. by south on beyond this.

Grass is very good above the sage plain, and but little fed down — below the bottom is narrowed to a few rods, and but little grass. The road on the other side rises on to a sage plain opposite this point, and runs down a long way before it strikes the river again. Camped half a mile above where the greasewood meets the willows, on the edge of an old dry channel, the road running on the river bank. Made eleven miles.

SEPT. 11, 1849. TUESDAY. Delayed this morning by the cattle getting scattered after the morning watch left for breakfast. The men have taken to card playing and neglect duty. A pack of cards should not be permitted in any train. Two of the men had a quarrel about them only last evening, and many a train has been broken up by them. From camp course S.S.W. one mile over a greasewood and sage plain; then one and a half miles to the river bottom S.W. by S; then one and three quarters of a mile to two clumps of bushes resembling thorn, from which I shall name the bottom Thorn-bush Valley; then two miles to the second of two bends in the river very near each other; then S.W. two and three fourths miles to the second of two similar bends the last of which affords a most excellent watering place; then S.W. by south, touching the bends of the river, and over the points of the greasewood plain, where it crowds down to the river one and a quarter miles; then W.S.W. by south two and a half miles, to the bluff of a sage plain elevated above this bottom about sixty feet, and bounding it on the east and south its whole length, stretching off south east between the mountains, broad and level, out of sight.

A similar plain, though more broken, and terminated by mountains on the west, ten miles distant, sweeping round south and east, bounds it on the west. The bottom itself is more than a mile wide here, and will average more than that above. It abounds in grass, most of which is now perfectly dry.

The road now travelled ascends the bluff near half a mile below this point, by a sharp angle to the left, and a few rods below the river washes the base of the bluff to a nearly perpendicular bank or wall of sand and clay: for the whole plain seems nothing more than a fine loose sand, the particles of almost every color. The road up the hill is of the very heaviest, and if we do not find the whole plain the same, I shall certainly mention it hereafter; so look out. Doubled teams. The road on the other side of the river appears to be from this point of view, as bad as on this; and if there is any difference, worse. Turning to the right down the river, we were happily disappointed to find ourselves only a quarter of a mile below, on the brink of the bluff, and down we went with a jerk on to the bottom again.

Course W.S.W. two miles past the sand bluffs again, touching the river before reaching them. Bottom one mile wide, and more in places. The sand on the bluff where we ascended is an excellent "writing sand," and enough of it to supply the world. One cannot hold it in the hand at all unless the back is down. The men finally left a good steer, not being able to find it.

Three o'clock p.m. The men came up with the lost steer. Found him in a train which drove him off intentionally this morning. Between the bend and the first bluff is a small pond, with rushes ten feet high and an inch in diameter. Here the road runs one hundred yards between the bluff and the river, which are not more than twenty yards asunder. Then they separate, and course continues the same several miles between the bluffs and river. Camped on the river some distance to the right of the road one and a half miles below the last point. The water in the river is much better than it has been, and the current wide, deeper and stronger.

Wood has been rather scarce for a few days, there being nothing to burn but dry willows, and another like emigration would sweep them all away. They grow very fast, however, and with a little management one may secure enough to cook with. A little more would be very desirable these cold mornings. Still one, by moving a little lively, may keep up the circulation. A little fly like a gnat is somewhat troublesome at times, biting rather sharply, and getting into the ears and eyes.

Lost a cow last night by the cattle hooking her into the river. Herd your beasts carefully here, or very likely some will be lost. Detached mountains may be seen in all directions. Teams and trains are coming down the river; fast crowding into the valley, pressing on and on, very few of the cattle being in a condition to pursue the route. Made nineteen and three quarters miles.

SEPT. 12, 1849. Course from camp S.W. two and a half miles to point of
bluff, where is only room between it and the river for the road; then S.S.W.
four and a half miles. At the beginning of this section the eastern or left
hand bluff curves off from the river, which runs toward the right hand one.
The road soon gets equi-distant from both, and bearing directly for the
farthest point of the left bluff. It then bends toward the right and takes a
course directly toward the lowest point where its bare white face (washed
almost all the way for two miles nearly perpendicular by the river, which
runs at its base) terminates.

When within half a mile of this point, the road turns a little to the left
and forks. One goes over the river bearing to the right, the other crosses the
bottom S. east nearly half a mile, and turns down the bluff, crossing the
river just below. The road so far on the other side of the river is reported to
be very heavy, and is certainly so below. The section we have just passed is
level, through a plain sparsely covered with grass and greasewood. There
has been feed, but none now. Bottom a mile wide; more water in the river,
though I cannot conceive where it comes from. The banks at this crossing
are lower, wide apart, and more sandy, with fine sandy hard bottom.

While sitting on the bank by the ford, Morse, the dentist, came up on a
pack mule, in good spirits and going ahead finely. Says he passed Cushing,
of Aurora, Ill., sick, this side of Green River, with no one but David Bellen-
ger to take care of him. Thinks he will die. I think that he will not. Morse
is an instance of what perseverance will do. He was disappointed in every
way, and at every turn, but finally succeeded in packing from St. Joseph on
the 20th of June, after footing it to Council Bluffs and returning. He says
that he has travelled most of the time alone, and some nights has camped
on the open prairie alone, with no team or human being in sight. He has
not been sick at all.

Took the right hand road, and crossed the ford, turning to the right;
passed up a slight hill, by a bend, into the sage plain half a mile S. west;
then S.S. east one mile to the junction of the two roads; then half a mile S.
west to a bend of the river. A road turns here to the right over the sage
plain, and comes in again twenty miles below on the river. We turned down
the river to the left, course S.S. east, passing on the way down a shallow
ravine, on the right bank of which are some of the thorn-like bushes, very
large; and down the bottom, which since leaving the ford has not been
much more than half a mile wide, and a little broken, to the point of the
right hand bluff, three miles, where is another ford, and a right hand road
directly to the right up the bluff.

The river from the ford above has, for the most part, run under the
eastern bluff, washing it down like the one above the ford to a point one
mile above this. Half a mile below this ford the road turns to the left on to
a greasewood plain, and runs down one mile on the east bank, very near,
and some fifteen or twenty feet above the water; then turning short to the

right, crosses the river again, and immediately turns down it south one and three quarters of a mile; then S.S.E. one and a quarter by the point of the right hand bluff, crossing an old dry channel, the river on the other side of the bottom; then south half a mile, crossing the dry channel again, and camped at the left of the road. The mountains passed on the left this afternoon are sprinkled with bushes, probably dwarf cedar. The road which turned up the bluff at the second ford above, descends to the bottom again in half a mile, and sweeping to the right, joins the other a mile below the next ford.

The Boston boys whom I saw on a packet in Chicago, bound for California, passed just before the teams came into camp. They, or the other branch which went by the way of Pittsburgh and Cincinnati, have lost four of their number, and among them an old gentlemen of the name of White. Cold this morning. Some clouds, but sultry hot in the forenoon. The wind breezed up a little, and gradually increasing, in the evening blew strong in gusts with an occasional sprinkle of rain. The wind abated before midnight and then there were a few light showers during my watch from twelve to sunrise.

The wolves are very bold, running all through the camp; but nobody minds wolves now. They have been "along side" every night, except two or three in the most barren mountains, and as many more in the Black Hills. The ravens have been in equally constant attendance by day. The road since morning has been crooked, and the last few miles there was a sprinkling of greasewood over the plain. Made fifteen and a half miles.

SEPT. 13, 1849. From camp road runs south one and a half miles and turns to the right up the bluff. The bottom, here not more than fifty rods wide, opens south directly on a mountain broken by ravines into sharp ridges and peaks, which are smooth and covered with grass, except a few places where masses of whitish grey stone protrude. One mile and a half below, the valley, gradually widening, sweeps round west toward the north base of the mountain. The sage plain is more broken, and the eastern bluff more sloping than above.

Ascending the bluff, neither high nor very steep, and curving round west through the sage plain, very heavy sand in one and a quarter miles the road descends to the river bottom again; source S.S. west; then across the bottom, crooked and sweeping round far to the right, S. west one and three quarter miles, past some of the thorn bushes on the banks of a channel, nearly dry, to the bluff. The valley sweeps round again from S. east of here, toward the mountain again.

Ascertaining that the road which rises on to the bluff here, and runs over the sage plain two miles S.W. is very heavy, deep sand, turned S. south east down the river one mile, the valley continuing on one mile farther, and ascended the bluff to the right, and across through heavy sand

S.W. three quarters of a mile, on to the river bottom again, which is a mile wide; then two miles W.S.W. to the bluff again. The ascent is easy and light.

The course is next S.W. by south one and a half miles through a greasewood and sage plain, part heavy and the sand drifting into heaps like snow, to a singularly beautiful bend where the river washes the bluff a few rods at the left to a perpendicular height of fifty feet, a little more than one half of the bed of the stream on the bluff side being white sand. The road turns now W.S.W. over the same plain to the valley again, one and three quarters miles, touching a bend in the river immediately after it leaves the bluff. The cut off or north road runs along the south base of the mountain north some eight miles distant. A few pack mules are now travelling over it.

The bottom is two miles wide here, and sprinkled over with greasewood, willows and thorns among the scattering grass. The road runs W.S.W., touching the river two or three times in two and a half miles.

From this point look to the right, and at the base of the mountain is a low hill, the whole face of which, two thirds of the distance from the bottom up, has the appearance of a flame of fire. It is more marked and striking when the sun, emerging from a cloud suddenly shines on it. There is a similar, but much brighter semicircular spot on the base of a hill at the west of it. From this point the road is crooked, and touching the river, runs a little south of west to the right hand bluff at the lower end of the valley, where is only space for the road between it and the river. From this the direction is west one and a quarter miles, running around a bend of the river north through the greasewood.

Thus far today we have travelled where has been abundance of feed, but it is now rather short, being dried or eaten out. Ascending the bluff, not very steep or heavy, by a very gradual descent S.W. through greasewood, not very heavy road, you reach the bottom again in one and a half miles. Then through greasewood by a very slight ascent and descent S.W. one and a half miles. On this or the last section, the cutoff road comes in. Then west one and a half miles on to the bottom, and camped at the left hand on the river.

Had a slight sprinkle of water from a doubtful looking cloud. I wonder if it ever rains here? The grass here has been literally devoured. It has been eaten down, trampled down, dried down, and the only process not down, and the last, which is to blow the fragments into, and let them float down the river, has not yet begun; but the weather is too faint and weak here, I reckon, to blow that hard, and so a little remnant of dry stems and roots remains. If—I say, if—it should take a notion to blow thus strong, "the last of the Mohicans" will have none to say grace over.

What a pity that cattle were not made to do without fodder. Well, well, I suppose it is all right. Everything but Eternity needs to be fed (that swallows all things) even to steam engines; and of the two, I mean oxen and engines, the last would have the least fodder in these "diggins." Made sixteen and three quarters miles.

FRIDAY, SEPT. 14, 1849. Cloudy this morning, and looks and feels like rain. Did sprinkle. Two and half miles from the foot of the hill back, west N. west you pass the point of the bluff, and directly half another, and again one larger than the first, all of them coming down very near the bends of the river, or its old dry channel. Just below the last, and half a mile from the first point, the road forks. One turns left and runs S.S.W. down to the sink; the other, or Lasscon's [Lassen's] Road, keeps right ahead half a mile W.N.W., passing a low sand hill on the left. Then W. by S. one and three quarters miles to the bluff across a greasewood plain.

From this point, the bluff some forty feet high, sweeps with a very regular curve to the north three quarters of a mile and comes round south to the next bend of the road back, forming a most beautiful circular level bottom. The base and the summits and points of this whole bluff are sparsely covered with greasewood, leaving a strip of white sand nearly the whole length of its face.

The southern side of the valley is bounded by a similar though higher bluff. Standing at the forks, and looking directly down Lassen's road, there is a mountain range ahead at the left, and a few peaks north of that. Directly at the right terminates the mountain range which yesterday lay at the north. Behind and at the left, terminates the south range passed yesterday, and below and west is a broad open space, on the west of which is a distant low range, extending and rising far on in the same direction, down behind the range just spoken of, as lying ahead at the left.

Ascending the bluff, here low and easy, the course is west, gradually descending through greasewood and a sprinkle of sage, a little of it heavy — four miles; then west by south, slightly ascending road, easy, and a little gravel four and a half miles; then west S.W., immediately descending into a ravine, and then gradually ascending toward the mountain gorge, road light and gravelly three miles; then south up a branch ravine one and a quarter miles, and camped.

One mile south of camp are several springs, the upper and left hand one affording excellent water. On the right hand of the road, some distance before turning south to camp, are some willows and singular rocks, where water has lately been found by digging about four feet. The plain we have just passed has no grass upon it, and is ten or twelve miles wide and forty or fifty long, north and south, with a southern inclination, and is broken toward the mountains. Our camp is enclosed by mountains, except on the N. east. Some of the peaks in sight today are high, abrupt, and crowned with rocks. At the north end of the plain may be seen a conical hill of some height, standing alone. The weather is very cool, and a sprinkle of rain all day. Evening cold.

The road side is not literally covered, nor strewed, nor even lined with dead cattle; but for a road travelled only a week or ten days, and only a part of the travel at that, it seems sadly in need of scavengers. The ravens may feast, the wolves glut, and loathsome insects roll and revel in mines of putrefactive wealth, with so little diminution that, soon, perhaps, the road will be abandoned or avoided, and the astonished traveller of after years, will look wonderingly though vainly for the slaughter house whose yawning gates have poured out so wide a flood of whitened skulls.

The valley we left this morning, I call Sand Ridge Valley, the spring and basin at camp, Golgotha. Fed out a part of our hay. All beyond here is uncertainty. We cannot give even a reasonable guess of the road, or grass, or water, as no reliance can be placed on any information we can get. Made seventeen and a half miles.

SEPTEMBER 15. SATURDAY. Watered the cattle before daylight. Rather a scanty supply. Had to dig it all up with a tin cup and water from a pail. Cold this morning but no ice. Forty teams here. Some rolled off in the night as soon as they got their cattle watered. Started off just as soon as we got through watering ours, some time before sun rise. Course west one mile and a little hilly, then S.W. one mile ascending, then W. by S. up a long easy ascent, good road one mile. Dwarf cedars on the mountains on the left. A very few on the right. Then one mile W.N.W. Ascent rather steep; then over to the left descending S.S.W. three fourths of a mile, then S.W. one and one quarter miles descending; then one half a mile W.S.W. then W.N.W. through a narrow valley to the top of the hill, in sight, six miles, where it passes down into another valley, at the left of some very fine shaped conical peaks. At the left of the road, there is a range of bare sand hills, some of which are crater shaped, and the nearest and largest seems lined with black basalt.

The valley is very pretty but small and covered with greasewood. The mountains are not high but broken, and the low peaks near the base of the ranges seem to prefer being alone as they stand or sit pretty well apart. There are neither trees nor bushes on any of them. From the top of the hill which is reached by some pretty steep ascents and descents, the course is west to "Point Distress" passing half way down along the southern base of the conical hills just mentioned. These are high, smooth and covered with a fine sand and earth like ashes, through which basalt of various colors appears in stripes and patches.

There are red, chocolate, purple, peach, blue, yellow, pink, green, etc. In the north part of this valley on the hill side is the resemblance of several abandoned lime kilns. The whole is on an extensive scale and the resemblance very close. I call this the "Valley of the Shadow of Death." On the south side of the road is another hill crowned with a rough mass of basalt, opposite are the striped parti-colored ones and between is the "Gate of

Desolation." Ascending this I have a view so entirely abandoned, so utterly desolate that the rugged barren deserts we have passed, rise up in the mind like green memories of departed joys. Mountains piled on mountains and rising in peaks on, beyond, and above another, till buried in the blue mist which covers but not conceals every distant object. Far to the west is the dim outline of a very high mountain range. At its base, apparently, stretches, right and left till its extremities are lost behind the mountain ridges, a wide, snow white level plain like a lake. On this are some patches and stripes of black or blue which may be water or anything beside.

At the north is a range of hills, white, very rough and rugged and appearing like an island in a lake. On this side is a broad valley, or rather plain, broken into hills, some of considerable height, and are colored like the mountain opposite me.

There are the same snow-white patches and the colors are many of them much brighter. There are several other white patches on the plain which look like soda ponds, as does the large one itself. Turning "Point Distress" the road runs down a broad ravine into a still wider one, two miles N.W. passing, near the terminus, some very interesting highly colored bluffs, which extending up the valley or ravine north, connect with similarly colored mountains. The whole is very picturesque and I turned back a score of times after leaving to give it the involuntary homage of a look. It is surpassingly beautiful, and the disadvantageous circumstances under which it was viewed in the midst of utter desolation could not wholly prevent me from admiring it.

Leaving "Point Misery" at the left, the course is 2¼ miles S.W. and ascending and turning over a low hill one half a mile W.S.W., winds S.S.W. down into the valley again, distance three quarters of a mile. On the right of the road half way from "Point Misery" to the hill is a scanty supply of water one half a mile to the right.

The valley terminates abruptly at the north at the base of a high mountain. On the brow of the hill where we begin to descend to the great valley or plain west are a number of wells with considerable water, where cattle may, with a good deal of labor, get some to drink. But they are surrounded by the stinking dead corpses of oxen and cows, even several have pitched into the wells and not been removed. They are in there now.

The course is next west N.W. three miles turning west across a ravine, then N.N.W., winding down and up and through and over the ravines and hills, not very bad nor steep, one and one half miles to the north side of a semicircular sand hill forty feet high. Then by a very crooked route N.W. by W. toward the south point of the island like range 18¼ miles. Reached the point 25½ miles, where some of the teams halted for supper and some rolled along. It was left optional with each team to stop or go on.

No grass. Not a blade nor a drop of water. After an hour, moved on, the first few miles over an uneven plain with two or three broad level places and sparsely covered with the smallest kind of greasewood. Travelled to 11:30 p.m. and halted on the edge of the level plain seen from the peak of the mountain today. The teams are scattered for two miles or more back. I have just come from the rear. There is no road to be distinguished, nothing but sand and greasewood. It is quite cool, foggy and no light but from the stars. The teams are not unhitched but lie down as they stopped, tired enough, for the last twenty miles has been heavy, a good deal of sand.

SEPT. 16, 1849. SUNDAY. 1 a.m. Most of the teams have crawled along so as to be in hailing distance of the front. The men thoroughly tired, have lain down beside the leaders or under the wagons or wherever they chanced to be when the halt was called. 3 a.m. All are sound asleep on the sand which is hot yet, from the burning heat of yesterday. I cannot sleep. So I write by candle light and think by the star light. 5 a.m. Seems that I have been asleep after all. I remember nothing in particular since 3:30 a.m. Roused the boys.

And now I begin to see though the light is not full yet, what the great white level is—merely a dried up mud hole. We are within ten rods of the edge. Now you know exactly. It is one hundred miles long and five to fifteen broad, with here and there a shallow channel through or rather across it where the water runs to the more depressed portions as it runs off during the subsidence of the waters after the melting of the snow. The water may average sometimes over the whole extent ten feet in depth, and at the deepest is probably less than twenty. It must be as a general thing very shallow. The sand mountain is only a collection of extinct craters of every color imaginable and stupendous size. The most southern point is a high isolated, very dark green or black rock.

Directly round the point on the west side a few rods from the base is an immense boiling spring or spring of boiling water. It is at least seven yards in diameter and no one knows how deep. There is a pool immediately west of, and connected with it and on the same level, several yards in diameter but quite shallow and serves as a cooler. The road around the point is quite rough to near the spring. Before reaching the point we passed a range of black hills over a sand hill. The mud plain is almost or quite destitute of bush or shrub or any green thing. We have passed 130 dead cattle this morning (by count in six miles and here are 40 lying dead on a quarter of an acre). Under any other circumstances I should take great pleasure in looking upon this scenery.

But to tell the truth, I am thoroughly disgusted with a sight so barren. So nothing but rock and sand and clay and ashes and dead animals—and who will object when they learn, if they will only believe, that I am travelling or standing in an atmosphere appreciable to all the senses. You ask, "Do you hear the smell?" If you don't believe, try it. Why, even the wolves hear it. Nothing but ravens and crawling worms are here from choice. I taste it. I

feel it. I smell it. Then I have had no breakfast this morning and for that
matter, no supper last night, and missed my lunch at noon yesterday.

Who cares for colors or rocks or craters or even trees (we have not seen
one in 200 miles) under such circumstances. I am hungry, tired and want a
drink of water. By the by, I have drunk but twice in 24 hours. And here we
are at the *Great Boiling Spring*.

SEPT 16, 1849, 10 a.m. I have just had my breakfast and things are putting on a different and somewhat better face. No so bad a place after all.
Plenty of water if we could only have it cooled. When the cattle first come
up to the stream which runs down from the Great Boiling Spring they make
a rush for it, and it is very difficult to get them far enough down to prevent
their scalding their noses.

Twenty or thirty rods below it will not scald, but is not cool enough to
drink. It soon spreads out, after the usual fashion in the country, and forms
a slough of several hundred acres where was plenty of course grass. There is
a crater of a volcano south east of Black Rock and partly connected with it
an immense hollow pile of loose stone and ashes which I attempted to
climb. Got up perhaps 25 feet and came down very suddenly in the midst of
an avalanche of ashes and blocks of basalt and other "debris." I was nearly
suffocated before I could get out of it. I gave it up. The stones kept rolling
down for several minutes and ultimately the movement reached the top, a
couple of hundred feet more or less. Some say 500. Don't believe it.

The teams are all in and watered. Report one sick ox left—supposed to
be dead. Missing none. There is said to be grass six miles from here—very
good. Shall be glad if it is not twelve. Leaving the springs, course N.N.W.
two miles we have the volcanic mountains on the right and a similar but
much higher range on the left, but several miles distant along the base of
which runs up to the north are arms of "Mud Lake," several miles long.

Passing along a nice, hard, smooth greasewood plain which, in its whole
length, gently descends to the arm of Mud Lake west, from the mountain
on the right, we cross an arm of the lake and rise again to a similar greasewood plain. The greasewood on the sides is growing on little hillocks beautifully rounded, from one foot in diameter and one foot high, to twenty feet
in diameter and eight feet high, and some are even larger. This arm of Mud
Lake or "Dry Mud Hole Plain" extends east to a gap or depression in the
right hand range, and the greasewood plain runs far off to the west, separating the two arms just described.

As we crossed the plain the men saw plenty of water along the base of
the western mountains. But, alas, it was only a splendid and most perfect
mirage. For a long distance from Great Boiling Spring, there were frequent
holes in the hard, almost brick-like surface, of all sizes from a few inches to
several feet, where the water comes almost or quite to the level of the earth,
but most of the water is hot or so alkaline as to be unfit for drinking. After

crossing the first arm of the lake our course was N.N.W. one and a half
miles over the plain to camp. This is a large level covered with grass,
apparently extending a long way west. It is nearly all fed off when we first
struck it at the edge of the arm of the lake, but grows better and better as
we go farther on to the plain. Directly ahead, west of the camp, is a high
rough peak in the mountain range, which is very conspicuous and covered
with volcanic products like the craters east of us. In fact, every thing about
here gives most indisputable evidence of volcanic action.

From present appearances I should judge that the mud which forms this
vast plain had been vomited from the craters in our vicinity or the great
boiling springs which abound here, or from both.

Six miles S.E. of the spring lies a mass of basalt apparently buried in the
earth. The part which projects would, if detached, weigh several tons. I got
the idea when I examined it that this plain was once a low depression
covered with mountain peaks, or that the mountains have gradually sunk
down and the mud had been poured from their sides and summit, until
they had been submerged, some more, some less, and that the black rock
craters, and this block of basalt are only the tops of those mountains just
projecting above the mud.

If they continue to sink they will soon be plastered over. The block of
basalt will disappear and even Black Rock will only just be discernable
above the mud. Even the greasewood plains seem to be formed by the more
recent vomitings as they are much the highest at the point where they are
and descend gradually from them. The little hillocks on which the greasewood grows so abundant are thus vomited up.

Though the surface of the plain is hard as a brick now at the surface,
yet only a foot below it is broken into square block an inch or two in
diameter and from that it begins to get soft and moist, and ten feet down is
so soft that a spade set on end soon sinks and disappears and a wagon
tongue dropped down end ways into the hole gradually sank and soon disappeared. The plain is covered, in the vicinity of Black Rock in patches
with pieces of lava which has once formed a crust more or less thick on
masses of basalt. I saw a round mass more than fifty pounds thus encrusted
over to the thickness of three inches. I have found pieces which are not
more than an eighth of an inch thick and probably came from a stone of
only a few ounces weight. The stones, large or small, probably drop into the
burning lava and are ejected, instantly, on account of their relative coldness. Thus a crust would be formed over them which, cooling rapidly,
would crack over the yet hot stone and shell off like a walnut shuck.

I saw many of the size and shape of small cast iron kettles, full as even
and thin and when stuck together they gave a metallic ring. All of them
were more or less broken but some of the segments would hold several
quarts of water.

Since we left the Humboldt we have passed a large number of living, dying and dead cattle abandoned by their drivers. At the base of the hill this side the Gate of Desolation yesterday, one stood with his side to the sun and his nose to the gravel bed on the side of the ravine, ruminating on his hard fate, probably, for he had nothing else to ruminate upon. Lying down on a gravel bed nearby (remember there was no grass there) I thought that by waiting a little I might see how philosophically an oxen could die.

I was tired and sleepy—drowsy and I sat listlessly watching his motions— or rather want of motion, his bones seemed to bend out and his wrinkled skin to swell, and a sound like the shrill whistle of the wind through a broken casement, changing to the low prolonged rumble and roll of a bass drum, became a low muttering articulation and ended in a tremulous tone of sad repining which said or seem to say:

> Too sure they've left me here to die,
>   An old and hungry ox;
> Where not a blade of grass can grow
>   Among the climbing rocks.
> They've left me here to starve and die,
>   Without a lock of hay.
> And they've burned my yoke and bows and gone
>   to Californ-i-a
>
> They took my yoke to fry their meat,
>   My bows to bake their bread,
> And left me here with naught to eat,
>   The dying with the dead.
> Near starved, without a drop to drink;
>   Without a drop, I say,
> They cracked their whip and rolled along
>   To Californ-i-a
>
> They cracked their whips and rolled along
>   And left me all alone;
> And "O Susanna" was the song,
>   That chased the rascals on.
> And O'Susanna, don't you cry,"
>   Was still the doleful lay,
> That cheered the rogues as they marched on
>   To Californ-i-a
>
> I know not who Susanna is,
>   Nor why she shouldn't cry,
> It's hard that one can't weep when left
>   Among the rocks to die;
> But I—I cannot weep, my brain
>   Is scorched and dried away,
> And rattles in my skull like gold
>   Of Californ-i-a

My hide grows fast unto my ribs,
    And my ribs are rubbed so thin,
That dirt alone keeps the day light out,
    When dust should keep it in.
I watched my shadow till it paled,
    And vanished quite away;
And I'm now a transparency outward bound,
        For Californ-i-a

I'm told on Sacramento's banks
    That broad green meadows lie
Where cattle nothing have to do,
    But eat and drink and die.
Could I be soaked but one night long,
    So as to hold some hay,
I'm sure I'd be strong enough to go
        To Californ-i-a.

O! Had they left me by some spring
    Or on a river's brink,
Where I might get a wisp of grass
    And half a pail of drink,
I would have dragged my load along
    And labored night and day,
Until they had stolen all the gold
        Of Californ-i-a

A sneaking wolf that passed me by,
    Drew back his lip and grinned,
Quoth he, "I'll see those old dry bones,
    Again when they are skinned."
A raven watched me all day long,
    And at night he flew away,
Quoth he, "His flesh with his shadow has gone,
        to Californ-i-a."

Next came a thieving hatless scamp
    Between an ass and goat,
A grizzly swamp was on his face
    "Susanna" in his throat.
And he punched me with a long sharp stick
    Then whistling, turned away;
Quoth he, "I can steal a better ox
        In Californ-i-a."

A weary life long road I pulled
    Their wagons on the plains;
And all I've got is kicks and blows
    And hunger for my pains.
If too fast they whipped, if to slow they kicked,
    And followed it day by day

As if kicking and beating would carry them through
To Californ-i-a.

They may kick and maul and beat me now,
But they'll find it is "no go."
For my neck will never bear a yoke,
Nor my shoulders press a bow
If an ox's ghost e'er runs at large,
I'll be revenged some day.
For I'll haunt the rascals as long as they live
In Californ-i-a

When cold, cold winds and drenching rains
Drown their unsheltered forms,
My breath shall chill their shivering hearts
Add terror to the storms
I'll stand by their couch when their fevered brains
See phantoms by night and day
And I'll stare on them till they rave to be free
From Californ-i-a.

I may have slept—I may not. Two hours after I sat down, I got up and left—the place, and the ox lying quietly on his skin. I did not examine him closely but he did not seem to breathe and I dare say he didn't. Still he might since the chest would hardly expand if the skin wouldn't hold air. It was only a pile of skin and bones after all. An animal, or rather a bovial collapse.

There are no directions for crossing the desert that will apply to every case. I can say that our transit was eminently successful and for the benefit of those green unfortunates who may hereafter wander here, I will describe the process.

Our cattle were in good condition. We took twelve pounds of hay from the Island Valley for each creature. More would be better if it could be found lower down, which would be done earlier in the season. From the "meadows," we took every advantage of the feed though still adhering to the rule of "short drives in good feed" and go ahead in short—we camped before we left the river as low down as possible and get any feed at all. Gave the cattle a chance before we left in the morning to pick the last grass.

Started late, 9:30 a.m. for Golgotha Springs, which we reached in good season in the afternoon. Fed, picketed and watered our cattle, by six p.m. and gave half, or six pounds, of hay to each. At 2 a.m. watered again and gave the other six pounds. Not a blade was lost. All licked up clean. At 2:30 the men took breakfast and moved off at 4:30 with orders for each team to take care of itself. No team was to assist another without special orders. They were to water whenever they found water not alkaline. Halt to rest occasionally. No team to drive within ten rods of another so as to avoid the dust, and not to unyoke under any circumstances till grass and water was reached.

At noon halted an hour and a half and as the hay had over run 1200 and odd pounds in weight there was more than 100 left in the wagon which was distributed, about a pound to each creature. The train being scattered in squads for two miles on the greasewood plain, each team having made the best of its time—all halted about midnight and awaited the light. Drove across Mud Lake to the spring as soon as we could see. After breakfast drove to grass.

MONDAY, SEPT. 17. The sick ox came in this morning. Left camp, course N.N.W. 1½ miles, part of the day through greasewood; then west one mile down to a grassy bottom, where is water, hot, warm, cool and boiling, and so it has been wherever there is grass between here and the Great Boiling Spring.

From here the road runs N.W. one mile and forks. We took the left hand which runs nearly west, across the plain. After going five miles began to come to patches of grass and holes of water. As you approach the mountains the grass gets better and more of it. The last lies in ridges of dried mud and sand, with sage and greasewood scattered over, and sometimes, very thickly.

Camped eight miles from the forks of the road west N.W. among patches of good grass and by the willows. The grass here will last some time. The whole distance of this desert route from when we leave the grass to where it grows again is 64 miles, and to passably good grass, 72, and had the whole emigration come this route it would have been more than 90 miles from grass to grass. It would have been next to impossible to cross under such a scarcity of feed, and the whole route would have been strewed with things that have been. The supply of hay even at the meadows would have soon been exhausted.

Many queer stories are told of the starving beasts. One lean ox, thinking, perhaps that his mouth and throat were sufficiently enlarged, was trying to swallow an iron cask hoop, rolling his tongue over and over it and that around his head. A hunter saw him at long intervals and the last report as the first—no abatement of his efforts. The mules eat bags and leather and "picket ropes" and for that matter everything but earth and stone, they could get their teeth upon. One man lay down with a nice leghorn hat upon his head, and woke up just in time to see the last of it going down the throat of his mule.

TUESDAY, SEPT. 18. Left camp. Course N.N.W. six miles to the main road. This whole section has the appearance of a great mud plain, dried down and covered with sand which has drifted into ridges, some of them ten to twenty feet high and several miles long.

Some are covered with course sand and some with fine gravel. And I frequently find gravel in the hollows between the ridges. The road is for the most part heavy on account of the deep sand. From "Warm Springs" the course by the main road is N.N.W. 23 miles to "Muddy Creek."

The first, generally very heavy—the last, says a paper stuck on a post by the road side, is first rate—a good road. I doubt it. But we shall see. No grass or water except at a great distance to the left. Road pretty level, the last part broken into long, easy swells.

The right hand mountain is quite lofty and diversified with rocks of every color. There are two remarkable black peaks at their base, about half way to Muddy Creek, which look enough alike to be twins. Soon after passing them the road becomes good, says the post office. Travelled over it and found a part sandy, most of it stony and quite rough and the last part very crooked.

To tell it just as it is, you cannot rely at all on any information you get on the road. Almost every man you meet and question proves himself a fool or a liar. If you get any knowledge of the road from any one it is purely accidental, and as to distance, I have known them not to come within four miles in five and a half. Asses, asses all; and but that their hat crowns were shed "long, long ago," their ears would thrust their hats off. Reached Muddy Creek late and camped. It was dark.

WEDNESDAY, SEPT. 19. We find ourselves this morning camped on a meadow surrounded by mountains, some of them very high. It seem to be a vast bog, some two or three miles in diameter and maybe twice that, partly dried down and covered with greasewood; partly moist and covered with grass and partly very wet and covered with rushes. It is a most singular formation for where the water stands upon the surface the earth two feet below is as dry as tinder, and so hard that we have to use an iron bar and pick to penetrate it.

There are more than 100 wagons here. Among them McClure and Ellensworth of Elgin—and the Kendall Co. train. There are some springs of good water but most of it is highly alkaline. Some of it red and like strong bay. The grass is not a good quality but abundant, probably for that very reason. Nothing but greasewood to burn.

THURSDAY, SEPT. 20. Did not leave camp. In trouble all day. Finally expelled Whipple and dismissed Van Wormer and Ballard. It ought to have been done long ago. They have all behaved scandalously. [C.B.] Dodson goes with them. He is a troublesome neighbor.

FRIDAY, SEPT. 21. Course from camp one and one half miles N.W. then three miles S.W. to a notch cut deeply down in the mountain at the west side of the valley. The valley itself is probably 13 miles in diameter. From the notch a ravine runs down to the bog, on the south side of the road we came in, but at some distance from it. This ravine is broad at the lower portion and abounds in springs and grass. The sides are generally precipitous and picturesque. It will [do] for a visit as it is a cut off for a footman. Indeed a very good road runs up from the bog two miles in it, and then, winding up the north bank, runs north a mile and enters the main road. The north of the base of which is the well hole in solid granite too.

The water discharged here runs down to Muddy Springs forming, no doubt, a lake there. And this accounts for the strange appearance of the soil and vegetation at our last camp. The scenery here is very interesting. Some distance east of the pass a road turns to the right and, passing round the other side of the hill, comes in again two miles ahead. From the north the course is S.S.W. two miles then west N.W. by west one and a quarter miles to a kanyon and up it in same direction three miles to camp, where is a spring. The whole distance through greasewood.

The valley we have just left is five miles north and south and two and a half east and west, and has near the middle a mud bottom, now dry like the great Mud Lake. In some parts is considerable grass. The mountains are of the same character as those around the Muddy Springs.

I have named it the "Valley of the Kanyons" as several open into it. A large extend of country must be drained into this valley, and in the spring the water must be from three to 25 feet deep all over it. It all has to escape through the well hole and runs down through the kanyon to Muddy Springs.

Where we camp or just below, commences a succession of remarkable cliff[s] or walls of red. Brown and black basalt, (excoriated) 300 to 400 ft. perpendicular height by measurement with a line. The first one is several hundred feet long and has a wide loam cavern in its base. The entrance is wide and very low; not more than three feet in the center.

The cave is 35 feet long parallel with the face of the rock, 14 feet deep and 11 feet high, very neatly arched, and the ceiling resembles in form the inside of the half of an egg shell. The wall is cut up into cliffs or sections, some 50 or 60 feet and some reaching 100, by perpendicular rifts, cutting down the base. Some of these may be ascended over loose blocks of basalt— having reached the summit there is nothing but high mountain peaks to be seen behind.

The cliff under which we are camped has a broad overhanging face nearly perpendicular, the base receding some twenty or thirty feet, with an enormous eagle's nest about half way to the summit. The kanyon here is for some distance four to ten rods wide. The wall on the left hand is much broken, very irregular and much less elevation. Two miles from the mouth of the kanyon we came to grass. From that point here it is smooth and grassy green as a meadow, beyond it was like a pavement, smooth and hard. There is an occasional sprinkling of willows wherever there is grass through this whole kanyon. A good deal of water must run through here in the spring. Ten to twenty feet would be a low estimate.

The report of a gun is almost deafening. A French horn is intolerable. A single violin is not unpleasant but it is no longer a single instrument, but a whole band, though if any particular instrument is represented more than another it is a "key bugle." But this is only when played soft. An organ played here would deafen the ear.

The face of the rock is grained, i.e., painted by nature to imitate knotty wood. The grain, or seams or colors of the rock wind and wave and twist and curl very beautifully; so much so as to appear sculptured. There are some immense scrolls and several surprising imitations of Corinthian and Ionic capitals. It has been quite cool for nearly a week except just before noon each day but today has been warm throughout. Made 12½ miles.

SATURDAY, SEPT. 22, Looked into some of the caverns which abound here. I ascended the cliff east of camp last evening but too late to see anything at a distance. This morning climbed up through the ravine again hoping to get a view of the "Sierra Nevada." Could not see more than twenty miles west any where and that only indistinctly on account of the smoke or haze which rests on every distant object.

There is a comparatively level space some distance back from the brow of the east wall of the kanyon. Thinking to get a better view, I crossed this and climbed the most available peak in the vicinity several hundred feet higher, with no better success. I saw a high table land on the west stretching away to the right and left and extending back or west ten or twelve miles, broken up by ravines and ledges of basalt. Beyond, nothing but smoke. North, east, and south, nothing but hills and mountains, rocks and kanyons.

The great kanyon through which our road passes, and which I can trace from this high perch as on a map, has a general course, N.W. but twists and turns to the east and west as regularly as a ravelled yarn. Springs abound and little streams from them run in all directions (i.e., it so appears from here). Whether it is so really remains to be seen, but there are threads and ribbons of what seems water, cutting the green sward like the figures in a carpet.

Opposite and a mile or two west of the kanyon is a beautiful grassy basin or bowl rather than a valley more than a quarter of a mile in diameter, containing several springs and small streams. A narrow fissure winding through the rock leads out this way into the kanyon. By raising my voice to the highest pitch I can [hear] eight distinct echoes, the first six very loud. Descended and went to the edge of the precipice and sat down with my legs hanging over the rock. Sent down a lead tied to a line. Found the wall by actual measurement 428 feet high and the plummet struck the ground 23 feet from the base, over hanging that much.

Left camp. One half a mile on came to water, then one and a quarter mile across a broad bottom, then a rough rocky place with a cave just ahead and high up in the rocks on the left. The grassy bottom like the road generally, half a mile passing through a narrow defile like where we camped last night. A stream of water runs through it. When through, the track turns to the left and six rods to the left of the road under the rocks are several cold springs of very good water. This is a luxury as most everywhere the water is both warm and alkaline. General course north. The widening here is of considerable extent. One mile and a quarter west nearly at its farthest extremity on the right under the point of a basalt cliff is a beautiful spring nearly as cold as the others but much purer. Plenty of stock water for thirty rods below when like all other streams in this region, it disappears below the surface.

Passing the spring the road turns directly north then at a right angle to the left, one fourth of a mile, then right one and three fourths of a mile N.W. by W. This section is broad and has some fine rocks on the right. They are whitish and bright yellow, shaded with light green. Stock water at the upper end, and beyond the yellow rock and under some white ones crowned with brown basalt is a fine spring. Just beyond on the right is the grave of "C.F. Woodin, Jefferson Co., Wisconsin. Died Sept. 2, 1849, Aged 40 years."

Course next one and a half miles N.W. by N. Gradually narrowing— bluff less high and some white rock on the east side. On same side about midway is a crater, which probably gave direction to the last expiring effort of volcanic powers. Everything is volcanic from the Humbolt here, even the men.

To see how the cattle stagger and how slow they travel one might think them an exception, but they are only exhausted one and the dead extinct ones, or craters (creatures?). A poor pun but better than none.

Water for cattle all along here.

Next course N.N.W. two miles, the bottom still narrowing and the sides gradually sloping more and more. Crossing a point or two of sage, where are some rock in the road, we strike into the bed of the stream now dry and covered with pebbles. Following it to the left a short distance it turns to the N.W. just where a ravine comes in from the south. The bottom here is uneven and about twelve rods wide from the edge of the grass one side to the edge the other. One half a mile on turns N.N.W. and the kanyon gets still narrower and crooks right and left, there being barely room for the road which is rocky most of the way. Here are some caverns on the left, one hundred perhaps, of different sizes, in a rock which looks like one great cinder from a blacksmith's forge. The holes or caves are scooped out deep and wide, with narrow entrances, like pockets. Some of them are ten or twelve feet in diameter. Just north, and above on the summit of a peak is a very exact caricature of a Californian done in red basalt.

He seems to be kneeling at the south end of a long block of stone. His body thrown forward, elbows on his thighs and chin on his hands. A pretty large nose, and a decently long chin, but neither are unnatural. He has a pack on his back, and appears to be addressing a multitude of objects a few yards north, among which I distinguish the head of an ape, and one of a dog. Two and a quarter miles on this course is a spring surrounding a large black rock, from which runs a stream that infringes much on the road. This is the head of Kanyon Creek. The road for the last one and a half miles is good, though ascending considerably, and has some grass on both sides.

Nothing worthy the name of hill is met with. Half a mile on from the spring the grassy bottom which here will average fifteen or twenty rods wide terminates abruptly at a low hill, and the road turns W.N.W. into a low kanyon several rods wide which, half a mile on, opens out broad with a grassy bottom. This nearly level plain is covered with grass through which the road runs one and a quarter mile N.W. It is bounded by sloping hills covered with sage—a relief to the eye which has so long gazed on basalt. Ascending gradually to the end of this section the road turns west and soon comes to the sink of a small stream, with low rough rocks of basalt at the right. Here opens a fine green meadow, half a mile wide, stretching off two miles west and finally narrowing into a ravine with low hills on each side and a mass of basalt W.N.W., indicating another fissured kanyon, on each side of which, extending a considerable distance, are high hills covered with basalt ledges. Drove up the meadow one and a quarter miles, course west bearing a little round to the south. Plenty of water here and there has been excellent feed, but it is much eaten now.

The running water is good, and not alkaline, coming down from a spring three miles above, in the side hill, on the right just below the kanyon. The water standing about in small pools is slightly alkaline. Nothing but sage for fire wood, but we have had no other save once since we left the Humbolt. Made 15¼ miles.

Twice lately we have had fresh beef. 1st, the Boston Co. killed a fat(?) steer driven expressly for beef, somewhere near Boiling Springs, and some other train on the Humbolt near Kanyon Ford had an ox spoiled by a shoulder sprain, and killed it. Very good beef, I reckon, don't you? Better than bacon, though. Killed a rattle snake today, the second living one I have seen on the whole route.

SUNDAY, SEPT. 23. Lay over. More than fifty wagons on the meadows. Ice half an inch thick this morning. I shall name this Great Spring Meadow. I have been up to the spring. It is very large; the water coming out of the side of the hill in a flood and rushing down 200 or 300 feet in ¾ of a mile into the bottom. The spring is surrounded by willows and poplars and the stream is lined with them part of the way down to the road. The road crosses this stream just before entering the kanyon, which should be called Great Spring Kanyon. From the heights west and north of the spring the country N.W. and south appears like a vast plain, cut up by ravines and kanyons, but the view is limited by the smoke so that the Nevada cannot be seen.

MONDAY, SEPT. 24. Cold but no ice. The days are uniformly hot. Ducks were flying in all directions before daylight this morning, and I heard wild geese in the night. Cloudy, and as usual, a slight breeze all around us, i.e., the wind, what little there is, blows from all points of the compass every five minutes, so that it is quite impossible to turn the stove fast enough to keep up with it or move into the broad grassy plain which from this point seems two or three miles wide and ten or twenty long N.E. to S.W. with a stream meandering it. Beyond is a beautiful sloping mountain range, lying in the same direction and covered with evergreens in patches. They look much like orchards and give it a very comfortable appearance. The trees on the ridge look almost like comb teeth, through the haze and smoke. I saw the same today, but did not know what it was, from the summit head of the great kanyon, where we began to descend west.

From the west side of this great sage level the road runs W.S.W. over some hills; past a mass of huge blocks of basalt, on the left, to a level sage plain and the south W. point of a short range that bounds on it then west three and a half miles. The middle one of the three peaks in this range is a handsome table mountain which I saw from the road several miles back. From the sage plain the course is W.S.W. toward a long range of mountains which seems to block our path. They extend out of sight north and south and are only dimly seen through the mist and smoke. It seems broken into long ridges rather than peaks, yet occasionally one of the last rears its head to get a view of its brethren. The distance to the base must be considerable, and by the line of dust rising, I should judge that the road crossed it in a due west course. Still it may turn north.

South and east the whole country is mapped out into broad, gently sloping hills and wide valleys, while north it seems but slightly broken. Bunch grass may be seen in all directions, indicating an approach to a better country; and surely we need it. Our cattle are weak and do not get enough of good quality to keep them in good condition. I have seen more dead cattle today in five miles than in any other twenty since we left "Muddy Springs." One week from now there will be no feed left within two or three miles of the road and then—they will have to camp off from the track and travel farther. There are families, men, women and children two or three weeks behind us. We need care little for the men for they are not worth a sympathy; but the women and children—(?). Camped at the right of the road just under the southern base of the table mountain range. The teams did not get in till after dark. Brought no water to drink as they are ordered to whenever we do not know that we shall find it ahead, and most of the men were as cross as—as, Californians. No supper—and to bed. Made 22¼ miles.

TUESDAY, SEPT. 25. Cattle fared well and filled themselves on the excellent small bunch grass. The guard came in at daylight and left the cattle as usual. There is no water here and as soon as the guard was well away the creatures made a move for water. They got off more than a mile and a half before they could be headed back. Moved off just after sunrise over an undulating sage and greasewood plain; a most excellent road gradually descending directly west towards the highest and smallest table mountain peak which looks as if it sat upon a broad table mountain but in reality it is beyond it. The road goes through at its north base and a little south of some large, fine looking white bluffs or rocks.

Two or three miles farther on I turned and looked back at the mountain we had left. On the west it presents a bold front of white rock, most singularly striped horizontally with yellow and orange. I never before saw anything like it.

Nine miles from camp came to a sharp descent of several feet down to a dry mud hole or lake one and a half miles long and three-fourths broad. The road makes a detour round the north end and returning nearly to its course on the other side, passes up into the mountain gorge. We turn to the right, after passing the lake, and camped two miles N.W. Made 13 miles.

A small stream formed by several springs at the base and on the side of the mountain runs down and irrigates several hundred acres of land—a handsome meadow covered with grass. Bunch grass of excellent quality grows to the mountain top as well as on the plain, but it is much dried up.

This valley is forty to sixty miles long north and south and of width varying from ten to fifteen miles. The north part seems covered with soda lakes, and others are scattered over it in all directions. There was a bat flying around the camp last night, the first we have seen since leaving the Missouri River. 13 miles.

WEDNESDAY, SEPT. 26. Ice this morning. On the mountains west are some large cedars branching from the very surface of the earth. The mountains are formed of white or grey sandstone on a base of dark brown and where high enough, capped with basalt. It is much washed away and into very queer shapes. The most common is one like the point of a diamond. On the mountain side and a little to the left of the springs is a very remarkable one. It is about sixty feet high and stands on a base forty feet high, which has a smooth red face. On each side are two similar ones, but much smaller. The right hand one quite small.

A mile to the left is a clump of immense masses with somewhat similar points, but the bases are much the largest part and are washed into plates and plain surfaces. Between the two and beyond is what is called the new "cutoff." As a specimen of the information we are constantly receiving I copy from a paper left in a split stick (post office). A few minutes before I arrived at camp yesterday morning: "Woodworths Cut off. This grand cut of across a spur of the Seravanada Mo A cut of 10 miles Coming by grass and water plenty taking the right hand road nown by the name of J.P. Woodworths cut off."

We have examined this "cut off" and find that we can save, perhaps five miles by doubling teams. Just before reaching the summit there are two tracks, one to the left and one to the right of the large mass of rocks. The right is the straightest and smoothest but a little the highest and sharpest.

From the heights I see nothing but mountains ahead, but back, especially at the left, the mountains which bound the immense plain. Slopes from the east have a bold high face with the appearance of being or having been washed at their base with water. On the whole this is a beautiful valley, and from their number might well be called the Valley of Mud Lakes. Most likely the waters that collect here have no way of escape and have to dry away.

Left camp at noon. Course S.S.W. winding to the summit of the first range one and a half miles. Then west by a gentle descent into the ravine intersecting the main road. Then winding up a grassy bottom with several fine springs by the road side. Road excellent and no place very steep. From the summit the course is W.N.W. by W. Winding down to the valley, with high sloping peaks covered in part with cedar and bunch grass and dotted in either hand with curious rocks. Some deep rough ravines run down into this valley and there is an immense excavation on the north side of the highest peak next beyond the summit on the left.

One mile down where the road turns to the right are some singular rocks. On the right they are irregular and rise some sixty feet; but on the left two thin plates of dark red or brown basalt run back and up from the valley. They lean to the east, and at the highest point may show 25 or 30 feet above the ground, like two walls. They are ten or fifteen yards apart— the top is irregular and broken across with a square shining fracture. The elements have no effect on it. At the base S.W. are a number of cold springs. These walls run parallel nearly two miles N.W. and finally plunge into the mountain side.

South of these springs, up in a large ravine are some small clumps of very handsome firs, and probably there are springs under them or near by as teams have turned in there to camp. Two and a half miles on, passing a very pretty cedar forest; on the right are some willows and springs where we camp. I call this "Bunch Grass Valley" from the abundance of grass and the width of the bottom, though it is not a valley properly speaking. Only a ravine. Just below camp it becomes quite narrow and turns to the left.

One mile south of camp is a very high "peak." From the summit we have just crossed I had a view of the "Sierra Nevada," the real "Simon Pure." In some places the range is very jagged. On others the ridge or crest is even for a long distance. The crest is for the most part covered with trees, which look like comb teeth, and on this points or peaks are isolated trees which

stand very conspicuous. There is too much haze to see very distinctly. Made
6½ miles.

THURSDAY, SEPT. 27. It was my watch, alone, from 12 p.m. to 6:30
this morning. Quite cool to 3 a.m. when the moon went down and a warm
breeze came over the hills from the west—soon blew quite strong and continued for an hour when it died away and some clouds loomed up both east
and west. It is now pleasantly cool, 6:30 a.m. This is the first really comfortable natural wholesome pleasant breeze I have observed on the route. It is
like a May morning at home.

I am on a steep hill which forms a part of the mountain base, and just
before the breeze sprang up, feeling very chilly, I built a fire by the root of a
huge cedar, which spread out its tongue horizontal from the trunk within
two feet of the ground. The bark soon took fire, and as dry limb after limb
caught the whole lower part of the top was soon in a blaze. A couple of
musquitoes here came in and were summarily disposed of. I presume they
came to get warm. I have little sympathy to spare for these rascals—Blood
for Blood. War to the Bill.

As I watched the progress of the fire, so rapidly devouring the food
which it had taken centuries to prepare, a feeling of regret came over me.
No matter. If the cedars of Lebanon did not escape, why should these? They
are abundant here and of no earthly use nor ever can be except to burn. It
was a beautiful tree yet, three feet in diameter with a top fifty feet across
and thirty high. At daylight it is a scorched and withered thing. A few of
the lower and outer branches remain, but the entire center has fallen in and
the glory thereof departed.

Left camp. Course ¼ mile west; then S.W. 1¾ down the ravine (for it
[is] nothing more) between two sloping hills sprinkled over with loose rocks
and occasionally presenting walls of basalt, loosely piled. Road cracked and
rapidly descending, with hills, and in places rocky: then W. by south ¾ of a
mile, two thirds over a slope descending into the bed of the ravine; the last
one third up a hill not very steep. Then W.S.W. three-fourths of a mile
down a long easy descent and up another easy hill: Then S.S.W. by S. one
mile descending into a ravine. Here the grass suddenly disappears, giving
place to a heavy growth of sage. The road turns here directly up a hill to
the right, not long, nor very steep and passes over W.S.W. by S. and down
into another ravine, and up a short, easy ascent one half mile in all and
then turns to the left, and runs down a long gradual descent S.W. by S. to
the bottom of and then down a deep broad ravine. Then turning to the
right again, up a short and rather steep ascent, on to a rocky ridge one and
one-fourth mile. The whole distance from where we left the grass to the
point is stony or rocky with the exception of the last one half mile, and not
much up hill but a great deal down.

From this summit the course is west by S. 3½ miles to a long ridge of basalt sloping from the north and quite crooked. The Sierra Nevada lies in sight directly ahead, stretching far away N. and S. and at its base is a broad level plain, apparently twelve to twenty miles broad, whitened with alkali and having a mirage in a hundred places. It appears exactly like water. Like a lake. South it stretches off beyond the limits of vision.

North it is hid behind some low mountains on my right. Between this ridge and the low plain looking like a string of lakes, is an uneven sage plain, gradually falling to an easy slope and finally merging into the first. From the ravines of the Sierra, which is half covered with timber, runs down rows of scattering evergreens which seem very large and tall and appear to grow on the banks of living streams. The general color today in the haze is yellow, with large and small and smaller patches of green. As seen with the naked eye it looks quite smooth and much of a color all over but with my glass I pronounce it a rather rough concern. The first part of this section is down a long, rather steep rocky hill; then a long easy descent; then down a hill, light but rocky. Then another long descent, some of it heavy sand—through a deep dry bed of a stream, very crooked, and out to camp on its west bank 2½ miles. Made 8¾ miles.

FRIDAY, SEPT. 28. Cloudy morning; pleasantly cool, like May. There is no water here, nor grass, except some tall bunch grass in the bottom of the dry stream bed. We drive the cattle to feed two miles up the ravine north, where is plenty of bunch grass and spring water. The place cannot be mistaken, as there is a low rough rocky hill at the right, just before you come to the dry bed. From camp to the point of basalt, one mile, the road passes over a rough rocky hill, neither high nor steep, and down a slope. Turning here W. northwest, it passes over a slightly descending greasewood and sage plain, in some places a little heavy, two miles; then three quarters of a mile north-west by west, to the point of a hill on the right.

The hills on the right have the appearance of having once been formed into terraces, with no covering but sage and basalt. On the left, at this point, is a long irregular mud lake, with a low rough ridge, probably drifted sand, covered with sage, between it and the great plain on the west. The road next runs west north-west by west three and a half miles, to the summit of a long slope which descends from the north, passing a meadow of 500 acres half a mile at the left, into which a considerable brook of hot water sinks. The spring which thus irrigates the meadow rises out the right of the road in a considerable grass patch, and must be boiling hot; for where it sinks to a quarter of a mile below, it is too warm for a comfortable wash, and has the pungent smell of chlorine gas.

The grave of John Bell, St. Louis, Mo., died Sept 22, aged 70, is within eight yards of the brook, at the edge of the grass, where it sinks. Probably this water is entirely unfit for use, and dangerous for cattle to drink. The section is somewhat sandy. No hills, but like the last section a slight ascent at the end. Distance, one and a half miles north-west by west. On the right of the last half of this section are more boiling springs and grass. A small stream of hot water runs down across the road, and forms another meadow, though much smaller. Next course north north-west by west, one mile on a high level. Then one and a half miles, same course, descending to near the end. Then west north-west one and a half miles, road crooked, and rapidly descending to the level plain. This is another mud lake, across the south end of which the road runs west three and a half miles; then north-west two and a half miles and then two miles south-west to camp.

You can reach the mountain by a number of different routes, according to the point you wish to strike. The best grass is as far south as our camp, which is where a ravine comes down from the mountain, sending a brook into the plain, lined with large pines to the distance of half a mile from the base. The largest of these trees is four feet and a half in diameter. The ground is rocky at the camp, but there is plenty of grass, wood and water of the very best quality. We are at the fourth row of trees, counting from the south, and the third, counting from the north. Besides the brooks from the ravines, there are abundance of springs from the base of the mountains, all of which sink into the earth within two miles, when, as the Psalmist has it, "the rivers are turned into a wilderness and the water springs into dry ground."

In front, or east of our camp, the ground descends with a gradual slope three-fourths of a mile, and the whole is covered with grass of the best kind. Then comes a level sloughy bottom, over half a mile wide, covered with rushes and coarse grass, intermixed with some fine, and completely dotted for a mile in length with hot and boiling springs.

These cool mornings the smoke rises from them as from the chimneys of a city. I counted 206, and I presume that there are double that number. They are of all sizes, from six inches to six rods in diameter; and of every temperature, from blood warm to boiling hot. Beyond these springs the grassy bottom is one and a half miles wide to the mud lake. There is a strip of grass under the mountains as far as I can see, (and that is thirty miles south and ten north), which extends out till it meets the lakes or the sage from the other side. The average breadth may be three miles, perhaps four. This great valley seems to terminate on the north, within fifty miles; the mountain there sending off a spur which sweeps round toward the east and stretches off south out of sight. This spur we crossed in coming into the valley.

SATURDAY, SEPT. 29. Lay over. Ascended the Sierra Nevada. We got up a bear hunt last evening, Ball and Stebbins captains, and of course the mountain heights and ravines must be the scene of action. Stebbins and I peeped up the first ravine south of camp, half a mile; and then leaving it, passed over into the second. Here we found a much denser forest of pine, fir and cedar than we had anticipated. The trees have fine straight bodies, and some of them are nearly 200 feet high. I noticed one almost six feet in diameter. A fine mountain stream rushes and tumbles down the bottom, over large and small masses of rock, along which is generally a tangled mass of different kinds of shrubs and briars; some of the latter very troublesome customers, sticking as close as though you owed them and did not intend to "fork over."

These with the rocks scattered about, compel one every few rods to take to the mountain side, which is generally loose earth, as dry and unstable as ashes, and filled with fragments of basalt. Sometimes, here, you realize the fable of the frog—for every step you take up, you slide down two. Following the ravine until we thought it time to be near the last summit, we turned to the right and ascended a high peak. We had before tried this experiment, and learned that "hills peeped o'er hills and alps on alps arose," but we were a trifle more successful this time. One mountain more, and then we reckoned we would be on the last and highest, and sure enough it was.

We reached the summit at two o'clock, having started early in the morning. We thought that we had seen mountains before. Nothing of the kind. They were only mole hills. The descent on the west side is very gradual; at least for three miles or more, smooth and covered with grass. At the base is a broad valley, stretching off south-west, apparently covered with grass.

There is usually a large body of timber where the slope begins to rise toward another peak; and from the ridge, or plateau, ravines make down on each side into the main ones, which run down to the plain from the last and highest summits. The ravines are for the most part timbered to the very crests of these summits, and all the peaks are more or less precipitous on the east. In most of them are perpendicular ledges, facing the east. Grapes, cherries, service berries and plums grow here, with many kinds of berries I never before saw, all now ripe.

Elder Wisner brought in a quart or more of plums, pitted and dried and of most delicious quality and flavor. He found them four miles south, in the second ravine from camp. We went to the same place again, and got four quarts more. Who pitted them, I know not; but they lay under the bushes, clean and nice, in halves and quarters; the pits with the meats out, commonly among them. If squirrels could and would talk, I reckon we might learn something about it. No matter, I wish for no better dried plums.

As for the hunt, some twenty men brought in a few peasants, and a lean gaunt sort of a red, black and grey squirrel, of very inferior quality; and thus ended the first bear hunt. Somebody saw three deer, and I shot a quarter of a mile at a running elk. The game is all frightened away. From this point it is only ten or twelve miles across to the road, and numbers pack over. It takes three or four days for the teams to get round, and the packers camp and hunt till the teams get up.

SUNDAY, SEPT. 30. Lay over. When we started from home I fixed on the first day of October to cross the Sierra Nevada.

MONDAY, OCT. 1, 1849. Left camp. Course north along the base of the mountain ten miles, to a springy place at the right of the road. Then northwest up into a mountain gorge. The mountain has fallen off several thousand feet here. There is a stream of water running down the ravine, and the road is smooth and easy for half a mile. In the next half mile are two short steep places, passing some pine and cedar to a clump of large pines. Passing through the pines, and up a steep ascent twenty rods, there is an easy and gradual descent into another ravine, or shallow valley. From this the road rises at an angle of 25 to 30 degrees, more or less and only one resting place 183 rods.

This is "The Hill," *par excellence*, and the only real hill we have been obliged to rise on the route; though we have descended some. If anybody knows the use of such hills, let him speak out now or forever after hold his peace as they say when they get married. A heap of folks are here inquiring, and the only reasonable answer yet brought out, is "to balance the world." Just think—we go up half a mile almost perpendicular, merely to go almost straight down again. The fact is, this going to California is a mere game of see saw. Go up, to go down—spend, to get and spend again—take from one pocket, to put not as much into the other—in short, to while away time, and change the location of a—fool.

As I came over into the ravine, at the foot of The Hill, I saw a man about half way up, whirling about and dashing himself to the ground. Directly a man came running down the hill, and then ran back like mad, seemingly without any purpose. Shortly word came down that a man was dead, and two others were dying on the hill. I went up instanter, and found John A. Dawson, of St. Louis, Mo. lying dead in the road. It seems he had been eating of the root of the wild parsnip, which grows in abundance in and about the springs here. The others vomited freely, and the present evil effects of what they had eaten vanished. They will hear from it hereafter.

Thus it is—full of life and vigor as any of us, he began to ascend the LAST HILL, as he jokingly remarked, expecting, nay, KNOWING, if one might credit him that he should look on the promised land from the summit; and though a short hour and little more than half a mile passed would place him where he wished—yet in half the time and space he was laid out still and soulless by the road side, like the "beasts that perish;" and ere the hour passed by, we laid him, like a dog, in a hole, without a coffin, a board, or even a blanket, unshaved, unshrived, and unannealed; and they who tarried to do the last work, shouldered their tools and went their way, only thinking that there would be one less to dig gold in California.

And it cannot well be otherwise. There is no board here except a bit torn from a wagon box, on which I graved the name of him who rests below; no barber to ply the keen-edged razor on the dead man's face, for even the living do not shave at all—no priest to render the last sad office to the dying—to pray, or give a word of consolation; for the dead know nothing, and the living care for nothing.

Even while the cold earth went rattling through the brush on his ghastly face, the cry of the teamster, the crack of the whip and the cheery laugh came up the hill, like the whisper of the cold wind through the sombre pines, wild and lonely, yet exciting a hope that the everlasting solitude which has reigned here from the beginning was about to be broken, and the wilderness made to feel the presence of man. It was too late to ascend the hill when the teams all got in, and we camped at the foot. Made 12 miles.

TUESDAY, OCT. 2, 1849. This is a beautiful place. The valley is fifty or sixty rods wide, stretching off south nearly half a mile to the base of the mountain, which rises very gradually on the south-east and south, but sharply on the west, and is partially covered with pines, some of which are four or five feet in diameter. North, it slopes easily half a mile and then descends rapidly to the mud lake. There are several fine springs here.

From the summit of the Sierra Nevada, looking west, we have on either hand a rough, rocky ridge, extending north and south, with little timber on the left, and some large pines on the right. At the base of the ridge, almost under your feet, is a beautiful valley running northwest, from one to two miles wide, with springs and streams which soon sink in the earth. From this, on the south, a beautiful pine forest rises to the top of a high mountain spur and extends from the ridge on the left to a lake, which may be seen spreading out, broad and blue, beyond the opening of the valley just described. Beyond this lake are low mountains, at a great distance. The whole scene is one of surpassing beauty; but one has not the heart to attempt a description after climbing such a hill.

Descending from the summit, by a way much less steep than the ascent on the other side, one mile brings you to the bottom of the valley, across which runs the road, gradually approaching the forest on the west, and passing springs four miles in that direction, where we turned a little to the left and camped by some beautiful springs at the base of the hill which bounds the valley on the west. The pines here are from a few inches to several feet in diameter, and the hill, which is fifty rods to the summits, and somewhat steep, is covered with large blocks of granite.

The grass is well fed down, except below toward the lake, and east under the Sierra Nevada, where it is plenty, though dry. This valley has sometime been another mud lake and the upper as well as a small portion of the lower part shows the process by which they become meadows. It would appear that the valley was at first a mere reservoir of water. The wear and tear, with the wash of the mountains on each side, fills it gradually, till the level is so high that it runs off to some lower level. Rushes now spring up, followed after a long succession of alluvial deposits by some warm water plants, or weeds and thin grass. The uper part of the valley is now mostly covered with a small valueless water plant, the rushes having almost disappeared. Muddy Spring is of the same class of valleys. Where the water cannot run off, but stands until it dries, or soaks, or leaches away, the mud lake is found. The east side of the Sierra seems to be lined with them.

North of the one we have just left behind is another; and a spur leaves the mountain south of it, stretching off east, and then sweeping round to the south, apparently forming a basin exactly like the others. If these miniature basins dispose of so much water, what may not the whole of the Great Basin do? Such rivers as the Mississippi or Amazon, might be swallowed with as little ceremony as a Jerseyman would use in bolting an oyster.

Today in crossing the mountain, the west wind blew very strong after 9 o'clock, covering the hill with clouds of dust, and somewhat hindering the ascent of the wagons. It wants ten or twelve yokes of cattle to draw up a load of 1200 pounds, and requires from one and a half to two hours to make a trip. We hear a variety of birds chirping and singing, among which I notice the familiar, well remembered voice of the robin. They flocked around the camp on the other side of the Sierra in considerable numbers. Made 5½ miles.

Chapter Six

October 3–October 26, 1849: California

———◆———◆———◆———

WEDNESDAY, OCT. 3, 1849. Ice three-fourths of an inch thick. Course from camp one mile and a quarter northwest; then, entering the skirt of the timber, W.N.W. by west, gradually ascending, at the last a little steep and rough, through a pine forest. From the summit the descent is gradual, but rocky, for a mile. Crossing an open valley half a mile in diameter, you pass up another slope among the pines, and over, and down a long descent to the edge of the forest, where you get a fine view of Goose Lake. Next turn left down a rather steep hill, into a deep ravine, with timber on the left bank, and cross a small stream at the foot of a very steep hill, four miles west; road good except the first part.

Goose Lake appears to be about thirty miles long and twelve wide. It may be much more, or some less. Still it is a fine looking body of water. The hill is twenty rods up and the teams should be doubled. From the summit, a plain, almost entirely destitute of timber, descends toward the lake. Through this plain the road runs west one mile and three-fourths to the bottom of a steep descent at its termination. Then over a level plain still considerably elevated above the lake; the last part rocky, and down a steep, long crooked hill, one mile S.W. by south, to the head of the lake where are some springs. Next S.S.W. half a mile, then S.S.E. two miles, turning two low rocky bluffs on the left, the lake only a short distance at the right.

From forty to sixty rods from where the water now stands, and on our left, is a beautiful gravel-beach, indicating the level of the lake during some period of the year. The intervening space is covered with grass. The waters of the lake appear brown, on account of the wind stirring up the fine sand

and mud composing its bed. When there is no wind, the surface from a distance looks blue, or rather deep blue. The shores are lined with a very large kind of gull; probably the only living thing inhabiting its waters at this season, for they are now rapidly drying away, and I should think, judging from the last wet beach, that it has settled a foot within the last ten days.

Next course four and a quarter miles south to a small muddy stream with willows. The mountain on the east of this section is covered with timber. Most of the grass ground here has been burned over as it has from the first point where we came down to the lake. There are at least eight thousand cattle behind us, and they will much need the grass. Crossed the stream and camped one mile and three quarters south south east, under a rocky hill just north of a basalt bluff, crowning a hill beyond. There is a small spring here among a mass of rocks, (not enough water for the cattle) and plenty of cedar and pine for wood. There is a low range of rocky hills in this section, and a wide timbered valley behind, before you reach the base of the Sierra Nevada.

We are now at the south extremity of the lake, but when the waters are high, they must cover a large bottom several miles farther on south and at least twelve miles wide. West of the lake there are no mountains to be seen; only a long, even timbered range of a few hundred feet elevation appears. It has been so cold that a coat was needed in the middle of the day. Made 18¼ miles.

THURSDAY, OCT. 4, 1849. There is less haze in the atmosphere this morning, and the low mountains south and S.S.W., are very distinct. Left camp. Course S.S.E. three miles, to the second of two fine streams from the mountains, whose sides abound with springs. Here we found a government man, who a short time since was wounded by the Oregon Indians, some sixty or seventy miles north of this. The captain [William H. Warner of the U.S. Topographical Engineers; reference Bruff & Holliday] and one man were killed [Sept. 26]. They belonged to an exploring party, and were surprised in a ravine. A company who have lost all their cattle, strayed or stolen, are packing here. They ask forty cents per lb. for flour, while it has never before on the route brought more than twenty to my knowledge. We bought for the last price at the foot of the mountains. Next course south five miles to another stream, where we nooned.

Here sent two men with the horse three miles up into a ravine to bring in a deer, which the men who crossed the mountains from the camp of Oct. 1st (in the morning) had killed, and notified us of by leaving a paper in a split stick beside the road, (i.e., the emigrant's P.O.). Next south south-east one and a quarter miles to another fine stream, beyond which the ground is springy and muddy. Then south south-west one and a quarter miles, crossing another stream, to the point of a mountain spur, one and a half miles, beyond which the road rises on to a slightly elevated plain, partially covered with cedar. Course the same on the west of this plain.

A kanyon takes the waters of the streams we have crossed out of the valley toward the south, and probably also the waters of Goose Lake. On the east the plain reaches the base of the great Sierra, which is in places covered with timber, but for the most part with grass, and sloping very gently. South it extends some distance, and is broken into ridges by the streams and ravines which rush down from the mountains.

Crossing the plain one mile south, you descend into a shallow ravine, which makes a wide break in the kanyon, then pass over a smooth swell, and descend into another ravine, down which you pass when three or four others enter, and make another breach into the kanyon, one mile S.S.E. Here is a handsome level and a stream of water. The west bank of the kanyon at this point is very steep, 200 feet high and crowned with pine and cedar. The two sections next the last are very rocky. The road, since we descended to the lake, has been in places a little sandy, and sometimes gravelly, or slightly stony; otherwise excellent, though the grass is mostly burned off. It must have been very abundant two or three weeks since.

Camped at the end of the last section, turning to the left up the stream on a low bluff. There are some willows here, but the best wood is half a mile west, on the cedar bluff. Colder today than yesterday, and wind strong from the east. Had some of the venison cooked for supper. It is very fat and tender, and has the exact flavor of a "two-year-old mutton." He must have been a noble fellow; but every deer as well as dog has his day, and I suppose he had all his. No longer will he have to endure the cold of winter, or fry in the burning summer sun, or fight the angry, blood-thirsty musquitoe, or dodge the searching glance of the wily Indian, or wind and turn to escape the desperate, reckless pursuit of the merciless wolf, or more tardy bear. He fell in the full vigor of lusty life, before the swelling muscles shrank, or the heaving lungs refused to swell, leaving him a panting, powerless, easy prey to the sneaking fox, or prowling mountain cat.

And such is life. It all passes like a shadow, and is forgotten. Does it matter when or how? "The dead know not anything." The hunters brought in a bushel of plums with the deer. They are not very good, having a bitter taste. Made 14 miles.

FRIDAY, OCT. 5, 1849. Cold, very cold; but before we left camp the sun rose warmly and cheerily above the eastern mountains, giving promise of a better day. Course from lower ford S.S.E by east one mile, along a level and up an easy hill; middle part of section somewhat rocky. Next S.S.W. by south, down through a deep ravine, and up to the top of a hill one [and] a half miles. The descent is not steep, but rough and rocky, as is the road part of the way across the bottom, in which is the dry rocky bed of a stream. The ascent is a little steep at the end, though the road is exceedingly smooth and easy. The whole section is crooked.

From the summit, one and a half miles S.S.W. by south, the descent is easy, crooked, and smooth, winding down into a ravine, and then into the bottom of Goose Lake Kanyon, the west face of which is here high and precipitous, covered with blocks, and crowned with a ledge of basalt. The grass is all burned off, and only a few scattering cedars remain. The stream runs at its base and is probably a branch of Pitt River.

Down the kanyon, or rather valley, for the bottom here opens to sixty rods width, and the sides fall down with a gradual slope, the course is S.S.W. by south. Half a mile on is a tall plate of rock, standing at the mouth of the ravine on the left. On the right of this are two rocks, the right hand one of which is a perfect cone in general outline, with the top slightly truncated. On the west side its base is broken off one-fourth its diameter; on the east, about half its height, is an excavation nearly through it. In a few years the work of destruction will be complete. It is even now tottering to its fall. The height is 34 feet, and diameter of base 18 feet. The other one is even more dilapidated. On the left of the central plate is another group of similar formation, and half a mile below, and at the left and beyond the ford, are a number of similar groups, some of them forty feet high. The composition seems to be a loose grey sandstone.

Nearly a mile below and just above the next ford, on the right by a large cedar, is another stone of the same kind, nine feet high, standing entirely alone. The stream will average two yards wide and eight inches deep, with gravelly bottom, and earthy banks covered with willows. Three miles down, the road turns a little to the left, over a very slightly elevated plain, covered with sage and greasewood, and skirting the bottom two miles, ascends another uneven plain, partially covered with cedars. Here, in the Post Office, is a notice of three mules and a horse having been shot night before last by the Indians.

This plain has a gradual ascent and is somewhat stony. Crossing it the road descends into a broad ravine by a steep hill. Here is a fine stream of water, three yards wide, Pitt River I suppose — distance one and three-fourths miles S.S.E. From this the road turns sharp to the right and then to the left, winding again to the right up a somewhat long and rather steep hill. From the top the descent is good, and very gradual, through a lusty growth of sage, to Goose Creek or Pitt River perhaps, one and one-half miles S.W. Next down the creek half a mile south; then S.E. a quarter of a mile; then up on to the bluff by a turn to the right. These bluffs are sandstone and beautifully striated. Since reaching the Sierra, we see grass growing almost everywhere, except on water, rocks, or among the pines.

Just as we began to ascend the hill, found the grave of Easterman, of Wisconsin, killed at three o'clock yesterday morning by an Indian arrowshot. The arrow was stuck in the grave, and without the point, measured two feet and a half. Two fifths from the point was a hard light wood, the other three fifths was a reed three eights of an inch in diameter, with three feathers nicely put on. The whole is fastened with the tendons of a deer. The workmanship is neat, and the weapon must be an efficient one, as the man was killed instantly. The Indian was probably from Oregon, judging from the length of the arrow. The hill is long, but not very steep, course S.S.W. and good road one-fourth of a mile. Then S.W. by south, down a long slope, up a short one and down a steep place into the valley again three-fourths of a mile. Next came one mile S.W.; then west S.W. by south three-fourths of a mile to the ford, and camped. It has been warm today in the sun, and cold in the shade. Made 16¾ miles. The river here has steep earthy banks on one side, generally ten feet high, and the current is getting sluggish. The men who came down the stream, report beaver dams recently raised above.

SATURDAY, OCT. 6, 1849. Very cold. Ice an inch thick. Crossed the river, which bears off southwest, and pushed on over a sage and greasewood plain, quite level, course W.S.W. five miles to a bend in the river, when it comes within ¾ of a mile of the base of a range of hills on the right. This range seems to be the south face of a high plateau, broken by ravines, and covered with timber, mostly cedar. It rises as it runs west until it reaches a considerable elevation. On this face, the cedars in some localities stand in dense forests. It is more broken as it gets west, and finally runs up into peaks. Course to next bend the same, one mile; then S.W. three miles (leaving the river a short distance on the left), to another bend, on the right of which is a high bluff, from which project some masses of handsomely striated sandstone. Here the road turns short to the left a few rods, and crosses the river, which has a swift current, several inches deep and ten yards wide.

On the left of the whole distance so far, today, we have passed low hills, and there seems to be a valley beyond them and on this side of a range of mountains, which stretches along from S.E. to N.W. The river bottom is sometimes only a few rods wide, and again a mile or two, but it is too much elevated to have much green grass at this season. The plain which we have crossed is very wide and partly covered with different kinds of shrubs, among which sage and greasewood predominate. The road is excellent. From the ford the course is S.W. two miles to the summit of a long easy ascent – a little rocky, the river on the right at some distance plunging through a rocky kanyon. From the summit down a steep hill, and along an easy descent, the course is S.W. by south 1¼ miles; then ¾ of a mile south. At the left of this section is a level covered entirely with coarse grass, and having the appearance of a slough. On the east are some isolated ragged rocks. South is a large, rough, square looking mass. Rising a little on to a plain, the road gradually descends S.S.W. one and a half miles. West of the last section an awkward looking mountain stands alone, in the middle of the valley.

One mile and a quarter beyond this, I found a camp of Uncle Sam's men, nooning. They are sent out to assist the emigrants. Among the hills for the last fifteen miles, Magnesia may be found in any quantity. It is excessively warm where we now are (at 1 o'clock p.m.) on the bank of the river. There is a broad level plain here. A slough comes down from the east several miles and is very bad to cross. On the right of the crossing, half a mile distant is the river, and beyond, the mountain. South and S.W. is the broken mountain range, sparsely, though in places thickly, covered with cedar and pine. A valley runs down at its base; a low long hill which terminates just below, separating it from the bottom here. West, broken mountains covered with timber seem to close the valley. The grass is mostly burned off at this point. The teams got a late start and did not come up. Went back one and a quarter miles to meet them and camped on the river bank. Some mountains directly across the river. Made 14½ miles.

SUNDAY, OCT. 7, 1849. Feed short; burned off. Moved on one and three-quarter miles, and crossed the slough. Several trains camped with us last night. Among them were the Washington division of Boston Packers, and the Washington city mule wagon trains. They are nearly destitute of provisions, which are getting very scarce.* Every few miles we see a creature with some portion cut out of its carcass. They generally cut from each side of the back bone. It is a great saving to eat cattle that die of themselves. It saves the time of killing and dressing; besides, they are good for nothing but to eat, when they are too poor to live.

Next course, one and one half miles S.W., directly toward the base of the mountain range; then west, sweeping round toward the south one mile; then west by south three miles, toward the southern base of a low flat mountain in the middle of the valley, with a high wall on the summit. The mountain slope on the left is pretty well timbered with pine. The river bottom is here several miles wide and earlier in the season abounds in grass, but it is completely dried up now. The willows are not as abundant here as above. River eight yards wide and two feet deep, and strong current—water not very clear. Next N.W. round the northern base of Wall Mountain, to a spring brook three feet wide and two deep, where we nooned.

At the bend, back of the mountain, the valley sends a branch up to the timber more than a mile, where are willows, springs, and good grass, but the P.O. warns us not to camp there on account of the Indians. Just beyond where we nooned, crossed a smaller stream, and continued west two miles, gradually ascending and descending till we gained a rocky elevation—the river bottom, here half a mile wide, at the right. Turning short to the left, the road, crooked and rocky, runs S.S.W. one quarter of a mile among the

*Compare to Bruff's Oct. 6 entry in his own diary (p. 179): "We passed the Batavia and an Illinois Company—last had killed an ox, and we bought some meat of them."

hills, gradually descending to the river bottom another one quarter N.N.W. The bottom here is of considerable size and occupies a great shore of the valley, which is two or three miles in diameter. One mile from the foot of the hill, turned south toward the base of the mountain one mile and camped.

There has been a gentle, warm, west wind today and it has been cloudy. This evening a sprinkle of rain, and a few gusts of wind. It has snowed on the Sierra today. I was alone on guard last night after 12 o'clock, and followed 17 head of our cattle three or four miles from camp almost to the foot of the mountains south-east. Not as cold as the night before. Stories of Indian depredations are rife, but no one knows what to believe. Made 11¾ miles.

MONDAY, OCT. 8, 1849. Cloudy this morning, but not cold. Looks like rain. This valley seems to abound in springs, and has good grass. The lower range of mountains south is covered with a thick forest of pines. Passed down to the foot of the valley three miles. The road through it runs west; and entered a kanyon, after crossing a rough, rocky hill, not high. This kanyon is rough, road crooked, rocky, and crossing a bad mud hole from some springs on the left. The sides are rocky, sloping, and thirty rods asunder at their bases. The river runs at the right of the road, under the base of the hill, and a considerable number of pines are scattered here and there. Course S.S.W. one half a mile, when the kanyon opens into a valley three miles long, and a mile or two wide. Course W.S.S. and very winding, crossing the river within a mile of the foot of the valley.

At its entrance is a dam of willows, covered with rocks made by the Indians. From the appearance of the stream, I should think that there has been a large number of such dams, but I have noticed no other recently built. The mountains on either hand are much broken, and those on the left are highest and covered with timber. From this point the road turns short N.W. by W., up a ravine by a spring with willows and scattering pines, one quarter of a mile; then left, up a short hill and over, and down a short steep place to the river, and down the river again W.N.W. one and a half miles to a ford.

The bottom here occupies the whole valley, though it is nearly forty rods wide. The hills on the right are covered with circular walls of basalt or granite, the left sloping and timbered, and both abounding in springs. From the ford, road rocky and crooked, and bottom only a few rods wide; in half a mile cross another ford, and then down to where a small valley opens, with a handsome grassy bottom, down which the road runs on the north side of a hill, and the river on the south. At the lower end of the bottom, one and a quarter miles from the ford, the road turns short left over the neck, which connects the hill with the mountain on the west, to another ford one half a mile S.W. Then down the river S.S.E. one half a mile; the road as in the last section, part of the way at the base of a steep slope, ten or twenty feet above the river, and rocky.

The sides of the kanyon, which is narrower, have a great many jagged, pointed rocks of basalt, and some scattering pines. Next course, S.W. half a mile through the pines, road better, and ford again. Then thirty rods, and another ford, and directly on, some fifty rods toward the base of a high rock, just before reaching which the road turns S.S.W. by S. crossing the river again in a quarter of a mile. This rocky bluff runs up perpendicularly from the south side of the stream, at least 130 feet, and stretches up the stream 150 or more.

As it stands from this point of view, it almost exactly represents the form of a hen's egg, split lengthways and half buried in the ground, the smaller end out. The color of a part of the rock is rose pink and the rest grey. The top is fringed with little sharp points of rock, which appear like ornaments purposely put on. There are many small cavities in the face, and some swallow's nests hanging to it. At the left, and a little back, are some similar rocks; which are almost concealed by the pines. This description is from a front view, immediately as we came to the rock. From the ford twenty rods below, it does not look the same thing. It is more rough and irregular, but still a splendid specimen of good-for-nothingness. The tall rock below is another specimen of the same kind. Next course is S.S.W. one and a quarter miles, passing some basalt walls on the right, nearly overhanging the road, and almost crowding it into the river. Just at the end of the section you pass a huge bluff, filled with fissures, and having some immense caverns beneath.

A hundred acres of such country as surrounds this would be a fortune for any man, near some great city in the east, but I have lost all interest in these things. I am heartily tired of being shut up among hills and mountains, with loose blocks of granite or basalt hanging over my head; and I believe that there are but few of my fellow-travellers who do not participate in the feeling. The only thing that makes it tolerable is the pine, which relieves the eye by its greenness, and the roar of the wind through its branches dispels the oppressive feeling of eternal silence and solitude.

Next course is W.S.W. up hill one-quarter of a mile, somewhat steep, but smooth. From the summit the road is steep into a ravine, then south down to and on to the crossing, three-quarters of a mile, road crooked. We have to go over this hill because the kanyon through which the river forces its way is impassable for anything but water fowl. On the east is a smooth overhanging basalt bluff, which is forty or fifty rods long and some (I know not how many) hundreds of feet high. I followed the stream down to it on the east side, and ascended to the summit. It was a rich scene even for a cloyed imagination. Who does not believe, let him come and see. Trees, trees, trees, in all directions—everywhere, except in the beautiful valley bottom, which winds and turns and twists among the mountains, garnished with the river's silver stripe.

The road follows the river around toward the east and then turns suddenly south and west. From the last ford or crossing, the road turns east three-quarters of a mile to a turn one-quarter of a mile, nearly beyond the next, and I hope, for the present, the last ford. It is said to be the last but one, when we finally leave the stream "for good."

When on the bluff, I examined the points which crown most of the rocks in this vicinity and found some of them very pointed, and several feet long. Many of them, however, are nothing but loose stone, or pieces of rock lying upon each other, the smallest at top and pushed off by a touch of the hand. They appear to be formed by the action of water on the softer rock below. There were literally hundreds standing around in all directions. This peculiar formation seems restricted to this immediate vicinity. A few cedars are scattered over the summit and sides.

To one not thoroughly satiated, this might, nay, must be a scene of surpassing beauty. I can be astounded, or something of that sort, but to be interested, delighted; to admire is a long way behind me. I might, perhaps; (I say perhaps), admire a whirlwind which was prostrating my house, or be highly delighted with the rushing avalanche as it pushed down the wreck of a thousand mountain storms upon my premises, or cry "Oh, pretty!" to the thunder bolt which drove the dust from my last foot print—but big rocks and high mountains and deep kanyons—never. When I hear of the latter, I feel just interest enough to ask, "Is the road rocky?" If it is not, I am thankful and walk on. It if is, why it is only what I expected, and so I am easy any way.

From the bend at the end of the last section, turned south one half a mile and camped under the northern base of a high smooth hill, with a few scattering pines, and directly before us. The river runs on east a considerable distance into a large and beautiful valley, and sweeping back comes in on the south side of the hill, only a short distance south of camp. Made 15¾ miles.

TUESDAY, OCT. 9, 1849. Passed on to the western base of the hill one-quarter of a mile, south: then W.S.W. over a rolling plain, somewhat elevated above the river, which is on the left at the base of the southern range, while the road runs a mile north and equi-distant from the base on either side. The southern range is broken, though the slopes are gentle, and being half hidden by the timber it is on the whole very beautiful.

In the valley are some low pine covered hills. Two miles on, the road descends to the bottom at a bend in the river, and then follows down under the base of the northern range, the river immediately on the left one and one-quarter miles; then west one mile, descending along a handsome plain, passing a pine covered mountain ridge, which viewed from the turn south of camp seemed to block the lower end of the valley—to the western extremity. Then S.W. down the river bank a short distance, and up a steep short hill, and over a rolling plain down to the river again; then over the slope of the right hand range, a steep descent, and touching the river bank, the road enters another kanyon, with handsome sloping sides partially covered with pine.

The river bottom thus far today has been very narrow, but the valleys are delightful. The hills on the right, a mile back, look like prairies—so smooth and grassy. The bottom itself is almost entirely covered with willows. Next over an elevated rolling plain, in one place a little rocky, down to a bend in the river where the road runs along a high rocky bank—in all four miles. Next south one half a mile to the next bend, then east one-quarter of a mile and ford the river for the last time.

The scenery of this irregular valley or congeries of valleys is not easily described. The river all along, the same as yesterday, seems to be a succession of ponds, formed by damming the river with willow bushes and rocks. The object probably is to catch fish. But for them, the current would be rapid, and the water much better.

At the last turn of the road and ford, the mountains on the right are low and sloping, and some of them heavily covered with timber; on the left they run up into peaks, except far ahead where is a most delicately turned, smooth, bare, large one, sloping off in all directions; and just north, though not seen from this point, another similar and partially covered with cedars. From the ford the course is S.S.E. by east two and a half miles, bending down toward the river to the right. Along the first two miles, on the other side of the stream, is a high rocky bluff, the upper one-fourth a perpendicular wall, the other three-fourths a slope formed of loose fragments of rock broken from the wall above. This slope is very steep and partly covered with scattering pines. The line of the plain above is smooth and no trees appear upon it.

In the distance beyond there seem to be some rough mountain peaks, but the fog which has covered every object today renders them very indistinct. It is difficult to distinguish anything, even a mountain, ten miles. The air is cool, and feels damp like a storm. At this bend the slope comes almost to the river, the road running between the two, one half a mile south, on the east bank of the stream. Halted at noon at the west side of the Bare Mountain [probably Lassen's Peak].

Next course S.S.E. one and one-quarter miles, passing some cedars, up on to a plain, the soil of which is purple, and on to the point of a low hill close to a bend of the river. From this point nothing but a broad valley appears at the south, where the river is lined with large willows, and a long low flat hill, with patches of white on the side, south east. There appear to be some tall pine clad mountains east, but so involved in mist and fog as not to be described.

Next course is S.S.E., toward a broad plain, and when there is no fog, a high hill with a few cedars may be seen far ahead, at the eastern base of which runs the road, nine miles to the camp, on the right of the road, one mile short of the hill. The plain is somewhat elevated, descending, has very

few bushes, and no trees. It is eight or ten miles wide, bounded on the east
by mountains, and on the west by the river. South-east it stretches off,
broad and level, as far as I can see. West of the river is a still higher plain,
and more uneven, with a few scattering cedars upon it. The road for the
first two and a half miles of this section is near the river, which then sweeps
round to the west three miles and back within less than one mile of the
road again at the camp.

Weather cool today and at 3 o'clock, p.m., the wind freshened from the
south a few minutes, and then chopped round east and blew a gale for fifteen minutes, then five minutes from the north, and subsided with a little
rain. It was almost dark for a while on account of the clouds of dust. It
cleared away the fog, however, and although it was very cold while the
wind blew, yet soon after it was very comfortable weather again. Water
three-fourths of a mile. Dry bushes for wood. Made 22¼ miles.

WEDNESDAY, OCT. 10, 1849. From camp one mile S.S.E. by E., passed
the point of the high hill leaving it on the right, sloping to the south, with
its cedars and rocks. Then one mile south by E. here is another flat table
hill on the left beyond which the plain opens broad and level, right and left
for a distance. West and south in the distance are mountains densely covered
with timber, and far away to the N.W. as seen from the table hill, broad
forests on each side of a grassy bottom, stretch away beyond vision.

The fog yet hid the south eastern prospect. Next course S. seven miles
across the plain, to the bend of the river, the low green willows indicating
its serpentine course, on the right for several miles.

About one third across are some pools of very good water in the bed of
a stream which comes in from the east and cuts the plain in all directions.
For up at the left a long line of willows indicates the presence of water.

There was a little rain last night, just enough to lay the dust and hardly
either, and was quite cool in the morning and is so now, at ten o'clock.
Some miles east of this bend is a large boiling spring as indicated by the
dense volumes of white vapor which it has been rolling out since day light.
It may be seen distinctly from the hill south of the camp of last night, and
so all the way across the plain any cold morning. On the last half of the
last section are large patches of greasewood with little or no grass among
them.

The river here is fordable though somewhat muddy. It is for the most
part sluggish, deep and narrow with high, steep, earthy banks and muddy
water.

Next course S. by E. four miles to the next bend of the river and halted
at noon. Here is a good place to water the bottom of the river being a flat
surface of impure carbonate of magnesia as level as the water. There are hills
if not mountains of this substance about us. Some of it is quite pure; white
like chalk.

Ball and I started off as usual to hunt a camp for the night. We had hardly travelled half a mile when Ball discovered some black objects about two or three miles west, moving about among the scattering trees at the base of the mountains whose sloping sides are densely covered with timber. I brought my glass to bear upon them and discovered a multitude of Indians rushing down onto the plain directly towards us and raising quite a cloud of dust before they disappeared in the tall grass. They appeared along the edge of the forest for more than a mile. There were several hundred of them. Every moment one would bob up out of the grass between us and the mountain and bob down again as suddenly. I could distinguish some in less than a mile. The grass of the whole plain seemed alive with them. They seemed trying to stretch out far enough on either hand to head us off and prevent our return, since they could not see the train, which had lain more than an hour on the lower level of the river among the willows. They manifestly meant us.

They had bows and arrows and other weapons, though I could not tell what. I sent Ball back to order the teams hitched up and to drive on immediately. They soon came up and halted. The Indians soon began to make for the mountains again. Kaup rode the pony across the river and then galloped across the plain toward them. He came upon one in the grass and fired a pistol over him. There was a general scattering for the tall timber at once. I counted a hundred entering the timber at a point between two trees not twenty rods apart. We saw no more of them.

Next course S.E. by E. four miles, then S. six miles to the lower end of the valley where the road leads up a hill. At the turn of the road is a spring on the left, raised two feet above the general level: at the end of the last section the road runs near the river, its first part sweeping round toward the east and the last, west. At the place where the road comes to the river is a fork, a road turning to the right across the river and up a long hill. We take the left and camp on an elevated level at the foot of a steep rock built hill, the first ascent of a long hill. There is some sage and a quarter of a mile off is some cedar, but it is green. Small chance for fire wood.

Papers in the P. Office at the fork say that, "The Wisconsin Train killed an Indian here four days ago and they are very troublesome."

Along the bank of the river ever since we found it entirely earthy or destitute of rock. We have found, every mile or two, deep pits close to the stream. They were originally of one shape and size, though some are now partly caved in and others almost entirely filled. The depth seems to have been ten feet, the length at the surface four, and the breadth two and a half, being oval in shape and growing gradually larger as they approach the bottom. They are probably root cellars or pits to catch animals or perhaps both. Cloudy all day and a little rain just at night. Made 23 miles.

THURSDAY, OCTOBER 11, 1849. Indians did not trouble us, as the guard was wide awake. It rained a little in the night and the air was very chilly and uncomfortable. Besides, the green cedar would not burn anyhow we could shape it, and the sage was too small to amount to anything very warm.

From camp the road turns south up the hill one quarter of a mile then S.E. two and a quarter miles to the summit. The first ascent is the worst — steep and rocky. It is a tedious hill — full half a day's work as you cannot start very early, the cattle having to be driven a full mile to water. All the feed is east of camp and the water west. From the top of the hill the view must be magnificent when there is no fog, mist or clouds. But the mountains are now completely hid by them. I can distinguish only their faint outlines in the distance. Next course is S. by E. one mile gradually descending till at the end there is a short steep descent. On the left of this section the summit of the mountain is covered with timber and from the road a rocky slope descends rapidly a mile to the brink of a rocky kanyon lined with cedar, and through this the river rushes on toward its final destiny — where we know not.

Beyond the kanyon extends, first a plain and south of that a broad, fine-looking meadow some two or three miles to the skirt of a body of timber. On the plain is a large round mass of basalt, and on the side of the mountain another, and on the south of it a high bare hill, beyond which and a little to the right are two similar ones with something like a meadow shining between. The east side of the first hill slopes down to the kanyon S.E. and has some scattering trees — cedars, on it. On the west side runs the right hand road.

Next course S.S.W. by S. one and a half miles descending except the very last, and some of the descents steep, and the whole rocky. The same scenery lies at the right of this and the last section. Next course S.S.E. by E. from the dry bed of a stream with a few willows — up a long ascent, rocky, but not steep three-quarters of a mile and halted for noon. On the right is timber. On the side hill on the left a ravine opens down, lined and faced with timber nearly to the road. Behind is the Great Kanyon. Next course S.S.E. one and one quarter mile. After the first quarter the road ascends but little. There is timber on both sides of the road and at the ends of the section it approaches within four rods on the right. Saw a number of live oaks this forenoon scattered among the pines — the first we have seen. Here found the following note in the post office.

"C.H. Bush.
I past hear tha third day at 8 oclock
I am not well I hope that yo ar well
Indians war githered ennto large crodes. be
Watch ful. At nit, Jonh E. Bush.
Mean near about 30 Indians saw yh
near last nit."

There you have it *verb. et lit. et punct.* "Lo the poor scholastic."

Next course—trees near on the right first part of the way, one mile south first descending and then an easy ascent to the summit. Then turn short to the right down a very steep, long hill and then along its base three-quarters of a mile in all, from the summit and rocky road. From this hill the view is extensive and very fine. N.W. beyond the three hills described this morning is a long, broad valley, apparently as level as a lake. West, south and east is a valley filled with low flat hills sloping down and covered sparsely with timber as is the valley bottom. Beyond the whole mountain rises above and beyond mountain, their high rounded peaks buried in the clouds which roll and tumble over them as if in sport. The river appears to come down south far into this valley and then turn far round to the north into the broad level valley beyond the hills.

But I must leave. It is too cold on this bleak hillside to sit in a west wind. Next course is S.S.W. down a ravine among the pines, very rocky road one mile—then S.W. road some better one and a half miles across a small valley—and ascend again among the pines, and pass a pretty meadow on the right. It contains about 100 acres and really deserves the name of meadow.

Then S.S.W. by S. one half a mile, road rocky. A descending, smooth, bare place on the right, and on the left pine and scrubby oak. Then S.S.E. down a considerable descent, the worst kind of a rocky road, and no mistake,—across a level and up a little and over and down the worst kind of a hill, same breed as the other but a great deal steeper, to a considerable stream one and three-quarters miles—then S.W. one half a mile, up and down among the large pines to an opening and turn up to the left one half a mile on to a beautiful meadow abounding in springs.

There has been plenty of grass but it is now fed down. A stream runs down on the north side of the meadow. It is very deep and hardly fordable for cattle anywhere. Plenty of wood all about. Plenty of grass on the hill side north but we are in too late to be benefitted by it tonight. The valley is surrounded on all sides by timber and mountains except the N. West. Made 14 miles.

FRIDAY, OCT. 12, 1849. Cold this morning and white frost, the first I have seen since we reached the Platte, and the reason is I suppose that no dew falls for it has been cold enough. Ice an inch thick. Some standing pines which Ball, Stebbins and myself set on fire in the evening fell with a great crash in the night and this morning lie off south on the mountain side burning and smoking like small volcanoes. Driving back to the road the first course is south three miles, rather easy of ascent, not near as rocky as yesterday, through a pine forest with a considerable sprinkling of large stately cedars. Except two places the first part is tolerably smooth, the last at the end steeper and very rocky. Double teams here.

Next course W.S.W. by S. one mile descending first through a dried up slough, covered with blocks and fragments of basalt, completely reduced to a black cinder—then through timber to the next turn course S.S.W. one and a half mile down into a ravine and up a steep hill on to a large rocky open space, with only a few scrubby pines and scattering cedars. The whole of the last two sections very rocky. Then three-fourths of a mile S.S.W. down is a rocky ravine and down it a little; then S.W. a quarter of a mile over a slope and down to a shallow ravine, road still rocky. Then S.S.W. down and over another low spur, rocky three-fourths of a mile into a narrow valley where are plenty of springs and brooks. Last half of the section has more timber, but road is crooked though less rocky. From the springs up a steep rocky hill, over an open rocky and gradually ascending plain, with scattering pines, and a ravine on the left to where the right hand road comes in from the west one and a quarter mile south. This road must make a long "detour" to come in from that direction.

Next course, S.E. A densely timbered hill on the right and plenty on both sides of the road. Passed on one half a mile and camped just before the road descends into a narrow ravine. The watch raised fires in all directions around camp and soon after the boys got a fiddle and a flute going and raised a regular stampede. They called it dancing cotillions. A strange place for a dance. The ground is so light and porous that you may thrust a cane a foot into it with very little effort. If the Indians are about they must think that our party is having a war dance over a hundred scalps. There is plenty of bunch grass among the pines, which are not as tall here as [at] a lower point. Made 7¾ miles.

SATURDAY, OCTOBER 13, 1849. We made quite an encampment and must appear very formidable to the Indians. There are 18 wagons in all. Here the road turns up a ravine to the right—thick timber and ascending about one mile, no steep place. Then it is nearly level a long distance south and only scattering cedars and pines; not very rocky, to a large space at the left destitute of timber. Then ascend a long hill, not steep, through timber after the first mile; road quite smooth but crooked like the whole road for the last two days. General directions, S.S.E. three miles to the first summit. The forest on the last hill side is composed of very large trees with handsome trunks though branching rather too low down. They are cedar, pine and fir. Next course south through timber, slight ascent and descent one and a half miles to a grassy ravine and springs on the right. These springs are surrounded by rocks, and they are numerous, but the supply of water is not large.

Course from springs, S.S.E. one mile, then E.S.E. two miles, gradually ascending, timber not dense except in patches. A grassy, sloughy looking strip running down on the left, and a timbered mountain beyond—the only one in sight on the right a similar sloughy patch stretches down and away

as far as I can see. The whole country at the right descends very gradually
until the slope becoming greater seems to fall into an immense valley. Last
one half mile has a little more ascent—timber dense and on the right, noticed
the grave of "John Hensley of Washington Co., Mo, age 73. Died, Sept. 22,
1849."

Next course, S.E. one mile, then E. by N. two miles ascending through
a dense forest of very large firs, road pretty good, then east descending
through the same forest, and then ascending again as much through thinner
timber two miles, then on into a large opening a mile long and a half a mile
wide through which the road descends. First course, E.N.E. one mile, then
east one mile and enter the timber again. On the north side of this opening
is a mountain densely covered with timber, stretching far away. N. and S.
on the east is a similar one.

Next course E. by S. three miles, first over a swell, then descending a
considerable distance, and ascending the balance. The S.E. three-fourths of
a mile—considerable ascent, to the highest point we have yet reached and I
hope the last. On this section, fir predominates and the trees are very tall
and large. There are a great many small ones which with the shrubs make a
dense and in some almost impassable undergrowth.

I stepped along from the root to the top of a fallen fir two and a half feet
in diameter, four feet above the root and found it 47 paces long: 141 feet. Next
course E. by N. rapidly descending into a ravine one and a half miles. Timber
same—then S.S.E. one half a mile down to a turn of the ravine; then E.S.E.
down on the S. side of ravine three-fourths of a mile and into the same
ravine again—and down it S. one mile into a grassy valley. At this point
turned east one mile and camped by springs. Did not get in till after dark.

Saw a grave today which had been dug open and a medicine chest taken
out, some Doct. all forlorn jaded, discouraged, disconsolate and worn; coat
in rags and breeches torn, oxen, horses, mules, stolen—dead—or gone in a
fit of desperation "cached" his medicine and like the famous Capt. Kid
sought to protect them by an appeal to popular superstition in the shape of
a headstone and the spirits of men which walk at midnight. It was no go.
Some wicked scamp has raised the dead and the Doct. will seek in vain,
when he returns. After all, it is no great loss to the world, and to bury was
the best use that could be made of them. Better exhume and destroy medicines than that they should destroy and inhume men. Better bury medicine
in a chest than in a patient, and the more you do of the first the less you
will be asked to do of the last.* Made 20¾ miles.

*This passage again closely resembles one in Bruff's account. His Oct. 12 entry (p. 188) in-
cludes the following: "On the descent, 100 yards from the trail, saw what appeared to be an
open grave. On visiting the spot, found that it was a cahce [cache]—and had been formed to
resemble a grave where a lot of medicines ahd [had] been deposited. An old chest, broken bottles, scattered pills, powders, papers and shavings. They had been exhumed through cupidity."

SUNDAY, OCT. 14, 1849. Lay over. This is a very pretty valley of considerable extent and surrounded by timber. The mountains are not very
high, i.e., above us for we are on the mountain tops. They lie in ridges on
the west, north and east and peaks on the south. This valley or opening is
several miles in diameter either way and only partially timbered and abounds
in grass. The wood is some distance from the spring.

MONDAY, OCT. 15, 1849. Rolled out from the springs—course S. two
and a quarter miles, level, through patches of sage, and destitute of grass to
a slight ascent—then to a higher level covered with sage—then S.S.W. to the
timber three-fourths of a mile. Only a few scattering trees at two places near
the road to this section. In the hollow just before rising to this level, may be
seen some mountain peaks to the S.W. covered with snow.

Next course, S.S.W. one half a mile—several piles of loose rocks on the
right and a slight hill. Then south two miles through a pine plain, timber
rather thin—then same course down on to a branch of the valley bottom we
left this morning one half a mile. Then S.S.E. just a little over into another
bottom and then into the timber again, a mountain on either hand—and on
the right a long strip of grassy bottom destitute of timber two and a quarter
miles. Then E.S.E. three and a quarter miles and turned a little to the right
among some willows and young pines—some dry and some green, and water
running from the west—and camped.

This is a large beautiful valley, and we are in the S.W. part of it. It is
four miles east and west and nearly two north and south, and is surrounded
by timber and low mountain ridges. The road has been tolerably good,
slightly descending and a little rocky. The stream on which we camp is a
yard wide and a yard deep and runs east. A second stream just beyond is
broader, shallower, and has a gravel bottom.

Another government train camped below us last night. They drive beef
cattle and carry provisions for suffering emigrants and are instructed to go
as far as they find any one on the road. Three packs came in just at dark
and said they had eaten nothing in the last 26 hours. We sent them down
to the relief train and there they got enough to eat. They report starvation
behind. The trains have just sent two men on to the north on their best
horses to give the sufferers notice of relief and cheer and hurry them along.
Hard freeze last night and cold this morning. The hardest freeze we have yet
seen.

TUESDAY, OCT. 16, 1849. Very cold this morning. Colder than yesterday. A pail of water brought from the spring just before sunrise had a skim
of ice over in five minutes after it was put down. As soon as the sun is well
up the days are very warm. From camp the course is S.E. five miles, sweeping round on the bottom to the east, to some lakes or ponds on the left of
the road. The road runs sometimes in the valley bottom, and sometimes on

a pine plain. Some of it in the rainy season, and after, must be very wet, as it appears sloughy, and has only just dried up. The lakes are in an opening about a mile in diameter, level and rocky. I suppose that the water stands for a greater or less length of time in most of these valleys, when the snow melts. The water is of course shallow, and in most, dries away very soon. The outlets of some have worn themselves channels deep enough to drain off all the water immediately.

Next course is south, through a pine plain into another valley one mile. This valley has no low water drain, and the ground is yet moist in the centre where it is but just dried up. It is ¾ of a mile wide and two miles long. The road runs obliquely across it one mile S.S.E.; then S.W. one half a mile up a steep rocky hill, and over into another valley, partly covered with a small growth of timber. The hill is very heavily timbered, some of the pines are nearly 200 feet high. We have passed some of the largest pines today that I ever saw. Some that I measured were more than seven feet in diameter, and I saw others at a distance much larger.

Next course S.S.W. one quarter of a mile to where the road forks. Took the right hand road across the bottom, in which is a large, dry stream bed lined with willows. On the right is a high bare ridge, terminating in a bluff of immense blocks of stone, many of which have fallen and rolled down even beyond where the track now passes. Course S.S.W. by S. one mile; then W. one and a half miles into a large valley, most of the way among small timber and by and through little openings, to a stream of pure water and a yard wide and one half a yard deep, which runs down to the left a mile and then turns east toward the timber, and sinks. This valley has a bottom four miles long and one and a half broad. Grass all fed down except on the skirts away from the water. Took in water, and turning south down the valley three miles camped on the left of the road in the edge of the timber. Good grass but no water. Made 13¼ miles.

WEDNESDAY, OCT. 17, 1849. Half a mile south from camp entered the timber again, a pine plain, at first rather open. Three and a half miles on, S.S.E,, came to a road turning down to the right, where is good grass and plenty of water within a mile through a very rough road, and six miles and a half beyond came to a little opening on either hand; turning across the left hand opening, east, two miles brought us to a small lake and springs, or rather to one great spring, with a considerable stream running from it; the first head of Feather River. The water is excellent, and there is some grass on the east side, on a kind of marshy shore. Above the level of the lake on the left as you approach it is a very large spring of excellent water. Before reaching the lake you cross a considerable opening, through which runs the dry bed of a stream, with willows. This stream bed is crossed by the road on the 6½ mile section, and runs on the right of the road through the whole of it, to the crossing. The whole of the two long sections are pretty well timbered, and without grass except on the stream bed. The road is crooked and rocky, and in some places sandy and rather heavy.

S. Hawley was tree'd by a bear today. He had a gun with him but did not, perhaps could not shoot. Made 12½ miles.

THURSDAY, OCT. 18, 1849. Ice this morning one inch thick. Course seven miles S.W. by S. to east branch of Feather River, all the way through pine forest, road descending and rocky. The descent to the river is very steep, very bad, very rocky and very short. The river banks and bed are a mass of huge blocks of granite tumbled together, through which the wild waters rush with the fury of a cataract. It is about 16 yards wide and two feet deep. Just above where the road comes to it is the outlet of some of the numerous springs which I have so often described as sinking. About ten feet above the river, rushes out a stream large enough to carry a sawmill constantly. There is grass some distance up the river but the road is almost impassable.

Next course is down the river, W.S.W. six and a half miles to a meadow, which appears at first sight to be very large. On the east side of this runs the river. The first mile on this section we cross two beautiful streams running south into the main branch and three miles on descend into a deep ravine by a very steep, long, rocky hill. The whole road so far today has been more or less rocky. Turning a little to the left the road ascends out of the ravine, by a very easy grade to a high pine plain; and here I first noticed a new variety of pine with a cone ten to sixteen inches long and three to six inches in diameter. Passing over this one mile there is another descent by a long and rather steep hill to a lower but similar one—and soon after another descent to a third level. The road is very good, and the timber the heaviest I ever saw; two or three kinds of pine and fir, averaging 200 feet in height and many of them eight and a half feet in diameter. In many places they stand so close that one can see but a short distance among them. Made 13½ miles.

FRIDAY, OCT 19, 1849. This valley or meadow is level, and surrounded with timber and mountains on the east, west and south, and probably on the north. The timber is very high, large and dense. I measured a pine today, two miles west from camp, and found it nine and a half feet in diameter. The whole valley must have been a lake at no very distant period, and is now full of spring holes and little lakes. In these the water is clear as crystal and thousands of fish may be seen swimming about; among them trout two feet long, though it is very difficult to catch them. In a dark night they sometimes bite at a hook. Some of our men built a raft and tried to spear them from it, but caught only a few, and a few others were shot in the day time. The water is so clear, however, that one can hardly judge of the depth to shoot well. At three feet they appear but a few inches.

There is a considerable lake at the left, up the timber one half a mile from camp, fed by a torrent, or rather river, rushing out from the base of the mountain. The grass is coarse, and grows in the water, and the ground is so soft that the cattle are constantly getting mired. Two or three from other trains have been lost today already. Two or three trains rolled in this evening, and among them the Armstrongs from Ottawa.

SATURDAY, OCT. 20, 1849. Cold morning. Had to haul a great many cattle out of the mire. The boys who were up at the lake fishing saw five Indians. Left camp and went down on the west side of the meadow, road crooking along as near it as possible, somewhat hilly and rocky at first. The last part is mostly on the grass, and excellent wheeling. Camped on the west fork of Feather River, where it comes in from a valley on the right, and the road turns round the timber up it. Here we cut grass. The east fork which comes in at the upper end of this great quagmire, forms a junction with the west fork three or four miles below this point, at the lower end of the valley. Our course from the camp of this morning, is S.S.W. by S. seven miles. The grass here is coarse and not very good. The river is thirty yards wide, and ten to fifteen feet deep, with a strong current and clear cold water. There is a detachment of the government relief party here, camped with a depot of provisions, and McClure, of Elgin, has hired to them until they return at $150 a month.

SUNDAY, OCT. 21, 1849. There are a great many wagons here now. Had preaching today. A Mr. Grael (I think his name was) from Iowa, Lee Co., a Methodist. His sermon was plain, practical and energetic; the right kind of a man for these "diggins." He was one of two men from the Mormons condemned to death in the city of the Great Salt Lake, for supposed partici- pation in the Mormon persecution in Hancock Co., Ill. They got notice from some friend of their danger, and left without notice, taking provisions, but no water. They crossed the Great Desert 83 miles without water, and lost their horse; saving their own lives by eating or drinking, perhaps, the blood of a dead creature. They suffered incredible hardships, but finally reached the St. Mary's and the track of the emigrants. After the first day in the desert they were unable to eat on account of extreme thirst; and when they got through, after ten days wandering, they could scarcely speak and were deaf. They were entirely destitute of water from Tuesday to Thursday, three days.

Two men are said to have been put to death by the Mormons for the same alleged crime, i.e., voting that the Mormons ought to be expelled from Hancock Co. I report from what I hear, but for myself do not doubt its truth. Indeed, I expected it; for a Mormon on Green River told me that none of their persecutors would be safe in passing through the city; and while he told of their wrongs, he ground his teeth so as to be heard two or three yards. Yet he was not naturally a violent man; rather the reverse.

Two Indians lie dead on the bank of the river one and a half miles below camp. They must have been dead some time, as the flesh is nearly gone. I suppose they must have been shot by the emigrants. The Indians are much sinned against as well as sinning.

MONDAY, OCT. 22, 1849. J.C. Rogers, a native of Virginia, now in the Quarter-Master's Department, has charge of the depot here. He is very intelligent, gentlemanly and obliging, rendering every assistance to emigrants which his circumstances and instructions will warrant. I spent several pleasant hours with him, finally took dinner and parted with a feeling of regret.

Got in the hay and rolled up the river at two p.m. Course W.N.W. two miles on the bottom to the ford, between the river and the timber. There is excellent grass here for cattle, and the bottom will average one mile wide. From the ford the course is W.S.W. one mile across the bottom, and then turns right through the skirt of the timber up the valley two miles N.W., passing some large springs, boiling up through large orifices in the solid rock. These springs form a broad, shallow stream, the head of which is just above camp. Bottom here from two to four miles and the head is four miles above or north, beyond which is a high broken mountain range, with some rugged, bare, snow-covered peaks. The ford is at the upper point of a small island, sixty or seventy yards wide and two feet eight inches deep at the deepest, with a strong current.

Coming up the broad spring brook, on the last section, I saw a wild goose, and off went his head, at 100 yards. This is a god-send for we are hard up for something fresh. Bacon is a drug and goose is a rarity, especially a young one like this. We have had Ball and McAuley ahead these four days after deer, and hope to come up with them tomorrow night on Deer Creek. This I call the Broad Spring Valley. The Camerons of the Oscaloosa train are with us now. Made five miles.

TUESDAY, OCT. 23, 1849. Left camp early. Course S.S.W. first part of the way rocky, through timber mostly, to the bank of a ravine, in the bottom of which is Butte Creek, a small, swift, clear water stream. Road all the way through heavy timber, with occasional grassy openings. It is very crooked and somewhat hilly, with a crooked and rather steep descent to the creek. Next course N.W. four miles on the east side of the creek—road crooked and a little rocky—and camped. The bottom is at first very narrow, but widens gradually to a mile at this point, and is covered with patches or clumps of small pines, with scattering ones in places and small grassy openings. On the south is a high mountain, only in part timbered. The streams here have a very abrupt beginning. We camped last night on one branch or head of Feather River, and one half a mile below the stream was fifteen yards wide and one foot deep; and one mile below that it is twice as wide and deep. The east fork is thirty to fifty yards wide, and three to ten feet deep, fifteen miles below its source. Made thirteen miles.

WEDNESDAY, OCT. 24, 1849. Moved on one and a half miles to the springs at the head of Butte Creek: road most of the way smooth. On the south side of the valley here is the source of a branch of Deer Creek. The valley is broken by huge piles of volcanic rock. Some of them have the appearance of irregular craters, and are circular: a part sink into the ground twenty or thirty feet, like basins, lined with rock. Some are oblong and thrown up thirty feet high. From this point the road is crooked and somewhat rocky five and a half miles, and descends down to the creek bottom by a short, steep, rocky hill; then down the bottom one and a half mile, smooth, level, and partially covered with small pines, and across a north branch of Deer Creek, and camped at the foot of a valley, which comes in from the west. General directions today west. The stream here is three yards wide and a foot deep at the shallowest. Passed some high, nearly bare peaks on the left, with patches of snow.

Just after I came on to the bottom, while lying beside the wagon of an emigrant, I saw a fine large doe coming down the hill from the north directly towards us. I kept quiet till she got within gun shot, some eighty yards, and then moved round behind another wagon and shot her in the throat just below the head, breaking her neck. This is the first of the Deer kind that I ever killed. We have some fresh [meat] now, without killing chipmunks. Ball and McAuley have been on the ground four days and killed nothing. They came into camp last night.

The middle of the day is still very warm, and the ice more than an inch thick in the morning, with white frost. I went two miles up the north branch of the creek this evening, and found plenty of grass land, all fed down beyond the first mile. This side it is tolerable feed. The emigrants have driven their cattle above, expecting to get better feed, and did for a time, but now there is none. They would not drive them back, and so the best feed is the nearest. Besides, the ground is miry. Such is human nature. Like the moon it has its phases, and has been true to them since the beginning, and will be to the end. On this route, where like a barrel of new beer it is constantly fermenting and freely working off at the bung, an observing man may most certainly foresee its specific course days and even weeks before hand. Made 8½ miles.

THURSDAY, OCT. 25, 1849. Lay over. Went with Ball S.W. down Deer Creek, on a hunt, and saw nothing but mountains, timber, rocks and bushes. It is a wild country. The snowy mountains on the south extend a long way in sight, dividing the waters of Feather River from Deer Creek. The bare snowy peak which we saw soon after leaving Pitt River, lies north of us about twenty miles.

FRIDAY, OCT. 26, 1849. Cold morning. Not as thick ice as usual, but strong cold north wind. Moved off late on account of delay in finding cattle. Course W.S.W. by S. five and a half miles. The whole road crooked, a little rocky and many trees in the way. Richardson broke an axle-tree here, through sheer carelessness. We made him a cart of the wheels and axle behind, and left him with young Hood to come into camp as soon as might be.

Next general direction is S.W. ten miles. The whole road is very crooked, hilly, and more or less rocky and rough. There has been considerable grass on the route, now all fed down. The whole country, except by the stream beds, is covered with a dense forest of pine and fir. Richardson came into camp long after dark, and says that he turned over the cart some distance back, and has brought in his team; a very unadvised move. Ordered the team back immediately, McAuley volunteering to assist, and they took with them the forward wheels and gearing of a wagon to turn the cart into a wagon again. It is a small matter to get a wagon here. Every few miles we find them standing entire, cover and all, ready for running, and the road side is literally strewed with wheels and other parts. Quite warm this evening. Made 15½ miles.

Chapter Seven

October 27–November 8, 1849:
Sacramento River

—◆——◆——◆—

SATURDAY, OCT. 27, 1849. Course S.W. up a long hill and down into a ravine for water two and a half miles and supply scanty. Road rocky. Next, a gradual rise five miles, a mountain immediately on the left. Went up it with Ball soon after leaving camp. Shot a doe through the head, running, 100 yards. From the summit, on the right of which is a ravine 2000 feet deep and a mile broad, the road descends rapidly and turns left to a bend in the same two miles, two miles, where we have a fine view of the great Sacramento Valley 24 or 30 miles west. This ravine winds down to it in a western direction, and rough broken ridges with similar chasms seem to occupy the whole space between the Cascade Range which we travelled down from Pitt River.

Beyond the Sac. Valley the dim, blue, high outline of the Coast Range stretches far away N. and S. Turning down on the S.E. side of the great ravine, and keeping a little on the south of the ridge dividing it from one on the left, the road descends rapidly again for about a mile. Here at the left in a shallow ravine leading down into the great left hand one I found water.

The road next ascends something of a hill and takes a more southerly course—crossing on a very narrow ridge where the two great ravines right and left nearly break into each other. Then up a long steep hill where teams have to double, and then west to camp, three miles. The water here is 3/8 to one half a mile north down in the great ravine, almost directly under our feet, but cattle may be driven down by a circuitous route with little difficulty. The supply is sufficient for only one team at a time.

After thirty head have drunk it requires an hour or more for the hole to fill again. The road today has been crooked and rather rocky in places and again very smooth, through heavy pine, fir, and cedar forests. The last four miles has an intermixture of oak. Deer are very plenty. I have seen thirty or forty but at some distance in the deep ravines. Made 14½ miles.

SUNDAY, OCT. 28, 1849. From camp course S.W. two miles to where the road turns to the left or south, down into a deep ravine, then up a heavy steep hill, and ascending gradually still through pine and oak, to a place where we see nothing but a long succession of barren ridges and deep ravines, covered with oak bushes and scattering scrubby trees two and a quarter miles S.W. Then along a ridge dividing two great ravines, road crooked and rocky to a very steep and very long hill where a wagon double locked will slide and drag a yoke of cattle after it, one and three quarter miles W.S.W. A mule path, turns to the right at the top of the hill, and crosses the narrow divide, with a sheet descent of a hundred feet on the left and a perpendicular wall of 700 [ft.] on the right—and only room for the path. It runs into the main road again half a mile beyond. This is the head of the ravine which rapidly descends towards the east and opens into the great ravine two miles distant, where is plenty of good water—but the road or path to it is bad, rocky and in many places very steep. We were well down into the head of it, and the mule path was a 1000 feet above us. Still it was judged by those sent down to look that the cattle would be more thirsty when they came back than now, if we should drive them down.

So drove out of the ravine up the hill to get on to the ridge again. It is steep, rough and rocky, especially near the top, where we wound round to the right—west. From the hill the road winds round north on to the divide again, and following it down three miles to camp where it is broad and comparatively level. No grass or water. Some oaks. Half a mile back is a spring on the right or west, half a mile from the road. Between our camp and the main road is a very steep hill but short which we descended to get here.

To get water for cattle, turn directly at the hill to the left and then go down on the ridge one half a mile to a smooth roll across it, or where it is nearly level and soon ascends. Here turn down to the left into the bottom of the ravine and over a low ridge into a shallow ravine. Follow this to its mouth and you will find water. All these ravines, and there are many opening into the great ravine on the left, in whose bottom runs among rock and bluffs a considerable stream of good water. There is water below here within a mile of the road as a rule but very inaccessible. There is also bunch grass in the ravines, and but for the rocks and the steepness it would be a very desirable place to lay over. This is the best place to get to the water and here it is one mile and as rocky as a stone wall.

There are several kinds of ripe berries on the creek in the bottom of the ravine, and plenty of frost grapes at the opening of the ravines into it. The Buckeye abounds here, and by the signs I should judge that deer are plenty.

Their tracks almost cover the ground here in the vicinity of the water but I can hardly get sight of one.

Doct. Collins of Iowa just now got a couple of shots at a black bear. Did not kill; only wounded him. The deer feed on acorns which grow on all the oaks from the largest to the smallest. Some only two feet high are covered with them, and they are of all sizes from a pea to the largest found in the States.

I notice a new variety of pine here which at a little distance resembles very much our weeping willows. The cone is almost spherical and very rough and contains seeds, similar to but much larger than those of the sunflower. Made nine miles.

MONDAY, OCT. 29, 1849. Lay over. Hunted most all day but saw no deer. It appears that they feed and run mostly in the night and lie still by day. The view of Sacramento Valley from here is magnificent. You can see it this morning for at least 100 miles up and down and the mountains beyond roll up like a wall in the morning sunlight. Between us and the promised land the long ridges and intervening chasms or ravines stretch down their winding tortuous lengths to mere points, and along one of the ridges we must pass to gain the lower, not the lowest level which is said to be but sixteen miles distant. Probably we shall not be able to leave the one we are on. A few miles due west would land us in the valley but that route is only passable for birds.

We are inexorably bound to this ridge as is a locomotive to its iron track. Have nothing but acorns to feed our cattle. They are abundant. A man can gather a bushel in a few minutes but if he picks them up clean and fit to feed it takes one half to three quarters of an hour or longer. Had to leave two of the cattle here; they were too weak to get up the first hill which was long and steep.

Started very early. It is about as well after all to drive on and not stop for water when it is so difficult to access. We got our cattle down to the water, it is true, and all but two back to camp in the morning, but greatly jaded and demoralized by a drive of two miles up hill at an angle of 45 degrees on an average,. They did not get down there till dark and were wandering about among the rocks and ravines half the night and started by 3:30 a.m. on their return. The first mile and a half is mostly descending and in places rocky, the ridge being narrow. The road may be seen for several miles ahead, winding down on the crest of the ridge, generally on the left side, or S.E. side. It seems to cross over, some distance below to the next ridge to the right. There is nothing here but sand and rock and a few scrubby oaks. Three miles on, turn to the right down a steep hill and up another, west, one half a mile, then gradually gaining the top of the ridge, road turns S.W. by S. and descends a little four miles, ascending a very little at the end of the section. Road rocky.

Then descends again, same course, pretty good road into a deep ravine which divides the ridge. Three miles to camp. Water here one mile to the left down, down, down, and one half a mile to the right in a frightful chasm, out of which a man can hardly climb with a canteen full of water. The liquid is current at two shillings a pint, and cheap at that. This is the original right hand Great Ravine, from whose brink we first saw Sac. Valley.

A Mrs. Pope lost her child here this evening. Dropsy of the brain. She has lost her husband on the route and now comes the second bereavement. Made 12 miles.

WEDNESDAY, OCTOBER 31, 1849. Left camp at 2 a.m. Cloudy yesterday and the wind blew a gale. Began to rain just after dark and continues till one a.m. when it partially cleared up and only left flying clouds—scudding over the face of the brightest moon that ever shone on mortal man.

I can easily read fine print. I presume there must be snow behind us after this, for the weather is wonderfully modified since we left the meadow. Every day's travel seem to have been equal to four or five degrees of latitude. The days are not as hot as up there. But the nights are warm here, and balmy, up there freezing. Yesterday it was cool, not cold, and the rain renders it a shade too cool this evening, or rather morning, as I write by moonlight sitting by the road side, watching the wagons as they roll with unwonted speed towards the valley, now only a few miles away. The teams seem invigorated by the moisture of the rain, as much as the shrubs around us.

Course S.W. by S two miles ascending a long hill not very steep and a little rocky. Then descending rapidly but no hill. The ridge is broad along this section, with scattering oaks, and the surface is quite smooth and unbroken. Very pretty on the whole. Considerable bunch grass on the last section. But it is too late to offer it now. We are bound for the valley, and can't stop for bunch grass, and so of all that preceded us. Else there would be no grass here now.

Next course S.W. to Antelope Creek, road descending and good—along the stream bordered by live oak, through which lies our road. This stream has a deep rocky bed, covered with boulders and furnishes abundance of good water, but the grass is everywhere fed down. Shaved smooth. Here we are in the great valley. The sun has risen to those who slept on the Sierra Nevada but they will never sleep in this valley. It is only light here though the Coast Range lies in a broad light and its towering crest begins to be gilded by the morning sun. It will not shine on us here this hour yet.

From this line, the ravines and ridges seem to run together and spread out into a vast plain intermediate, between the base of the mountains, i.e., when the long ridges terminate, and the Sacramento bottom or alluvion. This first plain is mostly a red earth, highly impregnated with iron and alkali, quite barren and destitute of trees, except where the streams cut through it, and covered with loose cobble stones. The whole is cut up by ravines which come down from the mountains, dividing it into sections, each of which is nearly level—a very little rolling north and south and descending gradually to the west. The ravines are, of course, shallow and merely furnish channels for the mountain streams. They are much like the marks across a cake of ginger-bread.

The scenery must be fine, viewed from the hills east, but it was dark this morning when we came down and so we lost it. The west side of the valley as seen from the mountains yesterday appeared like this side, and doubtless has a similar formation. After resting the cattle a while and congratulating and being congratulated on our safe arrival, we moved off south three miles, rising a few feet from the creek bottom to the broad level red land, which stretches off with an even surface to the next stream, south and south east. Our course nearly south. This stream is very shallow, and its bottom covered with smooth round pebbles, from the size of a pea to a large pumpkin.

Next course S.S.W. two miles to Deer Creek. The last mile sandy and a dead level. The oaks along here are the largest, by all odds, we have yet seen. There is quite a forest on the banks of Deer Creek. About noon I paced across the shadow east and west of one three feet in diameter and found it 41 paces. They all have immense tops. Some of the trunks are as much as five feet in diameter, but I saw no top much if any larger than the one I measured. It is not often that you see one more than twenty feet to the first great branches. Often not more than six or eight.

Crossing the creek which has a rapid current 25 yards wide and 18 inches deep the course is S.W. by S. two and a half miles to Lassen's, along a dead level, the creek a little at the right, lined with trees of different kinds, some covered with grape vines and interwoven with other vines and creeping running vegetation. The plain at Lassen's extends south and west to timber and east to the red land or higher plain, I have described. Lassen's establishment consists of a couple of houses built of sun dried brick and covered with logs and shakes or long split, oak shingles. He has a large enclosure south of it, irrigated by water taken down in a ditch from the creek at a point nearly a mile above. It is surrounded by willows but I did not see anything growing in it. It is said that he grows sweet potatoes, etc. there.

Found Warner of Chicago here dealing in groceries. 25 cents for a drink of whiskey, 50 for brandy, three dollars a pound for tea, sixty cents for pork. Sugar, salt, and flour and corn meal, 50; beef 25 to 40, and only six pence for a sugar. Plenty of barley growing wild here but the land in our immediate vicinity is sandy, and but partially covered with grass, which has been dry and fed very close. Is just springing up again and begins to look green. There has been a little rain here and an occasional shower this afternoon. There are a number of trains here but I sent our teams down onto the Sacramento four miles S.W. while [I] remain with Cameron's train on account of the sickness of Purvine's wife. Made 17 miles.

THURSDAY, NOVEMBER 1, 1849. At Warner's tent this morning got sight of N.Y. Tribune. It cost three dollars at Sacramento City—not a year's subscription, mind you, but a single copy. Warner is domiciled under a covering of colored cotton, stretched over three horizontal poles, and pinned to the ground on each side, forming a respectable roof and sides; but for the ends, one is open and the other (south) partially closed with brush and stakes. Half his goods would be stolen if thus exposed in Chicago or any country village, but nothing or next to nothing of the kind here. Judgment and sentence and justice are too speedily executed here to make stealing profitable.

A Wisconsin gentleman (?) was hauled up to a tree day before yesterday and thirty lashes with a braided rawhide rope, alias, lariat, applied by a strong arm to his bare back, for stealing a revolver. This keeps the evil thinkers and doers "in terrorism."

There are three principal buildings here; one of three rooms all occupied by a few goods and a heap of plunder of all kinds in store. They charge a dollar a package for one month or less and an extra dollar for every subsequent one. Another building seems to be a dwelling house where things look quite decent. At the south end is a blacksmith shop. The blacksmith was manufacturing spurs the points of which were two inches long and the diameter of the star six inches. It is all steel or iron. I asked the price. Forty to 150 dollars according to quality.

The third building I did not enter but from the number of Indians about it should judge that it might be for their use. There is plenty of liquor here. No lack of drink or drunkards, regular bloats. There are some dilapidated out buildings and a log house in course of erection. The whole establishment is on the bank of Deer Creek, which (the bank) is here 15 or 20 feet high and lined with alder, sycamore, willow, etc. etc. The enclosure I spoke of contains about 15 acres.

A sick man died in some of the houses last night. Poor chance here for the sick. Little attention: few necessaries, not many comforts, no luxuries, even where there is money—where there is none, the chapter is at an end. This whole concern is surrounded with filth. Bones, rags, chips, sticks, horns, skulls, hair, skin, entrails, blood, etc., etc., etc.

Quarters and parts of quarters of beef, hang on the trees and lie around on the logs. When most of the meat is cut from the bone, it is thrown away. The steep bank of the creek down which all must go for water, is paved with this offal. A fat beef of 400 to 500 pounds is worth 40 dollars.

The mountains east are covered with snow almost down to the valley this morning. We have just escaped our hoary friend, Jack Frost, and are truly thankful therefor. It makes me shiver now to look back at the white rascal. How he shines and glistens in the sun. I went down to the river S.W. over a fine sandy plain, sprinkled with large oaks having immense tops. One would think when at a distance that he was approaching a respectable forest, but there is more show than substance.

They will not average more than four to the acre. The Sacramento here is from 200 to 300 yards wide, very deep, with a strong current, and but few shoals. There are numerous islands covered with willow, sycamore, grape vines, etc. The banks are 15 to 20 feet above water and of clay and sand or mixed with gravel. In some places nearly perpendicular, again you find a handsome, sloping gravel shore. Some shallow ravines come in from the east; old river channels probably. They are filled and lined with the same vegetation as the islands. There is but little grass, but wild oats and barley abound, growing everywhere. The acorns are even longer than in the mountains, being 2½ to three inches, very nearly.

Followed the river down to camp four miles S. or below where they camped last night. By the road I came it is much farther. It turned off from the main road between Lassen's and Davis' ranch, about one half or three quarters of a mile above the former. The farther we go south the better grass we find.

Met an Indian packing two heavy bags of something on his head. These Indians seem to do a great deal of the labor here for I have already seen them performing all kinds of menial offices. They do all the work at Lawson's, the whites or browns merely superintending. They are illy fitted for hewers of wood and drawers of water for they [have] large heads, small bodies, big bellies and small limbs with little energy. Still they contrive to get a comfortable or rather a living, as their plumpness testifies. Seldom reach five and a half feet in height and it is difficult to determine whether one is 25 or 50 years old. They all appear about one age.

FRIDAY, NOVEMBER 2. Hunted nearly all day and saw only two deer. Found a ranch or village of Indians one and a half miles below camp. They seem industrious, having a large amount of acorns gathered in cribs and dried meat, salmon and other eatables. All but the acorns are stowed away in their small huts which are built of long grass thatched into slabs four feet by eight with willow or grape vine strings or warp. They display some ingenuity and did they like to labor a little more, might have large and convenient habitations of the same material. One man can carry one of these slabs on his head without difficulty. From the compactness of the weaving they must keep out most of the air.

The Indians are for the most part nearly or quite naked. Some have a shirt, coat, and pants. Some the two last—some a coat. Some only a shirt. Some a knit woolen under shirt. Some have a blanket, and very many nothing at all. One fellow sported a part of a blanket about a yard square, which he contrived to make answer all the purposes of all sorts of clothing. It was a mighty scant pattern when tried for a whole suit. Those that come into camp have something on if it is only a knit shirt coming down only to the hips.

Those who do not come are most of them entirely naked. I have seen no females yet, for none have appeared in our camp and I have caught none wandering outside of their ranches.

The weather was quite cold, with drizzling rain, the first part of the evening, with high wind. It then rained moderately, rather increasing and still rains, while the wind has increased to a furious gale. It rolls along like the waves of the ocean, roaring through the mighty oaks for half a minute or more, then gradually subsiding to be renewed with increased violence. 11 p.m. Gale and storm reign supreme.

SATURDAY, NOVEMBER 3. At day light, the storm which raged all night, abated and soon the rain ceased except a few light drops occasionally, and at 9 a.m. it cleared away and we have sunshine at intervals and light wind all day. Weather still cool but not uncomfortable. Evening pleasant and clear and so it is on the morning of

SUNDAY, NOVEMBER 4, 1849. Day before yesterday Elder Wisner shot a deer and today we got plenty of salmon from the Indians. It cost from one half a cent to a pound and most excellent eating is salmon. The Indians cut them up and string them on sticks so that one can hardly guess at the size of the whole fish. I should estimate the weight at from twenty to forty pounds. They catch them with a two-tined spear. The tines are made of wood, bound on to a small straight pole eight to twelve feet long. Ten cents will buy twenty to 25 pounds of fish. Or a cotton shirt, no matter how old if it be clean and have no hole torn or worn in it. By the appearance of what clothes they have I should judge that they were all obtained from the emigrants and probably most of them go entirely naked now. They seem careless, gentle and inoffensive and do not as yet manifest a thievish disposition.

Yesterday the river raised two feet and fell again one foot today. It is said to rise and fall very rapidly. There is abundance of snow on the mountains, and it seems to snow there every day. Cloudy and a slight rain here.

MONDAY, NOVEMBER 5, 1849. Rained moderately all night. Thick cloudy rainy morning. Prospect is dubious. Rain has set in two weeks earlier than usual, and though it is not positively cold yet it is a little too chilly to be exactly comfortable without houses. The trees are all dressed in green, and the grass and oats springing up in all directions, so that in spite of one's positive knowledge to the contrary, it seems neither more nor less than the May of Illinois. Glorious Old May! With its sunshine and showers, its smiles and tears. A little too much of the latter now for us, but it needs some moisture to atone for the dryness of an eight months fevered smile. Grapes are abundant. Larger than our frost grapes and sweet enough to cook without sugar, though some of the boys who have a sweet tooth add a very little. It takes but a few minutes to gather a bushel. Elder Wisner killed a deer today.

TUESDAY, NOVEMBER 6. Rain! Rain!! Rain!!! Splash! Splash!!
Splash!!! Whoever before saw such independent drops; and then they seem
to fall with such bullet-like precision; such deliberate malice, that one is
almost tempted to think them possessed of intelligence. There is no hurry,
no confusion, no crossing of lines. Each drop has its particular errand and is
bound to fulfill its destiny, and woe be to the luckless wight who puts his
trust in oil and rubber. It will not drive directly through, but it completely
mystifies one, so that he hardly knows whether his shirt is wet or dry. But if
there is the least crevice or break, it slips through with as much ease and
certainty as the lance of the knight errant might through the joints of his
antagonist's armor. Leave an inch of play between your cloak or coat and
the top of your boot and before you suspect foul play the last is half full of
water.

WEDNESDAY, NOVEMBER 7. Rained all night long, more deliberately—more maliciously, more unmercifully than ever; and but for the
splash, the big drops striking like bullets of quicksilver, might easily be confounded with the acorns which at every gust of wind fall in showers. This
journey is through extremes. In the desert we had no water. Dying of thirst.
We are now in danger of drowning. And but that we partly believe in the
old adage: "He that is born to be hanged, etc." we might despair, for we are
completely surrounded with water. The old channels and new, the bayous
and sloughs are all full and the river has raised ten feet and is still rising. It
cleared off partially between daylight and sun rise, and it does not rain now
here, but it is still raining on the lower mountain ranges and snows on the
highest.

This afternoon Elder W. killed another deer, and an Indian brought it
in on his head some two miles and more, wading two broad bayous, nearly
to his armpits in water. If you tell one of these creatures to do a thing he
sets about it at once. They evince a great degree of activity and energy and
considerable physical strength. They have been taught obedience by their
former masters. They gave them the skin for their labor, and added four
biscuits of hard bread. They took a hachet of ours and pounded the head to
a pulp and roasted after which they eat it, bones and all, except the largest
and harder pieces.

When they had finished it they bade us good bye and trotted off with
the skin, shanks and half emptied intestine, highly pleased with the fare and
pay.

There are numerous mounds in this vicinity which are said to be remains
of old Spanish towns or ranches. The sun-dried bricks have returned to
nearly their original state. Some distance below our camp is one 200 yards
long and 100 wide. It appears now as if originally some large deep pits had
been dug and washed partly full again by the overflowing waters.

I have seen several such but this is the largest. Two of these have been

dug into and a large number of human skulls, evidently Indian, taken out
and scattered round. From another mound a large quantity of other human
bones have been dragged. Some of them are half burned and I should judge
that these are only remnants of skeletons, most of them having been consumed entirely. They are probably waiting for these to dry and then they
will be burned too. This is all conjecture as I have no means of knowing
more than I can see.

THURSDAY, NOVEMBER 8. Cleared off in the night and this morning
only flying clouds and north wind. Cool, not cold. Indeed it has not been
really cold at any time, only chilly. The mountains, however, look bleak
enough this morning and well merit the appellation of "snowy." Some of the
peaks appear like great white clouds with a mellow yellowish tint. There is
snow on the Coast Range west, while here all the trees are clothed in green
and many flowers are scattered along the banks of the stream and "bayous."
The grain with the young grass is springing up in all directions about us.

If it only rained here in the summer as it does in Illinois, this would be
a delightful country for farming. The land of Egypt was never more prolific
than this valley might be, and probably it is as easily irrigated. But irrigation is a word that Yankees don't fancy. They prefer looking up for water,
rather than pumping it up. I said Yankees and I repeat it. If ever this land is
cultivated they will have to do it. There is much, however, to oppose and
finally prevent so desirable a consummation. I will only mention one now—
the Spanish Grants. I have no means of knowing their extent, but from the
number of the ranches and the apparent size of some of them, I should not
wonder if they are found, like the same kind of grants in Texas, to over lap
some portions, if not the whole country, like the shingles on a roof.

I suppose that government will recognize their titles, (though I do not
know, having never read the treaty in reference to that point) if only to
follow out old precedents. At all events the claimants and others deem them
safe else the former would accept the very liberal offers of the latter for their
chances. When these grants are disposed of, next comes the soldier's land
warrants, or certification floating off the remainder like a Mississippi over-
flow. The amount of these "floats" now lying in wait at "Frisco" abiding the
action of congress, is incredible. And a most stupendous scheme of land
monopoly is contemplated by the holders. No effort or outlay of money will
be spared to get a law at this session to make their scrip available. If they
succeed and the old claims are confirmed, the whole land will continue a
wilderness of tangled briars and vines and shrubs and weeds and grass
except where the fire and flood clean it off, or it will be held under a worse
tenure than the farming land of England or Ireland.

If men can get the land for nothing perhaps they may be induced to cul-
tivate it, but only an exorbitant price will draw it from these land sharks,
and that will not be paid—never. Probably the best town sites are already

seized upon, and then large prices may be obtained. But if the lands are not cultivated these towns will be but mushroom affairs. Lawson is now laying out a quarter section into town lots, and doubtless others are equally vigilant.

The mines cannot support them, at least steadily and permanently. Indeed the existence of country towns dependent on gold mines, must be sickly and precarious. You can take these rambling ideas of mine for what you judge they may be worth, and when I shall learn more I will give you the benefit of it. One thing, however, if congress and the people are not sufficiently awake to the subject of land monopoly, do not suffer them to sleep comfortably, at least tickle their noses with a straw.

Reports are rife this evening of extreme destitution and horrible suffering, among the emigrants in the mountains. The government relief party has come in, leaving mules and horses and everything for the sufferers. We have not yet learned many particulars and therefore I note none till they are more reliable.

Ball sent a deer into camp today by an Indian. I must give these fellows credit for a little more strength, for this one packed a large deer four miles; and for great honesty as he was offered clothes and food on the way, for the deer, but he shook his head and pushed along. Nothing could induce him to break his trust, though he might have done so and escaped, for he did not get in till dark, and Ball did not know him when he came in some time after.

I was at their village again today. They have a large quantity of acorns gathered and put in small cribs; also some oats and other seeds, and a quantity of grapes. They collect and carry them in a basket made of willow, funnel shaped and very neatly done. On the whole they yet retain much of the knowledge and skill imparted to them by the ancient "Padres" with the oats, barley and other vegetables if any there are which will grow without cultivation. There is a thick curtain of clouds over us but no rain yet.

Chapter Eight

November 9–December 21, 1849:
Rain! Rain! Rain!

———◆———◆———◆———

FRIDAY, NOVEMBER 9. Began to rain in the morning with constant drizzling rain all day and occasional showers. Today the Camerons bought a large yawl from some fellows who attempted to navigate the river to Redding mines. They are going to ferry the teams across the river and go down on the other side where the road is yet passable. I have engaged the boat to get over too and we have moved camp up three fourths of a mile.

SATURDAY, NOVEMBER 10. Rained all night, steady, deliberate pouring and the river has raised in that time seven feet and is rising fast. Cool: not cold. This rain makes the western bank also impassable. Next move is to build a raft, sell the cattle and take to the river. Rained steadily all day.

SUNDAY, NOVEMBER 11. River fell two feet last night and is falling fast though the rain fell at intervals all night. Wind north this morning and clear except a few floating clouds. The rain seems to come with a south E. wind and leave with a north. Perfectly clear this afternoon. The wild geese and brant are flying in clouds in all directions, day and night and have been ever since we have been in the valley.

Hundreds and thousands and tens of thousands may be seen at once and the air is filled with their screams.

MONDAY, NOVEMBER 12, 1849. Quite cool last night but no frost. Fine day today, and the sand hill cranes are flying toward the south in flocks. The river is ten feet lower this morning, and falling fast. We have

bargained away our cattle and the men are building a raft. If this weather.
holds only a few days (but it will not) we can roll our wagons into the
mines.

So the men have concluded this afternoon not to sell the cattle and the
bargain falls through. There is to be an election tomorrow and everybody
(white and 21 years old) may vote. I have seen the ticket and have a copy of
the new Constitution. It is very similar to that of Illinois: prohibits slavery,
niggers not citizens—but makes provisions for the legislature at some far
away future to extend the right of suffrage to certain Indians therein mentioned.

[Peter] Burnett [later installed as governor] and Sherwood are the candidates for Governor. As I understand, the Constitution is now up for
adoption or rejection. Cameron sold the yawl today. It is a common
schooner's yawl 25 feet long and brought 800 dollars. He gave 600.

They seem to care very little for money here. Sent up to Davis' ranch
for some molasses today. Had to pay eight dollars a gallon. We cannot make
a raft. We can't find a green stick that will float and dry timber is very
scarce, and I doubt that it will keep above water three days. This country
seems destitute of resources. Nothing seems available except grapes. The
timber in the mountains is inaccessible except by railroad and the oaks in
the valley cannot be rafted.

The water is fast running off and we can start tomorrow if we choose—if
it does not rain. A large dry cottonwood tree which we felled day before
yesterday and put in the river sunk this afternoon. No more rafts. 10 p.m.
Has been raining all the evening.

TUESDAY, NOVEMBER 13, 1849. Rain—rain all night. All the forenoon, and perseveringly continued to pour down till this afternoon when it
slacked up somewhat, and finally wound off this evening. We are now
engaged on some large canoes.

Jerry Armstrong had a "rencontre" with a bear today, and was rather
worsted. Knocked down or over at a single blow, his gun knocked from his
hands, and Jerry lying on his back with shut eyes expecting soon to become
a part of a bear. But his or her majesty left him untouched in that humiliating condition and walked (Jerry says ran) away.

In a bear fight trust not an arm of flesh, for Jerry's companions all
"vamoosed" and left him to the grizzly's tender mercies. The best thing in a
bear fight is a ball through the brain—of the bear, I mean.

Election today, but we do not vote although allowed to by the Constitution. The truth is we feel a deal like the old woman in the bear fight.
We know nothing and for that matter, can know nothing of the candidates,
and of course care but little which whips.

The truth is—I cannot—never will vote for a Constitution or law that
makes such arbitrary and invidious distinctions as does this, in regard to

citizenship, not even if it does prohibit slavery or is ever so good in other respects.

WEDNESDAY, NOVEMBER 14, 1849. Cleared off in the night, with no change in the wind except that it has blown fresher. Pleasant today but part of the time cloudy. Canoes are progressing slowly. Reports of great suffering come down from the mountains. Snow is deep and teams cannot move. Four persons were killed by the falling of a tree on to their tent when they slept.

THURSDAY, NOVEMBER 15, 1849. Cloudy all day but did not rain till nearly dark. High wind S. East.

FRIDAY, NOVEMBER 16. Rain nearly all night—continues this morning—not "right smart" but "powerful weak." Yesterday was the coolest day since we came into the valley, and yet it was not positively uncomfortably so. It is difficult to describe this sort of weather. It is to the feel like a week in Illinois, about the 20th of September—to the sight like a week of the first of June. In the mountains it seems to rain or snow, perhaps both at different elevations, most or all the time whether it is foul or fair here. Darling has come up from the mines and Whipple came with him (Whipple was expelled, you know, long, long ago). Darling says there is a great deal of suffering in the mines. Men work hard in fair weather and are shelterless in foul. Has rained but little here this afternoon. Misty and cloudy at 8 p.m. with high wind.

Rev. Mr. Stibbs has just come into camp this evening. Gives a sad account of affairs in the mountains. The company he came with left everything but their lives and clothes. He and wife came through from Feather River by the help of the Government train. Have only half a change of clothing left. He had a noble outfit and possibly might have pushed through but the Indians got their best cattle at Goose Lake and his load was originally much too heavy. He stops at Lawson's or Davis', I forget which and wants to get down to Sacramento City. I hope he will succeed, for he is the right kind.

SATURDAY, NOVEMBER 17, 1849. Company had a meeting last night and agreed to appraise all the property so that those who wish to leave may. Have been engaged all day in the business. It rained all night at intervals and river raised six feet. Cloudy and windy today. No rain, and not cold. Was rather chilly last night. Last night and early this morning was a little too chilly to be exactly comfortable.

Robert Horton, who is going down in our company, and travelled with us through the mountains, came in just now, almost sun down and reports a cow killed seven miles below—down the river. Did Bob kill it? If nobody owns the cow he did. If anybody owns it he didn't. It is probably a wild cow, and not marked and of course, not owned. No matter, we must have something to eat. Called in the men from work to go down and pack up the meat.

SUNDAY, NOVEMBER 18, 1849. We started at sundown yesterday a dozen or more strong to pack up the cow that Ben killed. It was dark when we got through though we made good time. Having secured what meat we wanted and hung the balance up high in the trees we started for camp. Each one had his rifle and other "fixings" and his meat in a bag thrown over his shoulder.

It was somewhat cloudy and rather dark, and when about half way up, three of the boys turned off to take what they said was a nearer route. Soon after I found that the balance of them were not following. I stopped and waited a while and not hearing anything of them, moved in, and soon came to a halt myself.

In going down we had the outlet of a large slough, or rather lake, in an old channel of the river, to cross by wading midsides or three and a half feet deep. Here three or four of the boys demured. They would not cross, because the water was ice cold and was rising fast, but agreed to wait till we returned.

We had started Horton, McCauley and Richardson for home nearly an hour before the rest of us left, so that they might be sure to get into camp if the river did rise so as to stop us. When they got to the outlet the water was up to their arm pits, but they waded it and found no one on the other side. They had left, and thus violated their word. But they (the packers) got into camp. When I came up the water had raised two feet. There was quite a current, the water cold as ice and the bottom had got soft so as to stick the feet. But I stripped, put my clothes, rifle, etc. on my bag of meat and went in. It was nearly eight rods wide now, and six or seven feet deep in the middle. I held my plunder above my head and waded till the water was above my eyes. Finding that I could not keep my feet much longer I turned back and got on shore again with some difficulty. I had about 60 lbs of meat and liver besides gun, etc.

I was thoroughly chilled. Would not go back and could not go forward. So I put on my clothes and went down the stream towards the river, found a clump of willows and camped. I first started a fire and this was rather difficult for every kind of fire wood was scarce and dry was out of the question. There had been a little drizzling rain for two hours, little more than a mist or fog, but enough to wet every thing. I succeeded however, in starting a fire and then I had light enough to get wood and make myself comfortable generally.

Cut some willow brush and made a bed by the fire. Hung up my meat on an oak limb out of reach of the bears and wolves, put my rifle in order and lay down with it under my head, on the willow bed and slept without blanket or any other covering. I waked two or three times and replenished the fire.

Was not disturbed, that I know of. It was rather chilly and a little too moist above and below, and around, for the most perfect enjoyment when awake, but it answered just as well to sleep by. The boys came in to my camp just as I was finishing my breakfast of broiled liver without salt, and roasted acorns. Gave them some of the same for breakfast and by that time the men came down from camp above with axes and ropes, and we built a bridge across the stream below, and just above where it entered the river, where it was only about 25 feet wide, though very deep.

These streams are old channels of the river and are some of them several miles long. At the upper end they are very shallow; some of them not more than a foot depression at the bank of the river. In the middle they are deep and generally there is standing water, in this one a lake half a mile long when the water is at the lowest. It is always at the same level as the river. At the lower end it is shallower and shallower from the lake till near the river where the channel suddenly deepens, gets narrower and pours its flood into the river. Many of these channels connect with each other and the upper end may be entirely cleared and level with the bank of the river. It is only when the river rises high enough to run over into these channels that there is ever any water in them except the lake in the center.

Under these circumstances it is evident that the river will fall a good deal before these bayous fall at all. So last night the river was falling rapidly and created such a current where I attempted to cross that I could not wade when the water covered my head, and this morning the river, having fallen four feet and more, there is a very strong current in the bayou though the water has not fallen six inches. Thus giving a fall of nearly four feet to a body of water six rods wide and six feet deep in a distance of 300 yards.

10 a.m. In camp. Find the men who did not go down and did not wait as they agreed debating and hesitating about going after the balance of the meat, some 250 lbs. Their excuse was, that it might be branded or marked though Horton assured them that there was no brand on it as he looked before and after he shot it.

Finally they concluded to go but when they got there they found that the vultures had eaten all but the bones. We have some men in the train who take every opportunity to delay, discourage, and impede every movement and operation. If it is wanted as in this case, to go on some expedition they contrive to delay and if alone are always too late. Among them is Morgan, one of the most lazy indolent men I have ever met with, and so far as he knows, a scoundrel and a hypocrite. He is a great talker and makes up in sound what he lacks in sense, and it amounts to a considerable sum. He was expelled from the company for neglect and laziness and insubordination. A week since he came back and by dint of talking and begging worked himself back again.

In making up a company, avoid great talkers. They are always a nuisance. Never do anything if they can avoid it. Now in this case we were out of meat entirely except a little jerked venison, which is at least as good if not better than bass wood chips. Dry, dry, dry! No fat. No salt. No relish. Best eaten raw, or without cooking: and yet these hypocritical rascals who have not one particle of moral principle, men of vicious practices and dishonest in deal at home, pretend they have certain qualms—scruples of conscience, forsooth?—and cannot meddle with such beef.

This is straining out a gnat and swallowing a camel. The fact is, as I understand it—There are a great many wild cattle in the country and those who pretend to own them catch and brand the calves when they are able to catch them. By Mexican law this makes them the property of the brander. If, after a certain age, six months I believe, one is found not branded, it may become the property of any one who can catch it, even though the calf of a branded cow. The brand is put on the left hip or shoulder, always, or if elsewhere is of no account. Each brander has his own mark or figure, and is easily seen at quite a distance. Lawson's brand is a bridle bit and can be seen 25 rods. Every rancho has its herders and a part of their business is to brand all the calves they can catch. No rain today. Some wind.

MONDAY, NOVEMBER 19, 1849. Rained all night long and blew a perfect gale; a sort of half hurricane. I never knew it to blow as hard in Illinois except for a few minutes at a time. This morning, after two or three showers, it cleared up again and the wind went down. It is quite cool today though by no means cool enough for mittens or overcoats. Cloudy and chilly again this evening with slight rain. E. Whipple is very sick of typhoid pneumonia contracted in the mines. They call it here, camp fever.

TUESDAY, NOVEMBER 20, 1849. Cloudy. Some wind and rain in the evening. Divided our provisions today.

WEDNESDAY, NOVEMBER 21. Cloudy. Rained all night and continued at intervals till this afternoon. Cloudy all day and misty, but no wind. Several canoes have gone by down the river today. Whipple gets worse. No rain or wind this evening, but cloudy.

THURSDAY, NOVEMBER 22. Clouded up thickly in the night and rained considerable, but fair and pleasantly cool this morning, and through the day. Grove came in from the mines and reports a scarcity of provisions, and much suffering for lack of shelter. The wind for a wonder has held on west all day and so continues—9 p.m.—all clear. Whipple no better.

FRIDAY, NOVEMBER 23. Fair and pleasant. Whipple better.

SATURDAY, NOVEMBER 24, Cloudy in the morning and slight wind, S.E. A sprinkle of rain and cleared off fine and pleasant, and continues so this evening—9 p.m.—slight wind N.W.

SUNDAY, NOVEMBER 25. Slight wind. Very pleasant, and quite warm, though the night was cool and heavy dew. No frost. Oats are three inches high. Leaves on all the trees green except sycamore which have become yellow.

MONDAY, NOVEMBER 26. Pleasant and warm all day. Clouded up this evening. Made a final division of property and part of the company withdrew by mutual consent. M.L. Wisner, J. Wisner, Ca Wisner, Darling, Ball, Sharp, Richardson and myself are the company now.

TUESDAY, NOVEMBER 27, 1849. Began sometime in the night to rain moderately and continued this morning. Our teams started nearly empty for the mines this morning, between eight and nine a.m. Leaving Ball, Richardson and myself to take down the goods in the canoes, and to boat up some provisions from the city. Robert Horton, a young man from Texas, wishes to go down with us and we take him. Rained most of the day and rather freely just at night but ceased before eight this evening.

WEDNESDAY, NOVEMBER 28. Clean night. Wind N.W. Fine all day. Quite cool in the night.

THURSDAY, NOVEMBER 29. Cool night and beautiful morning. Wind S.E. Started down with three canoes. The largest two and a half feet wide inside and 24 feet long, tonnage 30 Cwt. Two smaller, about sixteen feet long, were placed on each side of the large one and all securely fastened together, making a craft more than seven feet across and 28 feet long. On the center we placed a wagon box covered as we came across the plains. The central canoe was ballasted with the iron which we took from one of our wagons. The tire was cut and laid flat in the bottom after being straightened. We had a steering oar at each end and long oars with two rowlocks on each side of the boat to use in case of need.

We had to take Whipple with us as the other companies refused to take him though they had encouraged him to act as he did and caused his expulsion from the company. Bad luck to them. The river has all sorts of crooks, and turns. As a general rule it bends from a straight line a mile or two each way every three or four miles.

There are many large islands, and in places, many smaller ones, making the channels very numerous and giving one an insight into the manner of the process by which so many of those dry bayous are formed.

The current is generally three or four miles an hour but seems slower where it all runs in one channel. The large islands are for the most part lined and the small covered with willows. The main shores are mostly bluff on one side, with scattering oaks back, sycamore near the edge and willow lined, on the other, low like the islands. The bluff shores are nothing but fine sand and clay and are constantly being washed away. The western bank seems to be the highest and therefore has the best road. There is but little timber between the river and the mountains and the prospect is on the whole beautiful. There can be no serious obstacle to the navigation of this river at the present stage of water by steamers drawing three feet [of] water.

The few snags we have seen are easily avoided by such a craft as ours. We saw three otters at once as we passed a narrow channel between some islands. They seemed to enjoy themselves much, pitching and plunging after each other and tumbling across the stream. One swam up within forty feet of us. They are not as large as I expected to see. We passed four bends and camped on the east bank one mile below a deserted ranch which stands solitary and alone on the west bank. A most beautiful site for a residence but a still more desolate place now, a roofless little house with crumbling walls of unburned brick.

People at the east think that so imposing a name as Ranch must be attached to something very important. The truth is, that the most miserable log shanty in the "Big woods" in Illinois, is just as much entitled to be called a ranch as a majority of those I have yet seen—and a half decent log house such as you sometimes see in Kane County, with an inclosure for cattle is fully equal to the best. "A fico for the name." How people are gulled and humbugged by travellers who give only names while they should describe the things. Myers at Lawson Ranch has things quite ship shape, and as they say, does things up brown at $1.50 to 2.00 a meal, but he is a "rare avis," a very prince of public caterers in these "diggins."

In many places Indians are employed to cook. Bah!!! Soon after we landed, and while putting up the tent, Morgan Grove and Ben Wilson came in with two canoes. And here was a fix. We had taken but two days rations of meat expecting to kill a deer at our first camp. We were detained one day longer than we anticipated before starting. So breakfast this morning entitled us to the benefit of the bankrupt law by making a slight assignment of one pound of pork. There were eight of us.

Ball, Kaup and Horton went out for a deer. Kaup soon came back empty—literally so. The other two came in with five quails. These with hard bread, rice and a little of the pound of pork made us a grand supper; and we went to bed very well satisfied, heeding the scripture rule, "take no thought for the morrow what," etc.

The other three who do not belong to our mess killed nothing though Ben saw a black bear (grizzly) and wonders why he did not shoot as he was in fair gun shot—I don't though. The fact is Ben is very absent minded and

I wouldn't wonder if some day he shot himself and packed in a quarter before he found his mistake. Made perhaps 16 miles airline south or on our course, but must have run fifty or sixty.

FRIDAY, NOV. 30, 1849. The night was cold and this morning we saw the first frost we have had in the valley. The mountain glistens in the bright sunshine, white with snow, and looking cold, cheerless, desolate and dreary. The men came in again this morning without anything, but saw some wild cattle, and wanted an axe to bridge a stream in a ravine which they must cross to get to them. Had bread and rice for breakfast. Went out again, and came in after dark, with meat of a three year old cow; and now we are in fix again. Whipple worse.

Left camp and dropped down the river. Better navigation and fewer channels than the first day. Frost again this morning and the men complained so much of cold feet that we landed, took in wood, and set up the stove in the big canoe. This is comfortable, as the small ones are fastened stern and stern on each side, and the large one is so steady, that we do any kind of cooking on the stove. The bends of the river are more irregular every way, and the snags, which at one point, where were "rapids," were thickly set across the entire channel, offered no inconsiderable obstruction to the navigation. At a little higher stage of water, these snags could not be seen, nor be in the way. We steered clear, through a channel on the right.

At one o'clock, passed the mouth of a handsome stream coming in from the right, over a bed of fine, clean gravel. It may be thirty yards wide and one foot deep where it pours rapidly over the gravel into the river.

At 3 o'clock passed an Indian village on the left bank, and camped on the right or west bank, one mile below, where is a natural wharf of clay and stone, almost as hard as rock, and from two or four feet above the water. The earth bank is washed off to the depth of twelve feet, 40 or 50 feet back, leaving a handsome, level landing. The road here runs along the edge of the bank. West the view is uninterrupted to the mountains, without a bush or tree, after leaving the river, near which are clumps of large oaks scattered along at intervals, and sometimes extending half a mile back. The bends of the river are timbered with oak, sycamore, cottonwood, willows, aspen, etc. etc.

Just after dark we heard some one crying loudly, as if in distress, up at the Indian lodge. It sounded like the cries of some impatient sufferer, undergoing a severe surgical operation,—crying "O dear, O dear!" at regular intervals of two or three seconds, continued ten minutes and terminated in a long drawn groan, like one who finally yields up to his fate and dies, or is suddenly relieved from extreme torture.

SUNDAY, DEC. 2. About the same space before sunrise this morning,

as after sundown last night, the same lamentable cries were renewed, continued two or three minutes and ended in precisely the same manner.
Wonder what they are doing. They are a more miserable set than those
near our first camp on the Sacramento. Nearly one-third of the adults are
entirely naked. They beckoned us to stop, probably to trade, for I saw
several wild geese hanging on a post. The landing was difficult, however, to
haul up easily, and we had plenty of meat. Half of our men have a kind of
influenza, sore throat, heavy head ache, and pain and soreness in the flesh
and bones, with the head stuffed up as the men describe it. The river is very
irregular today in its course, and full of strong eddies and sharp turns. General course like yesterday, west of south. Made about 20 or 25 miles by the
river and camped on the east bank, perhaps ten miles below Neal's ranche.
Bread stuff almost gone.

MONDAY, DEC. 3. Cast off and found the river for the most part on a
pretty direct line. At 12 o'clock hauled up at Larkin's ranche, three or four
houses of sun dried brick, a miserably filthy place, but rather above par in
California. Did not see fit to buy anything, though somewhat in need. Flour
was $1 per pound, salt 50 cents, and other things in proportion. They had
no sugar, and were short of flour. Found Dickinson from Michigan there,
staying through the winter. Left the ranche at one o'clock and camped 25
miles below on the right bank.
     A number of Indians were on hand when we landed, and one of them,
a young coon who spoke Spanish, helped us get up wood and was quite
active. They were for the most part nearly naked, some of them entirely so,
and yet it is so cold that if one sits still out of the tent, and away from the
fire, he wants a great coat and mittens to be comfortable. Still it is only
chilly. Every few miles we see Indians on the bank, with the same scarcity of
covering. These they call wild Indians, those who wear clothes, tame ones.
The wild, for the most part, live under large conical heaps of earth, and are
hence called Diggers. The tame live above ground in such huts as I have
before described. We have passed abundance of grapes today. In some places
the river bank is barricaded with the vines for miles, and so closely interwoven are they that no one can get through them without a cutting instrument.

TUESDAY, DEC. 4. This morning, clear and cold. The earth is slightly
frozen on the surface; standing water had no ice. The lower range of mountains is covered with snow, and at noon oak leaves are turning yellow.
Wind so high that we lie over till it goes down. Bought some bows and
arrows of the Indians—two bows and 30 arrows, for three old shirts. They
are around our camp fire by dozens, like flies around a candle, all bare foot,
and nearly or quite naked. I have been up half a mile to their village. There
are some 40 men and big boys, but no women or children to be seen. Their

burrows are first dug four or five feet into the ground, the poles bent over
and coupled, and tied to the top, and covered with willows, grass, rushes and
earth. The opening into them is two feet wide and two and a half high, on a
level with the ground. They keep up the temperature in them with hot stones.

There are a large number of circular upright cribs of various sizes, made
of coarse rush mats, or grass, or willows, and shaped like a salt barrel,
though some of them are ten feet high. They are hooped with rope of small
grape vine, twisted, and some of them wound with bark. They all seem to
be full of acorns, out of which they are manufacturing meal and bread.
Heaps of acorns lie around and among the lodges, and bushels of the shelled
fruit lie under foot, drying on mats. Over the door of one burrow, sat eight
geese—as we supposed; but a close examination convinced us that not only
these, but those we saw back were only stuffed skins. They appear extremely
like life. Probably they are used as decoys, as no two are in the same position. They are very filthy even for Indians, as they tread on the drying
acorn meats without scruple. They use baskets as we use pails, or pans and
with as little leakage. Some of them will contain two bushels, and I have
seen one which would scarcely hold a quart.

WEDNESDAY, DEC. 5. Cold and ground frozen half an inch or more,
still no ice on water. Dropped down the river. The general direction to 12
o'clock has been a little south-east, when we passed some mountain peaks, a
few miles at our left, the river making some long bends, and coursing far to
the south. These peaks are barren, ragged looking fellows, but too low for
snow. There are several of them, and the range seems to be north and south.
We have seen plenty of ducks before today; here they literally swarm on the
river. It is, perhaps, somewhat singular, but I have not seen a wild goose in
the river, though thousands are flying about in all directions, and at all times
day and night.

We have passed any quantity of Indians today, naked as usual. Whipple
seems a little better, though he can not get well unless the weather is more
favorable. From 9 to 1 o'clock the weather has been quite warm. The grape
vines are more loaded, and the fruit fresher than above. I should think that
some vines have several bushels on them yet, though so many must have
dropped off. They are really black with grapes as they bend down under the
large clusters.

We are making good time, running before the wind which blows fresh
from the north. The river is no wider here than at Lassen's. From Larkin's
ranche to the Buttes, mostly on the right bank, are considerable forests of
handsome oaks. Some of the trunks will measure thirty or forty feet to a
limb. Generally, however, they are only fifteen to twenty, though they stand
densely enough to deserve the appellation of forests. Below the Buttes the
banks are lower, and most of the way both of them were overflowed at the
last freshet.

The timber is mostly sycamore and cottonwood, of small growth, with the usual quantity of willows for low grounds. Where the banks are high enough, are oaks of smaller growth than farther up the river, and they generally exhibit symptoms of decay. Camped on the east side, a few miles below the Buttes in a direct line, but by the river it must be not less than twenty miles.

THURSDAY, DEC. 6. Ground froze deeper than yesterday morning. Clear, and wind fresh in gusts from the north. Clouds of wild geese are flying about, yet none alight in the river. Probably the ponds, or lakes, which abound at a little distance back from the river, are covered with them, as they seem to rise and fly from these locations.

In the forenoon, the course of the river was south and east, pretty direct. This afternoon till 3 o'clock it was zigzag, south west at almost right angles; afterwards it was south east again. Landed just before sundown on the west bank. The banks are so low here that the last rise flowed over the whole. The timber is very scattering, and but little oak. A little back the land appears to be low and partly covered with water.

Whipple, who has been getting worse since the last cold weather came on, died soon after we landed, and we have just now, (9 o'clock) buried him. While digging the grave, a man from Oregon, last from Redding's mines, came into camp, with three Oregon Indians on horseback. They are going down the river, and got ahead of their train. Some of the cat kind, the Indian say panthers, are squalling fearfully some fifty or sixty rods down the river, in a thicket of willows and grape vines.

FRIDAY, DEC. 7. About 3 o'clock this morning I was awaked by several men who landed by our canoes. They were from Redding Mines (ten of them) in large pine canoes. They report that Conde, Holley [Hawley?], Stebbins and Dodge made shipwreck only a few miles below where they started from, on Sunday week, sinking canoes and wagons and all their plunder. The Redding boys helped them all day on Monday, in fishing up their baggage, and succeeded in recovering the most valuable part. The wagons were irretrievably lost, and they could not raise the canoes. They saved some portion of their provisions much damaged. This is sad news to us, and disastrous to them; but they must bear the loss alone, as they left the company voluntarily. Had they belonged to it, I should never have suffered the canoes to be so loaded down. After breakfast we took the large brands and burning logs from the camp fire, and piling them with wood and brush over Whipple's grave, left them burning furiously, and quietly dropped down the river.

Poor Whipple—to die away from one's friends and home is hard; but to die for want of proper shelter, in a strange land and be buried among the tangled vines of a lonely river's bank, with every mark of a grave obliterated by fire, lest the wild Indians should rob the grave, strip the last scanty covering from the dead, and leave his naked corpse a prey to the vulture and the wolf, is harder still. It cannot matter much, after all, and yet poor human nature shrinks from such a consummation. To know, *to feel*, that no little mound, no headboard, with name or age, no head stone with a "Here lies," shall mark our final resting place, is sufficiently humiliating. But to lie beneath a vulgar level, to rot undistinguished—unknown to the passers by— to be forgotten by the many, and scarcely remembered by the few; is, alas for poor human nature! the depth of earthly abasement. We nursed him to the best of our ability, and yet he died—delirious from the first, he never appreciated our sacrifices or kindness, and never knew to thank us. Richardson, who has had more to do with nursing him than any other, took the same fever day before yesterday, but is better this morning. I think, however, it is only in seeming, and he will be worse before night.

The river is very crooked part of the way, and then again quite straight. General direction south-east. Passed a ranche on the right bank, at about half an hour's sun, and they report five miles to Fremont. Pushed down one and a half miles, and camped on the east bank. Richardson much worse. High fever and delirium. The banks of the river have been getting higher all day. For the most part they were blockaded and barricaded by willows and grape vines. We are out of provisions and must pack up some from Fremont, or run down there, or starve. Though the nights are so cool, the middle of the day is warm, and at times the sun pours down uncomfortably hot.

SATURDAY, DEC. 8. Richardson delirious all night, sometimes furious. The symptoms are exactly those of delirium tremens, and yet he never takes narcotics, or alcohol. He is somewhat more rational this morning. The sun, as it rises, shines but bright and warm though there is considerable frost. Thousands of crows are flying about, among geese, ducks and brants. This whole valley abounds in crows, which troop about by thousands, and occasionally raise a clamor like the noise of 50 steamboats. The boys packed up some flour, sugar and salt from Fremont this evening, 34 cents a pound all round.

SUNDAY, DEC. 9. Left camp, and dropped down within half a mile from Fremont. The river is crooked, very crooked, and before we reached camp, we had to run almost every point of compass, and ten miles nearly though it is not more than four in a straight line. Cold night, warm day. Richardson rather worse. We can now procure necessaries for the sick, and may save him. Went down into town. The road from above comes in on this side. South, and towards Sacramento City, the country is a level plain, almost destitute of timber for a considerable distance, except on the river. It is a beautiful town site. The first building I came to was a school house. A balloon frame, of the slightest description, 35 feet long and 16 wide, covered with split oak clapboards, and the roof with canvass. Heard Mr. Cameron preach. There were 35 or 40 people in, nearly half well dressed females. There was good attention. I notice a great deal of bustle in town, though it does not reach here much, it being a quarter of a mile or more to the river where the principal business is done.

MONDAY, DEC. 10. The first sound that struck my ear on waking this morning, and one that fully assured me that I was in a land of civilization, was the sound of the hammer. If the sound of the hammer cheered the heart of Solomon as it does mine, he never would have allowed the temple to be built without it. Richardson no better. Pleasant day—cool and east wind.

TUESDAY, DEC. 11. Sent Ball into the mines for the teams to come down and haul up provision, luggage, etc. We cannot get the canoes far up Feather River, and the road is good on the west side down to within three miles of its mouth. Richardson no better. Had occasion to buy some eatables today. Molasses $2.50 per gallon, pork 50 cts. per lb.; dried apples 62½ cents per lb. It matters little what a thing cost originally. They sell every-thing by the pound here and for nearly the same price. Salt, sugar, flour, coffee, and pork, about the same price. Tea, fresh pork and potatoes, 75 cents each per lb. A sett of common cups and saucers, $5. Knives and forks, common, $12 to $15. Clothing from 50 to 100 per cent higher than in the States. Nails 20 to 25 cents per lb., etc. Four yokes of good working cattle and a wagon are in demand now at $600 to $1,000; three weeks ago they were slow at $300.

WEDNESDAY, DEC. 12. Rained from 12 last night to 9 this morning, with high wind from the east. Cloudy most of the day and cool; but warmer morning and evening than it has been.

Richardson died at half past eight this evening. The disease was typhus, and rendered fatal by the cold nights. We took the best care we could of him while he lived, and buried him as decently as we could when he died. Poor Nathan! He was beloved by the whole train, and we could better have spared some other man. He brought on the attack by his devoted attention to Whipple, became delirious almost immediately, and never again had his senses. Many, in this country, die and give no sign; but he needed not to give any. He was, living, a consistent christian and dead, I make no doubt, is a happy one. His troubles are passed, his fears ended, his hopes realized. Cold and heat and hunger, and sickness no more affect him, nor has the gold of California any charm. He is where gold glitters not and precious stones are as the dust of the earth, and even the bright sun pales and has no light.

THURSDAY, DEC. 13. Rained in the latter part of the night. Buried Nathan this morning. Cleared up in the evening; wind west.

FRIDAY, DEC. 14. Wind west. Continued so till 1 o'clock, when a furious storm came up from that direction, with hail. We had dropped down the river half a mile when it began to blow and when we got to the mouth of Feather River one and a half miles below camp by the river, it blew so strong that we hauled up on the Fremont side again, and waited nearly two hours, till it blew over. After it cleared off, we crossed to Vernon, on the opposite shore of the Sacramento, between the junction, and camped. Our teams must come down Feather River, and this side is much the most convenient. The evening is bright, cold and clear, and freezing hard.

SATURDAY, DEC. 15. Very cold morning, and continued so all day. Water froze in the pail. The "old ones" say that they never before saw it as cold here. I do not believe them. The Indians of Central America know as much about the weather in California as the inhabitants seem to.

SUNDAY, DEC. 16. Wind increased in the night to a perfect gale, and it rained towards morning. Some of the tents about town are blown down, and the canvass hawsers are more or less torn. Everything seems literally going to rags. The ragged Indians are out as usual notwithstanding the wind and rain and cold, after their whiskey. They are a mixed breed, Indian, Mexican, Spanish, and Apican, and seems much addicted to drinking. I have seen a number drunk already, and among those one squaw, and only one. They are all dressed "a la Anglaise" and a blanket like Joseph's coat, which they continue to wrap around them, leaving only the top of the head and the legs of the pants visible. They seem to have money enough, and the hell-bound rumsellers are getting it easy and sure—25 cents for whiskey, and 50 cents for brandy, which costs but little more at Sacramento than in the States. They are making up a long account to settle at the last day, whose items shall so appal them, that even in this world they "durst not seek repentance."

MONDAY, DEC. 17. No abatement of the storm. Rained some in the night. Cold, but water did not freeze in the pail. At 3 o'clock the wind went down, and the weather moderated a little. The steamer came in just now, one day behind her time, on account of the wind. The waves must have dashed about her in fine style if she had come up in the storm. Visited the only tavern in the place this evening. It is a building 35 by 45 made of joists and plank, the latter up and down on the outside, covered with shaved or planed oak shakes for clapboards, very decently put on, with a very well shingled roof. The inside is lined with dark calico and the ceiling is of cotton sheeting. The lower part is divided about equally across by two partitions. The middle room, probably is the largest. The north division is occupied as a groggery and grocery; the middle, an eating room; and the south a kind of bar room. On the back is a "lean-to" the whole length.

In the bar-room were people from almost every part of the United States, Oregon, South America, Sandwich Islands, etc., etc. They were playing at "Monte," where everyone who pleases put down as much money as he likes, loses or wins, and leaves when he chooses. The Sandwicher doubled almost every dollar he put down. One would think that almost everybody in this country gambled. More of this hereafter. They were offered $2,500 a month for the rent of this house, and asked $5,000 a month. The original cost was only half that sum.

TUESDAY, DEC. 18. Clear and cool this morning. A steamer forty feet long came up today. She is very pretty to look at, a perfect Lilliputian. The *Lawrence* [listed in 1851 Sacramento City Directory as 36 tons, Capt. Chadwick, travelling between San Francisco and Sacramento] is a good looking, apparently well-built boat of decent size for a young one, and has a stern wheel. The *Washington* is merely an old scow. There are here two ferries. One is free for citizens. The other charges fifty cents for a footman; $2 for a horse and man; for a team of one yoke of oxen and a wagon, $4; for each extra yoke, $1.50. The river is about 350 or 400 yards at the ferry. The boats are scows and run to a rope stretched across. Holly [Hawley], Dodge, Conde and Stebbins came in this morning in their canoes, with what they saved from the wreck. They brought in several hundred pounds of elk and venison. The market is not as good as yesterday. Several thousand pounds of meat have been brought in today, and reduced the price. It can be bought now for twenty cents on the average all around, except fresh pork, which commands 75 cents per lb.

WEDNESDAY, DEC. 19. Pleasant and quiet, though somewhat cloudy, till one o'clock p.m., when a tremendous gale came on. Rain, hail, and sleet tore around us like mad. At sundown the *Lawrence* ran down, and in rounding the point to run up the Sacramento under the tall willows on the Fremont side, fell into the trough of the sea and came mighty near a capsize. She made one lee lurch heavy enough to start her boilers, but probably ran in safe.

THURSDAY, DEC. 20. The storm of last night was beyond anything I ever before saw. Tents are down, houses unroofed, and everything seems going to wreck. Our tent ropes are very strong, and on the windward side have two stakes, one outside the other, and roped together. Thus double staked we outrode the storm in safety. There are only three or four out of a great many tents on this side, which pretend to stand at all; and those have extra ropes. The river which rose six or seven feet yesterday, has fallen some. Not as cold as yesterday, but uncomfortable yet. There must be a considerable loss of property by this rain. All kinds of groceries and provisions are exposed this morning. Near sundown, Ball and Elder Wisner came down from the mines, in company with a gentleman by the name of Camp, from Michigan of the Wolverine Ranger Company.

FRIDAY, DEC. 21. Rained all night, and some wind with it this morning. At one o'clock this afternoon, it began to rain with a rush. Wind south. Lest I should forget it, I will now describe these "diggins." The town of Fremont is located at the mouth of Feather River on the south side of the Sacramento, which comes in from the west and Feather River from the north north-west. From the junction the river runs almost east for a mile, and then turns toward the south. Vernon is directly opposite Fremont, on Sutter's great claim.

I have already described the tavern, and there is another building nearly as large, covered with pine boards—a passably good house for the place, and intended for a tavern. There is a storehouse, covered with pine, one story high. All the other buildings are small, and miserably done, except three unfinished ones, covered with shaved or planed shakes (oak). There are perhaps a dozen or fifteen in all. Rather hard counting, they go up so fast. Four stores of goods are kept open.

The side has until lately been covered with willows. It has a very gradual ascent from the water, perhaps 15 rods from the lowest mark. From this it runs back several miles, without anything to interrupt the view except a few willow bushes. These grow on the banks of Feather River and the ravines and bayous which cross the plains in all directions. Fremont has a bold shore, and the steamers can lie up close to the bank, which rises very handsomely some 12 or 15 feet from low water mark. The plain a few miles south and south-west is intersected by creeks or bayous lined with timber. It is said to be excellent ground for grazing. There are perhaps 40 buildings, great and small, none as large as in Vernon, nor as well built—three stores and one tavern. Almost every house is open for boarding.

Part III : Sacramento City and the Mines

Chapter Nine
December 22–December 30, 1849:
Sacramento Flood

◆ ◆ ◆

SATURDAY, DEC. 22. A little cloudy, but not cold. River has raised two feet more. Camp, Elder Wisner and myself started for Sacramento City in the big canoe, this morning before sunrise. The banks of the river get lower and lower as we descend and the course is south south-east. There are cabins and settlers at short intervals, nearly all the way; sometimes half a dozen in a mile. There is so much fog that we cannot see far into the country; but from the squalling of the geese I should think that it was low, and had plenty of ponds just back. About fifteen miles down the river turns nearly east, and the general direction to the city must be south east. The channel seems to be from three-eighths to one half a mile wide, and has a strong current. The banks are thinly lined with oak, sycamore, and willow, in part; and in part only willow, or entirely bare. The water does not yet run over the bank, though well up, until just above the junction with the American Fork, where it breaks over into the bottom north and runs into the Fork.

The whole country, on each side, is covered with water, and impassable. The only way by land is on the bank, which is higher than the country back. Shooting the canoe across the Fork, here 80 to 100 yards wide, coming in from the left, we dropped down astern of a large barque tied up to a big sycamore by the bank, and turning up an old channel of the Fork, over the end of a bridge which once served to cross it but is now twisted away, among boats, and logs, and tents, and groceries, half buried or overturned, in the muddy water, paddled our craft into a kind of pond, tied up to a tree on the right bank and stepped into the street, I think the one next [to] the principal business one.

Sacramento waterfront, ca. 1855 (California State Library).

The first view we had of the city was where the river turns round a bend a mile above the city. You first notice a long line of shipping, stretching along the river nearly a mile, and then a few small houses, looming mistily up in the fog among the trees, and so indistinct as to resemble a mirage. The ships are fast to the shore, and seem to be used as store houses. In the cabin of one, Dr. Burge, of N.York, has a hospital. The streets appear to be laid out at right angles, and there are some very good looking buildings. I am told that there were but three or four buildings here on the 4th of July last.

The first thing that strikes the attention of an observing man, is the want of order—the utter confusion and total disorder which prevail on every hand. The land is low and level, only two and a half feet above the present level of the water, which is said to be ten to twelve feet above low water—and the mud and water from the late heavy rains cover everything. Most of the buildings have canvass roofs, and many have canvass sides, which are splashed and daubed with the all pervading pigment.

The streets are not graded, nor is anything done to clear them out, except cutting down some of the scattering trees, which five or six months since, were the sole occupants of the ground. The whole town plot, except a few crooked, winding footpaths, among tents and through alleys, and a devious wagon way through the streets, and the ground occupied by tents and buildings, is covered with boxes and barrels, empty, or filled with all kinds of goods, in passable, indifferent, or bad order, or totally ruined, and wagons, lumber, glass bottles, machinery and plunder of all sorts, heaped and scattered and tumbled about in "most admired confusion."

In making side walks, (and mighty scarce are they, and of the smallest pattern) a most commendable spirit of independence is exhibited. The constructors seem to have adopted the sliding, inclined plane, shot-tower principle, that none but the upright and perfect man shall walk thereon; and he who is too "tight" to get off two and down two feet at once, had best take to the street with lead and line, or let himself out for a mud scow. The whole city is literally stuffed, crammed with eatables of every description, so exposed that almost every kind must suffer more or less damage, and hundreds of thousands of dollars damage is already done.

I saw at one establishment alone, over 200 boxes of herrings rotting in one pile, any amount of spoiled pork, bacon, cheese, mouldy and rotten, pilot bread, and almost everything else. The destruction and waste of property here is almost, or quite equal to that of the plains, with not half the necessity, and a thousand times the recklessness.

There are a great number of dealers in produce or rather eatables here but more dealers of "Monte." The taverns have usually a large bar-room in front— passing to which, you will see, on one side, more display of glasses, bottles, cigars and liquor, than in three or four of the largest liquor taverns in Chicago; and on the other, three or four more tables, literally groaning under piles of silver, with a supply of gold, and a man behind dealing "monte;" and this at all hours from breakfast to midnight. I know not yet how many such establishments there are, but I have seen dozens of them already.

In the next, or eating room, you may or may not, just as it happens, find them playing "brag," or "poker," or some other game. Even those who do not play stand by, and every few minutes bet on the luck, as they call it, of the other. It seems to be a perfect mania. Common laborers, mechanics, etc., will risk a whole day's earnings on the turn of a card, as if it was a pleasure to get rid of the stuff; and if they do curse, it is because they are chagrined at guessing wrong, rather than at losing their money. Almost every man who comes in contact with the insane, is more or less in danger of at least a partial aberration of intellect; and few or none escape, unless they have definitely settled two principles, to wit: that gambling is wrong, and that they will not do wrong for any chance of gain. The temptation to others must be great, indeed, as the odds certainly seem to be against the bank, and it seems easy to win twice out of three times.

Saw Hawkins, of Aurora, only a few minutes after I arrived in town. He looks well, and appears to feel well. While talking with him, young Tefft, of Elgin, came along, seeming well, and perfectly at home, as if a native. For a five months' old city, Sacramento is of the biggest kind.

SUNDAY, DEC. 23. Last night wandered about the city till 12 o'clock, through mud and rain, across streets, up side walks, and around others heaped with goods and lumber, and sometimes almost up side down, in the dark and fog and made no very great discoveries, after all, beyond what daylight revealed; for things are not done in a corner here, nor in the dark. In regard to gambling, what is the rule elsewhere is the exception here, and the exception the rule. Gambling seems to be the business, and not the pleasure of this place. Every open door, as I passed, displayed the same occupants, and occupations.

Drinking, smoking, playing, betting, swearing, lying, cheating, swindling, robbing, stealing, etc. piles of money, lots of drink, and cigars by the bushel. Some men seem never to stop smoking at all, except to eat and drink, for as soon as one cigar is out of the mouth another is stuck in. I am not aware if they smoke when asleep, or if they sleep at all. Boys whose mothers hardly "knows that they are out," make no exceptions to the rule; or if they do, are more reckless than others; perhaps because the smoke furnishes the amount of stimulus or intoxication their weak brains require, and they get along with less drink. Old heads, and dry brains, require more strong drink with the smoke.

One may easily misjudge, but a cursory survey might almost induce one to believe, in spite of any evidence to the contrary, that Sacramento City is one great gambling shop, and the population (not all citizens) swindlers, sharpers and gamblers—8,000 strong though they count; and I make no doubt there are that number, if not more, as some of the mines have poured all, or nearly all their population into it. A good evidence of this, if there was no other, is found in the fact that at some tables more dust is bet than coin, for miners usually "Come down with the dust." After all, the laborer as elsewhere, is the person least benefitted by labor. The table where he loses his money, I have been told, pays to the house $3 an hour out of that money, and a still higher per cent. in the immense profits on liquor and cigars at the bar must be paid from his hard earnings. When will the laborer learn wisdom enough to keep the stinted, grudged reward of his labor, and shun the swindler and social robber!

Attended meeting in a large, almost finished store room, on K street. By the by, the street next the river is called Front street, the next 2d street, then 3d street, etc. The streets running from the river are called I street, north, next to the pond, then K street, then L street, etc. The place for meeting was very clean and quiet for this city; 30 perhaps were present, all males. Probably the state of the weather and streets prevented the attendance of females, and many others. It is cloudy, misty and foggy, but no rain; and the only disturbance I had during service was from some hungry musquitoes. Of course the weather is warm enough to do without fire, when these insects are prowling about. Mr. Denham, a Presbyterian minister preached. A fine, quiet speaker, and well calculated to please, and be useful. They had a well played Melodeon, and excellent singing by several gentlemen, two of whom I heard sing at the great Island meadow, on the St. Mary's. I think that there may be some good in the city yet, and Sodom may be saved, some salt that has not entirely "lost its savor."

I have been introduced to some who appear, at least, to be of the right sort. There is as yet no Baptist church or society in the place, and the population is so transient and floating as to render such an organization impossible for some time, at least. Br. [Rev. J.] Cook, a Baptist minister who resides here, will bring it about as soon as possible, I have no doubt.

People die here, I reckon, for 28 were buried day before yesterday, and no body committed murder or suicide. When I went to bed last night, or rather this morning, I found a man in the berth at my feet raising blood from the lungs. There was at least 2 quarts in the pan before him. He is bound to die, and has been taken to the Hospital this morning. People can afford to employ physicians here. Only an ounce a visit, or $16. If they visit one in the house where they board, it is only an ounce a day. They are liberal, generous fellows, are the doctors.

I have been about the city a little, and find it much larger than I had first imagined. There are no well filled blocks, but there are several very good wood covered buildings, and two covered with zinc. On one corner two brick stones are going up. There is a large three-story fine looking building on Front street, opening for a tavern. The buildings, intermingled with tents, extend almost a mile east, and half a mile south, and the tents as much farther. Large trees still stand towering up in the streets, and among the buildings, in the heart of the town.

I notice one around which a tent has been pitched, or rather a canvass house has been erected on Front or Water street near the Elephant House.* It is kept by one Barlow of Chicago and the tree presents, when you look into the place, the exact appearance of a chimney and fire place. It may be used as such for ought I know. Saw Warner of Chicago and Squires of Aurora who went out with Hawkins. Foggy all day. About as much gambling and drinking today as any day of the week.

MONDAY, DEC. 24. Foggy and misty as ever this morning. I have been bit several times today by musquitoes. It can't be very cold when they circulate so freely out of door.

Nobody wears extra clothing and no one seems to need any. Were it not that the whole country about us is under water the business here would be almost unlimited. The only way now to get here is by water and the steamers are neither fast nor powerful nor large enough to do the business and then there are very few here.

There are auction sales on the "levee" at all hours of the day, where very many articles are to be obtained at greatly—relatively—reduced prices.

The great drawback is the damaged condition of most of the goods. There are hundreds here selling their "traps" at auction, and then bound for home. Some have made enough already and some are disgusted with the

The Elephant House was described as follows by James C. Kemp in the Sacramento Record-Union *on April 25, 1890: "The Elephant House, on the levee was the "palace" hotel of that day, a most imposing structure of stout Merrimac sheeting. It was one story high, 150 feet long and forty feet wide, with fifty feet partitioned off for a bar and office. There were three tiers of bunks on each side of the remaining 100 feet, and tables ranged up and down the center. The charge of $2 a meal, and four bits for either a cigar or drink."*

country and retire, homesick. Many are going to try their luck at San Francisco. Everything is afloat.

The thousand who are in from the mines are idly sauntering about. House carpenters are in good demand, the best for that matter, and most of them are employed at some price. Twelve to 20 dollars a day.

TUESDAY, DEC. 25. "Christmas Eve." and the "way they went it was a caution."—At the end of the dining table where I sat writing, till late in the evening, one fellow won 30 ounces of gold from the others "at poker," before I went to bed, and he was still winning. This morning, the floor around and under the table is covered with cards, two or three deep, at least half a bushel of them. Sometimes they played only one hand, and threw the pack away; then they would play several and again one of them would, in a fit of irritation, hurl two or three unsoiled packs on the floor at once. I noticed that the winner drank but little and used fewer cigars than the others.

There are several Express and Intelligence offices in town. I called in at Wood's and found that by depositing forty cents I could have a letter brought from San Francisco, providing always I had one there, and by the farther payment of one dollar could get the letter from their office. They said that it was useless to attempt to get a [news] paper from there, as they were thrown aside every succeeding mail, if not sooner and directly sold, thrown away, given away or destroyed. Probably they are thus disposed of on account of the want of necessary assistance to deliver them.

The profits of the office will not hire the help, at the enormous prices labor commands, and so there is not only an entire want of order, industry and regularity, but the most unlimited confusion.

The postmaster ought to be one who would hire clerks, rent buildings, work night and day, and charge $5 a letter, if necessary to cover the expense, and no body here would grumble at that; but instead of this we have, I will not say the fact, but certainly the evidence, of lazy imbecility. Time is everything here, and if a dozen men send an agent at $10 to $16 a day to the city, he will have to stay in all probability ten days to inquire for the whole; and then the fare down and back, and board from $4 to $8 a day, will reach a heap higher than $5 a letter. This morning I bought a second hand Tribune (Greeley's) of Warner, for fifty cents (market price 75 cts. to $1) the "California Delta," printed in New Orleans for this market, 50 cts., and a San Francisco and a Sacramento City paper at 25 cents each. I found no others for sale.

They ask one dollar for any kind of an 1850 almanac. I notice today a number of buildings going up, covered with sheet iron, and yet a short joint of common, rusty, bruised four inch stove pipe costs $4, and the new iron of which the "like of it" is made, $1.50 a pound. Sheet zinc is ten shillings a pound. Rents are extravagant. Water for a common boarding-house costs $20 per week.

As a kind of offset to this, I rather think that nobody pays taxes, as I am told that no one regards the city ordinances. All do as they please, amendable only to the common authorities and general law of the land; and the people from the States who came in last, have taken, or are taking possession of the land where it was not actually occupied by improvements, and are building and improving in defiance of all show of authority or law, except the natural and original right; and that in my opinion is not only the best, but in reality, the only one worth a straw.* Whoever wishes to build, gets his lot surveyed, and has it registered, and up goes a house at once. They are running them up rapidly on Front street, facing the river, and within a short "stone's throw" of the river and the shipping. A small house costing $2,000 will rent for $500 a month on this street. The city has increased in size since I came. Fifty buildings of considerable dimensions have been reared.

WEDNESDAY, DEC. 26. Took passage in the steamer *Lawrence*, for the Haystacks,† three miles up Feather River, leaving Elder Wisner to purchase and ship the rest of the freight on the steamer this evening. Distance thirty miles—fare $15—freight $4 per cwt., and everything weighed unless in sacks. Cast off at 10:30 a.m. and in dropping in to shore at the upper part of the city to take a scow load of lumber in tow, ran against the limb of a big sycamore and broke down the smoke pipe. I should think that they would cut down the nuisances. We now fell off into the middle of the river and anchored to give the hands a chance to set up the mutilated smoke carrier. I know not how long they worked; but they finally got under weigh and meantime I was occupied with recollections of the city, and the queer things which it contains.

Among them, certainly, not the least singular is the incongruous and in part grotesque character of the population. I wish to be impartial, and state only facts; and assuredly I had no predilections or prejudice to distort my vision in observing, or bias my judgment in noting down matters and things, saving and excepting a most implacable enmity to tobacco, whiskey, gambling and whiskers. Giving this reservation all the weight it deserves, truth compels me to say that I never before mingled with any considerable number of men, so few of whom were really intelligent, or rather intellectual and gentlemanly. I "nothing extenuate, nor set down ought in malice;" else

*Sacramento Transcript, Aug 21, 1850: "We are told that a gentleman who lives near this city called on the county treasurer, a day or two ago, and voluntarily paid over his poll tax. We do not state this to play upon public credulity. It may be a fact, but it is very strange."

†According to a July 1850 map of Brannan's Ranch drawn by A.R. Flint, Haystacks was not a town but literally a series of haystacks near the river bank.

I could tell on what circumstances my opinion is based. Not that it would
be but rather that it might *appear* malicious to enter into details.

I am told that the rains and melting snows bring yearly into Feather
River the scum and filth of eight months vegetative life and waste from the
mountain top and deep ravine with the bright and yellow gold—and while
the latter sinks and rests quietly in the deep water, the former goes rushing,
bubbling, whirling on, defiling everything they touch, and making the water
unfit for use of man or beast. So of this city. Occasionally you will find a
man of mind, a moral and intellectual man, and a thinking man; but they,
few or many, are hidden, overwhelmed by the putrid tide whose impurity
would contaminate the wash of the Augean stables, and push the reeking
impieties of Sodom a backward step from hell. The virtues here are all negative.

They refrain from—from—I hardly know what, unless it is common, vulgar stealing. I think there is less of what is ordinarily called stealing here,
than in any place I was ever in; and yet there can be little difficulty in stealing to almost any extent. A vast amount of property, easily moveable, is
daily and nightly exposed without a watch, or even a lock. This security
occurs, too, in a population composed of representatives from all parts of
the globe. Eastern and western men constitute the mass. The most interesting and singular to me, are the Sandwich Islanders and Chinese. The
former wear the common dress of American citizens in the States, and are
of the color of our Indians, though otherwise they appear more like mulattoes. They appear intelligent, and still they have a sort of staring, dreamy,
night-mare look, which, if one allows his fancy to wander, seems to say, "I
wouldn't mind taking a slice, if you was right fat." One cannot divest himself of the idea that, whilom, their fathers may have luxuriated in steaks of
good English—not beef—but sailors.

Everybody has seen pictures of the Chinese, and of course everybody
knows how they look. They cannot be caricatured. Their costume is absurd-
ity itself. It is too ridiculous to be singular, or picturesque. With their long,
skin tight pants, and the petticoat legs and bag seats of others, their jackets,
hardly longer than to the armpits, their long hair, done up in a pig tail cue,
drawing the skin away from their little eyes, and twisting them awry, their
twisted mustaches and the little, flat, shapeless mockery of a basket hat on
their little bullet heads,—to which you have only to add whiskers (an article
I believe they do not use,) you have a "tout ensemble" which defies pen and
pencil; a parody on humanity which even Cruikshank could neither invent,
imitate, or copy.

I was struck all aback when I saw them receiving and handling gold. To
examine the quality they go through with much the same manoeuvres that
the wheat buyers of Chicago do, when inspecting a sample of wheat. If it
looks clean and fair, it is poured into the scales and weighed. If it looks dirty
and has rock and sand in it, they take some in the palm, and stir it carelessly

around with the fore-finger, and determine its value. Very seldom, however, except in exchange for coin, is any deduction made. Every time it is weighed something is lost, and the business streets of Sacramento will, in a few years, be worth digging up and washing for the gold.* It is poured out and weighed almost as carelessly as rice or pepper in the States; and very few ever pick up any scattering flake, unless larger than a pin-head, and some pay no attention whatever to so small matters. In the large establishments, the dust is dipped about in pint tin cups. In a word, it is an article of produce, as easily got as wheat or corn in the States, and handled with much the same feeling, and comparatively with the same waste.

The *Lawrence* runs very slow. The current is strong, and she is loaded to the very last pound, and crowded with passengers; while the big scow is a heavy drag on her engine, which has not power enough at the best, and less now than common, as eight feet of her smoke pipe is off. The right bank, as we come up, is for the most part under water, and the left from a few inches to two feet above. Some day's morning sun will reveal a work of desolation from flood in this valley that will chill the blood of the listener, if one should be left to tell the story; unless, previously warned by lesser floods, proper precautions are taken. Just after dinner, the clouds thickened and it began to rain, and has continued till now, 7 o'clock p.m.

THURSDAY, DEC. 27. Hauled up on the Fremont side about one o'clock this morning; discharged some freight, and an hour after dropped off and ran over to Vernon, which seemed to be all under water. The principal tavern is entirely surrounded. Fremont is two and a half feet above water yet, though it crosses a mile or two back, leaving it an Island. Cast off, and steamed up Feather River without the old scow, making eight miles an hour. Mem. Never ride on a steamboat that has a scow in tow—*if you can help it.*

The whole country on the left, above the junction, and between Feather River and the Sacramento is covered with water. The inhabitants have abandoned the Haystacks, which is all under water, and camped on the right or east bank, which is two feet above, leaving everything to the merciless waters. I noticed a number of cattle, a sow and some fine pigs, several wagons, and a large quantity of flour and other provisions piled on a platform two feet above water. It is a pity for the hogs, as a good fat one of 300 lbs is worth $200. The right bank is very pretty, but a little more water *"and under she goes."*

An article in the Placer Times *on January 26, 1850, entitled "City Diggings" offered the following: "We saw a gentleman the other day who washed out about $10 in a few hours at the Embarcadero, and many others have been operating throughout the week in our streets, with some degree of success. The greater part of the dust has probably been spilt in the streets, although on the bank of the river may have come down from the mountains. P.S. We have been told that a man, on Thursday last, had the good fortune to dig out $21 on Front St."

Stopped at Nichol's ranche on the right bank, nine miles above the Haystacks, 12 above Vernon and just below the mouth of Bear River, said to be a little dirty, sluggish stream and now scarcely to be found, as the water runs all over it. Had our goods landed two miles above, on the opposite side, to save crossing a deep wide slough, which is dry when the river is down. On examination we found that we had not much bettered our condition, for a slough comes in above us and runs down into the one which we wished to avoid. We are high and dry, however, at least five feet above the wet, with a year's provisions, a good tent, and plenty of fire wood; *"away with care."*

FRIDAY, DEC. 28. Cleared off partially just before sundown last night, but before one in the morning the stars twinkled their very best, and the moon shone clear and bright enough to read by. The morning is cool, though not uncomfortable. The river, which rose 1½ feet last night, is falling again. At nine o'clock, some men came down in a boat for me to visit a sick man three miles up the river. Found one of the neglected, ill-treated fever cases which prove so fatal in this valley. Probably will die.

From this camp, which is on the west side, (the river having a general course, so far, southwest) the view is almost uninterrupted to the long blue line of the East Range on which no snow appears for 50 miles north. On this side, and apparently at the very Base, the eye falls on the long, low, thread-like black line of timber which shrouds the Sacramento and the broad silvery sheet of water, stretching far off to the north, and throwing its wavy ripple almost over our feet. A long line of timber, the skirt of an oak forest, commences several miles below, and very gradually receding from the river, sweeps round near this point and turns north. I cannot say how far it extends, but certainly out of sight. The plain covered with water is destitute of timber, and a little lower level than the broad plain on which the huge oaks stretch out their giant limbs and bid defiance to the storms. The plain above is not perfectly level, but seems left by the action of the floods in slightly elevated ridges, on which the oaks are more thickly planted, and sometimes run far into the watery waste, a long point of dense timber.

Occasionally I have noticed an area of 50 to 100 acres of rather low ground without a tree. With this exception, there seems to be no open ground on Feather River, above this point. Old and very extensive mounds indicate the past existence of by-gone Digger Burrows. They are green with a short, fine, thick grass, considerably elevated, and if the river ever covers the entire level, which it probably does, would make very desirable building sites.

Never land lay uncultivated, more captivating to the ploughman's eye, than this. The oaks would offer but little impediment to the plough, for they seldom number six to the acre, at the most. How it will produce without irrigation, I know not. The grass is growing as it does in the States the last of May, though most of the leaves on the trees are dead. The misletoe, which has a bright, deep green leaf, and grows in large bunches from all kinds of trees, covers many of the oaks to such an extent that a stranger would suppose they were rejoicing in their own foliage. The oaks here are large and low, with short trunks, and broad, spreading, craggy tops, and exhibit symptoms of extensive decay. Most of them are more or less burned at the roots, and some are lying on the ground, burned down. The banks of the river are like those of the Sacramento. Perhaps they are somewhat higher.

SATURDAY, DEC. 29. Another most beautiful morning. Did not return to camp last night. A little frost this morning. The birds are singing, and flying about in all directions, and the magpie, the noisiest of all, is chattering and mocking all the rest. The wolves are howling as usual at a little distance, and a drove of 300 or 400 antelopes are bounding across the plain within half a mile. The Sacramento Valley is one great Wolf Kennel. You can hear them screeching and howling at all hours, night or day, if you will only listen. After a little, one hardly notices them more than he would the barking of a dog in the States. At Fremont, and in Sacramento City, I heard them yelling often in the midst of the town. Went down to camp in the boat and sent up a load of goods to "terra firma." In the afternoon, Camp and Elder Wisner passed up the river in the steamer *Linda*, and hailed for Yuba City. Took the rest of the goods up, the last load by moon light, and got the cattle above the slough.

SUNDAY, DEC. 30. Dense fog this morning. At noon left for Yuba City, fourteen miles. The whole distance up is timbered, as I have described it below. The breadth of the forest plain increases as we go up, until we can no longer see through to the water on the left,—although one can easily see five or six miles, so level is the land and so scattering the trees. The Buttes have loomed up in sight at intervals all the way—ahead at the left. The whole is a nearly level plain until within three miles of Yuba City, where there is a steep short descent to a lower level, which is sometimes inundated. So much for generals; now for particulars.

Five miles after leaving camp, came to a deep ditch and embankment, part of a very extensive enclosure, which has the remains of a stake and pole fence on the embankment. A mile on, and just beyond a second ditch on the other side of the square, or whatever may be the shape of the enclosure, is a long one story building, of sun-dried brick, and thatched with rushes and flags after the rudest fashion. The walls are two and a half feet thick, and the whole is divided by two partitions of the same thickness into three rooms about twenty feet square each, and having no manner of communication with each other except by the outside door. One of the rooms has a chimney and fire place. I found it empty, but far from being swept

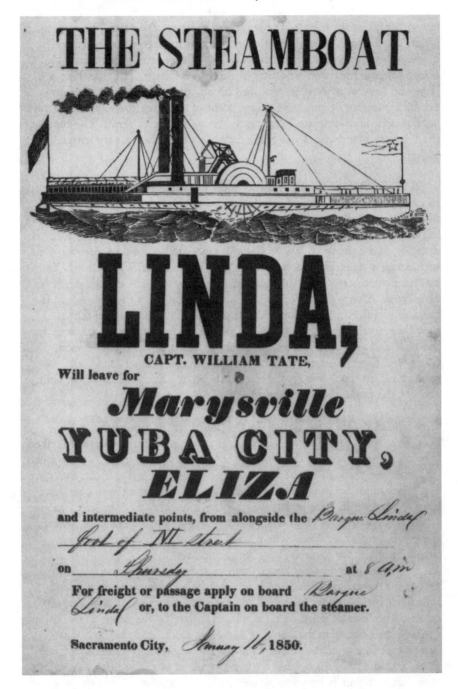

Ad for the steamer travelled on by members of Lord's party (California State Library).

or garnished. Dirt, and the smell of smoke, is all that indicates its ever having been inhabited.

Half a mile on are two enclosures, one on either hand, leaving a broad fine avenue of half a mile or more in length between them, and terminating at Sutter's house, where he now resides. The left hand one seems to contain several hundred acres, and some of it appears to be put into wheat, of which I noticed several old stacks, badly put up, and covered with the young grain growing green and luxuriant.

The field on the right extends no farther than the house, and is rather narrow, being bounded by the river; and is appropriated, so far as I could discern, to a herd of hogs and a flock of sheep. I could not determine the number of either, on account of the grass and bushes, though they count by hundreds. In front of Sutter's, one-half the avenue, on the left, is occupied by a large square enclosure, five feet high, used to shut up cattle in, and divided into several parts, or smaller enclosures. The inside presents one great mud hole, and the cattle must stand up the whole time they are shut in.

On the right is a long low house, forming half of that side or face of another square area of an acre; and directly opposite, forming part of the other face is "the House" or principal building, which is 25 feet by 75 or 80, and one story and a half high. It makes a very respectable appearance, the front showing as if white-washed, and is quite smooth as if plastered. It is, by all odds, the best building that I have seen on a "ranche" in the valley; and the out buildings and area, or court, have an air of neatness wholly unexampled in my experience of California. Beyond the house square, are a number of separate enclosures, probably for hogs and sheep. The inside presents nothing but bare walls and thin mud.

All the walls are of sun-dried brick, as well as every fence about the house, except that behind the last mentioned enclosures there seems to be a garden surrounded by a common picket fence, the pickets of split oak. It looks much like a Yankee garden plot in a new country. A short distance beyond is a village of Diggers, on the highest artificial mound that I have seen in the valley. The bank, from their lodges, slopes beautifully and rapidly to the river, carpeted with a mat of the finest, greenest grass, that the improvidence of savage life ever let run to waste.

The other side of the river is similar to this, only a little lower. The timber is mostly large oaks, widely scattered. The banks are twenty to thirty feet high, and the current smooth and strong, and perhaps 100 yards wide. The Indians must be very industrious, for in addition to their stock of provisions, they have several thousand feet of seine, hung out to dry and repair. The fabrics are about 100 feet long and four to five feet wide, and apparently made of some kind of grass. The twine is very fine, strong and even; and the cord seen, through the whole length of each edge, is of the size of a codline, or pipe stem, well twisted and neatly made. No part of the manufacture would suffer by comparison with anything of the kind made in the States.

Live oak grows scatteringly along the banks here, and above, until at Bennett's ranche, fourteen miles above, most of the timber, as I am told, is of that kind. The trees are small, several crooked dwarfish trunks starting off from one root, and spreading in all directions twenty or thirty feet. From Sutter's to Yuba City is seven miles, the last three on a lower level, the first part of which is covered with weeds and bushes.

Yuba City is four or five weeks old, and has about a dozen houses. It stands thirty or forty feet above the present level of the water, and the bank is excellent, sandy and sloping. The opposite side is lower, but dry, sandy and covered with oak. On that side, half a mile below the city, comes in Yuba River. This is at present considered the head of steam navigation, though steamers have been higher. Just below on this side is a village of Diggers, and another on the other side, immediately below the mouth of the Yuba. Eld. Wisner preached today.

Chapter Ten

December 31, 1849–January 29, 1850: Exploring the River

———◆——◆——◆———

MONDAY, DEC. 31, 1849. Left the city and rolled on up the river. The country a very little uneven, and the timber seems to extend from Feather River to the Buttes, a distance of nearly twenty miles. Before we reached Bennett's ranche, seven miles on, found the timber mostly live oak, except on the lower bottom, at the right, and lying in streaks where there is a slight depression like the bed of occasional running water. The land is less sandy, and the road not as good. The soil has a reddish appearance, and is mixed with fine flat gravel and broken shells. I noticed this more particularly three or four miles at the left of the road, towards the Buttes, where Ball and I made a circuit in search of deer. The grass grows in bunches, and covers but a very small portion of the earth, which in many localities is entirely covered with weeds, and small red willows, no more than two or three feet high.

Bennet has a double log house—no out buildings of any kind. The house has no floor, below or above and there were large cracks between the crooked logs. I felt no inconvenience from cold, even when lying on a single Buffalo robe on the bare earth. I stayed all night in attendance on a sick man, and the teams went up.

TUESDAY, JAN. 1, 1850. The wolves were howling about, within four rods of the house, nearly all night. About midnight, some of the men went out and killed an overgrown raccoon which the dog had driven up a tree. It began to rain this morning just before daylight, and there was some distant thunder. For supper; had fried beef and long cakes of poor flour, coffee, sugar and molasses. Breakfast—molasses, sugar, coffee, long cakes and fried beef. "Variety's the spice of life." This is only common doings, sometimes we come it on chicken fixings. That "coon" is in the kettle now, baking. It makes little difference, however. It is $1.50 here and no grumbling.

Bennett claims a handsome flat below, and between him and the river. It extends only a short distance above, and is several feet lower than the general level on which the road runs. This is in many places forty feet, or more, above the river. The road from Bennett's to where the teams camped last night, is rather bad now, though the ground is high enough. The soil seems to be red earth, mixed with fine gravel, sand, and broken shells, and holds water like a sponge. You frequently sink to the instep in walking over it where there is no water on the surface, and where there is, one must be careful where he puts his feet.

Live oak constitutes the mass of the timber, and nearly one-fourth of this has been burned down within a few years. They generally branch at the ground, half a dozen from a stem, and each trunk sends off innumerable small branches and twigs. They seldom reach a height of fifty feet. Thousands and millions of pigeons are congregated here, to feed on the small beautiful acorns which cover the ground.

Did not find the cattle till late, and only made about five miles—camping in a fine open level bottom, to which a new road descends, and across which it runs several miles. By the by, I lost a grand new year's supper—that "coon" was not done when I left.

WEDNESDAY, JAN. 2. Rained at intervals all night and showers this morning. Wind east, and a little cool. River banks here are high and current rapid. A mile beyond camp, turned on to the upper level again, and the country to the look is exactly like that between Nichol's and Sutter's—a broad level plain, and scattering oaks. The road is generally some distance from the river.

Eight miles above camp, came to Yates' ranche, having passed the road leading to the lower ford of Feather River without seeing it. The road for the last few miles is excellent, and good all the way up, except six miles this side of Bennett's. Passed several Indian villages today. They wear more clothing, build higher and better acorn cribs, and make smoother burrows than the Indians on the Sacramento. I notice no other difference. Camped early on account of the rain.

THURSDAY, JAN. 3. Cloudy, misty, chilly and foggy, with north wind. Camped in the vicinity of several tents, and a house body of crooked logs, some eight feet high, which gives promise strong of one of those splendid creations of the fancy yclept, a "ranche." The fact is, they are squatting all along the river, at short intervals, on both sides, and building shantees, and making brush fences; so give them whatever name you please, the things are still the same. From camp, the general direction of the road to Stout's, some eight or ten miles, is nearly east. The face of the country much the same as yesterday, about half the way, when it is cut into long narrow ridges by shallow ravines, formed by water running from the mountain, or from Feather River when it is very high.

Something more than a mile below Stout's struck what is called the "red land," and passing up a short distance, descended a steep place fifty feet to the present level of the river. At this point the high level which has been gradually approaching the river on our left for the last ten miles, runs up to its bank with an easy curve, and forms with it a high, handsome, smooth, but bold bluff of red earth, partially covered with pine, oak, and two or three kinds of shrubs of large growth, among which I notice red wood, [probably manzanita] now in full bloom. The flowers are white, and the whole looks very beautiful, with its bright red stems and twigs, and green leaves, embosomed in a mass of snow-white flowers. This shrub attains a diameter of six or eight inches on the red land, among the live oak about Bennett's ranche.

The road from the hill to Stout's runs under the bluff, where is generally room for wagons to pass each other, though not always. Above Stout's where by the by, wagons must stop, or cross the river by ferry, the banks are rocky and the hills rise rapidly into mountains. The teams were unloaded at Stout's, and Elder Wisner and Horton returned down the river with them, which Ball and myself remained to secure the goods and get them up to Long's,* six miles, where Darling, Sharpe and the two Wisner boys have fixed their winter quarters.

Towards night, left Ball and went up the river. Sometimes among the rocks near the river, and again on the hill side where the spongy ground saturated with water gives earnest warning to the weary wayfarer to move quickly. The general direction of the river, to a mile and a half below Long's is North and South. From Long's to that point, it runs west. It comes down, foaming and rushing and roaring through the rocks like a mad thing. I reached the hill above Long's just in time to see 200 or more tents and canvass roofs, shining like shells among the trees 300 feet below; and then the evening shadows fell, and the darkness came down so suddenly, like the closing of a curtain, that I was compelled to inquire and wander sometimes among rocks, tents, stumps, trees and ravines, before I could discover the Batavia Hotel.† Found them at supper, in a comfortable house of canvass and logs, with a cheerful and bright fire, as social and cozy as though 2,500 miles of desert did not separate them from friends and home.

---

*Long's Bar was one of the earliest settlements in Butte County. A store was opened by the Long brothers two miles above Ophir (Oroville) in October 1849.

†Since no record of a Batavia Hotel has been found, it seems likely that this was Dr. Lord's name for the tent in which he was living.

J. Wisner is just up from a sick bed, and Darling is confined to the house with scurvy, a disease very prevalent here. The evening is calm and pleasant. I did not speak of it at the time, but I met, in coming up, a number of persons with spade or pick on shoulder, a tin pan in hand, with a small heap of gold in a corner, returning from work among the rocks. I noticed several boys, one of whom, quite a lad, had as much as eight dollars. Some had two or three dollars only, and some fifteen or twenty. The gold was in thin flat scales, of all sizes, up to a kernel of wheat and mixed with ten times its bulk of black sand, as it is called (black sulph. terri.). This they blow out, when dry, at their leisure.

FRIDAY, JAN. 4. C. Wisner, Sharpe and myself went down to Stout's to pack up a few such luxuries as cheese, raisins, dried berries, etc. Saw nearly two hundred people actively engaged in washing for gold, among them Mansfield and McClure, of Elgin. They are getting at least an ounce each day. When I see the whole operation of washing complete, I will endeavor to describe it.

SATURDAY, JAN. 5, 1850. Rained all night—misty and foggy this morning. At noon went down to pack up some baggage. Returned just at night. Soon after a man came to notify us of a meeting to be held, on account of an assault committed on a man of the name of Nichols, in his own "diggings." After dark went down and found that a number of persons had convened, elected a magistrate and constable and adjourned to Col. Hamilton's house. Went over and found the house jammed full.

While the jury were out, a meeting was organized, and a Committee was appointed to draft resolutions to be reported on Saturday evening next, on the subject of claims. The trial was conducted with the best kind of feeling, the only aim being to establish the truth, and do justice to all. There were no lawyers to delay—no petty technicalities to obstruct the course of justice.

SUNDAY, JAN. 6. Rev. Mr. Stibbs preached today. The boys went, and I staid with Darling, who is worse.

MONDAY, JAN. 7. Rained moderately all night and continues today. It is not cold, hardly chilly, and I sit and write without a coat in a canvass roofed house, with very little fire. Although the sides of our house are not raised four feet, yet it is much more comfortable than a tent, and camping out, which I have so often spoken of; and now that I think of it I will speak definitely of what I mean all the way through by the expression "and camped."

We look out ahead for some place where is grass, wood, water, and dry ground or as many of these advantages as we can find combined. When the teams come in, the wagons are placed in position, and the cattle are unhitched and unyoked.

Now for the details of the mess. One brings out the tent and sets it up; another gets wood; another water; and a fourth gets out the stove and cooking utensils, and whatsoever else is wanted in the tent. Then one strikes a fire, another prepares the wood, a third wets up the bread, or mixes the batter for pancakes, a favorite way of disposing of flour, while a fourth assists the last in grinding coffee, washing dishes, etc., etc. One from each mess has usually to keep an eye on the cattle. When the bread is baked, or pancakes fried, the meat cooked and the coffee ready, or tea steeped, the table is set and supper eaten at leisure and in comfort, unless the wind which usually filled our breakfast with sand, should hold over and favor us with a sprinkling at evening.

In the first part of the journey, we had plenty of milk, and some butter, which added much to our camp comforts. Now, this fare will certainly keep soul and body together, as we have sufficiently proved; and more than that, it is really a scratch or two above the common mark. Only a small portion of the numerous messes which traversed the plain aspired to the luxury of a table; and as for civilized knives and forks, so genuine a sign of effeminacy was considered rather to compromise a man's character among the aristocracy of the plains; which spoons were put to unheard of uses if used at all, and tea spoons were returned "non est inventus."

I have dined and supped and breakfasted abroad, often and often, else how should I know all this? But hush! Were it not for violating the laws of hospitality, I could "a tale unfold," which, for aught I know, would turn over a piece of tripe in convulsions, to say nothing of a human stomach. Such cooking as I have seen, etc. We were fortunate in securing a good cook for our mess, in the tidy person of Sharpe. But, I repeat it, such cooking as I have seen would surprise any one who had not previously made a dirt pie, and accidently got a little flour and stewed apple into it.

If you have a good clean cook, the worst part of camp life is the crowded state of the tent, especially on a rainy night, and sleeping on the ground. We, for the most part, slept in the wagons, till we left them to voyage down the Sacramento. Thousands and thousands slept in tents the whole journey through.

If any one has lingering doubts respecting this matter now, before he makes up his mind definitely, I think he would do well to get a tent and camp out in July, with a Digger Indian and a mangy dog to cook for him; and if that does not satisfy, try it again about the time of the line storm in September. I would advise to camp by the side of some great thoroughfare, so that you can have the full benefit of all the dust raised in that quarter.

One thing I do aver, whatever may be the experience of others; I have eaten many a meal without daring to bring my teeth together on account of the sand. Sand wears away the teeth, and teeth are precious.

View of the Sacramento flood, January 1850 (California State Library).

TUESDAY, JAN. 8. Rained all day, and in the evening and the river is rising rapidly. The water runs down the mountain sides in torrents. Not cold.

WEDNESDAY, JAN. 9. The river has risen nearly thirty feet and whirls along with a rush.

FRIDAY, JAN. 11. Rain ceased a little after sunrise, and was all day clearing up. This evening there is not a cloud to be seen, and in the afternoon the sun poured down as hot as July in the States. The miners have improved the day and brought in a large quantity of gold from the different bars and ravines, where they have been at work. We have been building another and better house all the week, when the weather would permit, and hope to finish tomorrow. Next week we hope to try the wash bowl practice, and operate some in *the funds* with pick and shovel.

SATURDAY, JAN. 12. Almost cool enough for a frost this morning. Beautiful, pleasant and warm as soon as the sun was up. Ball was sick, and the house is not finished. On account of the favorable state of the weather, the miners' meeting proved a failure. The body of a drowned man was found at the ferry in the eddy today. Probably one that was drowned at the South Fork a week or two since.

SUNDAY, JAN 13. Rained a little in the night, but the day was quite pleasant, though cool. Rev. Mr. Whitcombe preached.

MONDAY, JAN. 14. Cloudy and cold.

TUESDAY AND WEDNESDAY. The cold continued, with rain.

THURSDAY, JAN. 17. Pleasant but cold. Ground frozen this morning. Ball and I went off north-west eight or ten miles to hunt antelope. Saw several hundreds. They are extremely shy. Ball and five or six others surrounded a herd and wounded several. One of them came round the hill where I stood waiting, followed by two Indian dogs. There were several Indians about, gathering earth worms. Two or three of these broke and followed the dogs and I followed the whole. The poor creature made for Stout's, on Feather River, some three or four miles across a nearly level plain. About half way over I came up with the Indians, who had caught it and twisted its neck so as to break it. This saves the blood in the flesh. I examined, and finding it quite lean, left it to the savages.

FRIDAY AND SATURDAY. Cold.

SUNDAY, JAN. 20. Mr. Taylor, of Lockport, Ill., preached today. Darling died at two o'clock this morning of hepatization of the lungs. He has been sick ever since we came back to our camp on the Sacramento. Fine evening. Cold but not freezing.

MONDAY AND TUESDAY. Cold and some snow.

WEDNESDAY, JAN. 23. Drizzling rain. Reports have been rife that Sacramento City was six to ten feet under water. Today they are fully confirmed, at eight feet. Strange that men should risk so much, in a case where they could arrive at an absolute certainty. There was not the least difficulty in ascertaining to what depth the land is usually flooded, and yet they seem to have paid no attention to it. Some lives are said to have been lost, and a vast amount of property destroyed. But for the great number of ships in the river, the loss of life must have been fearful, and of property almost total.

THURSDAY, FRIDAY AND SATURDAY. Cold, with some rain.

SUNDAY, JAN. 27. Fine, cool, pleasant morning. A Mr. Nichols preached today.

Chapter Eleven
January 30–April 13, 1850:
The Diggings

———◆——◆——◆———

WEDNESDAY, JAN. 30. Made our first essay at gold digging as a business. Six of us got only $18 for over half a day's work. Too bad.

THURSDAY, JAN. 31. Dug again today. Did considerably better than yesterday. The ground has been dug over three or four times already.

SUNDAY, FEB. 3. Warmer this morning. No frost and a little cloudy. Since the fair weather commenced, hundreds have gone up the river prospecting; i.e., examining the bars and ravines for gold. Fifteen miles above here the snow is several feet deep, and the air cold. It is generally supposed that the rainy season has closed. We shall see. Rev. Mr. Stibbs preached.

TUESDAY, FEB. 5. Everybody moving up the river to get into the mines. It may not be well understood by the uninitiated why we say "going up into the mines." I will explain. The whole western slope of the Sierra Nevada, down to the Sacramento valley, is broken into mountains and ranges of mountains, diverging from the great range at different angles. In the valleys and deep kanyons between and across these, run numerous streams and rivers. Of these, Feather River and its branches are the principal.

In following up this river, a few miles after leaving the plain you find only a table land, but little elevated. Then you enter a gorge between hills 1,500 or 2,000 feet high, some in ridges with steep slopes, some in sugar loaf peaks, and others with a table land on the summit, resting on a mass of rock, presenting a perpendicular wall down, from fifty to 150 feet. Between these are deep ravines, with streams running down in the rainy season, and occasionally one fed by springs which runs much later. All these streams pour into the river. Except where the ravines open the river itself is closely confined between the bases of these almost perpendicular hills, and runs in a channel that absolutely defies description.

It rushes and roars and whirls and pours and boils and rolls and races and dashes along between masses and walls and blocks and ledges and piles of a hard bluish grey rock, which seems placed there for no purpose whatever except to try the effect of water on stone. The whole of the wash of the immense ravines has been whirled off by the river, or formed into what are called bars; i.e., piles of rock, and masses of sand and gravel on the rock, which is here usually soft and shelly like slate. The gold is not scattered through or mixed with the whole of the earth alike, but seems confined to localities, and is washed by the water in the rainy season down the hills into the bottom of the ravines.

Some is deposited there, some is rolled down to the bars, and some into the river. Being heavier than anything else, it drops down and rests on the rock or compact bed of clay. These stop its descent; and on these it is found, sometimes under a few inches and sometimes a few feet of gravel, sand and earth. It is sometimes found under or among the loose rock, where the water has deposited earth, sand or gravel; and sometimes in pockets or holes worn in the solid rock by the friction of small stone whirled around by the water.

I noticed the point of a rock on the river today, with a square perpendicular face, ten feet in diameter above the present water line. On this face, equidistant from each other and the sides are the half sections of two huge drill-holes, sixteen inches at top and eight where they enter the water. These holes had some agency, probably in splitting off the rock, which no doubt contained thousands of dollars when it fell.

All the gold in the ravines is coarse, or has the appearance of melted lead, scattered in the sand, or thrown into water. It is found in irregular shaped pieces, from the size of fine sand to several ounces; some assert pounds weight. This kind is sometimes found on the bars, with the river gold, which is usually in irregularly oval thin plates, or flakes, the largest of the size of a large pea, the smallest a mere dust that will float on the water when it is dry. This flat or scale gold is no where found, as far as I can learn, except where the water of the river flows.

No one has yet been high enough to discover the localities which furnish it. Perhaps it is manufactured by the friction, grinding, and hammering of the water and rock in the river, out of the lump gold of the ravines. I think so. If not, there must be some place high up where it lies in large quantity, for every freshet deposits more or less in the bars. Some of them yield $10 a day per man, the fourth time working over. We are making eight now on one which has been thus worked.

Following up the gorge twenty miles, you find a large branch coming in from the north west. A few miles higher a large branch comes in from the south, called the South Fork. These principal forks are almost immediately divided and subdivided into a large number of branches, streams, and streamlets, draining in all probability 5,000 square miles or more, and yet the channel of the main stream is in many places not more than twenty or thirty yards wide, though nobody, I reckon, knows how deep.

The west branch of the North Fork has been explored, and the South Fork, some twelve miles from its mouth. The middle one is inaccessible, as well as the remainder of the north and the north or west side of the south; on account of the snow. It will be several weeks yet before that will be sufficiently melted to permit a thorough examination, though hundreds have gone up with bread, blanket, pick, spoon and pan, to prospect.

And now you know, or ought to, at least, what getting up into the mines is. The reason why they leave these "diggings" is, that they have been worked over and over until the average is less than an ounce a day. What the mines above will prove, I am unable to say, but I think there is little chance of making a large raise at once, unless by damming the river and taking the water entirely out of the channel. If the main stream could be dammed and "turned out of bed," I doubt not, the story of Aladdin's lamp would be eclipsed.

The untold wealth of a few mines near Long's Bar would make the richest of earth's nabobs comparatively poor. Tons and tons of shining gold lie quietly in its unfathomed depths, when 50,000 days' labor would lay it open to the gaze of rapacious man.

SATURDAY, FEB. 9, 1850. Clear, pleasant day. The Buckeye is just leaving out.

SUNDAY, FEB. 10. Another fine and warm day. Elder Taylor preached. There was a wedding just above us—a Mr. Lovelady to a Miss Morely, of Oregon.

MONDAY, FEB. 11. Left the river, where we have been making twelve dollars each for the last three days, and made a claim a mile and a half up a small stream, called Morse's Creek. In prospecting, I found several flakes or scales like the river gold, so I think the question may be settled as to the process by which the particular shape of the pieces is worked out.

Wherever the water moves with sufficient force to roll and tumble the rocks against each other, the bits of gold, falling between, get flatted and crushed and ground to thin scales, frequently light enough to swim on water, when dry, and there the flake gold is found washed up on to the bars. The heavy pieces fall into the eddies and bottom, where the water is still and deep, or are arrested by projecting rocks, or roots, or banks of gravel, liable to a notice to quit on any sudden rise of the river or change of current, unless firmly fixed in a crevice. Where there is water only while it is raining, or at most, for a few days after, and the rocks are not washed bare, and rolled over each other, the flake gold will not be found. Warm and pleasant all day. Benj. Wilson came in this evening from Fremont, where we left him weeks ago.

TUESDAY, FEB. 12. Somewhat cloudy today. Dug a ditch to drain our claim. Only a couple of dollars today for all hands. Tomorrow, or next day, expect to come to some. About eight o'clock this evening, we were startled by a most horrible discord of sounds from the other, or Longtown side of the river. A hundred or two pistol shots, and a cowbell, accompanied by a tin pan or two, beaten with sticks, seemed to take the lead, but I reckon didn't much get the start. Shout and scream, and song, and wild hurrah, filled up the intervals. It was really appalling for half an hour, and then all was hushed to silence. Had a dish of mashed Irish potatoes this evening. High living. Mem: potatoes 75 cents per lb.

WEDNESDAY, FEB. 13. Learned this morning that Mr. John January was married last evening to Miss Underhill, by Mr. _____, all of Longtown, at this present. So the uproar of last evening is fully accounted for. Why the wolves should be so much more uproarious than common, is not yet explained. Most likely they were aping their cousins, who recited the first act before nine o'clock. I have heard such sounds (not the wolves) before in the States, and I have often wondered why our sapient legislators, who would fine a man for passing a counterfeit one dollar bank note, have not before this made it a capital offence. Why a meritorious couple, when doing so commendable a thing as getting married, should be disturbed by a set of brawling, miserable, riotous, drunken blackguards, is past my comprehension; and why a civilized, half civilized, or even semi-barbarous – nay why it should be tolerated any where except in a wolf kennel, is to me an inexplicable mystery. Cloudy part of the day. Took out twenty dollars in opening up the prospect. Must do better.

THURSDAY, FEB. 14. Had to dig a deep ditch on account of an influx of water. Slightly cloudy – only nine dollars today.

SATURDAY, FEB. 16. Bought a mule, and horse fixings and furniture for packing. Price $450. On Monday we start for the mountains on the South Fork. Leased our claim on Morris Creek to Wilson. We furnish tools, board him and have two-fifths. Cloudy and looked like rain all day. Quite cool. Clearer this evening. McClure is getting better.

MONDAY, FEB. 18. Cloudy yet. Looks more like rain. Left for the S. Fork, the two Wisner boys, Ball, Horton and myself. Crossed over to Long-

town, and took a general direction south-east. Made about ten miles through
a very pretty looking country—gradually ascending easy slopes with occasional descents, and crossing and ascending small streams, running into
Feather River or the Yuba. There is a very good wagon road, the mule trail
crossing it at intervals, and shortening the distance. We did not follow
either, but took a route still farther round and easier. The leaves of the
Buckeye are about as much expanded here (at camp) as at Long's ten days
ago. There are many beautiful flowers and the grass is in its first freshness,
like the green sward of May in the Northern States. Camped in a delightful
valley by a clear mountain stream, at the base of the last summit before
descending toward the South Fork.

TUESDAY, FEB. 19. Fine cool morning. Birds singing or screaming
around; the water in the brook curling, rippling, and roaring; the raven and
hawk wheeling, whirling, diving, and chattering over head, while the sun
tinted nearest mountain peaks glow and flash in the sun's warm rays as the
snow-clad summits of the far distant northern Coast Range throw them
strongly back as from the face of a mirror. The parti-colored flowers and
grapes below, and evergreens and birds above, with the immense piles of
white flowers covering the huge evergreen red wood on every side—force
upon one the idea of spring in spite of positive knowledge that it is only
February.

Left camp, and ascending easily to the last summit, two miles, passed
down into a valley, a very considerable descent, and gradually ascending
again, reached a much less elevation two miles on and looked down on the
South Fork for the first time. The descent is one mile and a half from an
altitude of 2500 feet, rapid, rough, rocky, precipitous, slippery and sliding—
all are well represented here. Whoever ascends it on foot must pay old
Adam's penalty; and to ride up it, if not equivalent to a *felo de se*, would in
my estimation be a real *felo de mule*. I would sooner walk up it than describe
it, and yet wagons do come down, or rather are let down by ropes, though I
have never heard of one's returning. Doubtless they will, for nothing seems
impossible here, unless it is to be respectable and comfortable.

The river is from ten to thirty yards wide; in some places shallow, rocky
and rapid, in others deep and still. The water looks green, and is pure and
cold. There is generally a sand or gravel bar on one side of the river, and
frequently on both sides, and between this and the base of the mountain
you sometimes find a tolerably level area of considerable extent. The widest
that I have seen is at Stringtown, just above this point. It is nearly a mile
long, and twenty rods at the widest, generally very much less. The mountains present no rocky precipices or walls but are very steep. Four miles
above the peaks are more rocky and sharper.

The timber is live oak, white oak, pine, fir, cedar, alder and what
appears to be box wood. The pines are quite straight and many of them

tower to a height of 200 feet, though they are knotty to the stump. The firs and cedars are beautifully straight and tall, and split true and free. The box wood, an evergreen, sometimes attains two and a half feet in diameter, and sixty feet in height, but is crooked, and generally branches near the ground. The limbs are bare, like the sycamore, and yellow or orange color. In many places the pine, fir and cedar grow together in clumps. Generally however the timber is very scattering, though the spaces are in some measure relieved by the evergreen shrubs. There is very little grass after leaving the last summit. Camped on the river, and sent back the pack animals.

WEDNESDAY, FEB. 20. Much colder here than on the southern side of the "divide." Began to rain a little in afternoon and rained quite steadily till dark, with showers in the evening. No snow on the mountains so far as I can discover. Went four miles up the river today and found it lined with men at work, damming, draining, etc. Three-fourths of a mile above camp begins what is called Stringtown, which is some forty buildings strung along a pretty piece of ground for nearly a mile. Many of them are very well built, the cedar and fir furnishing excellent "materiel." I noticed several gardens, in one of which was a sturdy, fine looking young woman, raking over a bed for some kind of vegetable,—onions perhaps. The whole place looks quite neat, and on the whole more like living than anything I have before seen in California. Success to them.

FRIDAY, FEB. 22. Went up the river four miles, and bought a claim for 1,000 dollars, on which 150 days work has been expended. Our company now consists of the three Wisners, Sharpe, Robt. Horton of Texas, Mr. Woodman of Iowa, a young man, Murrell by name, E. Mansfield of Elgin, and myself. We have claimed a vacant place in the river here, the only one for twenty miles.

SATURDAY, FEB. 23. Showered in the night, but bright and cold this morning. The sun shines warm on the almost perpendicular side of the mountains, which rears itself 3,000 feet on the south-west and west. So cold is it here, (and yet not freezing,) and so comfortable and cozy does it appear aloft, that one feels inclined to wish for wings, to rise with the lark, and rejoice on the mountain's height in the genial sun-shine. By the by, this is not entirely a flight of fancy, for the lark does occasionally occupy that same desirable location,—desirable I mean for the winged tribes, but rather sharp for other bipeds.

SUNDAY, FEB. 24. Splendid day. Was called up to the Oregon Bar, three quarters of a mile, to sit as a juror in a claim dispute, where had been an assault and battery. After a short investigation, and hearing all the witnesses and parties who wished to speak, the jury brought in for the original claimants. They were somewhat in fault, and did not strictly comply with the letter of the law, by putting up notice every ten days, or occupying the premises. But they lived only thirty or forty rods above their claim, and the jumpers knew beforehand that they claimed and intended to work it as soon as the water would permit.

In equity they should hold the claim, but governed by the common, absurd, legal technicalities, those who hold no right whatever would have held it. The unsworn witnesses, no doubt, "told the truth, the whole truth, and nothing but the truth," which is more than I can say of them in any court of law I ever attended—and why?

The lawyers will not let them. Let a witness do his very best, and he can not but swear false—technically—if words have any meaning. If he attempts to tell the whole truth, and perseveres, he is incontinently "jugged" for contempt of court. Strange infatuation—to deem that the action of a legislature can raise the intellect of an ass, on the scale of omniscience, high enough to discern whether what a witness is about to say is pertinent to the case or not. A pretty compliment too is paid the jury, when they (the judges) dare not trust them with the truth, and let the lawyers talk three hours to exclude three words, which usually are slipped in some way after all, and left to the tender mercies of the dozen.

Law, as at present administered, is one of the mightiest humbugs of the age, and will shortly collapse, or, swelled with its own refinements and reduplicated reduplications, burst like a bomb shell, destroying all within its sphere of action, but clearing a space on which to erect a better system. Can't someone contrive to fire the fuse now?

In our case the jury was not sworn, and yet, I doubt not, did exact justice, which is more than the law, the judges and the lawyers will allow them to do in the States. The verdict was—for Plaintiffs—no costs—and recommended that this be the last trial on the Sabbath. Recollect that the jury here assess their own fees.

MONDAY, FEB. 25. Cloudy and cool this morning and began to rain sometime after noon and had rain with wind all the afternoon and two or three showers in the night.

26TH. Warmer this morning and occasional showers of rain and snow. Snowed freely on the mountains in sight ten miles above. Cleared off entirely this evening.

27TH. Rained all night and there is snow on all the heights above us, but none down the river below us, although some of the heights are much higher than where the snow lies here. Showers of rain all day but not cold. Some patches of clear sky and sunshine and rain at the same time.

THURSDAY, 28TH. Rained most of the night as in the day. Merely cool this morning though the snow which melted off yesterday almost over hangs us again. Only a single shower today. Very comfortable weather. Just pleasantly cool.

MARCH 1. Cold night, frost this morning and ice a half an inch thick. Not a cloud to be seen for the first time since we first came up here, except perhaps in the night. Clouded up again in the evening.

2ND. Rained more this morning and snowed briskly at 1,000 feet above us. Continued on steadily till afternoon when it cleared up, though there was an occasional flurry of snow on the heights above all day.

3. Pleasant and comfortable here though the heights are covered with snow which contrasts strongly and strangely with the green of the trees and warmth of the valley.

MONDAY, 4TH. Cold night and frosty Monday. Not a cloud to be seen.

5TH. Another cold night and frost. Ice a half an inch thick. About as cold as a frosty September morning in N.Y. or Ill. A few clouds scudding along. Began to rain in the afternoon and is rattling down now at 9:30 p.m. with gusts of wind. On the mountain overhead it is no doubt a regular wintry storm, A No. One and second to nothing this side of Behrings straits. I hear the wind roaring and rattling among the pines above and before night I could see the clouds up there white with shining snow pouring and dashing through them like a mountain flood.

WEDNESDAY, MARCH 6. Rained steadily all night and is raining still at nine a.m. Snow on the peaks around very steadily and freely down it poured all day and at bed time exhibited no symptoms of weariness. Very few people have passed today. Generally we see from fifty to a hundred a day—some with shovels and picks and pans, and packs and some packing mules and others Indians, alone or in companies. Some are ragged, dirty and unshaven, Oregonians or Missourians. Some are passable, and others respectable (almost!).

An old and very well dressed gentleman came along day before yesterday, who seemed to have lost his reckoning; and yet, I dare say, at home passed for a man of considerable sense. Here he was like a fish out of water. He said that he came from Mobile, seven months round Cape Horn, and brought out a full rigged house. Had come up into the mines, to pick up a cool thousand or two to pay freight and charges. Poor man! when he was in the mines, he could see no more gold to pick up than in the streets of his own native land. He was evidently disappointed, and evinced considerable anxiety as to the length of time it would take to reach Mobile again, with sundry misgivings as to what his house might be doing in his absence. Every minute or two he proposed this grave question "What had I better do?" He had better by far, have asked it before he started. I advised him to depart instanter for the Bay, rent his house and get a quarter in advance, pay charges, land and set it up, and then sell out, start for home and never be caught here again. He seemed to relish the advice and moved on. Yesterday he returned without any gold and was on his way back to his HOUSE.

SATURDAY, MARCH 9. Attended a miners' meeting at Boone's Bar, three and a half miles above. The country is much rougher than here, and the snow lies white and cold on the heights above. Nine miles above this the snow is three feet deep. The formation here is a loose granite-like sand stone, and piles and strata of milky quartz. Dr. Morse, dentist, from Aurora, came to us yesterday, sick. He is better today.

SUNDAY, MARCH 10. Report says that a company on the Youba have been "whipped out" by the "Diggers," and the men at Long's are turning out to go over to their aid. These "Diggers" are bound to be exterminated. If they would be quiet, they might get any kind of clothing, and plenty of food for their labor; yet they choose to steal, and that brings them in collision with the miners. There is a great deal of stealing going on at present, and some severe measures will have to be adopted to put a stop to it.*

TUESDAY, MARCH 12. Morse, the dentist from Aurora, Ill., who has been here sick three or four days, left for Long's.

THURSDAY, MARCH 14. The snow is reported to be six feet deep between this and the Youba, ten miles above here. If this fork drains any considerable surface of country, the melting of the snow will keep the water up two or three months yet, and delay our operations. In all probability we shall be ready to work in the bed of the river in about six weeks, if the water should not be thus kept up. Very few, however, will be ready in that time, though some think that a week is sufficient to finish their work. On most of the claims the projected operations are entirely insufficient to drain the river, and the working of its bed will be postponed to another year, or

*In an article dated August 1, 1854, the Sacramento Union wrote: "As an example of the decimation of the Indian population of our country, we need but refer to the Hock Farm Digger tribe, which consisted of over 500 souls a few years since—so we are informed by Gen. John A. Sutter. The same gentleman also says that of that entire number but fifteen are now living. The decrease has been far more rapid since the settlement of the State by Eastern immigrants."

Illustration of cradle rocking (California State Library).

be abandoned. Some, who will fail, are making extensive preparations, (in talk) and really doing but very little. Others are not making their estimates of required means and power high enough. The wildest schemes of human fancy are here mere common, every-day, matter-of-course speculations.

Many attempts have been made to improve upon the common rocker, or cradle, for separating the gold from the earth; and in my opinion all have most signally failed. The form is very similar to that of the article of the same name, used to rock children in, and here occasionally put to that use. Think of a cradle worth $55. The common size is four feet long, from sixteen to twenty inches wide on the top, and from six to eight inches deep. The bottom is laid down—from nine to twelve inches broad; next a piece five or six inches wide stands off on each side at an angle of 45 degrees; and then two pieces of like width perpendicularly above them, forming a trough with five unequal sides. These top pieces, at a point about two-fifths from one end, are slanted off, at about the same angle, towards each end; thus making the longest end, or foot of the cradle, the shallowest.

But this figure is only to lessen the weight, and make it a little more ship-shape. The short end, or head, slopes, perhaps, an inch and a half, and the long one, or foot, over two inches. A piece is next nailed across each end to close it up, the foot having an opening one and a half inches above the bottom, and two inches more or less wide, extending to within an inch and a half of the sides of the cradle. A cleat an inch and a half wide is nailed across the bottom at the junction of the two sections of the cradle, and another, midway between that and the foot. In each side (inside) of the head section, is nailed a thin strip of wood, slanting from near the top downwards towards the head, to within two or three inches of the bottom. On this is placed a thin frame, like the screens in a fanning mill, with a piece across the middle, on which is stretched a piece of strong cotton or linen cloth. This reaches to within two or three inches of the head.

A box five or six inches deep, and tapering toward the head to four, covering the whole upper section, with a bottom of sheet iron or zinc, punched with holes about two inches apart, and from one half to three-fourths of an inch in diameter, is hung to the head of the cradle by a couple of common three-inch butts. A handle is screwed to the side, and a couple of short rockers, with a short iron pin in the middle of the bottom of each, and the animal is ready to go. It is placed by the water, on a slight frame of two side pieces and two end ones, in the middle of each of which is a hole for the pin in the rocker to play in. These keep the cradle in its place.

Two lazy men sometimes work it, but usually one man is sufficient. He stands or sits with the left hand on the handle, which stands out more or less from the cradle, and in his right which is toward the head, a tin dipper holding two or three quarts. About a pail full of earth is thrown into the box, and the cradler begins to rock backward and forward, constantly throwing on water, until all is washed that will go through the holes in the metal bottom. The remainder is thrown out, by quickly raising the end of the box, and then the process is repeated.

Whatever goes through the holes is washed down the inclined cloth-plane, which lies under — and drops into the bottom of the cradle at the very head. From this point it is washed, dashing from side to side, traversing the whole length of the cradle, the bottom of which inclines toward the foot about four and a half inches, tumbling and rolling and whirling over the cleats, and finally rushes out at the opening in the foot.

Some of the gold usually stays on the cloth plane, unless it is very tensely stretched on the frame — most of the remainder is found in the upper section of the cradle, and some reaches the space between the first and second cleats — seldom lower. When the half day's or day's work is done the cloth is cleaned off into a pan, and the earth and gold in the upper section, and between the first and second cleats of the lower, are put back into the box and run through again. What remains in the same sections is drawn off through holes in the bottom (which at other times are kept plugged) into the pan with what was taken from the cloth and "panned out," such is the term used. This is sometimes quite a tedious process, on account of the quantity of fine black sand, almost as heavy as gold, which is, I believe, usually found with it. If the gold is coarse, this difficulty is obviated. By this process most or all the gold is saved, except the very fine dust, which is probably at least one-half in weight of all that in California has ever seen the light by the operations of nature; and without doubt some of the gold of Feather River has washed as far as the Pacific, though most of it stops far short of there.

With a quicksilver machine, the fine dust may be collected. These are not at present used above Long's, on Feather River, and probably will seldom or never be used on its branches to any extent. Though all cradles here are constructed on the same principles, yet some of them would make an eastern pig squeal, being the exact counterpart of that long snouted gentlemanly (?) animal's trough, well gnawed, battered and split. Verily, the world has never before seen such specimens of mechanical handy-work as are here every day exhibited, not only in cradles, but in every department of wood work. Surely I would soon entrust my work to a Yankee with a hand axe, saw and jack knife, than leave it to the tender mercies of a Missourian, with the best "kit."

SATURDAY, MARCH 16. Frost, and a thin scale of ice on the water—of course a little cooler, or cold for these "diggins." Still, cold as it is, the door stands wide open, and no one thinks of shutting it. Not so a few miles above. A party coming over from the Youba on Tuesday last, lost their way and struck this Fork on the kanyon nearly fifteen miles above where they intended. In the valleys they found the snow six feet deep, and after wallowing through it all day, they found themselves supperless at night, and camped.

Starting early in the morning they followed the heights down on the south of the Fork, and came in a mile below us, about two p.m. Not all, however, for a man by the name of Nichols, from Rock Island, I think, who wished to travel slower, was left behind at his own request, and has not yet come in. He may have descended to the valley as soon as he came to the foot of the kanyon—otherwise he has perished. So much for the lack of a pocket compass.

17TH. Cold night, ice one half an inch thick this morning. Cloudless sky, cool all day out of the sun.

18TH. Cold night and some ice. Two or three showers today mixed rain and round snow. High wind, cool, chilly. Sunshine everything by turns and nothing long. A nice dish of weather, a perfect salmagundi.

19TH. Slightly cloudy, chilly with frost and thin ice. After nine a.m. warm and almost cloudless till three p.m. when a thin cloudy curtain over spread the sky, threatening rain and it became too chilly to go without a coat.

20TH. Cool morning. No frost. A few fluey clouds but clear, fine and warm in the middle of the day and cool in the evening.

21ST. Clear. Frost one half an inch thick. Pretty cool though not really uncomfortable in your shirt sleeves. Warm from nine a.m. to three p.m. Circle around the moon this evening.

FRIDAY, MARCH 22, 1850. Began to rain before day light. Morning barely cool. No rain after breakfast till eight p.m.

23RD. Rained some in the night. Warm as May this morning but cloudy and misty till three p.m. when we had occasional gleams of sunshine.

24TH SUNDAY. Cloudy and misty. Warm and rained some in course of the day.

25TH. Cloudy mists and warm and rained considerable in course of the day, but partially clear in the evening.

TUESDAY, MARCH 26. Clear, warm day. Flying clouds. Just comfortably cool to go about without a coat this morning, after which the heat of the sun poured down like the hot air from a furnace. If it is thus warm in March, what will July be? The Buckeyes, from the Ohio claim, half a mile above, have been down for a chat and a sing several times. This evening they called on me for a California song, which I promised them the next visit. If they get it, I will send it on to you.

WEDNESDAY, MARCH 27. The snow above must be melting rapidly, as the river has risen nearly two feet. Pleasant but too warm in the middle of the day. Up to yesterday the weather has been much like April in Northern Illinois, or perhaps more like a wet May. The wind blows in gusts both warm and cool this afternoon and reminds one of June and the excessive heat does not lessen the reminiscence.

THURSDAY, MARCH 28. Another hot day. Ohio boys down for a song this evening—which I send according to promise:

THE SONG OF GOLDEN TOIL

Oh, that is not the work for me,
That delves the crusty soil,
For pittance yielded grudgingly,
To trouble care and toil;
But let me dig, if dig I must,
Where the rough rocks rise soft and free,

All crevice-lined with yellow dust;
   Oh, that's the work for me,
   Oh, that's the work for me.

'Tis not the work for me to hoe
   The corn that towers so high
And stretching off in endless row,
   Corn mingles with the sky;
But give me where the tall green pine,
Waves stately o'er the narrow lea,
And whispers to the golden mine:
   Oh, that's the work for me,
   Oh, that's the work for me.

Oh, ask me not to plow and sow
   Upon the boundless plains
Where poisoned waters sluggish flow,
   And fevers course my veins;
But let me work the mountain side,
The mountain stream that pours so free
O'er glittering gold its crystal tide;
   Oh, that's the work for me,
   Oh, that's the work for me.

Oh, doom me not to slave and toil,
   Beneath a master's eye,
Stripp'd of my title to the soil,
   And robb'd of Liberty;
But let me dig the mountain land,
No tax, no tariff for the free,
With beef and bread and golden sand;
   Oh, that's the work for me,
   Oh, that's the work for me.

Nor yet is that the work for me,
   Which yields six bits a day,
To toil and want and misery,
   In promises to pay;
But let me pick and pry and pull
The soft bed rock, where I can see
An ounce on every shovel-full;
   Oh, that's the work for me,
   Oh, that's the work for me.

Mind, I do not endorse every word of the above—but at least it is a good enough song "till after election."

FRIDAY, MARCH 29. Our canoe went down the stream last night— perhaps a quarter of a mile. It took nearly all the forenoon to get it up again. The fall in that distance is about nine feet, and of course the current

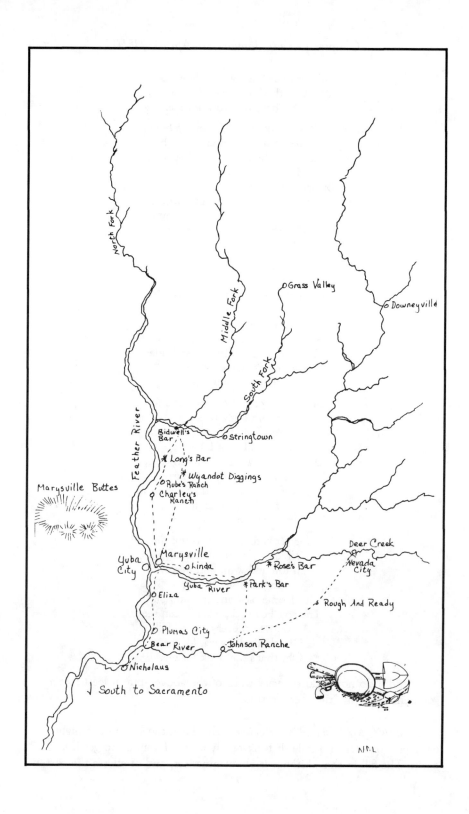

North Fork

Middle Fork

South Fork

o Grass Valley

o Downeyville

Feather River

Bidwell's
Bar

o Stringtown

*Long's Bar

*Wyandot Diggings

o Rube's Ranch

o Charley's
Ranch

Marysville Buttes

Deer Creek

Yuba
City

o Marysville

o Linda

*Rose's Bar

Nevada
City

Yuba River

*Park's Bar

o Eliza

s Rough And Ready

o Plumas City

Bear River

o Johnson Ranche

o Nicholaus

↓ South to Sacramento

N.M.L

is very strong. The river has risen something more than two feet in all, and still rises a little every day. The average depth of water on our claim, with a fall of two feet in thirty rods, is about seven feet, and the width thirty yards. There is evidence of its having been ten feet higher at some former period. It must have been seven or eight last winter. Heat as yesterday.

30TH. Cool again this morning and clear, but hot as June.

SUNDAY, MARCH 31. Cloudy this morning and cool. A sprinkle or two of rain in course of the day and some May showers crossed the valley above us in course of the day. Some sudden strong dashes of wind swept along and came down on our cabin this evening like eddying water.

The Buckeyes down again last evening. They sing several excellent songs in good style. Sharpe and C. Wisner also sing very well. This somewhat varies and gives zest to the monotony of cabin life – dig, eat and sleep. C. Wisner, Sharpe and the Elder attended meeting at Stony Point today – four miles up the river. Nichols preached, who, by the by, I at first took for a Methodist. He is a Baptist, as is also Smalley, a young man who preaches occasionally. So they have five preachers on one claim, in one company, at Stony Point. Verily, that ought to be the pattern company, and perhaps (?) it is.

But – that *but* is a forward fellow; always in somebody's way – I can say of our company of ten, that no one *smokes* – all faces are *smooth* once a week; the chewers of tobacco are – one, and if any one drinks he must do it so stealthily so not to be detected. I say nothing of swearing – for we are in the midst of reform; and Bob, (Texas Bob) [Horton] had to pay Sammy (Ball) four bits yesterday, on agreement, for saying _____ _____ no matter what; though after all it may be doubted whether it were swearing.

Four bits might be onerous in the States as an *oath forfeit*, here it is not thought of. It will only buy a mackerel, a pound of flour, or a quarter of a pound of butter; it takes two to sharpen one pick point. Only think, $2 for drawing and hardening the points of a pick. Yet honor is honor, I suppose, and Bob would like to keep his at par. Anyway, he is in a fix. He must stop swearing – or repudiate; for the fortune of an Astor would dwindle to a Bungtown copper* in the hands of Bob, at four bits an oath, unless he reforms. By our Constitution a man is expelled for gambling or drinking.

APRIL 1. Flying clouds and cool this morning and so continued all day.

*Bungtown Copper was a coin minted privately between the time of the American Revolution and the War of 1812. It was valued at less than a penny and was no longer in use after 1812 except as an expression denoting worthlessness.

Opposite: Map 4. California mining sites visited by Lord's party.

Just cool enough to work with comfort. This cloudy, just before dark. The river has raised only two feet in all and remains stationary. The snow is slowly melting in the mountains above.

TUESDAY, APRIL 2. Cloudy and cool this morning. I suppose that the temperature is much higher in Sacramento valley and that they have summer fifteen miles below, and perhaps ten. I learned that it has scarcely rained there at all since we left Long's, but the Sacramento is up again, and the whole valley will probably be under water again by the first of June. The rain and snow and cold seem to retreat through a well contested battle field to the heights of the Sierra Nevada, which they reach in July. There they maintain themselves against old Sol's fiercest attacks till October, and no sooner does he commence his southward retreat in sober earnest, than these persevering robbers sweep down the mountains slope into the plain below.

The South Fork, probably does not extend more than half way to the summit of the Great Sierra, and of course will run down much sooner than the other Forks, or the Youba, and yield us a sight of its golden bed. We are located on a bend of the river which has got the cognomen of golden. Our claim includes the bend, extending up the stream from its extreme point, 25 rods E.N.east, and down sixteen rods north north west. The whole bed of the river, at a medium stage of water, occupies about an acre.

Across the point of land projecting into the bend, we are digging a canal to take the water of the river through. It will be 25 rods long, besides the width of the river. The average depth is over twelve feet width at the top 28 feet, and at the bottom, seven to eight within the walls. Five feet at the upper end is granitic sandstone, at least half mica, which one man can pick down as fast as two can shovel out. The remaining twenty rods is sand and gravel filled with large and small boulders, seldom weighing more than 200 lbs. Many of them are worn almost as smooth as ice. This canal opens into and receives the water from one above, and that from a third, at the head of which is to be a dam.

The banks of our ditch, when completed, and it is nearly done, will be walled from four to nine feet high with the boulders, except where it is dug through the rock. When all this is finished, we have to conduct the water across the bed of the stream 100 feet to the head of the Louisiana race, and this we shall have to sink an average of three feet for twelve rods, through rock, most of it soft. Probably some of it will require blasting.

You will perceive that people who would get gold must not be idle. Without this last piece of work, we could not drain the bed of the river, and yet it will take a month to do it. The Louisianans ought to do it for their own good, but like slave-holders everywhere, they are idle, indolent; and honorable (?) as they are, like to avail themselves of the labors of others (unrequited.) They have two or three slaves with them now.

The second claim above us is owned by John Coburn, John W. Laird, and Jos. A. Farrington, of Lindon, Whiteside Co., Ill.; (if I mistake not) and Jno. McLeod, a Scotchman by parentage, though born in America. Gregg is the principal man in the claim above us. A Methodist minister by the name of Hobart belongs to the company. Each of them has a son, and there are three others whose names I have not learned. Cool and pleasant all day. The Elder has gone to Youba City after a beef. Farrington is sick of fever.

WEDNESDAY, APRIL 3. Ball sick this morning. Some of the men are out of sorts all the time. The climate is certainly unhealthy, decidedly so. Cramp is so common that a person can hardly hold his hand tightly closed for a moment and open it again, without a violent effort to overcome the spasm which is almost sure to follow a strong contraction of a muscle. Rheumatic pains are rife; scurvy as common as damaged flour, and diarrhea haunts the dwellers of this famous land, like the debts of a rejected applicant for the benefit of the Bankrupt law. And yet we seem to have pure air, soft crystal water, wholesome food, cooked well and regularly, and comfortable sleep. There have been a considerable number of deaths on the Fork since we came up, most of them, however, from scurvy, contracted before they came here. Weather much as yesterday.

THURSDAY, APRIL 4. Morning same as yesterday. Woodman and I went down to Long's to see Eno, of Fort Madison, Iowa, to whom I entrusted some money and business in Sacramento, more than a month ago. It seems that he went there, and then to San Francisco, where he was commissioned to get letters, and it is said did get some—but lost them. At Francisco he fell in with an old friend (?) who—but it is all as yet among the things unknown.

We do know, that he was a reformed drunkard, that he worked his way by some means to Youba City, minus $1,100 or $1,200, and was brought from there as he became drunk—a victim of the toper's hell, *delirium tremens.* We found him much reduced by that curse of the country, diarrhea. His life hangs on a thread. So much for liquor selling, and yet, temperance men (before they left the States) and church members have been, and are yet, engaged in it here.

Almost everybody drinks, and I verily believe that one-sixth of the whole male population will get drunk—dead, rolling down drunk. Some of the females certainly do drink more than occasionally, but I hardly dare risk a guess at the proportion. The moralocracy was on our side of the river at Long's, and yet we had three female tipplers out of less than twenty adults. The President of the Miner's Association, Price, was helped by our cabin on the Fork, the other day, so drunk that he went down every five rods, in spite of all that a man, hardly half as drunk as himself, could do. Some day, out of 100 persons who pass, twenty or thirty will go reeling. It is not uncommon for several hundred men to pass in a day, usually as many down as up. Eno was a Son of Temperance before he left home. He returned the money

I entrusted him with. How he managed to keep it when he lost so large a sum of his own, I cannot conceive.

How long will temperance men suffer these things, before they rush to the rescue and send swift destruction on all these hellish mantraps? Poor heartless fools, or hypocrites, are temperance men, or they would not long endure evils which might so easily be put down. The whole accursed system is now sustained—balanced by them, and will be until they open their eyes, and become honest and consistent, and value a principle higher than the good will of a poisoner, or rate the commands of God above the suggestions of the devil. These are grievous charges, but are quite as easily sustained as made. If anyone doubts, I am always ready for the proof, and with it.*

It seems like June, here at Long's; the nights are warm, and the white oak is fully leaved out. Coming down we saw abundance of most beautiful flowers, and some of the grass has already gone to seed, at a height of eighteen or twenty inches. The slope toward the Youba is completely covered with vegetation, to the very top of the divide.

The prospect from the mountain ridges is now magnificent, and but for the curse of deluge and drought, the country might be very habitable.

FRIDAY, APRIL 5. Returned to our mountain home. The distance from Long's is about sixteen miles, and yet there is a remarkable difference in the temperature.

It was cloudy in the morning but there had been no rain when we left at one p.m. Three or four miles up from Long's a few drops of rain spitted down upon us and the process was repeated occasionally till we struck the South Fork when it set in to rain with some thunder and is pouring down now at bed time.

APRIL 6TH. Rained the live long night—poured. The night is cool—25 miles above us they report snug winter weather and six to eight feet of snow. Here the Buckeye and black Raspberry are fully leaved out, and the buds of the white oak are ready to burst. Showers and sunshine all day. I recollect being troubled by a few vagabond musquitoes when at Long's and kept awake by a concert of rascally frogs. It is cool here.

7TH. Rained all night again and is raining this morning. Frequent and copious showers all day. Partially clear this evening. River rising.

8TH. Rained several times in the night. Cleared up just after sun rise this morning. Fine day. Cool and some wind.

*Dr. Lord's puritanism was supported by the Sacramento Daily Union on August 18, 1855 in an article about the Recorder's Court: "An attentive perusal of the cases of this Court will divulge the facts that nine-tenths of the crime committed is founded on rum. An armed inebriate is a dangerous concoction."

TUESDAY, APRIL 9. Cool night. Clear, fine, warm day. River falling.
A large number of armed men went up today to shoot the Diggers, who, it
is said, have been killing a few of the miners between this and the Youba.
These mountaineers are quite different from the Diggers of the valley,
though they have nearly the same physical conformation, and live in almost
the same manner. They are more daring, ferocious and deceitful. Their
word seems to pass for nothing. They sometimes make descents and carry
off the women of the lower Diggers. Since we have been here the latter have
usually recovered them, with usury; being furnished with a few guns and
pistols by the emigrants.

The other day they came up and gave the mountaineers on the Middle
Fork a thrashing; carrying off some of their women, and killing quite a
number of the men. Sometime since, they recovered some of their women
from the North Fork Indians, merely by a strong display of pistols.

APRIL 10. Weather as yesterday. Cannot finish our canal on account of
the water.

APRIL 11. Weather same.

FRIDAY, APRIL 12. Weather same. Eight of us got out $80 today. Small
business—hardly pays.

SATURDAY, APRIL 13. Weather same except a little hotter in the middle of the day. Took out $35 and the diggins ran into loose sand, which
would not sustain the gold. The men who went to chastise the Indians for
the depredations, have returned, and report two killed, and two prisoners,
who escaped from their guards in the night. Several villages were burned or
destroyed; and now we learn that the murdered (?) men left their clothes
and blankets at their overnight camp to prospect on a ravine some distance,
and before they returned the Indians cabbaged their traps. Not finding them
on their return, the men passed over to the Youba, where they now are in
health and safety, digging gold, while the Indians have been hunted like
wild beasts to avenge their supposed demise, their property destroyed and
two, perhaps two who have never offended—never been guilty of any overt
act, have paid the fearful penalty which fallible human (in)justice so frequently exacts from its victims.

Nor is there so material a difference as some imagine, when it is legally
administered. There the innocent are often punished, and the guilty much
oftener escape. The better way is, when the masses throw themselves on the
overwhelming flood of evils and wrongs which the law is powerless to
redress, for the wise and good to plunge in with the rest and guide the
chaotic, aimless, tumbling forces safely to the desired end, rather than timidly
shrink back from the raging tide, for fear of being implicated in its acts of

violence. He who guides the whirlwind and directs the storm—who taught a Franklin to paralyze the strong arm of the whelming thunder cloud, has given his image and representative on earth power over his fellows, and though he may not always stay the course of popular violence and fury, he may so guide and direct, as that it shall not result in positive evil.

Chapter Twelve

April 14–May 10, 1850:
High Water Contemplations

◆——◆——◆

SUNDAY, APRIL 14. Beautiful day. The earth is literally covered with flowers. The trees are full leaved, and the running and creeping vines have suddenly stretched their threads to yards. The growth of vegetation here is inconceivably rapid. The most barren places are almost in a night covered with green grass and beautiful flowers.

This is a wild land and no doubt if it was good for anything it might be good for some thing.

Nichols preached here today. But such abominable whiskers. He has had sense enough or some equivalent to shave his upper lip and around his mouth, which indicate progress and possibly, if the sequence is carried down, he may some day exhibit a respectable phiz. At present it is only a matter of private speculation and public conjecture as to when the race of omnivorous goats shall become extinct.

A few long, thin, veil-like clouds thrust themselves between us and the deep blue vault, ominous, no doubt, of a storm. The river rises every night and falls again in the day time; which indicates that the snow is melting high up the stream, as it takes from ten to twelve hours to reach here after it begins to melt in the forenoon.

Cool night as usual, but no rain. Quite warm in the middle of the day.

MONDAY, APRIL 15. Was in at Coburn's this evening, who is in high glee at the thought of his excellent cookery; and really he has just taken out a superb loaf of bread. (He wishes you to send the W.C. to Mrs. John Coburn, Linden, Whiteside Co., Ill. Send also to Frances Laird, Crandall's

233

Ferry, Dance Co. and send his there. Could get subscriptions here if I could
ever get the paper but we can hardly get our letters and I have not yet got
one from home.)

By the by, we don't eat common doings, altogether, in these diggins. We
have nice raised bread, excellent beef and pork, flour, pies and cakes and
now we have butter. We have likewise, the other *et ceteras* (to wit: dried
apples, peaches, and cherries) unless potatoes are therein included; and we
pay for them, you may be quite sure. Butter 15 shillings, apples eight shillings, peaches ten shillings per pound. Flour is lower, only 37½ cents a
pound. The first prices are remunerating to the trader, the latter entirely
ruinous.

WEDNESDAY, APRIL 17. Weather as yesterday except it was quite cool
about six p.m. and had a slight shower. This evening Bob and J. Wisner got
into a dispute over a chequerboard, when Bob split it and threw it into the
fire. This led to a quarrel, and Wisner calling him a thief. Bob swore he
would stab him with a large pocket knife he had in his hand (it seems that
he was whittling) unless he took it back; which he did, under protest, however, like a member of Congress when he votes against his—stomach. I was
about to say, or rather write, conscience; but we ought to be careful not to
speak of things which are not. There is a bull, an Irish one, though I hope
nobody will see it—and there goes another. Wisner now came in for me to
go into their cabin and settle the matter.

So it is, the world over. One half the humans keep the other half on
the "qui vive," either as arbiters, jurors or witnesses, officers of court, or
judges; and who is the wiser or better? Certainly not the fools who pay the
lawyers for helping them carry their specie through the world.

This resorting to violence for a *"spoken word,"* though advocated as prac-
tised by the mass, and many who profess better things, is most unjustifiable.
To strike a man for calling you a liar, is extremely absurd and ridiculous. It
is at least one step from the sublime. To say nothing of the more than
doubtful morality, one stands a fair chance of peeling his knuckles, sprain-
ing a finger, or dislocating a thumb, of getting his clothes torn, his body
bruised, his nose bloody, or his head broke,—through the perverse obstinate
and wicked spirit of retaliation by which some men are actuated and moved,
being, perhaps, as the indictments have it, instigated by the devil.

And then the figure a good Christian man cuts, beating God's image,
Cain-like, as though he was mauling out rails, or threshing wheat, or killing
snakes; and then such a wheezing, and puffing,—such a tugging, and hug-
ging so unlovingly, and such a do-like biting, and scratching and tearing,—
oh, it is fun for devils—a perfect feast.

It shakes off the dust and cleans off the scales with which the laws of
God, vulgarly called superstitions, have encrusted their most puissant
honor; and leaves it so bright and clean that they can at once recognize

their friends. It is a matter of comfort that there is some such excellent and commendable way to clean this troublesome honor; for it is but a dirty, scurvily conditioned thing, at the best—always getting tarnished, or rusty, or out of sorts in some way, requiring fists and guns, swords and pistols, daggers and knives, ropes and whips, to keep all square and tidy; and yet it claims to be the "sine qua non," the everything, for poor simple man, "creation's lord," and—fool.

Maybe it is; but in the material world, I see the copper become foul and the polished steel rust, while the gold shines out steadily from its muddy bed, and the diamond sparkles, though covered with filth. The truth is, if you tell your neighbor a lie, he has a most undoubted right to tell you of it; and it is not for you to prescribe the language in which he may choose to convey the discovery. He only tells you what is true, and you have no right to resent it. If he says "you lie," and you lie not,—you are innocent—unless you get angry and sin, or strike and commit a crime. Hard words break no bones; and he who, in trying to avenge mere empty sounds, gets soundly thrashed, deserves little sympathy.

THURSDAY, APRIL 18, Cooler last night than usual. No showers today. Rain falling. Received two letters from home. I cannot conceive why I did not get them sooner, as they date back to September and October and Eld. Wisner has letters of the same date, which he got in Sacramento City on the 25th of December. All were mailed at the same office, and directed to the same office.

19TH. Rained in the night. Cloudy and cool this morning. The first thing I heard in awaking was a robin. He seemed to enjoy himself wonderfully and sang in his highest key. Except this cosmopolite the feathered race here have as yet nothing to boast of. Was showery and quite cool till five p.m. and then rained till dark when it cleared partially and was entirely clear at bed time.

20TH. Quite cool. Cloudy and foggy this morning, but the clouds are broken and scudding towards the east. Pleasant and warm day.

SUNDAY, APRIL 21. Frost this morning and thin ice in the wash basin. Rain falling. Pleasant but quite cool all day, out of the sun. Eld. Whitcombe preached. Mr. [Elder Israel] Washburn, a Methodist minister, from Massachusetts, came down with him. He is located two and a half miles above.

APRIL 22ND. Clear, fair, cool morning. Warm day. Finished the wall in the race.

TUESDAY, APRIL 23. Cool night, warm and pleasant day. The boys got some milk this evening for stopping a couple of cows and a steer, which were following a drove of fat cattle up the river. The drovers told them to milk the cows, to pay themselves for the trouble of turning them back. This is the first milk we have had since our cows dried up on the road. It is just one year now since I left home. A lost year and one that will never return. Strange that we cannot believe without personal experience. Every pig must needs burn his nose, before he will be convinced that the swill is hot.

24TH. Night warmer and days same only warmer. Morse passed up today in health.

25TH. Same as yesterday only warmer. A few thin clouds floated along just before sunrise. The river rises by night and falls by day. Wind from the east in the night like a warm S. wind at home.

26TH. Warm and pleasant with an occasional slice of fleecy clouds. At noon several strong gusts of wind. Finished our work on the west side of the river today.

27TH. Rather cool this morning but soon warm enough. The musquitoes are becoming rather troublesome. They are quite small and mottled with black and very voracious and venomous.

SUNDAY, APRIL 28. Mr. Washburn was to have preached here today, but did not come, and but few attended. There seems to be little disposition to maintain religious worship here. The thoughts of the people are entirely pre-occupied with drinking, gambling, or getting gold out of the earth.

The finding of gold is the common topic of conversation, at all times, on all occasions, under all circumstances, and among all classes and professions, with very few exceptions in any of these items. The standard of morals is a sliding scale, without a thumb-screw worn so smooth that it stands no where except at the very bottom; and as every body knows where it is, nobody, or at least, few, take the trouble of looking to it.

With all this latitude, there is still a specious appearance of honesty, and a semblance of good faith, at least, in all business transactions, which prevents violence and outrage. I suppose that a common interest here answers to the legal restrains which the laws of the States impose on their citizens. We have here, at least, much less difficulty in business, every way, than there. If one refuses to pay, another might refuse to pay him, and thus the ball would rebound against his own head. I am inclined to think that, as a rule, all pay as soon as possible. As for "pure religion and undefiled," it is an article in small demand, seldom called for, and not often found. The Devil will make a speculation out of this California business, whatever the South may lose.

A worthy Dr. two miles below, keeps a trading post, sells whiskey, etc. through the week, drinks brandy freely, some say, and PREACHES on the Sabbath. Who cares? Not the Devil, you may be sure. I know of no trader out of Sacramento City in the whole of California who does not retail strong drink, and drink too. And why not? Brandy is nearly or quite as cheap at the city as at Chicago; and it retails for at least 25 cents a drink, and for the most part 50 cts. And then, when it reaches here, Feather River water is pure, soft, cool, handy and plenty, and mixes readily with brandy in the proportion of two to one—leaving quite a profit. I have heard that the highest proportion in which it can be mixed here is three to one. This I can hardly credit; for it mixes, if my memory serves, in almost any proportions in the States; and some of the Chicago combinations were once said to be as strong as six of water to one of *pure spirit*. Powerful weak must such liquors be, and yet strong enough, in all conscience, considering the size of the dose, and that it is mostly used as a medicine.

Yesterday, I saw at Dr. Powell's a very respectable looking loafer, probably quite a decent man before he left home, taking a common sized tumbler more than half full of brandy at a single dose, for an inveterate diarrhea. A severe case, no doubt—as he took a like dose in the morning, by the same token, that I saw him pay a dollar for the two when he took the last. And an inveterate case, by the by, as I have learned that he takes two doses every day, to say nothing of odds and ends, and gets worse constantly. Poor man! It (the diarrhea?) will be the death of him yet. Only think; $365.25 and a fraction, for liquor in one year.

This morning I walked up to the top of the mountain south east of us. It is nearly four miles and quite steep most of the way; at least one-fourth on an angle of 35 degrees, and some of it much steeper. From the summit I could see that immense bodies of snow still lie at the head of this fork, and on the Middle and the Youba, from twelve to sixteen miles distant. Judging from the form of the surface, the height of the mountains, etc. I should estimate the depth of the snow yet at from five to one hundred feet. In many places deep ravines seem completely filled, the tops of the pines only appearing above the snow. In others, large dense forests seem half buried. In others the red wood bushes had only the tops out.

The view was a fine one, with an excellent glass, on a field of pure snow. The limbs of some of the oaks were distinctly visible. I think that one can see distant objects much more clearly here than in Illinois. A person who has been up on the Youba, stated to me the other day, that the river ran through or beneath enormous beds of snow, and that he crossed several times where its muffled roar was so far beneath as to be scarcely heard. I thought at the time that it might be possible; now I do not question it, although I am aware that the Youba is a large stream, perhaps six times as large as this fork.

MONDAY, APRIL 29—River rising slowly. We are out of work, and can do nothing until it falls. It is somewhat strange that the fish do not come up. I had been informed, before leaving home that the streams were literally crowded, choked with fish; and here we are beside one of the most beautiful the world can boast and it is rare that we get a sight, much less a touch of one. I have seen a dozen small ones today; the largest a foot long. It may not be time yet. We shall see. Perhaps they have a presentment of the fate that awaits them and linger below for few or none that come up will be permitted to return.* The water is not surer of reaching the ocean than these unfortunates the stomachs of the miners if they are upward bound. Many an eye has become weary and dim with watching and, unsated from walking hunger, cried aloud at their tardiness. Still they come not.

True that they say that fish two feet long are caught above us. But what of that, it is ever thus. We neither get them nor ever see them and I much doubt if anybody does. Believe common report here and you are in for it. Everybody has fish except just around you. Plenty of gold everywhere except just where you are. Ants were never more busy in following instructions than the miners in following flying bullion. Both go criss cross here and there every way night and day. But the ants are seldom hum-bugged, miners seldom otherwise. Their movements remind one of a swarm of bees trying to settle after losing their queen.

TUESDAY, APRIL 30. Warm and pleasant. A few light fleecy clouds in the afternoon. I have been reading today, the speeches of Seward, Webster and Calhoun, on the California and slavery question. I am on the whole pleased with the first, and wish I had not read the others. I have made up my mind to rest a while; after years of political turmoil and moral strife; but the gross, glaring, rank inconsistencies, follies, and errors of the speeches of these two latter great *little* men, have so disturbed the equipoise of my mind, as to assimilate it nearly to the present condition of the Union; i.e., it seeks an "equilibrium," by removing the "disturbing forces." So Webster would not be foolish enough to vote for the Wilmot Proviso, *because the law of God makes it unnecessary,* and Calhoun asks if he will be *so kind as to remove the impediments* in the way of introducing slave chattels into New Mexico. Strange that slave-holders should wish to take their property where God will not have it, anyhow.

Why, this is the climax of mental imbecility—more puerile than a running trade with green plums and cracked marbles between two school boys.

---

*Or perhaps the rivers had been dammed, diverted and disrupted so thoroughly by miners that the fish found it impossible to survive, much less travel and spawn.

All the South wants, is to be let alone, and permitted to take property (slaves) into the new territories; and then they (the owners) will get a controlling influence in forming a constitution for a State, and slavery as a matter of course is incorporated in it, and then Mr. Clay would vote for it and Mr. Webster would certainly not refuse, and under certain very peculiar circumstances we may fear that Seward himself could follow suit. It is all stuff to talk about organic laws excluding slavery. Slave labor may be made as profitable here, as any where on the globe; and if I were *devil* enough to own, and were permitted to work 100 negroes, I could make their labor nett me $400,000 by the first day of November next.

There are negroes here now laboring for their liberty, having contracted to give what they can earn in one, two or three years, or for a specified sum. One on the Louisiana claim is to pay $10,000 for himself, wife and child; and yet he is a free man now, and knows it. His wife, like the wives of others, is held as a pledge of good faith. Had California been what John C. Calhoun would wish—had all impediments been removed, and the South permitted to occupy it as slave territory—be assured that slavery would have been a fundamental principle in the new Constitution, the free man of California would still be a slave, the gold of the free would have passed into the coffers of Southern tyrants, and free labor would have been excluded from half the mining districts.

No! No! Let there be no slavery here. Let Congress proclaim and send it to the world on the four winds, that the slave whose feet but touch the soil of its territories, stands thenceforth and forever a free man. Let justice be done, Union or no Union; and if fanaticism or dotage shall raise the cry that the cords are snapping, remember and rejoice that they are only the cords which bind the slave – the crack of whose parting strands should be music to the ear and heart of every honest man—every lover of his country, of his kind, and of freedom, and the world over.

Let the explosive force be applied again and again, until every cord is broken; and if the fabric shall be found rotten, and unable to sustain itself, let it fall, and another be reared in its stead. I for one, do not wish to live in a house that evermore threatens to tumble on my head; and when (if ever) reason shall desert us, may God give us at least the instinct of rats, and strength and grace to escape before the falling fragments block our way. To read the speeches in Congress, one would almost think their utterers esteemed themselves censors, at least, in the religious, and arbiters or sovereigns in the political world.

They may be so, while the people sleep. But will they always sleep? After all, they are men, mere men, hardly that—and when I see that a tornado only prostrates and defaces, and that an earthquake only cracks the earth or topples over a few buildings, I seem to feel that there is but little danger after all from the explosive tendencies of these moving, breathing torpedoes, unless the people should change to fulminating powder, Greek fire, gun cotton, or percussion caps. Until they are thus metamorphosed, the Union is safe from aught that these two and sixpenny earthquakes can effect, Mr. Calhoun's opinion to the contrary notwithstanding.

If he would only open his eyes, he would see that neither the action of government, nor northern fanatics, but his own cherished domestic institution is the cause, and, with the exception of its own proud, haughty indolence, the sole cause of all the evils and grievances complained of by the South.

For Calhoun, an ingenious—a very ingenious man, might, by a remote possibility, find or invent an excuse. But who can say as much for Daniel Webster? Oh, Daniel! Daniel!! "How are the mighty fallen?" Everyone but yourself, and that profane reprobate, James Gordon Bennett, can see the hand writing on the wall, which he that runs may read, "The days of thy political career are numbered, and the course of thy vaulting ambition finished: thy principles and thine intellect are weighed in the balances and found wanting: thine influence is divided and given to that illustrious "five," Bell, Cass, Calhoun, Clay and the Devil, and the Lord have mercy on thy soul."

TUESDAY, APRIL 30. As to the fate of our "Constitution," we are quite indifferent. I speak only of this section, having heard nothing from the cities, or the other mining districts. Very little is said about the action of Congress on the subject, and very little interest is manifested, above the passing inquiry, "Is California yet admitted into the Union?" If she is not; we are content. We have all the elements of self-government, and are ready and willing to use them to the fullest extent, even to the *entire exclusion of slavery.*"

If I do not greatly err, the popular vote, all polled, would stand, at least, as 300 to one against it. I have yet to see the first man here who would vote for it, when sober. If the States do not want us, we can take very good care of ourselves; and did the members of Congress know exactly the state of feeling which I believe to be general here, there never would have been five minutes talk on the matter in either House. Why, your Congressman is an inferior being; a mere common hireling, who gets only eight dollars a day, and boards himself. Nobody here will hire for that, unless he is boarded; and then he must be hard up.

If my vote could have determined the matter, California would never have applied for admission; and my opinion is, if she is rejected, it will be the last opportunity that Congress will have to reenact the folly. California, whether worth much or little, once lost, is lost forever. The people feel their own importance too much to be humbugged and a trip across the plains is a wonderful eye-opener. The new comers, too, are wonderfully apt in catching the tone and adopting the views of the old, while the circumstances which surround them, and even the face of the country, seem to stamp a common political character on all, and almost obliterate the faint impressions of the past.

The great, moving, impelling power here is money. Everything is estimated by dollars and cents, and to get an argument here, you must show the cash, and that must be paid in advance. Where potatoes are six "bits" a pound, a labor from ten to twenty dollars a day, with $100 "in prospect," it will be difficult persuading men to spend their time in electing officers and agents on the forlorn hope of some time or other being admitted into the Union.

Speaking of wages, I do not think that the miners are making an average of even five dollars a day, for at least half of them are lying idle, waiting the movement of the waters. They would sooner lie at ease than work under pay. Those who labor have various success. Sometimes, after hours or a whole day of toil, they can hardly make a show. Perhaps they have one, two, or three dollars; often they get ten or twenty; sometimes much more. A Mr. Collett, one and a half miles above us, took $900 last week out of a surface of less than the fourth of a square rod; and a man who worked with him part of the time, had for his share $500, making $1,400 in all. Last Monday they got out $300. If you work a week faithfully in one place, almost anywhere, if there is any gold, you may be sure of from five to twenty dollars a day, and may by chance make as many fives or tens. It all depends on whether or not you dig where it is.

WEDNESDAY, MAY 1. In the forenoon four of us took $21 out of a small place just below. Worked a little this afternoon and abandoned it. It has once been dug over.

THURSDAY, MAY 2. Petitions were in circulation yesterday, and again today, to exclude foreigners from the mines, and a meeting is called at Stoney Point on the 11th inst. I shall be there, and you shall hear the result.

MAY 3RD. Weather continues the same. Light fleecy clouds in the afternoon.

4TH. Cool nights—warmer today. Ben Wilson came up last night. Has worked out his claim below and got something over $600. Musquitoes are quite troublesome.

SUNDAY, MAY 5. Weather same, etc. River gradually rising. A Judge Mayfield, from Missouri, preached two miles below today.

MONDAY, MAY 6. Almost every plant is in flower; wild peas, raspberries and all. If the crop of wild peas is as large as the flowers promise, we shall have a surplus for exportation. A passerby today killed a rattlesnake in the path between our two cabins. He had twelve rattles, and was about the size of one of your prairie snakes of the same age.

7TH. Weather cooling. River still rising. Dandy this evening.

WEDNESDAY, MAY 8. Cooler with flying clouds and some wind. River at a stand, etc. A mule, packed with two small bales of cotton cloth, and a tin can of molasses, tumbled from the path which ascends the mountain spur, just west of us, and rolling over and over, a sheer descent of ninety feet, almost perpendicular, finally lodged among the rocks on the river's brink. As soon as he was released from the pack, he got up and began to browse the leaves about, as unconcerned as if nothing had happened. Indeed, except a scratch or two, and a thorough daubing with the molasses, he seemed to have escaped scot free.

9TH, MONDAY. Worked at the road today and improved the track so much that there is little danger of another fall. If all the miners would turn out they might in two days make a good road up the river.

FRIDAY, MAY 10. Morning like yesterday, almost cold enough for a frost. Thin clouds, etc. I have noticed several "bits" of backbone and ribs of pork lying about lately; and on the hint, I would suggest to some of your packers, that next fall they remove one source of considerable loss to the miners. From fifteen to twenty per cent of the pork brought here is bone. A barrel of pork is here always freighted at 300 pounds, unless you insist on having it weighed, when it usually overruns. Now 35 or forty pounds of this is bone, and lost. Of the first cost, we do not complain, but the transportation from Sacramento to this point is never less than 35 cents per pound, which, when you include twenty per cent of the barrel and brine, amounts to the nice little nett loss of $20 on a single barrel of pork. If the pork was put up and warranted, and the barrels branded, "WITHOUT BONE," no other pork would sell in a market while any of that remained. It is now packed on mules as soon as it reaches the mines, at least wagons penetrate, but a short distance into the mining district and when the mules can get no farther, it is transferred to the backs of men or Indians. The truth is, pork bones are utterly worthless here, and should be lain in quarantine at the bay, or sent back. Our dogs won't eat them. Warm day.

Chapter Thirteen

May 11–June 9, 1850:
Mining and Meetings

———◆———◆———◆———

SATURDAY, MAY 11. Went up to Stoney Point to attend the anti-
democratic meeting. We were almost the first upon the ground. In a few
minutes after our arrival there was a "monte" table, and a game of A.B.C.
in operation; but although every effort, even to the meanness of personal
entreaty, was used to entice men into it, only two or three could be induced
to play for the first hour or two. Stoney Point is a rough place, with a steep
sloping bank to the river's edge. A narrow sloping table land 150 feet above
the river supports a couple of buildings, one of them 55 feet long; the middle third occupied as a grocery. The river is crooked and rapid and no
doubt rich in gold.

The meeting was called to order between ten and eleven a.m., and
organized with Mr. Nichols in the Chair, and I.S.P. Lord, Sec'y. There were
only seventy or eighty persons present. A Committee of Business was
appointed and went out. There seems to be little feeling on the subject; at
least, little or none is yet manifested. I much fear that the foreigners will
thrust themselves forward, and disgust even their friends by too much noise
and bluster. Still, I hope for the best. If they only keep quiet, I think there
will be little or no difficulty in maintaining the democratic doctrine of
perfect equality, and giving the whole subject the "go-by."

It is strange that Americans are not willing to give foreigners an equal
chance, when there is so much labor required to secure the uncertain gains
which fall to the lot of the laborer here. One would be led to think, by the
talk of some, that gold can be picked up anywhere without trouble, and
belongs to themselves exclusively; that they had dropped or deposited it to

be reclaimed when they deemed most convenient. I, for one, contend that they have the same right to dig for gold here as in the older States for iron, or wheat, or potatoes. There seems to be no manner of difference. It requires hard delving in the soil to get out either, and whoever complains that an alien raises too much grain, or furnishes too much iron? The General Government has always encouraged men of every country, and all classes, to settle on and extract the products from the soil. In its very incipiency, it charges the King of England with "endeavoring to prevent the population of the States, by obstructing the laws for the naturalization of foreigners, refusing to encourage their migration hither, and raising the condition of new appropriations of land."

If these were grievances then, they are no less so now. If they violated the rights of men then, (and there can be no other political grievances than those resulting from violated human rights), they certainly do so now. All fundamental principles, or truths, remain ever the same. They are incapable of change; and The Declaration of Independence will be as true, when the last trumpet shall call its signers to their final account, as when with the sword of a powerful monarch's vengeance hanging over their devoted heads, they boldly and unflinchingly set their names to it in the Halls of the "city of Brotherly Love."

Stony Point
May 11, 1850

Pursuant to previous notice the miners of the South Fork of Feather River met at S. Point at the above date to take into consideration the rights of foreigners to work in the mines of California. Mr. Nichols was appointed chairman and I.S.P. Lord Secretary. The Chairman stated the object, moved by Mr. Whitcomb, that a committee of five be appointed to draft resolution to give expression to the sense of this meeting and for their further action.

Committee:

Carried—Mr. Taylor, Chairman, Committee
            Mr. Temple, Mr. Woodman, Mr. Lewis, Mr. Whitcomb

Comm. returned and reported between 2 and 3 o'clock

Chairman read report—moved to accept report of Committee: carried.

Moved to be read seriatim for action of the meeting: carried.

First Resolution: moved to adopt. Discussion, amended of inserting "according to laws of nations."

Second Resolution: carried with little debate on a call for the previous question.

The Third Resolution was debated a long time. The Fourth
and Fifth were introduced as explaining and qualifying the
Third, when a motion was made by I.S.P. Lord to amend by
striking out of the report all after the word Resolution in the
Third and substituting: "That in our opinion we have no power
nor jurisdiction in the premises and that we have no more to do
with it," which was carried—though the president seemed to
think that there was a majority of American citizens against it.

The Committee came in between two and three p.m. and reported the
following resolutions:

1. Resolved, That in the opinion of this meeting, American
citizens have (by the laws of nations) the exclusive right to the
public domain.
2. Resolved, That we the citizens of the United States,
residing on the South Fork of Feather River, in the absence of
any law or act of Congress, will endeavor to carry out what we
understand to be the views of the General Government, in
regard to aliens holding or claiming any portion of the mines on
said river.
3. Resolved, therefore, that said aliens shall be prohibited
from and after this date, claiming or holding any portion of the
mining district on said river.
4. Resolved, That all aliens who shall declare their intention
of becoming citizens of the United States, according to the laws
in such cases made and provided, shall enjoy all the rights of
citizens of the United States in these mines.
5. Resolved, That a Committee of three persons be appointed
in each of the districts whose duty it shall be to examine the
papers of such persons, and give permission to all such as shall
produce legal papers, or satisfactory evidence of citizenship,
within fifteen days from the date hereof, to own and work said
mine.

James H. Taylor, Ch'n

You will readily see that the last two resolutions are confused, and con-
flict with each other.

The first resolution was discussed very irregularly for some time, when I
offered that portion of it included in brackets as an amendment, and after
some farther discussion it carried; and the main question on the amended
resolution was then put, and the resolution adopted.

The second resolution was choked down with the previous question,
after a very few remarks from two or three—the opposition caring little
about it any way, as it was left open for every person to understand for

himself what action Congress had taken on the subject. I explained that as I considered that the General Government had taken no action whatever in the premises, although the subject had been often pressed upon their attention, they did not intend to meddle with it or allow anybody else to, and thus to carry out the views of Congress, we should let aliens alone.

The third resolution drew out an animated debate. Pending the discussion, I move, that all the report after the word "Resolved," in the third, be struck out, and the following inserted.

"That this meeting are of the opinion that they have no jurisdiction in the matter, or power to act in the premises; and deem it advisable to dismiss the subject, and dissolve the meeting without further discussion," and called for a division. The Chairman, on the division, acknowledged a majority for the motion, but complained that it was much increased by, if not made up of aliens. I believe that there were but five aliens at the meeting.

The Chairman made a bitter, virulent speech, chiefly directed against the John Bulls as he very classically termed them. The attack was direct, personal and unmanly, yet they bore it with great good humor, for those that win may laugh. I must say, that the foreigners evinced a degree of discretion worthy of all praise. They took everything pleasantly, and left their defense to their friends, or the friends of human rights; and their confidence was not misplaced, nor were their interests compromised, or their trusts betrayed.

I see that the battles of the weak are to be fought over in every land, where the son of freedom can find room to set his foot. The strong are always, as yet, oppressors. It is more for want of knowledge, however, than anything else. Did the mass really understand how much they endanger their own rights, when they aid the designing to usurp the rights of others, the reign of tyranny would soon close.

Could they see that the law for which this year they voted—to make the passing of a one dollar bank note a crime—is only a precedent which will next year be seized upon to disfranchise one class of citizens, and another class the next, and thus on and ever, until the power of the State shall be vested in the "upper ten thousand," as in South Carolina, or sink to the despotism of the "Autocrat," they would be more jealous, and resist to the death the first and very least invasion of human rights.

"Eternal vigilance is the price of Liberty." Caesar in crossing the Rubicon did not subvert the liberty of Rome. "Troja fuit." It was among the things that had been. The prevalence of slavery, the corruption and wickedness of the people, the ambition, avarice and duplicity of the public officers, had left nothing to liberty but the name: and the now slavish mass was prepared to hail, as master, the first man who had energy enough to protect their property and persons.

Notice was given for another meeting at Stringtown in two weeks. Perhaps they expect, by changing the ground, to be able to fight on more equal terms. We shall see.

Lith. & Pub.ᵈ by Britton & Rey S.F.

Prospecting on the Feather River (Bancroft Library, University of California at Berkeley).

TUESDAY, MAY 14. The Elder, C. Wisner, Woodman and I, took $103 out of the Louisiana Bar, or rather bank (of the river). This is the best day's work that any of our company have ever made on this Fork. If the water was down, it could be done any day.

WEDNESDAY, MAY 15. We four took out $93 today. Ball, J. Wisner and Murrell got $65 in a ravine below. It is not often we make such a raise.

Each man has what he can make, as we cannot work on the claim till the water falls.

THURSDAY, MAY 16. We worked in the forenoon on the Louisiana Bar, and in the afternoon on the ravine where they took out $65 yesterday. They got less than $10, and we something over $14, though, for that matter, we did not work very hard. One man across the ravine took out $187. The average here today is much less than $5, and it is considered rather poor diggins, as most are leaving. The gold is found on a narrow sloping plateau, from twenty to forty feet above the brook, whose banks are nearly perpendicular. They dig along the edge of the bluff, or bank, on each side of the stream, where the bed rock inclines back toward the mountain and from the brook. If the bed rock slants toward the stream the gold slides off. If the other way much of it is caught. The weather is as hot as hottest June, and the musquitoes very troublesome. River still rising.

FRIDAY, MAY 17. Very warm and light fleecy clouds have hung lazily about all day. The growth of vegetables is astonishingly rapid. Spots which appeared only as bare sand a week or two ago, are now covered with plants in full bloom. Some of the shrubs will send a shoot from six to twelve inches in 24 hours. Hill sides which were so barren as to have the appearance of clean sand stone, have now a luxuriant vegetation, and furnish abundant food for animals.

SUNDAY, MAY 18. Cloudy and cooler this morning. The housefly is a cosmopolite. I expected to get rid of them in the mountains, yet find them as numerous as in the States, and far more vivacious and troublesome. They fairly torment one whenever he sits still, either in or near the house.

SUNDAY, MAY 19. Thin fleecy clouds lying about this morning and a trifle cooler. More cloudy this afternoon. Heard from the other individuals of the Batavia Company. All alive but Van Wormer, who was killed on the Sacramento by a grizzly bear. Mr. Whitcombe came down to preach today, but nobody came to meeting. Elder Wisner preaches above. River falling.

MONDAY, MAY 20. Hazy and river falling. Cool Night. The rapidity and luxuriance of vegetative life here is only equalled by its variety and protean changes. In walking two miles, fifty different varieties of beautiful flowers may be collected within a rod of the path, and yet a great part of the whole generation will be swept away within five or six days, to make room for another, still more beautiful, if possible, to vanish and be replaced in its turn. Some varieties bloom on from week to week, the latest being the brightest, the colors most vivid, the growth most luxuriant; and yet the soil is almost as clean and barren as a granite boulder. It is little else than rock in its first stage of decomposition, washed by the rains of winter almost as clean as beach sand, and far coarser. In the ravines, and on bits of table land, there is considerable admixture of vegetable matter, and finely pulverized mica and quartz; but many of the hills, though covered with flowers, are nearly pure sand, with a sprinkling of ashes. Whatever vegetable matter may decay upon them, is mostly washed down by the rains of winter, as very little snow falls here.

Last week, the Indians between this and the Middle Fork had a fight. It seems the Rancheree below stole some acorns from the one above, whereupon the Indians above went down and made an attack upon them, killing half a dozen or such a matter. Both Rancherees are said to be deserted now, their inhabitants having left for parts unknown. After all, human nature is the same everywhere. This is only a miniature of our wars in Florida and Mexico, or any other; and it is not always easy to determine who stole the acorns. The tricks of diplomacy, oftener than otherwise, pass the credit to the wrong party.

When, think you, are the dreams of a millennium to be realized? I mean those regular Californian, Utopian crudities, which wander in the mazy brains of old cart-rut theologians, and some modern cut-and-thrust reformers, leading them to promise the entire, sudden or gradual, and perfect reformation of men, under their present mental and physical organization, and with the existing organization of the physical world?

Our ancestors may have been rude and uncouth; they may have made war and taken life without much thought—they may have been bigoted, perhaps cruel; have believed in goblins and witches, and persecuted each other in matters of conscience. Yet they had a kind of stern unyielding virtue, an inflexible integrity, a high-minded independent piety, and thorough, almost blind reliance on God, which led them to eschew vice, deal justly, make the Bible their rule, their Statute Book, and its Author their Supreme Head.

We, on the other hand are more refined and luxurious. We make war, take life, and preach against it. We disbelieve in witches, it is true, but are hot on the track of the Sadducee, denying the resurrection of the BODY, and doubting of angels and spirits, and still persecute as bitterly as ever for conscience's sake. Our virtue is the ozier wand, the sport of every breeze; our integrity an India rubber article, patent and hot pressed; our piety the trace of a rolling wave on the ocean's sand: and our trust in God exchanged for stock in steam engines and electric telegraphs. To sum up in a word, they were devilishly polite, and we are POLITELY DEVILISH.

A dark picture and the outlines drawn by (as you know) a bold hand. It is nevertheless true; and if you do not believe, come here and see. Come where the restrains of social life, of Christian fraternity, of church discipline are not felt; and you may fill out the picture with startling realities, the colors so vivid, so flashing, and the shades so deep, that the fires of hell shall for a moment pale when they shall ere while meet, as meet they must. After all, it is not necessary to come HERE. Save yourself the trouble and only cast a hasty glance into those sinks of moral pollution, those hot beds of vice, those slaughter-houses of virtue, our great cities—and our small cities—and our villages. God knows where vice and degradation and ruin and destruction are—but only in heaven it is not. "As it was in the time of Noah, so shall it be when the Son of Man cometh." Math. 24 Chapt.

MAY 21. Quite cool last night and hazy this morning. Pleasantly cool and a fine breeze all the afternoon, though sultry hot as usual in the forenoon. Cloudy this evening and a slight shower after dark. Cool this morning.

WEDNESDAY, MAY 22. Ball and I went on to the mountain southeast to get a shot at a deer. Wounded one in the shoulder, but did not get him. Found a man, or rather the skeleton and clothes of one, apparently 25 or thirty years old on the summit. He was near the path, in a clump of bushes, and probably froze to death, as his position and the length of time he has lain there favor the idea. I think that must be Nichols, whom I noticed in my journal of March, as being lost. Poor fellow! he must have been completely exhausted, for he was scarcely a mile from several cabins, and little more from ours. He might have seen the smoke from a dozen chimnies. Still, in all probability he could get no farther and dragging himself a couple of rods from the path, he lay down and submitted to his fate.

He might have thought of a father, or mother, or brother, or sister or nearer and dearer, of a wife and child, or "ladye-love;" and that thought must have added bitterness to death, in so desolate a place. The cold bleak wind, as it howled through the wild forest, whirling the wreathy snow over his prostrate form, could add little to the utter desolation with which the absence of, not only all he loved, but of all human beings, must have overwhelmed his flitting spirit. One hour at his own cheerful fireside would be precious beyond all estimate. All the gold of California, he would deem valueless, when offered as its price. And yet he loses all. In seeking what he never obtains, the vanity of which he now clearly sees, he loses that which he had; and thousands have already perished in the same pursuit. His last thought, who can tell? It must have been a sad one, at least, and mingled with a thousand tender regrets; and then, a confusion—a murmur, as of voices—an effort to determine what is, and what is not—and then—there is nothing more.

The lifeless body lies frozen on the snow, and the prowling wolf comes up only to drive off the stealthy cat, who watches till he leaves, to take her share in turn. The spirit cares little for the quarrels about the walls of its irksome prison house. It recks little what chains are gnawed off, what bolts broken, or breaches made. It needs not fire nor clothing, but freely, and, maybe joyously, speeds on to its destination. The earth, and its hopes and fears, its pleasures and pains, its strife, and trouble, and turmoil, are left behind; and on and on, and away and away, till there is nothing left around but God, and his broad universe, and his blazing central throne— the heaven of heavens.

So with the good man—and is the body lost? Is that most wonderful, most complicated, infinitely ingenious and skillful piece of divine workmanship to be annihilated? No—"for his saints shall he bring with him." "The dead shall be raised, (i.e., the dead body, for nothing else dies), and the living changed—so that we only throw common earth over that which may sometimes become "incorrupt" and "immortal"—"dust to dust." Will none but the "saints" come with him? There is no promise of more; and the soul that leaves its prison house unsanctified, "seeks its own place," or wanders over the face of the earth, seeking rest and finding none.

Alas! who shall answer for the dead of California? Not one in twenty can raise himself above the earth on which he treads. Their every thought tends downward, and their minds seem chained—glued to the earth—the bed rock, on which lies the sordid, soul-damning gold. How can a soul thus laden and fastened down, ever rise, even though the prison were thrown wide open? If gold is to drag me down to earth when I die, a weary, wandering, desolate spirit, without hope of the "better resurrection," rather let me, while living, have none of it. Let it be far from me. Rather let me be poor, hungry, destitute, forsaken, without gold, that I may soar to regions of moral purity, and intellectual joy, awaiting in hope a "glorious resurrection," and restitution of all good things.

23RD. Cool morning. Hot in the forenoon, cool in the afternoon and some wind with a smart shower.

FRIDAY, MAY 24. Quite cold rain. Chilling cold this morning but no frost. Mr. Buckingham, of Milford, Ct., came up from Stringtown this morning and identified the body we found as that of Isaiah Nichols, Harrison, Licking Co., Ohio. John Bowers, Noah Elliot, James Elliot and Nichols came in company. Bowers was drowned. N. Elliot died on the Youba, Nichols was frozen on the mountain and J. Elliot is now sick on the Youba. Mr. B. states that the Granville (Ohio) Company, to which he was attached, had 32 members, all of whom came through safe, and now more than one-third are dead. This is a fearful but not an uncommon mortality.

SATURDAY, MAY 25. Warmer this morning though the river is falling slowly as yesterday was quite hot. I suppose the snow must be nearly gone. If so, the river will soon run down. The meeting at Stringtown proved a failure; so the foreigners are safe and the right has triumphed. Twenty or thirty drunk men have passed us in a single day this week. Wonder what men get drunk for. Got the N.O. Delta and A.S. Courier today, $1 each. Queer things in them. The Delta says, on Mr. Wright's authority, that Col. Fremont has land worth six millions of dollars per acre, and that Government has land equally valuable. You may rest assured that is all a humbug. I doubt if any acre in California will ever be worth twelve tons of gold and any man would be a fool to give the owner twenty per cent of an untouched claim and dig it out himself. Some give forty to fifty per cent when all the ditching and damming is done.

You need not credit all the stories you hear or read as many of them are manufactured at home, and some written here are only to speculate on. A few traders will transport provisions, etc. to Trinity. They then write to somebody *confidentially* that there is plenty of gold there, that one man took out 6,000 in a week, another 2,000 in a day, another 46 lbs. in one lump. Away rush the miners to the new diggins. The scamps sell their goods at an enormous price and vamoose. The miner find the claims about as rich as the one they left while the expenses are greater and back they come, ready to run again at the first cry. I could today get one half the men on the South Fork 25 miles up into the mountains by reporting an eighty pound nugget as found there.

If Mr. Wright knew of any place thus rich, he would be in the diggins himself. He either never said it, which I am inclined to think, or he knows nothing about the mining region, or intends to misrepresent the matter. There are strange and incredible things enough here, without resorting to fiction. I trust that the time will soon come when I shall be able to state, with some degree of certainty, how much gold the South Fork bed will average to the square rod. But any estimate, from 100 to 1000 dollars, may be assumed with safety; and yet the highest mark is not a 36th part of six millions.

Still the old channels and present bed of the river are accounted the richest parts of the mining region, because they receive the wash of the mountains, and uniformly run immediately on, or over, the bed rock. I notice also that many are returning with large sums. Of those who have left these diggins for home, since I came into the mountains, very few dug out their "pile." Indeed, I have heard of no one who has carried away $4,000 of his own digging, because there has been no weather for mining, and it costs a great deal to live. Those who have taken more home, have probably made it by means that no honest man would resort to—by the sale of liquors, keeping gambling tables, gambling itself, or the more honorable employment of stealing cattle. Many such I know who are said to have carried away their thousands.

Next fall and winter, if the streams prove rich, you may chance to see or hear from a host of successful miners, who have amassed a "pile" honestly— by the sweat of their face. I am informed that many persons in the dry diggins on Deer Creek have dug what they want this winter and have gone home. I know not how it is. One can believe here, little more than he sees. The evidence of anything farther, depends, not upon the character of the reporter, but on its own reasonableness, as measured by facts we are daily cognizant of. I can readily believe that a man takes out from one to five hundred dollars in one day, and that another gets as many cents in ten days, though the last is the least likely—but when a man is reported to have returned from this section to the States, with five, six, eight or ten thousand dollars, honestly acquired, since the first day of November last, I beg leave to be excused from believing it. I do not dispute it, mark you; but you may just "post" such a man as the ninth wonder of the world.

26TH. Cool night. Warm, hot day. Stibbs preached.

27TH. D. Wisner, who went down to Robinson's Ranche for the ox, says the frost destroyed the vines, there, that is in the Sacramento valley. I have mentioned early frost we have had. Very hot day.

TUESDAY, MAY 28. We have been at work several days on our bar. Carrying off the gravel as fast as the water falls so that we may come at the bed rock at once when it is drained off. There is one-fourth of an acre and the gravel is from four to six feet deep. Though the mornings are cool, and there is a fine breeze up the valley till nine o'clock, yet it is excessively hot, and only a slight intermitting breeze from that till eleven; when it springs fresh again, and continues till one or two, p.m. Then it is hot—sultry hot an hour or two, and then fresher, finer, cooler and cooler till morning, which is sometimes chilly. Went up to Boone's Bar at noon, to visit, professionally, a young man from Western Virginia, of the name of Mills. His disease is catalepsy ("what's that"? cramp, cramp!) contracted on the overland route. The spasms are fearful, occurring once or twice a day.

WEDNESDAY, MAY 29. Remained at Boone's Bar all night. Took dinner at Stony Point, half a mile above, at a boarding house kept by a widow. It was "sliced up" in as good style (except the table, and quality of the crockery ware) as at a first rate boarding house in Chicago. We had sweet potatoes, fresh lobsters, and large, green marrowfat peas, as fresh and fine flavored as if just picked from the vines. The peas are imported in tin cans containing two and a half pints each, and sell for $4.00 a can. Lobsters are put up in the same way. The dining room is one story, double canvass roof and calico walls. It is airy and cool and there are fewer flies than I have seen at any table in a long time. Weather as yesterday, only cloudy towards night.

THURSDAY, MAY 30. Weather as yesterday. River falling slowly. Very hot. Mills better. Came home this evening.

FRIDAY, MAY 31. Weather same, generally clear. Hot in the sun, cool in the shade and a slight breeze most of the time. Nothing being done now, no travel. Webster was up again today, and we got from him Bennett's Herald and the Journal of Commerce of April 10th. There is very little in them of interest to us. The editorials of the Herald are the merest twaddle in the world, all about staving off legislative action by minority finesse; and its columns of Congressional proceedings, almost wholly occupied with the California question, would seem to bear on their face conclusive evidence, that the reprobate's advice is as needless as gratuitous.

But who cares? California goes her "own gate." She is a sovereign State and will remain so, the President of the United States—Cabinet—Congress, Army and Supreme Court "to the contrary notwithstanding." I speak advisedly. She asks admission as a matter of right, as an act of courtesy—from a dictate of feeling, and of interest—an impulse of instinct. Still, if rejected, she will shed no tear, nor ever ask again. No one ever dreamed of any other course than has been pursued, until our application was dishonored. Yet a feeling has since arisen, and is rapidly extending, which before another session of Congress will erase from the broad folds of our country's flag two embryo stars, and "the United States of the Pacific" will quietly take her place among the nations of the earth, without the hell-brewed stain of slavery upon her almost spotless escutcheon. Would that I could say,

> "Our flag is spotless white,
> Our Watchword, 'Freedom's right'
> To all be given."

The word "white" stains the fair face of ours, and that of almost every other State, except old Massachusetts—God bless her. It is useless to talk about force, for though the Government might wish it, the people would never consent. What! Allow navies and armies to be sent to slaughter blood relations? Brothers, fathers, uncles, cousins, husbands, sisters, almost every degree of consanguinity, for all are here? Never; and if they did come, we would laugh them to scorn.

SATURDAY, JUNE 1. Cool—warm—hot—sultry—hot—warm—cool, with a light breeze, is the history of another day. The river is now regularly falling an inch or more every day. This looks better.

SUNDAY, JUNE 2. Went up to see Mills. Find him much better. They are gambling and drinking in the grocery adjoining the room we sit in. Sunday is set apart by these reprobates for such purposes—desecrated. They gamble more on that than on any other day of the week. The liquor sellers furnish tables and cards, and the men sit down and play for drink. After one drink they must play another game—and the excitement of the play leads on till it goes round the four treats. Then they must have cigars, nuts, pickles, etc. etc., so that in the course of the day many will spend five or six dollars, and even more, at the bar; all which goes to swell the profits of the vender.

One dollar for four drinks, where liquor costs very little if any more than in the States, must yield considerable profit. The amount drank here is perfectly astounding—appalling. I noticed several, who took from eight to twelve glasses each, during the day. Old Alcohol, in his palmiest days, had not more faithful, loving subjects. I reckon that the churches and temperance societies will have something to do, if these recreants and rowdies ever get back. I say if; for half will never return, unless they quit drinking.

Simple Philanthrophy looks on disheartened; but the thorough student of revelation is taught to expect it; and regardless of appearances, and heedless of results, labors and toils on in his Master's vineyard, digging and delving, here a little and there a little, knowing it is "God who giveth the increase," and that he shall see the reward of his labors, and his soul be satisfied.

JUNE 3RD. Weather remains same and rain falling.

TUESDAY, JUNE 4. Weather same. River fell four inches the last 24 hrs. Ball has just received four letters, post marked, 1st Sept., 1st Oct., 3d of Dec., and 3d of March, respectively. They all came at once. Now where have these letters been, and what have they been doing all this time. Is there a billet-doux purgatory between here and the States? If so, who is at the head of the establishment? What makes it more singular, he has already (to wit: last February) received two letters from the same hand, one post marked at Batavia, Oct. 17, and the other sometime previous. The Department is GROSSLY NEGLIGENT in this matter. If it cannot manage the mail efficiently, let it be so understood. Individual enterprise can, and will ensure punctuality, and Government will be compelled to leave it to them.

5TH. Cloudy and feels like rain today. Not quite as hot through the day and cleared off towards night.

THURSDAY, JUNE 6. Clear, hot, sultry again. Still we will have the same breeze flitting and flaring and fainting about us. Soon after noon, a very fair, open-faced, fine-limbed specimen of the genus homo, rode up and announced himself as Mr. Catlett, a candidate for Sheriff of Butte County, and very politely tendered a stump speech, and in three minutes some twenty were on hand. "I feel some diffidence, gentlemen," said he, "in making a speech to those who are wholly strangers to me, and yet in this country we cannot expect to know one another. We are, in fact, all strangers in this country. We came, all or most of us, within the year, and many do not see the importance of a county organization. The law and order part of the

community can see the necessity of having officers of justice, to do away
with the necessity of "Lynch Law," which is now deemed necessary, and no
doubt it is. But there is no way to have the laws executed, only by county
organization, and then the laws of our Legislature will be obeyed and
executed; for I have no doubt they are constitutional, and Congress will
soon admit us into the Union. I hold the country, gentlemen, to be
sovereign and independent, and the acts of the people under the Constitution will be the law.

"Those who have not been South, are ready as I was, to give Fremont
credit for anything but truth in his representations of California. But I have
been down, and shall when I return to the States bring my family back with
me. Fremont has not said one word too much in favor of the country. Even
this part may prove much better than is now supposed, for agricultural purposes. Feeling this—in canvassing the country, I think the first—that is—I do
not deny that I want the office, for I acknowledge I am selfish as well as
every body else. We are all selfish; but I think the organization of the county
of more importance than for me to be Sheriff. Though I should like to be
Sheriff, if you can give me your votes.

"There is another thing which perhaps I ought to speak of, and that is,
our being kept out of the Union by the slavery questions. The Convention
thought to settle the difficulty by excluding it, when they ought to let it
alone; but unfortunately they made matters worse. It was done by a small
number in the North. I am a Southern man—a Kentuckian—that is, I was
educated in Kentucky, and of course was opposed to having anything to do
about it. I have opened all the bars until after 'lection, as I have to do as
the rest do, so you can call anywhere you please. A great object is to get
out the voters, and although, if I am Sheriff, I wish the expenses of the
country as small as possible, yet if it is not convenient to go away far to
vote, thirty voters can open the polls anywhere, and the first Judge of 'lection will carry the returns to Bidwell's ranche (forty miles) by the first Monday after 'lection, and there canvass them with the other Judges. He gets
one ounce a day for himself, $10 for horse, and 6 "bitts" a mile for travel. I
will cash all county orders as soon as presented. I believe I have no more to
say, gentlemen, and I must hurry along, as my competitors are close at my
heels, driving me up."

And thus endeth the first lesson. Slavery and Rum! Well, well! wouldn't
he have been surprised at the result of his eloquence? He convinced us all
that we could not by any possibility vote for him. Rum and Slavery! He was
a passably good looking fellow, and many of the crowd might have voted
for him but for the (to him) unfortunate introduction to these mooted
topics. Alas, alas! "he is a done over tailor." He may be Sheriff or pound
master or brothel-bully, but these votes never elect him whatever may be
his qualifications. It is quite a question after all, if the candidates are not all
of a feather. I shall expect to hear from others.

7TH. Cloudy and not as warm. A candidate for the Judgeship came along today. Said he had opened the Bars.* Go it Judge, you are one of them. It has been pleasanter working today than any day for a long time. Just breeze and cloud enough to be passably cool. Took in Jackson Lawrence from Missouri in place of Texas Bob, who gives Lawrence one half of his share and finds him. Lawrence was a slave at home. He is a great worker, worth two of Bob.

8TH. Partially cloudy and a pleasant breeze most all day. Lots of candidates straggling along. I shall endeavor to classify them as soon as possible.

SUNDAY, JUNE 9. Weather as yesterday. Went up to Boone's bar to see Mills. It was much quieter there than I had before seen.

> On the side of the mountain beneath a tall pine
> Stood a lone pale pink floret beside a green vine.
> Though surrounded by thousands more gay and more fair
> and a rainbow of flowlets was spread on the air
> Still unconscious of beauty its head was bowed low
> and enstamped on its frontlet the semblance of woe.
> The bill of the hummingbird was thrust down in vain
> And the sucker of honey came not thus again.
> For the warm breath of summer no aroma shed
> On the gay happy insects that played round its head.
> And the bright drops of morning were scattered in vain
> On the desolate stranger, this child of the plain.
> While I gazed on the shadows and tints it had nursed
> It curled like a vapor and rolled in the dust.
> Though the tooth of the cutworm no mark had left there
> and the green of its leaf was surprisingly fair,
> Do you ask why it perished—its bright colors fled
> Why it waved there so scentless, why drooped its pale head
> Why the warm breath of summer no life could instill
> Nor bright drops of the morning its empty veins fill?

---

*Candidates allowed constituents to charge drinks in the local bars in their names. Bars kept a tab and billed the candidate, win or lose, the following day—sometimes to the tune of several hundred dollars.

Chapter Fourteen

June 10–August 1, 1850:
Elections and Humbugs

———◆———◆———◆———

MONDAY, JUNE 10. Attended election at Stringtown this afternoon. Saw but few people, and very little excitement. The judges were quite decent looking men, with one exception, and were NOT DRUNK, entirely. This is rather singular—at least unexpected. There are a great number of candidates—six or eight for some offices. They are all, as far as I can learn, grossly immoral men, and such as I could not vote for under any circumstances. *I shall not vote at all.* The South, as usual, is fully represented. I can hear of but two among the fifty or sixty candidates who are natives of Northern States, though probably there are others. This is perfectly characteristic. These Southern chaps have a perfect mania for office, and why? *They love to rule.* and, I am told, the County Recorder gets a salary of $4,000 a year, the Judge, $8,000, and other officers in proportion.

This is what they like—what they are used to—living on the labors of others.

While I was sitting near the tables, the Judges got into an agreeable conversation, chiefly made up of old political reminiscences. They boasted of voting the party ticket straight through, year after year—right or wrong, good or bad. FOOLS!! By degrees it gradually ran into Martin Van Buren, and John [Brown?] and the Abolitionists. They finally came to the sage conclusion that the Great Magician and Co. stood no chance whatever in the end, as the time is coming, and that soon, when there will be a line drawn, and only one candidate for President in the North, and one in the South.

Then the North will be heard, and the South must abide by the Constitution, and will get only what the bond calls for. John, they thought must

258

coalesce with the Whigs to ever be any body again. There were three or four citizens of slave States present, who assented to most of the remarks—at least manifested no opposition. To judge of the calibre of the actors, or speakers, I listened to the whole very attentively. The President of the Board is pretty smart. One has nearly intellect enough for a pack mule—the other three seem to know enough, when sober, to keep what they do know to themselves. One of them was a mulatto. After the discussion, they all liquored up and took a smoke, and of course I left. Can't stand smoke.

I promised to classify the candidates. Well, there seems to be two classes. Class first is composed of worthless, drunken gamblers—and class second, of worthless, gambling drunkards. (Mem. "Gambler—one who plays or games for money." "Drunkard—an habitual drinker of alcoholic liquors." "Worthless—either of the above classes." Dict'y of common sense.) Probably there are some exceptions among all the candidates—and there are also some white crows.

11TH. Gusts of wind besides a cool breeze today as usual: all day. Every kind of cloth is used here for sand bags to dam the river with. The quality is of no account, the only question seems to be which will make most sand bags. The coarsest hemp sacking—common sheeting—drilling and jeans are all the same price here, six bits, and it is almost impossible now to get any in the city. The late fires have created a great demand for cloth and tacks, the last article being as high as two to four dollars a paper.

12TH. Cloudy and drizzly and misty all day. Cool and even chilly.

13TH. Cloudy most of the day and warm. A smart shower between sundown and dark and chilly.

14TH. Cloudy and warm till three p.m. Cool and chilly towards night and a shower at six p.m. Yesterday a piece of gold weighing $236 was found on a bar just below Boone's. Capt. Belfield has kindly promised me a sight of it the next time I come up. Mills is fast recovering. I give him no medicine, trusting the case entirely to *Animal Magnetism*. Elder Wisner has an attack of ague again. Received a letter from my brother in Batavia and with it one from my mother, mailed at Batavia, March 1st, three and a half months, when they ought to have been here in six weeks. We think three and a half months remarkably quick, after all.

15TH. Cloudy early in the morning but soon cleared. We worked yesterday in the Louisiana race and the head of it being at the lower end of our claim by sinking it to the bed of the river we drain our claim of water. Elder W. is up again and well.

SUNDAY, 16. Cloudy and looks like rain this morning. The river is falling two to four inches a day. The nights and mornings are invariably cool. Yesterday afternoon the water in the river was muddy and the water must have been turned through some of the canals. This morning it is nearly clear again. At Boone's today.

17TH. Night chilly enough for a frost but there is none. Weather as yesterday only more wind in the afternoon.

TUESDAY, JUNE 18. Great excitement about Gold Lake, at the head of the Middle Fork, or some other undiscovered locality. I believe it is all a hoax. They tell of getting from an ounce to a pound a day. Mansfield goes up tomorrow to see. I hope he may get something, but doubt it. Money is scarce here just now. Worth ten percent a month. Hard money country this. A month from this there will probably be plenty.

This is a singular state of things, still it is unavoidable. In working on their claims, and preparing to dam the river, the miners have expended all the earnings of last winter, and many of them are in debt. Not that there is no money, but the securities are not sufficient to induce the holders to shell out. Thousands on thousands are in the hands of cautious, miserly fellows, who love it too well to let it go out of sight, except for liquor. Large amounts are also held in hand, some pieces laid aside for keepsakes. And in conclusion, a thousand dollars is of no account here. It will buy nothing—absolutely nothing. Only think, a pair of boots that may be had in Elgin from the shoemaker singly for $3, are here worth $22.

19TH. No change in the weather. Mansfield has gone to the Gold Lake (humbug).

20TH. Weather same. Too chilly morning and evening to go without a coat.

21. Some warmer last night. Sick myself today.

22. Weather warmer. Flying clouds.

23. Same. Scarce a cloud.

MONDAY, JUNE 24. Not a cloud. Still it is not as hot as in Illinois in June. There is a report that Lassen has been robbed and murdered. The last has been long expected, as the emigrants led off on his route were highly exasperated, and his life has been threatened.*

*J. Goldsborough Bruff was staying at Lassen's Ranch during this time and makes no mention of trouble or rumor.

TUESDAY, JUNE 25. The days are getting hotter, and the nights decidedly warmer, though I have never yet, since I left Illinois, endured a regular sultry night, or even an approach to it. No, we can sleep here for all the heat, or the musquitoes; too cold for them. But the ants are everywhere; regular engineers—surveying out your pillow, or its substitute, or place, into town plots, bisected with rail road tracks in all imaginable lines of beauty. They are indefatigable. Darkness stays them not, nor does any impediment seem insurmountable. No sooner is your head or hand on one of the recent surveys, than these persevering creatures run their lines directly across the obtruding mass, and all is right again. It is always better to let them work on, for the moment you touch one, it exhales an aromatic, nauseous smell, strong enough to infect the atmosphere several feet around, and remaining on the hand or skin several minutes.

And then the flies—the flies !! (house flies). Not a word need ever be said to us again about the hard heart of that monster Pharaoh. The beast he had no heart, or the Egyptians knew nothing about California flies. Did I know of any Goshen here, I should be off directly. Alas! there is no escape. Even while I write, any number of ants (I can't stop to count) have been ranging undisturbed over my paper and not less than a score of flies, oftener fifty, are on each of my hands, apparently doing their very best to tickle them into convulsions. There are no green flies here and meat may be exposed without the risk of being crawled off with. They may say what they please, meat here so far has tainted just as soon as in the States.

WEDNESDAY, JUNE 26. We have nearly finished the La. race. I have not been able to do anything this week. Some of us sick all the time. Sad country this.

THURSDAY, JUNE 27. The country seems all alive about the Gold Lake humbug, though no one seems to know anything in particular. The Rev. Mr. Stibbs was lost last week, in returning from that region, and though diligent search has been made, no trace has been discovered. Perhaps one more victim to credulity.

FRIDAY, JUNE 28. Wm. McAuley and Calvert, of Elgin, called today. They complain bitterly of the mail Department. Have yet to receive the first line from home. I gave them all the news I had, and they were somewhat cheered. They wished their friends at home to know how entirely they were cut off from them, and Calvert seems quite anxious to ascertain, "If I did not think that I should be apt to know, if his wife was dead." I could only offer the negative evidence of never having heard of it, even this was some consolation. Pray don't laugh. When a friend's letter says nothing about any deaths in our own place, we infer that nobody is dead. It may not be exactly logical; but it is very natural, I assure you. Come and try it.

Today, on the works below, a Louisianian, of the name of Gale, struck
Hiram, a colored man (slave?) of the same company, on the head with a
stone and laid open his scalp to the skull. Our men are at work with them
in the same race; and Elder Wisner, being nearest, stepped between them,
and remonstrating with Gale, prevented his repeating the blow as he evidently designed on an unoffending man—one whom education and habits
has thus far rendered incapable of offering resistance to the personal violence
of a white man. It was a most dastardly act.

I was not present, but all agree that Hiram only said that he had carried
heavy stone, on the hand barrow several days in succession, with different
persons, and thought that he ought to be relieved. Gale told him to shut
up, when Hiram very mildly said that he should not be able to stand it
much longer. On this Gale made the brutal assault—used him just as he
would a slave at home. It was none of Gale's business, anyhow, who carried
or who didn't. The foreman should see that none of the men are over, or
unequally tasked. I was absent, and Doct. Mobley, the La. foreman, was
engaged below in drilling, and heard nothing of it until too late. Gale is
condemned by all, although his own company are mostly slaveholders.

SATURDAY, JUNE 29. Decidedly warmer today. No news of Stibbs. I
was invited to deliver a Fourth of July Oration at Stringtown. Told the
committee that I would give them an answer on Monday. A grog celebration no doubt. I have a free invite to the dinner anyway. So, also, has Elder
Wisner. How is it that these men wish to gain the cooperation of a man
who, they well know, is opposed to their every day business and practices? I
am now well known by almost every grocer from the kanyon to the foot of
the hill, as a "teetotaller," and bitterly opposed to gambling, swearing, and
Sabbath-breaking—known as well as in Kane County.

They have long since ceased offering to treat, even with lemonade or
soda; for I told them on the start that I never drank either, where alcoholic
liquors are kept, and quoted the injunction of the Apostle: "Abstain from
all appearance of evil." And now am I sent for, by these very men, to amuse
them on the Fourth. I will consider it well.

We have had no claim trials on Sunday, since the Sunday jury recommended other days; and yet I was for an hour or two uncertain in that case.
What an immense influence an ever-consistent moralist may exert. That is
the secret of success. But he must be consistent in the smallest, as well as
greatest things. He must "tithe mint and commin." Oh, what a glorious
being is a PERFECT moral reformer! We have had but one—Jesus of Naza-
reth. Would that we could all be nearer like him. After all, our intentions
are better than our judgment—or rather, our education, appetites, passions,
and prejudices, mislead the judgment, and we adopt wrong means to secure
our ends.

If I cannot settle a matter in my own mind so as to leave no doubt, I make it a rule not to act. "He that doubteth, is condemned already." If I am convinced that I must do a positive wrong, however small, to succeed, I am required to abandon the scheme altogether, as morally impracticable. No matter what are to be the certain results—how excellent, or how glorious. Be sure God has some other way to accomplish it, if he is ready to have it done, and set yourself diligently to some other work.

Ministers can be tested here, if anywhere. Shadrach, Meshach, and Abed-nego had never a hotter sitting room than they. It is a refiner's fire, fierce, glowing, flaming, roaring, raging and cankering, like the combined action of heat and acid; and when the heat is spent, the glow paled, the flame expired, and the canker has ceased to devour, we look, often and often, in vain for the gold. Alas! all dross—worthless dross—never anything but "sounding brass and a tinkling cymbal"—base metal—bogus.

As for soap, it won't save them—entirely out of the question. The personal appearance of many of them when they attempt to lead in public worship is filthy, disgusting in the extreme. Whisker-raisers, tobacco-chewers, beard-elongators, smokers, snuff-takers, whiskey drinkers and even card players—they look more like wandering Dunkers, and mendicant Mormons, who "lang syne" were wont to roam like vagrant maniacs over the country, than anything else I can now call to mind. No, no, it's too late for soap.

Elder Wisner occasionally preaches, and only occasionally. He is thoroughly discouraged, disheartened at the moral aspect. He says it is "casting pearls before swine." If the ministers were not as "thick as toads in a puddle," (excuse the coarseness of the simile for its aptness) I would preach myself. There are now sixteen or more regular preachers, besides exhorters, on the South Fork, in the distance of ten miles; and you can seldom find a meeting on the Sabbath. They complain that nobody will come to hear them. Were it not uncharitable, I could almost say the fault lies more with themselves than elsewhere.

Were I to preach, the people should come. I would say or do something that would bring them, whether they would or not, and when once there, I would tell them what they never before heard or thought of, so far as they can remember. I would seek and get a faith of my own; a belief that they would be there, and would come again; and they would. I have almost caught it now. It's no use, this sitting down where there is a difficulty, "a lion in the way," and crying, we cannot, we faint.

Anything—a rotten old scow boat, can sail in fair weather with a good wind. It is the storm, the tempest, which tries. In the moral storm, the strong (in faith) grows stronger, the weak, weaker. Could not Peter walk on his faithless footpath, as long as he believed that he could? Yes! yes! that is all: "according to your faith be it unto you."

A Camp-meeting was to commence at Powell's today. Elder W. returned this evening and says nobody attended. Where were the ministers? and echo answers, PROSPECTING!!

SUNDAY, JUNE 30. Hot, like a furnace today, and scarcely a breeze to shake the excessive heat from the air. The whole atmosphere glows, like that around the furnace of a glass factory. One day, and only one, have I ever seen like it; and that was on the St. Mary's River [now the Humboldt]. I am not well enough to attend the meeting today, and the Elder has a serious inflammation of the ear. I have not yet heard what has been done, but should judge, not much. There was to be a large auction sale of groceries, two miles below; and that, with the usual amusements of the Sabbath, will keep almost everybody away. The boys killed another large rattlesnake by the house today.

MONDAY, JULY 1. Hot as yesterday and warmest night of all. Mansfield returned today. Found some very good "diggins," but no Gold Lake. Those who went in search of Stibbs, send word down by him that they can find no trace of him.

2ND. Weather as yesterday. Perhaps not quite as hot and a fresher breeze. Bird, a colored man from Chicago, was here yesterday and again today. J. Wisner left today.

JULY 3RD. I wish I had a thermometer. Report says that, in the shade, in the afternoon, the quicksilver is skipping round from 104 to 116 degrees F. In the morning, at half-past four o'clock, it is almost cold enough for a frost. I will endeavor to ascertain what indications the thermometer really gives.

THURSDAY, JULY 4. Weather the same. The Celebration Committee have not called for an answer, and I have not been under the necessity of coming to a decision at all. Indeed, it has not yet cost me a thought except what you see written. I have been gradually improving, but am not well enough today to even ride to Stringtown, though I certainly am not sick. Everybody will be disappointed, and a number have already gone down expressly to hear the speech. Well, well, I do not certainly know what I should have decided to do; but I am now satisfied that I had no particular business there. That question seems definitely settled. This is some consolation for being half sick three or four days; for, really, I could not see on Sunday why I should not be able to work on Monday, and so of every day since. In fact, I have tried it a little "but it's no go."

The boys have been wasting powder this morning in trying to make a great noise. I told them that they had better keep it for blasting rocks, where it would make a heap more of noise, and do some good. I spent a trifle of breath and saved a little powder. This last article is getting scarce in this section. There has been forty pounds used in the Louisiana Race since we began work there. Some of the rock lies across it in compact masses, and there are many very large boulders. We have now only to cut the canal across the river bed, and unite with the one above. The water continues to fall about an inch a day. Not much will be done in the river bed this month.

George [Sharp] got up a very good supper. The Raisin cake was baked to a turn and frosted like the Shasta peak. Peas and potatoes would have made us glorious, but alas, the Stringtownites monopolized the trade. They had a dinner on the large side. Only $5 each. Dog cheap. After dinner – they (saith report) drank toasts, sung songs, and told stories till they were drunk. In this matter, California stands now where the Empire State did in 1824. All for drink and powder; not a dime for temperance.

5TH. Not as hot today. Cloudy at sundown and cool.

6TH. Cloudy and cooler this morning. Continued cool through the day.

SUNDAY, JULY 7. Clear and cool this morning. Elder Washburn preached here today, and a searching sermon it was. He is an original and close preacher. He means you, whoever else it may suit, and you cannot escape.

MONDAY, JULY 8. The nights get colder and colder and the days cooler. Still we have no dews and it is several months since I have seen any. Three loafers came and made a claim on our bar today. If they stick to the claim, we shall have some trouble. The law is, that if the bar can be worked at the lowest stage of water, without draining, anybody can lay claim to it; if not, it belongs to those who drain the river bed. Our Bar is the last condition.

TUESDAY, JULY 9. I have been informed by several persons, that, at Long's the thermometer stood in the shade at 116 degrees for several days. It was 107 at Stringtown. It is a fact that the fish do not come up Feather River, at least this year. So much for another California humbug. I shall be disappointed if we can keep the count of all we discover betwixt now and fall. I propose to call the State Humbugnia and that Fremont be appointed Governor "in perpetuo." It is a worthless country for anything but gold; and even for that, every day is accumulating evidence of its deprecating value. It would seem that the least sanguine, and I am one, have highly overestimated its mineral wealth. Time will decide and we, perforce, must wait.

WEDNESDAY, JULY 10. The loafers came back today, to look to their claim on our bar. We had 18 men at work yesterday, and twelve today, carrying off gravel; and they seemed much surprised and disappointed at not finding a foot of the original surface on which to sit down. After loitering around a while, they took themselves off, and left us to our own ways.

THURSDAY, JULY 11. Excessively hot in the middle of the day. I am just able to work a little again, and we have no one now on the sick list.

12TH. Hot as ever but a delightful evening. River falling slowly.

SATURDAY, JULY 13. Weather as yesterday. Just pleasantly warm this evening. We have been carrying gravel off the bar all the week. The average distance to carry has been about 100 feet. It is a great deal of labor, but will save time when it will be much more valuable to us, and we have now nothing else to do.

SUNDAY, JULY 14. Cool this morning. Eld. Washburn preached. Quite a number attended. Excessively hot in the middle of the day. It could hardly be endured, were it not for the cool breeze we have through the afternoon.

MONDAY, JULY 15. It is finally given up that Stibbs is dead, though his body has not been found. I believe that I stated, on my first acquaintance with him on the Missouri, that he came from Boston. He was an Englishman by birth, and resided in St. Louis sometime previous to leaving for California. He was a good man, and we could better have spared another. He leaves a wife, but no children.

There is to be an election today for two Justices of the Peace and a Constable. Our Bob, Texas Bob [Horton], is one of the four candidates up for the magistracy. Candidate, forsooth! Why, there is hardly a donkey in all California that is not as well qualified for the office. He is utterly ignorant of the elements of law, and the first principles of natural rights; and has not sufficient common sense to teach him the rule of right, or honesty or conscience to restrain him from wrong. He is now owner and keeper of the lowest kind of a doggery, and is a gambler by instinct, habit, profession and choice, and a slaveholder in the bargain. The other candidates are unknown to me. I have heard that one of them is a decent man. Strange, if true!

Forbes, who is trading in Stringtown, had a brother come in from the States today. He reached Johnson's on the 3rd inst., 80 days from Council Bluffs, (60 travelling) via Truckey Pass, with a light wagon, and four men in all. The team was five ponies. He left on the 13th of April, and thinks there was no one ahead. He is certainly the first overland emigrant we have had here for this year, though thousands have passed who came round the cape, or across the Isthmus.

TUESDAY, JULY 16. Weather same. Turned a part of the water into the race today. There is too much yet in the river. The miners are making a variety of dams across the streams. Sacks of sand and stone walls filled between with earth and brush, are most common. Some have already lost their claims by back water. One dam has thrown the water back over three entire claims and destroyed the prospects for this season of forty to fifty men. A decision before the Vice President of the Miner's Association, was to the effect that the oldest claim had that RIGHT (?). Everybody up this way says that the decision is grossly unjust, and that the Judges are fools. Nothing farther has been done. Those whom they flooded offered to dig their race deep enough to supersede the necessity of a dam, but they would yield to no compromise. If justice were done, their claim would be taken away and given to the others, and themselves expelled the district.

Bob is elected one of the just(asses)ices. Ca. is in a fair way to rival Ill. in filling their public offices. I can remember the time when in glorious old Kane the qualifications for a popular public officer and a candidate for the penitentiary were about which and 'tother. Thank God it is not so now.

17TH. The air seems like a furnace and is entirely destitute of moisture. There is no dew.

THURSDAY, JULY 18. Hundreds are, as usual, passing up and down, the up-ites for the most part clean, and tolerably decent; the down-ites as dirty as earth and grease can make them. Some will remain in the mountains for four to six weeks, and no change of clothing. Worst of all, they get very little gold.

19TH. No change in the weather.

SATURDAY, JULY 20. Reports from every direction come thicker and faster, of the leanness of the river beds. Few have tested them thoroughly, on account of the influx of water, but claims have assuredly fallen. Some men who have refused $1,000 or $1,500 are now offering for $500, and find no buyers. One share in a claim just above was sold a short time since for $3,000, and now it would scarcely command $300. Plenty to sell, but nobody wants. After all, it may turn out better than is now anticipated; though many after a slight examination have abandoned their claims altogether.

Am at Stringtown this evening, to see Dr. Powell, who is sick. He has two or three physicians already. They seem to know but little of what should be the treatment of fevers in this latitude. One of them can talk a great deal of nonsense about Pathology, and Tautology, and Doxology; but they can't break a remittent fever.

SUNDAY, JULY 21. Slept in the long low attic or lodging room of the boarding-house. Thirty or forty persons are lodged in the one room, and that none of the neatest. One half lay on the floor, the other in berths of no comfortable construction. There is a great deal of sickness in Stringtown;

and if they all lodge thus, I do not wonder. They do not all, for I now recollect that I saw several last night lying under the broad canopy of heaven, with a blanket beneath and one above. Plenty of air in that bedroom. Remained all day with Powell.

This is the principal business day here. I have heard several bargains made. One share in a claim was sold for $2,000; a house and fixtures for boarding, and a grocery for $2,000; (it might cost $200 in the States); and several lesser trades, besides packing for the mines, etc.

22ND. Sands and Mansfield left today, discouraged. Sands has one half a share which he loses. Mansfield will lose one half and perhaps all.

TUESDAY, JULY 23. We are prospecting our bar today, that is, trying to ascertain how far it is to the bed rock. The men reached it sooner than they expected, at a depth of three feet and took out 15 or 16 dollars in getting down. Too much water on as yet.

24TH. The atmosphere is filled with blue smoke.

THURSDAY, JULY 25. Was at Boone's bar today. On Fitt's claim, they are taking out $100 to each man; the only point on the river where they are making anything as yet.

FRIDAY, JULY 26. Was up the river again today and find three or four claims doing very well.

SATURDAY, JULY 27. A few clouds have been lying off north and west today. In the States it would portend rain. Here no one expects rain before November. Thousands out west eat, cook, and sleep under the evergreens or booths or a slight covering of brush like the temporary wigwam of an Indian. They can answer no purpose but to keep the sun off. We want to hire two men to supply the places of Sands and E. Mansfield who have left. There are hundreds and thousands in the country who are ready to work for five to eight dollars a day, but none for me, as I require that they do not drink or smoke a pipe. It is a shame, a disgrace to humanity, this filthy, disgusting habit of smoking. There is no smoke which I so much abhor, saving and excepting that which ascendeth forever and ever.

SUNDAY, JULY 28. Some clouds today. Washburn preached. Not many present, and yet they cannot reasonably complain of the preacher.

MONDAY, JULY 29. Men pass down every day who have abandoned claims above. Some have worked months, and when they got to the bed of the river, lo! there was nothing that they wanted. Long faces they have, but not merry ones. Barbers, if such things existed in California, would have their prices now. Luckily the race is extinct—gone with the mammoth and big lizards. They are about as useful here as would a penny whistle be under the fall of Niagara. A fine time for sad things when all these big whiskers get back to the States.

The mountains are brown again. The trees, not evergreen, retain their leaves, as also the larger shrubs; but the lesser vegetation, except in ravines, on alluvial deposits, is gone, dead and gone; all dried and withered, blasted and scorched, as when we first came into the mines; and the beautiful flowers have gone with them.

TUESDAY, JULY 30. Was at Stringtown all day. I am not yet able to work.

WEDNESDAY, JULY 31. Went up the river to Pleasant Valley. Our men began to work the bar today. Hired a man of the name of Cook, to work in my place. He swears not, drinks not, smokes not; and seldom speaks.

THURSDAY, AUGUST 1, 1850. Mr. Washburn takes Murrell's place in the company. David has been sick two or three times before and will not be able to do anything more. Returned from up the river this morning. Not much doing there. Most are discouraged and hundreds have abandoned the labor of from three to five months and gone to other "diggins." The bed of the river is likely to prove our entire failure and yet there is where it was expected to find the great deposits. What hopes have been crushed by this unexpected discovery cannot now be estimated. Some men have staked all and lost all—the labor of two years—everything they have, and run in debt on the single chance of getting this "Pile" from the bed of the river, and all is lost. Some will return home as soon as they can procure the means. Other will stay and try again, putting off to another year the sight of home and friends. Perhaps they will return. Perhaps they may leave their bones here, buried, without a mark to tell they the why or where or how, or mayhap bleaching like a wolf's on mountain side or desert plain.

Chapter Fifteen

August 2–September 3, 1850:
More Money in Medicine

FRIDAY, AUGUST 2, 1850. Left home to board at Stringtown for a short time. They are gambling and drinking all the time at the Hotel. It is really astonishing to see men with very limited, or rather no means at all, staking their last penny on the turn of a card, and as recklessly as though they had Aladdin's lamp in their bosom to replenish their exhausted pockets. If they have not discovered the Philosopher Stone, they at least have a philosophers coolness and are as imperturbable in good or ill fortune as marble statues. The only feeling developed to ordinary eyes is an evident though suppressed desire to cheat.

But whatever restraint they may put on their feelings they certainly seem to have no measure for their practices, other than to avoid a feeling that might lead to detection.

And why not cheat all they can, when the very first, indeed the great and only principle of the practice is cheating—taking your neighbor's money for naught. Gamblers talking about honor and being honorable men. They have no such thing as honor, even as they wish us to understand it, about them. They have no use for it. The gambler, like the drunkard, when hard up will steal the means of gratifying his favorite propensity. All. All. I cannot, will not make an exception. And indeed none need be made. It is all stealing and nothing else from first to last.

The majority in California being gamblers of course are essentially thieves, and the failure of the claims and consequent tightness in the money market and money matters, develops the true character of the people. We now hear of thefts committed at all times, and in every quarter. Nothing is safe unless well looked to. Men, who one month ago would have scorned to commit so base an act, will vamoos now and leave their board and tavern bills unpaid. Their honor has gone with the prospect of getting a "pile," and they appear what they really are, — scamps.

Honor! What is honor worth that requires so heavy a metal as gold to hold it down on a man's conscience. These last evils are limited as yet, and mark! I speak only of this section, though I presume that our section is morally equal to any in the state.

SATURDAY, AUG. 3. I think that the nights are getting cooler. This morning three miners came in from three different claims which have been abandoned. Every day men are coming in reporting such failures. Most of them look as if they would go home if they had the means. There are six Sandwich Islanders here at work on a claim in a dry diggins above, for Horton, Van Buren & Stevens. They are stout built, coarse featured, and have large mouths. They seem intelligent, speak English and seem like a mixture of Negro and North American Indian. They are accounted excellent for a day's work and so far as I have seen will not use intoxicating drinks at all (?).

SUNDAY, AUGUST 4. Was up the river to hear Washburn preach. The usual attendance. Sermon a good one. When I returned to Stringtown, found a California Sunday in full blast. Four tables surrounded by gamblers and a bar by drunkards, the whole swearing out of all time and measure, so that one might readily imagine himself in the "purlies" of hell. If this house was located over so suspicious a region as that where the great Boiling Spring of the desert sends up its everlasting smoke, I should certainly vamoos, lest the tragedy of sodom should some odd night be reenacted.

The utter recklessness, the perfect, "abandon" with which they eat, drink, gamble and swear is altogether astounding. You know nothing about it in the States; never did, never will, I trust. Their eating is, physically, their worst fault. They gorge themselves on beef and bread and stale butter and peppered pickles and stimulating sauces, like wolves or anacondas and the last thing before going to bed, must have sardines at three to five dollars a box, or a pie at one dollar as its equivalent, and then they lie down like swine and groan and blaspheme in this slumber of victims of gluttony and drunkenness now of disease tomorrow and the doctor the day after.

Of the three it is difficult to decide which is the worst, always bearing in mind that the last are not always like the first two — soul killers.

MONDAY, AUG. 5. At dinner Dr. Jamison told of a "row" in Marysville. It seems that a Dr. Wells or some name like it, went into a doggery and called for a glass of liquor. A colored man came in a moment after and called for one too. Both were placed on the counter at the same time and thereupon the Doct. retreated to a table in the back part of the room, asking the keeper to bring his glass there. The keeper asked the reason and the Democratic (?) Republican (?) doctor said that he was not accustomed to drink with "niggers."

"Nor do I," says the man touched at the insult, "often drink with mean rascally whites." Upon this the Doct. sprang up and struck the man, who was his equal, at least in vulgar wit, and proved himself his equal physically by flooring the valiant M.D. with a chair.

The democrat then went to his office and got a cowhide taking special care to arm himself with a pistol and followed the man, whom he overtook, and like a true slave owner ordered peremptorily to stop. The man went on his way paying no attention to his threats and thereupon the brave and chivalrous doct shot him in the thigh.

Such is the story, and probably the best side of it, as it is told by one who fully endorses the act, and declares that he would do the same for even a lesser offense. How he could do so, I cannot conceive, as the Doct. (Wells) was by his own (Jamison's) showing the aggressor throughout and where a man has done absolutely nothing, I really cannot see how he would well do any less. Jamison says they are all very quiet about it at Marysville though the negro is not expected to recover. Three men at the table joined in expressing the same views as Jamison. But Mark! they were all gamblers and drunkards, and I say it because I know it, I have not yet heard a man in all California advocate such doctrines and practices who was not both—nor one who was (to say nothing of being an advocate) even an excuser of slavery who did not drink brandy. The thing speaks for itself.

Its advocates themselves, by this single circumstance show of what mind they are, and have thus without advancing any other evidence affixed the broad seal of Hell to the whole system. Having given a few rapid strokes to be filled in a full final sketch of California character, permit me to observe, that if this country does not prove a curse to the United States, bringing commercial distress, individual ruin, national poverty, social and political revolution, immorality, vice, disease, and every concomitant evil, then cause will never produce effect, and the curses of Moses might have fallen among the Jews as gently as the Manna in the desert. If it leads to abolition of slavery perhaps it will pay.

Received a letter from my brother, M.N. Lord today. It was dated May 17, Postmarked 23rd.

TUESDAY, AUG. 6. The reports from the mines confirms all that we have heard before. A general failure. A very few claims prove rich, some are worth working, some have a little and some nothing.

WEDNESDAY, AUG. 7. George Sharp was down today to see my letter. The Elder and C. Wisner had each a letter. Among them all we are posted up to the first of June. We have N. York papers to June 14th. Queer things in them, too. The proceedings in Congress would disgrace a gang of school boys, playing at "leap frog." Strange that so many fools and knaves should by a coincidence of circumstances be congregated in one place.

A man came up from Marysville and says that the mule he rode down was taken from him at that place. This is not the first case of the kind by fifty. There is so much swindling now that if a man buys an animal he gets a "bill of sale." With this in his pocket he feels a certain degree of safety as they cannot make him a horse thief.

If a man below sees a horse or mule he wants, he immediately lays claim to it, and half an ounce will any day hire a witness or two to prove property. Time is worth too much here for an honest man to spend it in law, and he suffers the wrong if it should happen to be one, rather than pay twice the value of the animal to maintain his right. Such, at least, is the general belief and practice.* No doubt, some claim their own property for mules and horses are often stolen, but it is thought and probably with truth that most of these claims are fictitious and only sustained by perjury. What is singular and suspicious, that most all these claims are made by Oregon men backed by Oregon witnesses.

Yesterday Horton had a man brought over from the Middle Fork for taking a shovel from a claim, when he had disposed of his share. The whole proceedings were informal and illegal and plaintiff had to pay his own costs. My opinion of the J.P.'s judicial capabilities are fully verified by his own acts.

THURSDAY, AUG. 8. Was up at the old place. They only wait for the dam now to commence operations. Mansfield came up this evening and reports that Dr. Torry, of Elgin is over on the Yuba.

FRIDAY, AUG. 9. Left Stringtown for Rube's ranche, twelve miles down on the Marysville road. Tired enough to lie by though I did not get there till afternoon. Most of the way retraced the same road by which I entered the mines last February. This ranche was on a stream of water. It is now dry. Lies south of Long's bar.

SATURDAY, AUG. 10. Crossed over from Rube's to the Yuba. Kept just back of the first range of hill on account of the shade of an occasional tree.

*The Sacramento Transcript, *February 11, 1851, page 2, states: "We verily believe there are more than one thousand men in California who make horse stealing a regular business. In this city alone, it has been nothing very strange to recover from fifty to one hundred head of stolen stock in a single day; and of thieves detected, no fair proportion have been arrested. The Stockton Times, April 2, 1851, states that the "country is infested with horse thieves. . . . It may be esteemed by some as improper on our part, but our convictions urge us to say—lynch every man who may be caught in the act.*

The hills are low and easy, and sparsely covered with oaks with broad, spreading tops. About half way across came to a broad fine looking valley, where there is a large quantity of hay cut, and a herd of oxen grazing. There is now no running water here. The bed of the steam is for the most part dry, the water standing in pools at long distances. It will furnish stock water, probably through the season, but is now not fit for humans, though Missourians wouldn't mind it. On my right the valley of the Sacramento stretches off into the blue smoke or mist which shrouds every distant object.

On the left the mountains, some eight miles distant, tower up into the same blue vapor. The distance across from Rube's to the Yuba is 28 to 30 miles and I struck the last two miles below Long's Bar and five and a half below Parks. My destination is Park's or Segar's Bar. Took supper at Long's Bar at an eating house kept by two colored men. One of them, Coy, was second steward on board the ship Washburn came round the Horn in. They keep everything neat, and are scrupulously clean.

They have an airy canvass house under the shade of some broad spreading live oaks. In passing up the river I am struck with the general air of neatness, order, and quiet of everything. The houses are large and well lighted, and count by hundreds while the intervening spaces are filled with white tents. It is a day or rather evening of rejoicing as they have just closed the dam which turns the water through the race and is intended to drain the river bed a mile or more. Alas! Alas! for the vanity of human expectations. The dam, even while I write, has given way, and it will require a deal of labor to close it again. I suppose there are more than 300 men engaged in this work alone, besides the hundreds who are trading, doing nothing—at work on the "bar" above water, etc.

There are a number of taverns or eating houses and stores, and a great deal of taste is displayed in setting them off to the best advantage. The whole street as I passed up in the twilight, and darkness, the candles just lit up, had the appearance of a long street in the suburbs of a great city. The inhabitants seem mostly from the eastern states.

SUNDAY, AUGUST 11. The scenery here is somewhat like portions of the Rock River country, Illinois. The mountains begin to rise just above Park's Bar. Below, the hills are not high, and gently slope to the river. The valley is narrow, and the stream bed rocky. There are probably two or three thousand people on this river in a distance of five miles and an immense amount of labor has been expended here.

The bars were very rich, and the surface has been worked over by the acre. They are now digging below, on the bed rock, which lies from three to forty feet below the surface. I visited a place this afternoon where they are drifting beneath twenty feet of earth, along the surface of the rock. Most of the drifts are high enough to walk into without stooping much, and are generally supported by timbers. I followed one in sixty or seventy feet, and came to water. I think that I could see the terminus in the darkness beyond, but am not certain. These holes, or drifts, run across into each other, and probably the whole bed rock will be worked over in this way before it is abandoned. The gold is in fine particles, most of it imperceptible to the naked eye.

C.B. Dodson has a share in a claim (one-fifth of the whole) in the bank, which is accounted the richest in the Bar. The average yield per week is about $2,000 from the start, and as much as ten pounds have been taken out in one day. Only five men are employed, who have $10 a day, and board. They use a quick-silver machine. He has also a share in a race on the opposite side of the river. There are 52 shares in all, but no man can hold more than one. I think that Dodson is likely to do well.

Found Torrey in good health, and got all the news. He left Jerome Smith in Carson valley. Wm. McClure came through, and is in Marysville. Do write, says the Doctor, in such fashion to those behind, that no more of our friends shall come here. No use, says I, they won't believe, anyhow; so let them burn their fingers. Anybody is a fool to come here, quoth the Doctor. Amen, I respond, and so the matter rests for the present.

I should not be at all surprised, or rather, I should not wonder, I am slightly inclined to think that Dr. Torrey is a man of judgment, and has hit the nail on the head. I really hope that no one will be deterred from coming on account of what anybody else may say. The more fools the better – the fewer to laugh when we get back. Of course, it is wiser to believe stories trumped up in New York City by wicked wags, veritable stories, made to order in order to be sold, than the reports of eye-witnesses, who only feel, and see, and suffer, and believe and know nothing.

J. Wisner is here. Dr. Torrey returns with me. In coming over yesterday I saw several flocks of antelopes. They are very tame, and suffer the dog to run up within three or four rods. Two men, or things, were fighting in the streets today. They were too drunk to harm each other much, nothing more than mere scratches. One of them, however, got hold of a loaded musket, and would have shot the other down if Wisner had not taken it away. A California Justice of the Peace stood within eight rods, and quietly viewed the whole performance.

MONDAY, AUGUST 12. Crossed back to Rube's ranche with Dr. Torrey. My feet got very sore in going over, travelling in a pair of pumps. I could not find a pair of shoes to fit me on Feather River, and boots are too heavy. I obtained a pair of good ones on the Youba, but I was nearly used up before I got back to Rube's. The earth is so hot that the feet blister from the heat alone. Thermometer said to be 116 degrees.

TUESDAY, AUGUST 13. We were kept awake by that curse of California – gambling. Four of them were at it till three o'clock, when one was fast asleep, another a loser of all he had with him, and in debt nine and a half ounces, while the other two were (I think) in partnership, as they divided the spoils unseen by the loser. I am a competent witness, as my berth was in the second tier, almost over them, and they kept me awake by talking and swearing, drinking and smoking. Reached home again this evening after dark.

Mem: I never take another tramp in thin bottomed shoes, that's settled.

WEDNESDAY, AUGUST 14. My feet are blistered, inflamed, and swelling so that I am unable to walk, unless hitching across the room be walking.

THURSDAY, AUG 15. Cloudy this morning, and a sprinkle of rain. I kept my feet covered with cloth wet with cold water all day yesterday and they feel very comfortable this morning. Cloudy and cool all day and sprinkled several times in the forenoon.

FRIDAY, AUG. 16. Another day, hot as usual. The men have been taking out some gold, but there is too much water yet. The claim above has had four days grace. The dam goes in again tomorrow.

SATURDAY, AUGUST 17. Hot. Hot. Hot. They are putting in the dam and the water is fast running down. Very little left in the river bed this evening. The men cleared off a large space but on account of water only scraped some two square feet of bed rock, which yielded $17.50.

SUNDAY, Aug. 18. Eld. Washburn preached. No more hearers than usual.

MONDAY, AUGUST 19. Left with Dr. Torrey for Sacramento City, before breakfast, which we got at Stringtown. Found a Digger there who had been up at Nelson's Creek with Brookie, and came down yesterday on horseback. Some Indians from the ranche between this and the Middle Fork saw him just before he got in, and gave chase, bow and arrow in hand, and blood in the eye. The Indian jumped from his horse at the door of a trading house, and got protection from the whites till he could string his bow and get at his arrows, when he stepped among them, and defied the whole with as much confidence as Goliath. He at length became so frantic that the whites had to disarm him, and drive off the Indians, who sent a runner over to the ranche, and in a short time two or three hundred were about Stringtown, mostly across the river.

The chivalric Digger challenged the whole to come across, singly or in pairs, to fight, and walked unarmed up and down the river, sending across his defiance from time to time. The Rancheroes dared him to come over and fight all at once, which doubtless he would have done had he been permitted. Thus matters stood when we came to Stringtown this morning. There were droves of Indians all about town, armed with bow and spear, a rod less than an inch in diameter, seven feet long and headed with a stone point like that of an arrow and three inches long.

The whites were about to send an escort with him into the valley, as the Indians cover the hills by the way, to kill him as he passes. I offered to take him through with us, and had no doubt of his safety, as I had twelve shots rifle and pistol; but two men who were going down on horseback took charge of him and, as I learn this evening, were not molested. The Indians do not like to come in collision with the whites, who have the everlasting shooting irons. They dislike even one shot from the rifle, but a revolver they utterly abhor, and the third shot from the same instrument will put a hundred to route.

Arrived at Rube's ranch about one o'clock. By the by, the Indians are not the only ones who make trouble here. A day or two since, several men were brought or rather came, from the Middle Fork on a legal process, charged with a riot, or something like it, in tearing out a dam. They were committed for trial, and left yesterday in custody of Sheriff Wilbur, for jail, at Bidwells'.

TUESDAY, AUG. 20. Remained over, waiting for the team which is to bring my baggage from Stringtown. Torrey left yesterday for Marysville to find McClure, if possible, before I get down. The team was to be here by noon, but has not yet arrived, 9 p.m. There is no country in this wide world where so little trust can safely be reposed in man, as in California. They care not what they promise, and seldom intend to fulfil, unless it is for their interest to do so, and a big interest too. Mark me! I mean what I say, California is almost utterly destitute of good faith, of every kind and description.

There is a report that there have been serious disturbances at Sacramento City, between the squatters on city lots and the legal authorities. Some were killed. I shall endeavor to get the particulars when once there.

Barley is fed to horses and mules here instead of oats, and is quite cheap, only 25 cents a pound, while at Stringtown it is 50 cents. Hay is a bit a pound. I notice that of fifty men who have called here today, every one drank once, and many three or four times.

WEDNESDAY, AUGUST 21. Cloudy all day. Bellfield's team came down, and did not bring my baggage. Exactly—I expected it. About five p.m. a straggling team from the mountains brought it along. We started for Marysville about six p.m. and travelled till two a.m.

THURSDAY, AUGUST 22. Halting on a bottom, where we found the first green grass on the road about four miles below Charley's ranche. This

ranche, as seen by moonlight, is very pretty and kept neat. It is on a long
swell of land, with scattering oaks enough for shade, and has one very large
wooden building (i.e., for California) and two smaller ones, besides the long,
airy canvass building which they occupy until the other buildings are finished. I should like a daylight view.

Lay, for the second time in California, on the ground without shelter. It
was quite cool in the morning and there was some dew. Left at seven and got
a shocking bad breakfast at the ranche of a nondescript from the Cape of
Good Hope. His wife is neither fish, flesh, nor fowl, neither European,
Asiatic, African nor Indian, but most favors the latter, and seems quite a
decent body.

Arrived at Marysville at 12 a.m., and stopped at the St. Louis house. I
have passed a great many ranches on my way down. A part of the country
is dotted or sprinkled with oaks and the lower levels, next the river, generally
have green grass and weeds all over them. The next plateau has some. The
upper one, which is twenty to forty feet above the present level of the river,
gradually rises to the base of the hills which lie at the foot of the mountains,
and is dry and scorched as Nebachadnezzar's furnace. There are very few
trees at all upon this, except along the streambeds; which cut channels
down through it from the mountains.

I noticed a number of laid out towns as I came along this morning. The
stakes stand up as important and imposing as though they actually meant
something. It is really astonishing how completely the people are stultified.
Everyone of these paper towns for thirty miles along the river are, according
to the advertisements, at the head of steamboat navigation.

FRIDAY, AUGUST 23. If it was a pastoral or our agricultural country,
this madness would be less deplorable. But as it is—too little land moist
enough for cultivation without irrigation, and requiring one hundred acres
of the balance to keep one ox from starving during eight months of the
year. The infatuation of these monopolizing, moon-struck ranche speculators
and village plotters is ridiculously yet lamentably amusing. Incongruous
terms, you say—but I aver most characteristic for the wildest speculations of
1836 and 1837 were sober, legitimate business transactions of the very highest
characters, compared with the contemptible, swindling, rancheromania.

Job might, for aught I know, if he were alive, play at "Blindman's buff"
or "Button, button, Who's got the button?" with Solomon, Julius Caesar,
Newton or Thomas A. Kempis, but a farmers donkey would not have a
ranche in these diggins if he was any way smart. Faugh! One of these
fulsome lying hand bills about a town which has only two houses—a smoke
house and a one story doggery—would if fairly divided, make 200 emetics.

Marysville, which contained only two houses last fall, is a point of some
importance and has 300 now besides a number of tents. It stands just above

the junction of the Yuba and Feather Rivers and at present is built mostly on the Yuba.

The buildings stand upon the streets in a very irregular manner and furnish specimens of almost every variety of architecture, except a good one. Most of the holdings are occupied as hotels, stores, shops, bakeries, etc.

The National House is kept by a son of Dr. Arnold of DeKalb Co., Ill. if I am not mistaken. Found J. Wisner and S. Hawley here. Hawley has been sick a long time though he is now able to be about. I. Hawley has gone up the Yuba for a few days. Heard that the Gibsons are in Sacramento City. Latham has gone to Oregon. Wm. Latham is dead, and James somewhere in this region.

Only one steamer gets up as high as here at present. Several came up to Nicholaus' Ranche [ranch and trading post belonging to Nicolaus Allgeier, located between New Helvitia (Sutter's Fort) and Hock Farm] twelve or 15 miles above Vernon and three lines of stages run from here down and connect with them. One line runs through to Sacramento City. Yesterday the fare was reduced to ten dollars. This is quite reasonable, and the result of competition. I have shipped on the thing they call a "steamer" on account of the weight of my baggage.

I should, most likely, have gone on the stage to Nicholaus' and taken the *Gov. Dana*, but I could not find the agent nor ascertain how I was to get my baggage on board the stage, as I noticed that the coaches are all on the other side of the Youba.

Everybody here is independent from necessity. Nobody will carry your baggage. A landlord never thinks of touching a travellers trunk or carpet bag—even by proxy. Indeed if one can get a towel, to say nothing of a clean one, he may think himself too liberally dealt with.

But the boat. The reason why I called it a thing would be obvious if you could only get a description. I confess my inability to give an intelligible one. If you chose, however, you may imagine a large, awkward scow, of the very clumsiest build, primeval architecture 18 feet wide and 60 feet long. Next, some posts set up nearly perpendicular, a shabby floor spread over them for a deck and another set of posts and a rough framework covered with canvass, through the middle (or somewhere near) of which sticks up solitary and alone a long, rusty, rough, dusty smoke pipe. All propelled by a stern wheel at the rate of four miles an hour, or even faster possibly at times, particularly if the current happens to run three or four miles an hour. But can't tell yet, certain.

We left Marysville at 10:30 and if our speed does not derange the time pieces on board we shall probably know our average mileage when we get to the city.

The fare is five dollars deck passage with the privilege of being roasted between two naked boilers, and no escape only into the cabin where it is half roast. Cabin—?—only think. Six posts on each side, boarded two feet high, a bench on each side each 32 feet long. Whiskey and two berths at my end and dishes and four berths at the other. From these dishes we get our meals at 1.50 a meal. A long table meanders (nothing straight here) through the center or near the center of the—the—cabin.

Such is the Yuba. A yankee hen coop floating through some of the snaggiest places I ever saw mortal craft navigate. But she is under the protection of some buoyant influence; in other words she swims like a tub or we should have sank her before this, for she has been on a snag and unshipped her rudder once already and may be will half a dozen times more. However, it seems not to disturb anybody.

All right again after ten minutes. And two minutes after that the pilot ran her through the opening in an Indian fish dam not three feet wider than the stream—the scow I mean, without touching. The Indians have a fish dam across the Feather River just above the junction with the Youba.

11:30 a.m. Just passed a number of buildings on the left bank. One had as a sign: "Our House," another, "Sutter House," another "Old Virginy Shore," etc. Very pretty houses. I suppose it is some city. Daren't enquire. It would show ignorance. Better know nothing than expose your want of knowledge. Landed just below this city on the opposite side, for wood.

1 p.m. Got aground at Sutter's farm. Before we got afloat again, two gentlemen, two Indians and three squaws came along side in a boat and boarded us. I suppose they intend to take passage.

Were aground again from three to four a little below Plumas City [since vanished], which is on the left bank. An advertisement says it contains twenty houses. I saw three or four, but the bank is now twenty feet high and perhaps hides the city. Aground again at sundown two miles above Nicolaus. Part of the way the water is deep and the navigation unobstructed. The balance is either full of snags or immense bars of shifting sand like the Missouri or Platte. Should the river fall a few inches more this boat could not run if indeed it ever moves again.

SATURDAY, AUGUST 24. Sunrise. Aground yet. One consolation is, we know pretty near where we are, though we have no instrument to determine our latitude and longitude.

In two or three months also the rainy season will probably set in, and as the river rises then some twenty feet I suspect that the boat will be very nearly sure to float off. Still I question if our provisions will last, though we shall not have to be put on short allowance of water, unless the whole emigration should stop on Feather River and use it for culinary purposes.

Aside from these trifling annoyances, if they may be so greatly dignified, I deem our prospects lamentably flattering. Were I so disposed I could show all the fearful consequences which our prospective detention, would hustle upon the country, the United States, the world at large, and what future generations will probably say and think about—but I forbear. Would that all travellers were as considerate. I see no preparation for breakfast. Breakers ahead. Have enquired of the steward and pilot and one of the passengers and all report, "No provision." "No stores." "Nothing to eat." How scandalous and two miles to the nearest port. If we were not aground we could run into it in half a day. Am really disappointed. We got off at eight a.m. and was here before nine. But then the "engine had got well rested."

We had a scanty breakfast before we started. There are a dozen good houses here—taverns and stores. Two very considerable vessels that came round the cape lie here. One of them—a ship—rejoices in the name of *The Curtiss of N. London.* Stopped only a few minutes and put off again. This is at present the head of navigation, for where this scow goes up, all say, she will not return, and yet the cry is still "she comes." Probably these Nicolations would be pleased to have their predictions prove true. How selfish!

Was aground again some distance below Nicolous, and met the *Gov. Dana* a little above Vernon, which city we passed a little before noon. Only a few houses have been built since I was there last winter. The same of Fremont. By the bye, I had some fine melons at Marysville. They cost so, however. I helped eat a round, very fine flavored one eight inches in diameter. It cost $2.50. This fruit is cultivated here to a considerable extent. I have seen some very fine tomatoes and turnips. Onions are inferior, and potatoes small.

One of the gentlemen who came on board at Sutter's is a Pole: the head man, with an unspeakable name, of those who came to locate the lands granted by the U.S.A. to exiled Poles. He is sick with fever. I have this afternoon persuaded him to take some medicine.

One of the Indian women had her husband shot a few days since by a white man, and is returning from a visit she has just made to Captain Sutter, to whom she has applied for justice. Little will she get as her husband was drunk and the aggressor. The Captain has promised to investigate it. I believe that the Indians have great confidence in him, and probably it is not misplaced.

5 p.m. Landed in Sacramento City. How vain now are all my speculations in regard to the speed of the boat, her grounding, etc. The banks of the river are lined on both sides as far as I can see with vessels of almost all kinds and sizes. Everything has an active business appearance. In this city I notice as much activity as I ever witnessed in Chicago.

Put up at the Columbia House between I and J Streets. A great house where gambling is not allowed. I enquired for a temperance house and was met only by a vacant stare. They did not seem to know what I meant so I ordered the man to drive me here.

Portage for two trunks and one carpet bag three blocks only $1.50 – Cartage for self, $1.00. Board and lodging $7 a day. This evening it is much cooler here than where I left in the mountain.

SUNDAY, AUG. 25. Morning pleasantly cool, not chilly as in the mountains, or even at Marysville and one feels no need of a fire. Was out a little last evening and was surprised at the improvements made since I was here last January. There are three large hand bills for last evenings theaters. Stuck on pillars in the common sitting room of the Columbia House, besides a large one of "Herr Rossiter the Magician" for this evening, tomorrow and Tuesday.*

These strike my attention first as I enter the room this morning. Yesterday when we came in I noticed that the flags in the shipping were half mast, and a passenger suggested that the mayor, who was wounded in the squatter's affray, was dead.† This morning's papers are in mourning for the death of President Taylor, and so the tables are turned and 1841 returns in 1850 with a balance in favor of the Whigs, *but nothing for freedom.*

Then a Whig president dies and a hybrid steps in his place causing the Whigs to sing in doleful strains:

> "With Tip and Tyler, we bust Van's Biler
> With Ty alone we bust our own."

Now a mongrel president steps out an in comes a radical Whig. "Oh, who so happy as we." So the world goes. The Whigs are the people now and the Union of the "Hunkers and Free Soilers" premature. If the move had not been made the Hunkers would have been obliged to become Free Soilers in self defence.

They take the smallest drink here of any place I have visited in California. Called on John Gibson who keeps a house for "storing," "boarding," etc. Just below the mouth of the "American Fork." I think he is doing tolerably well. His brother is with him though not in partnership. About 12 a.m. I began to search for a meeting and though I readily found 50 gambling shops and palaces thronged with humans, it was a long time before I found the meeting house and then only by following some children who were dressed as though for Sunday school.

I at last found a congregation in a house, probably 24 or 34. It was full and many stood around the door and I among them. The voice of the speaker was so low that I did not hear much. Gibson called at three p.m. and we attended meeting where I did in the forenoon. It is a Methodist chapel criled with boards, has a very plain pulpit and no alter. There are two astral lamps on the desk. The steps are broad, easy and, of course,

---

Sacramento Transcript, Aug. 24, 1850: "New Exhibition—We understand that Herr Rosseter, celebrated magician, has arrived in town. He will give exhibitions in Legerdemain, Grecian Exercises and balancing feats on the slack rope. He has procured for a short time, the Tehama Theatre."

†*Harlin Bigelow, the mayor of Sacramento, was wounded in his thumb which later was amputated. He died of cholera in the ensuing epidemic.*

comfortable, but take up a great deal of room. The house is quite too much out of the way being half a mile back from the "levee" and a good piece down the river—between N & O streets. We were in time to get a seat. About 125 persons present, seven of whom were females. There were two ministers, one of them I should judge just across the plains—long hair and big whiskers. I do abominate whiskers on anybody, but on a minister they become intolerably annoying.

In returning, found a man preaching on the levee to 200 or 300 people. Took tea with Gibson and in the evening attended a temperance meeting in the same chapel. Judge Willis according to notice delivered an address [Edward J. Willis, Judge, Criminal-Probate courts, Sacramento, who presided over the "Squatter" trial in August 1850]. He is quite a young man, not more, apparently, than 30 [listed in 1850 census as 29]. Spoke very well but seemed not to have thought much upon the subject.

He was followed by a blacksmith in some very ludicrous remarks and he by a Dr. Deal [William Grove Deal, physician from Pennsylvania] or some such name—a very good speaking. The meeting adjourned two weeks without coming to any conclusion as to the best mode of operating on the drinking community.

MONDAY, AUGUST 26. Found Torry this morning. He came directly through and has taken an office on the corner of K and 10th street to which I moved my baggage. Met General Fry [Gen. Jacob Frye, of Ottowa, Ill., Senator, Placer County, 3rd Session, Calif. Legislature, 1852] in the street and had some conversation with him. He is delighted with the country and feels brilliant. I hope he will not get sick.

Came across Henry Northam formerly of Dupage Co. Ill., and had a long chat. He camps with the General about two miles down the river. His health is good. Like every new comer, he is at loss what to do. Has rather an itching for the mines; so with every one at first. Each thinks that he can find the lucky place and make his "pile." Probably he will go into some business here. The great difficulty one meets with is lack of capital.

Col. Bideman, an old acquaintance of the "plains" called yesterday. He has a store on I street between 9th and 10th. Is out of health and intends to return home soon. Bideman married Jo Smith's widow. We board at Mrs. Merrill's [Antartic (sic) House, K St. between 10th & 11th Sts., according to Sacramento City Directory, 1851, p. 48], formerly of Aurora. Very good house. $16 a week.

TUESDAY, AUG. 27TH. It was very cool last evening but this morning it is positively cold, and the dew is like the remains of a heavy shower. Everything not under cover is wet. Saw a number of people from Ill. Tomorrow will make up a list.

WEDNESDAY, AUGUST 28TH. Not as cold this morning. Saw Hicks—Leonard Hugunin and Marsh of Chicago just now. And Otis from East of Dundee is enquiring for Van Wormer. I told him the bears had got Van sure. Mr. Ambrose left Marsh's where he was boarding for Nevada City to be gone a week. Was expected back yesterday. Has not returned. Shall see him when he does. According to Marsh's report he has not yet made his "pile."

Two of the Hoveys, formerly of Hill Cottage and Chicago, are renting Lee's exchange on J St. It is fitted up like a palace and has a dozen or more tables for all kinds of "games." On one side is a counter, 30 feet long, behind which stands three fine looking young men dealing out death in the most inviting vehicles—sweet and sour and bitter and hot and cold and cool and raw and mixed.

In another corner is an office where everything eatable calculated to tickle the palate of the epicure may be had by presenting the great "open sesame" here—gold. Oyster and lobster and salad and sauce and fruit and flesh and fish and pies and cakes appear and disappear with so much rapidity and withal so little noise that it seems rather like a dream than a reality—and then this department is served by females. Again—elevated above the mass site a band of musicians playing—ever playing for the amusement of the spectators and gamblers and to attract the passers by.

Occasionally a good song is sung. The walls are covered with pictures, many of them, men and women, almost or quite in a nude state. Everything is got up, arranged and conducted with a view to add to the mad excitement of gambling.

The Lessees own the "banks" in the house and hire men by the day to tend them, i.e., to gamble. The pay is seven to twelve dollars and board. The second floor is occupied as a theatre. The gambling saloon below is very large. I do not know the size but 400 people (by count) moving about are not at all in each others' way.

Mr. Lacky from N. Illinois was just now in the office; also Dr. Obed Harvey, J.B. Smith, C.H. Pendleton, S. Wilcox, O. Wilson, Joseph Root and others from Elgin. Among them was Kent and William Root; Clarke from Cook Co., F. Kenwick & Bro., A. Plumes, A. Horner, G. Rosencrantz, Nathan Boyington, Henry Harvey, Wm. McClure, Hollis Sargent. Clarke of Elgin is here too and George Curtiss, Amos Tift and Lyman Black are at Dry Creek.

THURSDAY, AUGUST 29TH. The streets are thronged with mules and horses. They buy of emigrants in Carson Valley and anywhere this side the "sink," and after the beasts are sufficiently recruited, drive them here and put them in market. They give from one to six or eight pounds of flour for each animal and get from 40 to 120 dollars here. Every body rides at full gallop and, but that the animals know more than their riders, people would often be run down in the streets. Got two letters from home and one from H. Padelford, St. Louis. Sent six sheets of journal and a Sacramento paper to the Western Christian.

FRIDAY, AUG. 30. This morning very cool again, and smoky. Indeed it was more than commonly smoky yesterday. Cool today.

SATURDAY, AUG. 31. Cool morning and cool day. The only difference I can see or feel between the climate here and that of N. Ill. is that here from ten a.m. to five p.m. it is much warmer and the balance of the 24 hours it is a little cooler. It has been so throughout this month and I speak only of this month.

SUNDAY, SEPT. 1, 1850. Did not attend meeting, being quite ill.

MONDAY, SEPTEMBER 2ND. Election of Sheriff comes off today. More than a dozen candidates. No wonder, there are big stealings. Oftener than every hour a man comes round with votes—sometimes the candidate himself. Wagons with flags parade the streets to carry the voters to the polls.

E. Alexander and Joel S. Young were in the office this evening or afternoon. Mr. Loomis [Amasa Wightman Loomis, who prospered and returned home in 1853] of Lake Zurich, Ill. called also. He is keeping a boarding house on the opposite side of the street only a few doors above.

TUESDAY, SEPT. 3RD. Attended prayer meeting at the house of Judge Willis. Only eight present—all males. Mrs. Willis is expected out shortly. The judge and lady and both members of the Baptist church and he a good temperance man "a' that!"

Mr. James W. Capen, the Baptist minister is uncommonly prepossessing on a first acquaintance. He is young, tall, has a fine figure, is scrupulously neat and tasty in his dress, affable and easy in his manners, has not the shadow of a whisker, and above all, he appears unassumingly pious. If he is not I am greatly mistaken. I have seen him only once. He hails from Boston, Bladroin Place Church, and graduated at the Newton Theological Seminary. There is no Baptist church here yet, but they meet tomorrow evening to make the preliminary arrangements for forming one.

I learn from what the brethren said this evening that in my remarks, from time to time, on the sayings and doing of those who were professing Christians in the States, I have only given expression to the opinions of all faithful deserving thinking Christians. Still there are enough Baptists here who have "kept the faith" to form a church if it is only a small one. I suppose there may be a dozen who have letters from home and a character here. I have no letter from the church but I have been able to keep the character.

Chapter Sixteen

September 4–September 5, 1850:
President Zachary Taylor Funeral

———◆———◆———◆———

WEDNESDAY, SEPT. 4TH. Considerable more excitement than usual about the city today. There is to be a bull fight this evening. Gen. Taylor's mock funeral tomorrow, and the offer of 75 dollars a month for laborers on the Levee, raised the social thermometer a half a degree or so. Met at Judge Willis' this evening and concluded to postpone the Chh. organization till a week from next Saturday. There were but a few present and it was thought advisable to admit only those to membership who had letters or certificates. It is not certain what course will be pursued when all meet. I think that the decision is a good one.

Met Doct. John T. Temple in the street today. Found Capt. Hammond of Elgin at Marsh's store this evening. He is sick and returns home immediately.

THURSDAY, SEPT. 5. Was waked this morning by the firing of big guns. Truly man is of himself, intrinsically, a most significant creature, and knows it too, for he is always trying to make a great noise when he attempts to do even the smallest thing. Enclosed I send a programme of the fooleries to be enacted this 5th day of September, A.D. 1850. If I have time I shall report progress, and possibly it may differ somewhat from the printed one.

The streets of this town or city are in the worst possible condition, consistent with the possibility of moving at all. To obstruct them farther would be equivalent to complete embargo. I do believe that the like was never before seen anywhere, unless when some town taken by storm has been given over to sack and pillage.

On K Street they keep all the time a perfect jam of wagons, horses, cattle, mules, men and dogs and such a babel of sounds. It is the great cattle mart and sometimes as many as six or eight horses or mules will be "cried" by as many auctioneers at the same time, at the very top of their voices. Now there is no necessity for all this. A cross street that no one travels would be just as convenient for these purposes, and no one would have cause for complaint. When will men learn that other people have rights like themselves, that it is dangerous to teach them the contrary.

The Gen. Taylor procession was to form at 9 a.m. I was on the ground at 9:15. Saw nothing unless an occasional passer with crape on arm or hat or both. A crowd, however, soon gathered in front of the Columbia House, and men on horse back dressed in black coat and pants—colored pants and vests with white scarfs across the shoulder, secured under the left arm or on the left hip with a black ribbon. What this is for I know not as the sun is streaming down quite hot and they seem to have clothes enough on already. Probably they know. I see no difference in the conduct of these men—no gravity—sure it is not a funeral. They all drink and lounge and swear and talk as usual, even the scarf and crape men, six of whom are drinking at this moment, are no exception.

10 a.m. Not a store or gambling place—nothing—is closed except the Post Office, the very thing and indeed the only thing which should be open.

What now? What a burst! That's the Brass Band and the big drum. Oh! what a rush. Such a squeeze for a sight, and what a sight. He who makes the most noise is as black as the ace of spades. Go it Africa! They will be obliged to acknowledge your merits bye and bye. Bless your big bumps. May your time never be less or your tune wasted until you can sing the jubilee of a world's freedom. That's right. Hold up your head bravely; learn to know your own importance as you seem to feel it—they can't do without you. And you who puff and blow; go it! Crack your cheeks in honor of the great departed, and humor the vanity of those that have no other commodity to humour.

That's it! Livelier, livelier! Thousands will sing responsive to your strain. One half rejoice that the old man is gone and the other half are a little sorry. One party he permitted to do nothing and hindered the other from doing anything. Only those really mourn or even feel his loss who are unwilling to "fly from ills we suffer now, to others that we know not of."

And now the mounted scarfmen come in sight, "no banner waving o'er their desperate heads"—and these who follow? Why as I'm alive—men— grown up men, in blue and white aprons, with crape on arm and hat, shrouded in all the semblance of deep woe.

Their great black whiskers overshadowing quite, the mighty sorrows of their stricken hearts. What an assortment. Faster, faster, apron men! Legs, legs, little man! You beside the big one—only a difference of 21 inches in nett height—and that mostly in legs.

Trip it, trip it, short man! with the little apron, or you're distanced.
Neck and neck, no advantage, you sir, with one long leg and one longer. A
fair thing is a fair thing, so have in your "goose neck" a single considerable
lest you come in before you get there. Oh my! What a nose! No place that
for a rudder, friend, unless you're a regular Yuba scow with a steering oar in
the bow. And who or what comes now? A big chip hat and a little black
plume beside a big one. I can't for the life of me see what is under but judging by the motion I should guess it to be a man, or rather, a part of one.

And last and latest a little aproned man in black. There the crown
opens and a craped fellow, swinging his little apron by the strings, breaks
puffing through to take his place, and in the act ties on his bit of painted
rag as nice and handy as any washerwoman. I wouldn't wonder an' he was
one sometimes for _____. But the little man in black? Why he had a black
string round his neck, on which was slung, not himself, but something
before his beauty of an apron, which looked, for all the world, like a pie
and cake board, such as the pedlars use in hawking their edibles about
town.

I am thus particular as I suppose the productions to be indigenous. If
the like has ever been seen in the States I can only say, you will please
excuse me per account of ignorance and strike off − −Bang! That is the fifth
time that big gun has made me jump.−Strike off whatever you−−There
they go again. The procession is moving off. The scarfs and aprons are followed by the scarfs and ribbons: black ribbon and red, blue ribbon and
grey, tied in the button holes of the progressing bipeds−mingle, mingle,
mingle, mingle as they may. Black coats are there and striped coats and
blue, and fantasies of fashion and propriety too.

Oh what a mockery of human reason! What a gross perversion of social
instincts. A wolfish, hyenic longing to unearth the dead−the beggardly
desire of an anatomist jackall−a greedy, carnivorous, resurrectionist. To
chase, harass, torment, torture, flay alive, crucify an unoffending old man to
the death, and then unearth him under pretence of doing him honor. Bury
not the living, and let the dead rest; what say ye now, oh! graceless politi-
cians?

Well there they go, the motley crowd. I can only get a glimpse, but I see
two Chinamen in full dress of a sort of blue gown reaching to the ankle,
with clumpy, short shoes, no shirts, a hat like that which rode General Put-
nam down the rocks, a black fan to shade the sun from the face, the brown
(?) barbarian, and a long cue reaching from head to heel, for all the world
like a great black snake. How beautiful! I won't follow them. No, no. I can
do better. No doubt they will return some day and I will lie in wait by the
road side.

12 M. There they come, and here they pass. Scarfed horsemen music
and crapemen 56. And Legs and Shortie and Nosey and Plumes and Pie-
Board and queer things too incredible for relation or belief. Now I perceive

what the great white scarfs are for. The crapes and scarfs walk beside the hearse which is drawn by four big horses. On the chassis a coffin obliquely across which is thrown the flag:—Stars and Stripes. (Blood stains?)

Can I credit my eyes? Is that thing behind, with black housings and big pistols in a big black holster, and a hunching head "Old Whitey?" Who says it? He looks sorry sure—sorry—brown with dust—most wondrous story—and yet its not a bad nag. Still I question if he knows what he is sorry for unless the loss of supper and breakfast. No doubt he lost those that he might be more grave, and act beseeming the great occasion—and perhaps to save barley, who knows? Pops, the great farrier, has said, "act well your part there all the honor lies." Now honor to whom honor is due. Whitey acts Whitey to a charm, and if Whitey ain't a sorrowful acting and appearing horse, then those that left their bonus this year in the Great Basin died of excess of joys. Whitey is consistent and at least has shut up shop—fasted and drinks neither brandy nor whiskey, nor wears whiskers, nor smokes nor laughs.

I wonder if he knows that the rusty old boots stuck in his stirrups, or rather the saddles' "en reverse" are "bona fide" ones? It's queer though, but sure as you are a brown Whitey, those same boots are on the wrong track, toe backwards, and yet it's all right Old Hoss. The pie board man can explain, as he carries the documents under his nose, that those boots are the veritable boots that Jim Mosely nearly kicked his nigger Tom's posteriors to death with—last winter at Orient Bar.

And now they pass. Well, it's a small show after all to make such a fuss about. Two hundred twenty one all counted, from a population of ten or fifteen thousand and the post office closed at that. Yet all classes, clans, nations, facilities, families, politics, faces and principles except diggerism and Mormonism are faithfully represented. Only a few representatives from each, though, unless it be those whose scarlet faces never came honestly by their color.

And now for dinner while the upper 221 go to the theater to be bored with a grand oration about virtues that never existed, talents never discovered, glory which would shame the devil, honor which has long since retired from the public gaze, and liberty in whose praise ten thousand thousand empty skulled, bell tongued, brazen throated rogues are bawling, whose Iron heels are pressed upon her neck.

Oh! Col. Zabriskie! I could almost bear to hear you lie to the rascally hypocrites, from mere spleen, but that I do despise the humour of the cant.*

After dinner called on Dr. Temple. Really, I would not have believed without seeing. They have enacted the farce clear through, text, stage, directions, finis, blank leaf, and cover.

Col. James C. Zabriskie, formerly of New Jersey militia, was a Sacramento lawyer who was active in politics and who wrote a eulogy on Zachary Taylor which was published in the Sacramento Transcript, *Sept. 6, 1850.*

They are returning with the plumed hearse, but the coffin is safe under ground. Oh shame, shame! They boxed up when they should have set the Old Hero upright on his haunches, rifle in hand and bowie knife on knee, with his horn of powder and pouch of bullets—and parched corn for nine days, not forgetting his pipe. No use putting a warrior in a chest. But I forget.

He rests in his native land, and remembers his battles no more. Peace to his ashes. I have only witnessed the shadow of a night mare (horse?). Alas for poor Whitey. He too is gone, boots and all, vexed to death by the impudent graceless mockery of his long eared leather headed coadjutors, or starved out of breath by long fasting, or sacrificed at the grave of his pseudo-master's coffin by having his throat cut from ear to mane. Truly it would be a grand idea to get up a funeral for Nimrod or Zenghis Khan; and if it was enacted at the "Sink" in the "Great Basin," a thousand horses starved to epicurean nicety might be had for the killing—only think! A hecatomb! Splendid!

In connection with this subject, I would remark, that the musquitoes are not troublesome here, as we seldom see one, but the fleas are most pestilent fellows, playing all sorts of fantastic tricks to the great discomfort of those who desire to sleep. The rats, however, are the nuisance. I waked suddenly last night with the cry of "the Philistines be upon thee Sampson," and instanter two of the rascals went trooping over my face in full career.

We shall stop this soon I trust as Mrs. Merrill has hired a large new building, two and a half stories high on the opposite side of the street. It will be furnished in about ten days and then we shall see. Travellers report the musquitoes very troublesome immediately you leave the city to go below and down at the bay intolerable.

Chapter Seventeen

September 6–October 1, 1850:
Life in Sacramento

◆　◆　◆

FRIDAY, SEPT. 6. Oh, these mornings are so chilly, and the middle of the day so hot. Robinson, Esq., formerly of Aurora, Kane Co., boards here.

SATURDAY, SEPT. 7. Capt. Hammond proposes leaving tomorrow. Says that Jesse Spitzer and Capt. Slate of Naperville are over at Marsh's store on J St. Henry Northam called this morning with Wm. McClure of Joliet. Mr. Scott, of Naperville, is expected here shortly. Capt. Slate called this afternoon. He seems to have formed a very correct opinion of the country, does not think of returning at present.

SUNDAY, SEPT. 8. Jones, of Naperville, and James Pratt took dinner with us today. Jones returns to the mines immediately. Heard Mr. Capen preach this forenoon. It must be an embarrassing place to speak in, this court-room, being on 4th St. with a noisy hotel next door, and all kinds of noises and sounds but sweet ones in the streets. There is a bell, almost on the threshold; ringing, ringing, a brass bell of the loudest key and sharpest tone, and rung unnecessarily long, if it is only a call for dinner.

Still the sermon was a good one—plain, practical and spirited, and delivered in a natural easy, and graceful manner. It was on: "Come-outism," and he is a "come-outer," for he preached politics,—must vote conscientiously, and consistently with our Christian principles,—no Sunday, or exclusive religion, but one which reaches every business transaction, and requires us to do unto others as we would wish them to do unto us,—no overreaching in bargains—no cheating in trade—no selling of alcoholic drinks—or engaging in business or associating with any man in a business if its tendency is to injure any person whatever. In the afternoon he gave a beautiful and interesting paraphrase of the first Psalm.

Attended a Temperance meeting this evening. It was a very spirited one—but nobody, as yet, proposes any definite plan of action. The house was crowded, and what can such a room do towards containing the temperance audience of this great city?

MONDAY, SEPT. 9. Met Leonard Kimball, of Naperville, today. Wind blew fresh all day and strong this evening. Uncomfortably cool, or even cooler, and has been all day.

TUESDAY, SEPT. 10. Cold this morning. I think that I have seldom or never see it colder in the States at this season. There were a few clouds yesterday; today it is quite cloudy. A sprinkle of rain this evening or rather afternoon. Prayer meeting at Judge Willis' this evening. Brother Prevaux was present. He graduated at Newton, last year, with Br. Capen. He thinks of stopping at Coloma. Says that the prospect is exceedingly promising.

THURSDAY, SEPT. 12. Went up to Sutter's Fort this morning to see a sick man (Seth T. Walker) in the Sacramento Hospital.* The establishment seems to be very well conducted but there are too many patients (not less than 60) crowded into the principal room. They are mostly fever patients, or rather were; more than one half of them having diarrhea consequent on, or in connection with, fever. The floor is covered with flag, or rush matting, which retains all the filth and effluvia falling upon it. The air in the room is very offensive. The mortality is very great, and probably ever will be here, under almost any kind of management. In a hospital strictly private, the chances for recovery are much increased. This is only a public one, inasmuch as any one may enter, and if he has no money the city pays the bill. I understand it is eight to ten dollars a day. It was five dollars. I know not why the price is raised.

Sutter's fort is nearly or quite two miles above 10th Street and in the line of L. The situation is beautiful, and would be delightful if properly improved. It is now fast falling into ruins, and is the picture of desolation. It has been too often described to bear another description easily. There is a brewery, and a few famishing grog shops. Hot day.

FRIDAY, SEPT. 13. A little more cloudy, and not as warm. Jason Estis and Ai Sargent here today on their way home. Saw them off on the steamer *Fashion*. They go by Panama. Estis has been sick. Attended Bible Class at Judge Willis' this evening. Only a few present. Why is it that a Bible Class is seldom well attended?

*Walker, from New York, died in Sacramento on September 28 age age 25.

Sutter's Fort (California State Library).

SATURDAY, SEPT. 14. Met Rev. Mr. [Osgood C.] Wheeler at Doct. Temple's office today. He has come up by invitation, to assist in organizing a church here. This evening a considerable number of brethren met at Judge Willis', and formed a church. Only five letters of dismission were presented and these were constituted members. Enough letters recommendatory were than produced to increase the number to 15, and the bearers were then received by the church and thus we have the First Baptist Church of Sacramento.* Brother Capen was immediately called to preach to them.

Last winter, Brother Cook partly succeeded in organizing a Church. The principal difficulty seems to have been, the evanescent character of the population. That adjective better expresses it than any other. Tomorrow morning, Br. Wheeler will preach and give the right hand of fellowship. Br. Capen will preach in the afternoon, after which will be communion service. In the evening several ministers are expected to be present by invitation; and it is expected that the Congregational minister will give the charge to the church. Brother Wheeler was Moderator, and the business was executed with despatch, and yet "straight." The New Hampshire "Articles and Covenant" were adopted, with the addition of a strong temperance pledge, but

According to Thompson & West's 1880 book History of Sacramento County, California: *"A Baptist Society was organized in October (1850) by the Rev. O.C. Wheeler, then of San Francisco. There was no Baptist minister here regularly till about April or May, 1850, when the Rev. Mr. Capen took charge of the church."*

nothing was said about slavery. I am not aware that any of the members are slaveholders. It is possible, as some of them came from the South.*

There is great disparity of size and appearance between Br. Capen and Br. Wheeler. The latter is the shorter by six or eight inches and in appearance is far more assuming and positive than Br. Capen. But I should think him an excellent man for his present position, as he is constitutionally active, and does not hesitate to assume the responsibility if occasion requires.

SUNDAY, SEPT. 15. A man came into the office this morning with delirium tremens, and kept me till the afternoon service, when I heard Br. Capen preach. At the communion the usual invitation was extended when some 18 or 20, besides the church, were found anxious to avail themselves to the privilege. It was a profitable and pleasant season, I doubt not, for all. In passing, I would remark that the smell of what was intended to represent wine, was rank with the odor of the great liquid enemy of man. I wonder at this, as Br. Willis, who procured it, is an out and out temperance man. When will men learn to be on the watch for the first approach of the old enemy?

After meeting, our old friend, D.M. Kelsey, Whilom of Geneva and St. Charles, Ill., seized me by the hand. He has been sick, but is convalescent now. I did not at first recognize him, so changed. This is his first attempt to get out. Thunder, and several slight showers this evening. It has been cloudy all day, and seemed to threaten rain; only a few drops fell, however, in the day time.

MONDAY, SEPT. 16. Cloudy and warm today. Isaiah Goodwin of Lockport and a brother of Calvin Bristol called today. Doct. Bixby Dodson is in town, but I have not seen him. Justus Fordyce, a Harrison Elector in 1840, was in at breakfast. He says that he came for money, and intends to get it. He is carrying the express into the mines, and will probably do well enough—till he gets—SICK. He is almost sure to do so; else he is not made of the same stuff as other stragglers in these diggings. The mortality among the immigrants is much greater than last year, and hundreds of the sick, immediately when they get able, start for home in double quick time.

At least 300 persons leave every day in the steamboats. The fare to San Francisco is now very low, on account of the competition. Last winter it was $30 and find yourself. Four weeks ago, it was $15 to $20. Yesterday the highest was $10 all found, and the lowest $1—(on a little fippenny boat, the Jack Hays.)

The Senator, McKimm and New World are large boats for a new country, and about as long as is convenient. They would be medium size lake boats. *The California* I have not seen. *The Fashion* will carry 200 passengers. *The Hartford* is a propeller of considerable size—an old, black, scary looking ship. *The Gov. Dana*, is a pretty boat, and swift, running from here to Fremont and Vernon at present and to Marysville, when she can get there.

There are some scow boats (steam) playing round here and there; one running every few minutes across the river as a ferry boat, at 12½ cents for a footman, and I know not what for teams. *The Youba*, in which I came down, struck on a snag at the Hock Farm [Sutter's ranch on the Feather River, 8 miles below Yuba City, used as a stock ranch] a few days ago— broke up and sank in ten feet of water. (So says report, a liar.)

17TH. Some clouds today. Prayer meeting at Br. Willis' this evening. More than 20 persons. Ransom Clark, formerly of Warrenville and vicinity, here today. Alexander and Young both came in sick today. They are carrying on Blacksmithing here.

18TH. Hot day. Thermometer 100 degrees in the shade and the night warmer than I have before seen in California. The dust is flying all the time and the air is really unfit for respiration. The wind generally blows it off but there was none today.

19TH. Another hot day and warm last night. After 10 a.m. there was a pleasant breeze. Mr. Campbell of St. Chas. and Joel Young here today.

20TH. Cooler last night and this morning and all day, and cloudy this evening.

21ST. Showery in the night and this morning and then clouds and showery and cloudy all day. Some victim of delirium tremens ranging the streets today after threatening the lives of several individuals. Shot a negro and wounded him as I understand, severely. Rowley Wilson came in today. He says that Vandercook, James Champion and Chas. Van Epps with others came through with him. Sanford Van Epp was left this side of the desert to bring in a wagon. Ed Morgan and Mixer got to Hangtown where Mixer died of a diarrhea. Rowley intends going to work on the Levee a few days. This work is progressing rapidly and will probably be completed in a short time.

Wages are only $75 a month and more hands than they want at that. A strong effort was made to keep up wages but failed. I think they might pay $3 a day.

SUNDAY, SEPT. 22ND. Some cloudy and cool this morning but clear all day after an early sprinkle. The grog shops and gambling saloons were to have been shut up today, there being a city ordinance to that purport. I do not know if the city fathers will be sustained. I question such if they have the majority with them. We shall see.

Passed a new meeting house on 5th Street (as I came up from the afternoon service) where the minister was preaching with a great earnestness. It has been built within a week and I had not time to enquire what denomination worships there.

The colored people are building a new house. They have a preacher of their own color and will be in their chapel in two weeks at most. The Baptists are talking about building which here is equivalent to doing it and I would not be surprised if they had one up in three or four weeks. We have a Sunday School library of 280 volumes bought by a Bro. here at auction for ten dollars and we are now collecting scholars for a Sunday school. Bro. Willis thinks there will be 30 or 40 to start with. Among the new comers are many families. I should think there may be in the city at this time 300 children.

SEPT. 23RD. The grog shops were not shut yesterday. John Laueb of Naperville is said to be in town and Wm. Root of Elgin is in Hangtown. A heavy shower this evening at dark and continued to rain till 9 p.m.

24TH. Cloudy. Rowley Wilson left at noon for our "diggins" on Feather River. Torry returned from Phillips. The P.O. is closed today on account of the arrival of the great eastern mail. Hot day again and a few clouds in the afternoon.

25TH. Same as yesterday. The Vedders', formerly of DuPage Co. are in the city.

26TH. No change. The town is full of strangers leaving for home.

27TH. Joseph Ropps from St. Charles, Ill. called this morning. Very hot.

28TH. I have just learned that Col. Witt of Lockport, Ill. is dead.* He was at the City Hospital. I verily believe that a man is better off and far more likely to recover from the dysenteric fever that now prevails if left unaided and alone under one of the broad topped oaks on the mountains or in the valley than in the crowded wards of the City Hospital. This is certainly the filthiest city I was ever in and worthy of all execration.

There seems, however, not to be a great deal of sickness among the actual and permanent residents as yet. I think there is an increase since the

*John E. Witt, died in Sacramento Sept. 26, 1850, age 44.

little fall of rain. The rainy season, if it is warm, is probably the sickly one here. At the fort where the City Hospital is the ground is several feet higher than here but like everything in California, there is a drawback in shape of a long stinking pond in the bottom of a shallow and narrow ravine which forms a natural ditch on the north side of the fort at the foot of the wall rendering it inaccessible on that side. This sink is a breeder of pestilence and will probably ever remain so as it can only be abated by filling it with fresh earth. And that will hardly happen unless the rats take it in hand.

I would not wonder—and the rats had sole and undisputed possession of this city in five years, or a great part of it, and yet there are some very good buildings and several large and expensive ones are now being erected of brick. One on G street corner of Second is a splendid affair beyond anything in the brick line I have ever seen, that is, so far as general appearance is concerned. It is to be plastered I perceive as they are now lathing the ceiling of the basement, which is at least 18 feet high. This is all in one room. Nearly 100 feet on Second St. and 40 to 50 on G St., and will no doubt be a magnificent room. I do not know what use is to be made of it. The walls are very heavy and the work of the first class.

On the north side of G street between First and Second is a large gambling saloon to be opened immediately. The finish is superb—splendid beyond description. Opposite is the Empire kept by Keith formerly of Chicago—an immense room filled with gamblers and revellers. A brass band from their high "vantage" ground, a balcony at one end, inciting them to madness. Between Second and Third streets there are the Humboldt and Oregon in full career of crime. The last runs three bad alleys. Next is the great saloon under the theater—or Lee's Exchange which has been closed a few days and the Hoveys of Chicago have just opened. It is now finished up in a style that would astonish anything coming from beyond the Rocky mountains.

These are the great fashionable resorts but there are 200 or 300 other houses with from one to four gaming tables all in constant operation. And thus at any corner you may see a group of men betting about the twist of a string or the lifting a thimble or some of the thousand devices of gamblers to take money from fools. I saw one very staid grave looking man put down twenty dollars on the string game yesterday. He lost. Another lost 25 as foolishly. They said it was the first and last.

Angus Brown of Geneva was in the office today.

29TH. Hot. Very hot. C.B. Dodson called this evening.* Says that the

---

*Earlier in 1850, C.B. Dodson competed for Alcalde and Recorder of Marysville, CA. Dodson was defeated by nine votes by Judge Stephen J. Field. "Though he failed in his judicial aspirations for Alcalde, yet his continued exertions and marked influence caused him to leave a name richly associated with all the early history of Marysville and vicinity." Stephen J. Field, Personal Reminiscences of Early Days in California, De Capo Press, 1968.

dams on the Youba are destroyed or the races injured and water so high that there is but little chance of doing anything this year. Intends to return home. It is now certain that damming the rivers has proved a general and signal failure.

Hundreds of thousands—millions have been sunk there—literally swallowed up and no returns. Not one dam in 20 would pay cost if it did drain the river, and but few have. Now there has been a sudden, unexpected and probably unprecedented rise in the rivers and those claims that are rich cannot be worked at present and perhaps not this year—maybe never.

30TH. Dodson left this morning before I had time to get down to the boat. The cholera is approaching us slowly from both east and west. It will make a charnel house of Sacramento when it comes.* Hot day, wind north.

Oct. 1. Sultry hot and more dust in the air than I ever before saw suspended in it. I literally makes a dense fog, almost suffocating. The whole valley seems filled with and enveloped in it.

I have lately noticed a curiosity that had previously escaped me. The Californians seem frequently to carry an old rusty sword, or at least a scabbard and belt, on the saddle under the left thigh. It looks very ridiculous like every other part of California horsemanship. This business of riding is all a humbug. The people here are the most ungraceful I ever saw and yet they generally ride at a gallop—a good gait to show off. 500 times a day

*This is an interesting entry since there was no known case in Sacramento until October 18 when it is generally believed that cholera was brought to Sacramento on the steamer New World, which also brought news of the admission of California to the United States. Dr. John F. Morse's account, The First History of Sacramento City, states: "The first case that occurred was a steerage immigrant of the steamer which brought this disease. Early on the morning of the 20th of October a person was found on the levee in the collapsing stage of this formidable malady."

News of California's admission to the union came to San Francisco on October 19 on the steamer Oregon. Dr. Morse's partner, Dr. Jacob D.B. Stillman, left San Francisco for home in the east on October 19, 1850. His diary entry on that day states:

I was so far recovered as to visit the ship on which I had engaged passage to Realejo. While on board of her, I heard heavy guns down the bay, and, in a few minutes after, the steamer Oregon, her rigging crowded with her gala dress of flags and signals, rode by the town, bellowing forth to right and left the joyous intelligence, "California is admitted." The news was shouted from vessel to vessel of that vast fleet anchored in the bay, and the Stars and Stripes ran up to every truck, until the sky was ablaze with bunting, and every reluctant, rusty gun was made to proclaim, far over the waters and away into the rocky fastnesses of the mountains, that California had taken her place as a golden star in the constellation of States.

Also aboard the Oregon was the first case of cholera. The Gold Rush Letters of J.D.B. Stillman, with introduction by Kenneth Johnson, Lewis Osborne, Palo Alto, 1967.

men on horseback pass the office at a run regardless of the danger to themselves and others. You will frequently see two big men on one small mule. A real Spanish Californian will mount his mule or horse to cross Jary street.

Chapter Eighteen

October 2–November 13, 1850: Campaigns and Cholera

———◆——◆——◆———

OCTOBER 2ND. Last night there was an alarm of fire but it soon ceased. Fire out I suppose. Our supply of ice is scant today. Only a single hogshead came up this morning and that went to the gambling saloons. This ice is a cooling affair and comes from Boston, Mass. and is delivered at our doors at 30 cents per pound.

There is a great deal of noise and hurrahing down street. The 1001 candidates for office are gulling the people with blarney and making promises which they not only can't fulfill and never intend to but which they do not even understand. Among the many is Tom Spikens, a rough and tumble mountaineer. He is a customer. He is as ill looking as anything short of positive deformity can make him, worse dressed than visaged and more vicious than both: wicked as the "Wicked One" and more ignorant than wicked — dirtier than all together and drunk to boot. If his hands have been washed in twelve years it must have been through some accidental submersion. A touch of water without his knowledge or consent.

I should suppose, judging from this speeches, that they were "getting him up" and "taking him round," for sport and to get him to treat, but I am assured that he will get a great many votes and some would be glad to see him elected. He was arrested yesterday for brandishing his scalping knife about the heads of our peaceful citizens. I heard him say, "Gentlemen, I am a robber. I have robbed many a man," and I didn't doubt it. He looked like it, and yet I wouldn't want to meet a kinder, more helpful man in the mountains if I was there in trouble and couldn't extricate myself. Such is human nature.

300

OCT. 3. Heard Tom hold forth this evening and will send you a copy when printed as it doubtless will be. He is attended through the streets by one or two hundreds of yelling, shouting rowdies in the highest state of whisky political excitement. Stopping before some saloon they elevate on some barrel or box, and there he stands, bawling out at the top of his voice anything that happens to come into his head or those directly under him may chance to suggest. This prompting produces a strange medley as a specimen or two will show.

"No, Gen'lmen," says Tom. "I spec you'll vote fur me who fought—who—and bled—and,"

"Died," suggests some one.

"And died," says the veracious Tom, "for my country."

Again: "I'm a miner, Gen'lmen, I've mined in the Old States—I've mined in Illinois and I've mined in the whole United States—and—and—and—in Wisconstant State too—and in Old Calliforny—and in—"

"The Pacific Ocean," suggests a friend and true as an echo,

"In the Pacific Ocean," says Tom.

Each day is hotter than its predecessor. The air is full of dust and smoke.

OCTOBER 4. I inclose the promised speech. The reporter does not do Tom justice. He has made him merely ridiculous while he is infinitely below that. He never aspired so high. He is only maudlin, contemptible, idiotic. However, like the speeches of most great men the report is far beyond what was written while most members of Congress have the advantage of Tom, in being able to read printed matter and so an enabled to correct their speeches.

OCT. 5TH. Weather unchanged. The air is like a furnace and the heavens like heated brass.

OCT. 6. This is not Sunday, sure. The streets are blocked with loaded wagons, the stores and shops open. The gambling houses in full blast, while from the Empire the crash of the brass band is deafening. Dr. Wadsworth's son was baptised in the American Fork today. This is probably the first time the ordinance has been so observed in this river. I do not know however. There is quite as much noise as usual this evening. Tom Spikens is on the stump all through the city and tomorrow the election comes off.

MONDAY, OCT. 7, 1850. Died today at a quarter to 12 M. of heart disease—Col. Wm. S. Hamilton, youngest son of Alexander Hamilton who years by gone was swept from the political arena by the fiendlike malice of Aaron Burr. Take him all in all no worse man than that same Aaron Burr has ever polluted the American soil. Don't talk of Benedict Arnold. He was a meteor which glared and blazed and flashed and vanished. Burr was a

planet, dense, dark, portentous, madly yet steadily rushing on to jostle in its
errant course every other body within his influence. The one was the wandering uncertain "Will o' the Wisp," the other the fiery and certain stroke of
the winged lightening. Burr was terrific, Arnold only contemptible. Where
but in the bosom of Burr was steeped the germ that sprouted in Louisiana
and Florida shot up through the rank, corrupt, hot bed of Texas and grew
into luxuriance under the dewy moisture, the shining iniquity of a corrupt
administration, on the plains of Mexico and in the valleys of California.
The idea made even Jefferson forswear himself and in its growth has nearly
torn the Union in fragments. It still grows, on and up to curse—destroy and
perhaps annihilate. It killed the father and now the son. It has destroyed its
thousands and tens of thousands and when millions shall have perished it
will still be unsatisfied—destroying ever.

OCT. 8. Cloudy and quite cool this morning. Some thunder and a
smart shower at half past 2 p.m. Immediately after followed the remains of
Col. H. to their last resting place, and before we left the grave there was
another shower. Bessey died this evening.

OCT. 9TH. Clear and cool again this morning. So the rainy season is
yet in the future. Randolph Bessey buried today.

OCT. 10. Cool and cloudy this morning, but clear in the afternoon. A
patient, no convalescent, who has just got up a quantity of grapes from
below, presented us this evening with some beautiful clusters. Large quantities of grapes have been in market for weeks and sold until recently for
one dollar a pound. They are brought up in large rough boxes, in clusters,
some of them weighing two pounds. I was much disappointed in finding
them so juicy and with so little pulp, though the flavor is fine. The average
size is that of an ounce bullet. They can be had now at three or six bits a
pound. I notice apples in market but of very inferior quality. Scarcely larger
or better than crab-apples.

OCT. 11. The coolest morning yet and nearly cloudless. Buildings are
going on every side and the city is rapidly extending in anticipation of
the rainy season and yet there are 100 buildings for rent now.

OCT. 12TH. John Ross was in the office this evening. George Ross was
in the city two days ago. John Danforth is at the Trinity. Old Wm. Scott of
Naperville is sick on the road between here and Hangtown. I see so many
difficult to keep a memorandum of all. Saw Col. Anderson of DuPage a day
or two ago.

SUNDAY, OCT. 13TH. A beautiful day and not quite as much business being doing. Very few wagons loading in the streets though hundreds are leaving for the mines.

OCT. 14TH. Cloudy and cool and a sprinkle of rain. Hardly enough to say sprinkle. High wind.

15TH. Clear again and cool.

16TH. Cloudy again and coolish all day.

17TH. No change.

18TH. Warmer. Hawkins of Aurora left for home this morning. Went down to see him off and witnessed the terrible struggles of a man lying on the levee dying of cholera. This is the first case I have seen though it is reported that cases occurred the first of the week.*

19TH. Very hot and smokey. News of the reception of California into the Union received at 4 a.m. and hailed with firing of cannon which was kept up at intervals through the day and in the evening barrels of tar were burned in the streets, and all possible noises were made.

SUNDAY, OCT. 20, 1850. Hot day. A man died of cholera in the baker, back of our boarding house. People are just beginning to realize that cholera is here.

MONDAY, OCT. 21. Several cases of cholera yesterday, and all fatal. It seems to strike *dead* at once. A man was found lying on the ground in 11th Street, and died shortly after being taken into a house. Yet most of the M.D.s in town deny the presence of cholera. Surely they are the men, and wisdom dwells in their diggins. The Doctors are generally mighty smart before the scourge comes—ever ready to attack, and if you may believe them, conquer it; but once on them, and all their fine spun theories and speculations *sink with their* patients into one common grave.

The fact is, that when cholera has expended its first virulence, many cases become curable or get well, or rather do not die—under any rational mode of treatment. Till that time, the doctors will have to see their patients die, unless they trust to other methods than those devised by such as have

---

Although the cholera epidemic has generally been attributed to a passenger on the steamship New World, *this would indicate that there was cholera at least one day before the arrival of the* New World. *J.F. Morse, in* The First History of Sacramento City, *states: "Early on the morning of the 20th of October a person was found on the levee in the collapsing stage of this formidable malady. The cholera was now indeed in our city."*

written heretofore. I speak now of Allopathic practice. The city Council, however, in view of the extraordinary fatality of disease for a triplet of days, have passed an "ordinance," requiring the streets of the city to be cleaned out within 24 hours, under a heavy penalty. And sure they need it, though the cleaning of the Augean Stables was mere child's play compared to it. Hot; sultry, in the middle of the day.

Said to be seven cases fatal yesterday. I doubt if that is more than the half. This evening the streets are as filthy as ever, and the heated city is a living, moving toiling mass of men and animals, crawling like maggots in the filth, and breathing an atmosphere filled with poison and dust. The smoke and dust form a dense cloud, which involves everything in obscurity.

WEDNESDAY, OCT. 23. Seven more cases reported for yesterday. I suppose that it will not do to go beyond a particular number, or perhaps the cholera is confined to that particular sum. The corrected list gives one the 20th, when the truth is, all the deaths are not reported, and probably everyone reported was cholera. Pendleton, I KNOW died of cholera. Five on the 21st. Now the whole eight deaths were from cholera except one. Thirteen on the 22nd. There will be as many deaths today and many more every succeeding day.

There is considerable of a stir today.* A man walking down J street last evening, dropped suddenly, and lived only long enough to be carried into the nearest door. This, with the city ordinance and heavy penalty, has set the lazy Hombres in motion. There has been quite a clean up in J street, and cross streets, but the filth is burned in the middle of the streets, old shoes and boots and clothes by the ton, and cart loads of bones, and raw-hides, and putrid meat and spoiled bacon—so that the end of the matter is worse than the beginning. "The more they stir," etc., and our last state is worse than the first. The lurid fires, this evening, shining on the murky air, and the infernal compounds of noisome smells that salute the nostrils, might well remind one of that place Milton so well described. Not as much brimstone, but plenty of tar.

> Oct. 20. John Deidrich, Chicago, Ill., cholera; F. Candus, Abbot Co., Ind., unascertained; Amos P. Pendleton, Westerly, N.Y., diarrhea; Jacob Coates, unascertained; George Astley, Indiana, diarrhea; Henry Brown, (colored) unascertained.
> Oct. 21. Horace Harrison, Newark, N.Y., typhus fever; H.H. Train, cholera; Conrad Hage, (German) unascertained; Tringer, cholera; Wm.

---

*Morse, in his First History of Sacramento City, wrote: "Evidence of [cholera's] appearance created such a dread of its approach, such an inexpressible fear of the destruction which marked its progress, of the malignant and hopeless rapidity with which it hurried its victims into eternity, that the people watched its manifestations with an excitability of mind that can seldom be induced by any scene of earth."

Pitman, N.J., cholera; Joseph Keese, Miss. Co., Mo., typhus fever; Edward Ray, N.B., cholera; Nathan Wood, cholera.

Oct. 22. Davis, Boston, Mass., cholera; M. Frazer, (Scotchman) cholera; R.M. Richmond, Syracuse, N.Y., cholera; Thomas Edwards, N.Y. City, cholera; Smith Coman, Buffalo, N.Y., cholera; Kelly (Irishman) cholera; Edward G. Fowle, Boston, cholera; Alfred W. Rose, cholera; John Saunderson, Mo., cholera; Geor. B. Harvey, Ohio, cholera; Capt. S.W. Powers, Philadelphia, cholera; Charles Delany, cholera; Capt. Cook, cholera.

THURSDAY, OCT. 24. Hot as usual, and cloudy in the afternoon. A dozen or fifteen cases yesterday, though less reported. Mostly fatal. No reports of those who recover, because there are none to report.

FRIDAY, OCT. 25. Jacob Amick, of Chicago, died this morning.* Fifteen to 20 died yesterday—some dozen reported. Twenty had been buried today, between sun-rise and four o'clock p.m. and the cry was still, "They come." Charles Ballard was here this morning and P. Blanchard of Aurora, took breakfast with us. Cloudy this afternoon.

SATURDAY, OCT. 26. Twenty three cases of cholera certain, perhaps

---

Amick's case was recorded in Lord's book, Clinical Medicine, Vol. I on Intermittent Fever and Other Malarious Diseases, Boericke & Tafel, 1871. The date of death probably is more accurately the 25th, as the medical notes were transcribed several years later. There were few cases from Sacramento in Dr. Lord's Intermittent Fevers, and all of them malarial. It is certain that Dr. Lord did keep a medical journal in Sacramento, but whether it still exists or not I have not yet discovered. The following is the record of Amick's case:

Case 10 – Oct. 23 [1850], 8 A.M. Jacob A., 30. Cal. Typh. fever. A stool every twenty minutes; eyes red; face yellow, pale, cadaverous, ghastly; lips wrinkled; mouth and fauces dry; complains of a hollow roaring from the mouth to the ear; tongue dry with dark brown coating; can taste nothing; empty eructations; pain in the region of the heart, shooting up into the throat; pain in the hypogastrium; burning and pressing in the rectum and bladder during stool, and straining with sensation of chilliness; urine and stool at the same time; stool reddish, almost bloody and frothy; most pain after; constant urging to stool, skin hot and dry; extreme emaciation. Sulph. every half hour.

4 P.M. No heat; skin moist and warm. Cont. every hour.

7 P.M. Skin cold; slight hiccough, which ceased after smelling Camph/2D. Camph./2D one drop every hour

9:30 P.M. Stools are black, like tar, and very offensive. Carb. Veg. Ars. every hour.

Oct. 24 1 P.M. There was no change till 12 M. today, when he died.

This man was brought to a private hospital in Sacramento City by a friend, who knew him when at home. Was delirious and could give no account of himself, and seems to have been sick a long time. Only a few days after he died the cholera appeared in the city. Ars/30 should have been given at first with Not.Ac./3D. It would have availed nothing probably, though it would have looked better. It was the only chance. There was such a loss of nuclear action, that the epithelium of the rectum had slipped off, and there was so little functional power, that it could not be replaced. The burning, and tenesmus, and pain resulted from that cause; and so in part the frequent stools. After twelve hours Rhus should have been given.

thirty, for yesterday. The large saloon in the great brick building was opened last night. It is not as long as I described, a portion being cut off at the north end. It beats every thing in the city, except one, larger and more gaudy, opened this evening on 2nd Street. This has one immense saloon in front, and two very large rooms back; one with three billiard tables and the other a sitting room, furnished with dominoes, chequer boards, chess men, etc. The walls of the saloon are covered with paper, exhibiting modern Grecian scenery, in connection with the Turkish war, South American, etc., really splendid. And here the gamblers most do congregate.* A dress Ball is advertised to come off in the Bella Union tomorrow (Sunday) evening.† Surely they do not regard the cholera. Cloudy.

SUNDAY, OCT. 27. I suppose from 30 to 40 died yesterday. It is impossible to determine exactly; about half the number are published. I will send as complete a list as possible bye and bye. As yet, the epidemic proves exceedingly fatal. The Homeopaths are most successful, so far as I know. Most who are attacked die under other treatment. Most get well under that. I presume all their cases are predestined to get well.

MONDAY, OCT. 28. E. Alexander left for home today. Do. Scott of Naperville. There have been more deaths yesterday and today than any previous days. Cloudy and cool most of the day. Looks much like rain. P.M. clear.

TUESDAY, OCT. 29. Just before 12 a.m., Otis, of Dundee, Kane Co., came into the office with cholera. At one p.m. word came down that Dr. Torrey had the cholera at Mormon Tavern, 33 miles out on the Hangtown road, where he had gone to see Wm. Root, of Elgin, sick of dysentery. At quarter past one, I left to see him, and am now "en route" up the American River. The country is level, and mostly a *sort of pretty*, but generally worthless. The first ten miles, before the road leaves the river, it is lined with good buildings; some large, fine ones, and scarcely a road in the United States has as much travel. The timber is scattering oaks, stretching off a mile or two from the river, where the country is one wide barren waste as far as one can see.

Mormon Tavern, six o'clock p.m. Dr. Torrey died at one o'clock today. I have hardly spirit left to write it, and I have been here more than an hour. Oh! what an amount of misery, suffering, anguish, heart-breaking and

*These were the Orleans and El Dorado saloons, according to the Sacramento Transcript, Oct. 28, 1850.

†There is no listing of the Bella Union in the 1851 Sacramento City Directory. There was a Union Hotel as 217 J Street, and it is possible that Dr. Lord's wry sense of humor added the "Bella."

Interior of the El Dorado saloon (California State Library).

crime has this California humbug poured upon the world! It is a deluge of moral and physical evil. Would that the mines might soon fail, and people return to their senses. But the big stories which run through all the papers of the Union, spread the dire contagion, and all are more or less infected. If the truth, and the whole truth, could be told so as to be believed — credited, none but the most desperate men would ever come here.*

I find Root convalescent. A. Root, Hiram Cutting, Wm. Thompson, Isaac Wanzer, and Wm. J. Root of Elgin and Wm. Jones of Naperville are here. Jones was the doctor's nurse though Mr. Goodwin, of Will co., was with him part of the time. Jones, Wanzer, Thompson and Wm. J. Root, were present and assisted at his burial. Cutting is sick. Thompson unwell. Cloudy and cool all day.

WEDNESDAY, OCT. 30. Returned to the city today. Noticed a number of graves by the road side, not there yesterday. The fatal scourge is here,

---

*From the Sacramento Transcript: Who are the heroes of the epidemic? The faithful and educated physicians who rush with unfaltering determination and a total forgetfulness of self into the thickest dangers that malignant disease can possibly evolve. Never, never did the faculty exhibit a more noble, daring and beautiful courage than in this, the worse trial scene of firmness to which the profession was probably ever subjected in the world. They were falling like the foremost soldiers of a desperate charge, and ere this cholera season had subsided seventeen of their number were deposited in the sandhill cemetery of our city.

too. Six o'clock, p.m. Henry Pendleton, whom I left in health at the dinner table yesterday, lies dead upstairs. Otis is alive and may recover. Cloudy.

THURSDAY, OCT. 31. Very foggy this morning. The cholera does not abate yet, though half the population is gone. On the 19th inst. Levi C. Caldridge of DuPage Co., died at Hangtown, and James Johnson, of Naperville, at Mormon Tavern. He and Dr. Torrey are buried side by side.

FRIDAY, NOV. 1. Very cool this morning; almost a frost. Cholera yet very fatal and on the increase. Cloudy and cool all day.

SATURDAY, NOV. 2. Cloudy and cool all day. Morning chilly. The streets are almost deserted, the stores this evening shut, the auction rooms closed, and only three gambling saloons have any company at all. Many who survive this visitation will be ruined. They will be unable to pay the extravagant rents they have promised. The eating houses are almost empty, and all business, except some loading for the mines, and unloading of vessels, is at a dead stand.

SUNDAY, NOV. 3. Sick today. Cholera symptoms. Weather the same.

MONDAY, NOV. 4. Cold night. Frost this morning. Sick and "abed" today. They say that the cholera is abating. I doubt it, though two-thirds or three-fourths of the usual population are missing. I am told that some of the saloons are closing. It is time that something closed them; and yet I have no evidence that any one is any better for this visitation. There is just as much swearing, more drinking, and as much gambling in proportion to the population as before.

TUESDAY, NOV. 5. Frost again this morning. I feel much better today. The weather is much warmer, and this evening the air is loaded with vile and noisesome scents, and thick with smoke from the smouldering fires of half the filth of the city. A regular cholera breeder is today. Report says that Weaver and Hangtown have been attacked by 3,000 Indians. Another humbug. Might have been fifty. We shall know in a day or two. *Somebody wants money.*

WEDNESDAY, NOV. 6. Warm day and smoky. Report (the old liar) says cholera is abating. The people certainly are, three fourths to four fifths have gone entirely, and no one can say certainly where they are gone. Ask, and the answer is, "everywhere."

Dr. Harvey of Elgin is in today. Otis of Dundee is recovering. Sackrider of Geneva, ditto, slowly. Cholera both. Cloudy.

THURSDAY, NOV. 7. Cooler this morning—even chilly, though I do not notice any frost. The 3,000 Indians seem to have been only a small band of 45. Dr. Dickinson and a Delaware Indian were killed, and one drunken man wounded in the jaw. Can't swear any more till it gets well. A man was shot or stabbed—dead, at the horse market on J or K street, some 15 minutes since. The quarrel was all about mule stealing. The Elgin boys at Mormon Tavern are getting well. So says a friend direct from there.

FRIDAY, NOV. 8. It is said that there were sixty deaths yesterday. Frost this morning. Cloudy. Hot in the middle of the day, like yesterday. The Methodists began their Quarterly meeting this evening. Nine o'clock. Attended chapel. Mr. Owen preached. Not more than thirty present, though their meetings are generally well attended.

SATURDAY, NOV. 9. Uncomfortably cool this morning. Davis, who stabbed the man day before yesterday, was this morning bound over in the sum of $3,000. Cloudy most of the day. At half-past five p.m. there was a cry of fire, and this time there was no foolery. In five minutes the flashing, roaring flames were driving the sparkling meteors into the air, which was filled with sparks and glowing cinders. In fifteen minutes more the St. Francis and N.Y. hotels were involved in the conflagration, and their burning, naked timbers, stripped by the ruthless flames, plunged to the earth.

There was hardly a breath of air, else most of the city had been consumed. The fronts of the buildings on the opposite side of the street were more or less charred. The block is cleaned out. The corner, 4th and K street, a hardware store (brick) was saved by great exertion, though the window casings are much burned, the roof was often on fire, and the ends of the timber on the fire side charred. It is not generally known how the fire originated. A fire engine or two, which were lugged into the play, seemed to be of no use. Probably for want of water.

SUNDAY, NOV. 10. Mr. Capen preached. Last Sabbath he was sick. Cold night, and colder this morning. Warm day.

MONDAY, NOV. 11. Frost this morning. Partially cloudy. The steamboats are not crowded as they were. I suppose one reason is, and perhaps the principal one, cholera is subsiding here, or at least is supposed to be. Then it is said to be raging fearfully at San Francisco now, and that may have some influence. Again, many who would perhaps have left for home, stay in the mines, afraid to come to the city during the prevalence of the epidemic. The failure of the river beds set thousands adrift, who immediately left for home. This source of supply is exhausted.

The scourge, here, first made its visible, palpable "entree" on the levee, although for a number of days previous, some cases of disease would suddenly assume very anomalous symptoms, and run rapidly to a fatal termination. The fault was laid any and every where but in the right place. It was camp fever, inflammation of the kidneys, heart affection, brain disease, anything but cholera. One M.D. of some notoriety went so far as to say that this was no place for cholera, that it could not exist here, because it never did come here and because it was not a limestone formation, (as if cholera cares a fig for the limestone humbuggery) and because—because—it couldn't.

At the end of his learned harangue, I remarked that he had best wait, i.e., if he had no objection, till about the first of January, and that if he was alive and watching, he would probably see or feel it between now and then, if it did come. At which he seemed marvellously enlightened, as indeed he might well be. Possibly the idea of waiting had never before occurred to him. His theory had driven all the facts out of his head, if he ever had any in it. Limestone forsooth! Why, I should just as soon expect toad stools to hold consumption at abeyance, or horned toads keep off the small pox. I know all the arguments, the sophisms and fallacies, and I have seen that the facts do not sustain them.

"But," says Dr. Lime, "was there no limestone in Sacramento City?" Why yes—no—i.e., there has been "slacked" lime here in barrels and there are half a dozen or more plastered rooms. "Enough"-lime enough to keep cholera two seasons. Never any cholera in Sacramento City till lime was introduced.

And sure enough—strange as it may seem—cholera followeth lime as surely as a jackass followeth the dish of barley—toiled along up from the Bay by some ignorant fellows who were not aware of the mischief they were doing. Had they just dumped it overboard, the scourge in eager pursuit might have plunged to the bottom of the river and been drowned. Stranger things have happened. But they didn't and IT didn't and then it was on the levee, then up to 2nd and 3rd streets, etc.

I have been at some trouble to ascertain, as so far as I can discover or learn, it has only affected those who had some communication with the victims more or less directly. I do not believe that one single case can be certified in this city, where the person attacked had not been previously in direct communication with a diseased one, or some person who had been with him immediately before. The epidemic has been exceedingly fatal.

So far as my observation extends, the Homeopaths have been beyond compare the most successful. They cured at the outset, when the Allopaths lost ALMOST EVERY PATIENT. I might make that still stronger, but I forbear. Then to be seized with the pest, was to die. The chief and first action of the poison was directly on the nervous centres, and in very many cases there was no diarrhea or vomiting. They were stricken down—the vital energy suddenly depressed, exhausted as by the lightning stroke, and they ceased to breathe before they deemed themselves sick. In such a condition of the system, opium is contra indicated, at least in large doses. He who took it died; and as that was the basis of most cholera medicines, he who took them perished.

Saw James Pratt, Keefer and Boyce, formerly of Chicago today.

TUESDAY, NOV. 12TH. Cold morning. Very hot in the middle of the day. A woman died last night of cholera at the next corner above. Was apparently in good health three hours before. Another died this evening in the room opposite the one I occupy—killed by the medicine, I doubt not, for he had three or four doctors as did the woman.

How can mortal flesh stand so great an affliction or infliction as half a dozen M.D.s—and then such ones as we have here—stole their trade when and where they stole their medicines—on "The Plains."

Met Augustus Bryce today and saw James Pratt & Keefer of Naperville.

WEDNESDAY, NOV. 13. Had one warm night. I believe that I forgot to report the death of Thomas Wygant of Flag Creek, Lyonsville, Co., Ill. He died of cholera supervening diarrhea (chronic) on the night of the 1st inst. at Sacramento Ranche, four and a half miles down the river. Not quite as warm today. More people in the city.

The Fosters from Plainfield are here this evening. One of them is bound for home. They, i.e., the father and two sons have amassed some twenty thousand dollars or more, but not by mining. They have bought and sold and packed and ranched and dealt in any and everything that would turn a penny into their pockets. This I take from the mouth of one of the boys and in almost the very words.

It fully sustains my previous observation; and a little enquiry here by one who knows how to ask the proper questions, will convince any man who is willing to be convinced, that mining in the aggregate is a losing business and must eventually under the present system of labor, leave the operatives in debt, or at least sink all the capital invested and leave the source of supply—no matter where—minus 20 millions every year.

The truth is, the whole operation is deeply, irretrievably in debt, hopelessly in debt now, and so profoundly sensible are people here of it that they are loath to give notes for this indebtedness, anticipating that the courts at home will never give judgment on obligations which accrued here, to the extent of the demand; or if I may be allowed the expression "conventional liability" for such it is. And yet it is none the less real and imperative, and I doubt not, the courts will, in all cases, give judgment to the amount proved.

A singular idea, truly, that a man is to be released from a portion of his liabilities because they accrued where everything was estimated at a higher value than where the claim is finally enforced, i.e., I sell a man 100 pounds of flour at $1.50 per pound. It cost me $1.25.

His claim fails and he cannot pay and will not give his note, for the payment of that may be enforced in the States where flour is only $1.50 per cwt. and admits of no difference, while an account may be contested. Truly

the rogue always has had and always will have the advantage, (for the law
seems framed for their especial benefit) until they get where no coin is current and no badge allowed to pass but the word of truth and the garment of
righteousness.

We shall see whether roguery will flourish in this case, though as regards
evidence it has decidedly the advantage.

Chapter Nineteen
November 14–December 24, 1850:
Politics and Opinions

———◆——◆——◆———

WEDNESDAY, NOVEMBER 14. Ice this morning in a tub of water at
the door. Very hot in the middle of the day, the sun pouring down like
mid-summer. The evening air, in this city, is most certainly the worst in the
world. A dense cloud of dust and smoke lies in the city, for it hardly
reaches the tops of the buildings and suspends the most abominable smells —
all the noxious exhalations which must necessarily arise from the enormous
accumulation of filth, such as no American city ever before had. It is really
almost suffocating. One can with difficulty breathe. Oh! for the pure mountain air and the swift cold mountain stream.

Alfred Waterman was in today. Has a tumour on his neck. Came to
have it opened. Has had the cholera but has nearly recovered his strength
again. Is now living at Sutterville.

Got from the Post Office three months of the *American.* They were
exceedingly welcome. It is a long time since I have seen a religious paper or
learned anything of what was doing in the church. I should judge from the
tenor of the whole (for I have now, 10 p.m., read them all) that there has
been no great change since I left, at least, no improvement. Ministers are as
time serving, man worshipping simple, dishonest, unprincipled, inconsistent,
man-fearing, God-dishonoring, heaven-insulting as ever. These are grave,
serious charges but hardly include a moiety of the indictment.

They are merely picked, haphazard from the schedule and not only can
but will be sustained, and judgment finally executed. Unless they repent
God will some time spue them out as hateful, abominable things. I feel
indignant that humanity should be disgraced and religion outraged by those

who were formerly considered the ornaments of religious society, the bands of union in the church and the pillars of our denomination.

That such men should descend from their high position and sink to the dirty level, the foul arena where Henry Clay and Daniel Webster *et id omore gums* are wallowing in the slimy depths of politics and bartering away the rights of men with as little scruple as did the scourged ones in the temple of the Lord, their vagrant doves, is soul sickening.

Is not this "striking hands with the wicked?" Do not these men by all their public acts give countenance and support to the very principle, which carried out into action, strip men of their rights and violate the commands of God? And will God listen to the prayers of him who does these things?

What will, or does it avail such to cry, "Oh Lord! forgive our many transgressions and lay not these things to our charge," when they have not the remotest idea of reforming or committing one sin less. Do they think to cheat the Almighty by such open palpable jugglery? God is not to be mocked—neither can He be deceived.

One had better offend Daniel Webster, Henry Clay, Dr. Fuller, Sam Houston, all Texas and the devil "to boot" in the things nearest and dearest to their hearts, than incur the displeasure of the Lord by a single act of disobedience. I hope nobody will be offended at the above concatination of celebrities. "They are joined to their idols, let them alone." But what the word of God puts together, let no man put asunder.

If they choose each other's company I am not to be blamed for noting it, and I well remember an old saying which doubtless seemed a little hard to the original hearers but has lost none of its force by reason of age. "You are of your father the Devil whose works ye do."

I am right glad that their last abomination "The Fugitive Slave Law" is so entirely outrageous. Had it been a little moderate and so framed as to admit a variety of constructions, it might have lived and quietly worked out its own iniquity and the liberty of the nation.

But the last Congress has shown that its little finger is thicker than the old one's Loins, and if the people long submit to such unconstitutional, unwarrantable, heartless, merciless tyranny, they ought at once to return to the original state, which, according to some very wise men, is in the oyster shell, and beginning with all their past experience they might on emerging from the monkey tribes again, be somebody and have some slight idea of what is due to humans.

A most infamous proposition was made a few days since in the *St. Francisco Courier*, to wit: that our Legislature at its present session pass a law allowing one year for all those who have brought slaves here to take them away again.

I wonder if the editor belongs to the church. The chances are as one to a thousand that he is *not* a gambler, *not* a drunkard. I know nothing about him however, personally. There are a great many Blacks in the state who are claimed as slaves. They understand their position well and know that they are free. The would-be masters here complain that the free blacks give their quondam servants information and advice.

By the by, if some of the masters would only get a little information it could do them no great harm. They seem as ignorant of the power of the North and the strength of the Unionists throughout the States as was Old Black Hawk. They cannot be made to believe that any attempt to dissolve the Union by force would be only a second and greatly enlarged edition of the Black Hawk war. Something like the "rise and fall of the Diggers" a few days ago.

I notice a very distorted version of the late difficulty in the last no. of the Baptist. I came here the very next week after it occurred and was not an eye witness but I will collect and send documents on which you can rely. Suffice it, the one you have published has very little truth in it at all. For instance, Dr. [Charles L.] Robinson, who is said to have been shot through the head,* has been elected a member of the present [California] Legislature [Whig, Sacramento County] and is connected with the *Tribune* office, as is also McClutchy.

The difficulty arose from an attempt to monopolize the land on which the city is located. It seems that the squatters, as they are called, ascertained that Sutter's grant under which they claimed title only covered eleven leagues of land, which could only extend some 33 miles and that the Buttes were the northern boundary.

Now as it was ascertained that the Buttes were 45 or 50 miles north of the city, a grant of only 33 miles would not reach it. It mattered little whether the grant was valid or invalid as it did not reach the case. Under such circumstances they demand their right to the land equal to any other man's right and occupied the land accordingly.

When a legal decision pronounced against that right they were denied an appeal and this so exasperated them that it required only a spark to set their irritable feelings in a flame. A lack of wisdom and discretion and the precipitatancy of the public authorities brought the two parties in collision and the result we have seen.

Most assuredly the squatters were in the right. They had as much right to the land where Sacramento City stands as anybody (certainly more than the swindling minions of Sutter) and so took possession and built upon the lots. In fact, occupancy was the only title anybody could have and Sutter has a large farm, some 700 acres on Feather River and also a large tract two miles east of here on which stands what is called Sutter's fort with buildings on both places—and still more the 33 miles grant. Enough in all conscience for any reasonable man. The decision of the court was wrong in principle if

---

*J.F. Morse, in his *First History of Sacramento City*, wrote that Robinson was "actually wounded in the lower part of his body."

not in fact, for the squatters only claimed what they could and did then and there occupy, i.e., one or two lots at most for each.

Now as they had possession Sutter should have shown a better title or been non suited. That he could not show a title is evident, for he did not. It was only presumed—guessed at, that the grant would reach here though it was certainly and positively known that it did not. But even allowing that it did it is utterly worthless. The grant was never confirmed, though confirmatory document might be forged, perhaps have been as there is an immense amount at stake, and if I am not misinformed, the most unprincipled reckless gamblers in the state have the chief interest in the concern.

I predicted one year ago to these very gamblers what has taken place when they were telling how they had no objection to the squatters building for them. I told them that the people would take the matters into their own hands. One can hardly credit the simplicity and low knavery of some of these scamps.

For instance, when the emigrants with families first began to arrive in the city this fall, Brannan, a notorious gambler and pickpocket but great land owner here, stuck up a flaming hand-bill giving notice that he would lease for one year without charge a lot to each family which might apply. Now these lots were one and a half to two miles out of the city or at least from the levee where all the business is done, in short, where nobody then desired to locate.

One hardly knows which most to admire, the unblushing effrontery and consummate impudence of the offer or the infinite simplicity and ignorance it evinces.

Just as though the people would not learn in a few days how little respect is paid to such a rogue's claims and threatenings. If these men had their deserts (with the exception of Sutter) the keeper of the penitentiary would have to lay in a larger stock of provisions.

FRIDAY, NOV. 15. Cool day. Smoky and dusty as ever. The steamers have very few passengers down. The cholera has passed. Only here and there a case now. Cloudy part of the day, as it has been for some time—still it does not look more like rain than it did three months ago. The clouds, the air, the earth, all are dry and parched.

SATURDAY, NOV. 16. Warmer today. Called to see Dr. Brewer, who was staying at Miller's on 4th street, and was astounded with the intelligence of his death. Died, I believe on the 9th ins. of cholera. And thus they fall on every side. Only a few days after Torrey's death, Brewer, not having heard of it, called to see him, and was surprised at the news of his death—perhaps as much surprised as I am to find him dead, or some other inquirer may be to hear that I am no more. Dr. D.H. Brewer was from Fairwater, Fond du Lac Co., Wisconsin. He seems to have had a presentiment of his fate, as he wrote before he was attacked to his friends at home, with directions to send it when he should be no more.

Covenant meeting this evening. But few attended, some of the members being sick, or having sick friends or patients. The idea of building a house of worship is for the present abandoned. I believe that none of the church, and but one of the society, has died during the epidemic. The scarcity of money, and derangement in the money market on account of the cholera, will probably render it impossible to do anything till next year, and then, I am thinking, there will be such evident tokens of want of permanency in the mining and agricultural prospects of the country, that the idea of building of brick, at least, will scarcely be entertained.

There is nothing done in the burnt district yet, and I question if it is soon reoccupied. The fact is, that although a large number of buildings are now going up, yet they are mostly on J street, where they are immediately available, and where rent is so high that it amounts in a year to more than the cost of a wooden building. This state of things results from several causes; the principal of which are, the repugnance of landlords to lower rents, the extremely low price of lumber and labor, and the number of vacant lots up town, on the road to all the mines of the branches of the American, Youba and Feather Rivers. There are a considerable number of rooms on J street, constantly vacant, and lots of them every where else in the city except on the levee.

SUNDAY, NOV. 17. Ice again this morning. The saloons are all in full operation today. No more cholera. The coffin man's "occupation's gone." Best perhaps that 'tis so. Two or three of them have made some kind of a "pile." Cloudy and cool all day.

MONDAY, NOV. 18. Weather much the same as yesterday, only a little more so. Cooler and cloudier and the evening air feels much like rain. Wouldn't wonder if we had a sprinkle before morning.

TUESDAY, NOV. 19. Quite chilly this morning, but no ice. Rained a little some time in the night. Dark heavy clouds lie off low in the west, and scattered masses hang black over the eastern mountains. The air of the city would be materially improved by rain.

Three Common Council men to be elected today. Wagons, coaches, and carriages are parading the streets, in all directions, covered with banners and flags of divers colors, on which are printed the names of the different candidates. Almost every drayman has one or more on his horse or cart. There seems to be a very great anxiety to get votes, and a man may get a fine long ride in a carriage for his vote, and after all vote for whom he pleases. I notice that some one of the four avowed squatters are placed on almost every ticket, and there are at least twenty different ones, for the three vacancies.

How willing these self-sacrificing patriots are to serve the dear people for as much per day as they choose to vote themselves! One or two of the candidates are pledged not to take any wages, I observe, however, that this is an unpopular doctrine, and will not be sustained. The people, in general, prefer to pay their officers, an then they can make no future claim.

One of the carriages broke down in J street near the polls, and one of the voters was severely injured. A bone said to be broken. Didn't learn his name. The wind has been high, and from the South all day. Many of the rag signs and awnings are in tatters, and the rag houses are being stripped. The cloth of the more ancient ones is getting rotten, and a strong wind shakes them dangerously. A few drops only of rain have fallen.

WEDNESDAY, NOV. 20. Wind blew in strong gusts, and rain fell in showers all night. Flying clouds, fresh breeze, and cool this morning. The air is clear and bracing, and one can hardly realize that he is not in the western suburb of Chicago (if he has ever been there) on a fine May morning after a rainy night. The same sky, and air, and earth, and landscape, and green springing grass, and wooden houses, and board fences, and shantees, and haystacks. The telegraph posts and wires are lacking, and they only. Eld. Israel Washburn, of New Bedford, Mass., left for home in the steamer day before yesterday.

Considerable damage was done in the city last night by the wind and rain. A large quantity of flour was made into dough; the rats gnawing holes in the bags, and thus letting in the rain. These vermin damage or destroy a vast many articles, but mostly flour. Every morning one may see anywhere, almost, in the city (as most traders, except clothing and boot and shoe, keep flour) bags cut or eaten, or torn into with holes from two to eight inches long and from a few ounces to several pounds pulled out and scattered about each one of them. The usual place of storing flour (in the dry season) being out of doors. The rats have it all their own way; though, for that matter, their depredations are carried on in doors and out. They eat, drink, cut, or tear their way through every thing but brick walls.

Besides the tearing, and breaking, and slitting of awnings and signs and rag houses, the new Catholic church, which was almost enclosed was blown from its foundation (posts some five feet high) and much damaged. It may, and probably will be, raised and put in position again, but it will cost heaps of money, and will not be as strong. A large unfinished house on J street was blown down.

THURSDAY, NOV. 21. Rained a little before daylight; and it is like a cold, cloudy, rough, windy fall morning in Illinois. Began to rain about noon and drizzled and mizzled and dropped and sprinkled till near sundown, rendering it anything but pleasant. There was just wind enough to make a break into everybody's premises. It is worse than snow, by all odds. I prefer cold to a cool wet, and then an umbrella costs a small fortune here. I have not dared to ask the price since it clouded up, and didn't want one before. Wouldn't wonder if they had raised 500 per cent. Perhaps a very respectable one might be had for an ounce or two, "just to accommodate," "seeing it's you."

FRIDAY, NOV. 22. Cloudy, but no rain this morning, or since midnight. Rather chilly. The Erysipelas is getting waked up. Several cases have occurred about here, and a man died of it this morning only a few doors below. It is reported very unmanageable, though I had no difficulty in the two cases which came under my treatment. They have all, so far as I know, adopted the nitrate of silver treatment; which, I doubt not, will prove utterly inefficient; at least, in three cases which I have seen, it did not arrest the disease a single instant. I know not whose patients they are, but one of them is dead. The afternoon very pleasant and warm.

SATURDAY, NOV. 23. Cloudy, and rained early this morning, and something of a shower in the forenoon. No rain here this afternoon, but looks like plenty of it in the mountains. It cannot have rained there sooner than here, as the river has not yet raised. Got another number of the *American Baptist.* I notice that you make me to say, in the *Journal,* "The ducks literally swam in the river." Now there is nothing very singular about that. It is very common, and very natural, indeed, for ducks to do the like. A single letter would alter the whole complexion of it. Thus, "the ducks literally SWARM in the river." The picture of a hive of bees swarming was vividly presented to the mind's eye, in their number, noise, and rapid, wayward movements. I could liken it to nothing else. Without seeing, no one can form an adequate conception of the scene.

SUNDAY, NOV. 24. Too unwell to leave my room much today. Quite pleasant, though somewhat cloudy and densely so just at night.

MONDAY, NOV. 25. Cold this morning and clear, with frost. It is really uncomfortable. I was called over the river at five o'clock a.m., and suffered considerably from lack of an overcoat and gloves. Didn't think to take them along. No cold weather in California (?) A very paradise. This evening it is cold again, and the wind strong from the north, where it has held since morning, though it was warm in the middle of the day.

TUESDAY, NOV. 26. Cold, and heavy frost this morning, with considerable wind from the north. I do not discover any ice. At nine o'clock it is warm enough to be out and comfortable, without any extra clothing. The air is fresh, fine and bracing, i.e., if you keep out of the nucleus of the city. The river has raised some three or four feet in the last 36 hours. There must have been considerable rain in the mountains. there will not be enough water, however, to open the dry "diggins" to any extent, and money will be scarce till it rains more. For this, the present prospect is exceedingly dull. Never was there fairer promise of dry weather than now.

The principal streets of the city are almost impassable for footmen, as there is no provision made for crossing, unless in boats and tall boots. Still J street is as good, and two feet "better" than was Lake street, when I left Chicago one year ago last April. No entire team, to my knowledge, has disappeared in unknown depths of salvy mud. L street, where is very little travel, is almost mudless. And the levee, for fifty feet wide, is dry, and would be quite passable but for the plunder piled over it.

Some may be curious to learn how the goods get there. Along the bank of the river, fastened by chain and rope cables to the huge oaks and big sycamores, are a number of dismasted ships, on which are built store-houses, one or two stories high. A narrow plank bridge, thirty to fifty or sixty feet long, connects each of these with the shore. Two spars, one "fore and the other aft," brace from the ship's side against the shore, and keep her off and steady.

When the water is at its lowest point, you descend five to eight feet to reach the deck, and ascend considerably more at the highest. The steamers, and ships and other craft haul up on the outside and pass the goods over the decks of these store ships, on to the levee. From thence they are carted to the stores and mines. Lumber sometimes lies a long time unclaimed, and is finally sold to pay charges.

Vessels discharging here to pay wharfage; many, to save this, haul up on the other side, and land their cargoes as they sell them, or send them across in boats as they are wanted. Goods are sometimes stored in these ships, under what circumstances I am not aware.

When business is lively, and three or four steamers and twice as many other vessels are unloading every day, the levee is a tangled mass of men and rogues and Mexicans and Chinese and Chilians and Kanakas and horses and mules and asses and oxen and drays and lumber and flour and potatoes and molasses and brandy and pickles and oysters and yams and cabbages and books and furniture and almost everything that one could think of—except honesty and religion. These articles not being in demand here are not thrown into market.

WEDNESDAY, NOV. 27. Clouded up again this morning, though at day light it was clear and cold and a heavy frost. Dodge, Conde, and Stebbins left for home last evening. They have been in the mines almost a year. Will, with good luck and economy, get home with $1,000 each. All made by trading. By their own showing, they must have lost considerable in mining.

Like thousands of others, they were often within a little of a "big pile," and again the prospect would be mighty small. They are fortunate in saving as much as they have. Not one in fifty has done or will do it. All can't make their pile by trading, and the miners and diggers (not Indians) have to support the whole, at last, except what they swindle from the traders.

The roads cannot be very bad yet, as the city is full of teams, loading for the mines. Business is looking up again. The rain has not driven even the pudding and milk dealers from the streets. These fellows drag their savory wares about in covered carts, lighted with lamps in the night, and one can get a bowl of pudding and milk any time between daylight and ten p.m. They generally have fruit, cake and pies, also. It would look might queer in a Christian land, to see a grown up man eating pudding and milk in the streets. Here it is all right. Glad to get it so.

9 p.m. Had a smart shower and occasionally a slight sprinkle is course of the day.

NOV. 28. Cloudy and comfortable today and very passable in the streets.

NOV. 29. Cool again and cloudy. With an occasional sprinkle through the day and mist like rain after two p.m.

SATURDAY, NOV. 30. Misty, drizzling rain all day. The streets are so slippery that one can with difficulty keep right side up. The side walks, though planked, are no exception. It is really a break-neck business to get about the city today. The goods exposed on the levee look very much as though they couldn't help it. The original color of the packages and parcels will be remembered no more forever. The present is indescribable.

SUNDAY, DEC. 1. A glorious morning. The sun comes gliding over the eastern mountains in all its morning splendor, bright with the promise of a clearer, fairer day. Here it is quiet—all. I mean on the Washington [now Broderick] side of the Sacramento, where I have been staying the past week at the house of T.P. Cameron, (formerly of Oscaloosa, Iowa). In the city we usually hear the sound of the hammer, the rattle and rumble of wagons, the crack of fire arms, the racing of horses, and the squealing and braying of mules, confusedly mixed with all kinds of unearthly sounds, from the first breaking of day, when the kyotas open the concert, till sleep shuts the gates of the senses, and we are no more. There is very little business done in Washington, and as yet, there are only about thirty houses. (Fremont, some 25 miles above, is the "County seat" for this county.)

I counted nineteen graves in their burying ground, most of them, probably, cholera. Among the population are several families. The ground is somewhat higher than on the Sacramento side, and has not been overflowed in the memory of man, whatever the Diggers may know. Were it not almost entirely covered with bushes and weeds, it would be very pleasant. The air is pure, there is no filth, and then I get plenty of milk. Mr. C. keeps a great number of cows, and until the grass failed, was making money from the sale of milk. It has been from six shillings to eight shillings per quart, but for some time past only four shillings.

MONDAY, DEC. 2. Cold night. Chilly all day, and northwest wind. Cloudy this morning; bright sunshine most of the day after. Business has fallen off very much, and prices also, at the auction sales on Front st. I saw good sugar sold for 12 cents per lb., and first rate potatoes for nine cents per pound. One can now buy almost at his own price. Money scarce.

TUESDAY, DEC. 3. The coldest night and morning yet. The ground was frozen, and water congealed immediately wherever it was spilled, even after sunrise, and continued to do so in the shade all day. There has not been a cloud in sight since daylight, and in the sun it is comfortably warm, but cold in the shade.

WEDNESDAY, DEC. 4. Cold night. A tumbler of water in the window of my room, where was a fire till nine p.m. was frozen to the bottom this morning, but not entirely solid. Water froze in the porch almost as soon as it touched the floor. There was a fine lot of anchor ice in the pans of milk which were out in the porch through the night and yet I have killed half a dozen musquitoes this morning. They are, no doubt, tolerably quiet out of doors, but ferocious enough in here. By the by, they have been very troublesome to me since I have been on this side of the river. They have a long lease of life, and, maybe, are insured.

Was out on the plains west, and visited a lake which has the appearance of once having been *the* or *a* channel of the river. It is some five or six miles long, and from thirty to sixty rods wide, running nearly parallel with the present channel of the Sacramento River, some three or four miles distant. Saw plenty of pelicans flying, geese ditto, and any quantity of ducks and other water fowl, of which we killed several. Large quantities of fish are caught in this lake with seines. Most of this section is, or has been, covered as far as I went or can see, with a dense and almost impenetrable growth of enormous rushes and flags; some of the former an inch and a half in diameter and ten to twelve feet high. There is no grass among them, and the ground is very soft and wet, even now, though there has been very little rain yet.

Near the river the land is high and dry, but in these "tulares," or marshes, utterly worthless. I have said that there is no grass; I mean that I did not see a vestige of grass, in travelling several miles through them. The ground is now burned over in many places which I presume, does not occur every year. Last year at this time this whole section of country was one wide waste of water. We saw cattle in all directions, but what they find to eat here is more than I know. There is very little grass on the dry land, and that is coarse, and for the most part, dry. Still they do get a living, somehow, and many of them are fat. A few miles farther out, elks are said to bound. Certainly the tracks give evidence that not a few come down to the lake to drink.

THURSDAY, DEC. 5. As cold as yesterday. One wants mittens and overcoat to face the "raw norther" this morning. The snow on the eastern mountains looks frigid enough. It has been lying there glistening in the sun for a fortnight, but it didn't seem to chill one so to look at it before.

FRIDAY, DEC. 6. Cold night and ground frozen, or rather, it continues to freeze, not having thawed out yet. Over to the lake again, today, after ducks. Got only seven. Killed three times that number, but there was no wind to blow them ashore. It was quite warm after ten o'clock, a.m., and yet the southern extremity of the lake continued frozen all day. The ice was more than an inch thick, and the poor shivering birds stood around on the shore, gazing in silent admiration on the hard water, as it covered their best feeding ground. The contract for planking K street was let today.

SATURDAY, DEC. 7. Cold night and warm day. K street is lined with men grading it. Dry goods are selling over the river at auction for less than New York wholesale prices.

DEC. 8TH. Cooler today and a few feathery looking clouds around and about.

DEC. 9TH. Warmer this morning and too warm all day since. Cloudy and thunder. Rain.

DEC. 10TH. Same as yesterday.

WEDNESDAY, DEC. 11. Clear and cool. At three o'clock, p.m. left in the West Point for Benicia. The banks of the river are from six to 18 or 20 feet high, i.e., above low water mark, and the river about the same width as at Sacramento, till we turned into what is called the slough, or, as I suppose, an old channel of the river which turns off nearly twenty miles below the city. It was nearly dark when we entered it, to the right, and a few miles farther down, passed the Senator, fast aground on a sand bar. I should not know from appearances that we were not in the main channel of the river. They call it the slough, and I suppose that they know. The country so far, on each side, is much like the Upper Sacramento, only the great valley seems much wider, and there is less timber, and that more craggy, and covered with long moss.

At supper, we had four regular loafers, who ordered everything all kinds of ways, with much swearing. One made quite a handle of his bill ($1.50) for supper. The supper was much such an one as you would get on a Mississippi or Missouri steamer—several dishes of meat, potatoes, coffee, tea, etc. No kind of sauce and no pastry.

The West Point is a very pretty second class boat (here). Her cabin, aft, has two state rooms and 21 berths on each side. They are neat and clean, and the whole very well finished. We had just passengers enough for company, and no crowding; and all went off pleasantly except the supper exhibition of loaferism. There is no gambling for a wonder. At quarter to nine the boat, which had been running with fast and lessening speed for some time, suddenly choked down, tired out—the wheels ceased to revolve and we are merely floating broad on the water, which here seems to be from half a mile to a mile wide. On inquiry, I learn that the firemen are drunk, and have let the fire run entirely down.

Nine and a half o'clock. We are again "under way" (weigh?) having floated, citizens at large, three fourths of an hour on the waters as helpless as a wool sack. It is singular that the officers did not discover that the fire was failing. Were they drunk too? I don't know. I think that the Captain is sober, though he has very little, in general, to do with the fire. At 11 it became very dark and began to rain.

Half-past one, a.m. The word was passed for the Benicia passengers, and while they were getting ready, the boat ran against some part of a vessel lying in her course toward the store ship, and part of the hurricane deck was knocked into pi, causing a tremendous rattling, rolling, and slambanging over head. Most of the berths were emptied in the shortest possible time. Some very cooly asked what was the matter. One fellow, quite desperate, yelled out to know if the "biler was bustin." Another, struck speechless, made his "entree" in full Digger dress, to wit: one nether and nameless garment, and then made a plunge for the door and passed out on all fours over the chairs, verifying the old proverb—"Haste makes waste"—as he was pitching and plunging towards the boiler which he evidently thought was "bustin."

I was awake, not having lain down at all, and witnessed the whole scene with considerable interest, and no little surprise at the long continuance of the uproar (a minute or more) and my utter ignorance of the cause. On account of the darkness, the Captain would not leave till four o'clock, when we went on board the Store ship and remained till morning light. We had good, comfortable, and large arm chairs to sit in, and a fine large self-regulating parlor stove to sit by. The stove had a fire in it just after sunrise.

THURSDAY, DEC. 12. Left in a steam ferry boat for Martinez (mar-tenas), our destination. Thomas P. Cameron and lady, formerly of Oscaloosa, Iowa, were fellow passengers.

Martinez is on the opposite side of the river and two miles above Benicia. The distance between the two is some four miles, the river or bay being over two miles wide. The fare is one dollar. Looking to the east, up the stream, the water expands irregularly for a long distance into a bay, with an uncouth and, to me, unknown name. This bay is several miles wide. West and north, a broad expanse of water stretches off toward the north, forming another beautiful bay, and beyond, three or four miles, at the north end of it, the hills, smooth and covered with wild oats, crowd the river into a channel apparently less than half a mile wide, called the straits, through which I see the bay of San Francisco.

The scenery above the water level is made up of high, smooth, rounded hills, and shallow ravines, the whole covered with the yellow straw or stubble of the late crop of wild oats, dotted with oaks, a part of them live oak, growing in clumps in the ravines, and here and there streaked with a footpath or wagon track, and painted with patches of green by the wild oats just springing up, or blackened by the fire which has just swept over some portions of it.

In twenty-five minutes we landed in Martinez, which is very prettily situated on a beautiful plain or valley bottom, more than a half a mile wide and extending back, I should think, two miles or more. It is the most delightful site for a town that I have seen, occupied or unoccupied, in California—yes or ever saw—or ever expect to see.

The earth, where not occupied or tracked down, is covered with the fresh springing oats, green as a Yankee pasture in June. The trees are yet in the green and line the deep, narrow ravine, which runs down on the east side of the valley till within half a mile of the bay, when it passes diagonally nearly across it.

The houses, 75 in number, are all new, mostly painted, small and some of them brick. There seems to be no business here. Benicia is more in the way of the main road for ships and has deep water near the shore. On this side it is shoal and the bottom is sometimes bare 200 or 300 yards out.

A range of low hills on the east forming that side of the valley shuts out a view of the bay in that direction, though Mount Diavolo, which may be seen from Sacramento City, is distinctly visible above them, distant fifteen or twenty miles. The hills on the west and south are several hundred feet higher and much more broken.

On the Benicia side the hills are treeless, except a few acres some distance back of the United States Barracks, where the shore sweeps far away to the north—not a bush or even a weed anywhere to be seen—nothing but oats, oats, oats. The soil must be exceedingly fertile, to bear them thus, year after year. I shall take a closer look at the place, with its shipping line shore, than I can get from here.

FRIDAY, DEC. 13. Began to rain before light this morning, and rained most of the day, with high wind. The water in the bay has been in a constant foam. I am staying with Eld. Cameron, formerly of Oscaloosa, Iowa. He preaches here twice a month, and at "Santa Clara Mission" once. This mission is sixty miles below.

SATURDAY, DEC. 14. Flying clouds all day. It has rained in the Bay and on Mount Diavolo several times in the course of it. Went over the hills west, and had a most magnificent view of hill and valley and mountain. Cattle, singly or in squads, were quietly grazing in all directions, on the beautiful hills and in the long green valleys where I could get an occasional glimpse of them.

A broad valley seems to stretch along at the base of Mount Diavolo which rears itself beyond in gentle beautiful slopes of the same appearance as the hills here, only a greater show of timber. The soil, wherever I go, or can see, seems to be of the richest description; and the earth is covered with the standing straw of the last oat crop. The average height of the straw is about ten inches, generally closely set together and only a few grains on a stack.

Houses occupied by Spaniards who claim all the land under Mexican grants, are scattered over the country, but mostly in the vallies and not easily discovered from a distance. Some of these fellows hold a great many leagues and the yearly taxes amount to hundreds of dollars in some cases, even to a thousand. When they do not pay, and that is not uncommon, a portion of the land is sold for taxes. It may be redeemed in a year by paying 100 per cent. Doubtless the taxes and the "Yankees" will soon swallow up the whole and the title will finally rest in the hands of the more provident, who will not waste all their substance in gambling.

SUNDAY, DEC. 15. Mr. Cameron preached in the Court House, a story and a half building thirty by twenty feet. About twenty persons present, nearly one half females.

Cloudy all day, and cool. There is very little noise here; everything quiet. There are but few "monte tables" in town, and these small affairs. I am told that there is a "Billiard table and Ball alley." I cannot say how well they are patronized. I have already seen more Spanish women here than in all California besides. They dress every day in the richest silks or worsted, and stop for neither rain nor mud. The everlasting shawl serves for bonnet, umbrella, head gear, and sometimes for body and sleeves of their dress: thus, like charity, covering a multitude of—imperfections. More of these anon.

The Spaniards and others, perhaps back in the valleys, raise some vegetables—tomatoes, melons, potatoes and cabbages for the San Francisco market mostly. Cabbage heads here attain an enormous size. I should think

that some of them might weigh thirty to forty pounds, perhaps more. It may
be considered a "cabbage story," but to carry one half a mile is no small job,
and when there, it wants something more than a common doorway to let it
in whole.

MONDAY, DEC. 16. Rain, sunshine and clouds. Wind south as it has
been the last two or three days.

TUESDAY, DEC. 17. Rain and high wind all night and continues to
rain steadily at 11 o'clock. There is a rainbow in the north. This is the
fourth day that I have noticed the same phenomenon within an hour of 12
o'clock a.m.

12 M. Crossed over to Benicia. The tide is high and the salt marsh
which lies between the uneven, rolling, ascending plain on which the town
is built and the waters edge, at a medium stage, is now submerged. This low
ground, which indents the dry land nearly half a mile, renders it necessary
to construct "pikes" or plank roads across to the shipping. They have done
both. The lower, or down stream part of town has a bold, bluff bank of
sandstone or clay; above, the shore is low for more than a mile.

There are 160 buildings; some of them really good, and built with much
taste; but for the most part, only "so so," and hardly that; many of them
even worse. They are scattered over a square mile and exhibit a surprising
and truly commendable degree of independence. The inhabitants need have
no fear of a general conflagration.

About one mile back from the landing the surface rises rapidly in
smooth, beautiful, swelling hills, green with the new oats. I believe that the
taverns, like most of the houses, are only so so. I presume they have a
school house—don't know. Won't ask, lest they bring in a bill for the trouble of answering.

The Court House, or rather the Masonic Hall, in the basement of
which courts are held at present, is barely respectable. A Presbyterian meeting house is in process of erection, thirty by fifty feet. It was made in Boston, or New York, and is merely stuck together here. The work is of the
coarsest possible description and the whole in exceedingly bad taste. A fine
large bell stands near, ready to rise into its appointed place when that shall
be finished. I wouldn't like to stand under, the first time it is rung. If it stays
up there in that crow's nest of a steeple, it is a far quieter bell than I take it
for.

As regards durability, Jonah's gourd [Jonah 4: 6–10] was a fixture to this
Gothic nightmare. Nevertheless, I will warrant it to last, accident by fire
and sword and wind excepted, as long as the people of Benicia shall be
worth preaching to. I notice, away, away up, and toward the Barracks, a
meeting house looking concern, said to be half school-house. I can't afford
to pay it a visit.

Took tea at a boarding house kept by Samuel Ambrose, who is now gone to San Francisco. Waited on board the store ship till midnight, when, the West Point, failing her time, we went up to the Solano Hotel (the best in town) and took lodging. This house is built, fitted and furnished much like a second class hotel in Chicago, or elsewhere at home, to wit—beds, bedsteads, bedrooms, chairs, carpets, private rooms, plastered ceiling, etc.

WEDNESDAY, DEC. 18. The morning is fine and everything quiet. Benicia is a mighty quiet place(?). The parlor of our Hotel is neat, clean and carpeted, and has a mahogony sofa, and center table, a fine toned piano and on the table, a choice collection of books. Notwithstanding the house promised so well, the breakfast was meagre enough. Beef steak (lean), warm bread, coffee (poor), sugar, milk, butter (stale), and boiled potatoes (yesterday's) sliced and fried as hard as a boot heel, almost. I believe that short rations and Benicia are synonyms. It is certainly proverbial for poor fare. On a more specific survey of this "port of entry," I find a great many houses untenanted, among which are the very best in the place.

At 8 o'clock, p.m., took passage in the steamer *New World* for Sacramento City. Fare, $10, including berth. This is a splendid and fast boat; the cabins fitted up in good style, and everything all right, except the passengers.

Although there were several notices hung around the saloon of "No smoking allowed," yet two loafers (dressed like gentlemen it is true) smoked cigars and though gambling is prohibited in the same way, yet four or five were at it in a small way in the upper saloon. PERHAPS THEY CAN'T READ. Three ladies of doubtful reputation were among the cabin passengers. This must have been anything but pleasant to other lady passengers, for their conduct was somewhat too unequivocal to make it necessary to advertise.

The evening is delightful, and the moon shines out so bright and clear that Mount Diavolo is distinctly seen in all its lights and shadows on our right, as we shoot along up the river.

THURSDAY, DEC. 19. The rattling, splashing and groaning of the uneasy monster which drove our gliding palace so swiftly up the strong current of the muddy Sacramento, against wind and tide, ceased; and a quiet little thump against the store ship, at four o'clock a.m. gave token sure that we were safely tied up in Sacramento City.

Slept till daylight and then crossed the river, thankful to have escaped without a blow up or collision, or other small accident incident to steamboat rides. The morning is cool and the fog so dense that one can scarcely see five rods. The streets in the city are abominable. The planking of K street is suspended on account of the rain (some say want of funds). At 11 a.m. came off bright and clear, and the remainder of the day has been pleasant.

FRIDAY, DEC. 20. Some clouds and warm day. Tomorrow a member of the Legislature is to be elected, in place of _____ Dunlap, deceased.* They have an election for something almost every week. [John T.] Madden, the squatter nominee, has handed over his pretensions to Geiger, the Regular Democratic candidate, who has subscribed to "Free Soilism," "Homestead Exemption-ism," and every other good "ism" that the squatters asked him to — swallowed the whole, and no wry faces. They crammed the same wholesome doctrines down [Daniel J.] Lisle, the Whig candidate. Hope it will do them good. Geiger [Vincent E., Democratic candidate for Assembly], I understand, was a squatter anyway.

SACRAMENTO CITY, SATURDAY, DEC. 21. The election was the noisiest and most exciting I have yet seen. The polls were open in several places; and what with haranguing from the balconies, steps, and on horseback, parading the streets with bugle, drum, trumpet and sharp ringing clarionet, and the Babel-like jargon of hundreds of voices, in all languages, jabbering, chattering, huzzaing and yelling at the highest key, one could hardly realize that he was in the precincts of civilization, or that the reptiles thus foolishly wasting their breath were really humans.

SUNDAY, DEC. 22. Beautiful day, though the morning was pretty cool. After the forenoon services today, I visited the burying grounds south of the city. The first, containing from three to five hundred graves, is in a most uncivilized condition. As well might the dead have been buried among the moving sands of the Great Desert. A large majority of the graves are now level with the general surface, and can only be discovered by a bit of board or stake at the head or foot. Some of these have inscriptions, some not. The mounds are so obliterated that it is impossible to tell, without digging, within 200 or 300 of the actual number. The ground is strewed with bits of boards, inscribed with "here lies," "In memory of," etc.

The other ground, containing 1,039 bodies, is in tolerable order yet, and the gentlemanly sexton, A.W. Harlan, is endeavoring to bring order out of confusion. He is recording the names of all those who left names, and by a systematic numbering of the rows of dead, one may be able ever, hereafter, to find a friend or foe in any of the crooked lines, so long as a single grave in it can be identified.

A great many were buried in cholera times, in a portion where Mr. Harlan did not officiate, with so much hurry and confusion that it is quite impossible now to identify individual graves, and these of course must be left blank. Five, eight, ten or even fifteen have been piled together, awaiting burial; and although the names of all might be known, still they knew not the next hour which mound covered any particular person. Many an one

L.F. Dunlap was elected to the California Legislature but died before serving.

lies nameless now beneath these shifting sands, who came to California with high hopes and brilliant expectations; alas never to be realized! No tribute of respect or affection can ever be rendered to the nameless dead, except it be a thought, a sigh, or a tear. It is to be hoped that the city fathers will continue the present gentlemanly and communicative overseer in his place, as he is restoring the old graves, and doing his utmost to preserve the memory of the dead and the identity of their last resting place. The victims of cholera are about 800; 600 to 700 of which may be identified.

Heard Mr. Briggs, at the Methodist chapel this afternoon. He is the best sermonizer that I have listened to in California. They have been engaged in work on the levee and K street all day, and are at work as late as usual this evening.

MONDAY, DEC. 23. Another fine day. Saw at the *Tribune* (Squatter's) office, [James] Malony's sword; he who was the squatter leader in the "melee" of August last. It is a large instrument, with a rusty iron scabbard, and so very dull that nothing but sheer force would drive it skin deep. Truly, they that take the sword shall perish by the sword. Malony was shot, ["pursued a short distance up an alley and shot dead," according to Thompson & West, *History of Sacramento County, California*, 1880] and the Mayor, Hardin Bigelow, whose unadvised precipitancy caused the affray, died of cholera, after a long suffering from his wounds, and enduring the amputation of his thumb, and afterwards his arm—a just retribution. Apropos—There is a report that five or six men (gamblers) were killed at the El Dorado the night before last, or rather Sunday morning.

The stock auction has been driven by the mud to the public square. The citizens in general, and the inhabitants of K street in particular, at its former location, may congratulate themselves on the removal of this unmitigated nuisance. Mud to the axle is preferable to this Babel-like barricade. It ought to have been abated long, long ago.

TUESDAY, DEC. 24. Ground frozen this morning, and colder than yesterday. Lisle, the Whig, is elected by 150 majority. The vote was a meagre one, and either party might, in a few minutes, have drummed up ten times that number, who did not vote at all. The Democrats were SURE and were defeated. Hundreds in the city did not go to the polls at all, because they did not deem it necessary. There have been so many elections that sober minded people are heartily tired of them, especially as they perceive little change, except what goes into the pockets of the successful candidates—out of their own. How long, oh, how long, are laboring men to be a prey to those spoilers, political robbers, gulled, humbugged, tamely led about with a ring in the nose by these smooth tongued rogues?

Chapter Twenty

December 25, 1850–February 14, 1851: Last Visit to the Mines

————— ◆ ◆ ◆ —————

WEDNESDAY, DEC. 25. CHRISTMAS. Clear (but for the fog). Cold and frosty. Ground hard frozen. There has been yelling, and hallooing, and shouting and singing and firing of guns and crackers and bands of music playing most of the night. At nine a.m. left for Marysville in the *Gov. Dana.* The fog was so dense the first mile that we could, with difficulty, see fifty yards, and then we suddenly emerged into a clear, beautiful atmosphere. The aspect of things is essentially different from that of this same holiday last year. The water was then fourteen or fifteen feet above its present level, and rising; and the whole country under water. Now we are so much below the general surface that we scarcely get a glimpse beyond the banks, which certainly are monotonous enough. The greatest part if not all the valuable land is claimed (by squatters) and I notice some very good looking framed houses on the banks. Some intend to raise vegetables and others to ranche, i.e., go in for the stealings; at least, it is so understood in these diggins.

The *Dana* is a passably fast boat, and carries up a dozen and a half passengers, which, as it is cool enough to make it more comfortable to sit by the fire than in the open air, renders it more pleasant, for one has plenty of room. Last year, at this time, every "upward bound" craft was crammed with passengers and sometimes one could not get a passage at all on the same day he applied for a ticket.

Twelve o'clock, at Fremont. This place has improved but little since last year, and Vernon, ditto. I reckon that front lots will hardly bring $7,000 now.

Half-past one p.m. Landed at Nicolaus, and took the stage for Marys-ville. The river is too low for the *Dana* to go any higher up. The fare through, from Sacramento City, is $12. From Nicolaus up, $6. Reached Marysville just after sundown. Stopped with Geo. Sharpe, at the Wisconsin House.

George, I presume, has an interest in the concern, and his department is the washing and ironing. This brings in $50 a week, Marysville has enlarged a little, and only a little. Eliza, two miles below, has quite a number of houses, and appears thriving, otherwise, so so. Goods of all descriptions are very low here now. They are brought up from the city and sell below cost.

THURSDAY, DEC. 26. Cold morning for California. Footed it up to Park's Bar, on the Yuba, 18 miles. Some handsome looking farming lands, and some building going on. They seem to be making extensive preparations for farming. Long lines of unfinished fences stretch out in all directions, and the squatters seem entirely in earnest, in defiance of Sutter's notice to quit. Shouldn't wonder if they remain in spite, not only of the "old man" and the speculating harpies who have attempted to strip him, but even of the Government itself, should it unadvisedly interfere. The Yuba here is lined with miners. I did not expect to see so many at work after what I had heard.

FRIDAY, DEC. 27. Cold night and morning. Eld. Wisner is here, and Constantine, with Morgan. They take out here an average of six dollars, with quicksilver machines, in the old bank diggings. Some are washing dirt that was washed out last winter. This evening, some Frenchmen, a few doors off, are drinking champaigne, and rowdying largely. They sing in French, and make noise enough for a nail factory.

SATURDAY, DEC. 28. Too warm today for comfort. About as hot as June in Illinois. All kinds of wickedness in these diggins—drinking, swearing, swindling, litigation, quarrelling and fighting. One man was stabbed only a day or two since; now dead. No one knows here that he is safe for a moment, or whether some ruffian may not choose to make him acquainted with his knife blade, rather than waste powder and lead. Stealing is all the go. No one thinks of leaving exposed anything he cares a fig for—except his person.

The Frenchmen are at it again, even now, only two doors off, having a tremendous spree on some bottles of champaigne which they took by force today from a store, where it was deposited under the care of a man placed there by the Sheriff, who had seized it by virtue of some writ sued out at Marysville. There—there, now they are in for it. What a rush! I have been out to reconnoitre. One of the ruffians, perfectly frantic, has nearly cleared the house. Two or three only remain to pacify him. Well, for all that he has only a knife. A shot from one canvass house stops not at the walls of another. I have expected this long while to hear the crack. Miserable state of society this.

SUNDAY, DEC. 29. No meeting here today. I notice that one was appointed for Long Bar last Sunday. A Roman Catholic priest was to have preached. Rode with Hill a few miles down the river in his wagon and stopped with him, J. Wisner and Wm. McAuley, who are engaged in herding cattle on the south side of the Yuba. Beautiful day, only too hot. The grass from Marysville to the mountain is all fed down. The cattle can scarcely get enough to sustain life. It has sprouted two or three times, but the frosts cut it down and the coldness of the nights prevents its growing. It it does not rain very soon cattle will have to be driven to the mountains. Having no place to lodge, I walked down to Marysville, seven or eight miles, after dark.

MONDAY, DEC. 30. Went from Marysville over to Yuba City and called on Henry and Wm. McClure. The latter is sick, and the doctors are dosing him. Good luck to him, and may he live a thousand years. This city (?) has a goodly show of houses, scattered and stretched along for a mile. An Indian Ranche divides it into two parts. This is densely populated, but half of the houses in the city are unoccupied.

In passing, I saw a Digger Squaw, almost naked, doctoring a naked infant. It had inflammation of the lungs and really seemed to be dying. She held it on one hand with its face up, and dripped warm water from the fingers of the other into its mouth and over the face, so fast as almost to suffocate it. In about five minutes the child breathed freely, did not cough, and seemed entirely easy. Perhaps this practice may cure Diggers—might kill Yankees. Don't know. She finished by washing it all over and wrapping it in three inches thickness of cloth and fine slips of willow bark, cording it all round like a package of goods and handed it over to a young Digger to roll about the ground and play "toss and tumble" with, for ought I know. I waited half an hour to witness the result of the treatment and the breathing still continued free.

Some pegs in the soles of my new boots were making too free, for so short an acquaintance, with my soles, and I went to a shoemaker to get them removed. He had only an old, broken flat file to work with, and executed the pegs, my patience and very nearly my pile, for he only asked four bits for the job.

Mem: Always ask a shoemaker what he charges (by the by, I will add, for special reasons, the watchmaker) before he begins a job. Mem. 2nd: It's an even thing after all. It is worth 50 cents to tell of, and so I clear two bits at least in the operation. The boots, a good pair of heavy calf, well made, cost me $3.50 at auction; and 50 cents for cutting out a few straggling pegs. Huzza! for California. A beautiful day. Naked Indians about in all directions.

TUESDAY, DEC. 31. Left early for the Feather River diggins. Not much
travel on the road. Took dinner at Charley's ranche. The worst bread I
have yet seen in California. Too bad that. Looks better here in the night
than in the daytime. A large proportion of the trees about are "live oak,"
which give it quite a cheerful appearance. Musquitoes troublesome. Rather
too warm to travel with a coat on. Stopped for the night at Cuzard's ranche;
a new one, a mile farther in the mountains than Rube's, and 31 miles from
Marysville. Noticed a number of new ranches on the road up today.

WEDNESDAY, JAN. 1, 1851. Ground frozen and pretty cool, but a
delightful morning. The birds are singing about in the evergreens and the
grass is growing, notwithstanding the frosts. The little rain already fallen has
started it so that it is higher than in February (20th) last year. One can
hardly realize, in view of the general vegetable and animal greenness, that it
is "New Years' day."

Am winding my way up into the mountains, where it is altogether too
warm to travel with a coat on. Passed through the skirts to the Wyandot Diggins. They were opened in November, and *do not pay.* The city is being
deserted. Descending to the South Fork, I notice as I pass up on the south
side at the base of the mountain, that the ground is frozen and covered with
white frost like snow. At the old claim I find Ball, Woodson, Ferrington, and
I. & B. Coburn. They are digging in the bank and get only two or three
dollars a day now, each. These diggins look desolate. The houses are abandoned, and roofless—none of the shouting, hammering, singing, and firing of
guns, which indicate the presence of civilized man. A quiet, dreamy desolation seems to brood over the ditches, dams and flumes, where hundreds of
thousands of dollars in labor and goods have been sunk, never again to be
raised. Many a curse has been sent, with a will, from these mountain paths
into the depths below, where hopes and fears and joys and sorrows and property and prospects have been engulphed, and character blasted and reputation wasted, and souls ruined—all lost—utterly lost—and lost forever.

Which of the many, many mounds scattered about in the dark ravines,
contains a body which rests now in hope, or shall rise in joy? Alas! alas! for
California's dead. They lived as though they had no account to render, and
perished like the beasts—having a dog's burial. Priests and people alike have
gone astray, and none careth for the souls of the perishing. It is only, gold!
gold! gold!—no matter how acquired.

THURSDAY, JAN. 2. Went over to Indian Creek, two and a half miles
north, and found Benjamin and Rowley Wilson at work in very good diggins. They took out yesterday 23 dollars each. I think that they are averaging about an ounce. Returned in the evening. The nights are much colder
here than below; yet, to work in the sun, one has to strip off coat and vest.
Still the ground in the shade does not thaw out at all.

FRIDAY, JAN. 3. Cold night, about like the first of November in Illinois. Down at Stringtown. All desolate. No business. Some Indians.

JAN. 4. Cold morning and some cloudy with occasional gleams of sunshine. In the afternoon the frost under the mountain shadows melted and disappeared. Feels like rain.

SUNDAY, JAN. 5. Rained some in the night and occasional slight showers in the morning. The river has not raised. Rained all day with only short intervals.

MONDAY, JAN. 6. Rained all night and all day. The river has raised a little. Every body, almost, has been wishing for rain; now they have it.

JAN. 7. Nearly clear most all night but rained moderately all day.

JAN. 8. Clear all day. Ball and I went up the mountain for a deer. Returned with a fine large doe in about three hours. We went within less than a mile of the snow, and yet it was uncomfortably warm in the sunshine.

JAN. 9. Beautiful morning. Cloudy in the afternoon. On the mountain again in the afternoon. Saw only one deer. The frogs were having a grand concert at the mountain meadow where are some springs.

FRIDAY, JAN. 10. Went down to Stringtown and thence over to Indian Creek. The Wilsons took out $84 yesterday; today only $42. There are quite a number at work on the creek, and the average is not more than $3 a day. Beautiful weather.

SATURDAY, JAN. 11. Stayed over night, and worked with the boys part of the day. Took out $60. Delightful day. The Diggers have a number of "rancherees" on or near Indian Creek, and number nearly 1,000. They call themselves Nickees, and all other Indians Pikees and wage war with every tribe about them. Their arms are bow and spear. They appear about the cabins in the middle of the day, but bare footed, and frequently entirely naked, when the ground is frozen early in the morning. Indeed, except morning and evening, there is very little need of any more clothing than in July; yet they live from 1,000 to 2,000 feet above the Sacramento.
Several have been killed this winter, by falling from the trees into which they had climbed to gather acorns or pine nuts. One was killed by the falling of a bank under which he was "kyoting" for gold, and some have died of disease; but more than all these have been killed in skirmishes and battles. They burn all the dead at a place near the mouth of the creek, or rather they did—for the last one was buried Yankee fashion.

SUNDAY, JAN. 12. Walked over to the old cabin this morning. This place seems more like home than any other place in California. No meeting anywhere today. Silent as the grave, but for the hollow murmur of the rushing waters. The land where the Sabbath has been so desecrated is abandoned – desolate. No sound, human or inhuman, save that dull murmur, comes up the mountain slope as I descend into the valley. Found only Woodman at the cabin. The others have gone to Stringtown for the week's supplies – a universal practice in California. Saves time.

MONDAY, JAN. 13. Over at Indian Creek. Boys got out only $15. Slightly cloudy.

TUESDAY, JAN. 14. Weather as yesterday. Went down to Stringtown by the Indian burning ground. It is situated on a beautiful place on the Creek, and is nothing more than an area of three rods in diameter, slightly excavated, with a partial semi-circular bank of earth on each side north and south, two and a half feet high, and falling to the common level on the east and west, thus leaving an easy passage directly through the center.

These embankments are now covered with oak brush, recently cut; some of them stuck up, but mostly lying down. These brush, when they become dry, are probably used to burn the dead with. After the bodies are burned, the remains are scraped together and covered with earth, so as to form a little mound about one foot high and as much in diameter, nicely rounded and smoothed and covered with brush. They will soon have need of more fuel than they have here, unless they conclude to bury their dead, like the last. You can hardly see an Indian now who has not more or less a cough. I do not recollect to have heard one cough last winter. I suppose that their scanty and irregular supply of clothing is worse than to go entirely naked, as they have been used.

One day an Indian will be in camp, with two pairs of pants and two or three shirts on, maybe a vest, and perhaps a couple of coats; and the next, presents himself entirely naked – gambled all away. It is singular, that in adopting so many of our habits, they have rejected drunkenness. I have never seen an Indian in California drink, except at Vernon, and I suspect that they were more Mexican than Indian.

WEDNESDAY, JAN. 15. They took out a piece of gold at Indian Creek yesterday that weighed $35. Here they are not averaging $3 per diem. Beautiful day. Went over to Indian Creek for the last time, and returned after dark with R. Wilson.

THURSDAY, JAN. 16. Bade the boys good-bye and left with Ball for the Youba. We go by the way of Tolles' and to get there, ascend the mountain on the south, from whose summit I take a last lingering and yet in no wise reluctant view of the valley below from whose depths arises no sound save the hollow roar of the river, so long and to so little purpose listened to.

Yes, there below, so lone and dark and desolate now, the strength and bone and sinew and muscle, the life and breath, body and soul, and all the living energies of thousands have been wasted—frittered away in toil as useless, and labor as vain, as that of Sysiphus. "Woe worth the day" that staked the fortunes of so many needy men on so desperate an issue. It is past, never to return. Your pure waters may ripple down your mountain ravines, your roaring rivers rush through their narrow pathway, your shrubs and trees rejoice in everlasting verdure, and your tall pines wave a welcome to the distant wanderer; but few will hereafter disturb your solitudes. You have been inviting; but the days of your deception are ended. You promised much, and have given little. "Farewell, a long farewell to all your greatness."

Followed the crest of the mountain up some three and a half miles, and came to Tolles', (on the northern descent into a deep ravine which opens into the South Fork) seven miles from our cabin. Quite a number of respectable houses here, mostly for boarding or trading. Several hundred miners located here. A few are doing well, but the general average is hardly sufficient to cover current expenses. If it should rain before they all get out of patience and leave, they will probably do well for a while. Last night was quite cold down on the river, but it must have been much colder here, as the ground is frozen at the depth of two or three inches.

FRIDAY, JAN. 17. Cold night. Left for Tolles' new ranche. Our way lies over the mountains. Crossed several open places, meadows, in the bottom of the valleys, where the water was frozen over, and the ice strong enough to sustain our weight.

Arrived at the new ranche at two p.m., twelve miles. The road is only a mule trail, and although a mountain path, has no hills of any account, till we make the last descent into the valley where the ranche is. The whole country except the little meadows is densely covered with heavy timber, pine, fir, cedar and oak. One of the last I measured seven and a half feet in diameter. Some of the pines are large, and more than 200 feet high. Were directed—or rather misdirected, and struck the Youba at Frenchman's Bar, six or seven miles south west from Tolles'. About four miles from the ranche, we passed the frame of an immense building, ready for covering, intended for a steam saw mill, with a planning machine, etc. The boilers and some of the machinery are already in place, and the whole will soon be in full operation. Really, I cannot think what they will do with their lumber, unless they can keep it, for certainly they never can sell it.

SATURDAY, JAN. 18. We were very kindly entertained last night by Mr. & Mrs. Tyler who occupy the only house on the right bank of the river. The bar on the opposite side is very large and the river has been dammed. They are at work on the bar and average about seven dollars a day. It is accounted very rich. Left early for Park's Bar, 15 miles below. The path is over mountains and across deep ravines, the timber mostly oak and the craggy branching pines. Reached Mr. Nash's at one o'clock. Cloudy and a sprinkle of rain just before sundown. None of the ravines we passed today are working, probably for want of water. John Nash died of erysipelas this evening at 11:30. He was the son of James Nash, formerly of Plymouth, Marshall Co., Indiana.

SUNDAY, JANUARY 19. Park's Bar. A beautiful day. John Nash was buried without a prayer or a word except of simple thanks, though Elder Wisner was present and had offered his services. There was quite a crowd in attendance. Nash, the father, is an avowed infidel.

MONDAY, JAN. 20. Another beautiful day though it rained a little in the night. Slightly cloudy this evening and cool, too cool for rain.

TUESDAY, JAN. 21. Tramped to Marysville. Just cool enough for a pleasant walk. Queer winter weather, this.

WEDNESDAY, JAN. 22. Cloudy and chilly in the morning. No rain. Cool all day.

THURSDAY, JAN. 23. Weather as yesterday only very warm in the middle of the day. Very little business in Marysville. They are just beginning to move for the mines as the snow is clear high up and the prospect rather inviting.

FRIDAY, JAN. 24. At 9 a.m. left in a small boat with two other passengers for Sacramento. The steamers did not come up yesterday. Met three of them before we got to Nicolaus at 12 o'clock. Reached Sacramento City 75 miles by water at 7 p.m. Two of the men rowed from the time we left in the morning till we landed, without interruption except at Nicolaus, 15 minutes. The day was very hot, but they were "old salts."

SATURDAY, JAN. 25. Another hot day. K St. is not planked but very handsomely graded and wonderfully improved. A house was burned on J St. last night. The work of an incendiary.*

*This was the Prairie House, located between 10th and 11th streets. Mrs. Merrill, Dr. Lord's old landlady at the Antartic, had bought the house a few days before and was in the process of putting her investment in repair. The fire drew a crowd of 2,500 people, probably including Dr. Lord.

SUNDAY, JAN. 26. Cloudy and not as cool this morning. At dark it was thick cloudy and had a sprinkle of rain. At 7 p.m. it was quite warm.

MONDAY, JAN. 27. Fine day. Slightly cloudy. Rained some in the night. J St. was bad enough before. This morning it is one long mortar bed and stinks horribly: while K St. is passable everywhere. So much for grading. Most of the business today is through K St.

TUESDAY, JAN. 28. Cloudy today and pretty cool and clear all night. Clear again this evening. The steamers are now carrying passengers to San Francisco for one dollar and have been for a fortnight. It is 150 miles. The accounts from the miners are unfavorable. No water.

WEDNESDAY, JAN. 29. Weather continues the same. Long time since we have had any wind.

THURSDAY, JAN. 30. Left for Martinas in the *New World* at 2 p.m. It got cooler and cooler and the wind blew quite fresh as we approached the Bay. Very chilly when we landed at Benicia at 8 p.m.

FRIDAY, JAN. 23 [31]. Crossed over to Martinas. Very foggy and quite chilly all day. Old settlers say they have never seen any such weather here before. Strange that something new happens to the weather, go where I will. This is certainly a great country. The valley is as green as spring, the oats where not fed down being at least six inches high. The hills are not very green yet on account of the drought.

SATURDAY, FEBRUARY 1, 1851. Thick fog till afternoon and then too warm to exercise much in the sun. The Yankees are fast making an issue with the Spanish and original Californians and I should not be surprised if it resulted in the ejection of most of the latter from the country by one means or another, fair or foul.

Since I was here last they have had several of the scamps up for stealing cattle, and some of them indicted. One was severely whipped before he would tell who were his accomplices in the thefts, and his testimony agreeing with that of one who had told his story on being only threatened, it was considered conclusive.

The Spanish back in the valley took the whipping in high dudgeon; made a national affair of it and a few days after, an American was murdered and cut in pieces, shockingly mangled and mutilated only a few miles out of town. I believe that the general understanding now is, that if the like is done again, the natives must all leave or fight and no one doubts the result in the last case. It means extermination.

FEBRUARY 2, SUNDAY. No meeting today. Heavy fog till long after noon. There is a jail here built of stone at a cost to the county of $5000.00 and the stone and sand of which it was built may be obtained in any quantity within a mile of the building. The mortar is not cemented at all and crumbles at the slightest touch. I can with my bare fingers open a hole through the wall in ten minutes.

No man need stay in more than an hour even if he was left chained to the floor, for there is nothing but square blocks of coarse, crumbling sand stone between which is an equally rotten layer of some imitation of lime mortar. The rats had made their way up through it in thirty places, and thus they spend the people's money.

The state is in debt. The counties are in debt, the cities in debt if they could get trusted, and almost everybody owes somebody else and nobody cares to pay. The mines never did, do not, and never will pay. The whole concern is hopelessly, insanely, irretrievably, in debt and death and repudiation seem the only remedies.

MONDAY, FEBRUARY 3. Beautiful day but too warm. Went over to Mount Diavolo on an exploring expedition and to hunt. On the south and west, at the base of the mountain, is a valley some twenty miles long and from five to eight wide with numerous branches extend[ing] into the mountain.

Probably the valley really extends a long way to the north east, from the north side of the mountain. From the other end of the valley a narrow branch runs back and east bearing a little north to the extreme limit of ordinary vision. It seems to be very fertile and well watered. From Mount Diavolo itself the whole country seems only huge piles of mountains ranging for the most part east and west. Five-sixths of the whole land must be thus broken up and set on end. About one half the main valley is thinly timbered, with large scrubby looking white oaks with large branching tops standing generally on a barren soil, gravelly and baked hard unless immediately after a rain. Occasionally you find a patch of oats among the trees. The other half is covered with oats, the straws from two to three feet high as thick as they can stand. In fact, a perfect mat.

This makes a noble range for cattle. It must have been so used a long time. I noticed in one place several acres covered with bones and horns. Indeed you can see more or less of them scattered about in all directions. The whole of this beautiful country is claimed by half a dozen semi-savages under Spanish or Mexican grants.

The Yankees doubt the validity of these and from what I can now see from my present perch on the very peak of the mountain, I should judge that they are putting their doubts to a practical test for their own special benefit.

I notice a great many patches of recently ploughed land on the senor's extensive manor and woe to the unlucky land monopolist who attempts to maintain a little of this kind against the back woodsman's deadly rifle. The truth is, government ought to reduce every land claim in California to a limited quantity, say 320 acres, and only to actual settlers and if there are any legal claims on government for the land, let the government cash them. Almost all the arable land in California is claimed by a very few lazy, idle, worthless individuals, not particularly friendly to the government, and held at prices out of reach of the tillers of the soil.

If government sustains and confirms the title as claimed, it will virtually condemn the land to barrenness and leave it a desert unless, which is far more likely, the rifle and Bowie knife should settle the question of title in advance.

If government does not interfere and will only leave it to the people, there will be little danger of land monopoly here. It is very likely that through fear it will be disposed of at nominal prices, or at least most of it, before the courts are ever called to adjust it.

THURSDAY, FEBRUARY 4. Splendid day—though at noon it was as hot as July. Ranged over the mountain 20 to 25 miles and saw such sights as I have often dreamed of but never expected to see realized. No description, no paintings can give or convey an adequate idea of the beauties of the delightful valleys that branch off from the main one. The deer have been driven away from this vicinity by the hunters and are very shy. But with my glass I can see, within two or three miles, herds of them like flocks of sheep, feeding beside the mountain streams, or on the broad smooth hillsides, green with the young oats. I have seen only one kind of flower and that was a crimson poppy so very, so exquisitely beautiful, that I cannot remember ever to have seen its equal. It was abundant over a tract of five or six hundred acres and I noticed it in another locality.

The soil on the mountain, except some of the highest, sharpest peaks, is rich and in some places remarkably so. These barren peaks are more or less covered with different species of dark evergreens, and appear almost black from a distance. The mountain seems to be one great mass of sandstone which, on the rough sharp peaks, is hard and filled with fossils. I noticed one detached rock of a ton's weight, almost wholly formed of shells. Returned to camp tired and hungry.

By the by, slept out last night on the ground. The first time since—the last, really I can't remember when.

3 p.m. Left the delightful scenes probably forever and struck for Martinas. In returning through Susune Valley, saw thousands of wild geese feeding on the oats which cover the ground yet where it has not been burned over. Once vast herds of elk wandered over these plains and their bones may yet be seen lying around in all directions. In their place we have now large herds of cattle and droves of horses and mules, scattered all over the country quietly enjoying the rich pasturage.

Occasionally you will notice one of these living patches, which dot the country all over, begin to move and if you look very closely you will discover directly a mounted Californian on its trail—and away and away they go, faster, faster, helter skelter, neck or nothing. It is really singular that these fellows should possess so little sense, for they chase and frighten their cattle so much and so often that they can never approach them only on swift horses and materially retard their growth.

They will chase a whole herd of cattle or drove of horses or mules for hours just to catch one or perhaps drive 500 or 1000 head five or six, or even ten miles, on the run to a corralle just to catch one to take to market.

WEDNESDAY, FEBRUARY 5. 7:30 p.m. Left Benicia opposite Martinas, bound for Sacramento City. The wind blew fresh last night. Somewhat cloudy this morning.

THURSDAY, FEBRUARY 6. Woke this morning and found myself at Sacramento City in a berth in the steamer *New World*. Fare up five dollars. Berth extra $2.00. Cloudy morning. Left in the *Dana* for Marysville. Fare through five dollars but stage from Nicolaus. Seventy passengers. It was chilly all day and uncomfortable on deck without an overcoat. The night was cool with some wind and a sprinkle of rain. Stop at U.S. Hotel.

FRIDAY, FEBRUARY 7. Chilly but clear this morning. The U.S. Hotel is kept in very much the style of the Tremont House, Chicago, or any other of that class of hotels in the States. Rooms, pillows, feather beds, sheets, etc. There was a crowd at breakfast, whose "mustochios" certainly looked like a rooster's tail bedraggled on a rainy morning around the door of a grist mill. Left at eight o'clock in a real "coach an' four" for Long Bar, sixteen miles. Arrived at 10:30. From there started off on foot with R. Robinson, Esq. of Wisconsin and reached Rose's Bar, four miles, before twelve. Took dinner. Went over across to Deer Creek and up that on the Nevada [City] road.

Stopped with a Missourian ten miles short of Nevada City. He professed to keep tavern. Fare superlatively miserable, contemptible. Poor bread with tobacco leaves in it and fossil remains of rats. Beans half done. Meat frosted with "fly blows." Lodging worse. Five poles, two brush, one short stick for a pillow. Wherever you can find it. Supper $1.50, Lodging, $1.00.

SATURDAY, FEBRUARY 8. Concluded to climb the mountain before breakfast to get an appetite, and keep off the gout. A few miles on passed Newtown, a town of fifty or sixty houses all built in the last four weeks.

11 a.m. Entered Nevada City. The country we have passed through is much like that between Yuba and Feather Rivers. Nevada City contains several hundred (some say 600) houses. It has one long awkward crooked street built up for quite a distance on both sides. The buildings are for the

most part covered with boards split from the beautiful pines which abound here. There is a saw mill with steam power on the other side of Deer Creek, almost in the city, and is doing good business. But the lumber it can saw is wanted for floors and scants, and for other purposes than clapboard.

I suppose that shakes or split boards are the cheapest too. This may account for their common use. These 500 or 600 houses have sprung up like mushrooms or rather like Jonah's gourd and are probably destined to a like fate. A single spark would cause it to vanish in smoke.* In October there was but one house here. The tenth of November, three.

The diggins here are on a magnificent scale. All the ravines are dug up, and hundreds of shafts sunk and being sunk some of them more than one hundred and none less than sixty feet. They are now drifting in from the level of Deer Creek on the bed rock into the very bowels of the mountain and directly under the city. The dry weather has developed a new phase in mining operations.

Last winter is was nothing but ditch and pump and bail and drain to get rid of the water. Now they turn the streams from their beds and convey them to the diggins along the mountain sides, across broad valleys and deep ravines, over precipices and rivers. The dry diggins here are now supplied in part by water brought in that manner seven miles. It is taken from Deer Creek which here runs a thousand or two feet below. Hundreds of such ditches of only a few hundred yards in length are in operation all around us. I am told that they intend soon to take Deer Creek across the mountains to Rough and Ready, a distance of ten or twelve miles.

Water they must have and water they will have and if it don't come they are bound to bring it. This evening the gambling saloons look exactly like those of Marysville and Sacramento City. California cities are much alike. Gambling, drinking, swearing, etc. It has been very hot today and some cloudy.

SUNDAY, FEBRUARY 9. Cool night. Beautiful morning. Just after I got in bed last night there was a tremendous "row" in the street; yelling, sweating, and clashing of knives. It subsided in 15 or 20 minutes. I cannot learn that any one was killed. Night before last some body was nearly killed with a knife, and a night or two previous a man who was chasing another to stab him, fell and, sticking the knife into his own thigh, died in a few minutes.

Just a day or two before that a Dr. Lennox was shot in his own house through the window and died in five minutes. One [Lewis M.] Best is now under arrest in Marysville for the act. The opinion prevails here that he is guilty and but for the most strenuous exertions on the part of the lawyers and magistrates, he would have been hung on the spot.†

Within a year every house was burned to the ground.

†*The grand jury did not indict Best and he was released June 7, 1851, according to* Minutes of the District Court of Yuba County, *Vol. I, pg. 121.*

Left in a wagon that carries passengers direct to Sacramento City. No Sunday in Nevada City. Eight miles below passed through Rough and Ready. No Sunday. The people are at work, in the gambling saloons— groggeries—parading the streets, trading and amusing themselves generally as on any day. The town is built like Nevada on very rough ground and has 150 houses by count. The diggins must be very extensive and employ a great number of men. They appear more ruffianly here than in any part of California I have yet visited. Took a cane from a mansinnito [mansanita?] bush from the middle of the city. Put up before night. Fourteen miles below Rough and Ready with a very clever family and was well entertained and kindly used.

MONDAY, FEBRUARY 10. Left early and reached Sacramento City at four p.m. Saw several plants in flowers when we reached Sacramento Valley this morning and among them some beautiful violets. The Buckeye is leaving out, and the Redwood in full bloom among the lower ranges of hills. Strong wind from north east this afternoon.

TUESDAY, FEBRUARY 11. Went on board the *New World* at one p.m. and started at two p.m. bound for Benicia, which I have to stop one day. Fare, $1. Wind fresh and S.west. The nights are certainly cooler here than in the mountains or at Sacramento City. One gets quite chilly this evening (8 o'clock) standing on deck exposed to the wind on a craft running 15 miles an hour.

WEDNESDAY, FEBRUARY 12. In Benicia this morning. Crossed over to Martinas in the steam ferry boat. The wind blew fresh all the last part of the night and still continues to blow from the S.west. Was quite chilly and the Bay covered with white caps and very rough when we crossed. But there has been scarcely a cloud in sight all day.

THURSDAY, FEBRUARY 13. Strong wind all night, blew almost a gale this morning. Is as chilly as it was yesterday. Crossed back to Benicia and a fine tossing we got. The Bay was very rough and some cattle on board were jerked and tossed about very much to their discomfort, poor creatures.
    At eight a.m. left for San Francisco and was in at four p.m. Stopped at the Atlantic, [located at 10 Commercial Street] Long Wharf [Montgomery and Commercial Streets]; not the best house in California nor yet the worst. By the by, the Sawyer House has now the best table in Benicia.

FRIDAY, FEBRUARY 14. Took passage for Panama in the mail steamer, *Oregon*. No competition as the *Isthmus* is full to running over, at least it is so said, and people do not like to go in a "sail vessel" when they can go in a steamer for $125. Steerage it is true, but that is equal to a "sail vessel." All are anxious to get home and there are not vessels enough to carry all that wish to go. Indeed there is a perfect rush. Yet there are 300 to 400 vessels in port. There is a forest of masts. A squadron of vessels is now ready to sail, loaded with supplies, mules and miners for that great humbug, "Gold Bluffs."*

Took a short run through the city last night. The most prominent sights are the great gambling saloons. They are as magnificent as wood and brick and labor and gold and tinsel and paint can make them. Some of them are immensely large. The pictures which disgrace their walls are a most odious feature of the moral blotches, and yet they are wholly in taste—perfectly congruous. They certainly belong there if anywhere. Full length, life like, and life size pictures of naked men and women, done in oil, and some of them well done, meritorious as works of art hang against the walls staring at one from every side. It is rather startling at first, but one gets used to it after a little, especially when you look around and see a pretty woman sit facing a dozen full sized portraits of naked women in almost every attitude, surrounded by living gamblers and dealing "monte." Nobody seems to look at the pictures except strangers. Cool night and frosty morning.

FRIDAY, FEB. 14. 11 a.m. Am on the high hill west of Frisco, and sitting on the loose sand which gives support to a few scattering evergreens, my left side almost blistered by a July sun, and my right chilled by an October norther, which comes sweeping over Telegraph hill. I see spread out before me the narrow strait that leads the waters of the Sacramento into the great Pacific, which stretches off beyond the Golden Gate, blue, misty and illimitable; and on my right the Bay of San Francisco, with it windings, and turnings, and islands and steamers and whitened by canvass in all directions; while the pointed, tapering masts make it look like a huge hedgehog. At this moment, two ships, two steamers and one schooner are passing the straights, outward bound.

All around the hills and mountains, generally green and sloping; but these hills, except Telegraph hill, which is grassed over, are barren and composed of drifting sand. West of Telegraph hill, and in front of me, next the strait, the hills part covered with grass, and in a valley below are a couple or so of small gardens. The whole scenery, with the exception of the distant green hills (and they are for the most part treeless) is desolate enough. Nor does the city, which lies below at the right, add anything to the beauty (if one can see any beauty here) of the prospect; neither does it subtract one jot from the general desolation.

From this aerial point of view, it appears as if some fine city had been

Gold Bluffs was a beach along the ocean about 35 miles north of Trinidad, Humboldt County. Although the bluffs and sand contained a large potential of gold, extracting it never became profitable. Once again, Dr. Lord called it correctly a "great humbug."

blown up, and by some accident or design, the houses had all fallen here in a shower, where the land is utterly worthless for any other purpose; and thus dropped, they were shoved into lines far enough apart to admit the transit of a mule team with a sober driver; bringing in contiguity the palace and hovel, iron and wood, brick and zinc, circular and square, ellipsis and triangle, curve and straight, Gothic, Doric, Scythina, Digger, Yankee and Composite—all the colors of the rainbow without their brightness—roofs flat and round, roofs horizontal, roofs perpendicular, and roofs roofless. I can scarcely make out a single street, so narrow are they; and it is a man's work to travel them, when not planked. Most of them are so, or at least have sidewalks,—elsewhere the sand is loose, and ankle deep. The streets are kept tolerably clean, and an immense amount of labor has been, and is being expended on the harbor.

Wharves are projected several hundred yards, and Long Wharf is finished nearly to the deep water, near half a mile. But when the tide is out, one half the shipping in the harbor rests on the bosom of mother earth,—a soft bed, and not a scentless one,—all kinds of smells but roses. Every 24 hours, a hundred acres or more in the very heart of the city, and partly covered with buildings, is laid bare with all its filth and slime and often exposed to the burning rays of an unobscured sun, steaming, boiling, seething, reeking, and sending up its winged poisons to waste away human life, slowly it is true, but not the less surely. Such is Frisco.

What it will be, I am unable to say. Not much larger, I am thinking. Rents are falling; real estate, no sale; merchants selling at auction; small dealers, half their goods in the streets two doors off, selling at less than inside prices, and others disposing of their stock by lottery,—while the shipping is for the most part idle, or filled with goods which will not pay charges, nor for taking home again—neither ships nor goods. Occasionally they get up a Gold Bluff or Lake humbug, which gives temporary employment to a few vessels—but the number of ships in the harbor furnish no data on which to predicate the present amount of business. It only indicates what it has been.

Part IV : Panama and Home

Chapter Twenty-one
February 15–March 4, 1851:
Aboard the *Oregon*

—◆——◆——◆—

SATURDAY, FEB. 15, 1851. Cold and foggy this morning. I would much prefer snow and frost to this chilly, damp atmosphere. Went on board the U.S. mail steam Packet *Oregon*, at 1 p.m., the time designated by the agent at the office, as she is to start at four. She lies more than a mile out beyond the end of Long Wharf, and it is no small job to get on board. Why she does not anchor nearer, I cannot conceive.

She lies alongside the *Sea Queen*, a large ship, and as we dropped astern on the out side of the steamer we were ordered round to the other gangway between the two vessels, where the water runs through with frightful velocity, and were finally permitted to transfer our baggage to the deck. From this point we had some assistance from the steward. The impression which one receives on boarding is, "Come along, we can't hinder you. Help yourself; you won't get anything only what we have agreed specifically to do, and hardly that. Any part of the contract (meagre enough of itself) which we can avoid, be sure we shall."

The cabins are very fair, though nothing equal to the lake boats. Steerage is tolerable, for a steerage, roomy and clean. Supper at seven, and no fires started yet. They do not mean to go today. Why did they not say so, and then those that wished might have remained on shore. We had good reason to suppose that the most excellent, the United States mail steamer *Oregon*, would be off at the time. How fallible is human reason! She takes the place of the *California*, which is stuck somewhere down the coast, and perhaps could not get ready.

The fare in the cabin is only so so. In the steerage it is execrable, and the

347

passengers are fed like dogs. They won't stand it long, I reckon. Coal sacks occupy two-thirds of the table room, and the table had to be set three times. It has tin furniture, with knives and forks. I doubt if they can set a table for the whole 125. A piece of cold or hot fresh beef, or salt pork, a tin cup of tea, brown sugar and hard bread, was the sum total of fare, and not more than half enough at that—like a bad toast, to be eaten standing, and no chairs—(nor seats of any kind)—and so dark that only "by the taste or feel" could one kind be distinguished from another. Second table—ditto—variation—half of the dishes unwashed; third—ditto—variation—all unwashed.

The steward, as I understand, lays the blame on the cooks; and they claim that they were not notified that there would be so many to feed. If I mistake not, "it is for the interest" of the Company to have the "steerage" treated like dogs, and degrade them in their own estimation, if possible, and thus compel them to take cabin passage. There is no necessity for having the steerage stand to eat, or have two or three tables, or have their food get up in such a regular mad wolf fashion. They pay for better treatment, and should have it. It is very chilly on deck, and somewhat so everywhere; and yet there is no fire anywhere except in the cook's rooms.

SUNDAY, FEB. 16. Less complaint in the steerage about fare, and the second steward promises better things, though there is no more table room. No great reason for complaint in the cabin, and one who has been in the mines two years will hardly complain if treated half way decently. Cabins are very well fitted, though bed clothing is rather light. The steerage is furnished only with mattresses and pillows filled with fine hay or straw—no blankets.

Swung off and dropped astern of the *Sea Queen* at twenty minutes past four, p.m., and went rushing out of the harbor and down through the Golden Gate into the great Pacific, as fast as steam and tide could drive us. The long swell of the great waters, rolled up by the fresh west wind, soon upset the stomachs of a heap of the passengers. It looks black in the south and west. Heavy clouds and chilly.

MONDAY, FEB. 17. Cloudy, foggy and cold this morning. Seven sails in sight last night. All have vanished. Wind fresh, and dead ahead. Spoke to a small New England schooner upward bound. This evening the moon arose into an almost cloudless sky; a head wind quite fresh. The coast has been in sight all day, be we are gradually receding from it, and constantly passing islands, which are in general elevated from 100 to 600 feet, with bold shores, and apparently barren, though there is some show like grass. The main land presents the same general characteristics. Mountains, mountains, mountains, with deep ravines, and sharp ridges, and some few trees—small bushes—short grass, or more like oats—a barren, desolate country.

TUESDAY, FEB. 18. Warmer this morning, though the wind is the same and the sky half covered with clouds. Out of sight of the coast part of the day. Just at sundown entered the harbor of San Diego, 411 miles, and saw any quantity of black fish (small whales) putting out, puffing and blowing, in a mighty hurry, as if they disliked competition, or didn't care for such noisy company. Perhaps they have an aversion to smokers.

The harbor is a trifling affair, I should think, and the town equally trifling. A few houses about a mile above, where lie three vessels, and some show of a town three miles up at the head of the bay, is all that I can discover. Several boats came down where we lay in a little nook beside the *California* steamer, which put in here on account of a break in her machinery. We brought down some new pieces, and a few tons of coal for her. Her passengers seemed much pleased to see us, as they have been detained here near two weeks. The country looks better here than above. Left at dark, and soon after the moon arose in an almost cloudless sky.

WEDNESDAY, FEB. 19. Cool, as usual, this morning—no wind and cloudy. A heavy swell, and the ship pitches about so much that many a poor fellow has no appetite; or having eaten, parts company with his breakfast "sans ceremonie." Hot in the middle of the day. 12 a.m. Latitude 30° 12' north, long. 116° 10' west. Made 167 miles. In the afternoon the wind freshened from the north east, and we were soon rushing along driven by wind and steam.

THURSDAY, FEB. 20. Engine stopped two hours last night for repairs, and another hour this morning. Cloudy, but warm as May in Illinois, and most of the passengers are on deck. Wind N.W. and sails set, though they were furled for a couple of hours this morning. 12 a.m. lat. 26° 50', long. 114° 12'—made 227 miles. Saw a large whale making the best of his way from the ship. They seem to dislike such noisy neighbors as steamers.

At 3 p.m. spoke the *Carolina* propeller, upward bound, the most awkward, ugly looking craft I ever saw, on the "high seas" or low seas. She was crowded with passengers, and pitched like a gosling drinking from a sap trough. At sundown we were driving along with sail and wheel, dead before the wind. Cooler than in the morning.

FRIDAY, FEB. 21. Much as yesterday only a stiffer breeze. Added another sail, ("top gallan' sel") and away we go, faster and faster—and I believe that this is the only thing on board which pleases every body. With the mass, the more space they can put between them and California the better. Few speak well—or rather, most speak ill of the country. Most of those who intend to return, I would not be anxious to have for neighbors; and probably California is as suitable a place for them as any other. 12 a.m. lat. 24° 15'—long. 111° 45'—made only 210 miles. They claim that they have been sailing against a strong current running up the coast.

SATURDAY, FEB. 22. No wind this morning. They are taking in sail. The clouds are broken all around, but a thin grey haze covers every portion of sky and sea. Cape St. Lucas lies far away behind, indistinct in the mist, and probably never again to be seen by most, if not all of us. I presume that nobody cares, as much anxiety as been evinced to get past that point. People in the States will not make half as many sacrifices to get here as those here will to get home. 12 a.m. lat 21° 32', long. 109° 42'. Made 220 miles.

Out of sight of land all day, crossing the Gulf of California. Our monotonous existence was partially relieved by the sight of a few birds, among which was one a foot, or more, long with a single tail feather of three times that length, and a little pale green fellow no bigger than a wren, which boarded us in the afternoon. Have seen only one whale, which floundered along very awkwardly a short distance and disappeared. I might add a few flying fish. For the rest, some read, some write, some talk, and some few play at cards. Gambling is strictly forbidden, and the rule rigidly enforced. Today the water has been alternately blue, black, green and grey. This evening the "salt sea foam" sparkles most brilliantly in its own light.

SUNDAY, FEB. 23. A balmy delightful morning. Cloudy. The coast again in sight, covered with a blue mist. 12 a.m. lat 19° 46', long. 105° 25'. Distance 235 miles. The coast is very rough and shore generally rocky. Hills rise o'er hills, and mountains above and beyond mountains, in the distance, till the last blue, misty, cloud-capped ridge seems to split the sky. The lower ranges are covered with vegetation, probably cactus, which I am told grows here to an enormous size, from ten to twenty feet high. Fair wind and clear sky this evening. Passed an upward-bound barque.

MONDAY, FEB. 24. Hot enough below last night, and very warm today though there is a head wind. The sea is a most beautiful blue. 12 M. Lat 17.50°, long 102.08 — miles 225. To Acapulco 140. Today an awning was put over the whole deck. Without it the heat would be intolerable. Most of the steerage camped on deck early.

About 11:30 p.m. the cry of Fire! Fire! rang through the ship like a funeral knell. As the cry continued I roused up and, securing my money and papers, went on deck expecting to take a swim for it, and calculating on the chances of being interrupted in a precarious navigation of 15 or 20 miles by the sharks, some of which we occasionally get a glimpse of. There was a fearful excitement for about ten minutes and when it did subside there was a heavy ground swell left, heaving up the living masses. Many were greatly frightened as they had reason to be and I think that if the fire had not been subdued, one half of the passengers would have jumped overboard before there was any danger of burning.

ACAPULCO, FEB. 25. All kinds of American and other goods are kept here in the stores, and sold at reasonable prices. How the women can tolerate these tattered senors, I cannot conceive; and yet they seem as current as any. Most foreigners who live here may be found swinging in a hammock at all times—the lazy vermin. They would swing higher if they had their desert. I see no reason for such indolence, as it is not hotter now than it usually is in Illinois in June and July. Hammocks are swinging in every house, and seem to be in the same demand here that chairs are where people use such trumpery.

The bells of the Cathedral have been ringing at short intervals all day. At sundown, a large funeral procession left the house and proceeded at a rapid pace out of the city. At the same moment a chain gang is passing along the pavement, down the point toward the fort, guarded by almost their own number of redoubtable Mexican soldiery. As far as looks are concerned, the men are, many of them, absolutely hideous—generally passable. Some of the women are good looking; generally ugly, sometimes as sin. I did not see a handsome feature one in the city.

As regards their morals—I am of the opinion that they are, on the whole, somewhat exceptionable. But mark, it is only an opinion, and an opinion is all that I am able to give, as the facts will hardly bear transcribing into a public journal. I saw no woman in the whole place that wore more than a single nameless garment above the waist, except the universal shawl (in the sun) and they take special care that the skirt, which generally hangs from the hips, shall be long enough to cover the bare feet. These, by the by, are none of the handsomest—the toes spreading wide, as if in a transition state to the order amphibia—and the whole race, for that matter, take to the water as readily as ducks or frogs.

After all, a salt water bath in the surf here is a great luxury, as I can testify from experience. It is somewhat singular, but I saw no aquatic bird here, saving and excepting half a dozen awkward, half plucked pelicans, which really seemed half inclined to dispute the empire of the surf with us as we rolled over its rushing crest. It is well for this creature that it cannot see itself as others see it; else it would some day drown itself for very shame of its awkward, shapeless figure. The Dodo has become extinct, and the Dodo was a dandy bird, compared with this crooked disgusting deformity—this slovenly compound of stupidity and ignorance; of big bill and little legs— coarse feathers and stinking flesh.

A sort of slaughter yard above the fort furnishes food for a kind of turkey buzzard, so tame as almost to be in your way, and thick as grasshoppers—to which the above description will apply, with many additions and amendments, as the booksellers say when they issue an abridgment of a work which never existed.

Our quartermaster left us here—shipped as first mate on board a ship of 700 tons, now lying in port discharging a cargo of coal. He is quite a young man and shipped before the mast on the steamer, leaving it a quarter master. So much for promotion in California.

The country back is said to have many beautiful and fertile valleys, which supply the market of this barren place. Their cattle are small, and beef none of the best; turkeys and hens, of which they seem to have an abundance, very fine; sheep, miserable excuses for mutton; rabbits, wrapped in a leather apron; vegetables, too numerous to mention; indeed, I hardly knew the names of half of them. One article exposed for sale, and to the invasion of a million and a half of flies, is perhaps as characteristic of this people as any other thing—to wit: cattle's entrails, nearly half cleaned, strung up like drying pumpkins in Yankee land. Pigs are good looking, small, and fat. They live, or rather feed, better than the people; otherwise seem to have common rights and habits—a community of feeling and goods.

One singularity more, and I have done. In trading, they use cakes of stamped soap for change, (so it seemed to me.) I did not inquire its value, but I am sure it is hard soap, and it is emphatically a hard currency. The cakes are two and a half inches square and three fourths of an inch thick, when new. It is not a bad idea after all; for it has a real value, and when below par as money, they can use it to wash their garments.

On board again at four o'clock, everything and everybody covered with coal dust, and the poor natives whom we left dragging the heavy coal sacks across the deck this morning are still on the jump, naked and blackened with dust and sweat. About dark they wished to quit and there was quite a "row," and any quantity of Spanish swearing. However, I believe they had to work or lose all their wages, as they were still rattling the coal down to the ship at nine o'clock when I went to sleep. We came near not getting any supper at all.

WEDNESDAY, FEB. 26. The big guns on board were banged off, as usual when we leave or enter a place, and we "put out" at half past one this morning. We have now lots of hens and beeves and pigs on board, and the passengers have full supplies of fruit. Great times ahead. Wonder how those will feel who came on board drunk last night? Mean, I reckon. Out of sight of land most of the day. Cloudy, and a thin gray haze spread over everything. 12 a.m. lat. 15° 56', long. 98° 32'. Distance 100 miles. Very hot. Wind west and fair.

THURSDAY, FEB. 27. Somewhat cloudy. No haze. No land in sight. Wind ahead. A large bird was caught on deck yesterday, plagued awhile, and kicked overboard. This morning he is flying about, and trying to get on board again. The butcher killed and skinned a pig this morning, and hung him up on the guard over the place where the firemen throw down ashes, and cooks the offal. Directly the cord which suspended little piggy broke, and down he went for a salt water bathe. Some lucky shark had a dainty breakfast, though he could have dispensed with the skinning; and the butcher must be at the trouble (no small one) of skinning again. Mighty well for the pig, though, as he saved his skin by leaving it behind, and the sharks had to make "two bites of a cherry."

Hot, hot, hot in the sun, and but for the awning intolerable. Kit Carson's brother is on board: a big, burly, good-natured fellow, near sixty years old. He has been a mountaineer 27 years, and in all that time has never attended a religious meeting. Is on a visit to Missouri, and divides his time about equally between swearing, making sport, and sleeping on deck, stretched out in the coolest place.

Sleeping below is almost out of the question now, so hot is it. Half the passengers have colds and cough, and yet are constantly perspiring night and day. Even the night air is not cool enough to chill one, though he might be naked. a.m. 12. Lat 14° 23'. Long 94° 38'. Distance 225 miles. Very little wind this afternoon and the sea almost as smooth as glass; though there is a heavy swell pitching the ship backward and forward like a hobby horse.

FRIDAY, FEB. 28. Still warmer this morning and wind fresh and dead ahead. A quarrel last night among the firemen. One, it seems, by accident got another's liquor. Whisky originates most quarrels. A great deal of liquor was brought on board at Acapulco, and several passengers have been pretty well sizzled every day since. Still, at that place, we have the name of being the civilest set of fellows that ever landed. Maybe so; and maybe they have soft soap for change, on occasion, as well as hard.

If they had known how many revolvers went ashore, it might have changed their private opinion at least. Spaniards, as well as Irishmen, have bulls—as we discovered after we landed and went into the American Hotel and read a notice by the biggest man there, forbidding any person landing with any description of fire arms. There we were, armed to the teeth, and never dreamed of the horrible offense we were committing. However, no trouble came of it, and probably it is much better so than to let them know it before hand, as in that case every man would be sure to go armed.

Showery around. A mere sprinkle of one passed over the ship. a.m. 12° 44', Long. 91° 30'. Distance 228 miles. San Francisco time at 12 today is nine and twenty minutes. Heavy clouds low in the west and south at sundown. Everything about the deck is very damp this evening. The ship rolls and pitches more than she has done before.

SATURDAY, MARCH 1. Warmer, cloudy, and showers at the South. Heavy swell, and wind ahead, and strong in the afternoon, with rough sea. A school of porpoises ran along side, pitching and rolling and tumbling and leaping for half an hour, much to the amusement of the passengers, and I suppose porpoises too. 12 a.m. Lat 11° 26'. Long. 88° 55'. Distance 170 miles. Cool and wind increasing this evening. Rough night, I should think.

SUNDAY, MARCH 2. Cool, and sea rough, with strong head wind. About midnight it blew almost a gale, and the passengers who had camped on deck were completely routed, body and blankets, and driven below. They say that the ship behaved handsomely and I dare say she did, and after all only acted out human nature, wood and iron though she is. She treated the "canaille," which tumbled past, with the utmost contempt, while to the "upper ten" which came rolling and swelling along, she bowed and court'sied like a Broadway belle; polite to a charm. But occasionally, when a bloated million- aire came towering, sweeping along, I noticed that she seemed a little flurried, and ducked rather than bowed, sometimes getting a cap full of brine dashed over her to check her presumption; rather amusing, than annoying to most of the passengers. Yes, she is very polite, on the whole; very polite indeed, and no doubt deserves great credit—but it makes one's head dizzy to see it, and turns many a stomach wrong side out just thinking about it.

The greatest annoyance I have on board is tobacco. The deck, not the quarter, is drenched in spittle, and literally choked with old quids and half smoked segars. How a human being can so degrade himself as to use tobacco, I am unable to see. Can't do it. He is less than human, somewhere between a thumbscrew and a coal pit; a mere instrument of torture, with too little sense to be accountable,—a kind of sleepy unconsciousness—the embodi- ment of a fuddled dream. Look at them. Faugh! How sickening! It is only drunkenness in another shape. There may be ten persons on the ship who do not smoke nor chew; not as many who do not drink brandy; and swear- ing is so common that one can hardly say who don't swear. Strange that the ship swims at all. If every sin committed by this people were now on board, and rated at two grains each, I verily believe that the ship would find bot- tom, though ten thousand fathoms deep.

12 a.m. Lat. 10° 1'. Long. 87° 5'. Distance 175 miles. I cannot see by what process of admeasurement the captain makes it so much. Fresh breeze from the north-east and heavy clouds in the south-west every few minutes gleam- ing with lightning. Warmer.

MONDAY, MARCH 3. Heavy clouds hang lazily about the horizon and before daylight were often illumined with lightning. Land in sight on the larboard quarter, none ahead. The ship behaves a great deal better, at least on my estimation, than she did during the "blow." Goes on her way, minds her own business, bows to nobody, and scarcely rolls at all.

The sea is a most exquisitely beautiful blue, wherever you can look directly down upon it. Thousands of flying fish are in motion. Every moment they rise in flocks, from the bow or from before the wheels and dash off or glance away above the water. Some drop into the flashing waters directly while others glide along several rods. I noticed one that sustained itself 200 yards by occasionally touching the surface with its wings. I did not believe before that one could fly so far.

I have not yet seen one three feet above the general level of the surface. When they fly on board a ship as they sometimes do, it must be from a wave whose top is nearly on a level with the deck. They are a small affair. I do not think that I have yet seen one more than eight or nine inches long.

12 M. Latitude 8° 19′, Long. 84°. 196 miles. Islands in sight all day. Cloudy. Cool this evening. Such an appearance of the clouds would indicate rain to a certainty in Illinois, but it clears off entirely in the night however much it may threaten in the day time, yet the air is full of moisture in the evening and linen clothes feel very damp after sitting out a while.

TUESDAY, MARCH 4. At sunrise this morning was on deck and the first thing I saw was land—hills covered with dense forests of towering evergreens. We were passing between a small island on our right, and the large one of Quibo on our left. A few perpendicular rocks rise boldly from the water near the shore, which in many places is a high rocky bluff.

The air is cool and balmy and pure, and reviving fresh though blowing right in our teeth. Last night about eleven it kicked up quite a fuss, and dashed the spray all over the decks, much to the annoyance of those who would rather sleep than laugh. And this is the entrance to the Bay of Panama from the north. Glad am I, and I doubt not all participate in the feeling. The steerage certainly has good reason to desire once more to stand on "terra firma" if there is anything clean there to eat. The fare without a question has been abominable. The provisions are damaged, the attendance infamous and the cooking execrable. The chief steward is directly accountable for it all. The steerage steward is a perfect "non pariel," attentive, indefatigable, accommodating, kind to the sick, polite to all and always on hand.

But the company—the owners of the "line" are all, after all, to be held accountable. I am sure that no ship steward without positive instructions, would ever think of being so mean, so little, so half souled, so penurious. None but a rich man would ever think of starving the poor to increase his gains; of making money by cheating a man out of his dinner after he had paid two pieces for it.

No. Neither a poor man nor a fat man would do it. He has no skip jack of a starveling dried up herring skin flinty gizzard and misnamed a soul rattling round in his mortal body. No, no, I say again, the poor man's soul in the quality of hospitality would fill the hide of an ox. In food and drink he is liberal to a fault. He never lies awake nights to contrive ways and means to swell by dirt and mould and fermentation and loathing, the stomachs of 15 men with the scanty ill-selected rations of three. Some of the hard bread was good quality, some mould and much of it was infested with black bugs burrowing into it like wood chucks in a sand bank. A cold water soak would drive them out of their holes and cause them to vamoos, and you had the supreme gratification of knowing how many escaped, but you get no satisfaction as to how many remained to be eaten.

It was altogether better to soak them in hot water or in your tea as they cooked as easily as oyster and you didn't have to eat them raw. They were not numerous enough to be a full substitute for fresh meat, but there really seemed great danger of some specimen crackers following the example of the riches spoken of in scripture, taking to themselves wings and flying away.

If the hard bread has been bad, the pork has been worse. Not that it was wormy. No, no, it was too strong for that. Worms know what is palatable and take good care not to get into such pork barrels as ours. A very few barrels of the pork has been passable; but bad as was the bread and pork, there was strength enough in the salt junk to redeem both. It absolutely stank so bad that after a few days one had no nose for the pork and no eyes for the bugs.

Many and many a savory ten pound morsel of the ox carrion has been tossed overboard that must have proved a vomit for a shark. If not disposed of in some such effectual way it would appear at the next table in some other shape, nobody could tell what, or name the slush tub scrapings, the protean vomiting of a dozen meals on its advent to a new and untried existence. It seemed to delight in the amphibious, and its habits were much like those of the frog, always swimming in dirty green water, slimy with paste and accompanied by a few small bits of potatoes, which seemed to have an instinctive dread of their rotten hearted neighbor, darting off whenever they came in contact like a tadpole from an electric eel. The cooks call the stuff wet hash, and wet it was sure, and harsh enough for certain. Nobody will dispute that.

The rotten mackerel, done up *secundum artium* with shrivelled half dried abortions from the onion tribe or caricatures of leeks were the chief d'oeuvre of the cooks. I have assisted in dressing a cancer in a close, warm room, have eat my dinner on the desert, that great Golgotha, when every proximate object was a rotting carcass—and I have been in a Sacramento City hospital, so give me credit for some experience in subtle strong "effluvia," but never say stink to me till you have cooked rotten mackerel with onions. It is a perversion of the very first principle of gastronomy and the cook who invented it must have his nostrils lined with Platina.

I would suggest, though with great diffidence, as additions of sauce of grass hopper jam or cricket jelly and a salad of skunk cabbage—served under a rotten egg and sprinkled with sour molasses and sulphur. It is doubtful if gun powder and asafoetida would make it any more agreeable.

Another favorite dish, at least with the cooks, was Indian pudding, and such as would be hard to beat. Indeed with a single exception it was unexceptionable. It was too thin—a very little. I am sorry to say it but so it was. I allow that certain lewd fellows slanderously reported that the meal was sour, nearly one half in mouldy lumps and that it would be better for being sifted as it would be likely to take out the lumps and bugs and worms, etc, for the cat had been in after the rats which had just got out. But nobody minded what they said, as everyone could see for himself that it was exactly so. Who cared when dark (I do not say dirty) molasses would hide the mould and strangle the bugs, and tangle the worms.

The curse of sourness might be blessed with vinegar and the vinegar might be made of this or that or the other, no great matter what was once in it. Nothing like straining. And it was not bad looking after all, and might be improved by a pinch of mustard while a good sprinkle of pepper likened all the little black bugs to itself unless they crept and then the less said the better. In fact that trite saying will apply oftener than many are disposed to think. Possibly I had better hold my peace in this matter. The flesh is willing but the spirit is weak.

Speaking of flesh puts me in mind of the tough beef we had sometimes. I do not wish to be censorious and surely the Lord is not to be blamed because the Mexicans raise such little, tough, sinewy, cock fighting bundles of rattan and rubber done up in calf skin for beef, or that they tie them by the heels like a doomed chicken, and after two or three days of torture, release them on a ship board to starve or be killed to keep them from starving.

But surely their excellencies, the Great Pacific U.S. Mail Steam Company, need not buy or even steal such miserable shadows, such stringy phantoms to feel passengers on. A wolf could scarcely make a living in a pantry filled with [it]. To say it was tough is to say just nothing; a perversion of truth. A sturgeons nose, boiled cottonwood, steamed leather, or India Rubber are its real representatives.

Nothing in all creation its equal in the beef meat or beast line if one may except the gizzard case of a Pacific U.S.M. Steamship Co. I should not like to institute a post mortem in that diggins. It would be a filthy job. Too dirty a place to search even for the truth though you had searched every where else in vain.

At Acapulco we got one very good "beef" and some that could be eat. So there is eatable, chewable, digestible meat in the country and nothing but the sheerest avarice would seek or buy any other. In the whole voyage there has been but one palatable, wholesome meal and that was a "pot pie."

It is said that there is abundance of flour on board but we have had no soft bread but twice and a half and that was sour and mouldy. The truth is they are too stingy to employ help enough, (though they can get enough for their board) to make bread or do the work as it ought to be done and the cooks just throw the pork, beef, fish and small potatoes about as chance may mis-direct, and dirt and slop is a regular part of the fare as the other. The coffee is burnt, black and muddy, strong and very bitter and withall more or less greasy; generally more. The sugar is "common," or rather "uncommon Brown" and often buggy; always dirty. The dishes are all tin and the soup and tea and coffee and water are all drank from the same cup. Coffee in the morning, Soup and water at dinner, tea at night, so that they

are always more or less greasy being washed in sea water (to save salt?) and
without soap, I reckon.

Those who are at all squeamish never look into their cups. The knives
and forks are of the roughest workmanship and patterns and appear like the
refuse the remnant of twenty auction sales every cuttery establishment in
the world and probably some out, being fairly represented; and then even of
these there are not enough on board to furnish both tables, so that a dozen
or two have to wait at every meal. Sometimes we find them covered handle
and tine and shank and blade covered with crumbs and rust, and often
with the threads and shreds and tatters of the worn out dish cloths, looking
much like a thorn bush in a sheep pasture.

In serving, the cooks set the pans and plates of meat, hash, etc., on the
dirty deck and then the waiters pile them on each other, and, of course, the
dirt on the bottom of the upper falls into the food, or mess rather, in the
dish below, just as though the cooks did not know how much dirt to put in
at first.

The tables are none of the cleanest though covered with "oil cloth," and
during the performance the audience remain standing. That men under
such circumstances should always keep between two proprieties is hardly to
be expected. Especially if we take into the account the fact that for a long
time there was seldom enough on the tables to eat.

Towards the last there was always enough, but for days and days in the
beginning it did not average three ounces of potatoes per man per day, and
not more than one half got any at all. Once we had some dried apples stewed
and apple pudding six times, but the cook ought never to brag of his skill,
and certainly no one will ever brag for him.

There is nothing more to find fault with except, perhaps, the rice and
we had plenty of that. Yes, the rice, and such rice. Let me see. O, I have it.
Take a very poor article of rice; moisten it, let it heat and ferment and get a
very little mouldy, add "quantum suff." of dirt, bugs, husks, pebbles, etc.,
like the currants in the fruit pudding, half boil all together in greasy water;
say, dish water: without sorting, or picking or sifting or washing and serve
on a square tin, to be eat "ad libitum," without salt or with if you choose.

12 M. Latitude 7° 08', Long. 8° 46', 200 miles. 155 miles to Panama.

> In 'Frisco Bay
> the miners lay
> The number 81
> Thinking to sleep,
> on the bonny deep
> That night in the *Oregon*.
>
> For the agent, he
> said they must be
> On board at 1 p.m.
> And never knew,

the humbugged crew,
That the agent would lie to them.

They waited awhile
for "the bilers to bile"
But water don't "bile" without fire
And the chimney was cold
as an iceberg's "hold"
And proclaimed the fellow a liar.

And night came down,
both gray and brown
As cold as an April fog.
And a little bell
like a funeral knell
Led us up to the grub of a dog.

The smutty skin
from many a shin
That night was rubbed away,
For the coal sacks thick
as a 1000 brick
In the gang-ways scattered lay.

One third of all
in coal dust hall
Beside their dog meat stand,
While the rest for their sins,
with battered shins,
Wish themselves again on land.

No light is there
save the murky glare
From the cook room gleaming out,
And the waiters seem
like a nightmare's dream
As they dodge and flit about.

The tea is as strong
as a bondman's wrong
And greasy's the head of a whale
And the bread as hard
as the teeth of a "pard,"
And tough as the string of a flail.

They cut at the meat
and chewed to eat,
And cut and chewed again
And the more they chew,
the tougher it grew,
Their toil and labor in vain.

Is it flesh or fish
in that big tin dish?
Pray roll it along this way
But none can tell
by the taste or smell
If 'twas fed on worms or hay.

It might be mule
or the leg of a stool
Or the horn of a mountain sheep
Or a Spanish hide
or cork chips fried
Or a sword fish from the deep.

They rattled the tin
and then turned in
and dreamed of the ticket they'd cashed.
When another set came
and did the same
Though but half the dishes are washed.

They munched and chewed
and twisted and screwed
Till their jaws got into a lock
Then muttering they sped
to a checkered hay bed
With a curse for the steward and clerk.

The night was brief
and the tough bull beef
Came back with the morning sun
And the hard tack too
with its mould so blue
And the bugs that through it run.

And stomachs strong
were turned that morn
That never turned before
And loathing souls
sat on the coals
And wished themselves ashore

For buggy peas
and slushy grease
And stinking pork were spread
Beside the meat
so tough to eat
And mouldy buggy bread.

While coffee black
as chimney back

And strong and bitter too
Was served milk warm
lest it should harm
The stomachs of the crew.

Day followed day
as on the way
For Panama we scud
And various were
the bills of fare
Upon the table spread.

Potatoes scant,
supplied the want
Of those who loathed the bread.
And a pig would squeal
at the mouldy meal
Of which the puddings were made.

And many a dish
of rotten fish
Went steaming by the nose,
And twice a big
piece of a pig
Like Samuel's ghost arose.

The knives and forks
like unfledged storks
Full many a dishrag tore
And tattered tags and
threads from rags
Blades, prongs and handles bore.

Long may she live,
long may she thrive
The good ship *Oregon*
And Aspinwall,
the great mogul
May he live just as long.

And long nose he,
who came to see
The rotten stinking meat,
Dressed out so neat
and called it sweet,
The passengers to cheat.

Long may he live
and learn to thrive,
On rotten beef and mouldy meal,
And when the rats

rob him of that
God grant him grace to steal.

6 p.m. Are passing a mountainous cape covered with the densest foliage, a tangled mass of vegetative life. The crew of the ship are used much as are the passengers. One of them was knocked down by the second mate merely for eating a mouthful of "duff." Poor fellows, they are hard worked, kept awake, made to do unnecessary jobs just to keep them busy, half starved and treated like dogs generally, and all for money. 200 or 300 dollars more or less, a trip, could make them a great deal more comfortable. But no matter, they only shipped for their passage and get nothing else.

Indeed I am told that very few hands can be got to ship both ways at any price. Money, money, money. Grind the soul out of the poor. But there is a day of reckoning and the tables will then be turned. Some day the monopolist will howl and weep. There is now an extra dinner getting up in the cabin, and as compared with the steerage it is a striking illustration of Dives and Lazarus. And yet the men who are to riot there and drink champaign pilfered the money from those who are to eat the steerage dinner, wrung it from their hands; drew it from their pockets by lying, fraud and deception. Took seven prices of everything and ten for grub; borrowed and never paid. Bought on credit and sold for gold. Kept the gold and lost the credit when it was not worth keeping.

So the world goes, and such for the most part are the cabins—all the rogues and gamblers can afford it. Very few of the latter in the steerage.

3:45 p.m. Spoke to the *E. Randall* of Cambridge with sixty passengers from Frisco, bound for Panama. Been out nearly two months and hanging out in the Bay fourteen days. On short allowance eight days and only enough for 24 hours left. The Capt. of the *Oregon* would not take her passengers on any terms, but sent a boat load of flour and pork.

Glad to see the stinking meat go, but sorry for the *Randall's* passengers. The Capt. seems to think that they had grub enough and only wanted to get their passengers off their hands. I don't know.

Quite cool with a fresh head wind. I had anticipated excessive and dead calm here and find it pleasantly cool with plenty of wind. Let no one make up his mind for any particular weather, or doubtless he will be disappointed. I would not be at all surprised to hear from the next traveller that he was detained by ice a fortnight or so. If a man has no other business this way than to see the sights, he had best stay at home as there is nothing else to come for any way.

Chapter Twenty-two

March 5–March 9, 1851:
On the Isthmus of Panama

◆ ◆ ◆

WEDNESDAY, MARCH 5. Going on deck at sunrise, saw several small, rocky islands, peering out of the grey mist directly ahead. We are still driving up against stiff breeze. The wind seems to head us at every turn. A brig, or barque, with her tall white towers of canvass, is bearing down upon us. The islands are rocky mountains, covered with tropical vegetation, like all those we have passed the last few days.

Ran between a couple of islands on the right and the island, harbor and town of Tobaga on the left as one of our guns bellowed forth its rude good morning at 9:15 o'clock. The town, which is situated on a low beach, looks much like Acapulco, only more compact; and crowds up into a little ravine, piercing the mountain side, as though it liked to be squeezed. The island is one small mountain, the steep side of which has scattered patches of cultivation—pine apple, plantain, banana, etc. It looks mighty slovenly and Spanish like—and now we are standing direct for Panama, and the passengers are getting the baggage on deck.

Half past ten o'clock dropped anchor. Twenty seven sail moored around us. Great harbor this—open as a ten acre lot without any fence. Panama lies three or four miles in front of us, and a few little jagged rocks, sticking a few hundred feet above water, on our left, dotted with little patches of cultivation. I reckon they don't need fences, else they would be too lazy to raise anything.

There are already three or four boats at the gangway, waiting to take passengers ashore. Price, $1.50. But the gangway is up again, and a little steamer belonging to the Company comes alongside, and by dint of lifting

and tugging and lugging on the part of the passengers, the baggage is transferred to her deck and all on board. She is a very pretty affair, after all—
and not so small either—and quite an accommodation to the travelling
public, as they only have to pay $2.00—only 50 cents more than anybody
else asks.

Joseph Belcher died on board just as the anchor dropped. He came on
board at Frisco, just gone with bronchitis, and no one thought that he
could ever reach this port alive. He did, and that was all. I believe they
claim that some port regulation connected with this death required them to
cut off communication with the shore. Mem: If you don't wish to pay more
than the common price, go in a boat where nobody dies. Belcher was from
St. Louis. One evening, on the passage down, I saw him give his purse and
papers to the surgeon of the ship, to hand over to the Consul at Panama.
He stated the amount of money at $800. What will become of it, I can't say.

The coast toward the east stretches off low and flat in the distance, west
it is mountainous; and inland, or north, it is broken into peaks and ridges.
The city from here looks like a motley collection of gray and reddish brown
houses, here and there parched with white, and the cathedral towers, two of
which are very prominent, rear themselves high in the air after a very awkward, ungainly fashion. I trust that a nearer view will give a more favorable
impression, as I would like to be pleased with ancient Panama, though, for
that matter, I am told (I do not vouch for its truth) that this is rather a
modern affair, the site of the old city, which was burned, being three miles
distant.

The mail bags have been shipped without difficulty or danger, and I
cannot see how they can be lost in this operation. Any quantity of different
sized and shaped boxes sealed with more seals than the book which John
saw, were next trundled on board and stowed away. I wonder what is in
them? Gold dust, likely. At one p.m. tried hard to leave the *Oregon*; but,
true to her instincts, she played the grab to the last, and as a parting token
took the top of our wheelhouse off with her starboard anchor. If that ship
keeps afloat and don't pay her way, then everything "goes to pot"—if she
can't play the California game of "grab," nothing can.

As we approach shore, I see a crowd on the narrow beach, under the
walls, most of them seemingly nearly naked. The moment the steamer comes
within hail, a score of boats shove off. And now the anchor drops, and they
are about us. "The Philistines are on thee, Sampson." All want a chance to
take us ashore for two bits, but we are to be taken in the four boats of the
steamer. The rascals all pretend to belong to the company service, so that
one of the steamer officers has to be on hand all the time to prevent
imposition.

It is thirty rods to the beach; and there go four boats, deep with
passengers, sixty or seventy of them, and the brown and black and yellow
rogues crowd down to meet them. The boats ground and are instantly

surrounded, three or four deep; and such a pulling and hauling and yelling and singing and swearing. They seem to want to carry the passengers on shore on their backs, and sure enough, there goes one on an ass ride. I pity the trunk handles unless they are proved to be quite destitute of feeling for such tugging must weary even leather.

And now they go over the bows like a flock of sheep. Splash! there goes one fellow into the water, knee deep. Waited a trifle too long, or jumped a shade too quick. The big boat has grounded too far from dry land, and there they lie, thirty of them, and can't get ashore. Now comes our turn.

Well, we have got out of that scrape, but such a scene. We ground on between the big boat and the shore, and all its passengers went teeming over us, while the natives surrounded us and seemed disposed, not so much to help as to tear our baggage in pieces. They were kept off by some well applied punches of canes, some threats, and a vast deal of the biggest kind of swearing; and we had our traps once more on "terra firma."

Then we were in another "fix." The tide was coming in, and in half an hour would be up to the city wall. We had to move our trunks twice and each time half a dozen rogues wanted two bits each for moving each parcel that we moved ourselves. They attached themselves like leaches to each particular thing, and seemed to regard it as their property for the time being. They wanted a dollar for carrying each parcel into the city, and kept telling us that the water was coming—a fact so obvious that we were little inclined to dispute it, or if so, only for argument's sake. In fact, it was too inconveniently obvious to admit of direct contradiction, already wetting the trunks for the third time.

I paid two fellows fifty cents each for carrying my two trunks. Passengers generally took their own baggage. They made no great spec in carrying mine after all. The trunks weighed together 220 pounds and made them sweat. Fifty cents, however, is more than they can get for a whole day's work; indeed, they can't get anything like steady employment at any price, as near as I can find. Many of them are entirely naked, and mostly only clothed at.

From the narrow beach where we landed, we held our devious way under the city wall among the tumbling ruins, spiced with every sort of filth, and ascended a few feet to a dilapidated platform of stone masonry, 100 feet long and 15 to 20 feet wide, which seems "*lang syne*" to have been something; as there are a number of stone columns facing the water, and the remains of others, distinctly showing the whilom existence of an arcade front to a boat landing at high tide.

The whole was once roofed over and must have had a very pretty, if not grand and imposing, appearance. How are the mighty fallen! Its arches have tumbled in ruins, its pillars rolled in the dust and that shattered fragment of a roof which once sheltered the proud, lordly Don from sun and rain, now only overshadows huge ranges of greasy looking bar soap, piled against the wall, as though the city itself were soap walled—and all kinds of tropical fruits, and cheap trinkets, and fancy goods and Bolognas and watches, hats and shoes, beads and cakes, red peppers and ribbons, knives and cattle's entrails, men and women, dogs and babies, parrots and monkeys, and non-descripts.

"Want anyting?" "Buy dis," "Buy dat," "Buy tuder," "buy anyting?" "Buy noting." Oh, Babel! where are thou?

Passed through the wall by a big arched hole, with a sort of twist. The old Spaniard never went straight forward to anything but bloodshed. Found ourselves suddenly in a narrow street, right and left set up edge ways and paved with stone. Stone behind, stone before, stone above; stone stairs, stone battlement, stone roofs, all stone, stone, stone and mortar every-where—no there is a patch of blue sky above. Thankful to see a hole out any where. Right ahead, we go through a channel in the stone, much like the tunnel of the Harlaem Rail Road. If that narrow blue streak over head is sky, it must be only a slice laid away for some poor fellow who has never seen any. It ought to be labelled to be known surely.

And here we are on the Plaza; a rough square mortice in a great block of granite. Let me get on to the balcony of the Mansion House on the left hand corner there, and I can tell better what I think. Haven't many ideas to spare just now. I see before me, on the far side of the mortice, a New Grenadian ant or two, tugging something about on the shoulder that looks a heap like an old British musket.

Have washed and been to dinner. Glad it was not of stone, though the very next thing to it. Six bits a meal, four bits lodging. Great Hotel. First story canvass ceiling; second story no ceiling. Partitions ten feet high, when nothing 40 feet to the criss cross crotchety timbers of the roof on which the tile are laid. Sleep on canvas berths. Queer everything and strange and now from the window I will take a good look.

Across the Plaza some twenty rods, is a huge front flagged by two huge towers. On the left hand one is a dial plate that points to half past two. This is the main front of the great cathedral and is fast going to destruction. The design and ground appearance is imposing, but the workmanship of the main wall is of the roughest character. The front between the towers is almost covered with workmanship of a different kind entirely. Probably imported from Spain. Row above row of fluted columns with well wrought capitals are there displayed in great profusion.

Niche above, niche highly ornamented and filled with well carved and gilded images. Must have some day tickled the gravity of the solemn Don and at least astonished the natives into adoration. How often elsewhere has wonder been mistaken for worship and admiration for devotion.

It is past now. The wonder is that the columns stick on the wall at all as their bases are broken away, their capitals crumbled or crumbling away and some entire sections partially displaced by what means I cannot conceive unless jostled aside by an earth quake. That the gilding of the images has not

The cathedral at Panama City, ca. 1850 (Bancroft Library, University of California at Berkeley).

been restored for now it only specks them over here and there like the spangles on a courtesan's dress or the mould on a side of rotten bacon: that their noses and hands and heads and feet have not been replaced, for some of all these things have fallen away and been changed in the gutters to common dirt and nobody seems to care. Poor, harmless, inefficient, shadowy, lame, maimed images of Paganism! How long will ye stand then staring and staring, ye that have eyes to stare, after your departed, mutilated, dishonored members, before you shall follow them, and pitching down from your high places where ye have been worshipped by millions, lie crushed in broken fragments on the pavement, to seek communion with your better halves in the mud and filth of the common sewers.

Shame! Shame! You ragged naked hombres! to let your graven images and gilded gods thus perish, crumble and fall, and be no more, while the poor headless trunks and handless arms and footless legs and eyeless, noseless heads, silently and vainly, oh! how vainly implore your aid—ask again and again for help. Alas! there are few to pity and none to save.

If they are worth making, surely they are worth saving and as there are now only two or three cathedrals in the city these might, one would think, be kept in repair. There are several very large cathedrals in ruins, crumbling to their fall—overgrown with vines and shrubs and walled in to prevent any one entering lest the tumbling fragments should fall on them.

On the left is the calaboose or prison, a great awkward stone structure with a few soldiers walking about it. On the right is the French restaurant.

The streets run at right angles or nearly so. The city is twenty or thirty feet above the level of the sea, and built altogether of stone.

There goes a priest across the Plaza. A tall, gaunt, upright, black silk gown, a fine ancle, foot, and slipper, an enormous broad brimmed black beaver like a corn fan rolled on itself, tied to the crown on each side and raking for and aft like a patent gimlet handle or a pea pod on a thorn. Altogether he looks much like a gimlet stuck into the pavement. His step is light and mincing as a city belle or the pith ball of an electrometer, and the cloud of smoke that issues from beneath that enormous incubus, would indicate that the craft went by steam. I have seen no priest yet without the everlasting segar in his mouth. Shall make a note of it when I do.

Dropped into the cathedral this afternoon. Five priests were reading very busily sometimes all together and then in turn. It is difficult to convey a correct idea by words, of the inside. The lofty roof, with its long tapering naked rafters, net work cane, and long rows of concave tile supported by immense arches resting on the long, rough, plastered, white washed columns. The lattice work of mahogony around the alter and choir, towards the front entrance, itself large as [a] big house. The sculptured, columned, gilded imagery at the far end of the house, with the saints staring at you from all quarters and the hum of those buzzing voices, waving and wandering and trembling through the great void present such a diversity of object and excite such a tumult of ideas that one scarcely knows what to think.

The huge doors, each ten feet by twenty and six inches thick, made of rivets and oak plank, are rotting down, the varnish and gilding wearing off, the carving wasting away, holes worn into and often through the flagging, and yet the cannon which lie unused and useless on the city walls would sell for more than enough to restore the whole to more than pristine beauty.

There are six or eight of these cannon, very large pieces, 24 or 32 pounders, of some very valuable metal compound and said to be worth many tens of thousands of dollars. Any way they are highly polished and very beautiful, though they have been exposed to the weather and salt sea spray more than 200 years. They are all dismounted and are about twelve feet long and 22 inches in diameter at the breech.

The shape of the walled city is probably a mystery to all living men and never known except to the engineers who designed the works. A great deal of useless labor has been expanded in the fortifications, the walls, ditch, etc. Better have put it in school houses. The natives are for the most part crowded out into the great suburb. It would require very convincing proof to make me believe that this city contained 8,000 inhabitants.

The whites are very indolent, lounging in their hammocks all day, and the browns are lazy. Some few are very busy a part of the time. The drinking water is brought in jars or pots on mules from somewhere out of the city. Many of the stores are well supplied with goods of most descriptions.

Panama hats are a great article. Some are as high as 32 dollars and one is said to have been ordered for Santa Anna worth 60 dollars.

They are manufactured farther south down the coast. Eight dimes are a dollar here and the natives are eager to exchange American, Spanish, Mexican and other dollar coins into dimes at that rate. The hotels are shocking bad.

I can find no one who has yet succeeded in any place in getting a respectable meal. The streets are narrow and some of the[m] none of the cleanest, while the alleys, courts, and by places are filthy beyond description. Licentiousness walks the streets unblushingly and is the rule.

Attended service in the great cathedral this evening. 300 to 400 mostly females present. They come in through the great entrance on the sides for there is one on each side, dip their fingers in the font, a great stone trough fixed on the side of one of the great stone columns, and filled with water — cross themselves on the forhead, then give a flirting motion with the fingers, and then walk forward and kneel down somewhere in the main body of the house.

I notice that a servant often precedes and lays down a piece of carpet or rug or a low stool a half a yard square, richly upholstered, and directly the mistress follows and kneels on that. Sometimes the servant goes back and brings one for herself or himself and kneels on that but most kneel on the bare pavement. Sometimes of a short kneel they sit. The service lasted nearly three hours, till all seemed weary. One old fellow perched up thirty feet in the air in a basket shaped nest on the side of one of the columns, gave us a long discourse in Spanish in praise of one of the saints, who I thought seemed to give very particular attention to every word and gesture, and once when he was apostrophized with great feeling and fervor, I fancied that he gave an approving nod.

This was doing a great deal for a chiseled bit of stone. The Spanish [language] was made to scold with. A Spanish seems always scolding when she talks. Snaps out her words like a fire cracker. I forgot to say that there were several thousand people in the cathedral before the services were ended. It is an immense structure. There were three speakers holding forth at one time and no one interfered with another. A half a dozen country churches might be put into it at once and room for more.

PANAMA, THURSDAY, MARCH 6. Waked this morning at five by the heavy bell of the great cathedral. By the by, they have a dozen there, I should think, and occasionally ring a cracked one, which gives out a horrible sound. I can see the great front now from my berth, and the two giant towers looming out of the receding darkness, for the door of our room is like — as if they had forgotten to put in that side of the house when they made it — so broad is it, and it has been open to the balcony all night. Indeed, I am not sure that it is ever shut. It is much like a California bed room; and yet, here, anything but disagreeable, so warm is it; and as for safety, it is a smart thief that climbs up here—and then the fear, or at least the walls of the calaboose must be directly before his eyes, unless he turns his back to it. There are the dwarfish soldiers, now standing in the broad open doorways, with their rough old flint-locks and clumsy bayonets of the American and British infantry, long ago thrown away as not worth carrying about. These homicides are mostly negroes, or half-bloods at least. The prisoners must be somewhat numerous, as their heads fill the grated openings, few and far between. No determined American could be long kept, unless ironed, in that big pile of stone, brick and mortar and timber and tile and flimsy lattice work within.

We are called to an early breakfast—six o'clock—and the mules (which so abound that one would almost think them the natives and that the natives were mules—at least cousin germans) begin to congregate around the main entrance to the Mansion house, and all is bustle and noise and confusion. All colors and frizzles and dresses and undresses, running and dodging and twining and tumbling about.

Most of the packing is now done by the Americans, who hire all the mules and pack them through, making only a dollar or two on each one for their trouble and risk. This is designed to prevent a heap of mistakes, and many difficulties, as a foreigner with three or four words of Spanish usually deems himself a "brick"—fit for government interpreter, at least, and never stops to consider whether the natives understand him or not; and if any difficulty arises, a revolver always comes in for a concluding and conclusive argument.

It is as current and as cogent as that great revolver of the metaphysician—an axiom. Well, at eight or nine—time is of small account here—we move off, up a narrow street, a long, straggling train of mules and men and women and children and natives and horses, very small ones, and dogs, etc. Some of the men and muleteers and the women and children ride.

Mrs. Purvine of Iowa has three little girls. She carries one on her lap, and the others ride together on a mule and do it bravely and safely, too. We soon pass out at one of the gateways of massive stone masonry, and crossing the broad ditch, emerge through a semi-circular road with a heavy wall on each side into the suburbs—bigger by half than the walled city, but not half as heavy. It seems to be inhabited entirely by negroes, and mixed brown races. They dress for the most part in white, generally sprigged with blue or pink; short below and short above.

There is very little of en bon point in these diggings—short rations, probably. The women are generally tall and gaunt as Don Quixote's dreams, and have a most manly stride and masculine, impudent bearing. A blind ballot from the ranks would give a respectable representative for a company of lath makers, or a fish pole manufactory. The houses are, if possible, more dilapidated than in the city, and were never so substantially built.

A gradual descent on a paved street brings one to a level with the bay, where the road is lined with houses of the most flimsy construction – reeds, poles and leaves. Excuses for fences, broken down gates, tangled vines, and small trees of twenty different kinds, all strange to me, and any quantity of dogs and a few hogs and pigs, bound the vision on every hand, except directly backwards and forwards, along the narrow, slightly raised street. The soil is a red or yellow clay, and does not look as though it could produce anything – hardly sorrel or mullen. Still, the most slovenly cultivation is repaid by abundance of delicious fruits. But if any one thinks that he is to pick what he wants at every turn, and eat at his leisure, he will be disappointed. You will see no fruit suitable for eating, except in market; and for that matter, the market of Panama is miserably supplied, or rather unsupplied. The people are too lazy to work, even for money, and but for their mules would be useless and penniless.

As we pass on the houses are slighter and slighter, the people more and more naked, and the road more out of repair, while the land is more uneven, and on the left is a considerable mountain. At short distances you find warm water, liquors, and sometimes three or four kinds of unpalatable bread. Many a good (?) temperance man here finds, in the bad water, already poisoned, an excuse for taking some dirty poisonous spirit, to neutralize it, I suppose. There is a slight cooling breeze, and a few clouds lying lazily about, which render it quite pleasant, on the whole.

A few miles out, the street runs almost imperceptibly into a paved road, seven feet wide, with rough curb-stone on each side. It leads to Cruces, and we are to follow it several miles before we turn off to the left for Gorgona. It is generally very well preserved; in some places much broken, and in some places almost obliterated, nothing but the mule trails showing its course. The way is now shaded nearly half the time, and gets better as we progress. The trees are small, seldom reaching one foot in diameter.

A dime will buy as much liquor as one can put in a very small glass. By the by, tumblers grow less and less as we leave California. At Acapulco they were small, at Panama smaller, and here most of them are less than half a gill.

We see very few men – any quantity of women – and what is to me remarkable, their scanty clothing, though white, is very clean. Certainly they have no excuse to have it otherwise, though they do sit on the ground, for we pass the gravelly bed of a brook every hundred or two yards, and most of them have water standing in pools on the clear pebbles.

The last three miles has furnished running water, which, were it iced, would be excellent. Very good as it runs, especially at this moment, as we have just passed an open place where the sun poured fiercely down, and the breeze failed us entirely. Still it is not hotter than many a July day in the northern States.

And now there is lingering, and lagging behind, and not half way yet, sore feet, and lame legs, and weary backs, though the road is now all shaded and the timber larger. The hard pavement with its wash board surface and broken grade is passed—plenty of water—more hilly, and road rough, often descending rather rocky places, neither steep, deep, nor dangerous, as the ladies ride up and down the worst of them without difficulty, and even the children seem to have no fear. Sometimes we find the path cut down almost perpendicularly on each side, ten feet or more, ascending and descending through banks of red or yellow clay, now crumbling off in flakes after the long drought, as this is past the middle of the dry season. The half way house ought to be here, and yet they say that it is a mile farther, and it is two o'clock.

But we must have dinner—and such a dinner! No matter, still I must say that these fellows take the "rag off" any cut throats I have ever met. Never mind they will get their deserts—probably have already for they (these Yankees) look as though they had had the ague half a century and had just taken a dose of lobelia to keep them from vomiting.

Poor lathy, weakly, lazy reptiles lying in wait by the way side, like starved toads, offering their villainous compounds of poison and fire, hard bread and stinking ham, rotten mackerel, pickled sundries and muddy coffee.

Yes, yes, they have it good—yellow white and blue in the face, they appear the very incarnation of feverish dreams fainting away. I have seen no native sick and never in any country have I seen so large a proportion of old looking people. Most of the native males go naked. One fellow who would not deem himself slandered if he knew I was "writing him down naked," just now came stalking out of the timber and is crossing the road not two rods off. He carries a huge "machette" in his hand, is at least six feet, six inches high, and the finest figure I have seen in many a long year. His step is as military as that of the emperor Nicholas of Russia. He crosses the street and enters a house of one story made of cane having three sides and a roof, in which three very decent looking women sit.

He did not even look at me as he passed, not at the women as he entered nor they at him. But he went to the back of the room, took down his pipe from a small shelf, filled it and sat down on the ground, very composedly, by the side of the youngest and prettiest of the women (the villain) and smoked away the same as any smoker would. Cool isn't it. By no means. The thermometer must be 115° in the shade and yet he smokes on and the women work on—and there as I am alive that the woman turns and speaks to him and actually smiles as if pleased when she ought to lay the broom stick—by the by, they don't use brooms only some little twigs tied in a bundle. Well, really, I never! Well there is nothing like getting used to a thing. They are talking all the same as if he were dressed in a full winter suit with fur on.

If all the men are like him they can afford to go in Adam's fashion of the year one B.C. But the women cannot and will not probably for they are greatly inferior to the men physically. They are tall enough any of them, but so gaunt, lean, bony. I have yet to see the first one that has an ounce of flesh to spare. A couple of pounds taken would leave many of them with only bare bones.

The Simon pure "half way house" has an American woman for a mistress. There is nothing to brag of here, though I saw some boiled eggs. They bring all their bread from Panama and miserable stuff it is. The first house on our route having a sign on it was the "Pic House," or Pacific more property. I went into it and saw nothing to eat or drink except Brandy and some dirty looking stuff labelled wine. I was not there a minute before the landlord began a serious quarrel with his feminine "help mate" for letting an old rotten earthen gallon jug half full of water fall and break. I vamoosed, thinking it misnamed the Pacific House. That landlord is a reprobate of the first class. A red whiskered old villain who is only kept from robbery and murder by his cowardice.

At the Panama half way house (there are several half-way houses) we saw under arrest one of the fellows charged with the recent atrocious murder on the Chagres River. He is guarded by a real native soldier, and has his arms tied loosely back. If he wished to run away he has only to try and if he only gets into one of the hundred trails leading through the tangled forest without being seen, it would be exceedingly difficult to trace him. Indeed without a cutting instrument, one can hardly get more than a yard or two from the paths which penetrate the forest in all directions. It is one maze of tangled vines and thorns and trees and leaves.

The view is generally bounded by the sides of the path from two to twenty feet wide and the curves a few yards before or behind. Occasionally from some barren place on the summit of a hill one gets a glimpse of the valleys and mountains which lie around, most of them densely covered with trees. Some of these are not in full bloom. I notice two or three, perhaps more, very large ones whose spreading tops are covered with a deep yellow flower. Indeed there seems to be no leaves.

In the rainy season the roads must be very bad, as the streams cross the road so often, and sometimes the bank must be very miry and slippery, where it is cut down into a narrow ditch, deep enough to hide a mule or a horse in and only wide enough for him to pass. These straits are dry now and of easy descent.

The highest and roughest hills are in the middle of the route and the last part of the road is rougher than the first. In the dry season it is a pleasant enough route if one could only get anything fit to eat. The mules all have to be led, and some of our boys were green enough to take halters and offer to "spell" the drivers. Now as sure as you do this the rascals become invisible at once and as long as the packs are right remain so. Always keep your eye on your mule. He will some times dart off into one of the hundreds of paths that intersect the main one and you may be unable to find him. But don't meddle. Only make a note of the place and time.

You pay ten dollars for the use of a mule and an "inhuman" to take your baggage to Gorgonas and let them do it. Don't lift a finger to help, only keep your eye skinned, and don't give them anything—nothing—nothing. If you give them a dime they will ask more directly, next will demand something. No satisfying them. They are a begging and beggarly race. They are accountable to you in Panama and these fellows to them. Never pay till your work is done and if you employ two of them to do anything, never pay one alone but pay to both when both are present, else you will likely have to pay twice or use your revolver. Keep with your baggage. If you have more than one mule can carry, see that both are owned by one man or driver, and above all, make sure that they understand that you are the one to whom the baggage is to be delivered at Gorgona.

A great many wayfarers stop at the "half way house," fagged out. I presume that not more than one half will get through to Gorgona, 28 miles from Panama, tonight.

Gorgona, 6:15 p.m. Ball and I have just got in, not very tired. Bathed in the river. A most beautiful place. Got supper and very good lodging at the R.R. House, kept by one Miller. Very good fare and scrupulously clean, that's one comfort, at least. The last six miles today we were rather short of water, otherwise the day's trip has been far from unpleasant.

Have just learned that there are alligators in the river in which I have been bathing in the dark. They didn't meddle with [me] though. Much obliged to them for the present.

One p.m. Good night; for I must try those nice clean sheets and that luxury, a feather pillow.

GORGONA, FRIDAY, MARCH 7, 1851. Miller sends us down this morning in a long flat bottomed boat on our way to Chagres—I do not say to—for we have not got there yet. The number is limited to 30. That Miller looks the rogue, or I don't read aright. After breakfast had our baggage (by the bye, our bill is $2) down to the landing, a beautiful gravel bar or beach of some 30 or 40 acres on a bend of the river where the boats lie. One to two dimes postage on a trunk here. After a great deal of getting on board and off board, and moving and shifting, and fretting and crowding, and scolding and swearing, (some men will swear anyhow, even with a thumbscrew on), we finally shoved off, and before we got ten rods ran ashore again.

The boat does not mind her rudder more than a spoiled child does its mother. This is a fair beginning and I fancy only a prelude, a fore-taste, a shadowing forth of strange things to come. We were told that the boat had an awning—true to the letter, there is a sort of awning covering half the length of the boat, and maybe we shall get along very well, as the clouds are rolling up in our favor, promising shade and coolness. All five of the boatmen have curly hair, and one prominent virtue, sticking out beyond everything else—to wit: independence.

Indeed, they pay no more attention to each other, or to the orders of the captain than they do to the lizards which are sometimes seen crawling on the banks of the river. If each were running a separate craft there would be as much seeming community of feeling and interest. If the current of the river was as much divided, we should sail in all directions at once. I am not sure that they do not intend to break her up on the first snag, and each one have a separate command.

Twelve miles down we were turned ashore at a miserable place on the right bank, and the "dog fare" suffered some for a few minutes. We have now been out four hours, been aground three times, passed a steamer fast on a bar, tugged and twisting with steam, rope and pole, to get loose, been turned round and ran down stern foremost awhile, and on two or three snags—all nothing to what we can do. Expect to burst our "biler," and smash some craft, perhaps our own, in pieces before night. Shortly after leaving they ran the boat on a snag. (I say they, because she would not run on it herself.) And now we leak—the boat, I mean. Landed, caulked and tallowed the smash and split, and off we drift again; for to call it sailing is an abuse of words. Passed a tent town on the right bank, with a large wooden building where the Americans are at work on the Rail Road.

Twenty four miles from Gorgona, passed a wooden city on the right bank, another rail road depot, where the grade lies directly along the river bank, for a mile or more and mostly done, except the culverts. I suppose that most of the road is graded from here to Navy Island, and the whole will soon be done to the crossing above Gorgona—if not, then never. We have met a number of boats, but none of them have passengers. Lots going down, but none coming up. I suppose that the tide will turn the other way when the steamers come in.

I thought so—that Miller is a rascal. We have ten passengers more than the agreement—only half an awning—a crew that care not how soon the boat is snagged, and are restrained only by fear of present punishment—a captain without authority—and have got to be out all night, whereas if they had only rowed well, we might have been in at ten p.m.

We get along so very slow with all the steam that the natives can raise, that the passengers, weary of delay, are now at the oars themselves. Precisely what the rascals have been waiting for. To this point the river is full of rapids, shoals and snags, and has many short turns—the banks, ten to twenty feet high, are rock, or yellow or reddish brown clay, and generally on one side or the other is a clean gravel bar. The whole country is densely covered with tropical vegetation, grass, shrubs and trees, of which the palm bears off the palm of beauty. An enormous trunk, with leafless branches and smooth reddish brown bark, occasionally uprears itself from the tangled mass like a huge column. I cannot learn its name. Every half or quarter of a mile, is a beautiful open space on one bank or the other. It is almost impossible to break into the forest anywhere else.

The stream varies from thirty to eighty yards in width; the water is clear, and on the whole it is the most beautiful stream I ever sailed upon. Flocks of parrots have wheeled and whirled and swept around us, screaming and squalling; birds have sung to us from the trees, and sat on the water, and stood on the land, gazing at us for their own amusement and ours; and the lizards have crawled up the bank, much to our satisfaction, for some of them are three feet long and quite a sight, but no alligator has gratified us with a view of himself, and I am beginning to think that they are out of town—gone to the mines. I wish that one would show a part of himself, if no more.

Strange that everybody but me can see the great sights, and wherever I go they all vanish. The trees won't fall on me—the bears avoid me—nobody steals my purse, or shoots at me—the boat keeps right side up—nothing uncommon or worth telling of. How unfortunate! Well there is one comfort yet. They snag boats on the Mississippi, and blow them up too, and I can go that way. A little risk in the last operation. Prefer on the whole not to be blown up. I would sooner imagine it, or dream it. Well, I'm in no danger of being hurt, if I meet with none of these strange things to tell of. Below this Depot the river is clear of snags, the water smooth and deep and no short turns.

About sundown, came to Murderer's Point, a low sand bar on the left bank, where a party of eight persons were murdered last week,—four men killed and thrown into the river, and two women and two children buried in the sand. The buzzards, or some other vermin, have dug them up and picked the flesh off their bones, which now lie exposed in two piles on the bar.

The banks are here twenty feet high and for some distance there has been no improvement—no houses upon them, as above. We have in several places passed neat cattle, pigs, and goats. Some time after dark the Captain ordered the boat ashore on the right bank, where, from the lights, there appeared to be several houses; and as all were willing, ashore we went, and after wandering round a while, found two places where they keep something to eat, or pretend to. All Spanish—looked still farther, and beyond discovered a large one story building, or shed, kept by an American. This we seized and claimed (the law of nations) by right of discovery, though a dozen had discovered and taken possession before. I waited a while, and seeing a small chance for supper, went over to the Spanish house and drove as close a bargain as possible for a "snack." Made my way nearly through a cup of most execrable coffee, and the seventh part of a common butter cracker, and gave it up. Couldn't stand it—sour, mouldy crackers for bread, on dry land, and yet it is not so dry as one might think.

It sprinkled a trifle before dark, and is now raining quite sharp. Indeed, our landlord (Americano) says that it has rained almost every night since— well, for three months; and that the rainy season is not to be looked for till

June. Took his word for that, and the more willingly, as he put a ticket for supper with it. Sure our baggage will get wet, with half an awning, and one that would hardly keep out a shower of feathers. Feel quite independent, as I am labelled for the next table—number of tickets limited—very exclusive.

A young Irish looking, rather slatternly woman was preparing the tables for the sixth time, while the landlord was prospecting in the pantry (end of the room) and being well fagged out, scolded those who were in her way much less than, from the scowl on her face, one could reasonably expect. I reckon that she smiles sometimes. Sure am I that she tried it once, twice and thrice before she gave it up.

Human nature won't stand everything, and seven suppers with a prospect of more, and a crowd of hungry men and women and children, and no help save a worthless puppy all the time under foot, would pucker the beautiful mouth of sweet patience herself. And the landlord, who looked like the fag end of a three months' yellow fever, bustled and tumbled and dodged about, as though we were to be his last customers, and he was bound by something stronger than an oath to cheat every mother's son of them.

Some wag of our company told him that there was a "chiel amang them takin notes," and he was exceedingly polite; couldn't do too much. The credit of the house was at stake. Everything was done up to a T. I was asked to take something. Wine was urged; "Sure I wouldn't refuse?" "Cider?" No! and finding that I was really in earnest, he put away his bottles and remarked that his liquor was good and he would like that some good judge should try it. Anyhow, he had barrels of it under the counter and wouldn't tap it for any body now. Wouldn't sell any more tonight. He was tired and too much trouble. And true to his word, he was soon stretched on his own counter asleep, and no one could get liquor.

There are quite a number of passengers here from New Orleans for California; several women and some children. We gave them some idea—a faint sketch of the animal they kept for show on this route. Supper was served at least decently, and the ham, for a wonder, was eatable—yams ditto—potatoes good—coffee passable—butter not bad, and bread and pickles very good; and the rest might have been extra—we did not see it.

The only serious drawbacks to all these luxuries were no beds—hardly decent bunks, and a most loathsome, all-pervading smell of fowls about the premises, as though it had been an aviary since the time of Nebuchadnezzar. A few of the men slept on the boat. I staid with mine host the Americano most of the night, watching his nose to discover a solution of the important questions—how is one to determine if he does or does not snore in his sleep? sitting up to keep from lying down, and keeping awake to keep from getting asleep, and a busy time I had of it you may be sure—steady business and no pay. Preferable, however, to lying (can't sleep) with Spanish vermin, and looking at the roof to see where the rain is coming through next. Occasionally visited the boat, and waked them up for a change.

SATURDAY, MARCH 8. Raised a "row" at four a.m. and all is instantly bustle and hurrah, and very soon we are again drifting down the river. Soon after sunrise it rained powerfully some time, and our awning proved of no service at all, as the water poured through it as through a sieve. Miller knew when we started that it rained nights, and that the awning would not shelter us, the scoundrel. If it had been well put up, it would have shed rain. Those who had umbrellas fared best. I was wet to the skin, but suffered no particular inconvenience, as the sun came out shortly and dried all again. There are some pretty plantations on this section of the river, and the country around for some distance seems nearly level.

One must not expect to see here the clean cultivation of the States. All vegetative life grows so rank and luxuriant that it looks more like a forest than a field, and all the fence needed is across the footpaths, as nothing but a snake can make its way through the forest which surrounds every patch of cultivation. They are too lazy to clear away just for the prospect.

Ten miles down we come to the rail road again; and here the rails are down, and the road in operation, for just as we dropped along side, a hand car came rattling along the track, and was loudly cheered by our passengers. There are quite a number of Yankee houses here. But they tell us that many of the hands are sick. Our informants were sitting on a low ledge of rocks fishing and looking sickly enough, sure. They said that they catched salmon and—I did not hear what else, for we shot past the end of their fishing poles like a turtle from a clay bank.

We have seen one monkey hanging or lounging across a dry limb, as carelessly as though it was not fifty feet to hard ground or water. Heedless creatures are those, and if they fall in the water it is to drown, as I am told they never try to swim. A flock or two of parrots flew around and above us just now, squalling and screaming; and an alligator, perhaps ten feet long, lying on the opposite shore at a turn of the river, took French leave on receiving a shot from the rifle of a passenger. His alligatorship was before slightly and very slowly moving his awkward and unwieldy carcass, but gave no promise of the activity which so suddenly seemed to animate him.

We have met a steamer too—much such a looking boat as one sees on the Illinois or Missouri rivers. She runs up to the rail road depot. As we descend the banks get lower and lower and the thickets lining them appear absolutely impenetrable. Occasionally, a path opens down to the water, giving evidence that somebody has been there. Doubtless they lead to plantations back in the forest.

We saw bananas (the fruit) growing on the bank in one place where no house was visible. The tree or plant on which they grow is a splendid affair. It stands eight to 15 feet high—the long stems of the leaves bending or curving gracefully out and over from the large smooth stalk, and on it hangs the green leaf, like a long narrow strip of satin on a bent rod. I have seen a stalk eight inches in diameter, with leaf stems ten to twelve feet long, almost reaching the ground again, and the leaf fringe on each side ten inches wide, tapering towards the point or end of the leaf. The fruit grows of the size of common cucumbers, in a large cluster around a stem one and a half inch or two inches in diameter. This stem springs from the top of the stalk, or trunk, and sometimes has as many as 80 or 100 bananas, and will weigh 30 pounds. It is a delicious fruit – better I think than the plantain, which is twice the size, and of the same shape, and grows in the same manner.

Oranges grow here in the forest. The banks are lined with trees and shrubs and vines, many of them in full bloom. The "morning glory" is the most conspicuous. To a person just from the States, going up the river, the whole must be exceedingly novel and interesting; but after passing over the "plains," living or staying in California and crossing half the Isthmus, one cares very little for any sights or sounds that may arise around him. A single glance of home is worth them all, though one lived to look as long as Methuselah.

We have met a few boats coming up with the passengers of steamers just in. They report only a limited number. Glad of it. I could wish that no one hereafter might be fool enough to leave his home, to go to California. I notice some women and children among them. They are to be pitied, because not to be blamed.

Landed at Chagres, and put up at the Irving House. "Mock turtle soup," "baked Pig," and "ruta bagas" were among the curiosities of the table. A woman superintends the establishment, which is kept by Buncker, Miller & Co. The cooking and serving is clean and ready, and the sleeping apartments airy, but the sheets are not changed often enough, or at least washed. There are several houses of about equal calibre here, where one can be quite comfortable. There are four steamers in now, one to come in tomorrow, and one the next day. The competition for passengers is very great. Fare, in cabin to New York $55 – steerage $20. To New Orleans $40 and $15. Cool and rained awhile this evening.

SUNDAY, MARCH 9. Beautiful morning. Cloudy and cool breeze. Chagres is located on both sides the river at its very mouth. The left, or American, or "shingled roof" side is on a low point, or sand beach. There is no lath nor plaster, that I can find, in the place. There is no business done here, except in passing passengers and goods back and forth, and this will cease the instant the R.R. is finished to Gorgona, and Chagres cease to be.

The cocoa grows here among the houses, as do the oaks in Illinois. The beach is covered with the wreck of vessels. There are no regular streets, and what are used for such are filled with all kinds of timber, lumber, etc. etc. A large sign in one part is very conspicuous, and reads thus: "Commit no nuisance!" The schoolmaster is surely out.

West, or up the coast, the country rises gradually into hills, densely timbered and a small stream of fresh water running down from them empties into the ocean at the base of a rocky point, one mile and a quarter above town. There the inhabitants go to wash their clothes, and bathe—at least some of them. I have been there for the last purpose and found a most beautiful sandy bottom, though the water is of no great depth or extent— perhaps two or three rods wide. The drinking water is said to be brought from a small stream some distance up the river. It is very palatable, and with ice, good enough. That article is a "luxury" here, and mostly used to mix their poisonous drinks.

The shores on either side of the river, which is here 200 to 300 yards wide, are lined with boats and canoes of all sizes and descriptions, covered, half covered and open. The Spanish side is built on a low piece of ground, has two or three large houses covered with tile, one uncovered and 50 to 100 thatched.

On a high rocky point between it and the ocean is an old fort; a minia- ture Gibraltar, on and in the solid rock. It must have cost a mint of money, but is now in ruins—everything crumbling down. The cannon are there, but useless; and the town is there, but not worth defending if anybody should be foolish enough to want it.

I do not now wonder, as I once did, why the gold of the New World should beggar Spain. It would reduce any nation to beggary, whose people could not make a fair living on an iceberg floating in the tropics. Such a people as the Spanish, once strapped are strapped forever; but the Yankee is never bankrupt long. He has no "Don"ish pride to sustain his dignity in rags. He knows too well the value of money and the consequence it confers on one to be idle when work will bring it; and will perform, cheerfully, the most menial services for pay, and deem it no disgrace unless the pay is too small—and as for beggary, he has no idea of any such thing. In extremity, he would sooner steal; (I hope that is no slander;) or, what is equivalent, run in debt without any expectations or intention of paying.

These wandering Yankees are not very numerous here, and most of them are pale enough. They say that few remain over a month or two without having the fever, and many of them two or three attacks. The hands that are brought to work on the rail road get sick immediately and have to be sent home if they live long enough. They say, and in this case, I learn from the surgeon of the *Philadelphia*, say true—that 20 or 30 are to go on that steamer to New Orleans. I have seen some of them. They appear to be used up—seem to have lost all courage and lie about like inanimate things. It must be a great place, this, to make money; but no one can stay long enough to make much, without great risk of life.

The mass of the inhabitants in the American town (and there may be a daily average of 800 to 1,000) are natives, who are mostly negroes, the descen- dants of Spanish slaves, a mixed race—and negroes and mulattoes from different parts, mostly Jamaica. These last are as saucy, impudent, active and strong as white men, and know as well the worth of money. They are the workers of the country, though the R.R. employs some of the natives (a very inoffensive race) at 50 cents a day; so I am told.

The great manager and prime mover here is the Yankee, i.e., the citizen of the United States. Much of the smaller business is carried on by foreigners, mostly Jews. The best table, judging by the looks, in Chagres, is kept by a mulatto.

I feel sick this evening—have fever. The whole atmosphere seems poisoned, and yet there is a cool breeze most of the time. It may be all fancy, and yet one can give a pretty good guess whether or not he is sick. I feel perfectly sure in my own case, though no one could have persuaded me 12 hours ago that the climate would have affected me thus suddenly.

Chapter Twenty-three
March 10–March 20, 1851:
Through the Gulf of Mexico

MONDAY, MARCH 10, 1851. Cloudy and cool this morning. Feel feverish and sick. Passengers down the river are constantly arriving. They complain of hard fare, and being swindled at every turn. A little before noon there was a "big row" at the boat landing. Clubs, pistols, guns and fists were in sudden requisition.

It seems that three Frenchmen, with their wives and children, had just arrived in a canoe from Gorgona. One of the women started to go ashore, (their husbands, or the men, being already on shore), when the Captain, a Carthagenian, threatened to beat out her brains with a club unless she stopped. One of the men at that moment stepping on board, interfered, and the Captain immediately seized a gun, when a Yankee jumped aboard; and then such a knocking overboard, and climbing up, and knocking off, and tumbling in, and the gun was discharged, and such a swearing in French and Spanish and German and Yankee and English, and the crew were driven from the canoe, principally by the Yankee, who finally fell overboard and was dragged in again.

At this moment the levee was swarming with the representatives of all unions. It was a splendid time for a painter. Every eye was turned upon the boatmen who were swimming in the river. One of the Frenchmen raised a huge horse-pistol and deliberately fired twice at one of the swimmers, a distance of ten or 15 steps, and just missed his head each time. At this juncture a new ingredient was added to increase the disorder. Separated from the boat where the "row" originated only by a single boat, were two canoes, loaded with the treasure brought down in the *Oregon* from "Frisco," and guarded by a dozen of the redoubtable native soldiers, who were in the highest state of excitement, thinking that the whole was a preconcerted scheme to seize on the money in the confusion of a street fight. One of them became perfectly frantic; and leaping ashore, attempted by threatening, scolding and swearing, to frighten away the crowd. Altogether it was one of the most ridiculous scenes I ever witnessed. And yet the spilling of a single drop of blood by the military would have been the signal for a grand massacre – 500 shots might have been fired in less time than one could count a score.

There must have been prodigious excitement on the Spanish side of the river when they saw what was going on, as 200 or 300 were directly assembled, and with my glass I could see the senoritas haranguing the men with the most furious gesticulations. They seemed to wish their dear lords to come over and have a hand in the fight. They, however, seemed very well satisfied to remain at that distance, had very little curiosity. Doubtless it would have been a profitless expedition; and a gentlemen who knows them well remarked that if two small boats loaded with Americans were to start for that side, the entire crowd would disperse like a morning fog.

Directly the Alcalde and a priest came over and everything was quiet at once. The goods and women were transferred to a surf-boat, and on their way to the ship; and the Padre was on his way back with a fine green parrot on his shoulders – a present from one of the Frenchmen.

Just before 12 a.m. started to go on board the steamer *Philadelphia*, bound for New Orleans. She was to have sailed this morning. They take passengers to the anchorage, two miles, in boats – costs two dollars. The *Philadelphia* pays for carrying her passengers by agreement. The *Crescent City* steamer has just come in. From the shore, the passage out looks perilous, but I believe it to be safe with a sober crew.

There is real danger, however, in getting on board – the boats rising and falling some five to ten feet, and the ship rolling and pitching, sometimes bring the iron stairs with a crash on the bow of the boat, nearly overturning it.

In discharging for ashore, the women are let down into the boats in a kind of arm chair, and most are hauled up in the same way. Some of them are much frightened, and all more or less disconcerted by their novel and rather unexpected elevation. Children are handed from the steps into the boat and sometimes a "little thing" is handed two or three times before the boat gets a favorable position – every failure drawing a shriek of terror from the mother, who will smile at her fears when she at length receives it safely in her arms, and sees with what ease and safety it was finally passed. No woman or child ought ever to go to California. The man who does it is a fool.

The *Falcon* steamer has just come in and anchored outside of us. She carries the mail. Boats loaded with passengers are coming to or going from

the different ships all the time, though the wind is quite fresh and the surf
rolls in strong, so that some of them are two or three hours in rowing out.

TUESDAY, MARCH 11. Rained some in the night. Cloudy and warm
this morning. Somewhat better and can eat some breakfast. There are more
than thirty on board who have, or are just recovering from, the Chagres
fever. Boats are still coming, and the passengers who come down from Frisco
on the *Isthmus* (steamer) begin to come in. Cabin passage is reported, from
shore, at twenty five dollars; some say, twenty; yesterday, paid thirty-five.

Half past 12. The *Mexico* (steamer) is just coming out of the harbor
where she has been lying (in more seases than one) the only boat which has
now entered the mouth of the river. She anchored when fairly out, and
more than half a mile within the other ships. Went on shore. When I
returned at four o'clock, p.m., she was out on her way for New Orleans—
and hull down—just see her smoke pipe. In a few minutes the *Crescent City*
fired a gun, and began heaving at her anchor, and they are now loading the
sta'board gun on our ship. These guns make a great noise, and I wonder
how human beings can take delight—Bang! there it goes—enough to deafen
one, and yet it is in this case, indirectly, rather agreeable; or rather, not
very disagreeable; for it associates with itself the idea of motion.

5:15—under way, and moving slowly, gracefully sweep past the three
steamers which we leave at anchor, their decks crowded with passengers.
Behind us stretches off the low shore, with hills in the background. On the
right the sun is fast sinking into the waste of waters; on the left a bold,
rocky indented bluff meets the eye for several miles, and the bright evening
sun shining directly against it, shadows forth its every nook and corner. Its
deep caverns are overshadowed with vines, and its heights rising and stretching back, are crowned with a dense growth of evergreen trees and shrubs.
Before us we have the broad ocean for our pathway, and ask no aid from
the free wind but to fan our fires.

The ship! The ship! Onward she rushes, fearless and free, dividing the
crested waves like some huge monster, and dashing the spray from her shining side like a thing of life. Thus mayest thou ever be—no stronger wind; no
higher wave. But no—one breath of the tornado shall shatter thy form, and
mar thy beautiful symmetry—and when the angry sea shall rise in its might,
and come roaring and foaming and rolling on in liquid majesty, thy
strength shall vanish, thy glory be swallowed up, and all thy fair proportions be scattered wide and sunk in the deep, deep waters.

About sundown two sailors on the "fo'cas'le" had a fight about—nothing.
They performed very much like dogs or cats, mere animals as they are. The
mate parted them very much after the fashion that he would two dogs—i.e.,
if the mate would part dogs at all.

Distance and darkness will soon hide from our eyes Navy Bay; which
lies misty and indistinct, on our left; (i.e., as we look astern or toward the

south); and now its grey and now its white building vanish, and very few of us will, probably, ever see them again. And who wishes to? That land, fair as it looks, is as the valley of the shadow of death, morally and physically. Though the inhabitants of Sodom were to be saved, and California pardoned without repentance, still, there is no hope for the Isthmus. The vices of every nation there riot in rank rottenness, and the distilled scoundrelism of the globe seems to have eddied into that narrow place; and, but for the pestilence that walketh at midnight and wasteth at noonday, one would be far safer in passing along from Jerusalem to Jericho than from Panama to Chagres.

None but the natives and inhabitants of the neighboring provinces expect to live long here; and they seem to have an eye on the command which Judas received, "What thou doest, do quickly." And surely, if a fair and impartial parallel might be run between characters, it is here. It only fails in the winding up—"and Judas went and hanged himself." If justice is done, and they get what they deserve, that will be all right; and then ropes will take a rise in Chagres.

The mortality among the Railroad hands is fearfully great, and two or three weeks is generally sufficient to put every fresh importation on the sick list, or into their graves. They have been mustered on deck, i.e., all who could come up, and such another looking set can hardly be scared up. Poor fellows, they wanted to go to California, and the doctor has sent them back home. Well, if they can only be satisfied to stay at home, they will have made a lucky hit, for they would have made nothing there in California and fewer still would have returned.

WEDNESDAY, MARCH 12. Cloudy and light head winds. It is much rougher than the Pacific, with the same wind. The *Philadelphia* is shorter than the *Oregon*, and pitches about more. Thousands of flying fish are rising around us. Nearly half the cabin passengers are sea sick.

THURSDAY, MARCH 13. Cloudy. Stiff breeze all day from the east. Sea somewhat rough. Most of the passengers complain more or less of sickness and very few really enjoy themselves. I have had some fever and headache every day since I came on board. One comfort—there is much less smoking than on the *Oregon*. Query: Is sea sickness a remedy for profanity, or do men restrain themselves more as they approach home?

FRIDAY, MARCH 14. Cloudy still, but much less wind. We are carrying a "jib and main sail." If the wind would alter a trifle, we would be much sooner in Kingston. We ought to have been there this morning—but a head wind, a (not) fast ship, and (I suspect) a slightly disordered engine, render our progress slow. I suppose that we have not averaged more than six or seven miles an hour. Dragging business for a steamer, when everybody on board is anxious to get home. Some have been absent only a few weeks, others months, and others, again, years.

Here is Josh. Carson going back after an absence of 27 years. To him everything must seem new, but not strange. Nothing is strange or singular to him who has seen the mighty changes that have sprung up in the "far west"—a rushing, living tide of men and animals, sweeping across the trackless deserts and wild mountains; the bowels of the earth ransacked, and the rivers turned from their courses; their banks uptorn, plundered, ravaged, deserted—villages, towns, cities rising like Aladdin's palace in a single night, vanishing at noonday, and forgotten at eventide—rivers choked with all the various craft of every people, and the harbor of a city, but yesterday a miserable hamlet, not even a faint foreshadowing of its today's existence, crammed with shipping enough for a nation's commerce.

And yet, after all, it may seem strange to him that so little change has taken place at home. He visits the Crescent City—twenty seven years have wrought no wonders to his unmicroscopic eye. The banks of the Mississippi are almost unchanged, and St. Louis, he sees it, and is in doubt. His idea of progress, caught from the wandering emigrant or vagrant trapper, would lead him to seek the suburbs five miles out, while only here and there a house dots the wide waste. It does not fully meet his notions of extension, and yet he is not exactly disappointed. It is rather an indefinable feeling of vacuity, as though one was seeking, indifferently, what he never expected—only imagine that he hoped to see.

Yonder is a gambler. At Panama, Gorgona and Chagres, he staked and won or lost hundreds, perhaps thousands of dollars, at monte. His place is the first cabin. She who is with him and seems to have his love and confidence, is not his wife. A few weeks or months at most, and she will be deserted, and such as it becomes not us to speak of; while he, probably, will be penniless, a vagabond and a wonderer over the earth. A few days in New Orleans will suffice to strip him of his ill gotten gains, and then he can hang, drown, blow out his brains, or go to California. There is but little choice. Perhaps he thinks that he will gamble no more after he gets home. Poor fool! He is wedded to the vice. As well think to escape death when the appointed time is come.

And yonder tall gaunt man—the incarnation of sick and hungry disappointment! He has, or had, a small farm, neat buildings and a small stock, and was prosperous. A desire for more drove him to California. Sickness and knavery prevented his getting or wrenched from him his hard earned gains. Sick and disheartened he returns, borrowing money from some more fortunate or less scrupulous rogue (?)—to pay his passage home, where for a short time he may forget in the joy of meeting a wife and children, that in a few days he has to meet a mortgage that he can not raise, and that his homestead will pass from under him like the foundation of a dream, leaving him afloat on the world's wide waste just where he was twenty years ago—

but not as he was. The strength, the vigor, the hopes of early manhood are gone, and only the wreck of all remains.

Who is that with the goat-like whiskers and beard, and the swiniform upper lip—half human and all beast—a cigar in his mouth, and an oath on either side of it—crowding against everybody like a pickpocket—nosing his way into every company, and making his "gab" heard in every place—sound without sense—words without knowledge—smoking in every man's face, spitting on everyone's shoes—his nose red and eyes scarlet, his teeth black and worn, and his breath reeking and steaming with the fumes of brandy like one of the vent holes of the pit—a blue shirt, never—and never to be washed, and yellowish brown pants stuck into boot tops that never knew their own color? Who is it? He holds his head as high as though he was somebody— was a man created in God's image, and when gnawing a bone at the cabin table, didn't drop it (the bone) from his mouth on to his plate, and forget what forks were made for.

Who is it? A puke from Missouri, who never saw a door to a house till he got to Council Bluff—a puke—brought up on corn dodgers and bacon, till squealing is as natural as breathing. A puke! taught nothing but to sing, "O Susanna" and "Jim along Josey," and break and drive steers with a Ho! Jube! and a Yoa! Dave! a compound of impudence and ignorance, smut, tobacco smoke and profanity, who rolled along to California, and while two thirds of his company died of scurvy from living like dogs, kept singing, "Poor Miss Lucy Neal," and digging out the dust, and now returns as independent as a lame skunk, to do—the Lord only knows what with his $2,000.

Well, success to him. Let God's curse rest on the man who would defraud him of it. He got his money by the sweat of his face, which is more than I can say of him who passes next.

He too, brings $3,000 home with all the vices, less of the filth, but none of the honesty of the Puke. A sucker is he, and he sucked his money from the lusts of the victims of appetite. His money has the stain of blood upon it, and the curse of God will follow it to the third generation. He kept burning the fires of hell, though others might have kindled them. In his trading house might have been found almost everything but the Bible. All that could pander to man's appetites, or stimulate his worst passions, was there. Strong drinks and spiced meats, poker and the monte table, and—she whose way leads down to hell. Well—he swaggers now and boasts of his wealth, and rejoices as though there was no God. The day of retribution is forgotten, and he never expects to meet his victims again. His hand is red with the blood of his fellows, and he has no care. Reckless, heartless, heaven-daring he goes his own way, and his way perish with him.

There goes one! A Christian man, who went to California for gold. He wanted $20,000 and he would give the Lord half. Poor man! He little knows what a snare he has escaped, the trouble that wealth confers—inflicts—how avaricious it makes one. He labors hard, and strives much and long to get it honestly, but it is not for him. The wicked ruffian, the profane reprobate can find it, but he digs in vain. A merciful providence hid it from him, and he returns a wiser and a better man. The Lord can get money enough, and will hardly risk spoiling those he loves by trusting them with money at the halves. When a man feels that all that he has is only held in trust, and is willing to give it all, not half, if it is wanted; then and then only is he fit to be trusted with the Lord's money.

FRIDAY, MARCH 14, 12 O'CLOCK. The dark blue mountains of Jamaica are just bursting upon our sight, through the thick clouds and heavy mist, directly ahead. It resembles the Pacific coast which we so lately ran down.

As we approach the blue seems almost equally divided with the patches of lighter color, white and yellow, which seem to be barren peaks and mountain sides, divested of soil and destitute of vegetation. Large portions are at times partially obscured, or entirely hid by blue mist or rain, and clouds hang like the folds of a curtain over the mountains.

Half past one. It is hardly more distinct now. I seem to see, far off on the left bow, a tract of level country at the base of the mountains, with houses and improvements but, it may be all fancy. No it is not fancy. It is a long sloping table land, stretching from the shore to the mountains, and some of it must be highly cultivated. There comes the pilot, in a little cockle shell of a boat, sixteen feet long and three and a half wide, and so light and frail that two men might easily carry it. The very shadow of a boat, and yet, we are ten or 15 miles from land. Of the four ragged fellows in that little gourd shell which is the pilot? Oh, there he goes up the rope on the la'board quarter, like a cat—and his is one of them—a Spaniard maybe, and maybe not. His color is dark olive, hair curly, countenance intelligent; feet, bare; pants, linen; shirt, calico; and coat, black bombazelle, with one sleeve off above the elbow, the other just below.

Half past three. The Harbor which we are just entering is a deep indentation of the coast, and on our left is a long stretch of low land, gradually ascending and then falling back again, as though the broad valley of a river lay behind. Beyond, I see nothing but mountains.

We have passed a red buoy on our right, and now are running in smoother water. There, broad on our left, is a long low rocky range descending steep to the water's edge, except at the point where it is a perpendicular bluff. The other or further extremity, toward the main land, seems to be occupied by a cluster of large buildings and some are scattered along on the slope between them and the point.

Directly in front, right and left is spread out a broad green plain, in places gradually ascending to the base of the mountains, which rise peak above peak behind. This plain which is the one which attracted my attention when we first made the land, stretches off behind the first range I spoke of, into the valley north. From this point the plain looks exceedingly beautiful, and seems highly cultivated, and dotted with houses in all directions. The mountains are steep and appear barren. Bang! goes the big gun.

Here we are, stopped by a little boat with only two negroes and some officer in uniform on board.

That beautiful little low point of land, or island on our right, (only a hundred yards or so) covered with a couple of hundreds of low buildings, with verandahs of all colors and dotted with beautiful palms (cocoas I presume) is Port Royal. Oh, what a nice, tidy, peaceable looking place. Half a dozen ships are lying here at anchor. Now we are moving again, by the permission of their graces, the two darkies and almost whitey. Oh! how it slams and echoes against and from the barracks and the big buildings, and that great ship, which has five awful guns now thrust out of her ports. How dare they send such a note of defiance against the ugly, old, black, rusty man-killer? She has only to be waked up and one sneeze from her black, swelling hull, and we are all to smash on the bottom. It's no use to try to escape. Before one has time to turn he pops on another of the "varmints."

A low fort lies directly on our left, and an ugly customer, for all its apparent humility. My! but wouldn't they riddle us if they had the notion. It is just stuck on to the point where the cluster of houses is; or rather, the whole concern seems projected out into the water, just as though the land was too good to be used for such purposes. I am thankful that they have no grudge against us. Port Royal is an island sure. We turn to the right, run between Port Royal and the mainland and Kingston is directly ahead. In fact, we have kept turning and turning to the right ever since we entered the harbor, till we are completely hemmed in by the land.

A long low, narrow slip of land, but just above water, stretches off from the town of Port Royal to the mountain coast, several miles south of Kingston. Between this and the mainland is the bay, which may be from two to four miles wide. The Harbor, proper, is marked out by high, white stakes or posts, and the passage out with buoys. A steeple, and the high chimney of some manufactory, are the most prominent objects in sight. I notice some square or round towers, and several domes. Red seems to be the pervading color.

And now we move slowly past the end of a wharf, projecting out on our left, on which stand forty or fifty women, of all colors and characters, probably, except good ones, giving cheer after cheer to the "Buenos Americanos," and swinging hat and handkerchief, till the escape pipe of the steam can't get a hearing at all.

The engine stops, the wheels cease to roll, and we glide gently up to a wharf burdened with 500 tons of coal, one half of which is to be transferred to our ship's hold; and there beside it stands the bone and muscle and life that is to move it. Canoes and other craft, loaded with fruit, are crowded

together beneath us the length of the wharf. I thought that I knew the
meaning of jargon, and could define confusion, for I have been in a nail factory, attended a stock auction in Sacramento City, seen Babel out-done,
and "confusion worse confounded." But never trust experience in these
matters — anyway, never express an opinion till you visit Kingston.

It is not the yelling and scolding and squalling of those who have
oranges and bananas and limes and cigars and bundles of sticks and lots of
things to sell, nor the begging and talking and jabbering and hallooing of
those who are to shift the coal — but it is that all make every kind of hideous
noise at the same time, and nobody thinks of stopping. Noise seems to be
their life, and confusion their element. They breathe only to emulate a
thunder storm.

The ship is no sooner fast, and the plank put down, than up comes a
long string of women, yellow and black — each one having a third of a barrel
filled with coal, upon her head, and the crowd singing nearly the same tune,
in nearly the same time, and using nearly the same words; though each one
keeps a word or two behind her leader and the clear, loud rattling ring of
their voices rises above the din, like a cracked bugle in a concert of frogs.
The meaning of the song, if it has any, is unfathomable — past finding out;
but the burden or chorus is sensible, something to the purpose; and when
sung by a hundred voices at a time, amid the tramping of feet, the rush of
the multitude, the roar of mirth, the howl of drunkenness, the crash of coal
falling on the deck, or dashing and rolling in huge lumps down the long
iron tubes leading into the vessel; seems music run mad without a lariat,
and never expecting to be catched — and this is the fashion of it:

> O! come along; come along,
> Take along, I go,
> Come Along, Tat-e-rat-tu
> Rat-tay Rat-tay.
> Why don't you come,
> Come along, come along,
> Tam-ma-ray-no
> Tarra-lallah
> Tat-te-ra-hu: how do you do?
> Chickery-chee
> I go away, why don't you come?
> Tarry-lallah, cherry-na-chee
> Yah-py-ro lo
> Py-ro-lo, Tarry lallah
> Py-ro-lal, py-ro-lallah
> Yah py-ro-lah, yah-py-ro-lah
> Py-ro-lallah, py-ro-lallah
> Sally mi chee, Salley mi chee
> Lally-lallah lal, lally-lah
> Tunny-ra-ting - tum! tum!!

> Hum-me-ry-haw - hold-e-jaw,
> Come along, come along,
> Now come along -

Some people might object to cumbering your columns with poetry, but it is well enough to know something of the condition of the fine arts in foreign countries, and Jamaica should not be neglected; besides this is only a short chorus, for none but a reporter from a pigeon roost would dare attempt the song.

From the ship one sees hardly anything except wharves and coal and a few ships and machinery and brown or gray house roofs—no high buildings. The U.S. Hotel, a big awkward house on the left, is the tallest, and that sits on the ground like the cover of a Chinese basket.

Went ashore, and by a circuitous route through a great building stored with all kinds of goods and refreshments and liquors, got into the first street, from which a noise had been rushing as I advanced, that bid fair to rival that of the wharves.

Here is fun alive and abroad. Everything to sell but no one can get a chance to buy. Before you say "how much?" half a dozen traders have you by the elbow on the other quarter, with "here massa, buy of me." - "Now massa, take mine." - "Very good oranges, one shilling massa." - "Any cakes?" - "Massa want?" - "What you know 'bout dat, nigga?" - "Only one dime, cheap, massa." - "Yes." - "You get out." - "Shell box, massa?" - "Six dollars." - "Cheap as dirt, massa." - "Two shillings." - "One shirt." - "Wanta drink?" - "Four weeks, massa" - "shirt?" - "Two dimes" - "Can't make it quicker nohow." - "here" - "there" - "worth six dollars, massa." - "you get out" - "stop there, nigga" - "can't come it" - "now don't" - "yah! yah! yah! haw! haw! haw!" - buzz - hum - hum - rattle - whistle - whizz - and I drew my upper lip across my teeth like a band of rubber, looked up the long narrow street and trotted, looking neither to the right nor left, and so far from thinking of Lot's wife, my mind was wholly occupied in the thinking how many more pulls right or left it would have taken to abstract my purse, and I felt greatly indebted to my poverty for a very cordial feeling of security, seeing that the most lucky rogue if perfectly successful could only get two or three dollars at most; and then it would half compensate the loss to anticipate the rascal's disappointment when he found that instead of English shillings, he had only stolen French francs. How they would have shoved them then as they will me now.

Once out of the din I look back, and there they are yelling like 10,000 Indians, humming like a locomotive, buzzing like a thousand circular saws, and swarming like a row of beehives in June. Who says that Kingston is not a busy place. So the blacks and yellows can't take care of themselves? Better look out for them or they will take care of you—and such excellent care, that ten to one—yes a hundred to one, nobody but themselves shall be able to tell where they left you last.

After all they are probably much like the lower class of whites in our large cities—they will do anything and when I say anything, I mean *anything*, for money, while with us, they want the money without doing the anything. As a general thing I should that they are respectful to those who treat them civilly and only importunate and annoying in the way of trade.

They are saucy I doubt not to those who treat them uncivilly. These impressions are taken from a single survey and hardly reliable. If my mind is changed by further observation I will so record it. Mean time, we shall see.

Went into a heavy wholesale establishment with a man to assist him in getting a few hundred dollars in gold exchanged for coin. The head man is a Jew. He tells me that he has not in the last 17 years sold anything or done any business on Saturday, or on Sunday. He is a Pharisee stricter than St. Paul. Now I will lay a hypocrite's head agianst a puff ball that he cheats us in spite of wit or wisdom. He has bothered and bantered an hour and finally agrees to give $17 per ounce in American gold. Will he do it? I counted the gold for the man. All right. He let it lie on the counter a moment, while he arranged his purse. The Jew stole five dollars then.

When we got to the ship he found fifty dollars in California coin slipped in. Now this coin is at ten per cent discount—four dollars minus. Five and four are nine. So the Jew cheated him out of nine dollars. He went back directly but the store was closed. Tomorrow is Saturday and next day Sunday, of course. The Jew has done no business on those days for 17 years. He won't break over the rule now for a paltry nine dollars—not he. Oh, most pious Jew.

Returned again to the ship and there bedlam seems to have broken loose. The lungs that furnish that hubbub must be made of rubber and can never tire, the old Homer never could have visited Kingston till after he invented that fable of Stentor's throat and lungs being line with brass. Why there are fellows here that would run old Stentor off the track though backed by a Chinese gong.

And now the shades of evening descend and the bright moon looks down on the high mountains and strives to peer into their deep recesses, and on and over into the plains below, and over palaces and broad fields and gardens and tiled roofs and through the branches of the cocoa nut and down upon the ships and out upon the smooth bright waters, and so it was lost in the great west. Here the tumult has half subsided. And now a hum like the rush of a passing wind in the forest rises from the narrow streets of the town. Anon it swells to the clamor of riot, the din of battle and the thunder of furious strife. There is trouble there. No matter; here we are safe.

12 p.m. Hour after hour has passed. Midnight has come. All is still here. Silence reigns. The tumult of labor and the song of toil has ceased. The tubs stand by the coal pile and the men no longer place them on the heads of

the women. All have left to enjoy the rest promised to the weary. Bless me what a "row" on deck.

The cabin waiters and steward have come back drunk and there is a fight. Slam! Bang! and down they thunder on the deck. A lone cry of "take him off! Take him off! I don't want to hurt him," winds down into the cabin with most ludicrous effect.

"Take him off! Take him off I say," and then somebody did take him off and down into the cabin they came, the steward doing his best to make the men believe that he was sober.

SATURDAY, MARCH 15. Took a run through the town. If Panama is a great stone pile, then Kingston is a great brickyard. Its narrow streets 15 or 20 feet in the clear are walled in with low brick walls having iron grated windows and doors like jails. A great many stores are closed. The best use they can be put to. The city is well supplied with water from some source and is conveyed on ship board in pipes. There are iron hydrants at the corners of the streets all over the city.

Negroes and mulattoes seem to form the mass of the population, though I saw a great many English; but they are well housed today, and yet it is not very hot. Indeed it is pleasantly cool in the shade as there is a fine breeze from the ocean.

The gold fever has raged some here and the mountains have been ransacked for the poverty bearing dust. A gentleman connected with a copper mine speculated in the Island showed me a collection of 300 or 400 specimens of minerals and fossils gathered from various localities and was very anxious to learn if there might not be some gold in some of them. He seemed much disappointed when I assured him that there was not only no gold in them, but none where they were found. Some Galena has been found and a copper mine has been worked some but a heavy pecuniary loss. They will not be cursed with a gold mine!

KINGSTON, JAMAICA, SATURDAY, MARCH 15. Many complain that the negros are very saucy, impudent—but I can see very little difference between them and the "hewers of wood and drawers of water" in the great commercial emporiums of "the States." And even if they should put on Sunday airs, and assume that they are of some little consequence in the world, it ought not to be regarded as particularly wonderful.

They have been slaves—degraded, held as beasts, chattels, not men, and now they know that they are equal, at least legally and theoretically, to any biped who may chance along. And they want not only to know but to be sure of it, and more than that—to make others recognize and feel sure of it too; and lest it should be forgotten, they let no occasional slip to impress the fact upon strangers. They have discovered that they are men, and wish

all the world to participate in the benefit of the discovery. The man who
treats them decently, as though they are equals, will be treated respectfully
in turn. If he treats them as inferiors or slaves, they fire up at once and
stand their rights.

Where is the blame? He who has a just regard for the rights of others,
will estimate properly and overlook this perhaps overweening jealously of
new fledged liberty; but he who cares not for the rights of others and knows
nothing about his own, will curse the honesty that set them free, and ask
with the muddled complacency of tallow-headed soap-brained idiocy, if "that
don't cure you of abolitionism" "of the idea of freeing niggers?" The idea of
universal freedom!—and then with what infinite satisfaction he chuckles
over this invention of superlative folly till it stretches his mouth in a broad
grin—a grin, which, opening in Little Delaware and running from lip to lip,
terminating in Texas, stretches out wide and long and fathomless enough to
swallow—engulph the politics, religions, morals and wealth, body and soul
of the entire nation!

Well, grin on my masters—the time is coming when some real live
Yankee teacher will bring your mouth to a pucker when you don't want to
whistle. The negro must be free, or he, or the master, or both perish—and
the hand of mercy, so white and fair now, extended to save both, will some
time, ere long, be plunged deep in the sanguinary tide, to rescue even a
moiety of the innocent from the red sea of revolutionary blood.

It is amusing, and yet it vexes one, to hear bipeds who really appear a
heap smarter than the half dozen monkeys chattering about the deck, talk
about the falling off of exports and imports, and the evils of emancipation;
just as though it was left to them to say what this people shall produce, or
that consume; what shall be exported and what imported; who shall raise
coffee and how much, and who shall drink it. Suppose that we look about
us at home, and try this same (want of) principle.

The people of Indiana might raise much more corn than they now do,
for export—why don't they? Ask and you will directly learn. Talk to a
Hoosier about the great benefit to the country of his producing more—how
it would enrich the State and that it is his imperative duty to do it, and all
such verbose humbuggery—and you will hear—

"Wall, now, strange-er, you're a heap smarter than I purtent to be, and
no doubt you understand all about the politics, and tariffs, and pat-rot-ism,
and all them other curosities; but, I reckon I know when I git pay for raising
corn; and when I don't get the stuff rite down, I don't raise it, no how you
can fix it, and you'll al'wers find me thar, strange-er. Now, there's that are
colt—I call her Bets—I can take 50 dollars for her any day and she didn't
cost me 20 all told, sure as you live. Raise corn for a fin? No, strange-er
don't talk to me of raising this or that or t'other thing—only offer a price for
I'm tetotally busted if I don't raise what I like, and that I call the 'golden
rule for No. one.'"

Now, that's the talk, exactly. A free people do not like dictation in their domestic affairs, and are not likely to be well pleased with any attempts to coerce them in the direction of their rightful pursuits. Indeed they will not tolerate it in the U.S.A. and why should they in Jamaica? Are not the rights of the freeman of Jamaica, and the Hoosier, one and identical, each to raise what he chooses, and sell when he pleases? Indeed, will any man, who has the least regard for human rights, or even common decency, attempt to restrain him in its exercise, or by coercion give it an unnatural direction? Surely, if ever fanaticism ran mad, and needed a straight jacket, it is here.

These Southern and Northern aristocrats are so accustomed to be obeyed, that we may soon expect to see them turning out young Joshuas, and commanding the sun and moon to stand still. It would be hardly less Quixotic. No, no, wiseacres! if you want the people of Jamaica to export any particular product, offer a remunerating price, and you will get it, sure. Abolish slavery in Cuba, and elsewhere, and the price of sugar will take, and probably for a time, sustain a rise. Then Jamaica will export sugar, and when there is a surplus the price will come down again, and less will be produced, and so with all the products of slave labor. People, if they know it, will produce only what they get paid for.

There is one article, however, that now grows in the Island almost spontaneously, and in great abundance, if I can credit the testimony of several respectable gentlemen here who certainly ought to know. It was never a staple, or article of export, in slavery's palmiest day. Indeed it is said seldom or never to have reached the green leaf and never to have brought forth fruit. I believe it is not exported now, there being as yet only enough for home consumption, no surplus. It is happiness—a plant which never grows out of the shade of the liberty pole. The once slave is now the owner of land, and has his own hearth-stone. He has wife and children and neighbors around him, and works as anybody would (being permitted?) where he can best enjoy himself and get most pay.

What does he care whether we want coffee, or sugar? All he wants to know, is what will be the market price. If any hollow-headed, empty-hearted politician wants coffee to supply his lack of brains, or sugar to fill his rotting veins, and cannot buy, let him go and raise them, rather than speculate on the cause of their decrease or absence from market—or attempt, by legislating, to increase or bring them back again. The best legislation is to let these things entirely alone, and leave people to raise and sell what they please, and when they please, so long as no general injury results from the use of their products.

There was a shower this afternoon. It would seem that they have one every day. Under weigh again at six o'clock.

SUNDAY, MARCH 16. Cloudy, and showers at a distance. One passed over the ship. There is very little wind and the air is just pleasantly cool. We have a great many discussions in regard to Jamaica affairs, particularly its present condition. Some pretend to believe that the whole Island is like Kingston. But all know that such places furnish a harbor for the most abandoned and reckless and that there the vicious are most likely to congregate. One might expect beforehand to find just such a state of things as actually exists. There is not a whit more cheating, stealing, quarreling, fighting, or impudence, and far less swearing and more begging, than in Albany, Buffalo, Detroit, Chicago, or St. Louis. I speak of the masses in the streets. Not yet dark, and the Island has disappeared in the thick blue mist far, far behind on our right.

MONDAY, MARCH 17. Cloudy, and showers at distance. Something of a breeze from the N.E., but little change in the temperature yet.

TUESDAY, MARCH 18. Weather as yesterday, only much cooler at night. The wind has increased so much as to raise a heavy sea, and many of the passengers are sick.

WEDNESDAY, MARCH 19. Quite cool this morning and sea rough. Wind still ahead. About 7:30 p.m. the crank on the end of the middle shaft broke; the wheels suddenly ceased to move, and here we are in an instant left helpless on the wide waters. Bisby, the Chief Engineer, will doubtless take us into port as he is one of the indomitables and never says give up. His resources seem inexhaustible, and his energy is measured only by possibilities. He never stands to query whether what is to be done is probable. If he deems it possible, he sets about it, and instantly, and with his own hands.

When the *Philadelphia* was crippled at Chagres, and the Captain expected to be obliged to lay over and send home for the broken pieces— Bisby said that he could mend all these, and mend it he did, though everybody else said it was impossible, and the ship sailed on her day, and made the regular trip. For this service he received from the owners something more substantial than thanks, and he has just shown me a valuable gold watch, presented him by the passengers in the *Philadelphia*, in the great storm a couple of months since. The machinery of the ship seems very defective—always breaking. Two o'clock a.m.

THURSDAY, MARCH 20. There, the wheel turns again, and again we are in motion. A part of the starboard wheel has been stript of its buckets, the larboard shaft disconnectd, and we are running with the wheel of that side, like a crippled duck. If the wind only blew so that we could use our wings, we could go yet; but there is no wind for us—or only a head one.

The sea was quite rough, and the engine labored considerably before it broke. At sunrise it was almost a dead calm, and somewhat cloudy.

12 a.m. We have made 190 miles in 24 hours, against a head wind with one wheel crippled. Lay rolling about six and a quarter hours, and finally ran the remainder of the time with only one wheel.

I have been reading a book entitled, "Jamaica in 1850," by Bigelow, of New York. I had designed, before seeing it, to write out in full all that my short stay in Kingston would warrant, and had made the most of that short time in collecting information from every available source. As this book gives in detail what I could only have given in synopsis of, I would advise everyone who has any desire to learn the present condition of the Island to procure and read it. I think that all his statements are reliable, and not only so, but the causes assigned for its present unenviable state, and the arguments and facts adduced to sustain them are essentially the same that I had from intelligent residents of Jamaica.

I say again, read that book, and don't let southern men or their toadies humbug you with the stupid idea that emancipation caused the pecuniary distress of the Island. Make yourself master of the facts, the arguments and the statistics, and then you are prepared to meet them on their own ground, though, after all, it is not relevant to the main question.

The slaves should have been freed; though the inevitable result would be a universal bankruptcy. The liberty of one man for an hour is of more real value than the combined wealth of fifty such miserable, sordid, mean, calculating nations as the U.S.A. – a nation whose great, everlasting dollar-lined mouth, pours forth in one continuous thunder burst; a flashy foggy, foaming, frothy, misty, flood tide of liberty, while its thousand hands are, on the one side, busily employed in surveying new landed acquisitions, and on the other tightening the manacles and adding weight to the chains that bind one sixth of its whole people to the most crushing, brutalizing servitude that man has ever yet enforced or submitted to. I have said, meet them on their own ground, and where is that? I am indignant when I think where. Indeed, a Freeman cannot be otherwise.

To think that man (?) freemen (??) Democrats (???) Whigs (????) should rejoice that the apparent result of emancipation is disastrous, and exert themselves to prove that it is real, and not only so, but a necessary and unavailable one. Out upon such starveling, hypocritical reprobates! Who that looks upon these yelping curs of the Black Demon can help imagining that he sees the tiger, though the spots and stripes were by mistake laid upon other backs?

When I look about me on the quarter deck, I am no longer surprised at the support which slavery has received in the several short discussions which have been elicited. They are all tobacco chewers, smokers, rum drinkers, swearers, card-players or gamblers. Much more might be added; and I know of but two exception, if they be such, and these are a Georgian and a Louisianian, and they smoke and chew—than which there are scarcely greater abominations (if we except slavery) and they will add much, even, to the horrors of that. I am ashamed of them as men, advocating human oppression, and for that matter, I should be ashamed of such company even in a good cause. Here is a dilemma. Smoker, get out of it.

Chapter Twenty-four

March 21–April 3, 1851:
The Mississippi River and Home

———◆———◆———◆———

FRIDAY, MARCH 21. Cloudy and pleasantly cool. Made the light house at the mouth of the Mississippi at one p.m. and at the same time were boarded by a pilot. The pilot boat, a beautiful craft, has just sent one on board the *Georgia*, which was in sight this morning and passed us a few minutes ago. We have seen several sail today. The water, which has been changing color since sunrise, is now quite muddy.

Two p.m. Just passed the *Georgia*, stuck fast in the mud. This entrance to the Mississippi is exceedingly intricate. I believe that there are several. The channels pass among low broken banks of earth, deposited on immense fields of drift wood, which sticks above the water between the banks. The banks themselves have some vegetation. Went down to dinner, and when we returned, we had a regular river bank on each side of us, and the stream, about half a mile wide. I do not know the name of this channel.

We are now passing, on our right, a pretty village situated on both sides of a Bayou, where the Pilots live. There may be some 50 houses, some of them quite large, and the whole looks very neat, though now on a level with the water. There are a great many men engaged in this business. Here we took a river pilot, and discharged our Balize man.

Above, on the opposite side, is the telegraph office, I should think, as the line of posts and the wire terminate there. Several tow boats lie about at the different landings, some distance above there is a plantation on the left hand, where the American flag is displayed, and the health officer resides. Here the land is higher, though only just above the waters of the Gulf, except for a short distance below the Doctor's. Indeed, it is only a few rods across in many places. Bisby says that the banks here are sometimes three or four feet above water. From this point the banks and bayous are lined with willows, and we pass another large channel of the river, running into the Gulf on our right.

A little fly somewhat larger than a gnat is troublesome an hour or two before sun down. For an hour after sundown, there has been only a narrow slip of land on either side between us and the salt water bays, running in from the Gulf.

SATURDAY, MARCH 22. Up at four a.m. Everything on deck dripping with dew, and the deck flooded with water. The banks seem timbered, and here and there is an old house. We are running, or rather moving very slowly, with one wheel, two and a half miles an hour. Went below into the main saloon, and there the musquitoes "are upon thee, Sampson." I soon succeeded in putting a quietus upon some dozen or so. These are petty annoyances, it is true, and most annoyances are such; though, like the forces which disturb the motion of the planets, they make a heap of difference; gyrating one here, and another there, like a crazy sky rocket; never exactly right; crossing and re-crossing its appointed orbit, and coming round into the same track only at long periods.

Well, well, if we can only start right and hit our point of departure at every successive revolution, we may thank God and take courage. They say that experience confers wisdom. I don't know how that is. Some very great fools have had vast experience. But I do say, that California is entirely out of sight of the right track, and if any one catches me skylarking or grub-hunting on those diggins again, I'll just thank him to lasso me like a regular "long ear," and tie me up at the first hitching post that he may chance to run against.

After running a few miles, the wheel stopped again, (tired out), the anchor dropped, and the steam was blown off. Then the boiler, which had sprung a leak, was mended and at ten a.m., we are in motion again. Both banks are lined with hamlets—one or two large houses, and a large number of small ones around; i.e., on both sides; beyond which fields are fenced out from half a mile to two miles back from the river. Most of the back ground is a dense growth of heavy timber, seemingly impenetrable. A levee runs along or near the edge of each bank, and prevents the water running over into the fields, which are now several feet below the surface of the water in the river.

Indeed, the water is nearly at the top of the levee, and in many places the people are mending it where the water is breaking over. Eight or ten inches more rise would drown them out. The plantations are on both sides, from half a mile to a mile apart, and most of them seem highly cultivated. The buildings are for the most part of wood, and in very good preservation, though some are much dilapidated, and whole plantations going to waste, and the houses and fences to ruin. Some fields have just been reclaimed from the forest, the surface yet black with burned stumps. Each establishment has a large space inclosed with palings and filled with vegetables and trees. Among the latter, the bitter orange is most conspicuous, loaded down with its golden fruit.

Occasionally we see a white man riding up or down the levee, in a turn-out which would expose him to ridicule in the north. A very high cart, of a very clumsy construction, with an awkward, very ill-looking black cover, drawn by two creatures, very much resembling a blood horse that has crossed the great desert, or a caricature of that good knight, Don Quixote's Rosinante. To go the entire truth—I have no where seen such sorry nags, except in Kingston, where the fast and fat (?) cab horses seem never in a hurry—and lean to leanness.

The negro quarters, or small houses are to all appearances comfortable, and with some exceptions have a general air of cleanliness and thrift. A few "hands" are at work in the fields, weeding out the long rows of sugar cane, which is now only a few inches high, and looks much like broom corn. They seem to take it very leisurely, and well they may, for their enormous hoes are enough to bring a harlequin to terms, or steady a weathercock.

And this is slave land; and here the hand of the oppressor is strong, and there is none to deliver. Here, none heeds the great and imperative law, "Do unto others, even as ye would that they should do unto you." Every body knows the law, though they never heard or read the words. All recognize the principle, immediately they are wronged. It's no use talking about it. The judgment is set, and the doom is pronounced, already, at that dread tribunal from which there is no appeal; and the damnation though long delayed, is sure. Let us be silent—Ephriam wants to be let alone.

At four p.m., passed the battle ground of Old Hickory. It is a broad plain on the right, and has nothing peculiar as a slaughter yard. There are several beautiful plantations on the ground now. Yonder is a broad-spreading oak, which is pointed out as that under which Packenham was laid after being wounded. Thirty six years have passed away, and the rains and the dews of heaven fall in vain; for though the blood and stains may not be apparent, yet they are indelibly fixed where nothing but the last great conflagration can remove them. When shall wars cease? Now we slowly pass the United States' barracks on our right, immediately south of which is a large square, enclosed with a brick wall, flanked on each corner with enormous round towers. And here, perhaps the city may be said to begin.

As we move leisurely up, the bank on our left presents a beautiful appearance. Every 200 yards, more or less, are large fine houses—palaces, almost—with out buildings of all descriptions, surrounded by grounds in the highest state of cultivation. Evergreen shrubbery and trees make it look to a northern eye exceedingly—surpassingly beautiful; and the more so to us now, as it presents the desirable medium between the luxuriant waste of the tropics we have just left, and the stinted barrenness of March in the north, which we are soon to see. Elegant carriages and fine horses are taking the place of the ugly vehicles and ragged nags below—and here is the city. What an awkward ugly looking tower that is—rising like Saul, head and shoulders above the city. It appears much like Chimney Rock. St. Patrick's church? eh? Well, if St. Patrick had any taste in these matters, he'd knock that steeple into "pi." Couldn't help it.

The harbor is as active as a bee-hive. Steamers of all sizes running up and down, around, straight and in curves, and ships gliding from place to place without any ostensible power of locomotion, until a close survey discloses some little bit of a steamer on one side, tugging it along, very much as an ant would a gad-fly. And now we pass ship after ship, till they count by scores and long lines of huge steamers, like flocks of sheep at a feeding trough—and now the city is almost behind us—and the gun has been banged off again, and five o'clock is come, and everybody (I mean on board) is in hopes that we are not to stop—when by some process at present unknown our (want of?) speed became reduced a little, a very little, and we didn't go at all. And next we are to wait for the custom house officer—and wait we did—a short time, when they turned us loose. I am sure that nobody is sorry, though we have to run the gauntlet and be cheated again, "regular," by the land sharks for the next 24 hours.

NEW ORLEANS, SATURDAY, MARCH 22. The cabin fare has been good. Some failures in the cookery, as the chief cook has been sick. I should think the steerage fare better than on the Pacific side, though the steerage itself is far inferior. The provisions were better cooked, better served, and of better quality. The Captain and Steward are fat men, both. That accounts for it.

As I was leaving the ship with some boxes containing some fancy shell work that I bought in Jamaica, a young man began with, "What have your there, sir?"

"Shell boxes."

"Where from?"

"Jamaica."

"Well, sir, I am an officer of the customs and you may save yourself trouble by leaving them on board till morning, which I would advise you to do."

"Thank you sir, and much obliged for your advice, but I don't care whether there is any inspection or not. If there are any duties, inspect them and say what is to pay, but they go ashore, you may be sure."

"I can't do it, I'm not the Inspector, sir; he will be here in the morning."

"Very well, I shall not, and so shall lose the pleasure of seeing him; besides, if he is very anxious for an interview, he should be on hand."

"How the h_____ can he be here till the ship reports herself?"

"She did report below, sir, as my almost deafened ears bear testimony."

"Better leave them, sir, or you may get into trouble."

"Obliged to you, sir, but I would sooner get into anything than remain here; and as the gangway is now clear, I bid you a good evening."

"Yes, sir, and I'll have different works when another boat comes in."

"Hope you'll improve, sir, and succeed in all laudable undertakings," and so we parted for the first, and probably, the last time.

I do think that it is a most contemptible oozing out of meanness for a great people like ours to support a central government by searching people's trunks, like a set of rusty bum-bailiffs after stolen goods, or a gang of mail robbers. One feels degraded—lowered in his own estimation, when entering a port of his own country, to anticipate the prying search that shall disclose to the argus-eyed officers the astounding fact of a most extraordinary and unheard-of fraud, about to have been perpetrated upon the Customs—to wit: the introduction into the country of two dirty shirts—the threads in the stitching thereof being supposed to be of foreign manufacture, in violation of the laws and ordinances of Congress (not the people). This is but one among the many things, equally infamous, equally violations of natural rights, and which the people are outright fools to tolerate.

Speaking of the government, it is sheer nonsense, with us, to talk of the power being in the hands of the people; nor has it ever been; or if it has, certainly not in their brains. It is, and ever has been, in the heads and hands of a few designing individuals, with little exception, and always will be till the people take the trouble to think for themselves. They will then learn that the most expensive way of supporting a government is by a revenue derived from customs, and one most dangerous to the liberties of the people. It is a way that tyrants first taught, and all oppressors learned, but which no free people can ever practice safely, nor will they, unless unthinkingly.

A man cannot by any possibility be either a revenue or a protective tariff man, and a sound Democrat. The two are incompatible. The most that can be said for it is, that it is a queer way to collect money, and a rare way to spend it. However, the sovereign people have the name of doing it, and only make them believe that they are somebody, and they will submit to about anything.

A Revenue Tariff? Puts the idle and lazy in a way to steal in gross, and thus protects the pockets of individuals. A Protection Tariff? Takes a dime each from the pockets of ten men who need it, and puts a single dime in the pocket of one man who needs it not—and the remainder, like the remnant of a coat pattern, or a half side of leather at Crispins, goes into the stealings, and never appears on the balance sheet. I know that these notions won't please—but they fit like an India rubber shoe. That's enough.

Let me see; where am I? Ah! In a private boarding house, on Tchoupitaulas St., (which of you will pronounce it?). Well, they call it here—

Tchop-tu-la. The fellow who named it was never tongue-tied, or if he was, had it cut down to his palate. It is a mile and a half below where we landed, two blocks back from the levee; and in the immediate vicinity of the up-river steamers. I wonder how they intend to cheat us; for sure am I that they not only design, but will do it—though twelve of us came here together on one coach, and have a special contract to pay one dollar apiece, neither more nor less—coach fare included.

I have been out. It is quite dark. Some of the streets are lighted, and some not. Gas lights I suppose. This is one of the principal streets, and yet very few people travel it on foot. Carriages are constantly passing. In coming down, I noticed that the streets were narrow, the houses low, and not built with much taste. We saw many fine horses and carriages as we rattled down the pavements. Quite pleasant and barely cool this evening.

SUNDAY, MARCH 23. A little chilly this morning. Three or four boats are going out this afternoon, and then no more go till Tuesday or Wednesday; and it was determined by the company to take passage on the *Pawnee*, which is to leave at one o'clock. At half past eleven, a.m., left the hotel where we have had good fare and treatment. Knew they'd cheat us. Charged the day we came one dollar—only had supper and lodging; and today one dollar, though we only had breakfast. All right; these are great sinners, and must get all the cheat out of them, if possible, before they die.

Boat moved off at 1:30 p.m. There is a poor fellow lying on the levee with his leg just broken. I wonder how he did it—or if he has a family in the city. No, they take him to the hospital. Maybe he will get well after a long time—perhaps not. Does anybody care? Perhaps this accident has saved him from a greater danger. Who knows?

We are passing the Marine Hospital (they say), a noble building on our left. Warm enough in the sun, but quite cool in the shade. The city and vicinity does not appear as well above as below. A few miles up on the left there is a break in the levee, through which the water is furiously rushing, inundating the country in all directions. A host of people are laboring to fill it up. Good luck to them.

By the by, I did not see much of New Orleans. St. Patrick's church—I was in it this morning—nothing very attractive, inside or out. The furniture is not magnificent, and from the entrance where I stood one does not get a good view enough to judge of the merit of three great paintings at the far end of the house—and yet that should be the most favorable point of view. Perhaps the light is bad. A great many people were constantly passing in and out. Some went through the ceremonies, dipping the finger in holy water, crossing and kneeling, with great fervor; others, particularly the children, with infinite grace; and others, in the most awkward and ungainly manner.

Two old women came in and besides the ordinary and extraordinary performances, each secured a little square vial or bottle full of water (holy?) and not content with that, one of them dipped her rosary in it and quietly slipped it in her pocket. Had she been a worshipper of all the gods of "Heathen Ind," I could have pitied her—but I was only astonished. I had room for no other feeling. I presume that she would have been more astonished, that I did it not, had she noticed me. I have never seen its parallel in real life—Macbeth's witches were perfect "flats."

There are some very good buildings in the city. I had anticipated much pleasure in taking a look at the St. Charles Hotel, but that is only a huge mass of ruins. The fire did its work thoroughly. The Atchafalaya Banking House once had a very fine front but the columns are crumbling down, the capitals mouldering away, and the cornice so broken that the doves have entire possession of it now. The Bank was probably one of those swindling concerns, the operators in which should be punished as other criminals are (ought to be?). How slow men are to learn the principles or practice of right.

Legislators, mis-called the people's representatives, by virtue of an assumed power to do wrong, guarantee to certain ones the exclusive legal (?) right (?) to swindle the community for forty years with their worthless paper, and in the very next section prohibit under stringent penalties any other person or persons making or uttering any species of paper intended or calculated for a circulating medium—alias, swindling too; and not satisfied with that, they must next prohibit any one from passing a note which even the legalized swindlers have made, under their own (the legislative) authority, provided its denomination is less than five dollars. Now why not punish crime when it is committed, rather than foolishly attempt to prevent it by invading the clearest right of individuals? The making or passing a bank note, or any other, as an equivalent for money, or representative of value, may in the minds of some raise the presumption of criminality; but it is only a presumption; and if every man who is fairly presumed to be a rogue is to be punished, a weary and a thankless task awaits the few who are to inflict it.

They had better follow the example of Lot, and "vamoose." No, no, our great men with their long faces and owl eyes and shaking heads and all their reputation for SAP-(ience,) have not a bit of wisdom to spare—not enough common sense for home consumption, nor any wit for export, nor honesty enough to loan a dime's worth at a Shylock usury, and less consistency than all these put together.

There's a Pat-lander for you. Let there be no law for enforcing the collection of debts, no imprisonment for debt, nor penalties for selling anything, unless it should be necessarily noxious or hurtful to the buyers, or the community; then if a man does, (not is presumed to) get in debt for the purpose of swindling, or without the intention of paying, or sells his paper with similar design, let him be treated as a criminal, for such he is—i.e., be imprisoned and put at hard labor, and then he will produce something for the support of his family or the public. Cheaper fifty times over than to support him in idleness, with all the cumbrous mechanism and almost intolerable burdens of law courts for the collection of debts—a motly medley of incongruous machinery—weights from Nimrod and Nebuchadnezzar, wheels from Egypt, and regulator from Judea; bells from the Roman Emperors and springs from the Pope; a bloody handless dial-plate from Greece, gilded in Revolutionary France, and covered and concealed by an English case, polished and varnished by the Yankees who sell it to the highest bidder. It is a time-keeper that never kept time; a machine that never moved unless carried; and varnished with bird lime, to which everything with which it comes in contact adheres.

It always will be—ever has been increasing, (it is its nature), and will continue to do so, until demolished, annihilated; for, like a snow ball, if it be moved it rolls, and rolling it is sure to accumulate. Every bad law calls forth half a dozen others to remedy it. I would like to hold the match to the train that is to blow the whole "sky high." One single cry of stand from under and up she goes. There would be something of a fuss and a smoke (so much dry dirt), and then the people would settle down quietly again, and 50 years would elapse before the rogues and fools would be able to get another monster into operation.

Now in all this you will perceive no design to make war on the banks. They would not mind it if I did. May they all prosper in all honesty (its no use wishing the other way, they'll take care of that) for paper is a cheaper and certainly a more convenient currency than silver, or even gold; and does not entail half the loss on the holders, as I can testify. In the last two years I have seen more loss per cent on gold and silver, than on paper under the glorious old wild cat system of Democratic, Whigocratic, Rogue-ocratic Michigan. One of the men in our company was cheated in Jamaica; one was defrauded in the say way of $150 in New Orleans, and another of $200, and so on, ad infinitum. No one gets money changed, as far as I can learn, but gets cheated in count or weight or both. A great many carelessly brought pieces of gold of private coinage from California, which is worth no more than bullion here. The loss is ten per cent, or more. These coin all look like Uncle Sam's and one who does not know might take any quantity and not find it out till too late.

And then in the mines, in the great game of grab, false weights figure large. A man walks up to a counter, calls for a drink, and perhaps treats his friend, then throws his purse on the counter to have the dust weighed out. If the purse is small and the man sober, and not much engaged, the honest bar keeper will only put in a four dollar weight instead of two. If he is drunk and careless and the purse big enough, there is no stint in the process. I have seen cases when I am satisfied that at least 150 dollars were weighed out for five drinks and then the whole company were "treated gratis" by the liberal thief, all who would drink—and it was not common to refuse. A nice trick was to wet the bottom of the scale basin with spittle, which holds it to the counter, and if it is done dexterously, they get the reputation of being very liberal—not requiring down weight, while in reality they get two to four dollars more or less, clear.

It is easy to conceive that one might prevent such imposition, but one finds it very difficult on account of the diversity in the weights. They are of lead, brass, copper, zinc, tin or other easily fused metals—flat, round, oval, oblong, square cubes and all kinds and sorts of shapes and then there is a great difference in the relative weight of different piles of dust as compared with the bulk. The only sure way to escape robbery is to have your dust accurately weighed before you leave home, and put up in small parcels. This will detect the rascals, but not so as to shame them, as they immediately excuse themselves, by saying "A mistake, sir." "Meant to have taken to'ther weight." "This is the two dollar weight, sir." "They look exactly alike, you see, sir." "It agrees with your weights exactly, sir." "Oh! I knew it would." "If you had been dealing with Dobbins, now, you would have lost two dollars, but I always try to make sure of my weights." He might have added, "and your gold, too."

Another branch of the game is to catch the ring of the gold side over the end of the beam as it is raised, thus shortening that arm and requiring more gold to balance the weights. One may easily detect this, and it often happens by mistake, but in small scales it is usually overlooked. I intended to perpetrate a chapter on the "Grab" and I may as well finish it now. I pass over *the grab direct of the footpad* and, hardly less so, of the gambler, the *rake down of the land monopolist* and the *sweep clean of the landlords and boarding house keepers* and those *canker worms* the Jew-*pedlers* and small dealers and those locusts the teamsters and steamboat agents and come to the blood suckers.

"Well, who are they, stranger?" Trust a man in California and you directly learn. Lend a man a few hundred dollars or ounces, and you will never again be at a loss to distinguish a leech from an earthworm. California has three kinds of debtors—indigenous, that never pay. They are the fortunate, the unfortunate and the misfortunate—or the "won't pays," the "can't pays," and the "never can pays," which include about nine-tenths of the whole population.

We begin with Class 3rd. They came into the country strapped or nearly so—and sick and discouraged and mad. They must be taken care of, and of course, get in debt. It is their misfortune to be trusted and yours to trust them. They try hard to live, for it is bad to die. You try hard to save them, for it is hard to lose them—and your pay too. But its no go. It is their misfortune and yours, and no help for it. People can't live always and Methuselah never was in California, or had a chronic diarrhea. Note that down as a fact.

Next comes Class 2nd. Those who arrive destitute but in health. They run in debt for provisions and everything they need or want. They work hard and strive to make something, but it don't do. The gold won't be found and the necessity recurs for further credit. They are clever fellows— will pay sometime—you can't refuse, and there goes another hundred or two. They are unfortunate, and it is unfortunate for you that they are so. They will promise anything, and certainly intend to pay, but they don't— can't pay—and then the unfortunates often pass into the misfortunates. And now for Class first.

These seem at first to belong to Class 2nd and certainly have a queer way of paying off—liquidating their debts. They "will hand it over in a few days." You call again. They "Paid it to one of your company. Can't recollect the name."

"Which one was it?"

"Anyway he wore whiskers and his hair was—of some color."

Call the third—"It must be a mistake—certainly paid it." Will see and if he can't find the man, will pay over.

Call the fourth, a year after. "Strapped, sir. Don't pay any man a cent. Been cheated. Dammed the river. Damned everybody and everything and going to stay in California. If you think you can get anything, go ahead; I don't think you'll make a big strike."

Now it is fortunate for him that he has nothing, else he might be troubled with the calls of Constables and Sheriffs and you are fortunate in having such a debtor, you know exactly what to do. You get rid of trusting him any more, and save paying lawyers and costs and wasting money and time, as you do in trying to collect of the unfortunates. Now, at least three-fourths of the debtors of California are fortunates, unfortunates, or misfortunates. Besides the California gold coin, you are shaved on the Isthmus by the local currency of 80 cents to the dollar, four two-real pieces of 20 cents each being a dollar, while four 25 cent pieces are worth no more, and eight dimes the same, and twelve and a half cents is only a dime.

At Kingston a British shilling is worth twenty-five cents, while a two-real piece is a drug—worth only twelve and a half to 15 cents at most. At New Orleans the British shilling is only twenty cents and hard at that, and thus it is nothing but shave and grab all the way.

There is another great nation (disgrace) shaving machine going up in the midst of the city. I refer to the Custom house. The staging alone is worth going some distance to see. The main wall is only the first story high. Its area is only to be measured by acres, and its height, judging from the staging, only by the clouds.

The Odd Fellows Hall is a noble building—just going up. The lower story is arcade—of stone—the rest brick—to be plastered. Over two of the doors I noticed three huge links of a chain, carved in the stone. Very suspicious. I don't like chains, though in this case, I reckon, all depends on the meaning one attaches to the symbol. It would be a fit emblem for a slave pen, or a dog sausage (link?) market, but what use the I.O.O.F. have for chains, I can't imagine. Sure they can't intend to fasten a fellow after that fashion, as it would not be odd at all. If the chains were broken, and the oppressed to go free, I could hail this emblem as one of the queerest – entirely out of fashion – odd as honesty and strange as silence. It's no use, however, to be particular here.

New Orleans is going ahead with her narrow, and wide and clean and dirty streets; her brick and stone and wood and iron houses; her black and brown and grey and yellow population; her manufacturers and trade and commerce and everything that constitutes a great city but freedom. Cool, or rather cold this evening, so that one needs an overcoat.

MONDAY, MARCH 24. Chilly. The air has more sharpness than with the same degree of cold in California. We have, the whole day, been passing a long village, or city, or rather all the people and houses of a State seem to have been collected and stretched along in two rows, scarcely interrupted or broken by a space – and here, on our right, at half past three, is Baton Rouge (bah-tun-roosch) – one great, white, awkward looking affair, which they call the State House, being the only thing as yet worth looking at.

We miss the telegraph posts and wires which accompanied us all the way from the Balize to New Orleans. There it crossed over to the north side, and was to be seen all day yesterday on our right – one line of tall round posts, another of sawed square posts. This is the first natural land surface we have yet seen, as high as the surface of the water in the river. The land is here elevated from ten to thirty feet – and here we have the telegraph again. Wonder where it has been. There is a narrow slip of land at the base of the bluff, and now almost on the level with the water. A few houses are built upon it.

The plain on which the city is built is some fifteen or twenty feet higher, and is a beautiful location. The streets run directly from the river. I do not notice any very good buildings, except a hotel, the barracks, and the State House. The latter is a fine – a very fine building – and but for its being stuck on the very edge of the bluff, and surrounded by most miserable "shantees," would appear well. Its models may be found in France and Germany, perhaps – and it would be a heap more at home at Paris than there, where it looks as if it had just sprung out of the ground – clean as a mushroom and staring from its great circular windows as if in doubt whether to stay or go back. Indeed, so strong is the illusion and so "outre" is the entire thing, that I should not be surprised in the least to see it descend at this moment and disappear in the earth. It really has no business there. When the ground around it are laid out it will no doubt appear to better advantage. Still it is too near the river.

Took in a lot of sugar here. The country for some distance above is not all under cultivation, and the bank on our right is covered with water back, I suppose, to the bluff. Warmer this evening.

TUESDAY, MARCH 25. Warm night and warm all day. The bank on
our left, through the day, has been low and more improved than that on
our right, which has occasionally presented high, yellow or whitish bluffs,
with enormous "slides" lying at their base, partly under water.

The plantations are much more recent, as a general thing, than those
we have passed before, though some of them are ancient enough. Generally
one bank, and often both, are covered to the water's (or rather bank's) edge
with a dense growth of small timber, appearing from a distance like a forest
of well trimmed hop poles, though they are covered at the top with leaves,
now nearly of the full size.

Sometimes the heavy timber makes its appearance on the bank, and it
may be seen almost anywhere at the back of the plantations, and in the
most recent ones, hundreds of them stand dead and dry, blackened with
fire, or rearing their enormous barkless trunks and leafless limbs, high and
white into the air.

Three o'clock, p.m. Stopped at Natchez a few minutes. Some large
building, just burned to the ground, lies a mass of black and smoking ruins.
Very few buildings under the bluff, which appears to be two hundred feet
high. The city, of which we have only a glimpse, is on the bluff, and is
reached by a very easy carriage way, dug along the hill side. There are two
of these roads. The country, on the whole, today, has looked rather thrift-
less and desolate. In some few places I noticed peach trees in full bloom.

WEDNESDAY, MARCH 26. Cloudy and just comfortable this morning.
Ten o'clock at Vicksburg, the most active business place we have seen since
leaving New Orleans. The town is built mostly of brick and appears new. It
is on the top and slope of a higher bluff than Natchez stands on and to
appearance unlike that city very rough and irregular. The low and almost
inundated land between the bluff and the river is occupied by store houses,
saw-mills, etc., etc., and every spot not put to other use is literally piled,
heaped, or stowed with logs, shingles, boards, and all kinds of lumber; half a
dozen or more of steam saw-mills are in active operation.

A large, new brick church on the bluff (probably Episcopal) is a fine
looking building, and I notice two or three other pretty looking domes or
steeples. The country has been the same as yesterday till this afternoon,
when the land is somewhat higher, the levee more perfect, and the timber
much larger. Indeed, this evening we are passing some of the heaviest I have
ever seen, except in California. The plantations exhibit very great recent
improvements. The banks are lined with long piles of beautiful split (cotton)
wood and everything appears flourishing except the trees, which are for the
most part leafless. Nothing but the want of foliage indicates our rapid
approach to a colder region, as it has been rather warm today.

A lad of ten or twelve came on board at Plaquemine, and, telling a pitiful
story of his orphaned condition, persuaded a passenger to pay his passage,

(deck) and give him money to buy provision, etc., promising to go with him and be bound to him till he should be 21. Just as the boat was leaving Vicksburg today, he stepped on the old hulk which serves for a wharf, store house and grogery, and "vamoosed." Thus is charity imposed upon, and young scamps trained for the gallows.

The Californians are fair game for anybody. Hear all the stories, and you can only conclude that there is but one safe place to sell gold in New Orleans. Try it and you will call in question the existence of that one. Else, why are all cheated? Some of the tune of ten or twelve ounces. As in gold, so in everything. Cheat covers the whole routine of business transactions. I wonder if New Orleans is the worst place in the United States of America.

THURSDAY, MARCH 27. Cloudy this morning, and some rain. Came where two large scows were loaded with wood. Ran between and took both in tow, and in a few minutes, without a very perceptible diminution of speed, both loads were transferred to our deck, and the scows sent adrift. We have had several boats in tow before, but never two at once.

Four p.m. We are now at Napoleon, just below the mouth of the Arkansas. The river is falling and the place, just coming up out of the water, is one row of wooden buildings on the bank, with a broken plank side walk in front. Street there is none. The town may be fifty or sixty rods long. In the center, a wharf projects eighty yards into the river. We hauled up and tied to a covered scow several rods below—a little farther down, lie two vast steamer hulks, now used for landing. In the upper part of the town is Marine Hospital, a large new brick building with a cupola. They are now putting on the roof, the rafters already there. The Arkansas seems to add nothing to the Mississippi. No particular difference in the banks or country today.

FRIDAY, MARCH 28. Just pleasantly cool this morning and somewhat cloudy. The river has fallen enough to leave the banks for the most part above water—a very great improvement. At two p.m. passed a large scow or ark, hard aground, probably snagged and leaking, as they were tossing the ice overboard, and pumping with "might and main," apparently to keep her afloat.

It was dark when we reached Memphis and we coud see nothing of the city. The plantations passed today look a little more thrifty, and I noticed several large apple and peach orchards and plum trees in full bloom. The water has fallen eight feet here.

Came very near being run down last night. On turning a sharp point, the *Grand Turk*, coming down at the rate of twenty miles an hour, ran within four feet of us. Accidents on the river lately have been almost too frequent to be called by that name. Certainties would be much nearer the mark. Our Captain had his boat (not this) blown up and burned a short time since. I reckon that he don't intend to be blown up again, unless cold weather does it, for we never have more than a third, and generally only a quarter, of what the boilers would safely bear. Slow business, but sure. Better go slowly up the river than rush into the air. No danger.

Haven't seen one of the crew drunk, and the officers don't seem to drink at all. Very queer that all should keep sober. I wish that I could say as much for the passengers. We have some of the veriest loafers that Arkansas and Missouri can "scare out," of whom two or three have been drunk all the time. The same old customer that couldn't find his berth one night on the *Oregon*, was looking for it two or three hours last night, and didn't find it at last. Since the first night out, a set of some half dozen professed gamblers have been playing night and day—more or less or all of them at once, keeping the other passengers awake. One comfort—they haven't made much. One of them got twenty or thirty dollars out of an Arkansas chap; but he earned it, for they played three days and nights, steadily.

SATURDAY, MARCH 29. Cloudy and pleasantly cool. Country well timbered, but appears desolate. Occasionally we pass a plantation that looks better. Passed several steamers this morning, bound down, all in a few minutes.

SUNDAY, MARCH 30. We ought to have been at St. Louis today; at least we do anticipate, and we are now, eight o'clock a.m., only at the mouth of the Ohio. This is Cairo—the drowned and shrivelled bantling of overgrown speculation—a city of thirty houses and three old hulks—hardly equal to Yuba City. It will be a long while before you outgrow St. Louis (?) or Cincinnati. Half past one and thirty miles above the mouth of the Ohio. "Commerce" is on our left. What a libel on trade! Why, Commerce has only one craft in harbor, and that is a skiff with two yards of canvass. The town is just above high water mark, and just below a low rocky bluff, which spreads and rises back and up the river, into hills. There may be thirty houses here. Opposite, in Illinois, is a little huddle of buildings under a hill, where something seems to be about to be done in the lumber trade.

Passed a steamer on our left, sunk guards under. A lot of people are engaged in getting out her furniture, etc. She probably ran on a rock, or snag, only a day or two ago. The country has been rough for several miles, and we have passed two or three small towns. One on the Illinois side appeared thriving. There are orchards scattered along, and the peaches and plums are in full bloom. The Red-bud looks much like the peach, and abounds in this section. I have noticed it frequently for two or three days.

Four p.m. Here on our left is Cape Giradeau—a very pretty and apparently thriving town. It is built on a fine bluff, far above the highest rise of the Mississippi, I should think. The houses are mostly of brick, and appear very well—more like Peoria, Ill., than any town I ever saw. I can see no steeple here, though the population must be a thousand or more. A heavy thunder shower down the river. The lightning streams down, and the thunder rolls heavily—the first thing of the kind I have seen in a long time—and now it is passing over us. How chilly!

A man preached in the Saloon this afternoon. The machinery and steam pipe made such a noise that I could not hear very distinctly. His sermon was not very satisfactory. Indeed I could hardly tell, when he was through, what he had been, or would be, driving at. What a pity that so many fine words should be so entirely destitute of meaning, at least to common minds. Crude thought-germs, bursting from an uncultivated soil, to perish instantly for want of nutriment. I have heard a heap of such in California. Sick of them. The moral man, after leaving the States, seems to become as barren as the soil he treads upon.

MONDAY, MARCH 31. 8 A.M. ST. GENEVIEVE, an old, scattering town, of wood, brick, and stone, red, white and yellow, with green blinds. Any quantity of iron and lead here, from the mines thirty or forty miles back in the country. Raw, chilly air this morning, seemingly colder than when it freezes in California. Next, on the left, passed Jefferson Barracks, a very pretty looking piece of ground, now covered with green grass and leafless trees. The leaves are not yet out, though the plums and peaches are in full bloom. Six miles above, on the same side, passed a considerable huddle of new houses; then the arsenal; and now, at a quarter past three, we are at St. Louis. The Illinois side of the river, today, has been low and heavily timbered—the Missouri side, light timbered, hilly, with high, rocky bluffs. Both sides have some good looking farms. The bluffs are very beautiful, much like some of the scenery about Chimney Rock.

Left St. Louis at five p.m., in the *Ocean Wave*, bound for Peru. Through some little mismanagement in working the boat out we were detained twenty minutes. There are two boats just starting for the same place, and doubtless we shall have a fine race, if we don't take a flying leap into the air.

St. Louis has changed wonderfully in two years. The fire has caused great improvements. The diminutive, irregular, rough, uncouth, ill-looking buildings on the levee have been replaced by uniform, solid blocks of brick, which gives the street or front a really fine appearance. If a few more buildings were in some way removed and thus replaced it would improve the view still more. There are not as many boats lying at the levee as two years ago. Perhaps they have left—for we have met between here and New Orleans 30 boats which I counted, besides those that passed in the night or when I was not on the watch.

One feature of the river trade calculated to strike the attention of a stranger, is the immense number of great flat boats, or arks. They are mostly great scows or boxes, covered with boards like the hurricane deck of a steamer, and literally swarm on the river. They are deeply freighted with every kind of eatable, drinkable, or "usable" raised above; and often the banks are lined with them. You will frequently see a dozen, or twenty, or even fifty, at once, afloat and ashore. The boats at St. Louis are lively enough. Half a dozen started out, and some came in, at the time we left. Passed Alton in the night.

TUESDAY, APRIL 1. Chilly, with rain this morning. The boat is crowded with passengers. She has been under a fearful pressure of steam all night. Wherever there was the least chance of escape, it would sing, and whistle and shriek as if impatient of confinement; and then it would surge back upon the wheels and make them fairly buzz and the boat would leap forward like a frightened horse.

There are two boats just ahead to beat or be beaten, and though we hauled up for something, or to leave something, every half hour, yet no steam was wasted; and fine coal, mixed with powdered rosin, was shovelled in to increase the madness of the fire monster. Perhaps there was no danger, but I would much sooner be beat by an hour or two, than be hustled along at such a mad rate.

Nobody knows when the iron may become too weak to restrain this terrible agent; and however funny it might be to be hoisted half-sky-high in daylight, it is anything but desirable to be tossed out of a warm bed, on a dark night, into the water, to say nothing of cold and rain, and hot steam. I am, on the whole, disposed to think that I didn't sleep much. The trees are leaving out, and the springing grass has a strong smack of the greenness of spring.

The water is somewhat up, and considerable land on each side of the river, at intervals, underwater. Some of the numerous towns we have passed today appear quite thriving; but the river banks, to the eye of an agriculturist, must seem an awful blank. Broken fences, waste fields, timbered bottoms, no barns, and rotting log cabins, evidence a fearful proximity to diggerism. Wouldn't wonder if the tendency downwards continues, as they cannot well have schools under the present dispensation. The only congregations I have yet seen are the children of pigs, dogs and turkey-buzzards.

WEDNESDAY, APRIL 2. Landed in Peru at eight a.m., and took stage immediately for Aurora, deeming myself almost home. No such thing. We were to be in Aurora at ten p.m., so said the driver, so said the agent, so said everybody, that said anything about it. Well, before we were two miles out, a horse dropped in the harness and was dead before they could strip or loose him. It was quite cool and a couple of us bipeds footed it on to keep up the animal heat. Two and a half miles on the conveyance overtook us, where we had stopped to examine some coal diggins, a living horse supplying the deficit occasioned by death.

I wonder what is to break next. Glad they have no cranks, and can't blow up. I won't add anything to the category, for I am half disposed to think that they can do almost anything else.

Took dinner at Ottawa, and left at 3:30 p.m. So we are in for a night drive. There, I knew it—here it is; dark and only 14 miles from Ottawa, and we have been stuck fast in a big slough, two mortal hours. I thought that all danger of being drowned was past when we left the river; but one lives to learn, and learns to live. The last can be done with a deal of pleasure, with such a supper as we have had—chicken fixins and all; and as to the first, one must learn to wear water proof boots, or take a conveyance that won't get stuck in a mud hole. The perils of the land are far greater than those of the high seas; and we have been jostled and misused, bodily, today, more than in all the journey besides. Truly, we are left to the tender mercies of wicked drivers, who seem determined to know how hard a thump of the wheels against a rock it requires to break—something. We have broken one bolt already, and a slip of two inches more back, would have left the "fore wheels" with the horses, and us with the hind wheels. We worked some ten minutes, with hands and nails and rails, to set matters right; and then the driver, to console us, remarked that it was nothing—"He had broke a hundred before"—Didn't doubt it all from his manner of driving. Indeed I shouldn't have disputed him had he said a thousand.

THURSDAY, APRIL 3, 1851. 3 A.M. Landed safely at Wilder's in Aurora. Rolled myself in my blanket, a California indispensable, and lay down on the floor. Waked just before sunrise. Can't say what happened in the interim—suppose that I was asleep. In a couple of hours was on the track, and in 20 minutes stepped from the car on to my own premises, glad to get home, and with a heap more wit than I had two years before.

If I should get time, I will give you my reasons why I think ninety-nine out of every hundred who shall hereafter go to California, are either madmen, fools—or radically unprincipled, and of course, dishonest. Meantime, I remains as ever, yours,

I.S.P. LORD

Appendix A

Contemporary Biography of Israel Shipman Pelton Lord

The following is taken from Cleave's Biographical Cyclo-paedia of Homeopathic Physicians and Surgeons, *1873, pp. 195–196.*

LORD, ISRAEL SHIPMAN PELTON, M.D., now resident in Brooklyn, L.I., was born in Hadlyme, Conn., September 16th, 1805. His parents were of high respectability, and in very easy circumstances. His mother, whose maiden name was Beckwith, was descended from Admiral Sir Francis Drake, whose name and deeds are conspicuous in the annals of the British navy.

In 1811, the family removed from Connecticut to Sag Harbor, Long Island; a year or two after to Utica, N.Y. then only a small village; and in 1818 to the town of Collins, in Erie county of the same State; and in 1818 to Middleburg, Genessee county, near Wyoming. In Middleburg, he entered the academy, and continued his connection with it until his graduation in 1826.

In that year he began the study of medicine with Dr. Frederick Fitch, of LeRoy, N.Y. From 1828 to 1830, he attended lectures in Fairfield, N.Y. In the spring of 1830, he took charge of fourteen students in medicine, in the office of Dr. Elijah Park, of Vernal, Genessee county, and though comparatively young, gave direction to their studies. Here, having plenty of patients, with horses at his command, he made himself familiar with the details of practice, of which, as there was no clinic at Fairfield, he had known little experimentally. At the County Medical Society's annual session of that year he read a paper, "On the Use and Abuse of Blisters;" and sub-

417

sequently, one "On the Use and Abuse of Emetics." Treatises on these subjects were greatly needed at that time, when blisters and emetics were considered as the most useful appliances of a physician's treatment of his
patients.

In February, 1831, he settled in the town of French Creek, Chatauqua
county, N.Y. arriving there on the day of the great total eclipse. On September 19th of this year he married the fifth daughter of the Hon. Isaac
Wilson, of Middleburg, Genessee county, N.Y. Suffering from the ague,
which threatened to undermine his constitution, he removed to Attica, and
entered into partnership with Dr. E. Park.

In April, 1834, he started for the West, and reached Chicago—then a
bed of mud, with but a few scattering houses—in May. Passing on, he made
a claim on the Dupage River, twenty-nine miles west from Chicago, at a
place since called Warrenville. Here, where ague and fever of their worst
types were very prevalent, his labors were incessant by day and by night: he
riding from thirty to forty miles in all directions. He had no competition in
this field, but his practice was too fatiguing, and concluding to circumscribe
his field, he went to Chicago, which was then growing rapidly, and had
almost attained the dimensions of a city. Here he purchased eligible lots,
and, erecting a house, prepared to commence the practice of this profession.
But the lack of patients, followed by the financial crisis caused by the great
fire in New York, compelled him to leave, and he removed to Warrenville,
where he resumed his old practice.

In 1838, he discovered a method of reducing quicksilver for blue mass,
by trituration, at one-tenth the cost of the old method. After manufacturing
a ton and a half of blue pills with a machine of his own invention, he abandoned it, and the secret of this discovery he has never disclosed.

An alarming attack of illness, in which his attendant physicians were
unsuccessful, confirmed his belief that the fewer and simpler the medicines
in use, the better. He now confined his practice to a very limited number
and quantity of the drugs in use, and was virtually a homeopathist. He was
indebted to Dr. D.S. Smith, of Chicago, for a copy of Hahnemann's
"Organon," which was accompanied with some very valuable advice. He
read the book, but did not follow the advice, and had almost made up his
mind to abandon the profession. His friend, Dr. Smith, advised him to continue, and to use the homeopathic remedies. In these he was successful.

In 1849, he started for California. The cholera was prevailing fearfully
along the overland route; and so successful was his treatment that but one
case died, and that was an infant. In California the disease was exceedingly
fatal. In its treatment the homeopathic practice was uniformly successful.

After travelling in all parts of the State, he sailed for the Eastern States
on the 15th February, 1851, returning to his old place and practice; and in
1861 went again to Chicago. Here in five years he built up a large and successful practice; but suffering greatly from a persistent cough, he removed to

Poughkeepsie in 1867; and in 1872 removed to Brooklyn, where he is now engaged in successful practice.

Dr. Lord is a thorough homeopathist, repudiating in his practice all blisters and emetics, and giving the finest attenuations which will reach the disease in hand. A temperance man from principle, he never, under any circumstances, uses or prescribes intoxicating drinks, and carries out his total abstinence principles in the matter of tobacco.

In his ecclesiastical relations, he was a member of the Baptist Society for twenty-five years; and in 1853 transferred his membership to the Society of the Disciples, or Campbellites.

Dr. Lord's contributions to medical literature have been quite numerous and very popular. Chief among them are an essay on the "Abuse of the Obstetric Forceps;" one on "Alcohol;" a review of "Hale's New Remedies;" a report on "Materia Medica," presented to the Illinois Homeopathic Medical Society; and a paper on "Typhlo-Enteritis," contributed to the *United States Medical and Surgical Journal*.

In 1871, he published an octavo volume of 350 pages, on "Intermittent Fever." This work, which is largely clinical, is based upon notes and data accumulated during many years' experience. It is an original and invaluable monograph. Dr. Lord's intense hatred of shams has led him to gather a large storehouse of facts upon which his ideas of practical medicine are founded.

For twenty-three years he has taken a verbatim phonographic report of every case of every disease for which he has prescribed. All the conditions and circumstances pertaining thereto, as well as the medicines given, their attenuation and repetition, have been carefully noted down *at the bedside*. These have been as carefully copied by his own hand, so that he now has seven large folio volumes, or 4000 pages of manuscript, which it is hoped will one day be available to the profession.

Appendix B

Letters from a Member of Lord's Party

The following letters were written by M.L. Wisner, who accompanied Dr. Lord on his travels, to a newspaper editor in Missouri. They were published in a Kane County, Illinois, newspaper, The Western Christian.

St. Joseph, Mo. May 10, 1849.
Br. Walker:

We are now at the extremity of civilization, on the western bank of the Missouri River, where we have been three days waiting for "our turn" to be ferried over; having journied, since I wrote last, about three hundred miles, through a part of Iowa and almost the whole length of Missouri. We have gradually wound our way along over high hills, through deep valleys, and across the muddy streams of Missouri, with very few bridges, until at last we have reached the greatest stream of mud I ever saw. Whoever has noticed a puddle of water in a clay bed, after a heavy shower of rain, can form something of an idea of the appearance of this river; and the appearance of the inhabitants, with some exceptions, resemble the rivers of the country.

Never was I more sensible of the present benefit of the Christian religion than since I commenced this journey. Every thing corresponds. You may commence with the Eastern States. The air is pure; the water is clear and sweet; schools flourish; society is elevated; the Sabbath is observed; religion has a strong hold upon the affections of a majority of those who roll the wheels of improvement along. Travelling westward until you pass through the State of Ohio, you will hardly perceive the change; but travel on, and before you have passed the centre of Illinois, you will find yourself among those who have few schools, few or no Sabbaths, very little religion, and the great majority of them exceedingly vile and profane.

When we leave this place we leave the white man's habitation. We shall probably not see as many drunken Indians as we have seen white men reeling about the streets of this village; yet I should think, from what I can learn, that there are some who are followers of the Savior here. There are several places of worship in this town, and I learn from one merchant, a brother Newman, who resides in this place, that the Baptists have a church numbering some seventy and enjoy the labors of Elder Williams a part of the time. This being an important starting point through the Indian country, at this season of the year, emigrants throng the streets, and one would think from appearances that the whole world were moving to California.

I have tried to satisfy myself as to the probable number of those going this season by the South Pass, but I cannot tell, and dare not hazard an opinion. I can compare the movement to only one event of which I have ever read, and that is the children of Israel going from bondage to the land flowing with milk and honey, only making this difference—the one groaning under bondage, and seeking for the enjoyment of man's God-given rights; the other leaving a land of comparative freedom and plenty to seek for earth's hidden treasures. You may cast your eye to the right or left, and you can see the various colored covered waggons, drawn by mules, horses, oxen and even cows, and the white tents scattered all over the hills and valleys. Very little contention is known among the emigrants. Occasionally a quarrel of words rises, but there are generally enough who are in favor of good order to quell disturbances, and see that every man has his rights.

The United States armies were never armed as these emigrants are, every one a little afraid of the Indians has prepared himself, if necessary, to force his way through the uncivilized country. My impression is, that if the emigrants treat them civilly, they will not make war upon us; and if they do make war upon the Californians, it will be death to hundreds of them—for there is hardly a wagon but what can give out from six to thirty shots from rifles, revolvers, pistols, etc. without even halting to load.

Hundreds of families are moving with women and children to California, while thousands of men are going without. Some are selling their outfit and going back, but the number is comparatively small. Very few instances of the cholera have appeared among them, and almost always among those who come around by water. Last evening, the steamer *Mary* landed at this place some Welch Mormons, on their way to join their brethren at the Salt Lake—forty-three had died with cholera on the passage from St. Louis to this place. I tell you, the news made some sober-looking countenances.

My health is improving very fast, and the prospect with me is, that I am

to be a well man again. This outdoor life, living in the woods, along the
road, cooking my own victuals, washing my dishes, my clothes, making my
bread, sitting frequently flat on the ground to eat, sleeping in my wagon,
dreaming along after an ox-team—a singular kind of medicine indeed it is—
but if it only gives me health, and drives away the ague and fever, I bless
the Lord for it, and take courage.

M.L. Wisner

Fort Kearny, Platte River,
June 6, 1849—Wisner letter

Brother Walker,

When I wrote you at the Missouri River I did not expect to send again
until I had finished my journey to California—but as I have an opportunity
to send from this Fort, with pleasure I embrace it.

It is now fifteen days since we left the river for this place two hundred
and sixty miles. We have traveled it in thirteen days. Rested in camp two
Sabbaths.

The first circumstance which interested us more than usual was the paying to "Caesar his dues," or in other words we came to a small Indian
village, when the old Chief and some half dozen of his men presented a
written certificate from Col. Vaughn, at the missionary station, certifying
that they were very friendly to the whites, had not stolen anything from the
emigrants, timber scarce in their country, thought it proper to give them a
little money for the game, firewood, pasture, etc., which we would naturally
use in passing through. We gave them three dollars for the company and
were glad to get rid of them at that rate; for though we had seen some hard-
looking cases among the whites, yet these savages look worse.

Seventy-five miles brought us to the station where I was informed the
Presbyterians have quite a Society, made up of Whites and Indians. Some of
the whites (or rather half-breeds) were planting corn. It is a pleasant place.
Mr. Hamilton preaches to them. There is a small shaving shop, alias a store
of goods to trade with the Indians, some half dozen blockhouses, and very
fine looking fields of wheat. It resembled civilization.

The next important circumstances attracting our attention was the new
made graves where the emigrants had camped. We undertook at first to
count, but soon finding them very numerous, and frequently half a mile or
a mile from the road, where water and wood could be obtained for culinary
purposes, we abandoned the idea of counting and came to the conclusion
that they would average if all were counted to one a mile. Thus you see,
death is on this track. The cholera was carried up the Missouri River on the

boats and the emigrants carried it with them along the road, and sad is the havoc which has been made. The most ungodly men you ever knew have generally been the victims. Drunkards have died by hundreds on this route, and sixteen men professing to be skillful physicians have been buried between St. Joseph and this place in one month past.

We are about ten days behind the crowd. We have not had the symptoms of cholera among us; yet we have been exposed to it if it is contagious. We have been within a few rods of the dead and dying. Doct. Lord watches every movement—he is our physician. He says he can cure every case if taken in season and I think he can cure the most of them. Last week we passed a man by the side of the road who had been attacked by the cholera when his company, panic struck, inhumanly left him to die one hundred and fifty miles from any house. He had a sack of provisions by his side and lying on the ground could hardly speak. I went to him, gave him some cold coffee and the Doctor gave him some cholera medicine; but what could we do for him? The Doctor said he could not be moved, die he must—and all I could do for him was to bring him one of my pint tin cups full of water and leave it close by his side. It was a mild, pleasant day, and with the assistance we gave him, we learned by a man on horseback the next day that he had recovered and was on his journey. Much will be the suffering no doubt on this road; "for man's inhumanity to man makes countless millions mourn."

Today we were overtaken by a company of mules and ox wagons which had crossed above St. Joseph, and taken a different road to this place. They were among the unfortunate too; though they had lost none of their company, they had been attacked by 18 Indians, who attempted to plunder them. They numbered 40. The Indians shot an arrow through one man's leg and shot down one of their animals; when they fired upon the savages and killed five out of the 18 the first shot. The rest ran off before they had time to reload. The Indians will find hard fare this summer if they attempt to plunder the emigrants. The soldiers of this fort tell us that about four thousand teams is all that have passed this place this season. They will probably average three to a team. About one thousand have gone up on the north side of the Platte, so that we calculate that if the savages are disposed to be ugly, they will have to contend with fifteen thousand riflemen, well armed and the most of these good marksmen.

This Fort is a new post, only commenced last fall, with a few turf and mud buildings put up to winter in, though government has erected a saw mill moved by horse power, and they are now making brick, erecting buildings, etc. There are one hundred and fifty soldiers here. They have no one to preach to them on the Sabbath; probably do not want any one. I see much for the matter of reflection on this journey, but have a few religious privileges as yet, except in private devotion. If this was well timbered, it would be a delightful country. Probably it is as healthy a spot as could be found. My health has greatly improved enough to compensate me for much of the toil I have had.

Adieu,
Yours in the Gospel,
M.L. Wisner

June 7, Reached Fort Kearney, 260-miles from St. Joseph last night, and the mail goes so early that I was obliged to enclose at once.

Appendix C

Letter from Israel Lord to Monroe Nathan Lord

Letter from Israel Shipman Pelton Lord to his younger brother, Monroe Nathan Lord in Batavia, IL, who apparently had some financial investment in Lord's gold rush adventure.

———— ◆ ———— ◆ ———— ◆ ————

Long's Bar
Feather River, Cal.
Jan'y 22, 1850

Dear Brother,

I have finally got leisure to write you. You will have heard before this from my letters home and to the West. Christian; the only ones I have written, what we are about and how doing. If the citizen does not publish you can get the manuscript at their office. If you are acquainted with matters and things you will doubtless be somewhat surprised at the divisions in our company and their present position.

To understand this matter in general you have only to learn that ours is almost the only company that kept up an organization into Sacramento Valley. Hundreds of companies, which left St. Joseph, Independence, and other points on the Missouri with the most complete outfits and fairest prospects; buried their men, lost their cattle, quarreled, separated and became disorganized; dropping into the valley in fragments, hungry, ragged and destitute. And almost all this destruction of property, suffering and loss of life is fairly to be attributed to insubordination among the men.

I know of no train that started with as light teams as ours and yet cannot learn of any which came through with as little loss. If we had been 2

425

weeks earlier we should have lost nothing to speak of—for then the feed would have been good in comparison to what it was when we did come.

To understand in detail requires more. I shall give a few particulars after all and you must judge of the matter for yourself. Doubtless before this you may have received letters from Van [Wormer] and Charley [Ballard] and I doubt not some kind of version of the whole matter. Passing that however as though it had not been and will give a statement of *the facts*. From the very start Van Wormer appeared restless under any kind of control. I did my best to make as little show of authority as possible and to conciliate him in particular as I clearly forsaw a spirit of insubordination which would prove troublesome before we got through. I found a like disposition in Whipple. He fell out with me at St. Joseph and he being *wholly* in the fault.

It seems that George Sharpe borrowed a wooden pail of him somewhere on the road which he would not take back but demanded of George one of his tin pails. When I got to St. Jo. he demanded the tin pail. I told him I would see to it and learning from George and others how it was I ordered a new wooden pail to be bought and given to him. He would not receive it and whether or not he ever did I never asked.

From this time to the end he took every pain to make dissatisfaction among the men and because the Elder [Wisner] sustained me, he became so bitter as to take every opportunity to abuse him and not only so he made opportunities and went out of his way to disturb him. His conversation at times was absolutely blasphemous and savored of insanity.

Sometime near the beginning of the journey he played some trick with the Elder about the eating fixings—the Elder was then helping George to cook. He played back the same trick on Charley supposing it would hit [E.] Whipple. This enraged Charley and from that time he abused the Elder as long as they travelled together. If I had thrashed them both soundly on the start, it would have been better for the train and all concerned.

[Ed] Morgan is one of the laziest men I ever saw. I had to stir him up two or three times and he became one of the disaffected. Isaac Hawley is a complete shirk and I was obliged to reprove him. All these united to do all the mischief they could and retard the train as much as possible. If I ordered at halt at 5 o'clock they grumbled—we ought to drive till sundown. If we drove till sundown we ought to have stopped at 4 o'clock. If we turned to the right for feed, we should have gone to the left, if to the left, nothing but the right would answer. If we went away from the road to camp I was a dam'd fool and a d____der one if I camped on the road. If I halted at noon it was a dead loss of time, if I kept on till night I should kill the cattle.

The night we camped on the Big Blue, Van Wormer stopped 3 miles back and swore he would not go any farther. He kept two teams back with him. (I think it was two.) This hindered us at least one day. It was strictly contrary to orders, and I have no doubt that he stopped simply because it was so. Had I been with the teams he would not have stopped, but I was ahead all the afternoon. Two or three times when I was behind the train he told some of the men that it was time to halt and we should not find so good a place to camp if we went on. At this moment I passed the word to halt and he immediately turned and swore that I was a damned fool for stopping so early and where there was no wood or water etc. This shows that it was merely for opposition. Indeed I have ascertained that the project was to make Van Capt.

After crossing the South Fork of the Platte we camped at night where was no wood and in the morning moved on a few miles and I called a halt for breakfast as there was willow enough for fuel. Van however went on and I sent to him to stop but he went on a mile farther. I did intend to have him expelled but thinking that you might deem it a hasty movement, I passed it over. I have no hesitation whatever in asserting that he delayed the whole train, by stopping at different times contrary to orders, getting the men disaffected, losing cattle by dividing the train and weakening the watch, etc at least ten days, directly; and indirectly by consequence as many more.

This may not seem probable to the uninitiated but to any one who has come the overland route it must be a matter of knowledge. For instance, one day I left the train with orders to Van not to halt till he got to certain springs though it should take till three o'clock. Before noon he halted 3 or 4 miles short. On starting the train fell in behind or became entangled in the rear of 3 or 4 other trains and thus came to the Springs. The cattle were thirsty but the water was warm and they would not drink until they had been in it several minutes. The teams which came in first had covered the whole ground and even then half of them were not able to touch the water. Of course, ours had to wait. Two hours were thus lost and few of the cattle had time to get any. That night we had to camp in a spot almost destitute of feed and halted the next day before noon to repair the error in good feed by a delay of at least 24 hours.

But this is not all. Besides injuring the cattle and rendering them unfit for business just in the degree that they suffered from hunger and thirst, there is still another loss to be brought into account. In many places had we been only *one* day earlier, we should have had very good feed where we found it very poor. In many localities the difference of 4 or 5 days made the only difference between getting through with the whole team or losing the whole. One can hardly credit how rapidly all the grass disappears before such a locust like emigration.

At Muddy Springs, 20 miles this side the Great Boiling Spring, Whipple became so violent and abusive that he was expelled–Charley and Van immediately applied for dismission and it was granted. A committee was appointed to settle with them who were so intimidated by Van's threats about looking into his wagon that they did not ascertain how much Van's wagon had in it. We have since ascertained that they had considerable

property more than the committee knew of and that the company were
cheated in the settlement. They kept a wagon cover which was taken from
Hill's wagon I think and when we found it out they refused to give it up. I
did not know at the time but what the committee were in the wagon and
examined every thing.

He had a good team and yet was always grumbling about his load.
Before we reached the St. Mary's River, at the Hot Springs, nothing would
do but he must stop the whole train and have the loads weighed. The day
before or day but one he had thrown out some of his load which the
Wisner boys brought along. When the whole was weighed his load included
the weight of that which he had thrown out was 300 lbs less than the boys
team had drawn all along. In fact, he had one of the lightest loads in the
train. At Raft River he left the train and went off in my absence and camped
by himself. He tried to get the other teams to go with him. We did not lose
much by this operation but by the other we were delayed at least 2 days
without any necessity.

To enumerate all the delays and vexations occasioned by the scamp
would occupy several sheets. After he left us instead of laying over and
hunting better feed, etc. he almost invariable followed us up closely, usually
camping with or very near us though we gave him, intimation gentle, that
we did not need him any longer. By the by, he rode in his wagon more
than any well man in the train and beat his oxen most unmercifully—Dodge
beat his more but not as cruelly. To sum up the matter, he is a kind of half
good natured, half lazy, unprincipled, quick-tempered, obstinate, ignorant
scoundrel. I do not know but he and Charley will deal honestly with you. It
is possible. You had best look well to them, however.

McCauley is something of -- of -- an -- Irishman. He maintained all
along that an order ought not to be obeyed nor would he obey one unless
he thought it was a proper one. And it must be given very politely or
nobody was bound to obey it. No matter how important it was, the least
show of authority, simply saying "do it" instead of "will you do this?" was
sufficient to nullify the order. Nobody was bound to obey. He is a great—I
was about to say ass—but I will say Irishman—is that McCauley. He is a
thorough going worker after all, and wants to go ahead, so one can get
along with almost anything.

If Van Wormer and Morgan had not been in the train I think we
should have the whole company together now. If we had we could work to
very great advantage. But you will soon hear more on that point. As for the
chance of making money here by trading, it depends entirely on a man's fore-
sight and activity. Boots are now worth 2 oz ($32). Round pointed shovels 5
to 6 dollars. Picks very light steel ones, 8$ to 10$. Common sized bake kettles, 12$. 1 sheet of zinc 30$. 1 sheet of iron 40$, &c &c ---- Let me copy a
bill we have just bought at Yuba City, Jan 24th, the transportation to which
place by steam is 8 cents per lb, & from there to here .17¢ lb.

2500	lb	flour	26½¢ lb	selling here for	6/	to	8/	lb
800	"	Pork 3	9 & 44¢ lb	"	"	"	do	"	do	"
50	"	Candles	$1.00 lb	"	"	"	14/	"	16	"
50	"	Soap	.20 "	"	"	"	10/	"	12/	"
54	"	Peaches	.30 "	"	"	"	12/	"	14/	"
31	"	Potatoes	.40 "	"	"	"			8/	"
9½	"	Tea	1.00 "	"	"	"	20/	"	24/	"
113	"	Hard B.	.22 "	"	"	"			6/	"
30	"	Beans	.10 "	"	"	"			5/	"
55	"	Pears (dried)	.75 "	"	"	"	12/	"	16/	"
50	"	Figs	.70 "	"	"	"	12/	"	16/	"

Everything goes by the lb "& so they goes" as Hank Hood would say. An active man can turn every word & thought and breath to money here and a lazy one will get nothing. All that is wanted here is something to eat, drink, wear and work with. Round pointed shovels, light and strong, light steel picks and strong tin pans holding about 2 gallons are in most demand. The tin wants to be of the heaviest kind. When made on purpose a strip of tin about an inch wide and made convex outward is soldered under the rim or wire on the outside making a smooth round projection to take hold of. Imagine this fragment of a pan in diagram to be bottom side upward you can see the roll of tin on the outside. Such pans bring 6 dollars here, plain ones 5, old, worn, bruised, light ones 3-½ to 4. Best picks are worth 8 or 10$s. Common ones 5 – A round pointed long handled shovel 5 to 6$ & 7. Tacks of all sizes are called for every day at 8/ per paper and nails 6 & 4 & 3s are 8/–lb. Easy a horse shoe magnet like Phillip's smallest is worth 6 to 8 or 10 $s here. It is used to take the sulphuret of Iron out of the gold in the form of a fine black sand. Good cowhide boots that reach the knees are worth here 32$ a pair & if they cover the whole leg and are of kep & the leather prepared so as to keep the water out the present price is *big*. I was offered 90$ for mine but I reckon I want dry feet as much as any body.

A gold washer is worth 50 to 60 dollars & a man can make one easily in 2 days. It requires only about 10 or 12 feet of lumber, a few nails and a piece of sheet iron 18 or 20 inches square. I sold 2 such pieces a day or two ago for 8$s apiece and was offered 10 for another & 12 for a 4th. We want to use them. I could sell 200 here immediately if I had them. Clothing is not very high except India Rubber and a first rate article of strong oil cloth that won't rip, nor tear. Sal Eratus is good for 3$s here (a pound I mean.) Ground spice 4 to 6$ lb & pepper 3 to 5$s lb. A pie is currently at 10/ – & a night's lodging bursts a dollar. Cooking stoves at the city Sacramento No 1, Jew's harp 125$ & 25$ more every number up, other patterns, same Nos 30 to 50 per cent higher. Balances to weigh gold small ones such as apothecaries use & worth 6/ to 8/ in Chicago, are 8 to 12 $ here & large ones that will weigh 1000$s are worth 50$.

But I may as well stop. Provisions are for the most part injured before we get them. Apples are bitter unless brought in liquor casks. Flour from the States is generally lumpy and musty or sour and oftener than any way all three. Chili flour is tolerably good & Oregon is good when you can get it. They break the lumps and sift the flour from the states and palm it off for Chili & Oregon. The process of getting gold, the surface of the country &c &c I shall communicate to the Westn Christn immediately & you will find it there.

You will hear many very exaggerated stories of gold diggers. You may rely upon it that the man who has gone back with his 20 or 30,000 do not dig it & none but a gambler can make a 100,000 in a year. There are many drawbacks in digging gold. The weather, the difficulty of getting about, the high prices of everything, the health of the country &c – prevent a man from making his jack in a day but whoever has his health is sure to get a reasonable amount in 2 or 3 years. Medical business is good what there is of it, but the Doctors are as thick as they are in – in – in a place I seldom speak of since we came by the Big Boiling Spring – a pokerish hole and a hot one was that.

I heard from Morse the dentist today. He lies sick down at Yates Ranche. He is now reaping the reward or rather harvest of his improvident exposure in packing through. Cushing I cannot hear from at all. The Gilsons are at the Yuba or some mines below. [Samuel] Ambrose is in Sacramento. Mr. Latham is up in Redding's Mines 150 or more miles above Sacramento. So far as we are concerned immediately, Darling is dead. Otherwise we are right side up. Darling left with Whipple & came to the mines from 50 or 60 miles beond the pass of the Sierra Nevada. He left without any liberty or giving any notice. They suffered incredibly in packing through for want of provisions, sleeping in the open air &c. When they reached the mines they had little or no shelter and were exposed to the early rains. They returned to us in camp up at Lassen's on the Sacramento, both sick. Darling had a very bad cough night & day with fever & diarrhea. When the teams left for the mines Darling was fast recovering & nearly well but he got worse in going down & before I got round into the mines more than a month elapsed. I found Darling with some cough, diarrhea & bloated all over, with one leg swelled full. He had applied to a doct. & got salivated. He called it Scurvy. I began to treat him after 3 days & he became better for a time but there was too much disease about the lungs. It progressed very rapidly & finally the lungs became Hepatized or filled up & stopped his breath. Doubtless the old

disease of Asthma which I noticed had troubled him all through hastened
the fatal termination.

We have now only – The Elder, Sammy [Ball], George [Sharpe], Tine
[probably Constantine Wisner], Dude & myself with a young man named
Robt Horton left. The others are scattered to the 5 winds. McAuley, Morgan
& the Holleys are in partnership doing – not much – Hoods, Stebbins &
Dodge, doing a heap less & Condes is doing *less that all 8 together* & what
are you doing?

Why, we have a good house worth 400$s, provisions which cost 1800 $s
& will sell here for 3000 or 4000 dollars or more. Our teams are in good
order & worth from 100 to 150 dollars a yoke. We have 12 yokes & 2 or 3
cows. We have all our baggage & traps & rifles. I was offered yesterday 80
dollars for my rifle. I ask 100 & shall get it I think. I bought Morgan's
revolver & shall not think of less than 125$ for it. Gave him 30$s. Those
boys are hard up. Grove & Hill are at work for 50$ a month. They are the
boys.

You see a man can do nothing alone. He can make 5 or 6 $s a day at a
great risk. A company can haul their own provisions, build their own house,
& build dams across the river when the proper time comes. This is the way
to get gold fast. The bottom of the river is covered with gold & a company
strong enough to dam it frequently will take out several 1000 dollars in a
day – I want you to show this to Makepeace as he wanted some of the information which it contains & I may not get time to write him these 3 weeks.

Remember me to Mrs. Makepeace, Miss House & Ellen. Tell Ellen there
is not gold enough in California to pay her father for leaving home & coming here. Let nobody come the overland route. It is a long dismal weary way
which no money can pay for travelling over – It is fit only for a highway for
wild beasts & Ravens. The whole country from the Missouri to the Sierra
Nevada is not worth one picayune.

I have no letter or news from home yet. California is a miserable place
in the winter, though the weather is only just cold enough to scare away
the musquitoes & the grass on the ground & the leaves on the trees are
green, & some of the shrubs are in flower & some have a splendid red
berry. The flowers are scentless & the berries bitter as John's little book, so
there is no comfort in that or this & the green puts one in mind of a
greater degree of verdancy &c &c.

I am far from being home sick but to rain, rain, rain, when one has not
heard from home in almost a year is intolerable. I reckon when this country
was made, they concluded it wasn't worth anything as it is & as it would
not pay for altering, it was determined to leave it to chance. The Indians
have maintained a precarious existence until now warring with various success, against fire & flood & cold & heat & malaria; building on artificial
hillocks & burrowing like wild beasts in the ground. Now comes the white
man to face the angry elements. Well, well, time will show, but if there are

not more fleshless bones in California by one year from today than one would like to read of, then wet & dry & cold & heat have ceased to effect humans & poison has no more power.

When you write directly to Sacramento City California (in full) for they are to lazy to call C.a. California anyhow. You may remember me by the bushel to all enquiring — in general — in particular, to Jane, Mother, Fred, Albina, Elizabeth, Almira, Ben, *Laren* (I wish I had him here to make a machine to take the fine black sulphuret of Iron out of gold & it adheres to a magnet like iron filings.) The Cols & wife. Alfred. Resk, Arthur, Joseph & families. See mother Wilson [Lord's mother-in-law] & tell her there are heaps on heaps of gold here but mighty hard digging. I wish you to see Whiteman & let him read what I have written about Whipple. Tell him that Ben is doing nothing. I tried to keep Ben but could not. He took all the money W. had. Not much. See Whipples friends also. I shall write if I can get time but I have already written to my wife about it & they will see that. I have secured some articles for keepsakes which I shall bring home with me if I ever live to return. Do not let Polly [ISP's wife, Mary Pollydelia Wilson Lord] or the children want for anything in your power to assist them to.

Polly will doubtless like to see this letter. Though I may send her one by the same mail. I have written already & it must be half way there by this time. Give my best love to her & the children & remember that I remain truly your brother.

                                        (Signed) I.S.P. Lord

M.N. Lord

Index

433